KARNEVAL 3

Touya Mikanagi

STORY

A YOUNG BOY NAMED NAI JOURNEYS IN SEARCH OF THE MISSING KAROKU, ACCOMPANIED BY GAREKI AND THE AGENTS OF CIRCUS WHOM HE ENCOUNTERED ALONG THE WAY. AFTER EXAMINING NAI'S BODY AND DISCOVERING THAT HE IS NOT HUMAN, CIRCUS HAS BECOME DEEPLY INTERESTED IN NAI AND KAROKU, THE ONE WHO CREATED NAI. WHEN NAI AND FRIENDS HEAD TO THE ICY CITY OF RINOL DURING A CRIMINAL INVESTIGATION, THEIR WORK IS INTERRUPTED BY THE APPEARANCE OF A MYSTERIOUS PAIR THAT SUDDENLY ATTACKS THEM...! DURING THE BATTLE, YOGI ABRUPTLY UNDERGOES A VAST PERSONALITY CHANGE AND ALL BUT DECIMATES THE AREA. WORSE YET, DURING THE CONFUSION, TSUKUMO IS CAPTURED BY THE ENEMY!

CHARACTERS OF KARNEVAL

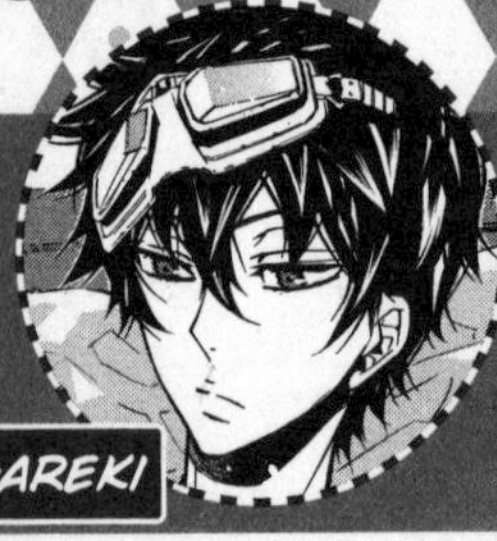

GAREKI

HE MET NAI INSIDE AN EERIE MANSION THAT HE HAD INTENDED TO BURGLARIZE. INTRIGUED BY THE BRACELET NAI CARRIES, HE HAS JOINED FORCES WITH THE BOY.

RESCUED →

← ATTACHED

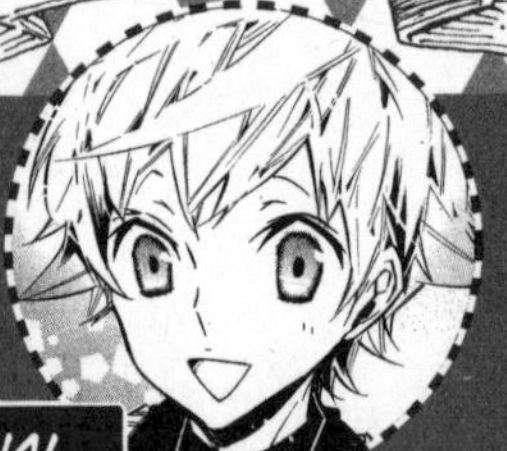

NAI

A BOY SEARCHING FOR "KAROKU" WITH A BRACELET AS HIS ONLY CLUE. THOUGH HIS ABILITY TO SURVIVE ON HIS OWN SEEMS VERY LOW, HE HAS AMAZINGLY SHARP HEARING.

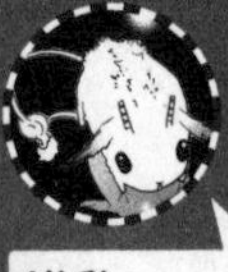

NIJI

THE ANIMAL FROM WHICH NAI WAS CREATED. THEY EXIST ONLY IN THE RAINBOW FOREST, A HIGHLY UNUSUAL ECOSYSTEM THAT ALLOWED THE NIJI TO EVOLVE AS THEY DID.

ON THE TRAIL OF

GUARDING

HIRATO

CAPTAIN OF CIRCUS'S 2ND SHIP. NAI (AND GAREKI), WHO BROUGHT THEM A BRACELET BELONGING TO CIRCUS, ARE CURRENTLY UNDER HIS PROTECTION.

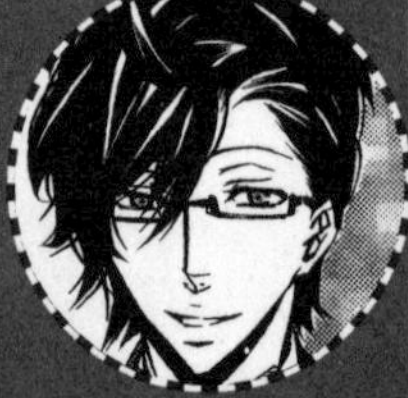

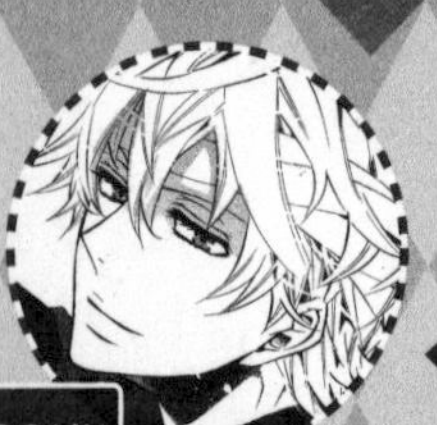

KAROKU

WENT MISSING, LEAVING BEHIND ONLY HIS BRACELET IN A POOL OF BLOOD BEFORE VANISHING. HE SEEMS TO BE ABLE TO CONTACT NAI TELEPATHICALLY...

← ? →

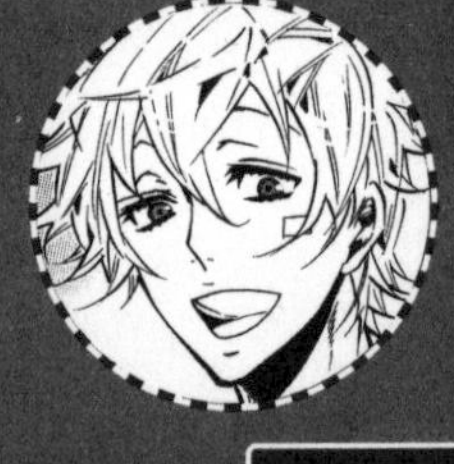

YOGI

CIRCUS 2ND SHIP COMBAT SPECIALIST. HE HAS A CHEERFUL, FRIENDLY PERSONALITY. FOR SHOWS, HE WEARS AN ANIMAL MASCOT SUIT.

TSUKUMO

CIRCUS 2ND SHIP COMBAT SPECIALIST. A BEAUTIFUL GIRL WITH A COOL, SERIOUS PERSONALITY. AS A SHOW PERFORMER, SHE IS VERY POPULAR DUE TO HER DAZZLING ACROBATICS AND BEAUTY.

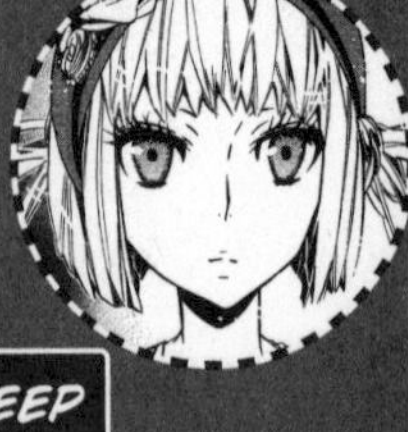

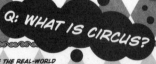

Q: WHAT IS CIRCUS?

A: THE EQUIVALENT OF THE REAL-WORLD POLICE. THEY CONDUCT THEIR LARGE-SCALE "OPERATIONS" WITHOUT FOREWARNING TO ENSURE THEIR TARGETS WILL NOT ESCAPE ARREST, UTILIZING COORDINATED, POWERFUL ATTACKS!! AFTER AN OPERATION, CIRCUS PERFORMS A "SHOW" FOR THE PEOPLE OF THE CITY AS AN APOLOGY FOR THE FEAR AND INCONVENIENCE THEIR WORK MAY HAVE CAUSED. IN SHORT, "CIRCUS" IS A CHEERFUL (?) AGENCY THAT CARRIES OUT ITS MISSION DAY AND NIGHT TO APPREHEND EVIL AND PROTECT THE PEACE OF THE LAND.

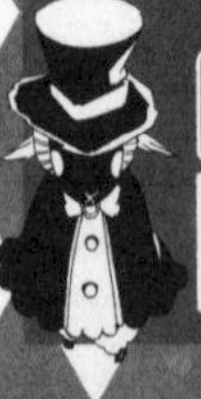

SHEEP

A CIRCUS DEFENSE SYSTEM. DESPITE THEIR CUTE APPEARANCE, THE SHEEP HAVE SOME VERY POWERFUL CAPABILITIES.

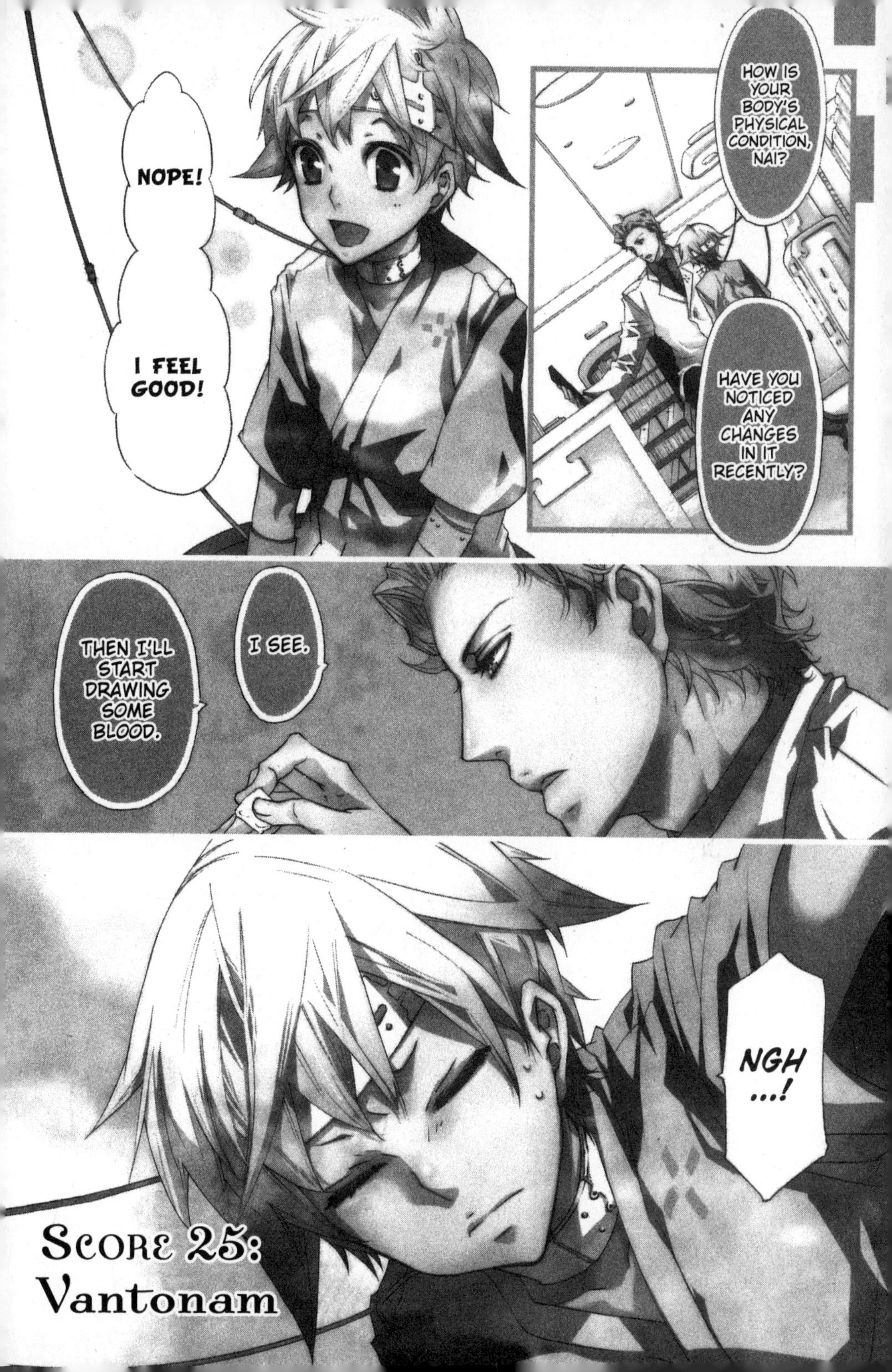
HOW IS YOUR BODY'S PHYSICAL CONDITION, NAI?
HAVE YOU NOTICED ANY CHANGES IN IT RECENTLY?
NOPE!
I FEEL GOOD!
I SEE.
THEN I'LL START DRAWING SOME BLOOD.
NGH ...!

Score 25: Vantonam

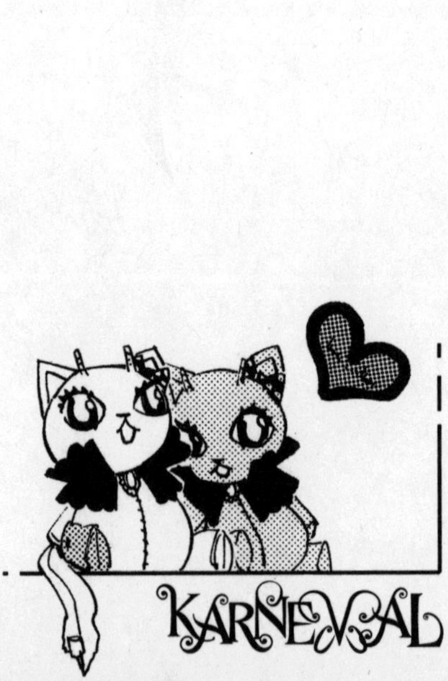
KARNEVAL

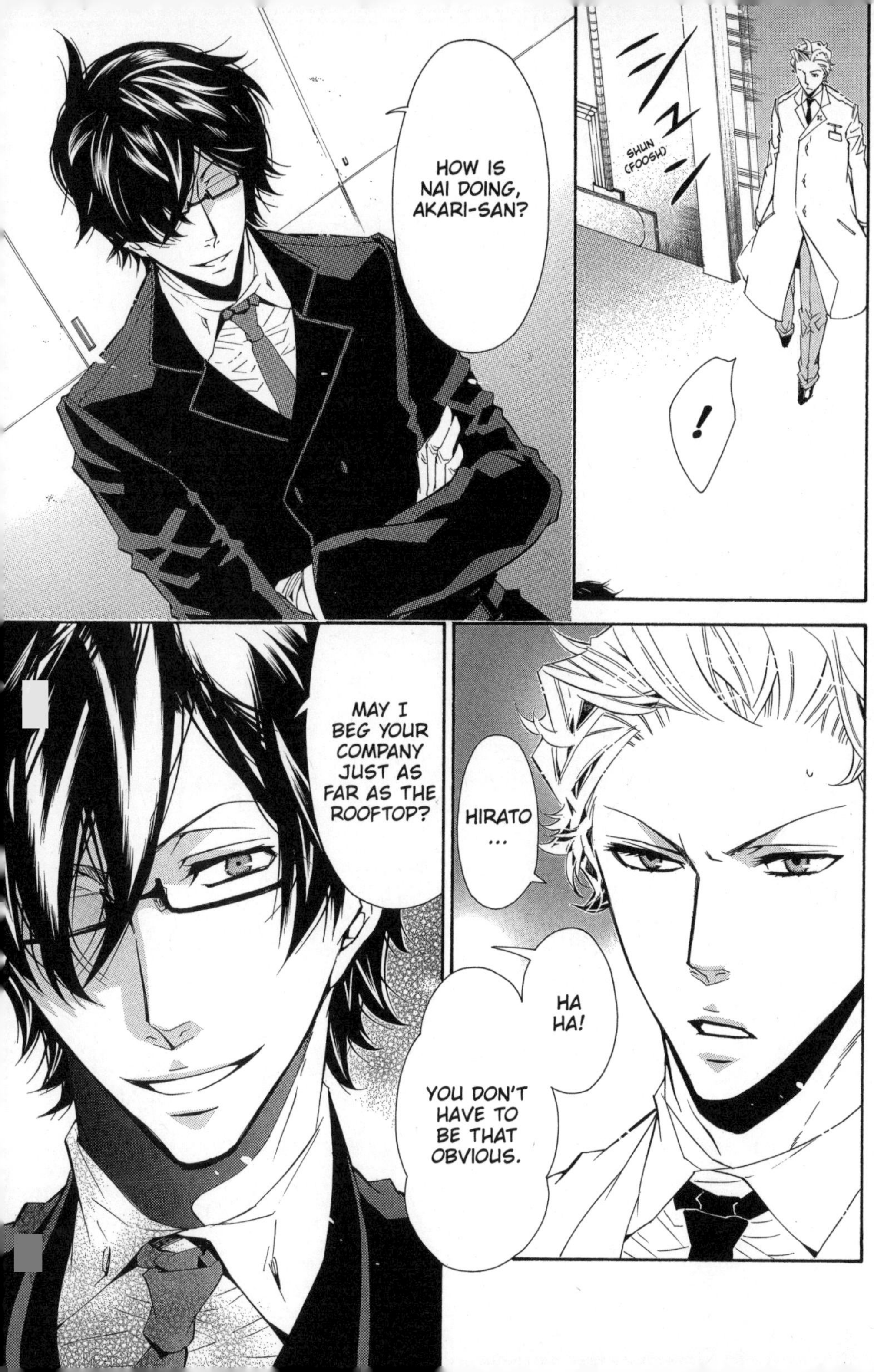
SHUN (FOOSH)
!
HOW IS NAI DOING, AKARI-SAN?
HIRATO ...
HA HA!
YOU DON'T HAVE TO BE THAT OBVIOUS.
MAY I BEG YOUR COMPANY JUST AS FAR AS THE ROOFTOP?

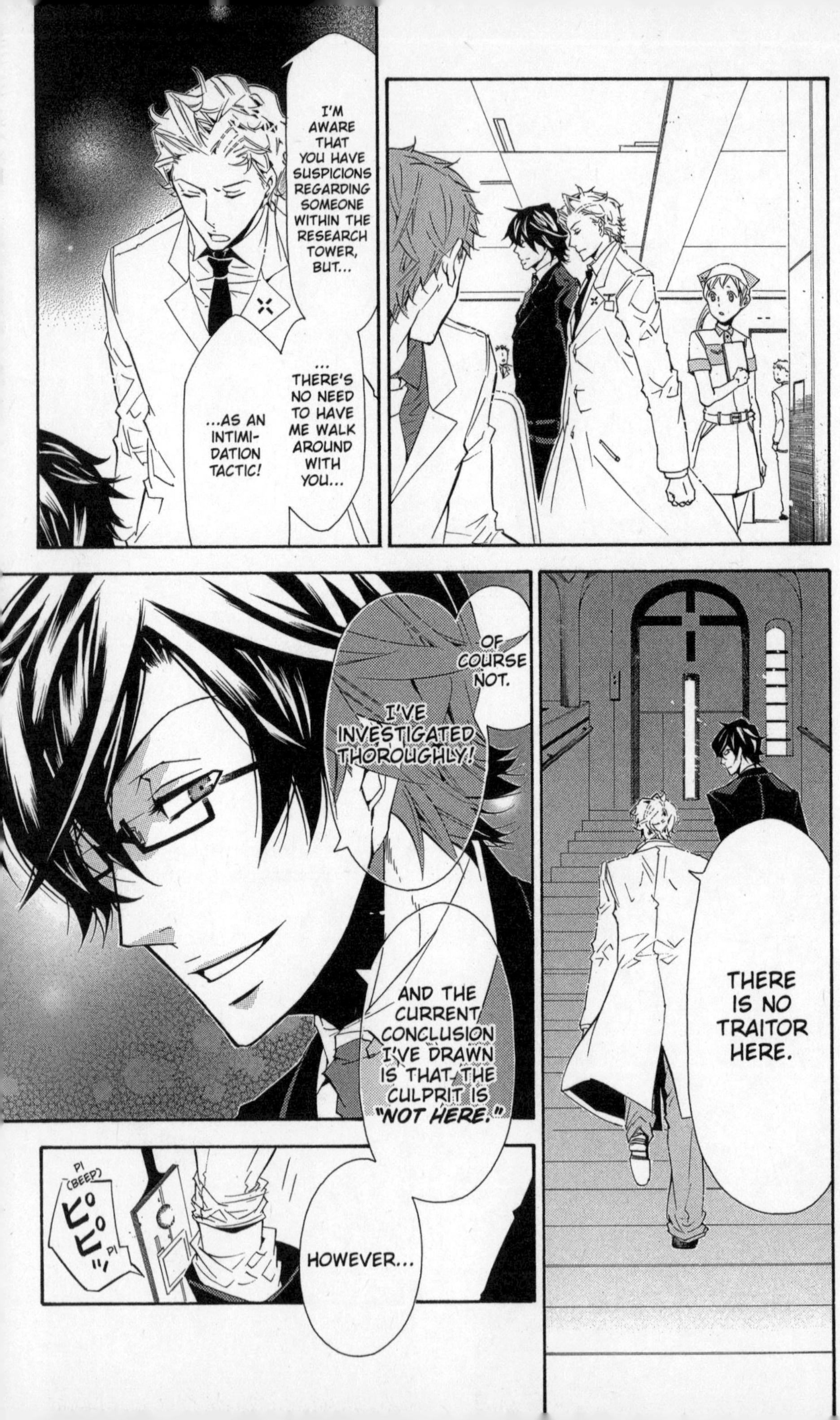
I'M AWARE THAT YOU HAVE SUSPICIONS REGARDING SOMEONE WITHIN THE RESEARCH TOWER, BUT...
... THERE'S NO NEED TO HAVE ME WALK AROUND WITH YOU...
...AS AN INTIMIDATION TACTIC!
THERE IS NO TRAITOR HERE.
OF COURSE NOT.
I'VE INVESTIGATED THOROUGHLY!
AND THE CURRENT CONCLUSION I'VE DRAWN IS THAT THE CULPRIT IS "NOT HERE."
PI (BEEP)
PI
HOWEVER...

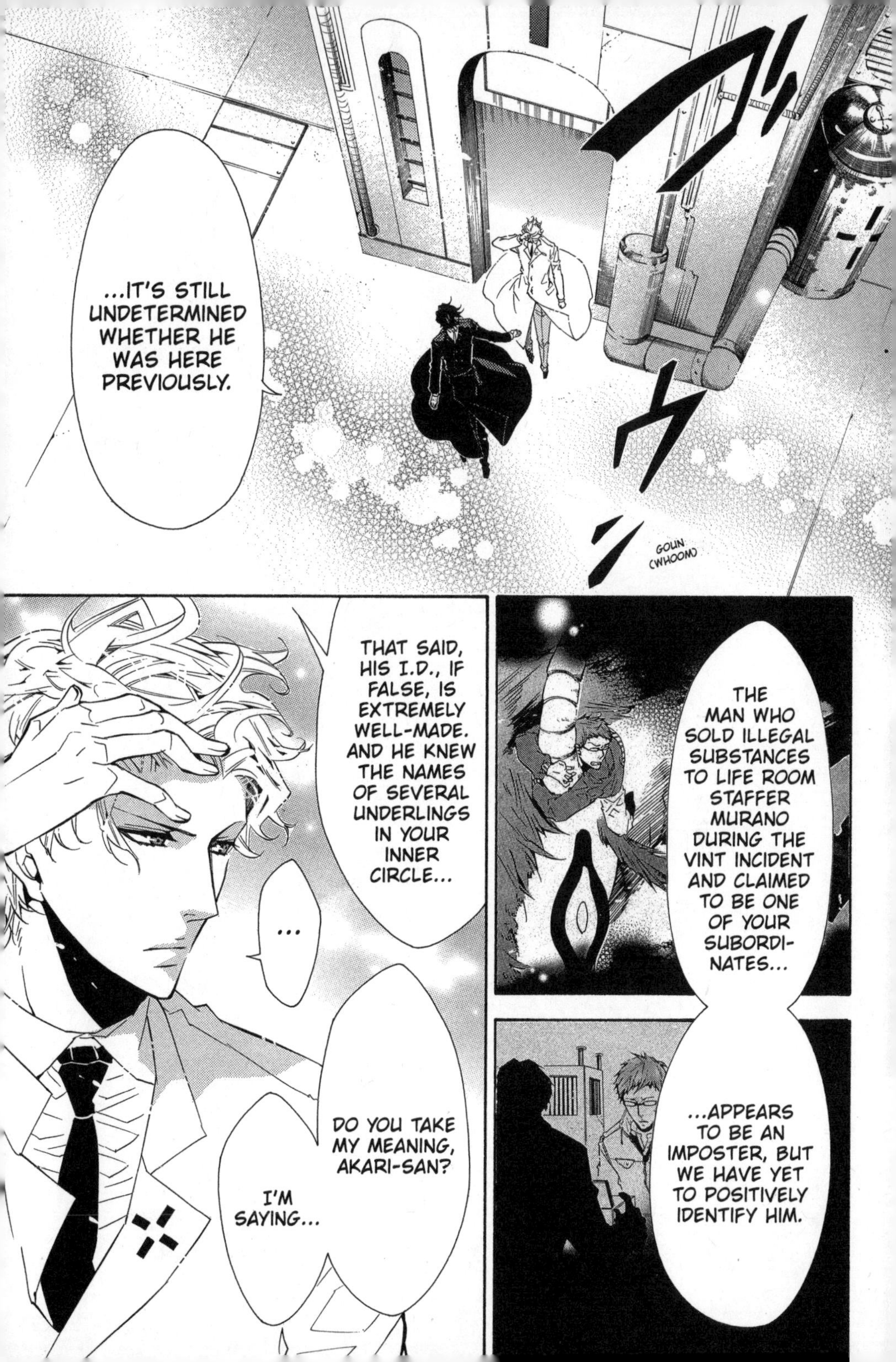
...IT'S STILL UNDETERMINED WHETHER HE WAS HERE PREVIOUSLY.
GOUN (WHOOM)
THE MAN WHO SOLD ILLEGAL SUBSTANCES TO LIFE ROOM STAFFER MURANO DURING THE VINT INCIDENT AND CLAIMED TO BE ONE OF YOUR SUBORDINATES...
...APPEARS TO BE AN IMPOSTER, BUT WE HAVE YET TO POSITIVELY IDENTIFY HIM.
THAT SAID, HIS I.D., IF FALSE, IS EXTREMELY WELL-MADE. AND HE KNEW THE NAMES OF SEVERAL UNDERLINGS IN YOUR INNER CIRCLE...
...
DO YOU TAKE MY MEANING, AKARI-SAN?
I'M SAYING...

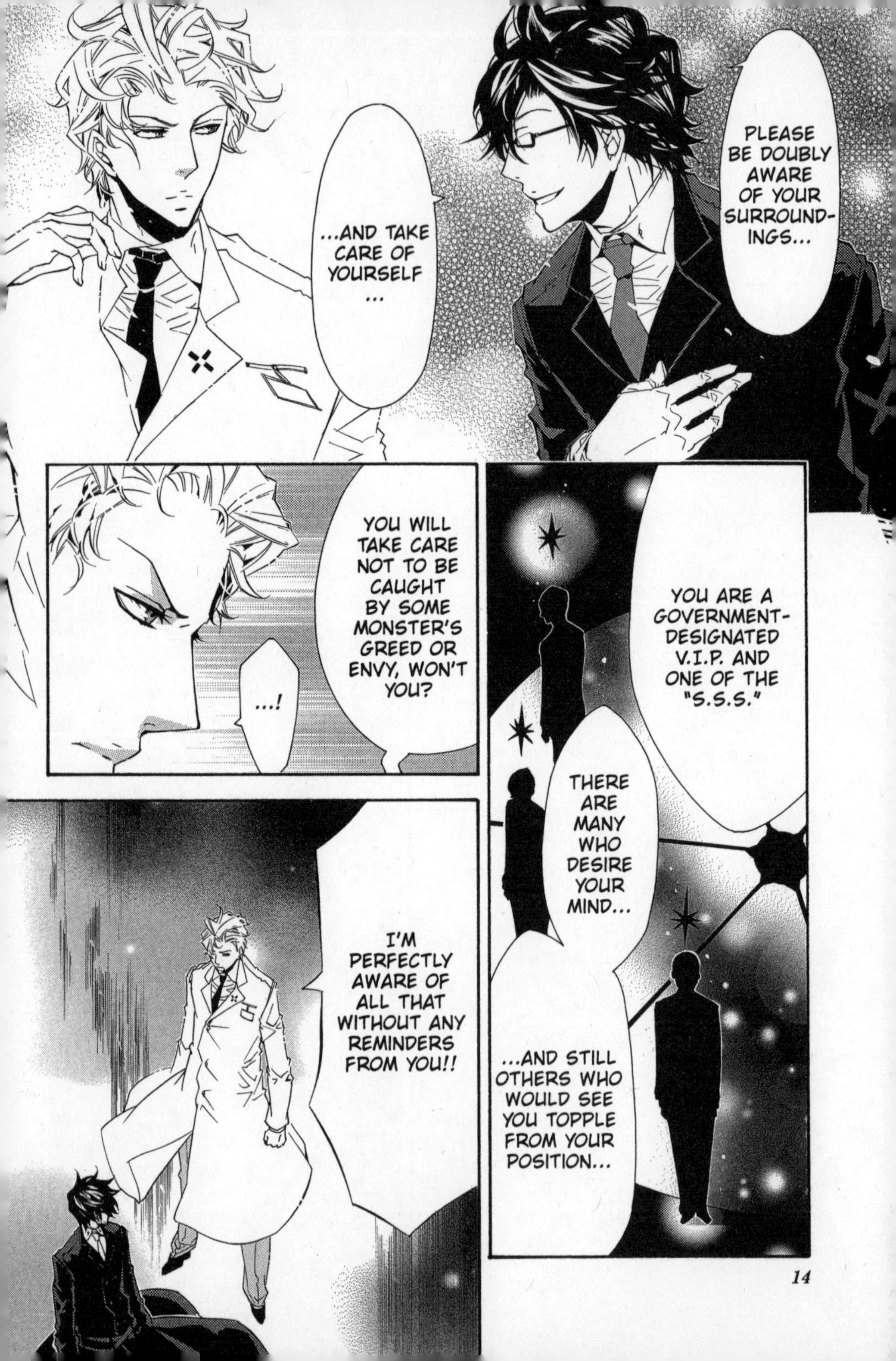
PLEASE BE DOUBLY AWARE OF YOUR SURROUND-INGS...
...AND TAKE CARE OF YOURSELF ...
YOU ARE A GOVERNMENT-DESIGNATED V.I.P. AND ONE OF THE "S.S.S."
THERE ARE MANY WHO DESIRE YOUR MIND...
...AND STILL OTHERS WHO WOULD SEE YOU TOPPLE FROM YOUR POSITION...
YOU WILL TAKE CARE NOT TO BE CAUGHT BY SOME MONSTER'S GREED OR ENVY, WON'T YOU?
...!
I'M PERFECTLY AWARE OF ALL THAT WITHOUT ANY REMINDERS FROM YOU!!

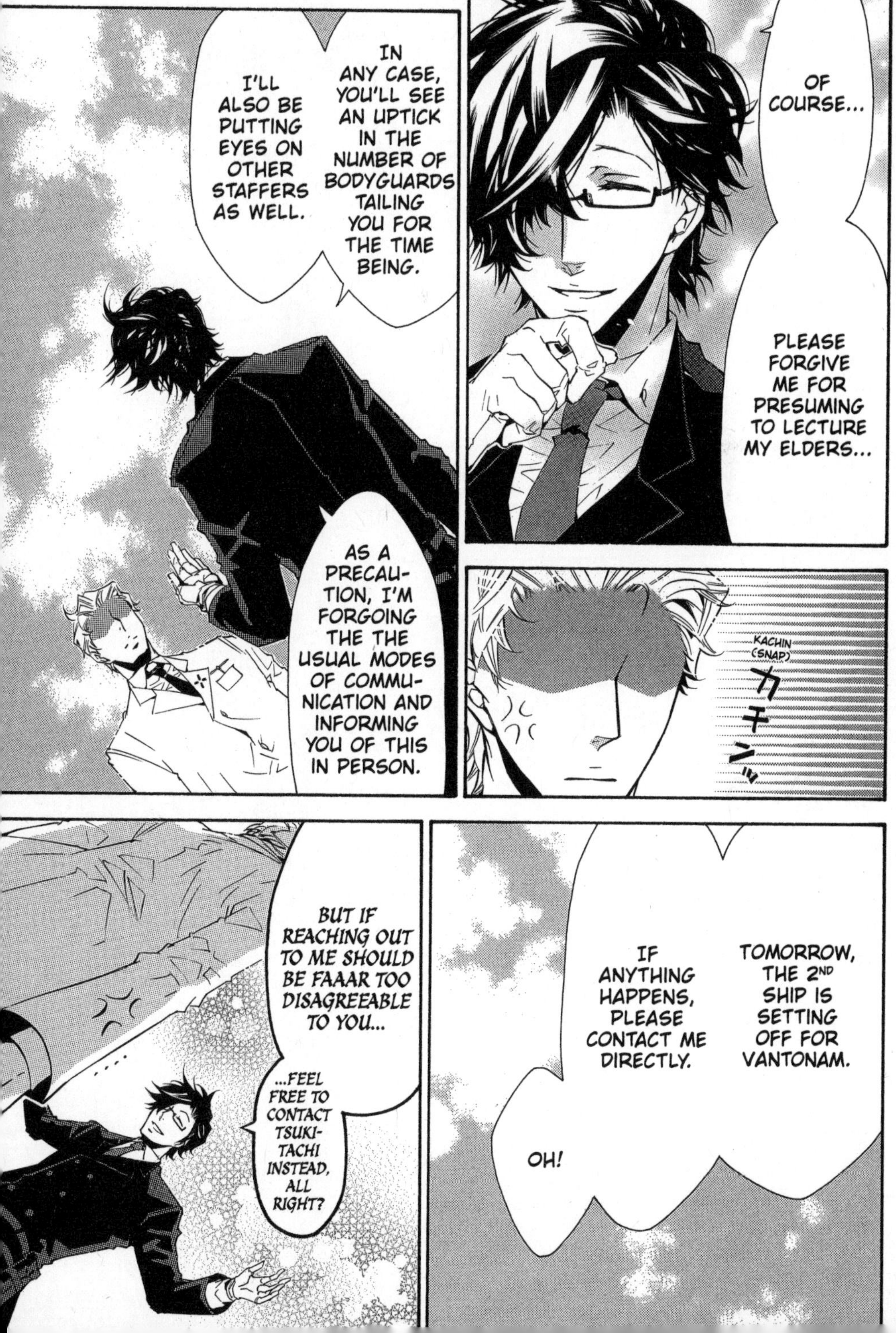
OF COURSE...
PLEASE FORGIVE ME FOR PRESUMING TO LECTURE MY ELDERS...
KACHIN (SNAP)
カチン
IN ANY CASE, YOU'LL SEE AN UPTICK IN THE NUMBER OF BODYGUARDS TAILING YOU FOR THE TIME BEING.
I'LL ALSO BE PUTTING EYES ON OTHER STAFFERS AS WELL.
AS A PRECAUTION, I'M FORGOING THE THE USUAL MODES OF COMMUNICATION AND INFORMING YOU OF THIS IN PERSON.
TOMORROW, THE 2ND SHIP IS SETTING OFF FOR VANTONAM.
IF ANYTHING HAPPENS, PLEASE CONTACT ME DIRECTLY.
OH!
BUT IF REACHING OUT TO ME SHOULD BE FAAAR TOO DISAGREEABLE TO YOU...
...FEEL FREE TO CONTACT TSUKITACHI INSTEAD, ALL RIGHT?
....

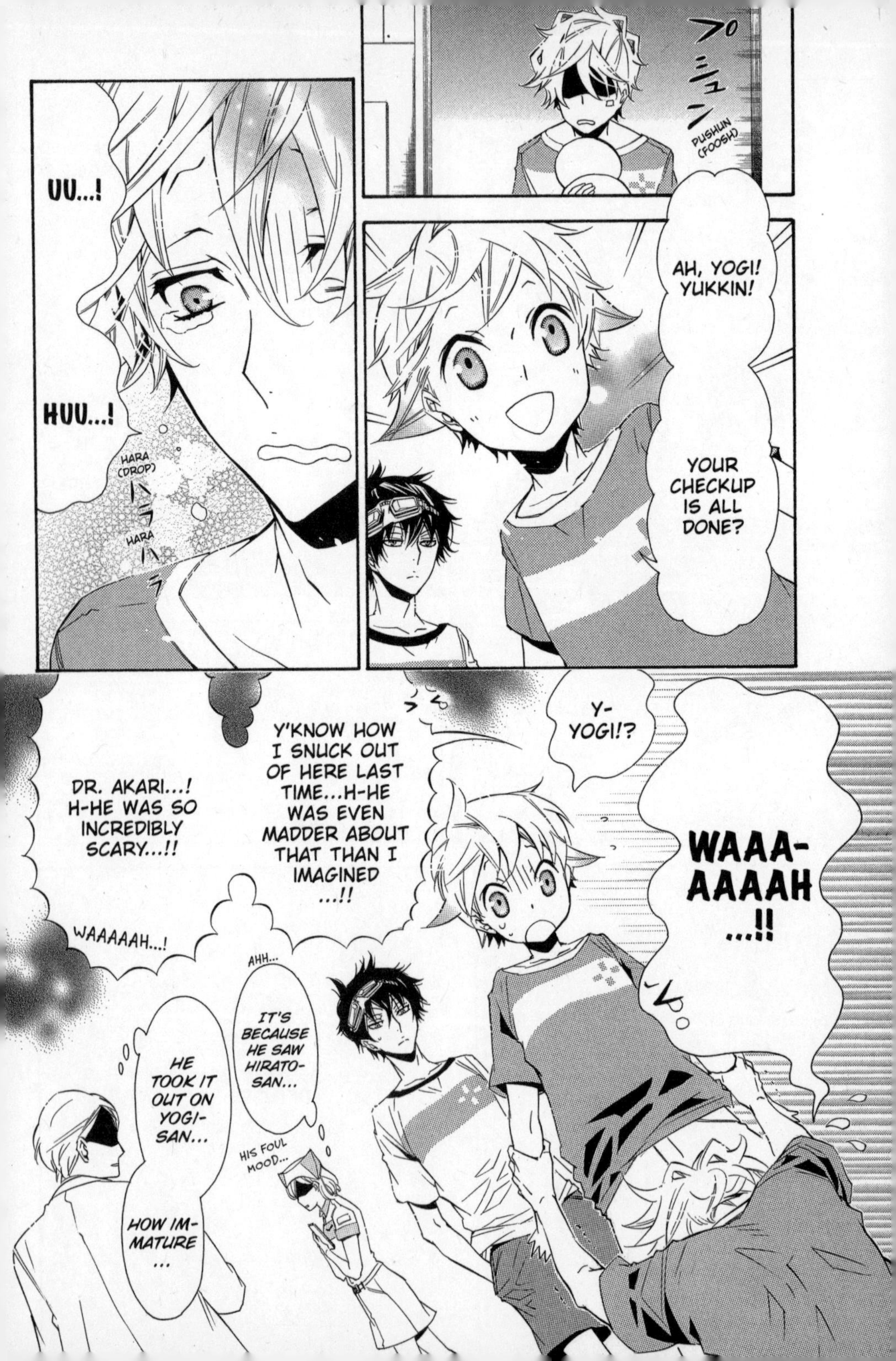
PUSHUN (FOOSH)
AH, YOGI! YUKKIN!
YOUR CHECKUP IS ALL DONE?
UU...!
HUU...!
HARA (DROP)
HARA
WAAA-AAAAH ...!!
Y-YOGI!?
Y'KNOW HOW I SNUCK OUT OF HERE LAST TIME...H-HE WAS EVEN MADDER ABOUT THAT THAN I IMAGINED ...!!
DR. AKARI...! H-HE WAS SO INCREDIBLY SCARY...!!
WAAAAAH...!
AHH...
IT'S BECAUSE HE SAW HIRATO-SAN...
HE TOOK IT OUT ON YOGI-SAN...
HIS FOUL MOOD...
HOW IM-MATURE ...

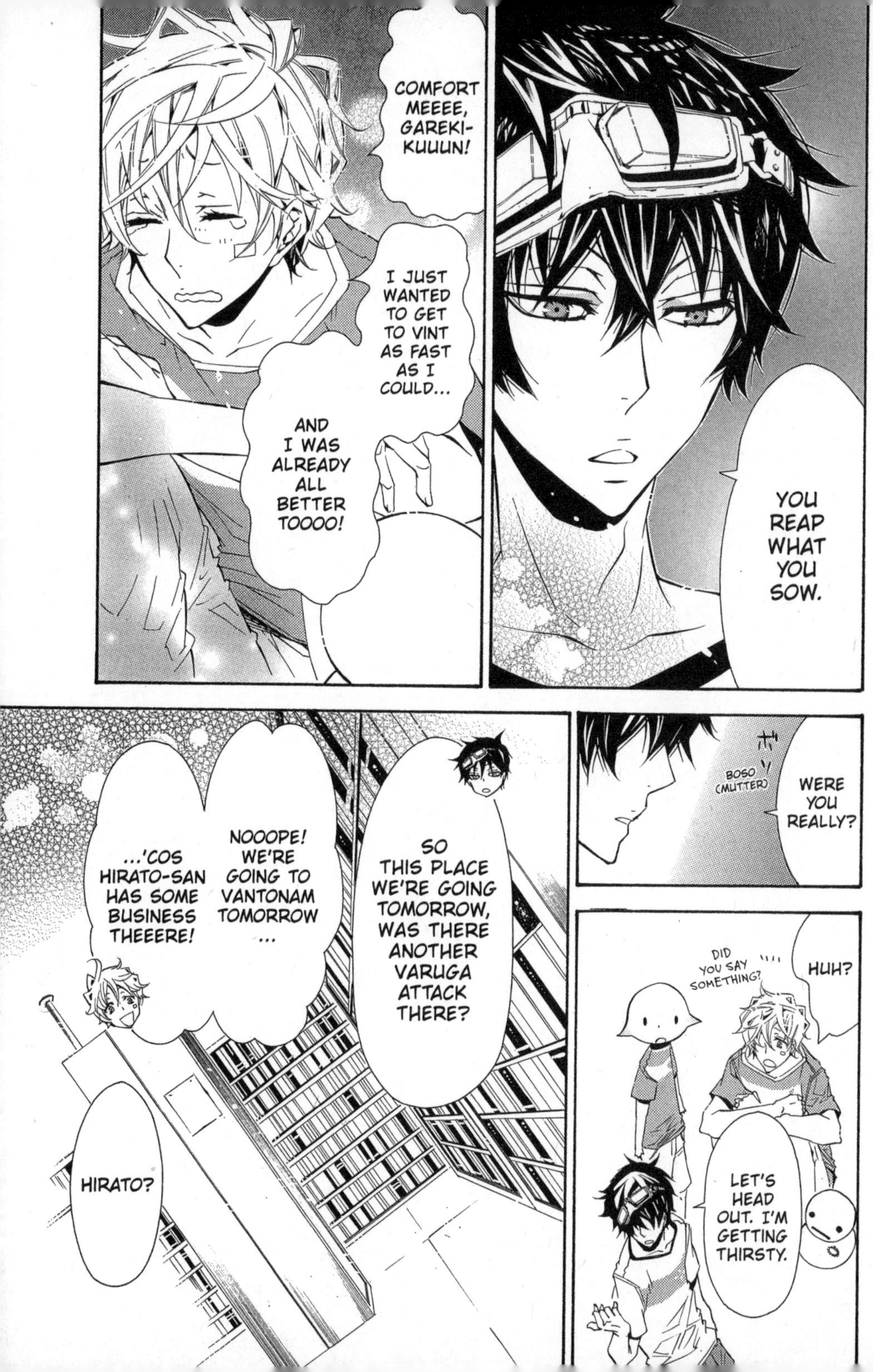
YOU REAP WHAT YOU SOW.
COMFORT MEEEE, GAREKI-KUUUN!
I JUST WANTED TO GET TO VINT AS FAST AS I COULD...
AND I WAS ALREADY ALL BETTER TOOOO!
BOSO (MUTTER)
WERE YOU REALLY?
HUH?
DID YOU SAY SOMETHING?
LET'S HEAD OUT. I'M GETTING THIRSTY.
SO THIS PLACE WE'RE GOING TOMORROW, WAS THERE ANOTHER VARUGA ATTACK THERE?
NOOOPE! WE'RE GOING TO VANTONAM TOMORROW...
...'COS HIRATO-SAN HAS SOME BUSINESS THEEERE!
HIRATO?

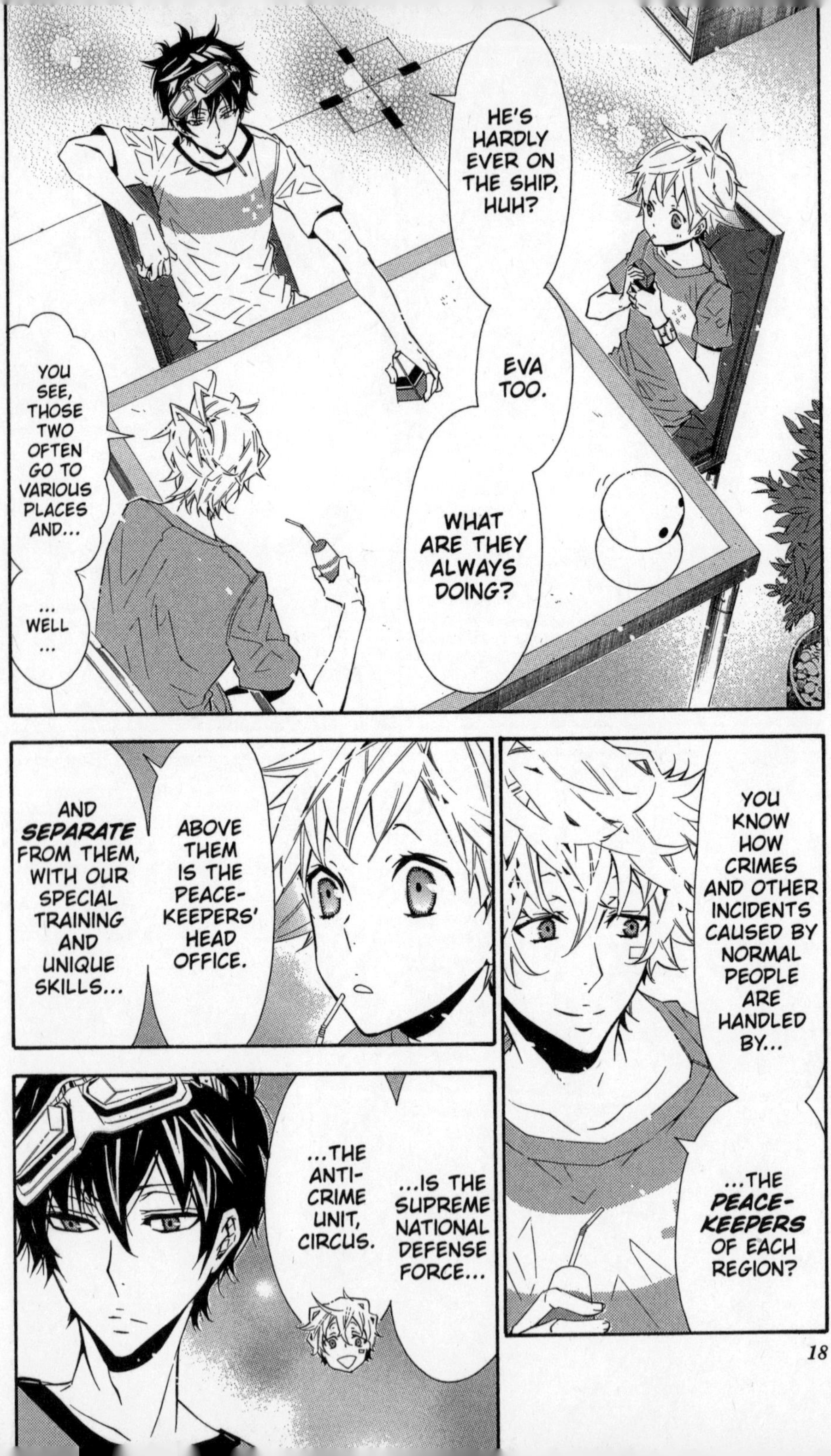
HE'S HARDLY EVER ON THE SHIP, HUH?
EVA TOO.
WHAT ARE THEY ALWAYS DOING?
YOU SEE, THOSE TWO OFTEN GO TO VARIOUS PLACES AND...
...WELL...
YOU KNOW HOW CRIMES AND OTHER INCIDENTS CAUSED BY NORMAL PEOPLE ARE HANDLED BY...
...THE *PEACE-KEEPERS* OF EACH REGION?
ABOVE THEM IS THE PEACE-KEEPERS' HEAD OFFICE.
AND *SEPARATE* FROM THEM, WITH OUR SPECIAL TRAINING AND UNIQUE SKILLS...
...IS THE SUPREME NATIONAL DEFENSE FORCE...
...THE ANTI-CRIME UNIT, CIRCUS.

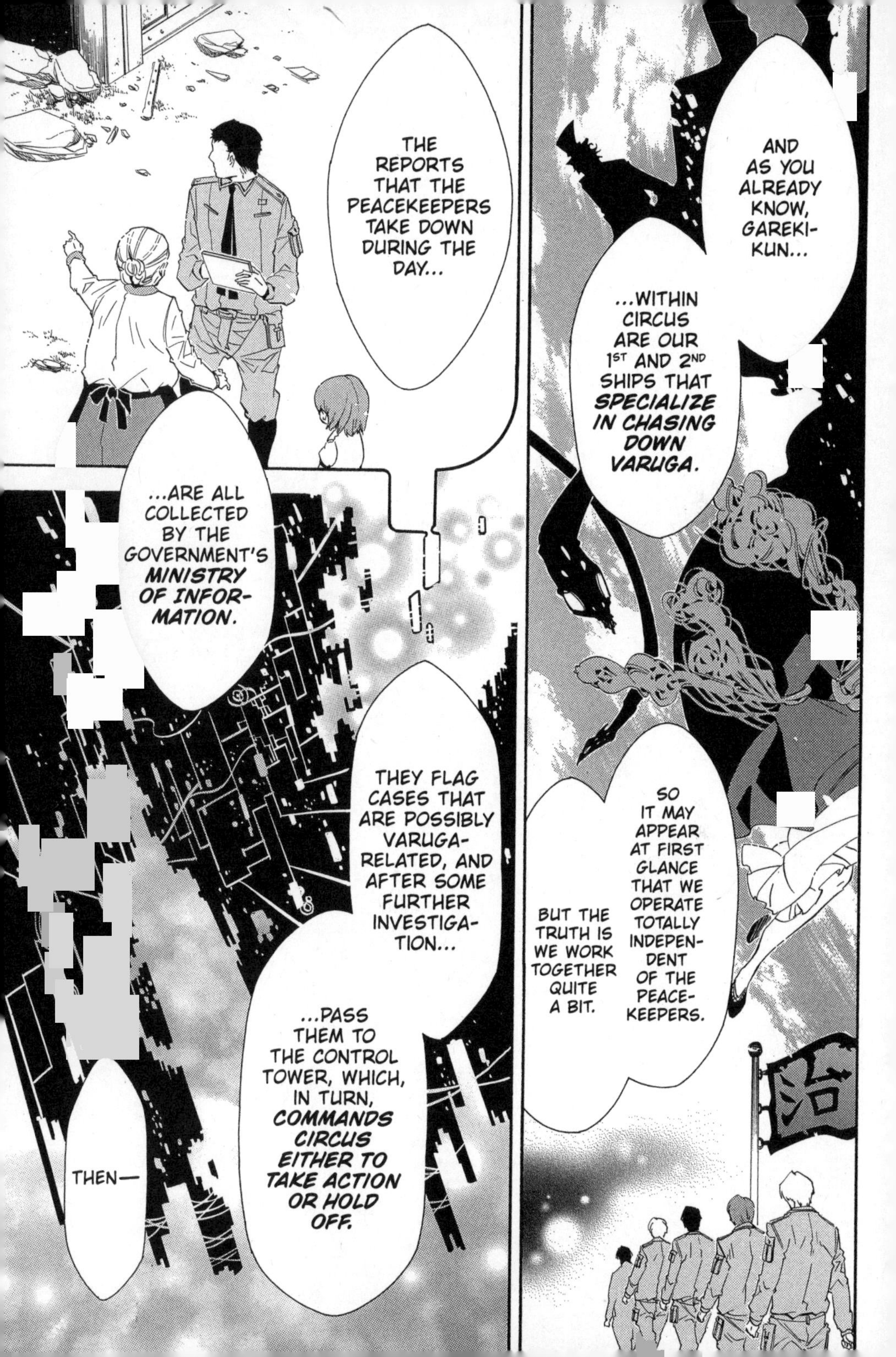
AND AS YOU ALREADY KNOW, GAREKI-KUN...
...WITHIN CIRCUS ARE OUR 1ST AND 2ND SHIPS THAT **SPECIALIZE IN CHASING DOWN VARUGA.**
SO IT MAY APPEAR AT FIRST GLANCE THAT WE OPERATE TOTALLY INDEPENDENT OF THE PEACE-KEEPERS.
BUT THE TRUTH IS WE WORK TOGETHER QUITE A BIT.
THE REPORTS THAT THE PEACEKEEPERS TAKE DOWN DURING THE DAY...
...ARE ALL COLLECTED BY THE GOVERNMENT'S ***MINISTRY OF INFOR-MATION.***
THEY FLAG CASES THAT ARE POSSIBLY VARUGA-RELATED, AND AFTER SOME FURTHER INVESTIGA-TION...
...PASS THEM TO THE CONTROL TOWER, WHICH, IN TURN, ***COMMANDS CIRCUS EITHER TO TAKE ACTION OR HOLD OFF.***
THEN—

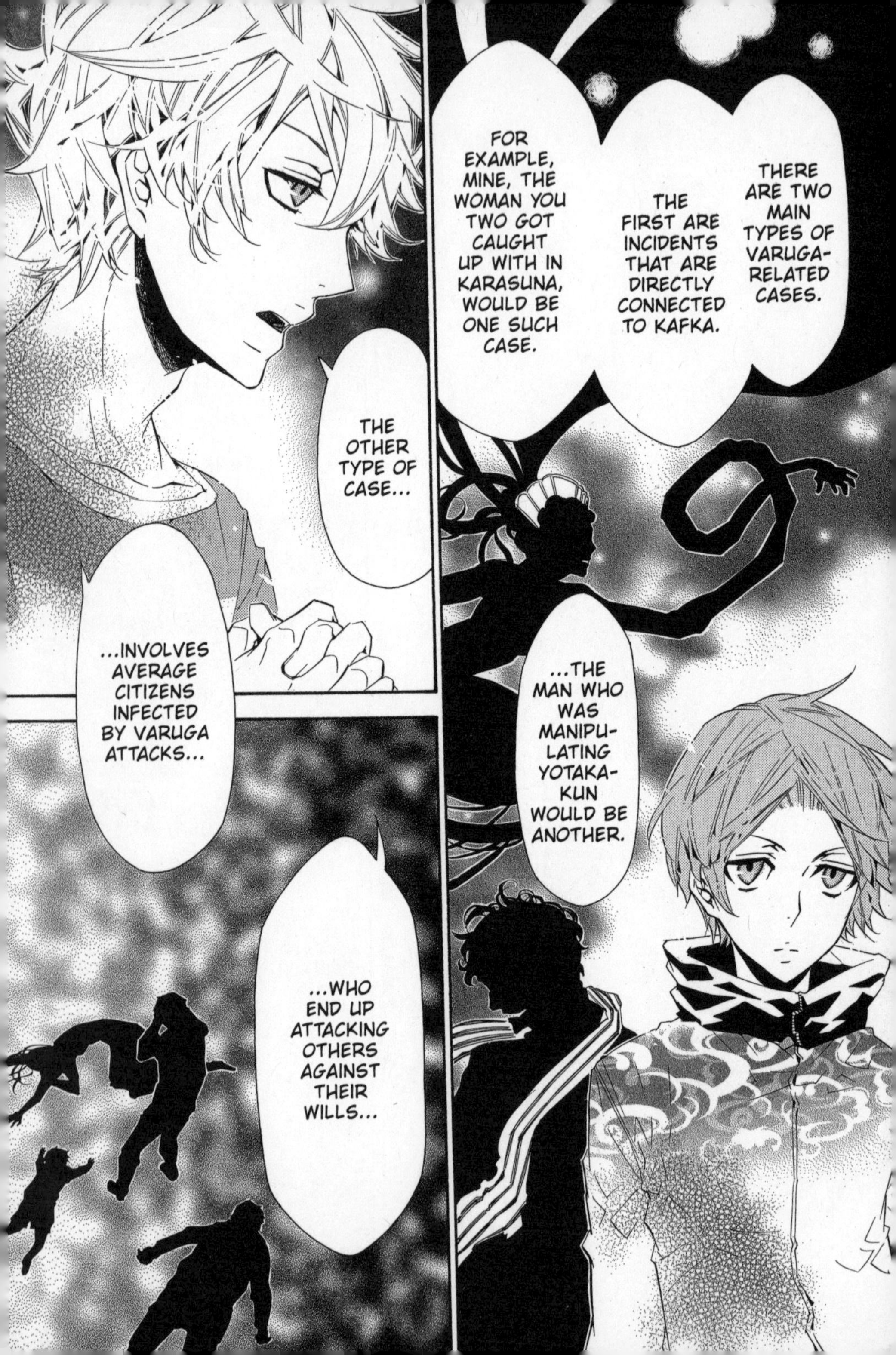
THERE ARE TWO MAIN TYPES OF VARUGA-RELATED CASES.
THE FIRST ARE INCIDENTS THAT ARE DIRECTLY CONNECTED TO KAFKA.
FOR EXAMPLE, MINE, THE WOMAN YOU TWO GOT CAUGHT UP WITH IN KARASUNA, WOULD BE ONE SUCH CASE.
...THE MAN WHO WAS MANIPULATING YOTAKA-KUN WOULD BE ANOTHER.
THE OTHER TYPE OF CASE...
...INVOLVES AVERAGE CITIZENS INFECTED BY VARUGA ATTACKS...
...WHO END UP ATTACKING OTHERS AGAINST THEIR WILLS...

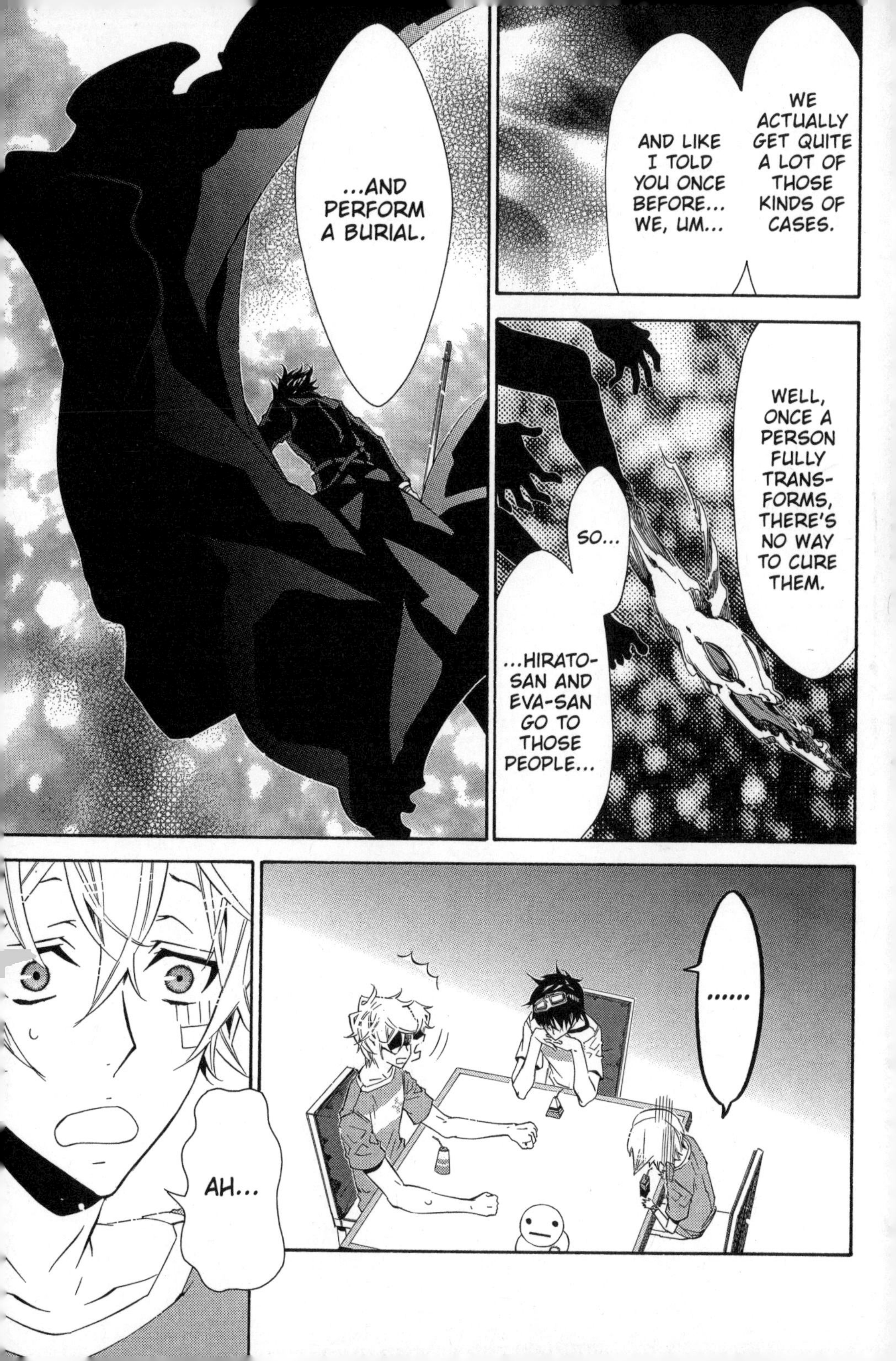
WE ACTUALLY GET QUITE A LOT OF THOSE KINDS OF CASES.
AND LIKE I TOLD YOU ONCE BEFORE... WE, UM...
WELL, ONCE A PERSON FULLY TRANS-FORMS, THERE'S NO WAY TO CURE THEM.
SO...
...HIRATO-SAN AND EVA-SAN GO TO THOSE PEOPLE...
...AND PERFORM A BURIAL.
......
AH...

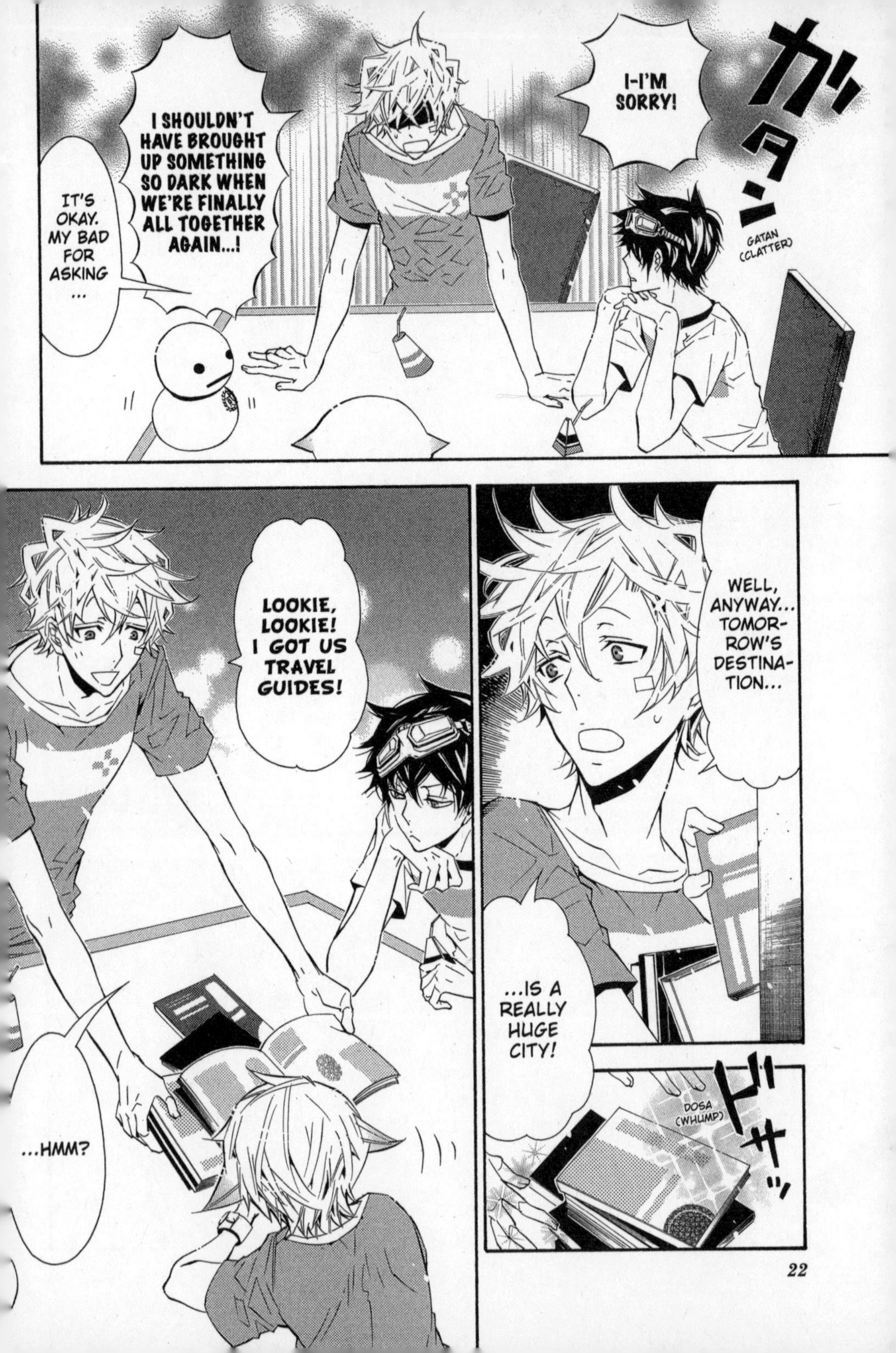

GATAN (CLATTER)
I-I'M SORRY!
I SHOULDN'T HAVE BROUGHT UP SOMETHING SO DARK WHEN WE'RE FINALLY ALL TOGETHER AGAIN...!
IT'S OKAY. MY BAD FOR ASKING ...
WELL, ANYWAY... TOMORROW'S DESTINATION...
...IS A REALLY HUGE CITY!
DOSA (WHUMP)
LOOKIE, LOOKIE! I GOT US TRAVEL GUIDES!
...HMM?

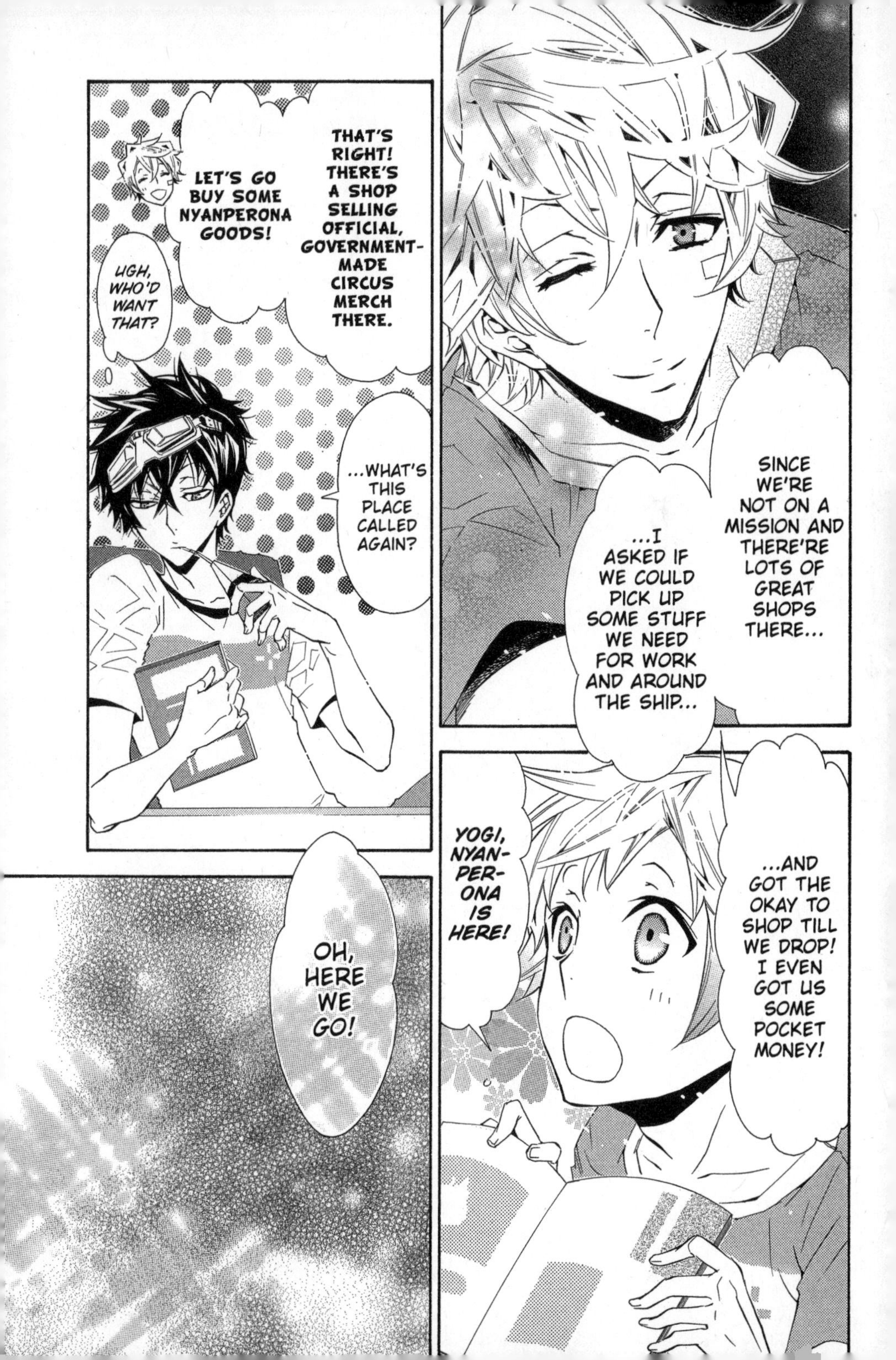
SINCE WE'RE NOT ON A MISSION AND THERE'RE LOTS OF GREAT SHOPS THERE...
...I ASKED IF WE COULD PICK UP SOME STUFF WE NEED FOR WORK AND AROUND THE SHIP...
...AND GOT THE OKAY TO SHOP TILL WE DROP! I EVEN GOT US SOME POCKET MONEY!
YOGI, NYANPERONA IS HERE!
THAT'S RIGHT! THERE'S A SHOP SELLING OFFICIAL, GOVERNMENT-MADE CIRCUS MERCH THERE.
LET'S GO BUY SOME NYANPERONA GOODS!
UGH, WHO'D WANT THAT?
...WHAT'S THIS PLACE CALLED AGAIN?
OH, HERE WE GO!

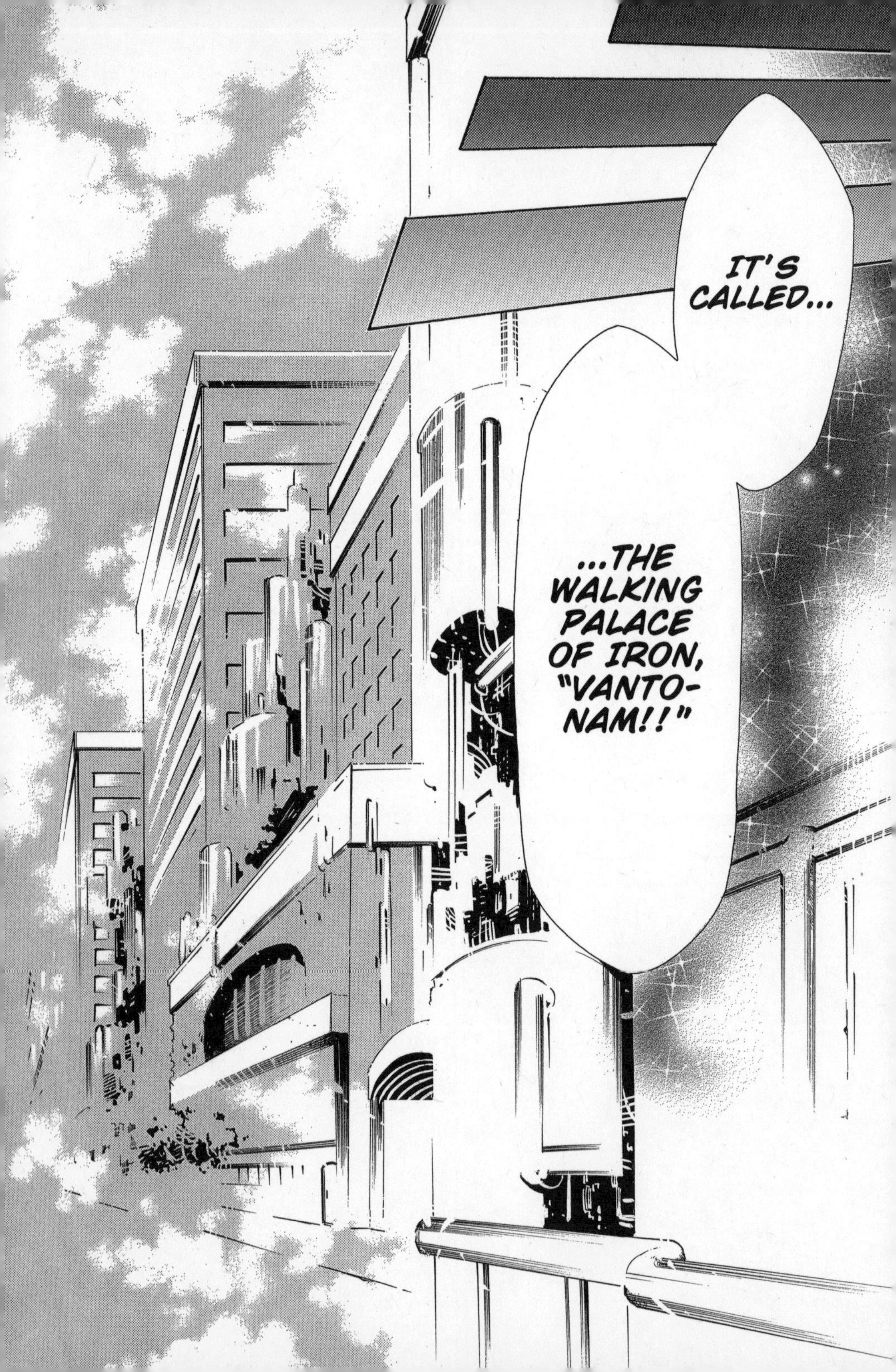
IT'S CALLED...
...THE WALKING PALACE OF IRON, "VANTO-NAM!!"

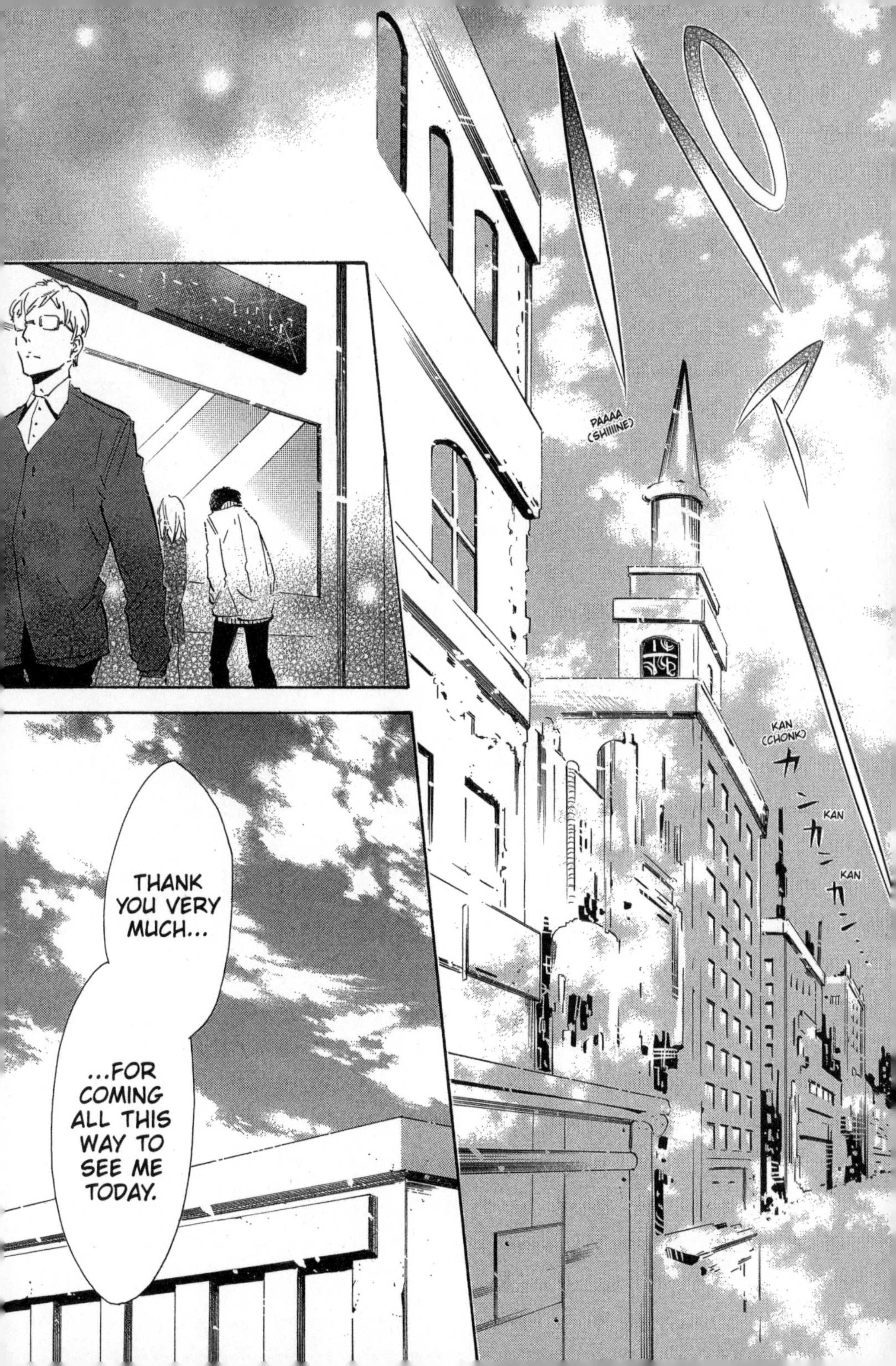
PAAAA (SHIIINE)
KAN (CHONK)
KAN
KAN
THANK YOU VERY MUCH...
...FOR COMING ALL THIS WAY TO SEE ME TODAY.

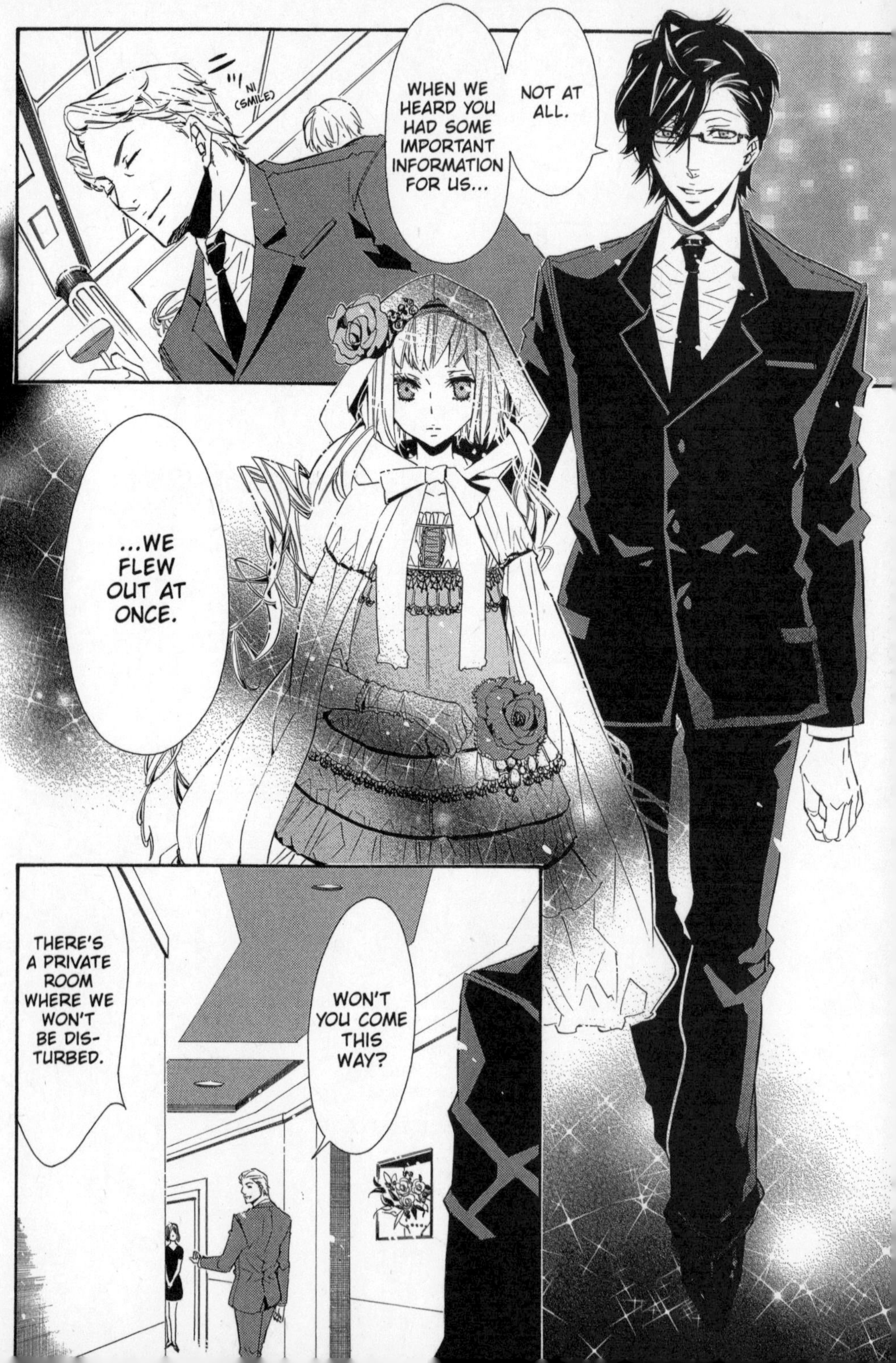
NOT AT ALL.
WHEN WE HEARD YOU HAD SOME IMPORTANT INFORMATION FOR US...
NI (SMILE)
...WE FLEW OUT AT ONCE.
THERE'S A PRIVATE ROOM WHERE WE WON'T BE DIS-TURBED.
WON'T YOU COME THIS WAY?

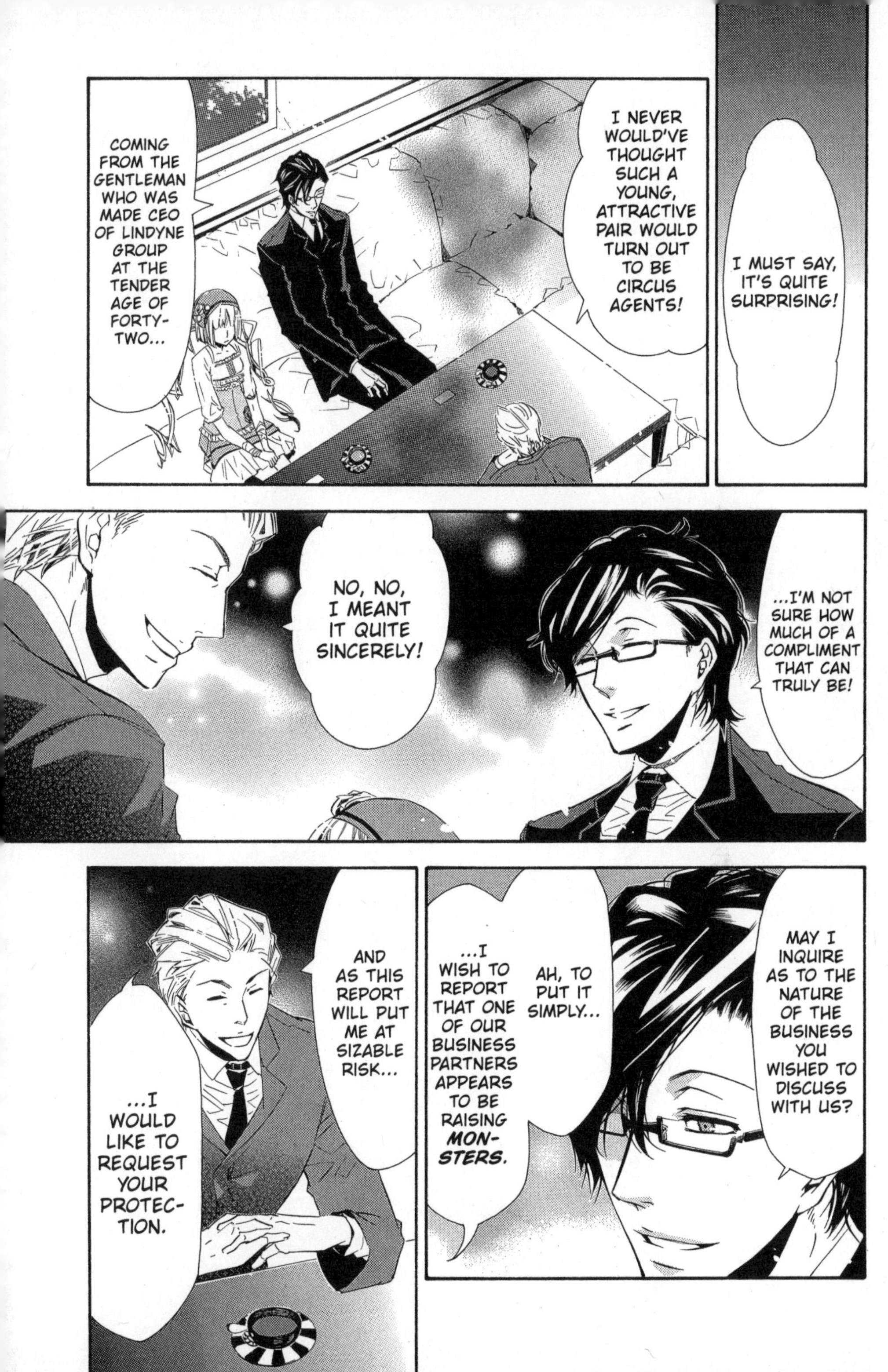

I MUST SAY, IT'S QUITE SURPRISING!
I NEVER WOULD'VE THOUGHT SUCH A YOUNG, ATTRACTIVE PAIR WOULD TURN OUT TO BE CIRCUS AGENTS!
COMING FROM THE GENTLEMAN WHO WAS MADE CEO OF LINDYNE GROUP AT THE TENDER AGE OF FORTY-TWO...
...I'M NOT SURE HOW MUCH OF A COMPLIMENT THAT CAN TRULY BE!
NO, NO, I MEANT IT QUITE SINCERELY!
MAY I INQUIRE AS TO THE NATURE OF THE BUSINESS YOU WISHED TO DISCUSS WITH US?
AH, TO PUT IT SIMPLY...
...I WISH TO REPORT THAT ONE OF OUR BUSINESS PARTNERS APPEARS TO BE RAISING ***MONSTERS.***
AND AS THIS REPORT WILL PUT ME AT SIZABLE RISK...
...I WOULD LIKE TO REQUEST YOUR PROTECTION.

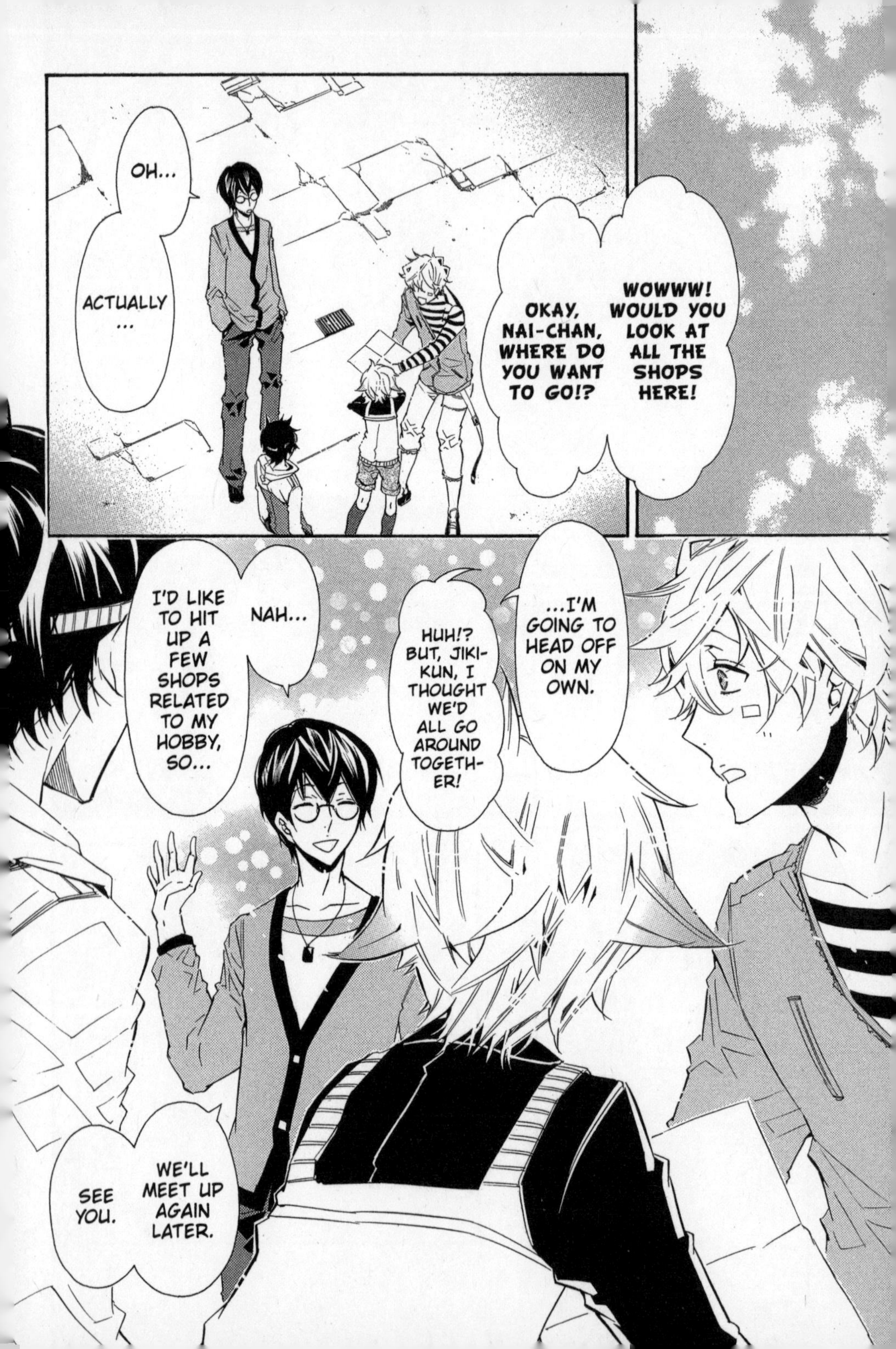
WOWWW! WOULD YOU LOOK AT ALL THE SHOPS HERE!
OKAY, NAI-CHAN, WHERE DO YOU WANT TO GO!?
OH...
ACTUALLY...
...I'M GOING TO HEAD OFF ON MY OWN.
HUH!? BUT, JIKI-KUN, I THOUGHT WE'D ALL GO AROUND TOGETHER!
NAH...
I'D LIKE TO HIT UP A FEW SHOPS RELATED TO MY HOBBY, SO...
WE'LL MEET UP AGAIN LATER.
SEE YOU.

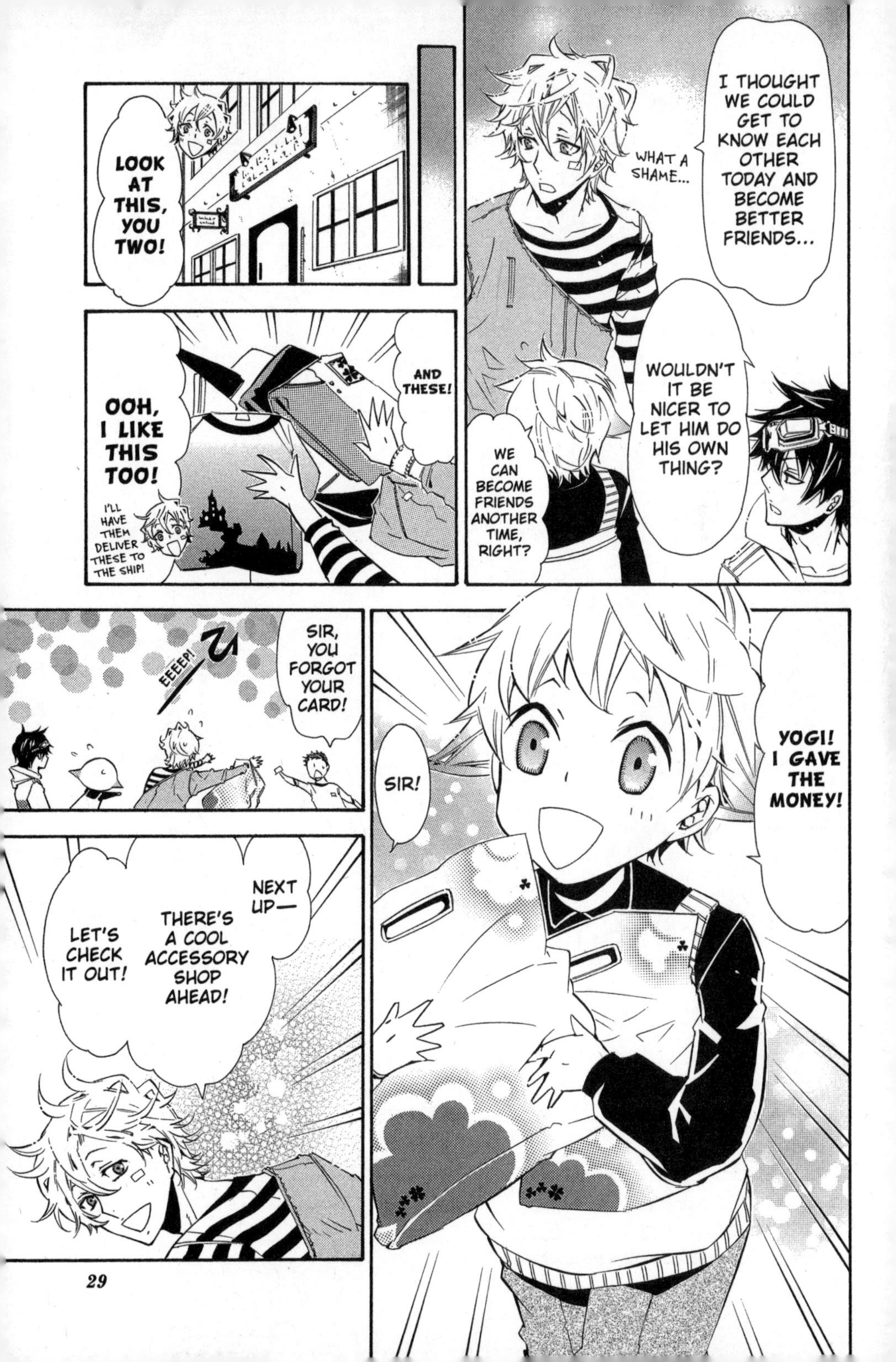
I THOUGHT WE COULD GET TO KNOW EACH OTHER TODAY AND BECOME BETTER FRIENDS...
WHAT A SHAME...
WOULDN'T IT BE NICER TO LET HIM DO HIS OWN THING?
WE CAN BECOME FRIENDS ANOTHER TIME, RIGHT?
LOOK AT THIS, YOU TWO!
AND THESE!
OOH, I LIKE THIS TOO!
I'LL HAVE THEM DELIVER THESE TO THE SHIP!
YOGI! I GAVE THE MONEY!
SIR!
SIR, YOU FORGOT YOUR CARD!
EEEEP!
NEXT UP—
THERE'S A COOL ACCESSORY SHOP AHEAD!
LET'S CHECK IT OUT!

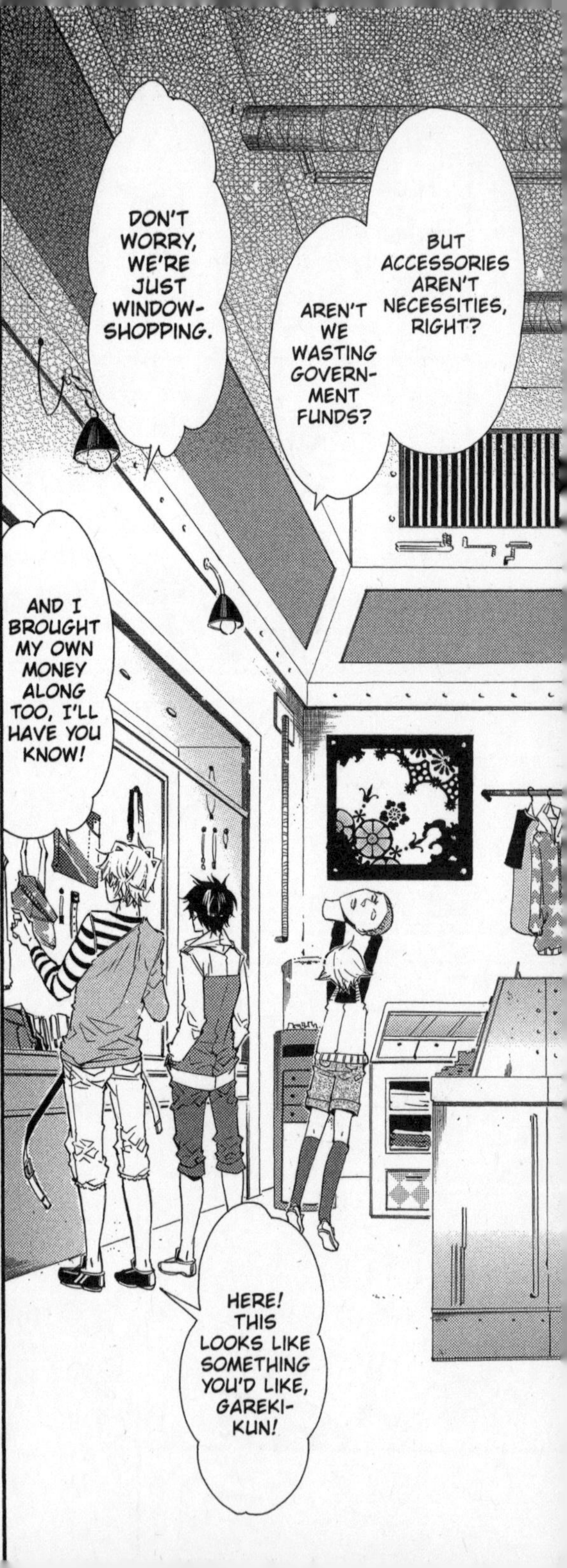
BUT ACCESSORIES AREN'T NECESSITIES, RIGHT?
AREN'T WE WASTING GOVERN-MENT FUNDS?
DON'T WORRY, WE'RE JUST WINDOW-SHOPPING.
AND I BROUGHT MY OWN MONEY ALONG TOO, I'LL HAVE YOU KNOW!
HERE! THIS LOOKS LIKE SOMETHING YOU'D LIKE, GAREKI-KUN!

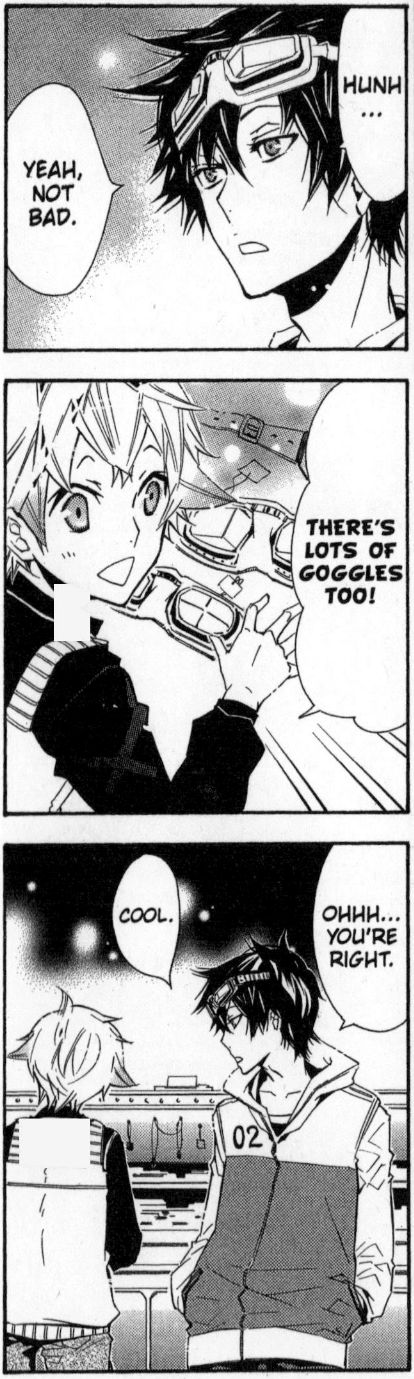
HUNH ...
YEAH, NOT BAD.
THERE'S LOTS OF GOGGLES TOO!
OHHH... YOU'RE RIGHT.
COOL.

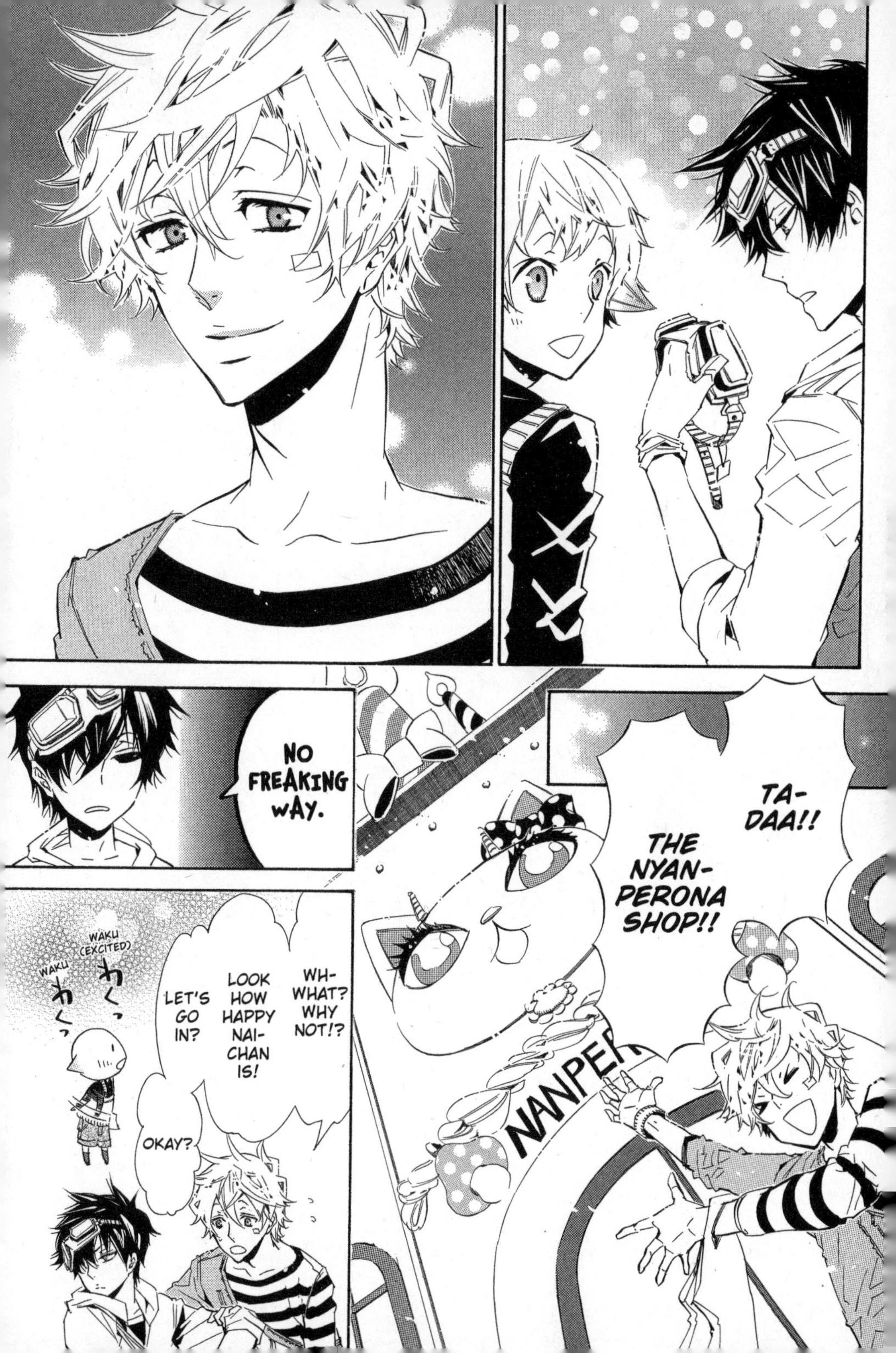
TA-DAA!!
THE NYAN-PERONA SHOP!!
NO FREAKING WAY.
WH-WHAT? WHY NOT!?
LOOK HOW HAPPY NAI-CHAN IS!
LET'S GO IN?
OKAY?
わくっ
WAKU (EXCITED)
わくっ
WAKU

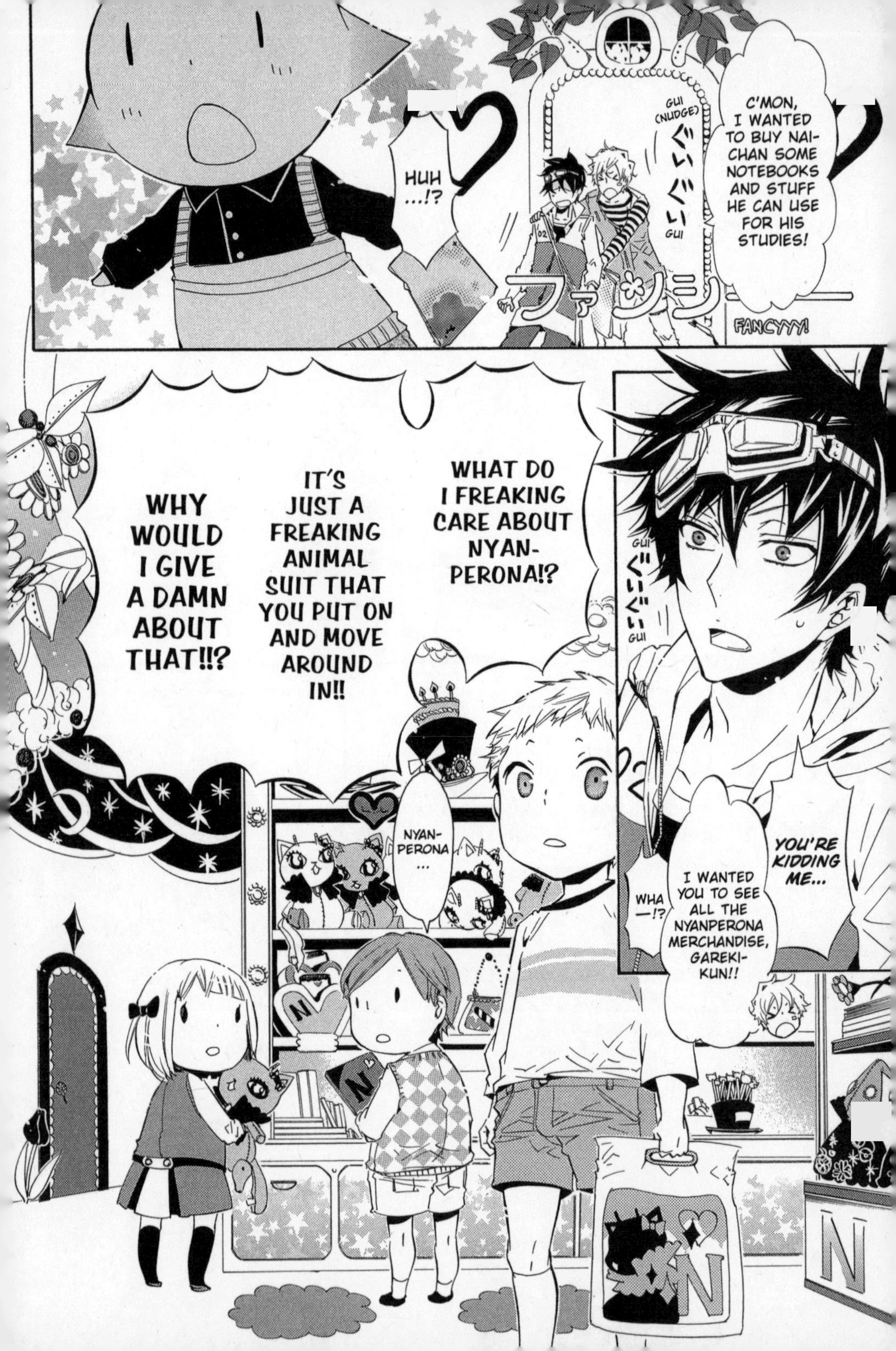
C'MON, I WANTED TO BUY NAI-CHAN SOME NOTEBOOKS AND STUFF HE CAN USE FOR HIS STUDIES!
GUI (NUDGE)
ぐいぐい
GUI
ファンシー
FANCYYY!
HUH ...!?
GUI
ぐいぐい
GUI
WHAT DO I FREAKING CARE ABOUT NYAN-PERONA!?
IT'S JUST A FREAKING ANIMAL SUIT THAT YOU PUT ON AND MOVE AROUND IN!!
WHY WOULD I GIVE A DAMN ABOUT THAT!!?
YOU'RE KIDDING ME...
I WANTED YOU TO SEE ALL THE NYANPERONA MERCHANDISE, GAREKI-KUN!!
WHA—!?
NYAN-PERONA ...

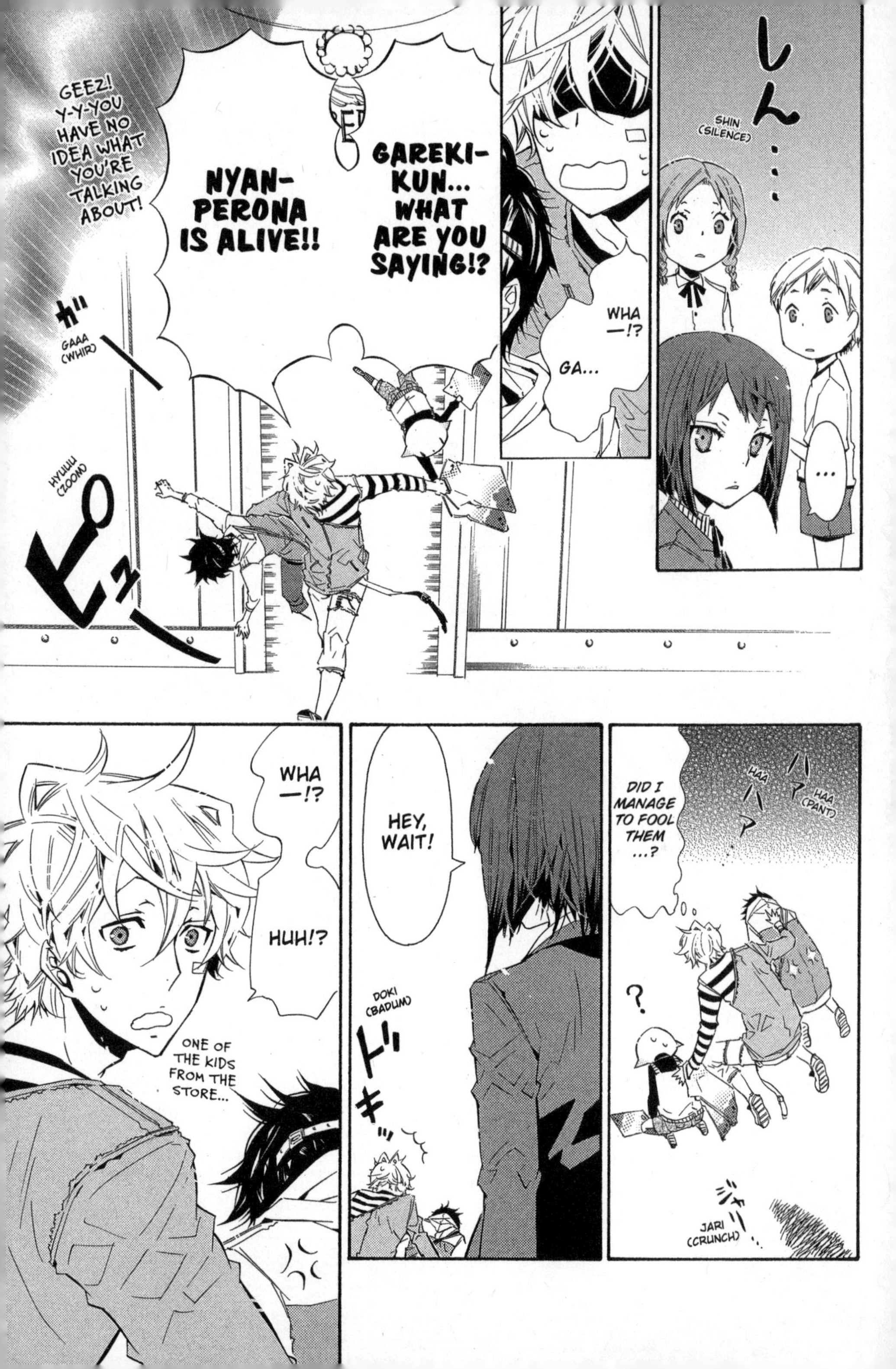

しん…
SHIN (SILENCE)
...
WHA—!?
GA...
GAREKI-KUN... WHAT ARE YOU SAYING!?
NYAN-PERONA IS ALIVE!!
GEEZ! Y-Y-YOU HAVE NO IDEA WHAT YOU'RE TALKING ABOUT!
GAAA (WHIR)
HYUUU (ZOOM)
ハァハァ
HAA HAA (PANT)
DID I MANAGE TO FOOL THEM ...?
?
ジャリ…
JARI (CRUNCH)
HEY, WAIT!
ドキ
DOKI (BADUM)
WHA—!?
HUH!?
ONE OF THE KIDS FROM THE STORE...

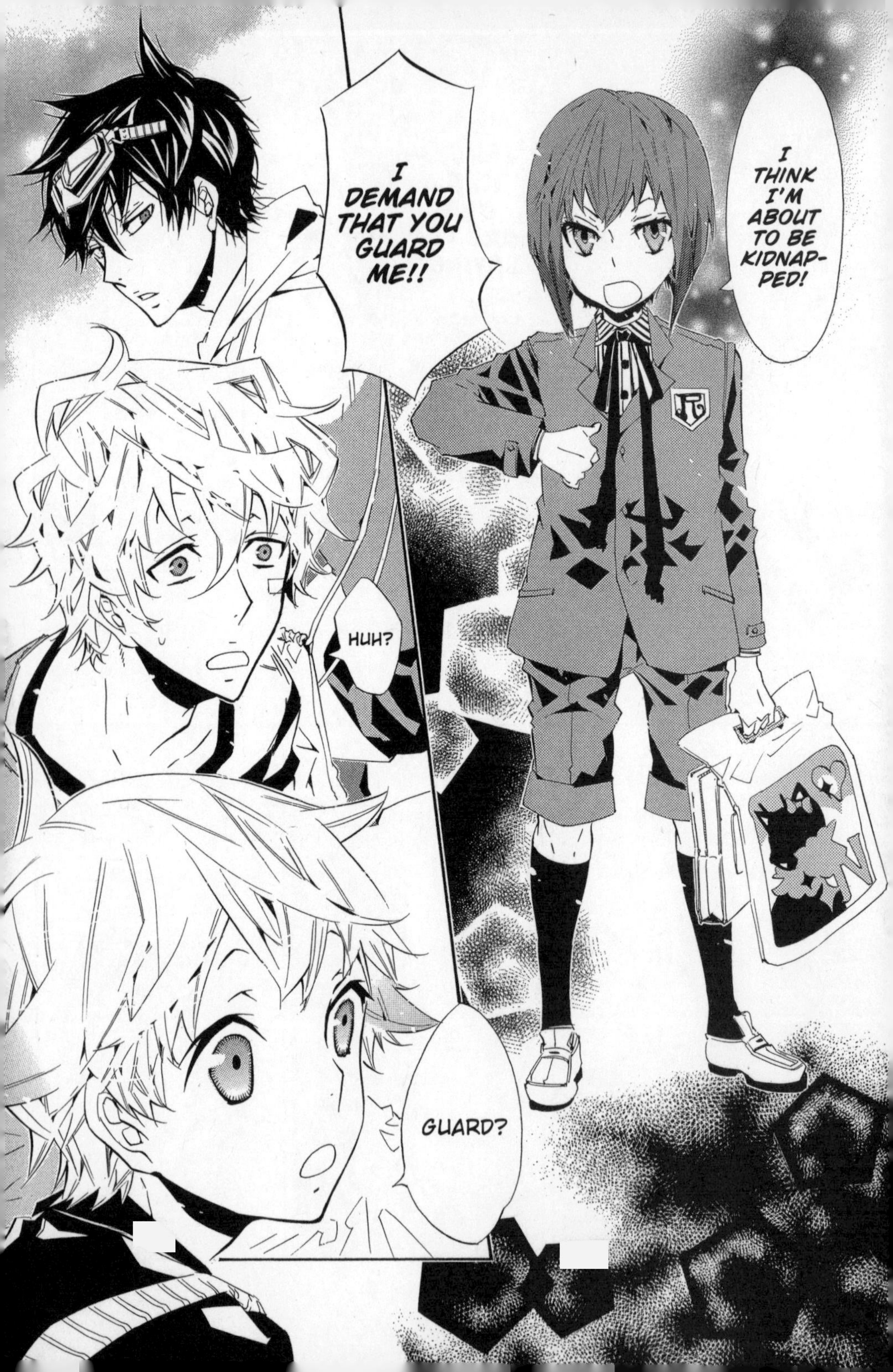
I THINK I'M ABOUT TO BE KIDNAP-PED!
I DEMAND THAT YOU GUARD ME!!
HUH?
GUARD?

Score 26: Yanari

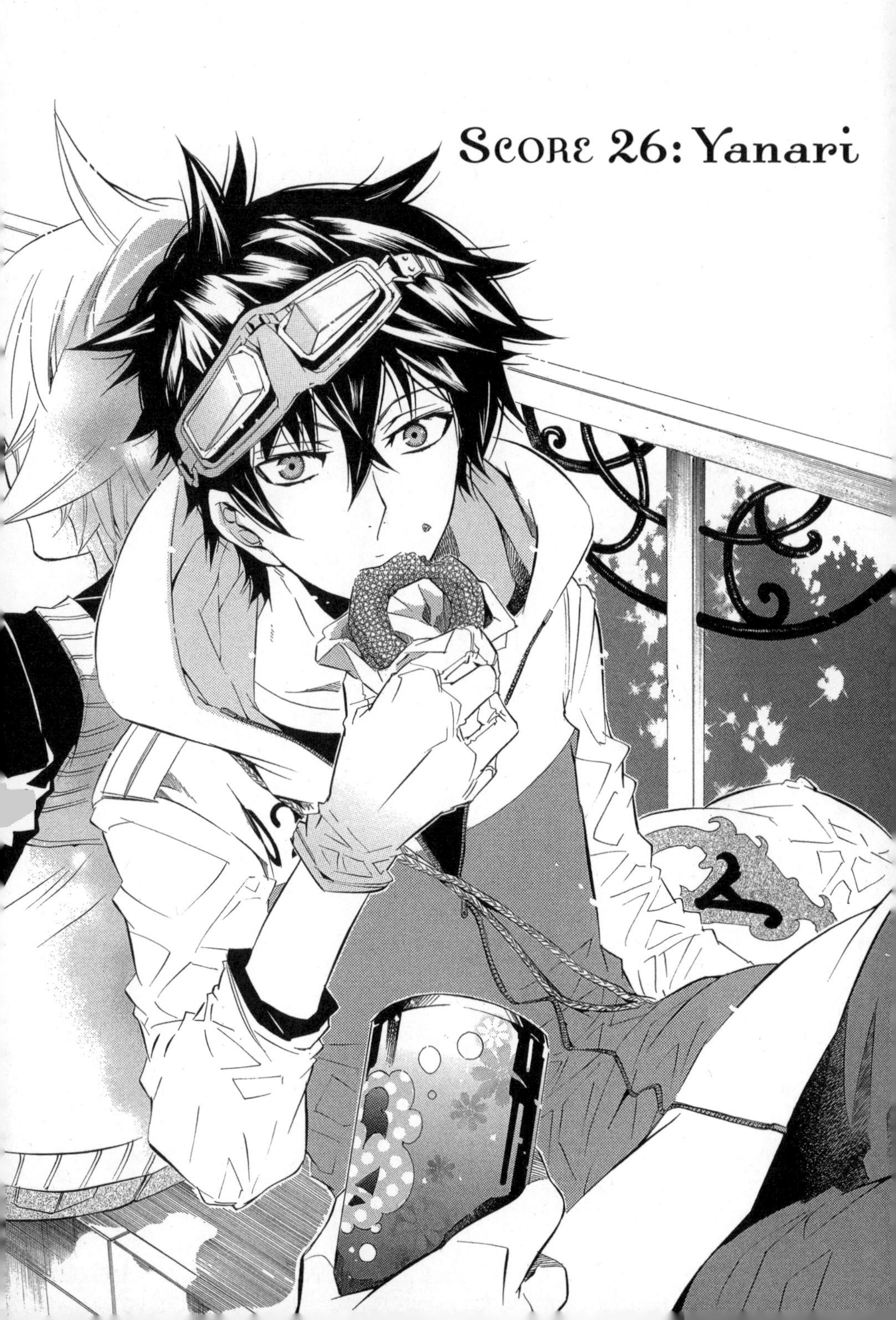

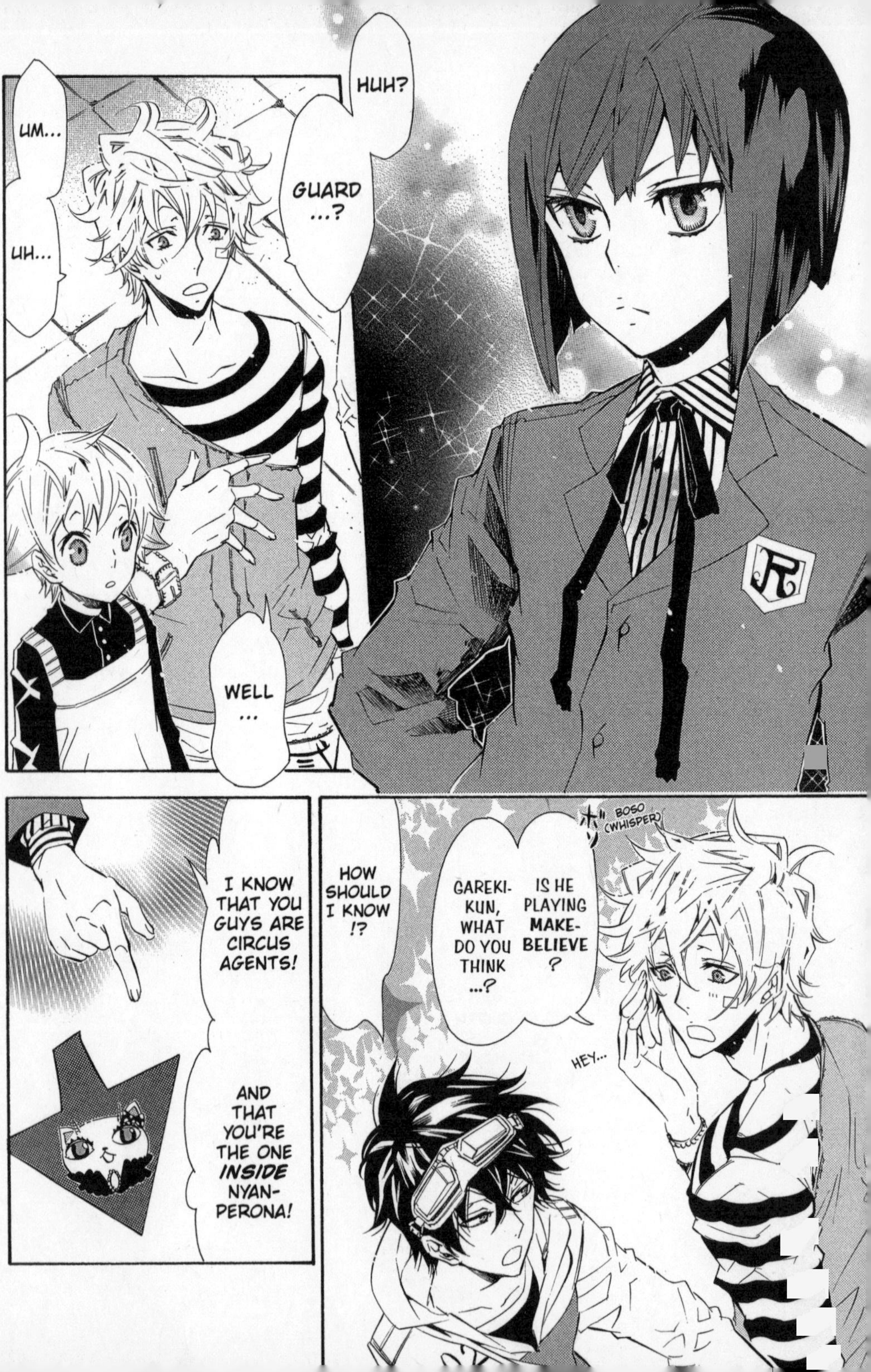
HUH?
GUARD ...?
UM...
UH...
WELL ...
BOSO (WHISPER)
IS HE PLAYING MAKE-BELIEVE?
GAREKI-KUN, WHAT DO YOU THINK ...?
HOW SHOULD I KNOW !?
HEY...
I KNOW THAT YOU GUYS ARE CIRCUS AGENTS!
AND THAT YOU'RE THE ONE INSIDE NYAN-PERONA!

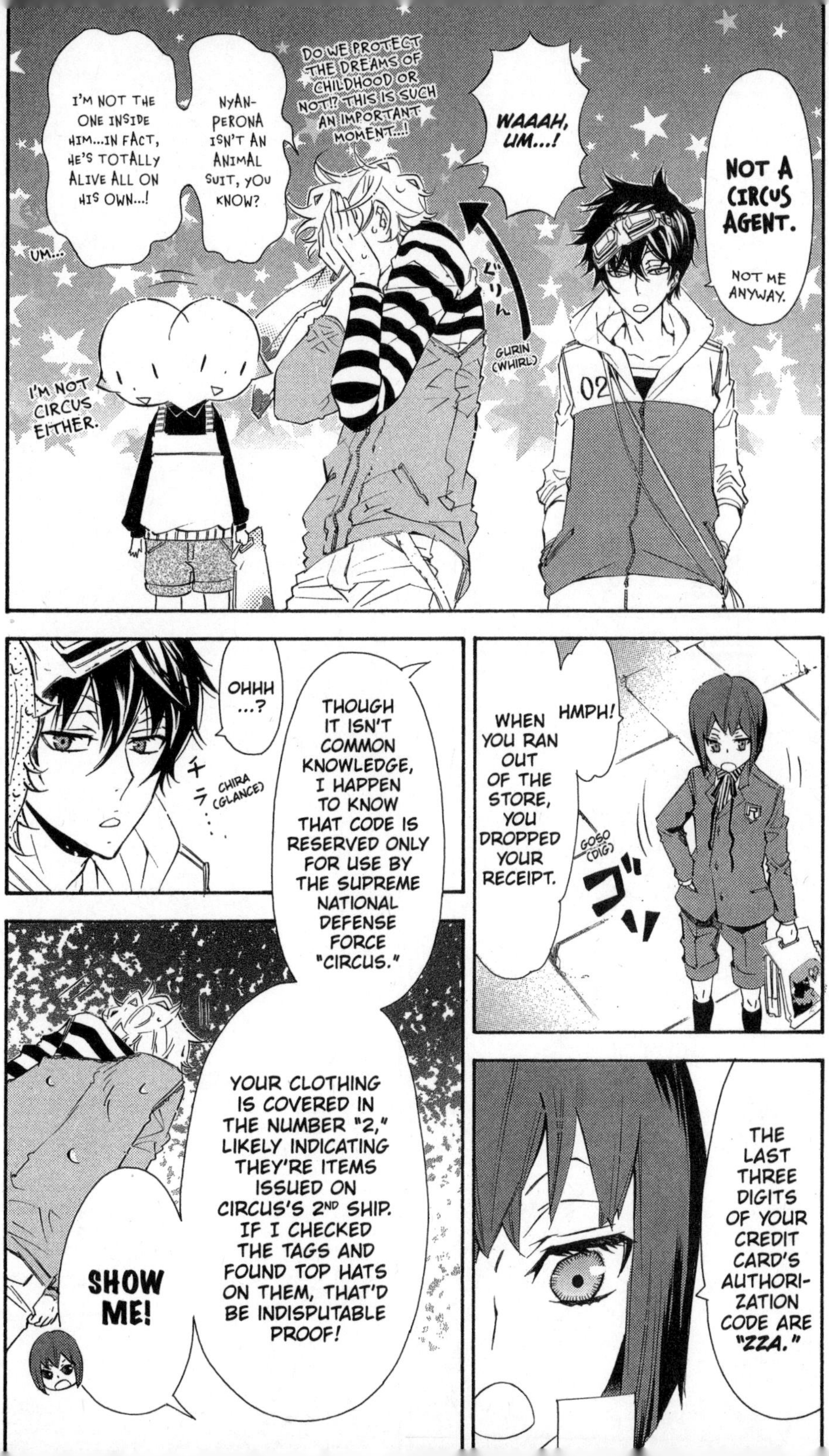
NOT A CIRCUS AGENT.
NOT ME ANYWAY.
WAAAH, UM...!
ぐりん
GURIN (WHIRL)
DO WE PROTECT THE DREAMS OF CHILDHOOD OR NOT!? THIS IS SUCH AN IMPORTANT MOMENT...!
NYAN-PERONA ISN'T AN ANIMAL SUIT, YOU KNOW?
I'M NOT THE ONE INSIDE HIM...IN FACT, HE'S TOTALLY ALIVE ALL ON HIS OWN...!
UM...
I'M NOT CIRCUS EITHER.
HMPH!
WHEN YOU RAN OUT OF THE STORE, YOU DROPPED YOUR RECEIPT.
ゴソ
GOSO (DIG)
THE LAST THREE DIGITS OF YOUR CREDIT CARD'S AUTHORIZATION CODE ARE "ZZA."
OHHH ...?
チラ
CHIRA (GLANCE)
THOUGH IT ISN'T COMMON KNOWLEDGE, I HAPPEN TO KNOW THAT CODE IS RESERVED ONLY FOR USE BY THE SUPREME NATIONAL DEFENSE FORCE "CIRCUS."
YOUR CLOTHING IS COVERED IN THE NUMBER "2," LIKELY INDICATING THEY'RE ITEMS ISSUED ON CIRCUS'S 2ND SHIP. IF I CHECKED THE TAGS AND FOUND TOP HATS ON THEM, THAT'D BE INDISPUTABLE PROOF!
SHOW ME!

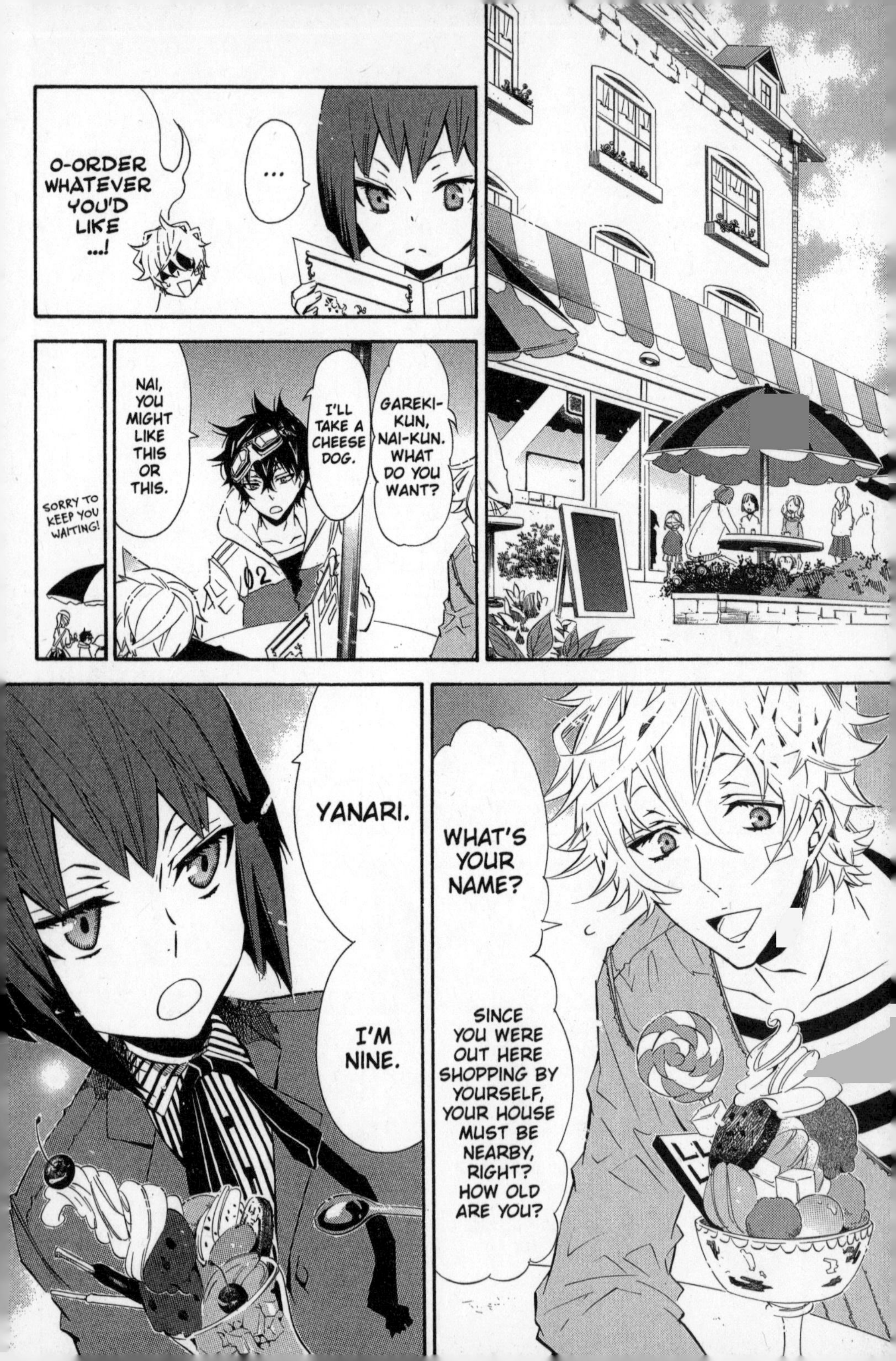

...
O-ORDER WHATEVER YOU'D LIKE ...!
GAREKI-KUN, NAI-KUN. WHAT DO YOU WANT?
I'LL TAKE A CHEESE DOG.
NAI, YOU MIGHT LIKE THIS OR THIS.
SORRY TO KEEP YOU WAITING!
WHAT'S YOUR NAME?
SINCE YOU WERE OUT HERE SHOPPING BY YOURSELF, YOUR HOUSE MUST BE NEARBY, RIGHT? HOW OLD ARE YOU?
YANARI.
I'M NINE.

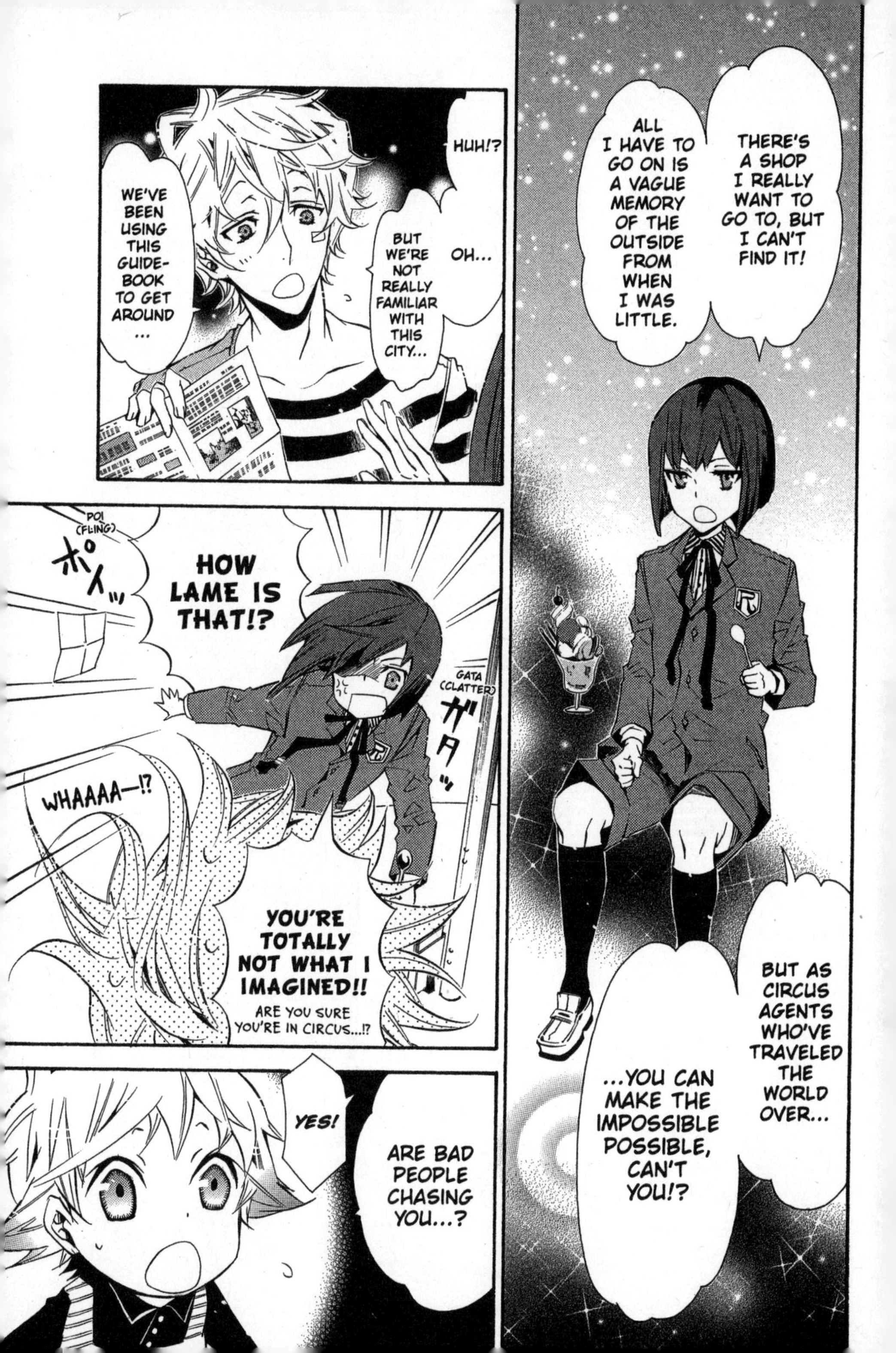
THERE'S A SHOP I REALLY WANT TO GO TO, BUT I CAN'T FIND IT!
ALL I HAVE TO GO ON IS A VAGUE MEMORY OF THE OUTSIDE FROM WHEN I WAS LITTLE.
BUT AS CIRCUS AGENTS WHO'VE TRAVELED THE WORLD OVER...
...YOU CAN MAKE THE IMPOSSIBLE POSSIBLE, CAN'T YOU!?
HUH!?
OH...
BUT WE'RE NOT REALLY FAMILIAR WITH THIS CITY...
WE'VE BEEN USING THIS GUIDE-BOOK TO GET AROUND...
HOW LAME IS THAT!?
GATA (CLATTER)
ガタッ
POI (FLING)
ポイッ
WHAAAA—!?
YOU'RE TOTALLY NOT WHAT I IMAGINED!!
ARE YOU SURE YOU'RE IN CIRCUS...!?
YES!
ARE BAD PEOPLE CHASING YOU...?

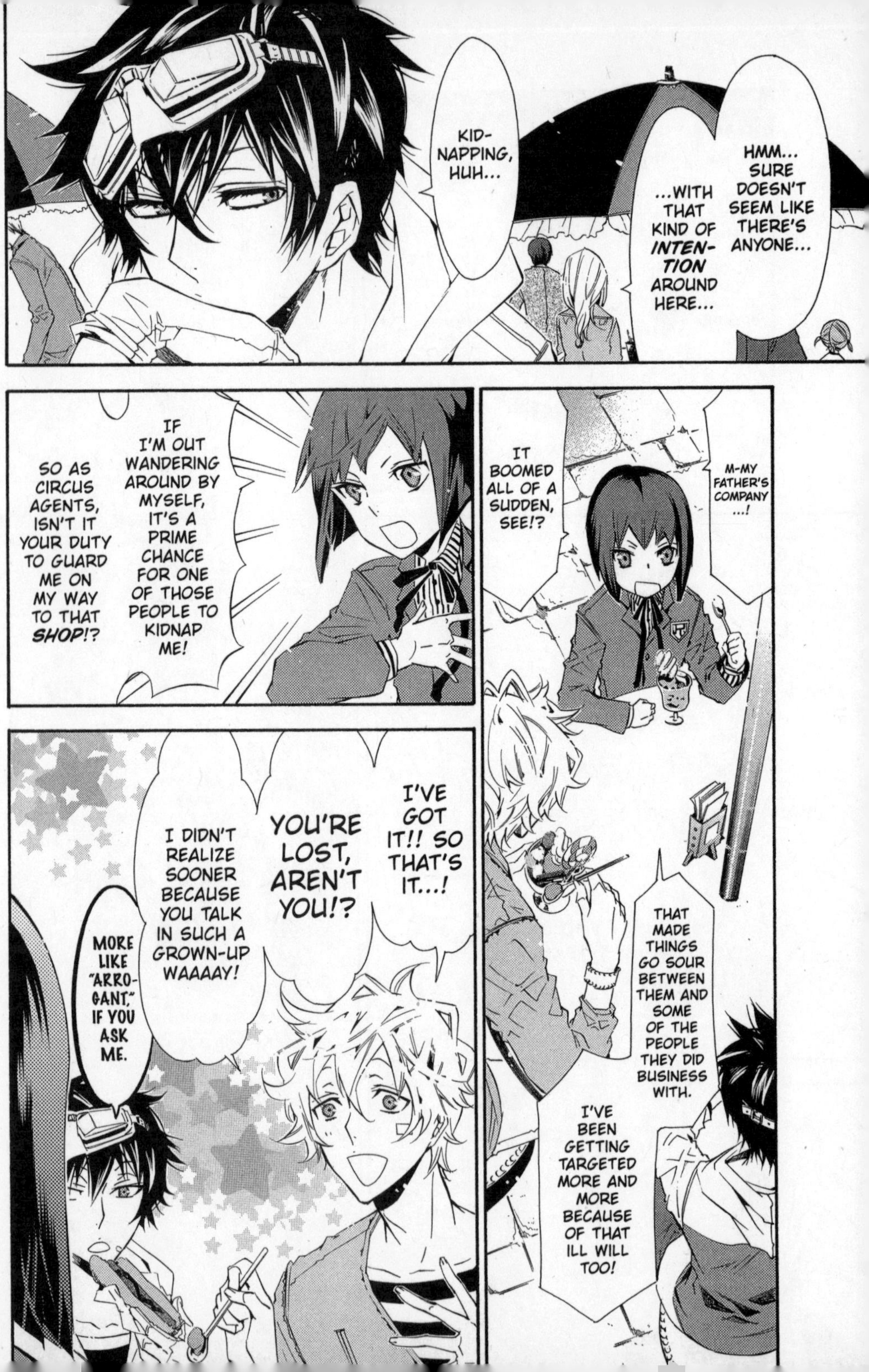
HMM... SURE DOESN'T SEEM LIKE THERE'S ANYONE...
...WITH THAT KIND OF *INTENTION* AROUND HERE...
KID-NAPPING, HUH...
M-MY FATHER'S COMPANY ...!
IT BOOMED ALL OF A SUDDEN, SEE!?
THAT MADE THINGS GO SOUR BETWEEN THEM AND SOME OF THE PEOPLE THEY DID BUSINESS WITH.
I'VE BEEN GETTING TARGETED MORE AND MORE BECAUSE OF THAT ILL WILL TOO!
IF I'M OUT WANDERING AROUND BY MYSELF, IT'S A PRIME CHANCE FOR ONE OF THOSE PEOPLE TO KIDNAP ME!
SO AS CIRCUS AGENTS, ISN'T IT YOUR DUTY TO GUARD ME ON MY WAY TO THAT *SHOP*!?
I'VE GOT IT!! SO THAT'S IT...!
YOU'RE LOST, AREN'T YOU!?
I DIDN'T REALIZE SOONER BECAUSE YOU TALK IN SUCH A GROWN-UP WAAAAY!
MORE LIKE "ARRO-GANT," IF YOU ASK ME.

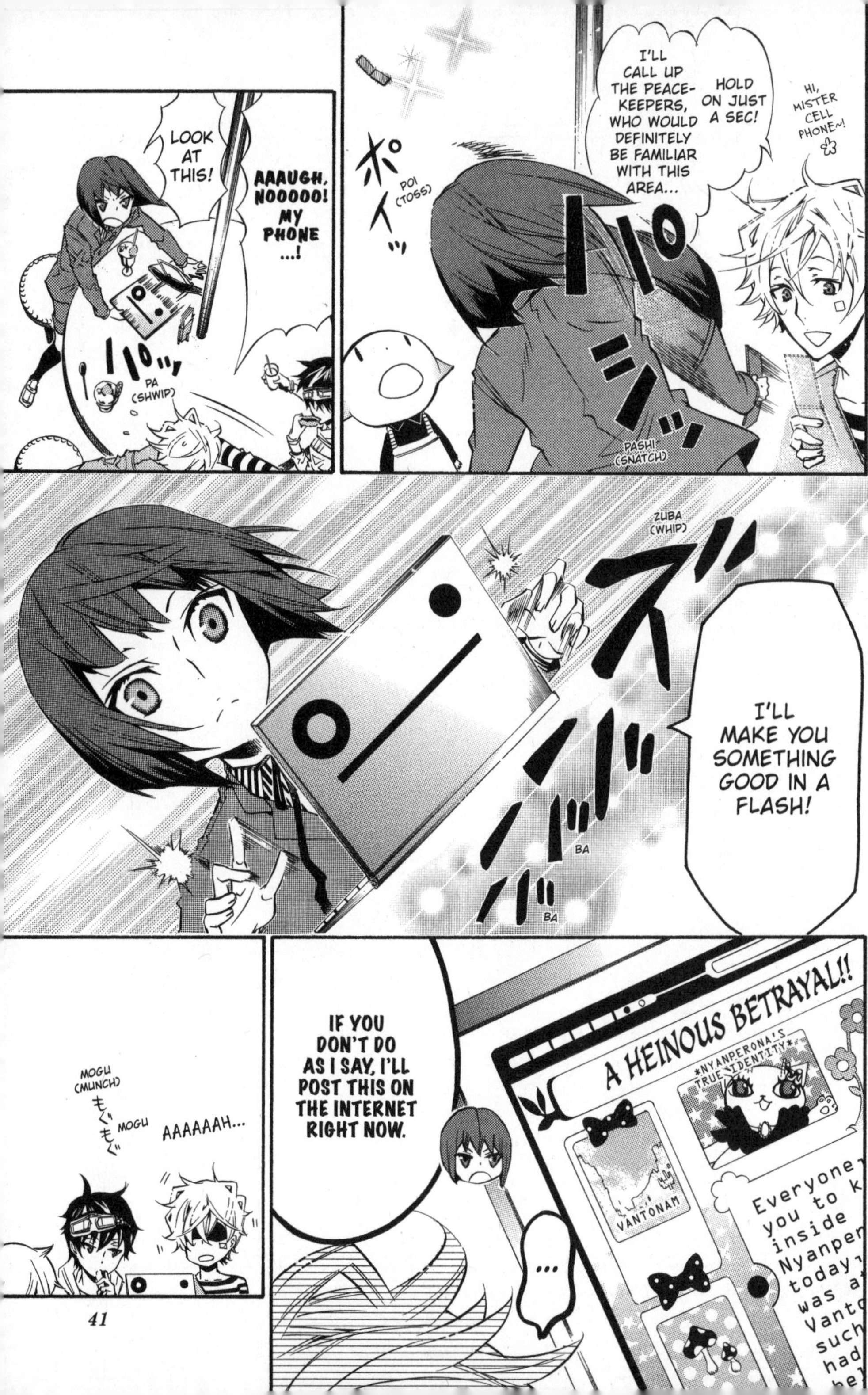
HI, MISTER CELL PHONE~!
HOLD ON JUST A SEC!
I'LL CALL UP THE PEACE-KEEPERS, WHO WOULD DEFINITELY BE FAMILIAR WITH THIS AREA...
POI (TOSS)
PASHI (SNATCH)
AAAUGH, NOOOOO! MY PHONE ...!
LOOK AT THIS!
PA (SHWIP)
I'LL MAKE YOU SOMETHING GOOD IN A FLASH!
ZUBA (WHIP)
BA
BA
A HEINOUS BETRAYAL!!
NYANPERONA'S TRUE IDENTITY
VANTONAM
IF YOU DON'T DO AS I SAY, I'LL POST THIS ON THE INTERNET RIGHT NOW.
...
AAAAAAH...
MOGU (MUNCH) MOGU

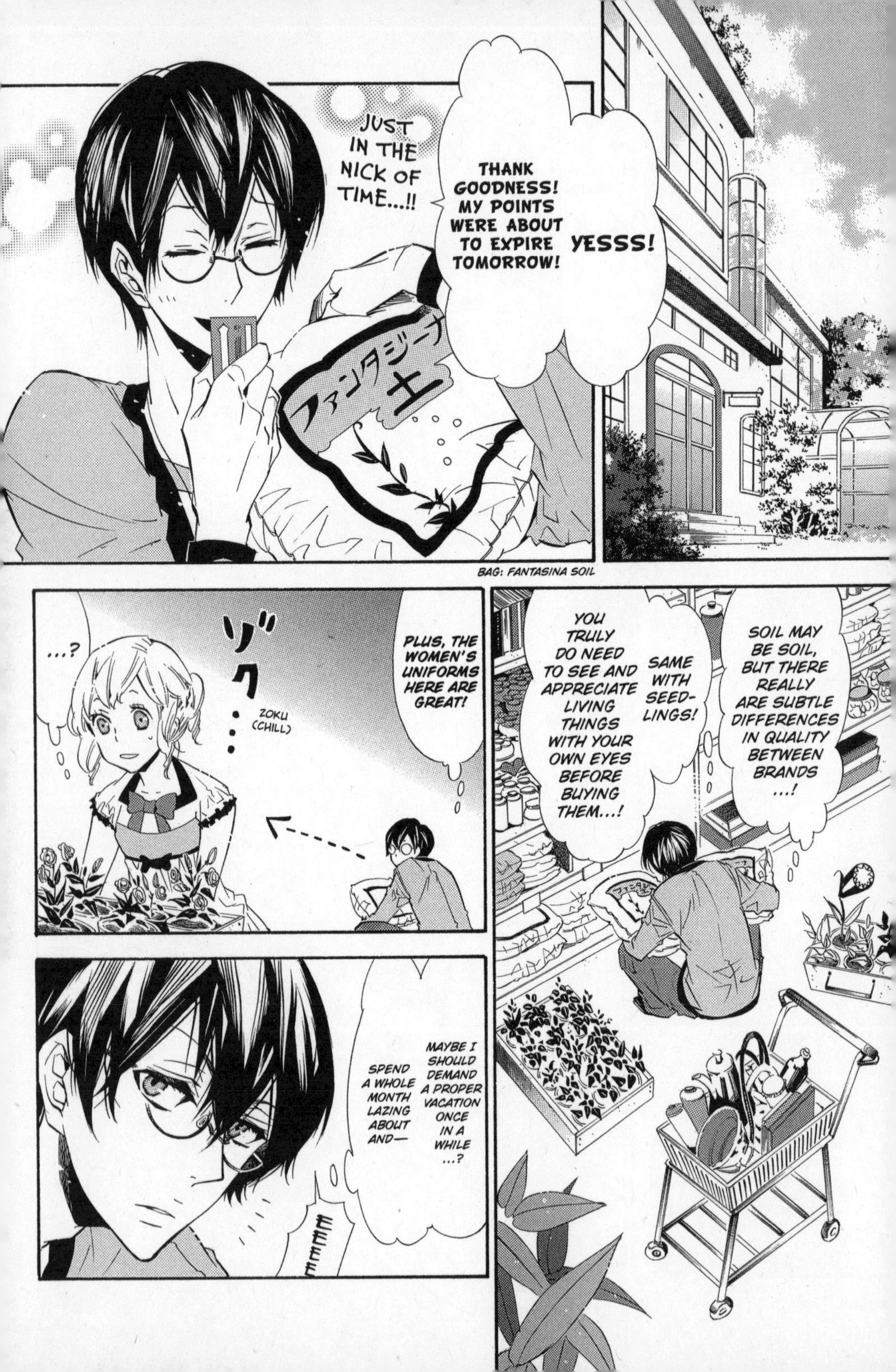
YESSS!
THANK GOODNESS! MY POINTS WERE ABOUT TO EXPIRE TOMORROW!
JUST IN THE NICK OF TIME...!!
ファンタジーナ 土
BAG: FANTASINA SOIL
SOIL MAY BE SOIL, BUT THERE REALLY ARE SUBTLE DIFFERENCES IN QUALITY BETWEEN BRANDS ...!
SAME WITH SEED-LINGS!
YOU TRULY DO NEED TO SEE AND APPRECIATE LIVING THINGS WITH YOUR OWN EYES BEFORE BUYING THEM...!
PLUS, THE WOMEN'S UNIFORMS HERE ARE GREAT!
ゾク...
ZOKU (CHILL)
...?
MAYBE I SHOULD DEMAND A PROPER VACATION ONCE IN A WHILE ...?
SPEND A WHOLE MONTH LAZING ABOUT AND—

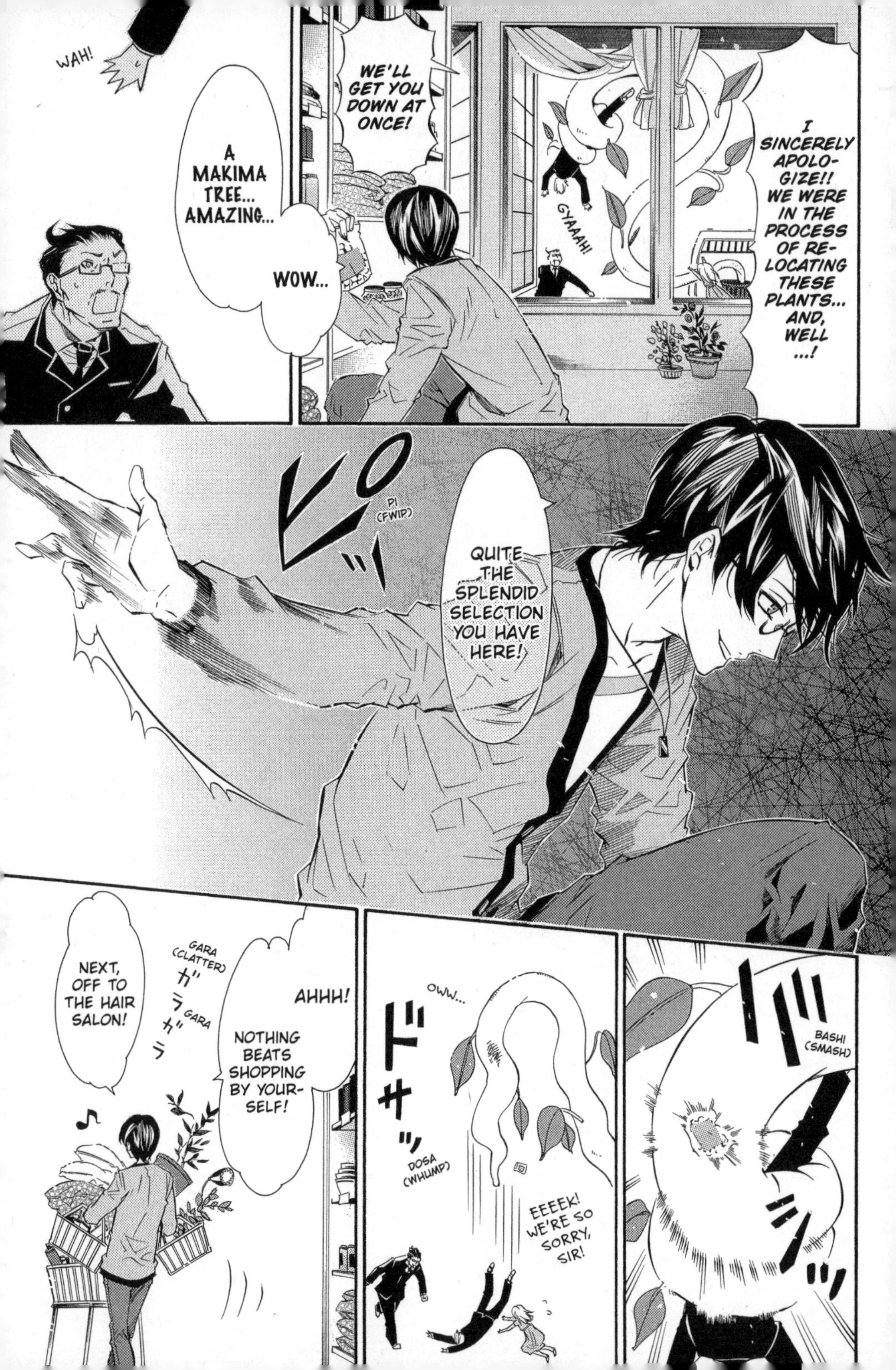
I SINCERELY APOLOGIZE!! WE WERE IN THE PROCESS OF RELOCATING THESE PLANTS... AND, WELL ...!
GYAAAH!
WE'LL GET YOU DOWN AT ONCE!
WOW...
A MAKIMA TREE... AMAZING...
WAH!
PI (FWIP)
QUITE THE SPLENDID SELECTION YOU HAVE HERE!
BASHI (SMASH)
OWW...
ドサッ
DOSA (WHUMP)
EEEEK! WE'RE SO SORRY, SIR!
AHHH!
NOTHING BEATS SHOPPING BY YOURSELF!
ガラガラ
GARA (CLATTER) GARA
NEXT, OFF TO THE HAIR SALON!

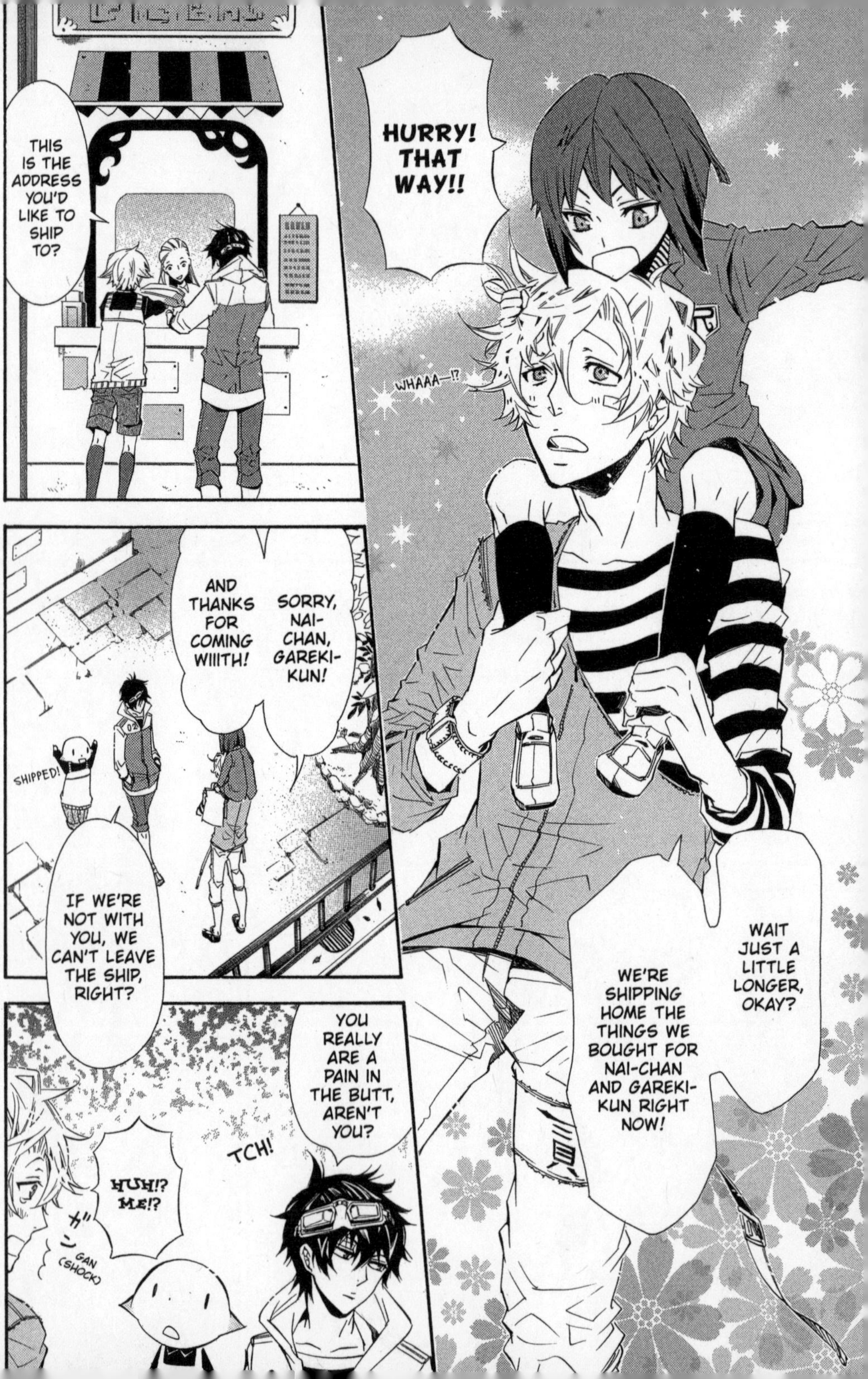
HURRY! THAT WAY!!
WHAAA—!?
WAIT JUST A LITTLE LONGER, OKAY?
WE'RE SHIPPING HOME THE THINGS WE BOUGHT FOR NAI-CHAN AND GAREKI-KUN RIGHT NOW!
THIS IS THE ADDRESS YOU'D LIKE TO SHIP TO?
SORRY, NAI-CHAN, GAREKI-KUN!
AND THANKS FOR COMING WIIITH!
SHIPPED!
IF WE'RE NOT WITH YOU, WE CAN'T LEAVE THE SHIP, RIGHT?
YOU REALLY ARE A PAIN IN THE BUTT, AREN'T YOU?
TCH!
HUH!? ME!?
ガーン
GAN (SHOCK)

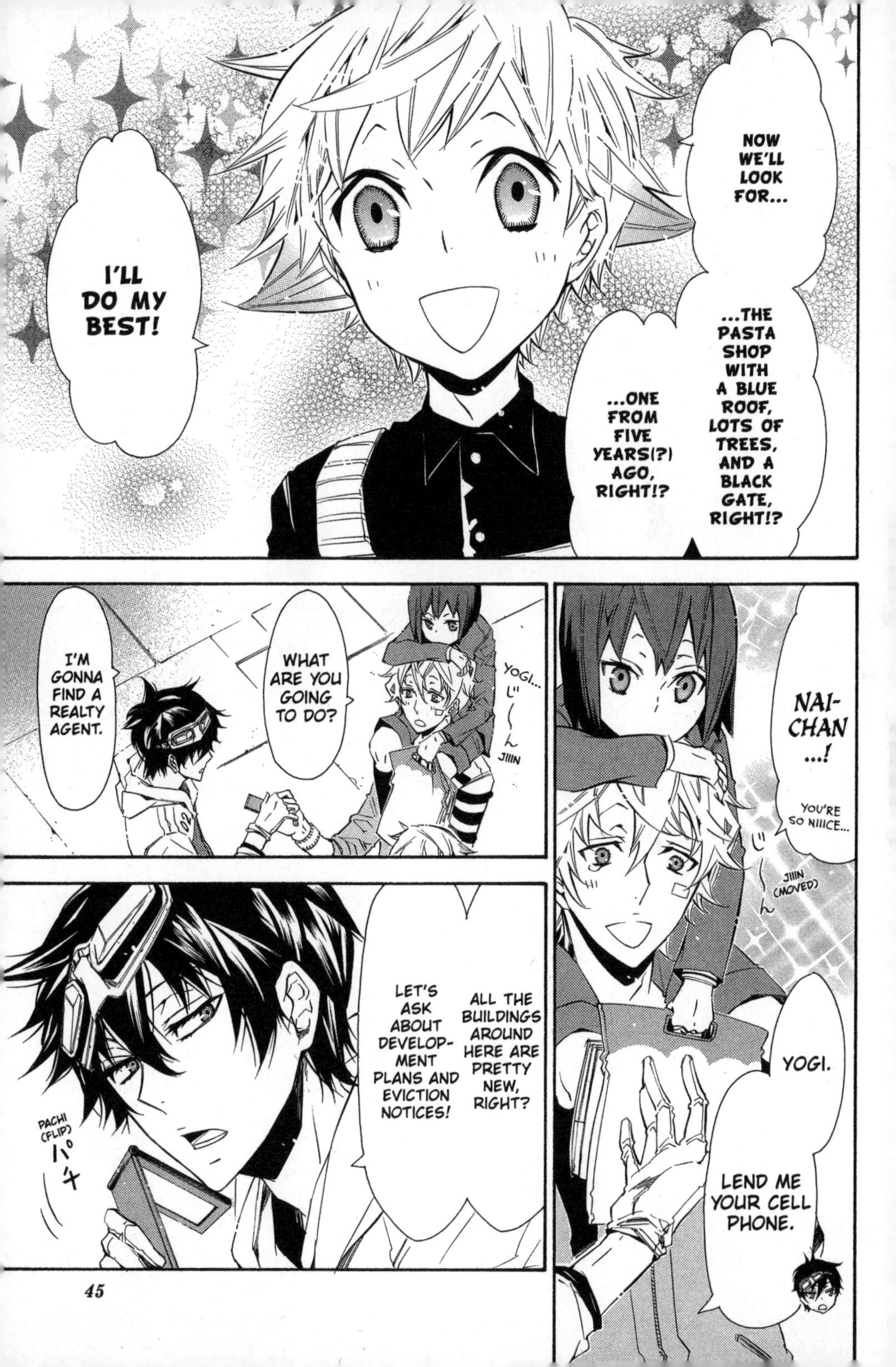
NOW WE'LL LOOK FOR...
...THE PASTA SHOP WITH A BLUE ROOF, LOTS OF TREES, AND A BLACK GATE, RIGHT!?
...ONE FROM FIVE YEARS(?) AGO, RIGHT!?
I'LL DO MY BEST!
NAI-CHAN...!
YOU'RE SO NIIICE...
じ〜ん
JIIIN (MOVED)
YOGI.
LEND ME YOUR CELL PHONE.
WHAT ARE YOU GOING TO DO?
YOGI...
じ〜ん
JIIIN
I'M GONNA FIND A REALTY AGENT.
ALL THE BUILDINGS AROUND HERE ARE PRETTY NEW, RIGHT?
LET'S ASK ABOUT DEVELOPMENT PLANS AND EVICTION NOTICES!
PACHI (FLIP)
パチ

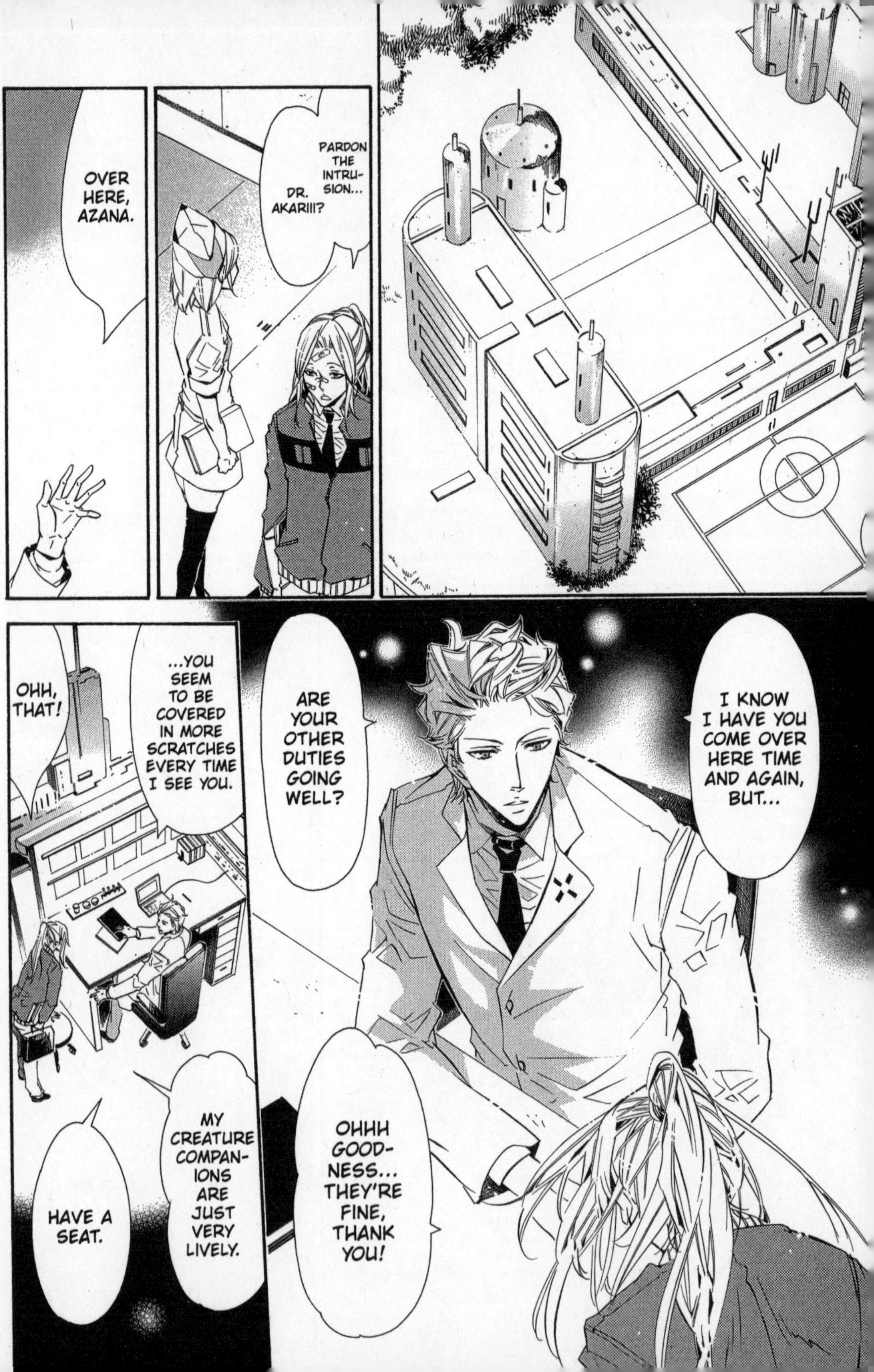
PARDON THE INTRU-SION... DR. AKARIII?
OVER HERE, AZANA.
I KNOW I HAVE YOU COME OVER HERE TIME AND AGAIN, BUT...
ARE YOUR OTHER DUTIES GOING WELL?
OHHH GOOD-NESS... THEY'RE FINE, THANK YOU!
...YOU SEEM TO BE COVERED IN MORE SCRATCHES EVERY TIME I SEE YOU.
OHH, THAT!
MY CREATURE COMPAN-IONS ARE JUST VERY LIVELY.
HAVE A SEAT.

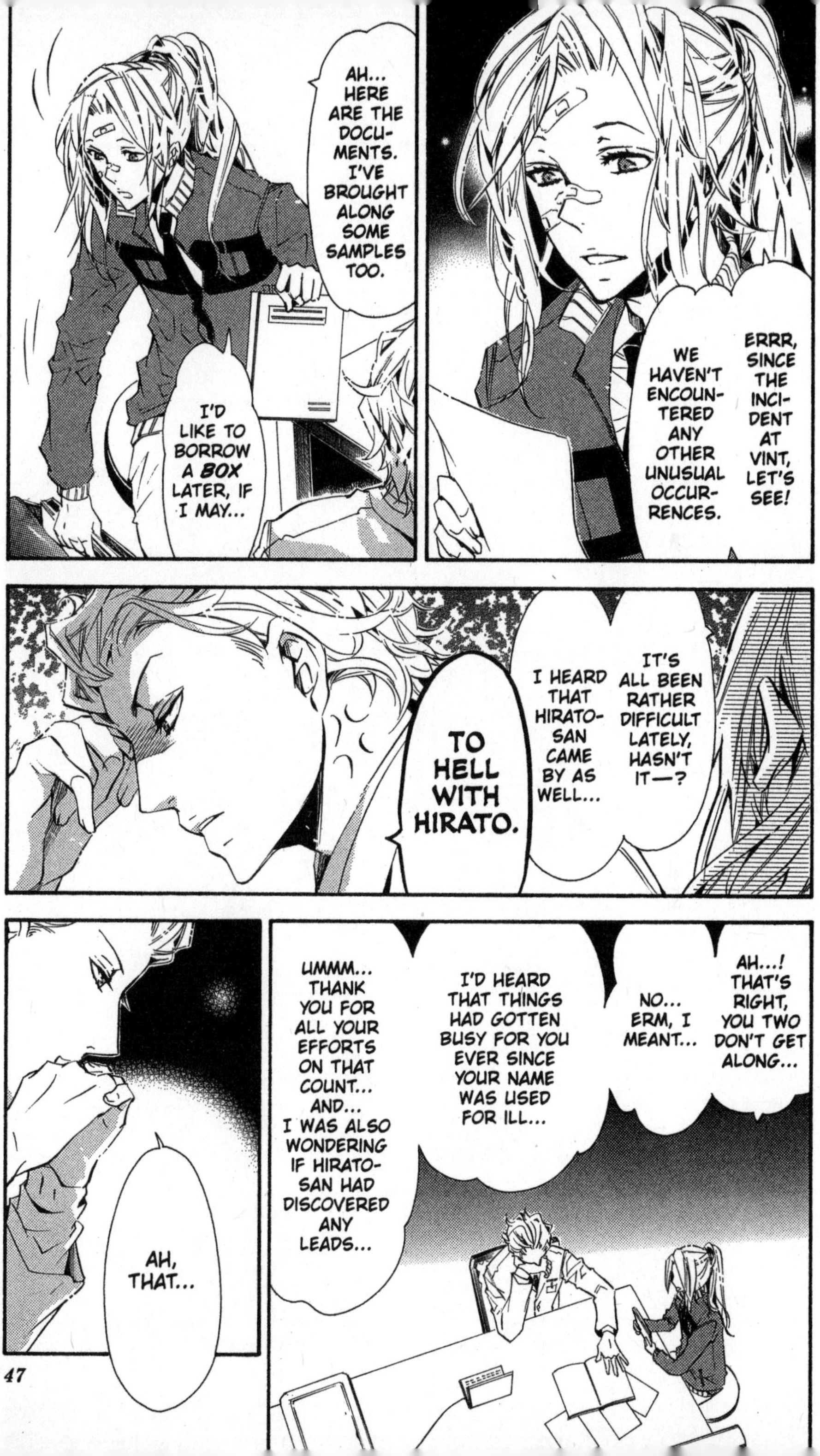
ERRR, SINCE THE INCIDENT AT VINT, LET'S SEE!
WE HAVEN'T ENCOUNTERED ANY OTHER UNUSUAL OCCURRENCES.
AH... HERE ARE THE DOCUMENTS. I'VE BROUGHT ALONG SOME SAMPLES TOO.
I'D LIKE TO BORROW A *BOX* LATER, IF I MAY...
IT'S ALL BEEN RATHER DIFFICULT LATELY, HASN'T IT—?
I HEARD THAT HIRATO-SAN CAME BY AS WELL...
TO HELL WITH HIRATO.
AH...! THAT'S RIGHT, YOU TWO DON'T GET ALONG...
NO... ERM, I MEANT...
I'D HEARD THAT THINGS HAD GOTTEN BUSY FOR YOU EVER SINCE YOUR NAME WAS USED FOR ILL...
UMMM... THANK YOU FOR ALL YOUR EFFORTS ON THAT COUNT... AND... I WAS ALSO WONDERING IF HIRATO-SAN HAD DISCOVERED ANY LEADS...
AH, THAT...

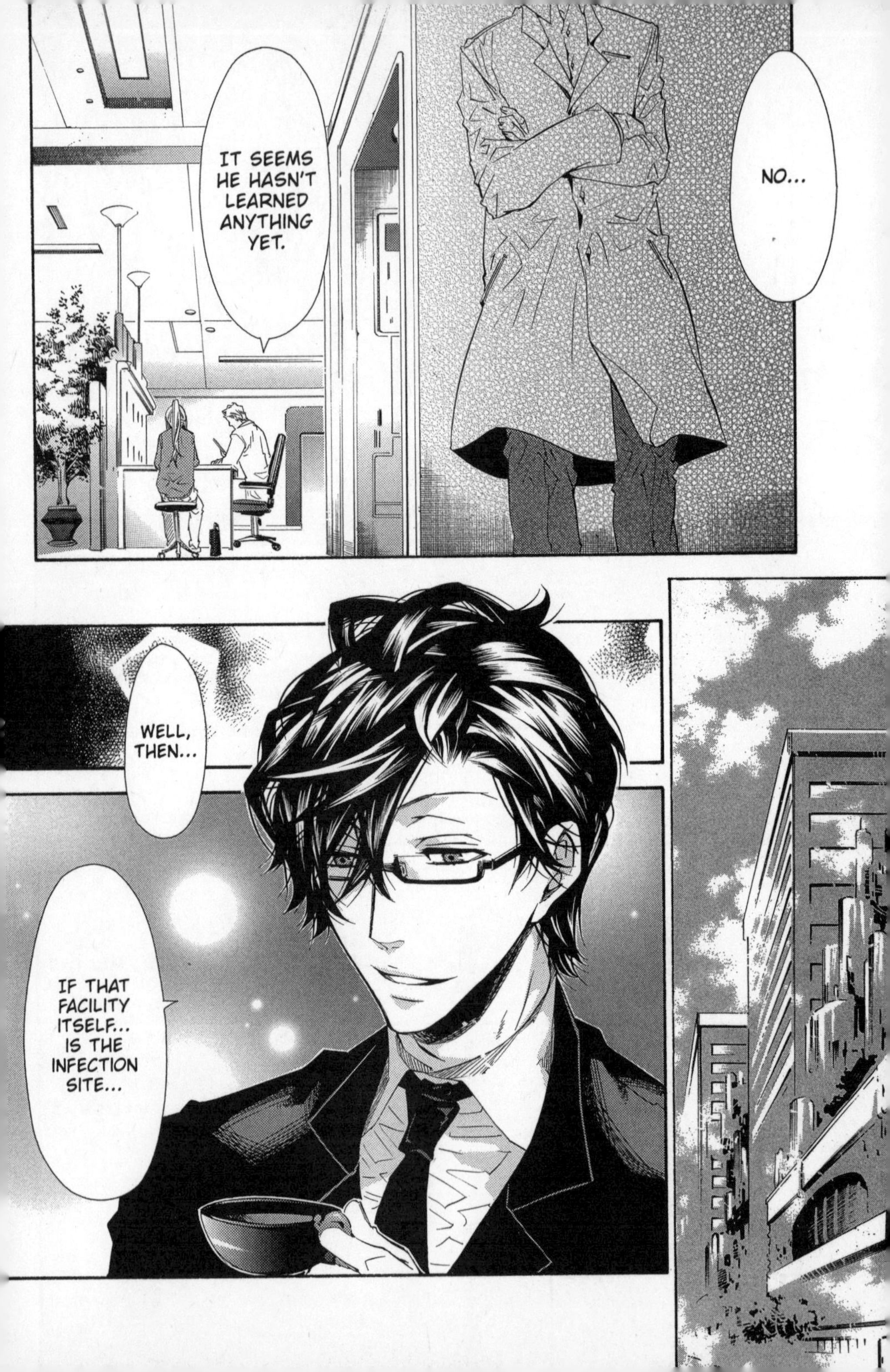
NO...
IT SEEMS HE HASN'T LEARNED ANYTHING YET.
WELL, THEN...
IF THAT FACILITY ITSELF... IS THE INFECTION SITE...

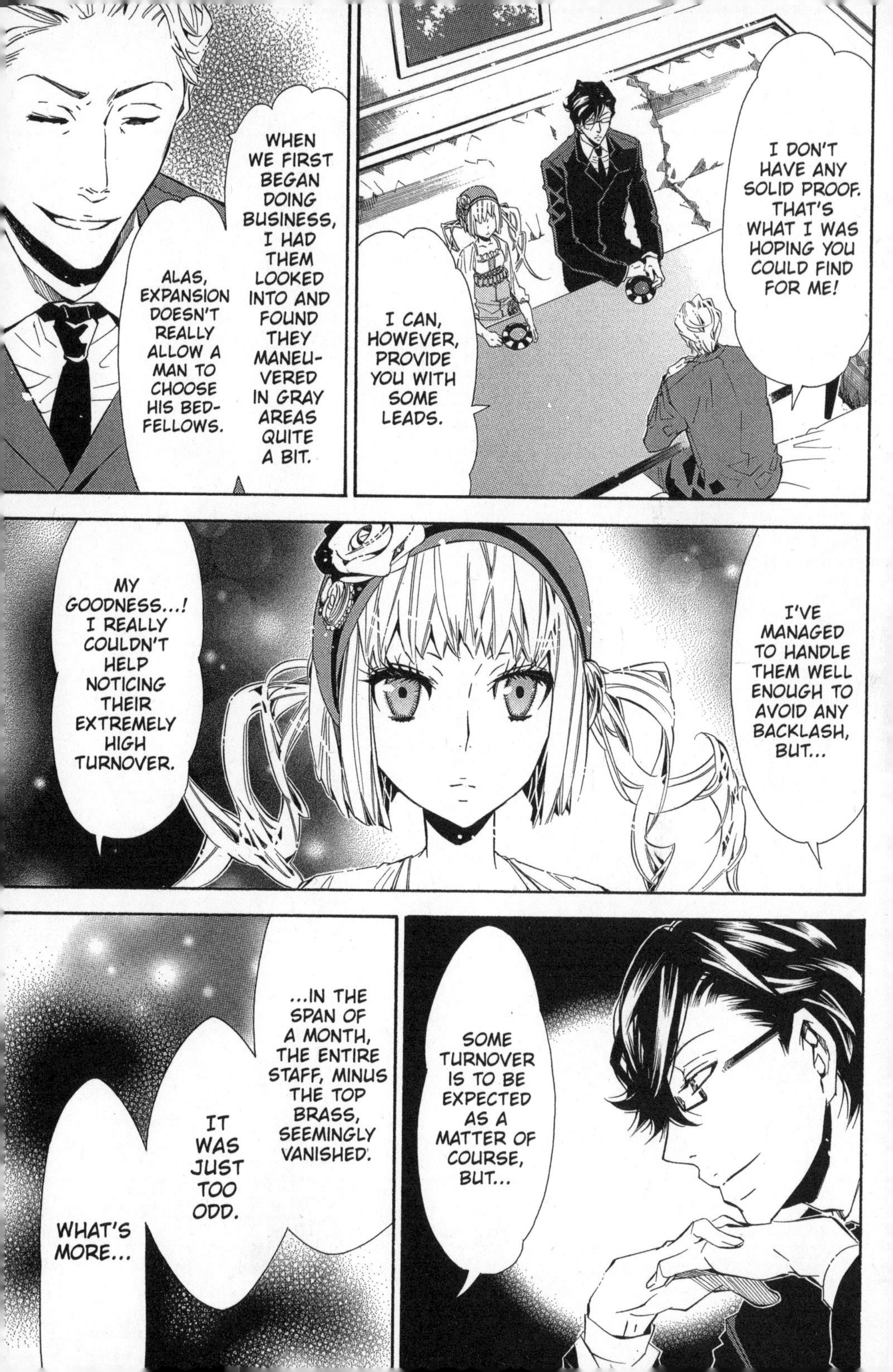
I DON'T HAVE ANY SOLID PROOF. THAT'S WHAT I WAS HOPING YOU COULD FIND FOR ME!
I CAN, HOWEVER, PROVIDE YOU WITH SOME LEADS.
WHEN WE FIRST BEGAN DOING BUSINESS, I HAD THEM LOOKED INTO AND FOUND THEY MANEU-VERED IN GRAY AREAS QUITE A BIT.
ALAS, EXPANSION DOESN'T REALLY ALLOW A MAN TO CHOOSE HIS BED-FELLOWS.
I'VE MANAGED TO HANDLE THEM WELL ENOUGH TO AVOID ANY BACKLASH, BUT...
MY GOODNESS...! I REALLY COULDN'T HELP NOTICING THEIR EXTREMELY HIGH TURNOVER.
SOME TURNOVER IS TO BE EXPECTED AS A MATTER OF COURSE, BUT...
...IN THE SPAN OF A MONTH, THE ENTIRE STAFF, MINUS THE TOP BRASS, SEEMINGLY VANISHED.
IT WAS JUST TOO ODD.
WHAT'S MORE...

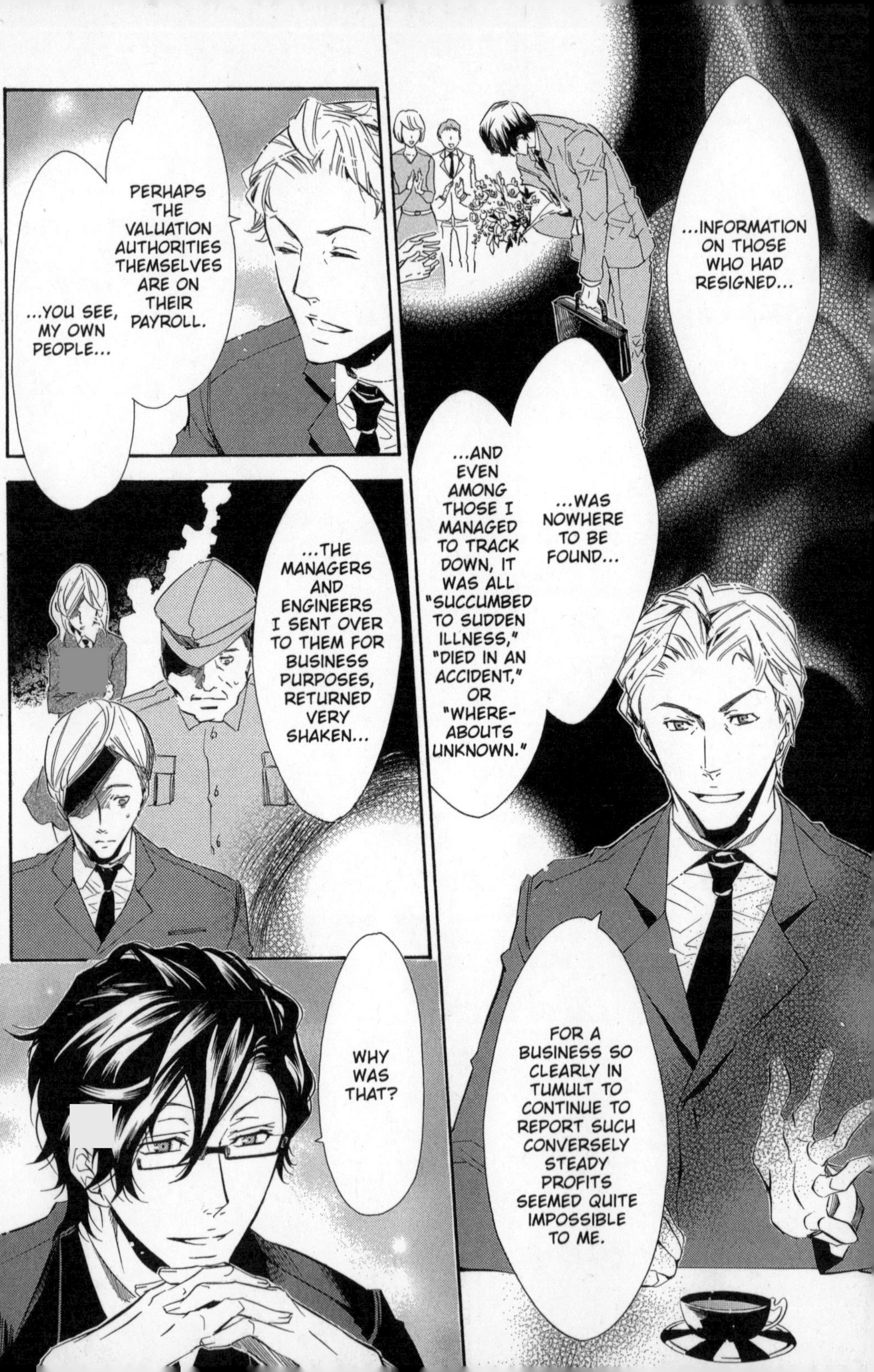
...INFORMATION ON THOSE WHO HAD RESIGNED...
...WAS NOWHERE TO BE FOUND...
...AND EVEN AMONG THOSE I MANAGED TO TRACK DOWN, IT WAS ALL "SUCCUMBED TO SUDDEN ILLNESS," "DIED IN AN ACCIDENT," OR "WHERE-ABOUTS UNKNOWN."
FOR A BUSINESS SO CLEARLY IN TUMULT TO CONTINUE TO REPORT SUCH CONVERSELY STEADY PROFITS SEEMED QUITE IMPOSSIBLE TO ME.
PERHAPS THE VALUATION AUTHORITIES THEMSELVES ARE ON THEIR PAYROLL.
...YOU SEE, MY OWN PEOPLE...
...THE MANAGERS AND ENGINEERS I SENT OVER TO THEM FOR BUSINESS PURPOSES, RETURNED VERY SHAKEN...
WHY WAS THAT?

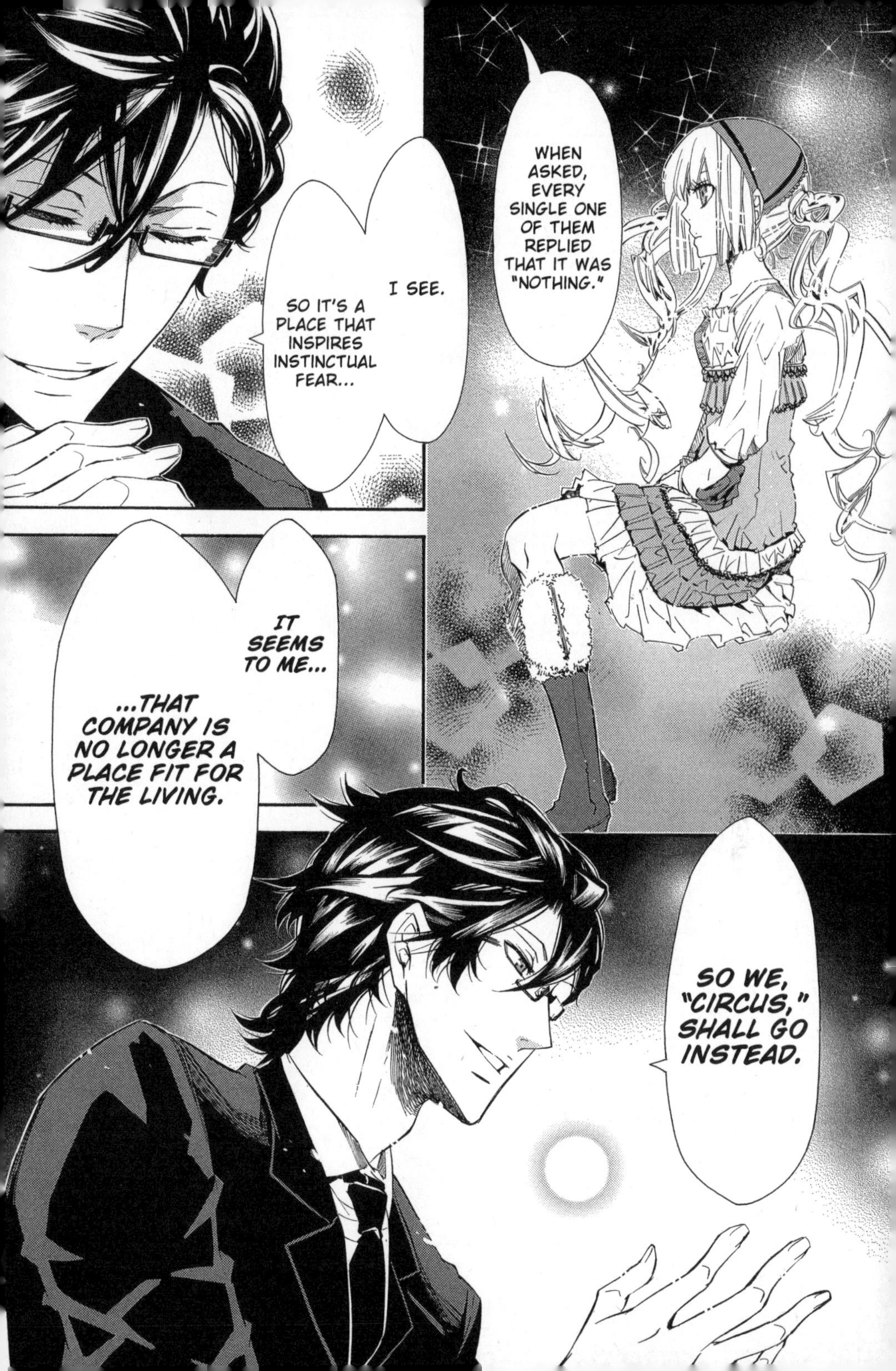
WHEN ASKED, EVERY SINGLE ONE OF THEM REPLIED THAT IT WAS "NOTHING."
I SEE.
SO IT'S A PLACE THAT INSPIRES INSTINCTUAL FEAR...
IT SEEMS TO ME...
...THAT COMPANY IS NO LONGER A PLACE FIT FOR THE LIVING.
SO WE, "CIRCUS," SHALL GO INSTEAD.

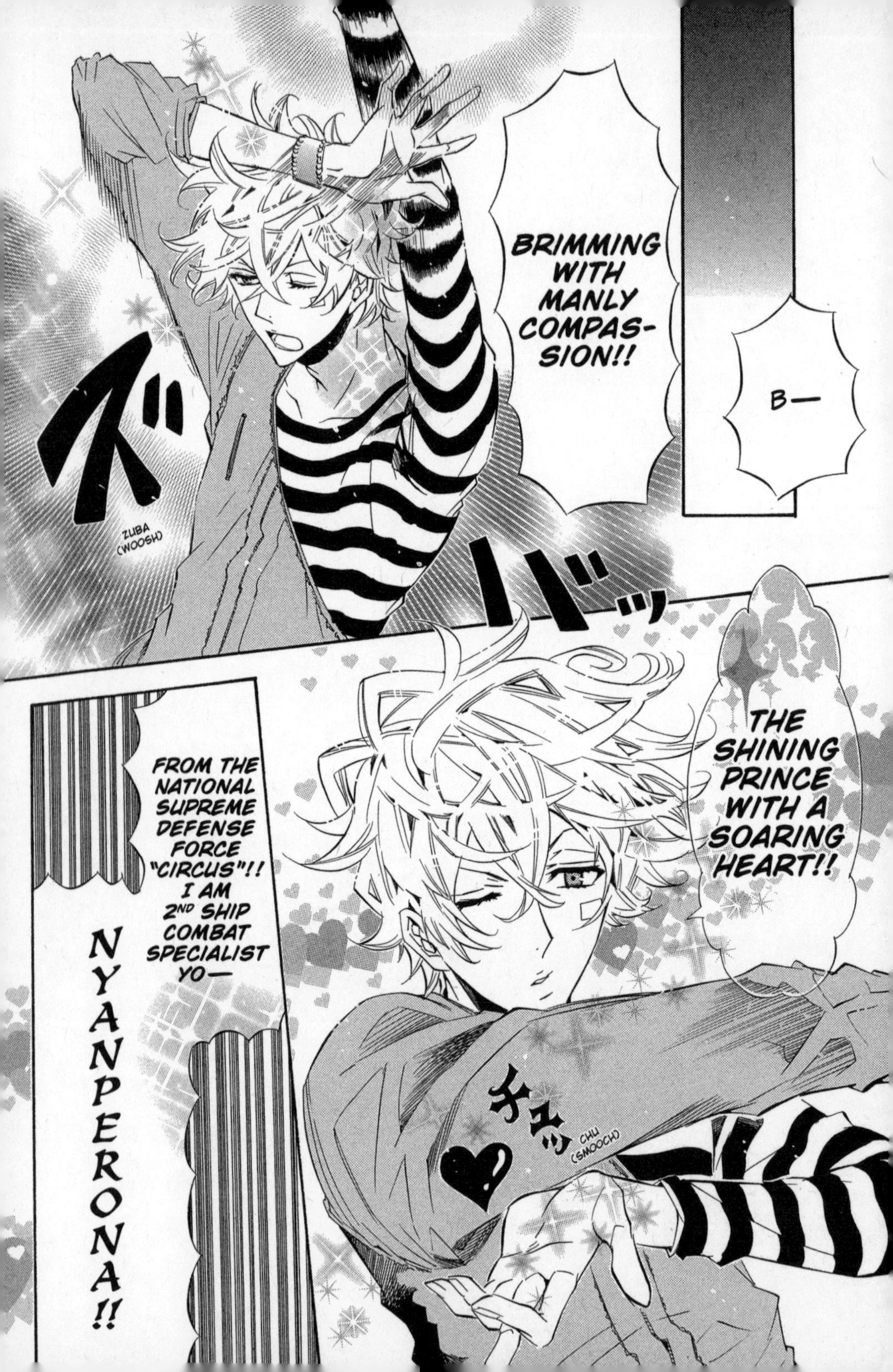

B—
BRIMMING WITH MANLY COMPAS-SION!!
ZUBA (WOOSH)
THE SHINING PRINCE WITH A SOARING HEART!!
FROM THE NATIONAL SUPREME DEFENSE FORCE "CIRCUS"!! I AM 2ND SHIP COMBAT SPECIALIST YO—
CHU (SMOOCH)
NYANPERONA!!

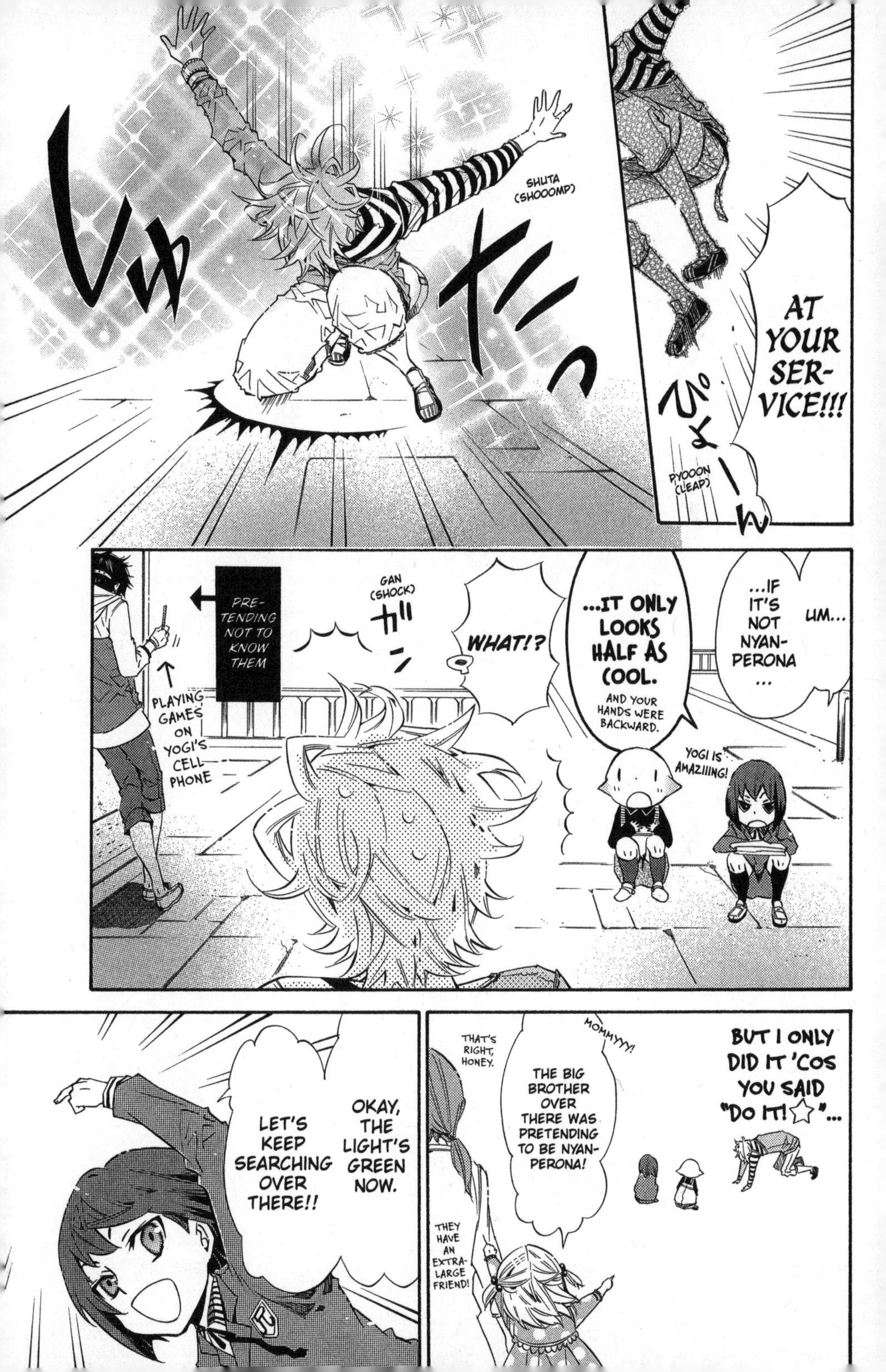
AT YOUR SER-VICE!!!
ぴょーん
PYOOON (LEAP)
しゅたっ
SHUTA (SHOOOMP)
UM...
...IF IT'S NOT NYAN-PERONA...
...IT ONLY LOOKS HALF AS COOL.
AND YOUR HANDS WERE BACKWARD.
YOGI IS AMAZIIING!
WHAT!?
ガーン
GAN (SHOCK)
PRE-TENDING NOT TO KNOW THEM
PLAYING GAMES ON YOGI'S CELL PHONE
BUT I ONLY DID IT 'COS YOU SAID "DO IT!☆"...
MOMMYYY!
THE BIG BROTHER OVER THERE WAS PRETENDING TO BE NYAN-PERONA!
THAT'S RIGHT, HONEY.
THEY HAVE AN EXTRA-LARGE FRIEND!
OKAY, THE LIGHT'S GREEN NOW.
LET'S KEEP SEARCHING OVER THERE!!

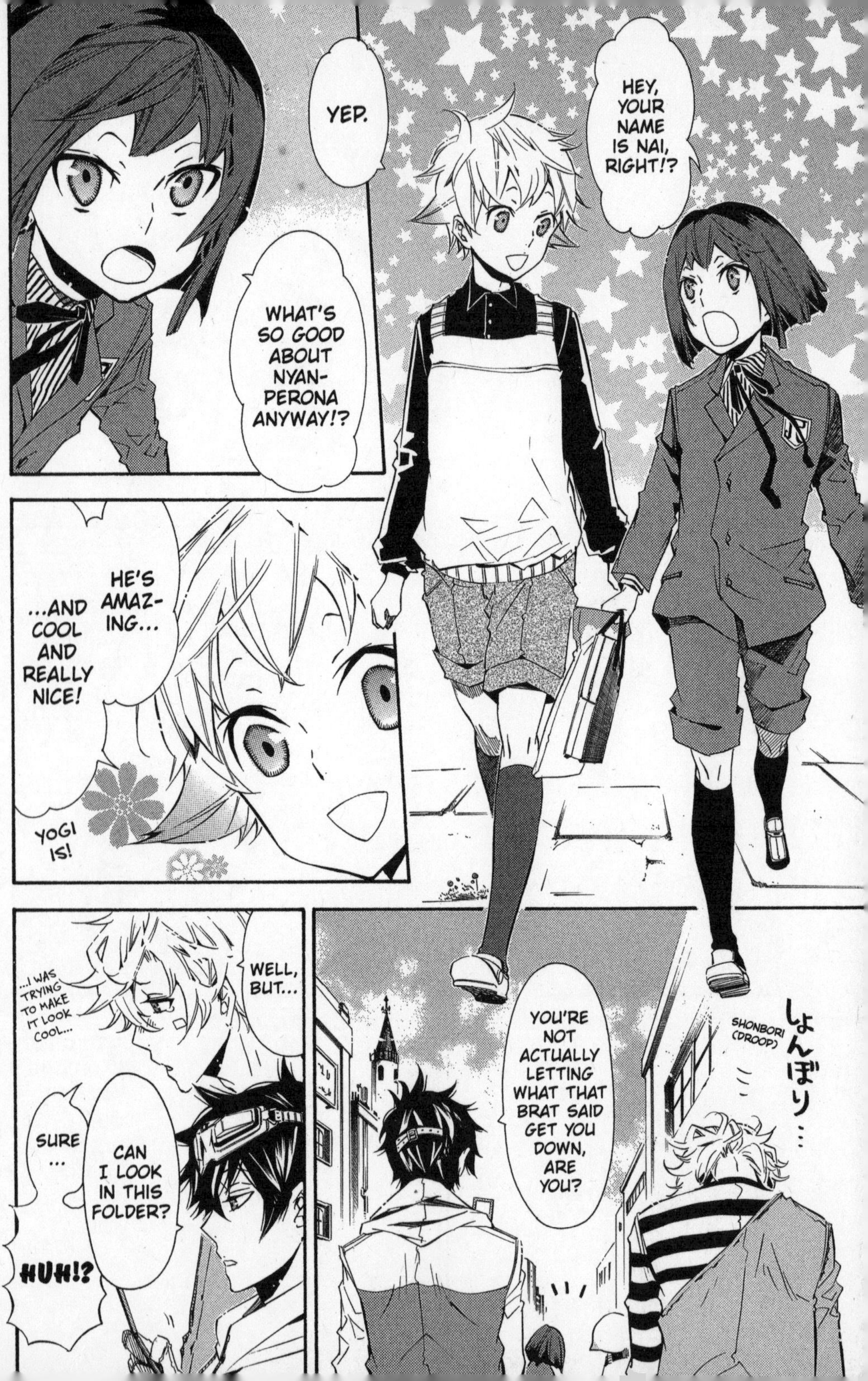
HEY, YOUR NAME IS NAI, RIGHT!?
YEP.
WHAT'S SO GOOD ABOUT NYAN-PERONA ANYWAY!?
HE'S AMAZING...
...AND COOL AND REALLY NICE!
YOGI IS!
しょんぼり…
SHONBORI (DROOP)
YOU'RE NOT ACTUALLY LETTING WHAT THAT BRAT SAID GET YOU DOWN, ARE YOU?
WELL, BUT...
...I WAS TRYING TO MAKE IT LOOK COOL...
CAN I LOOK IN THIS FOLDER?
SURE ...
HUH!?

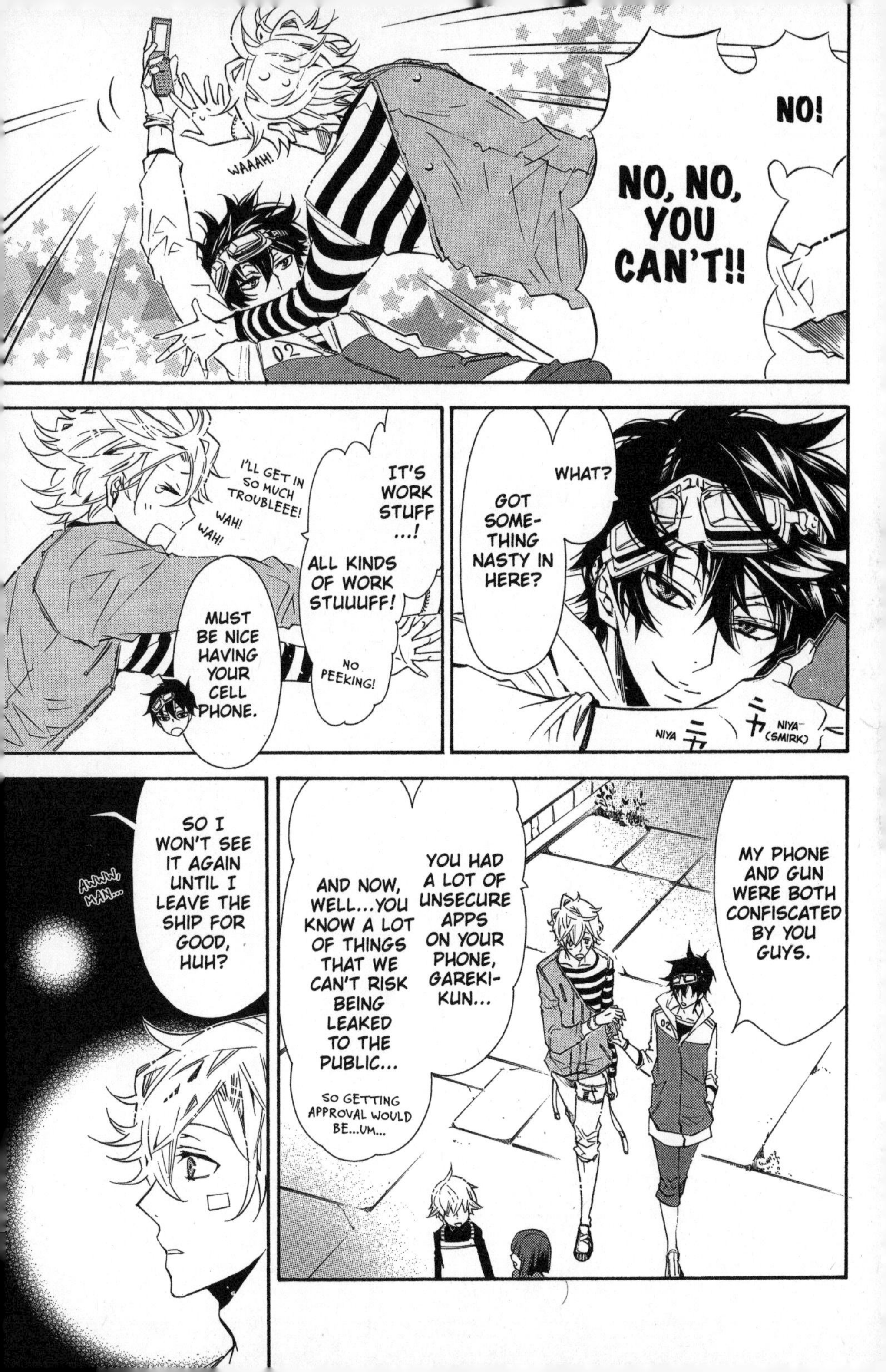
NO!
NO, NO, YOU CAN'T!!
WAAAH!
WHAT?
GOT SOMETHING NASTY IN HERE?
NIYA~ (SMIRK)
NIYA
IT'S WORK STUFF...!
ALL KINDS OF WORK STUUUFF!
I'LL GET IN SO MUCH TROUBLEEE!
WAH! WAH!
NO PEEKING!
MUST BE NICE HAVING YOUR CELL PHONE.
MY PHONE AND GUN WERE BOTH CONFISCATED BY YOU GUYS.
YOU HAD A LOT OF UNSECURE APPS ON YOUR PHONE, GAREKI-KUN...
AND NOW, WELL...YOU KNOW A LOT OF THINGS THAT WE CAN'T RISK BEING LEAKED TO THE PUBLIC...
SO GETTING APPROVAL WOULD BE...UM...
SO I WON'T SEE IT AGAIN UNTIL I LEAVE THE SHIP FOR GOOD, HUH?
AWWW, MAN...

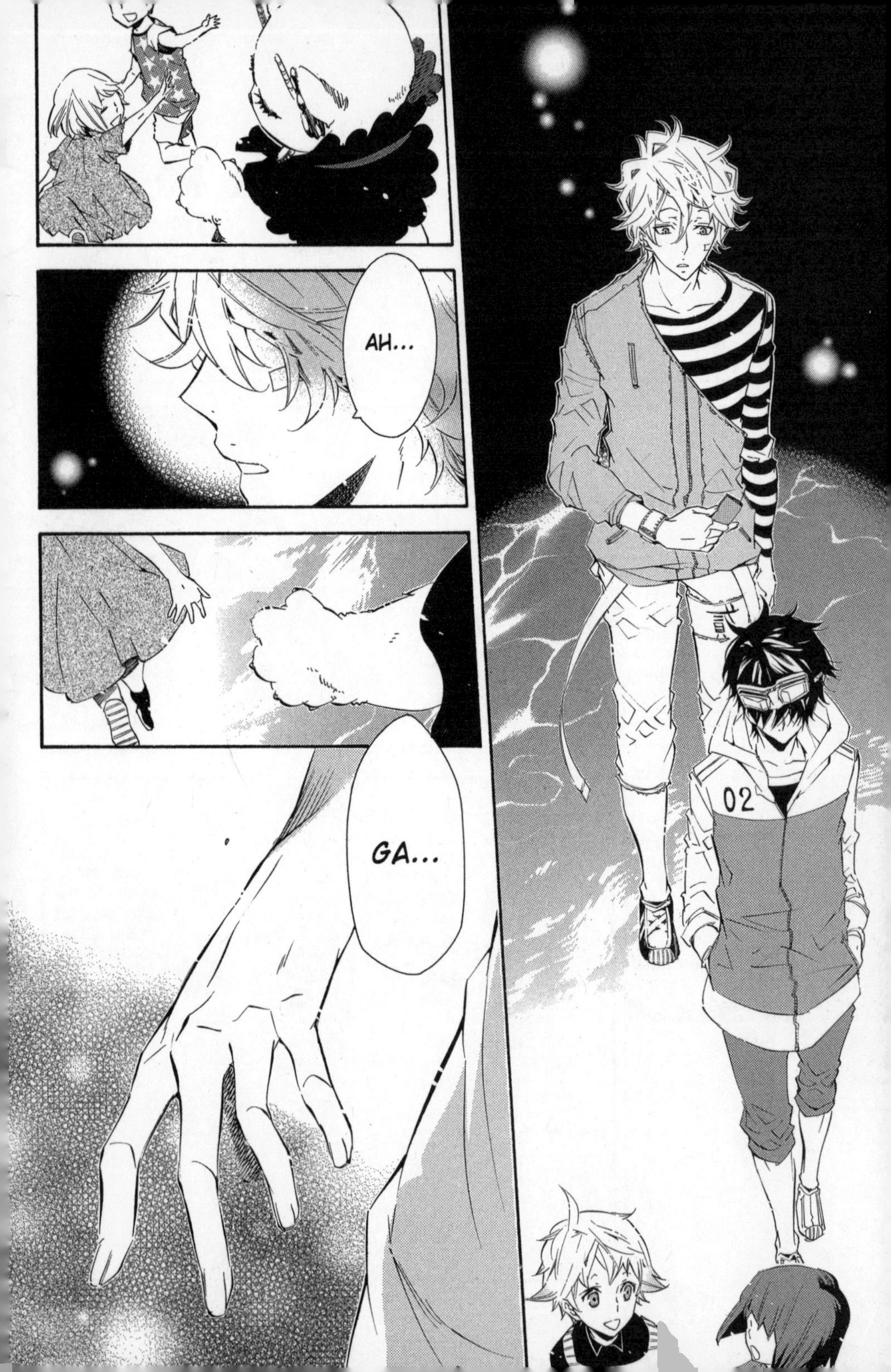
AH...
GA...

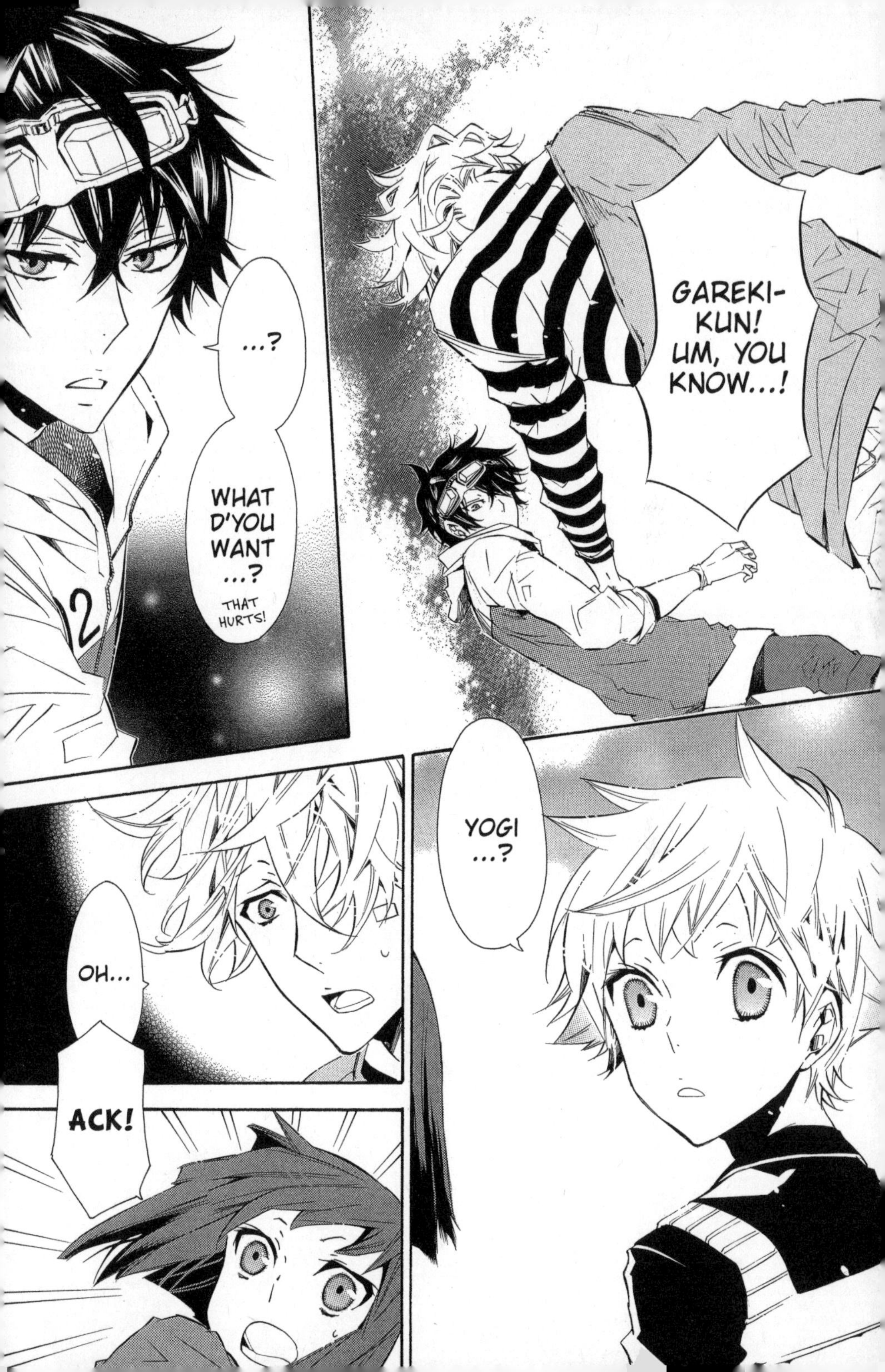
GAREKI-KUN! UM, YOU KNOW...!
...?
WHAT D'YOU WANT ...?
THAT HURTS!
YOGI ...?
OH...
ACK!

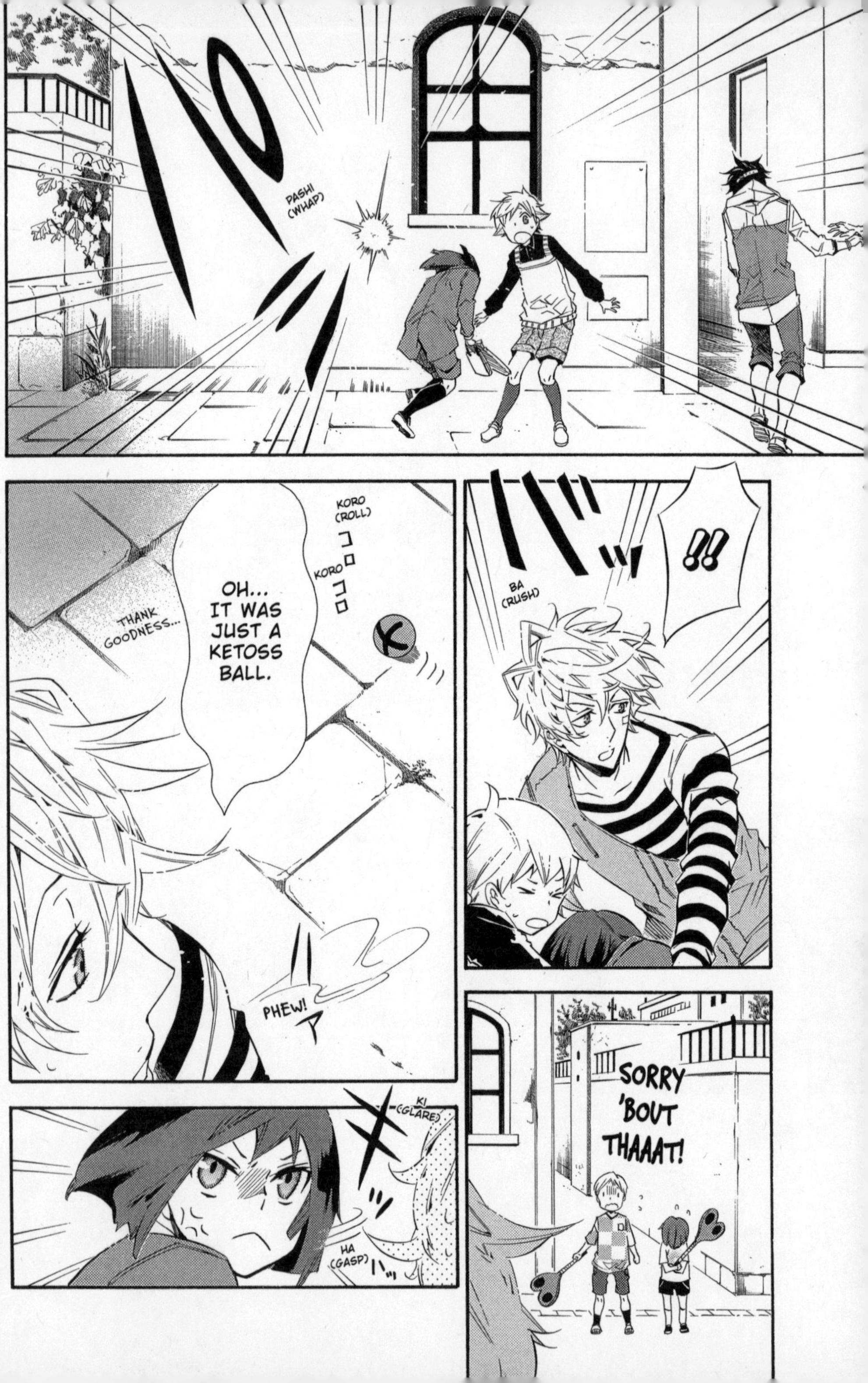
PASHI (WHAP)
!!
BA (RUSH)
KORO (ROLL)
KORO
OH... IT WAS JUST A KETOSS BALL.
THANK GOODNESS...
PHEW!
SORRY 'BOUT THAAAT!
KI (GLARE)
HA (GASP)

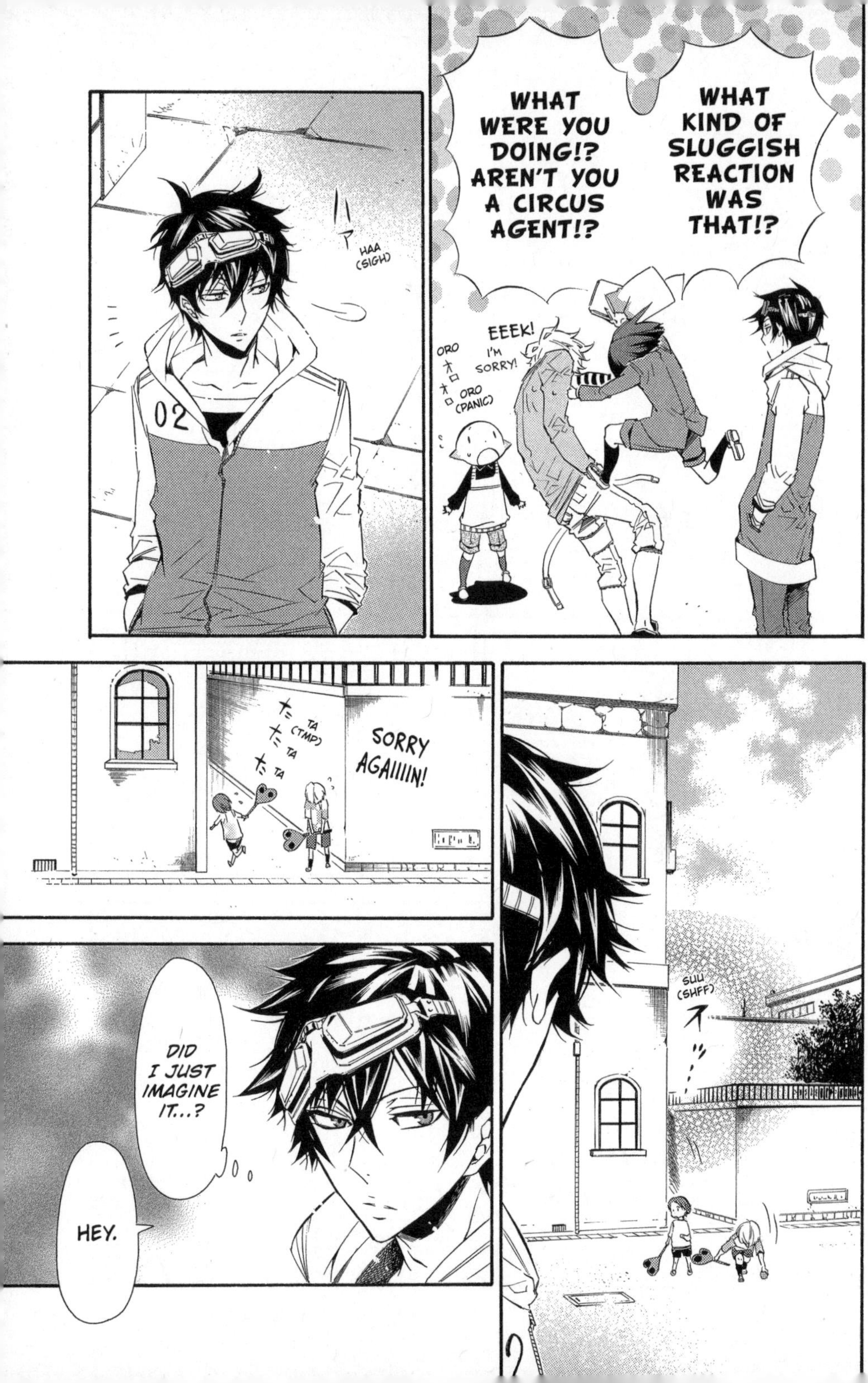
WHAT KIND OF SLUGGISH REACTION WAS THAT!?
WHAT WERE YOU DOING!? AREN'T YOU A CIRCUS AGENT!?
EEEK!
I'M SORRY!
ORO ORO (PANIC)
HAA (SIGH)
SUU (SHFF)
SORRY AGAIIIIN!
TA (TMP) TA TA
DID I JUST IMAGINE IT...?
HEY.

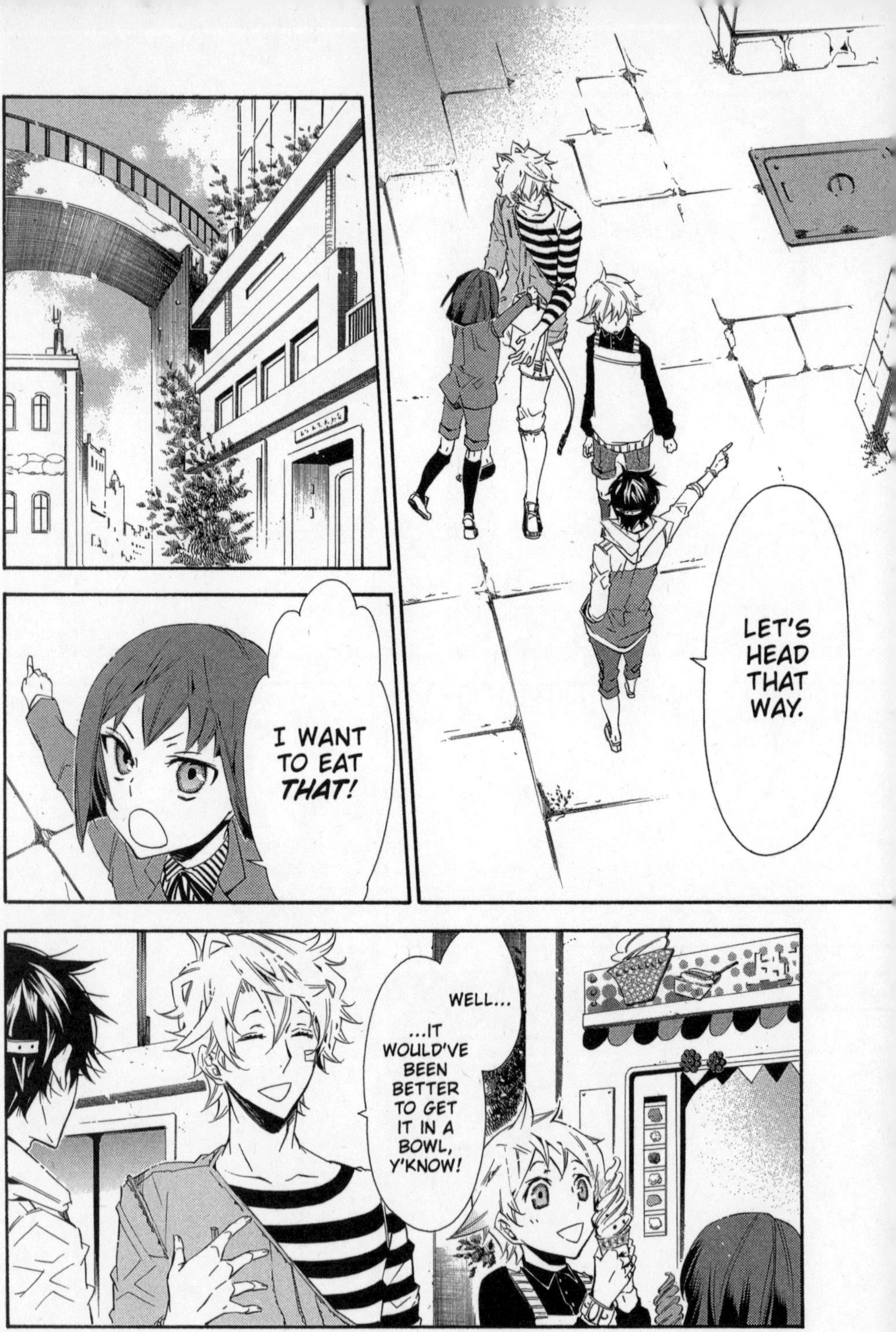
LET'S HEAD THAT WAY.
I WANT TO EAT THAT!
WELL...
...IT WOULD'VE BEEN BETTER TO GET IT IN A BOWL, Y'KNOW!

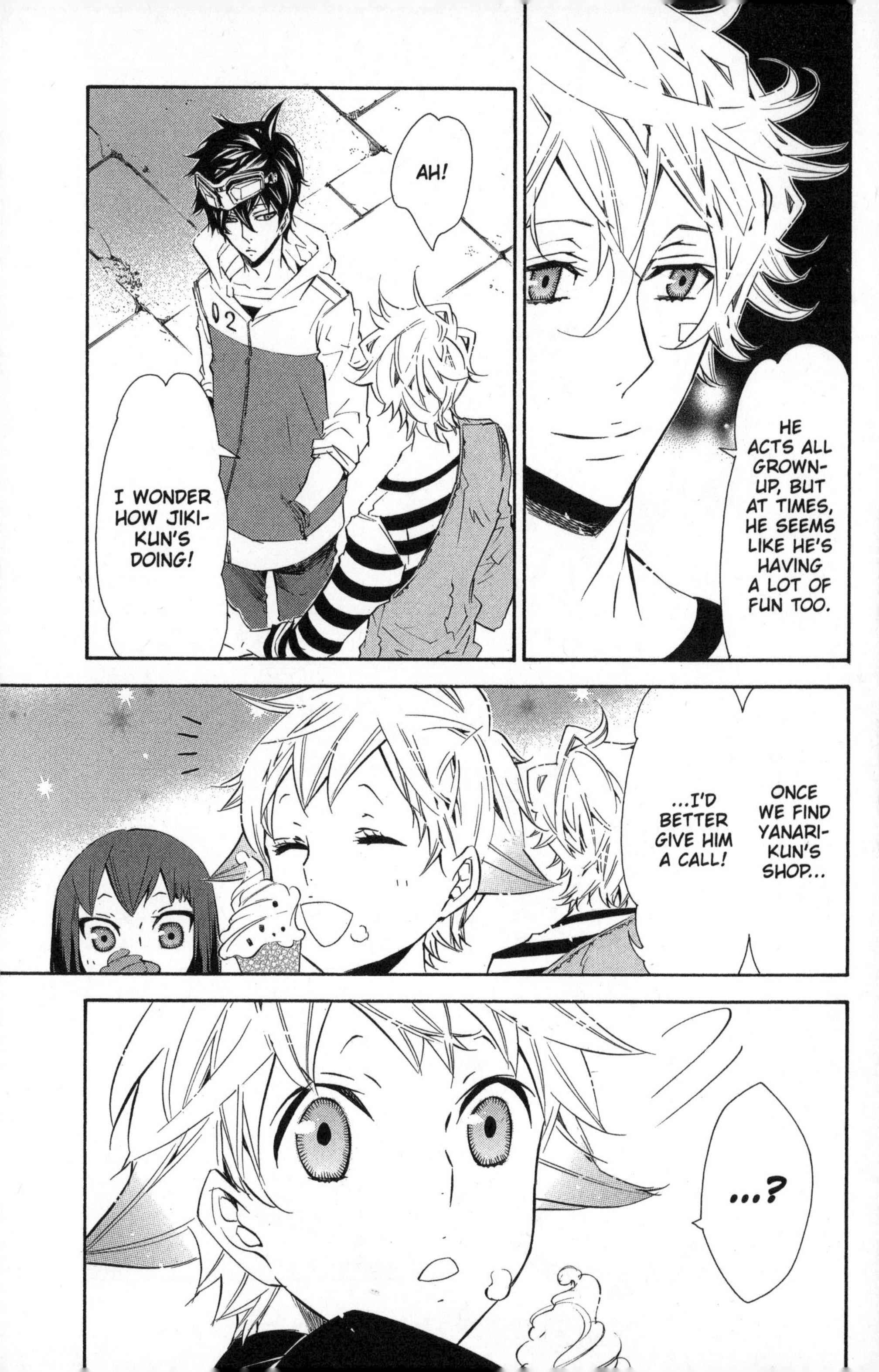
HE ACTS ALL GROWN-UP, BUT AT TIMES, HE SEEMS LIKE HE'S HAVING A LOT OF FUN TOO.
AH!
I WONDER HOW JIKI-KUN'S DOING!
ONCE WE FIND YANARI-KUN'S SHOP...
...I'D BETTER GIVE HIM A CALL!
...?

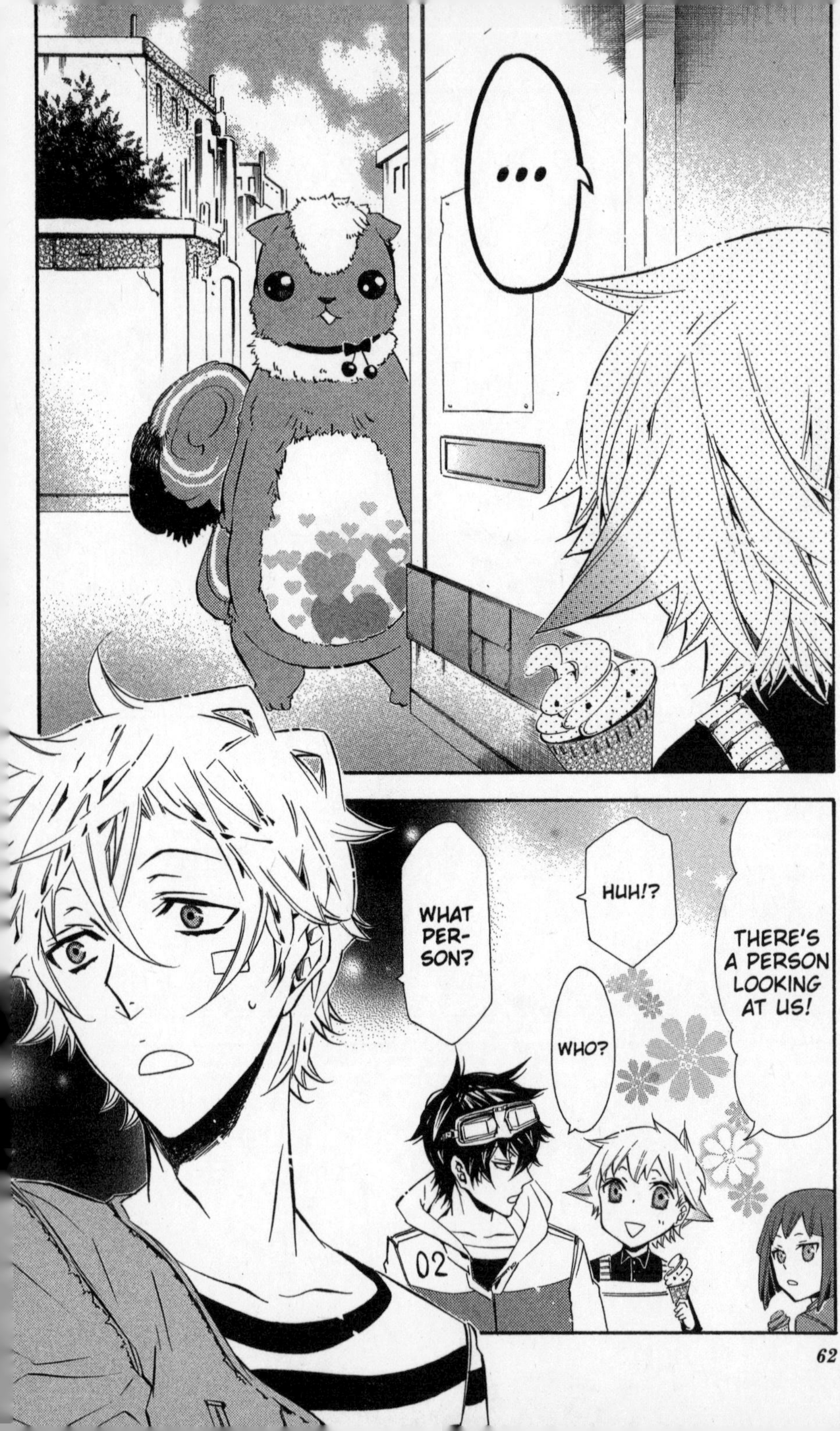
...
THERE'S A PERSON LOOKING AT US!
HUH!?
WHO?
WHAT PERSON?

KARNEVAL

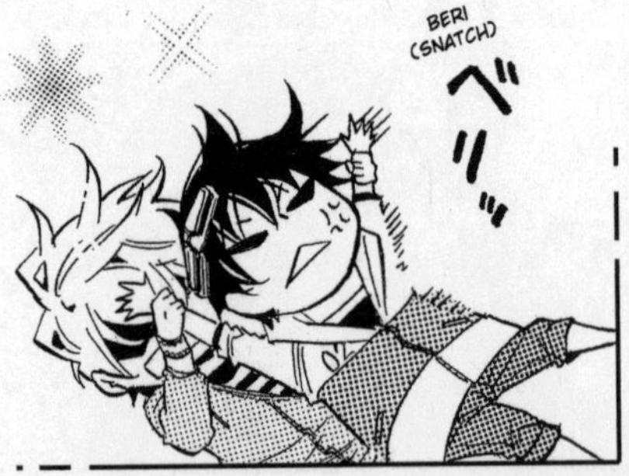

BERI (SNATCH)
ベリッ

KARNEVAL

Score 27: Kidnappers

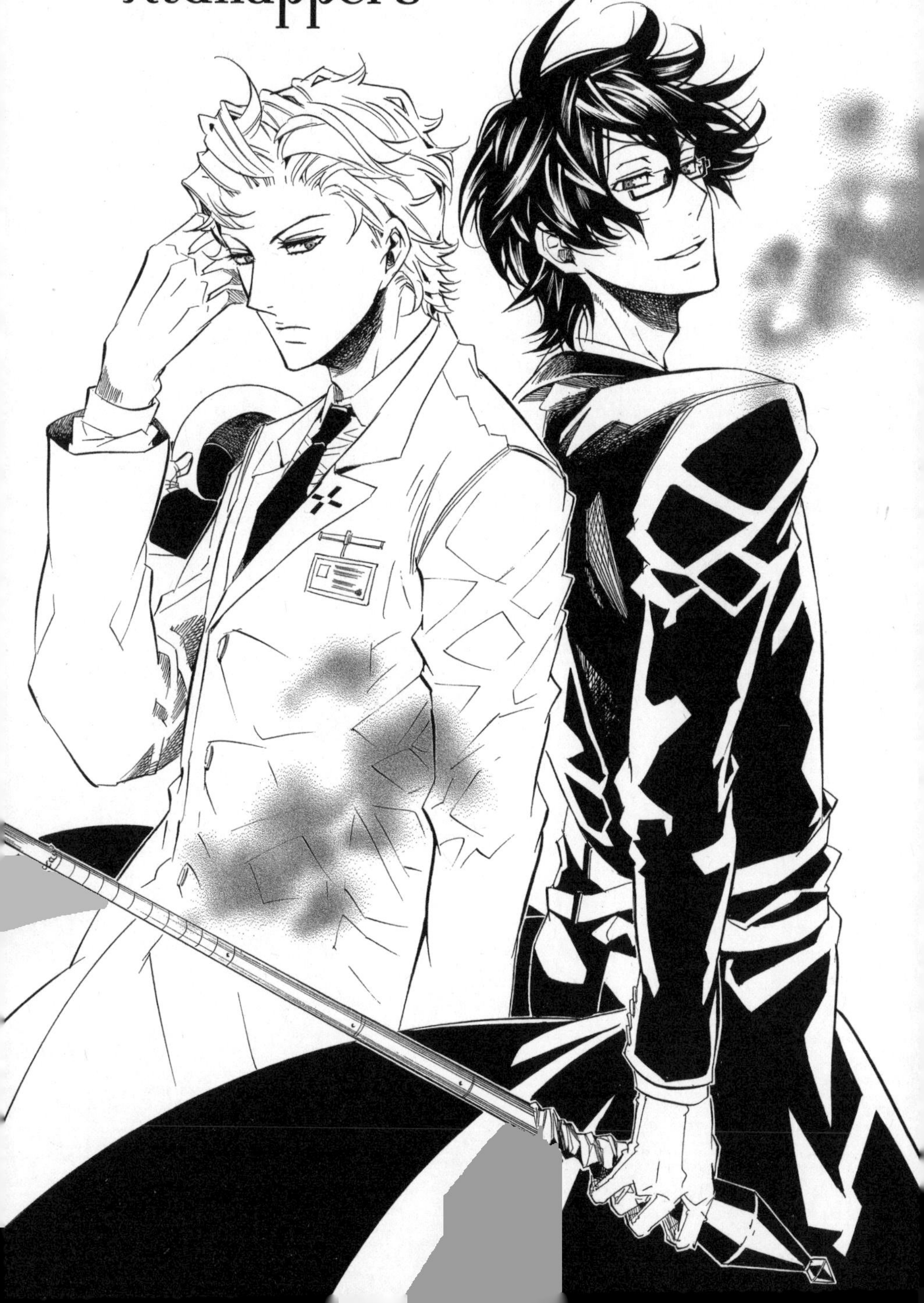

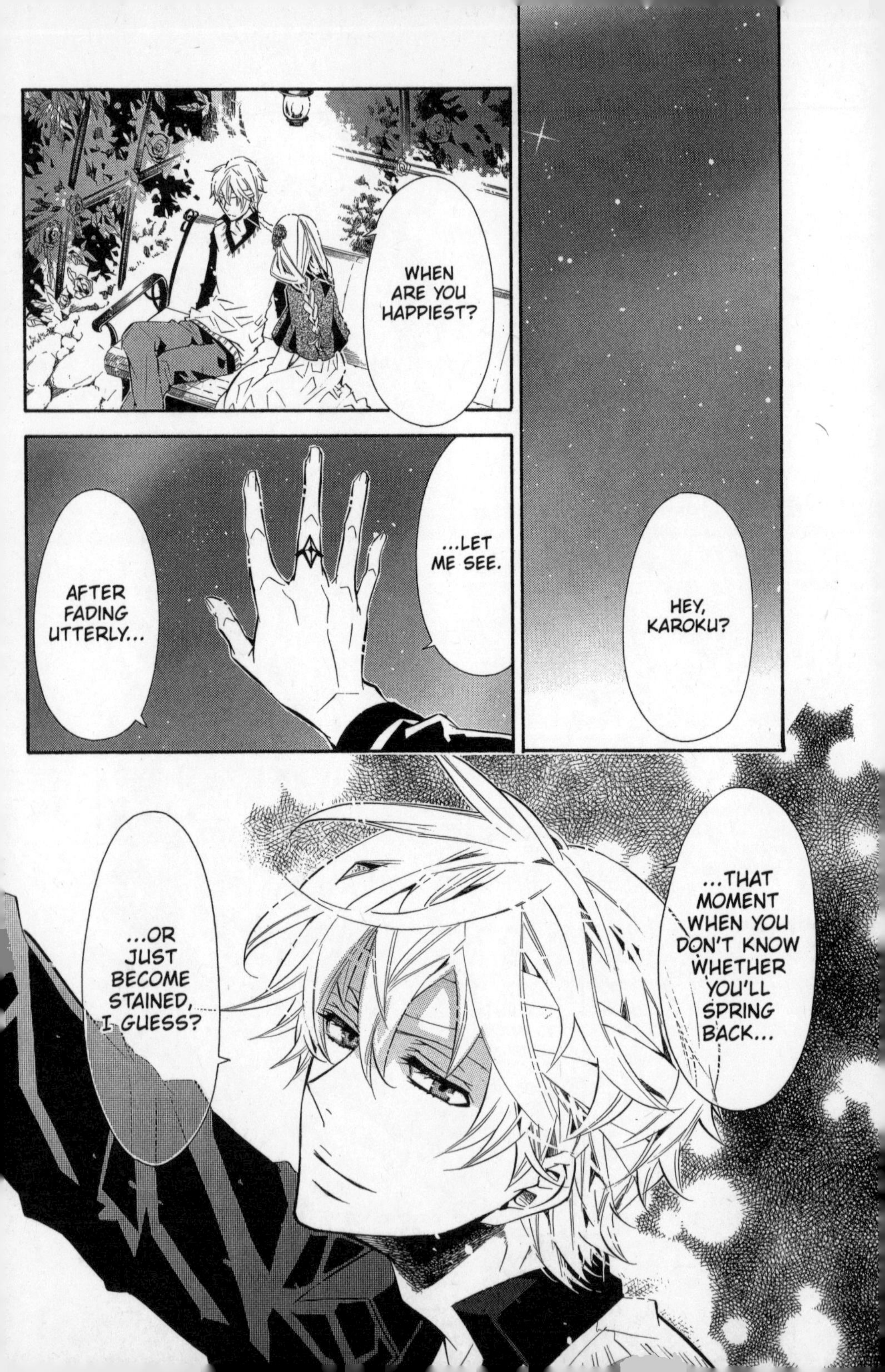
HEY, KAROKU?
WHEN ARE YOU HAPPIEST?
...LET ME SEE.
AFTER FADING UTTERLY...
...THAT MOMENT WHEN YOU DON'T KNOW WHETHER YOU'LL SPRING BACK...
...OR JUST BECOME STAINED, I GUESS?

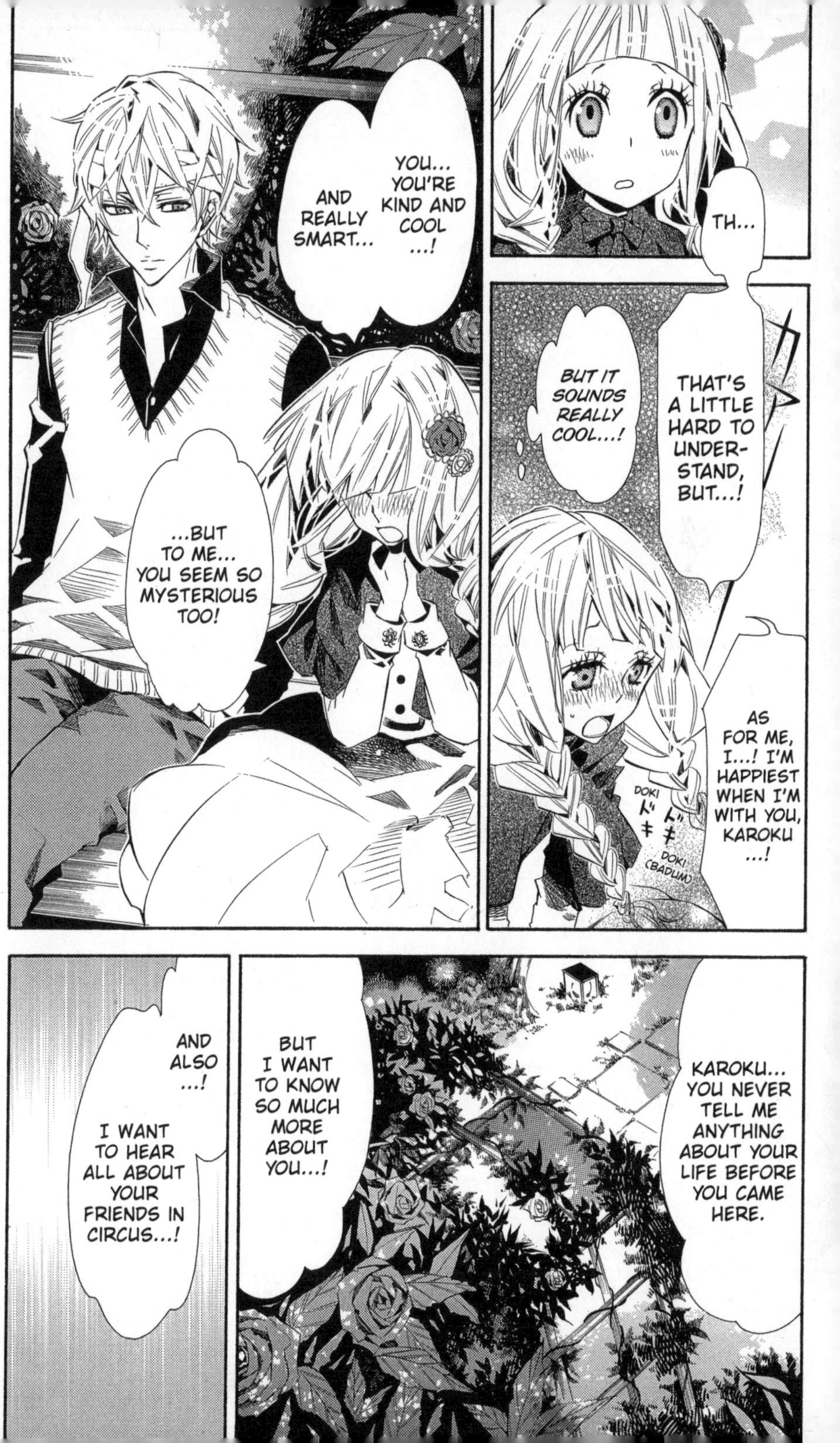
TH...
THAT'S A LITTLE HARD TO UNDER-STAND, BUT...!
BUT IT SOUNDS REALLY COOL...!
AS FOR ME, I...! I'M HAPPIEST WHEN I'M WITH YOU, KAROKU...!
ドキ DOKI
ドキ DOKI (BADUM)
YOU... YOU'RE KIND AND COOL...!
AND REALLY SMART...
...BUT TO ME... YOU SEEM SO MYSTERIOUS TOO!
KAROKU... YOU NEVER TELL ME ANYTHING ABOUT YOUR LIFE BEFORE YOU CAME HERE.
BUT I WANT TO KNOW SO MUCH MORE ABOUT YOU...!
AND ALSO...!
I WANT TO HEAR ALL ABOUT YOUR FRIENDS IN CIRCUS...!

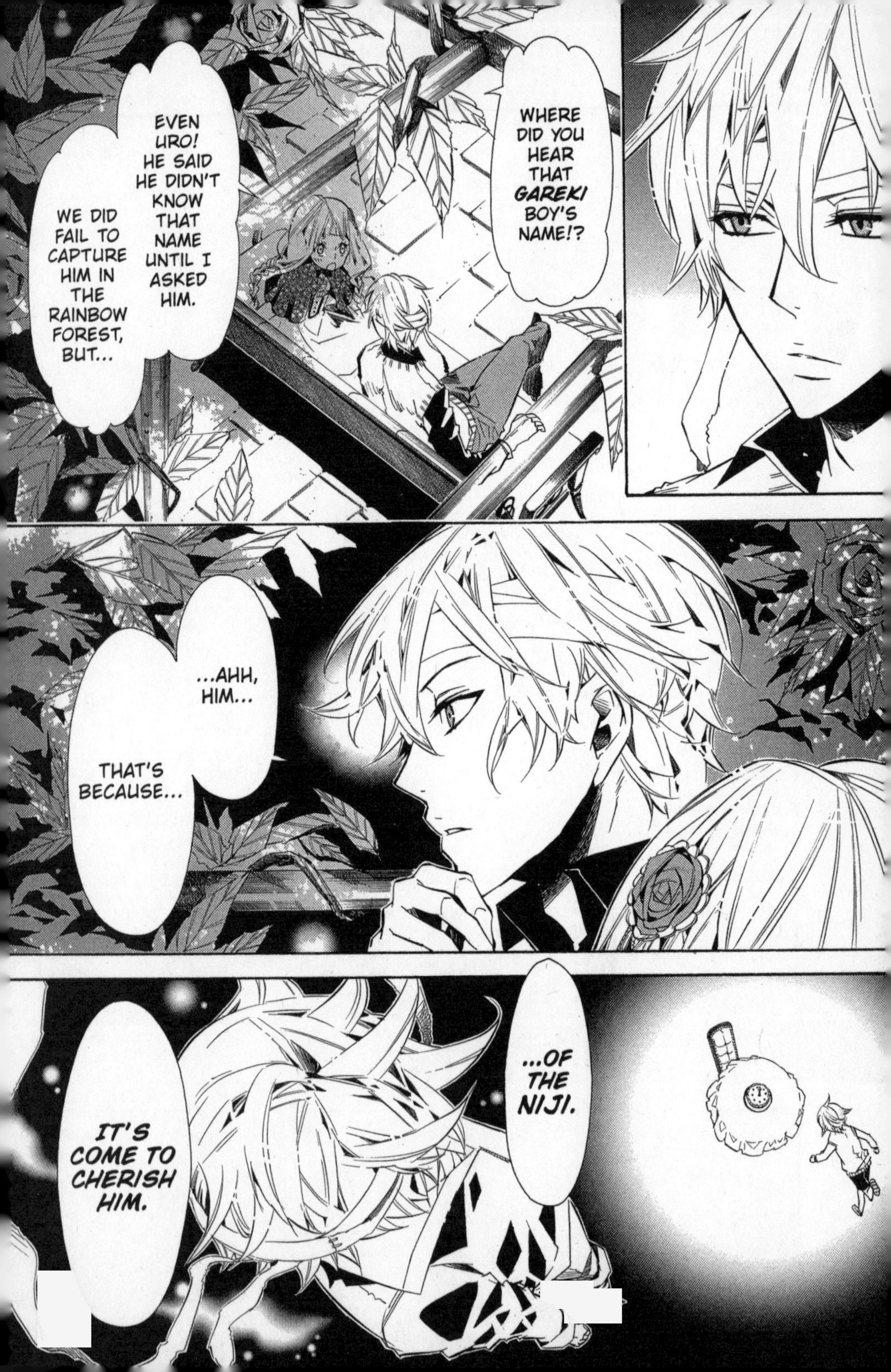
WHERE DID YOU HEAR THAT *GAREKI* BOY'S NAME!?
EVEN URO! HE SAID HE DIDN'T KNOW THAT NAME UNTIL I ASKED HIM.
WE DID FAIL TO CAPTURE HIM IN THE RAINBOW FOREST, BUT...
...AHH, HIM...
THAT'S BECAUSE...
...OF THE NIJI.
IT'S COME TO CHERISH HIM.

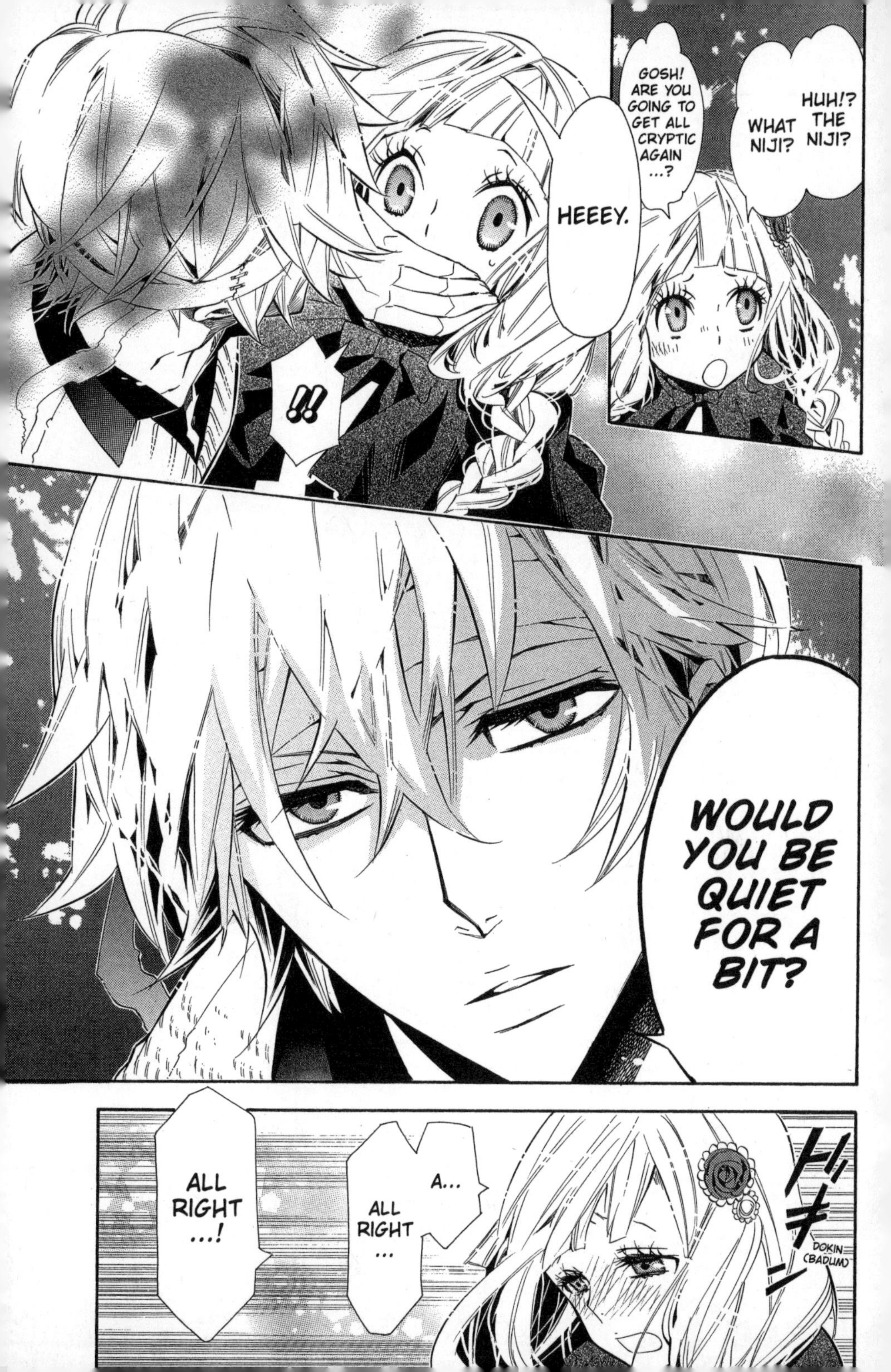
HUH!? THE NIJI? WHAT NIJI?
GOSH! ARE YOU GOING TO GET ALL CRYPTIC AGAIN ...?
HEEEY.
!!
WOULD YOU BE QUIET FOR A BIT?
DOKIN (BADUM)
A... ALL RIGHT ...
ALL RIGHT ...!

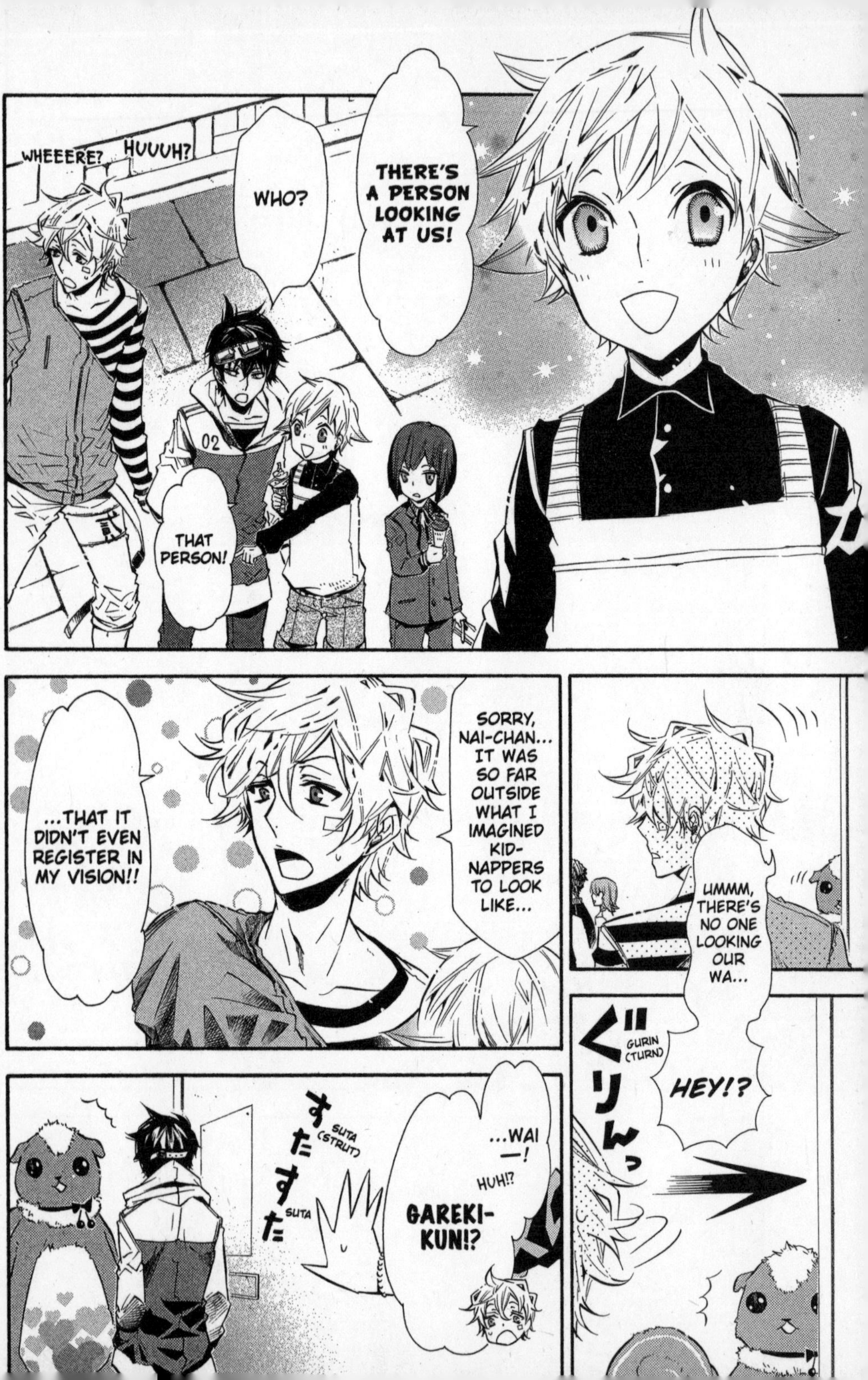
THERE'S A PERSON LOOKING AT US!
WHO?
HUUUH?
WHEEERE?
THAT PERSON!
UMMM, THERE'S NO ONE LOOKING OUR WA...
SORRY, NAI-CHAN... IT WAS SO FAR OUTSIDE WHAT I IMAGINED KID-NAPPERS TO LOOK LIKE...
...THAT IT DIDN'T EVEN REGISTER IN MY VISION!!
HEY!?
ぐりんっ
GURIN (TURN)
...WAI—!
HUH!?
GAREKI-KUN!?
すたすた
SUTA (STRUT)
SUTA

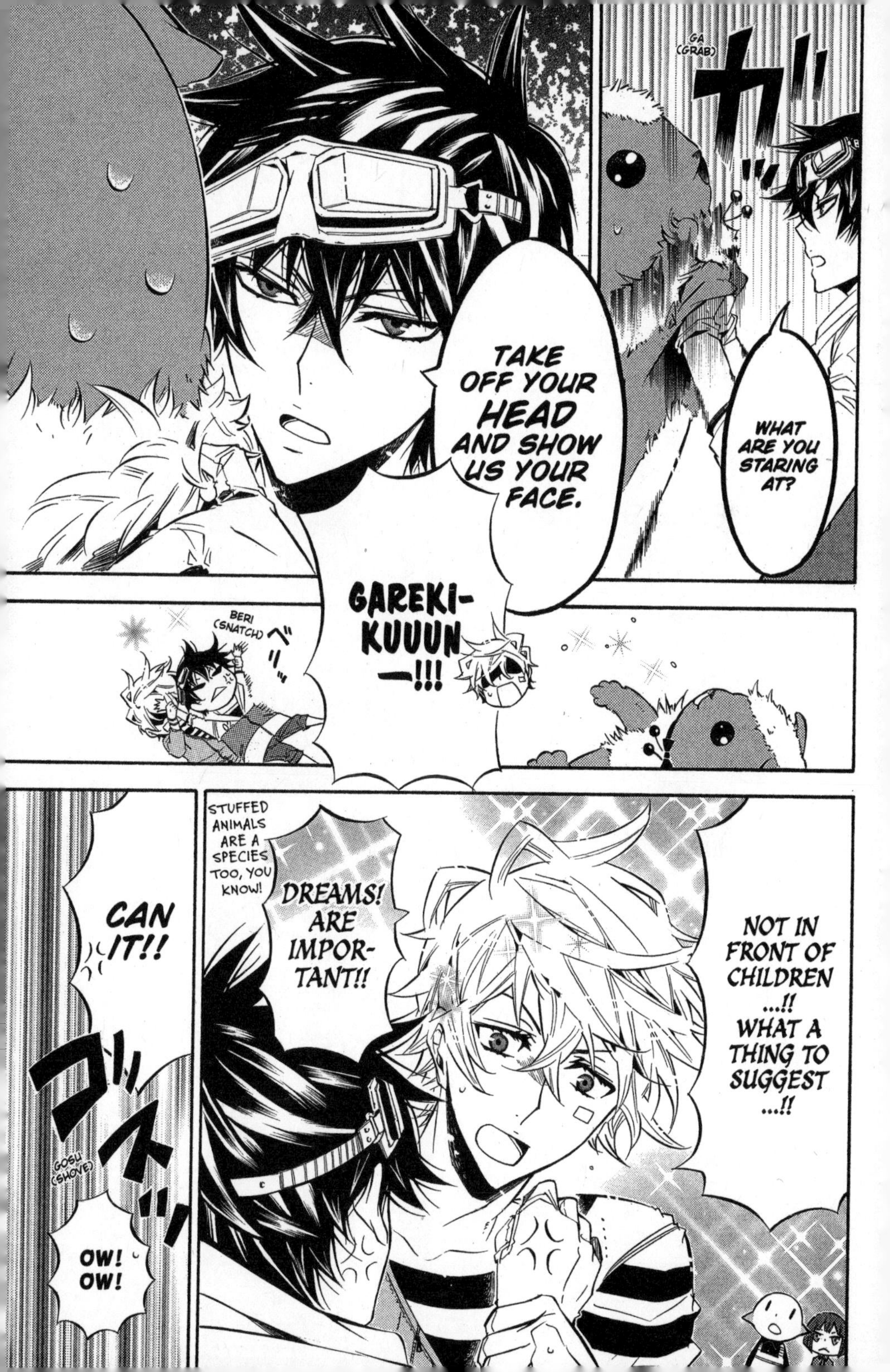
GA (GRAB)
WHAT ARE YOU STARING AT?
TAKE OFF YOUR HEAD AND SHOW US YOUR FACE.
GAREKI-KUUUN—!!!
BERI (SNATCH)
NOT IN FRONT OF CHILDREN ...!! WHAT A THING TO SUGGEST ...!!
DREAMS! ARE IMPORTANT!!
STUFFED ANIMALS ARE A SPECIES TOO, YOU KNOW!
CAN IT!!
GOSU (SHOVE)
OW! OW!

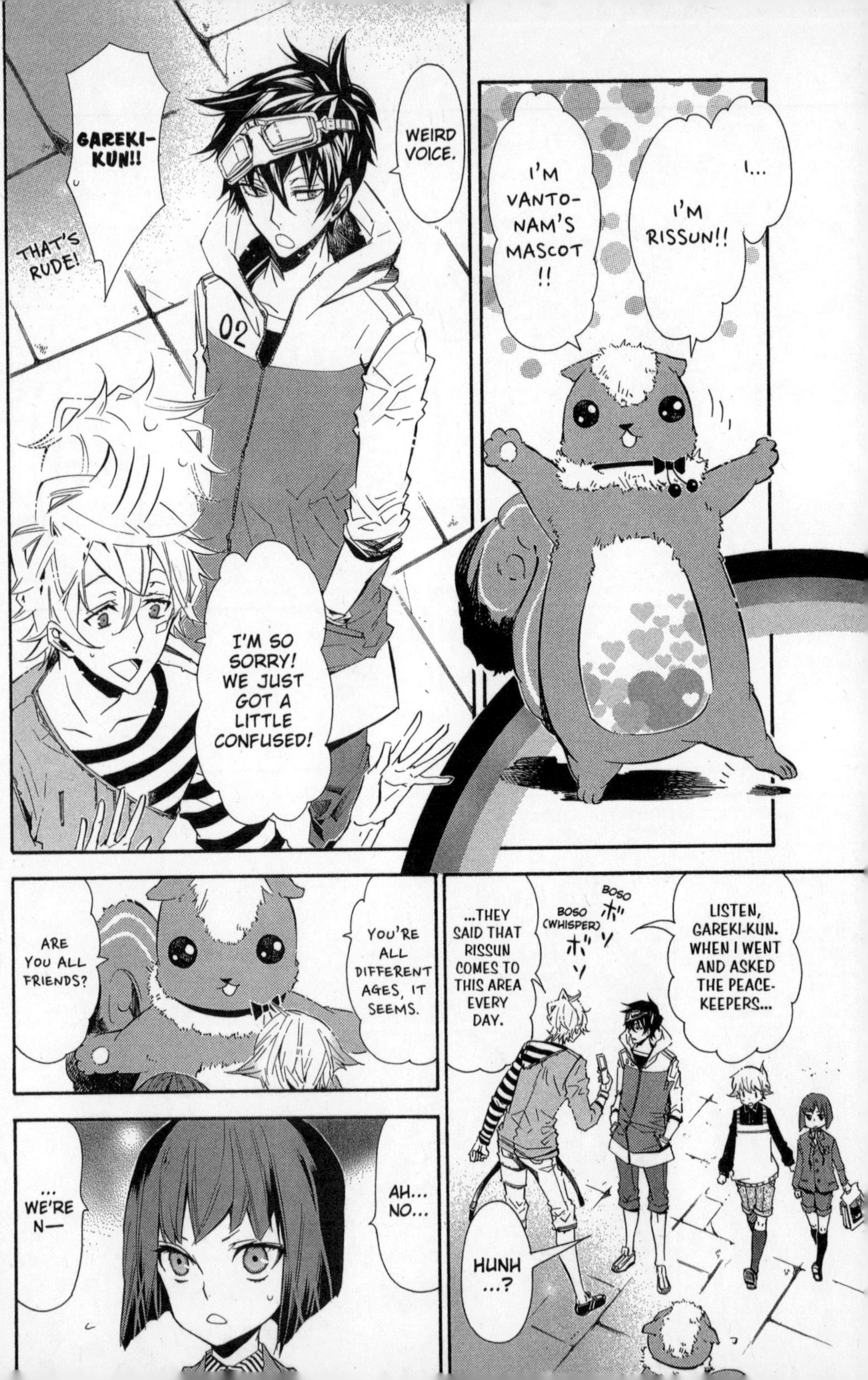
I...
I'M RISSUN!!
I'M VANTO-NAM'S MASCOT!!
WEIRD VOICE.
GAREKI-KUN!!
THAT'S RUDE!
I'M SO SORRY! WE JUST GOT A LITTLE CONFUSED!
LISTEN, GAREKI-KUN. WHEN I WENT AND ASKED THE PEACE-KEEPERS...
BOSO ボソ
BOSO (WHISPER) ボソ
...THEY SAID THAT RISSUN COMES TO THIS AREA EVERY DAY.
HUNH ...?
YOU'RE ALL DIFFERENT AGES, IT SEEMS.
ARE YOU ALL FRIENDS?
AH... NO...
... WE'RE N—

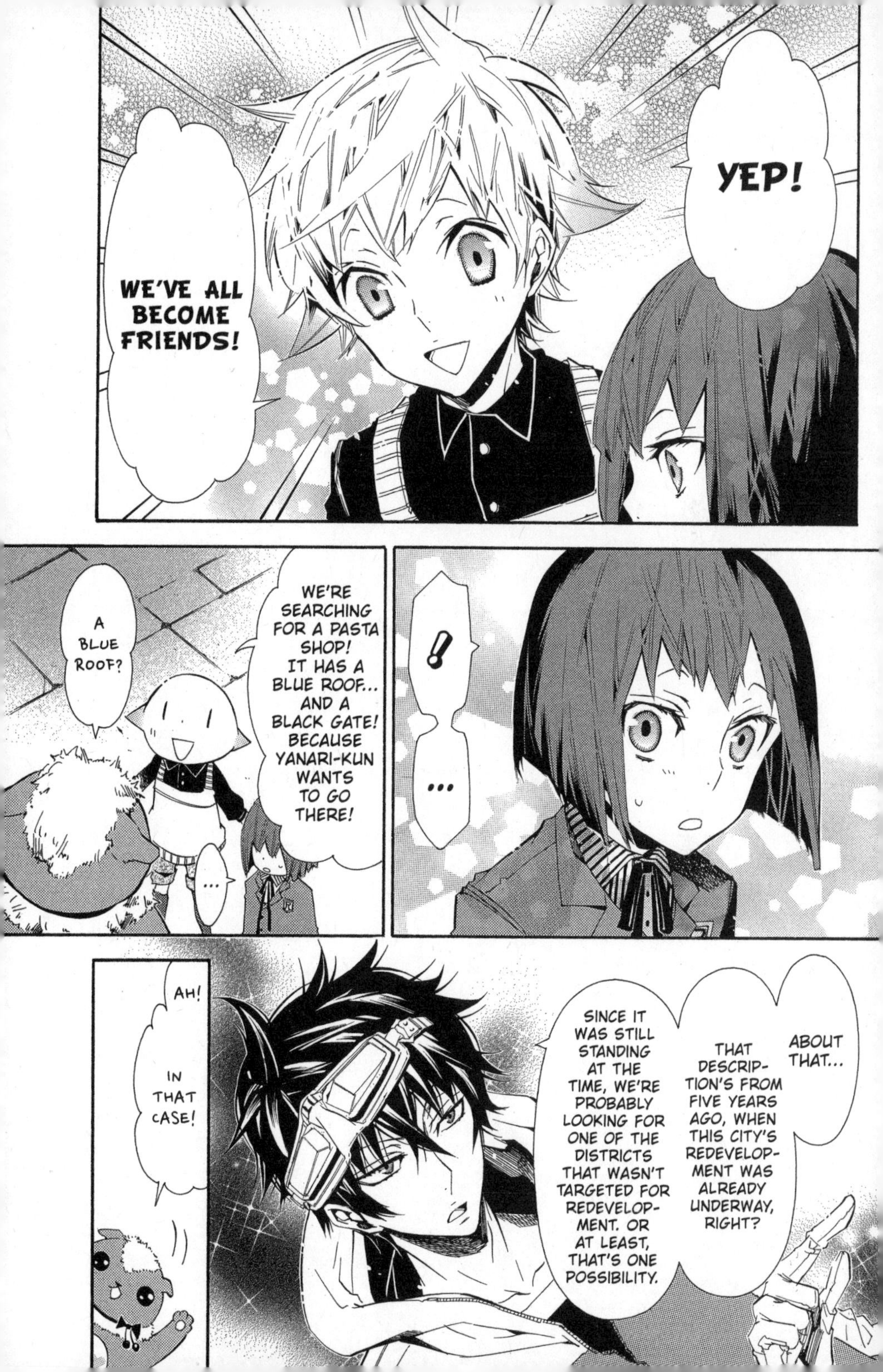
YEP!
WE'VE ALL BECOME FRIENDS!
!
...
WE'RE SEARCHING FOR A PASTA SHOP! IT HAS A BLUE ROOF... AND A BLACK GATE! BECAUSE YANARI-KUN WANTS TO GO THERE!
A BLUE ROOF?
...
ABOUT THAT...
THAT DESCRIPTION'S FROM FIVE YEARS AGO, WHEN THIS CITY'S REDEVELOPMENT WAS ALREADY UNDERWAY, RIGHT?
SINCE IT WAS STILL STANDING AT THE TIME, WE'RE PROBABLY LOOKING FOR ONE OF THE DISTRICTS THAT WASN'T TARGETED FOR REDEVELOPMENT. OR AT LEAST, THAT'S ONE POSSIBILITY.
AH!
IN THAT CASE!

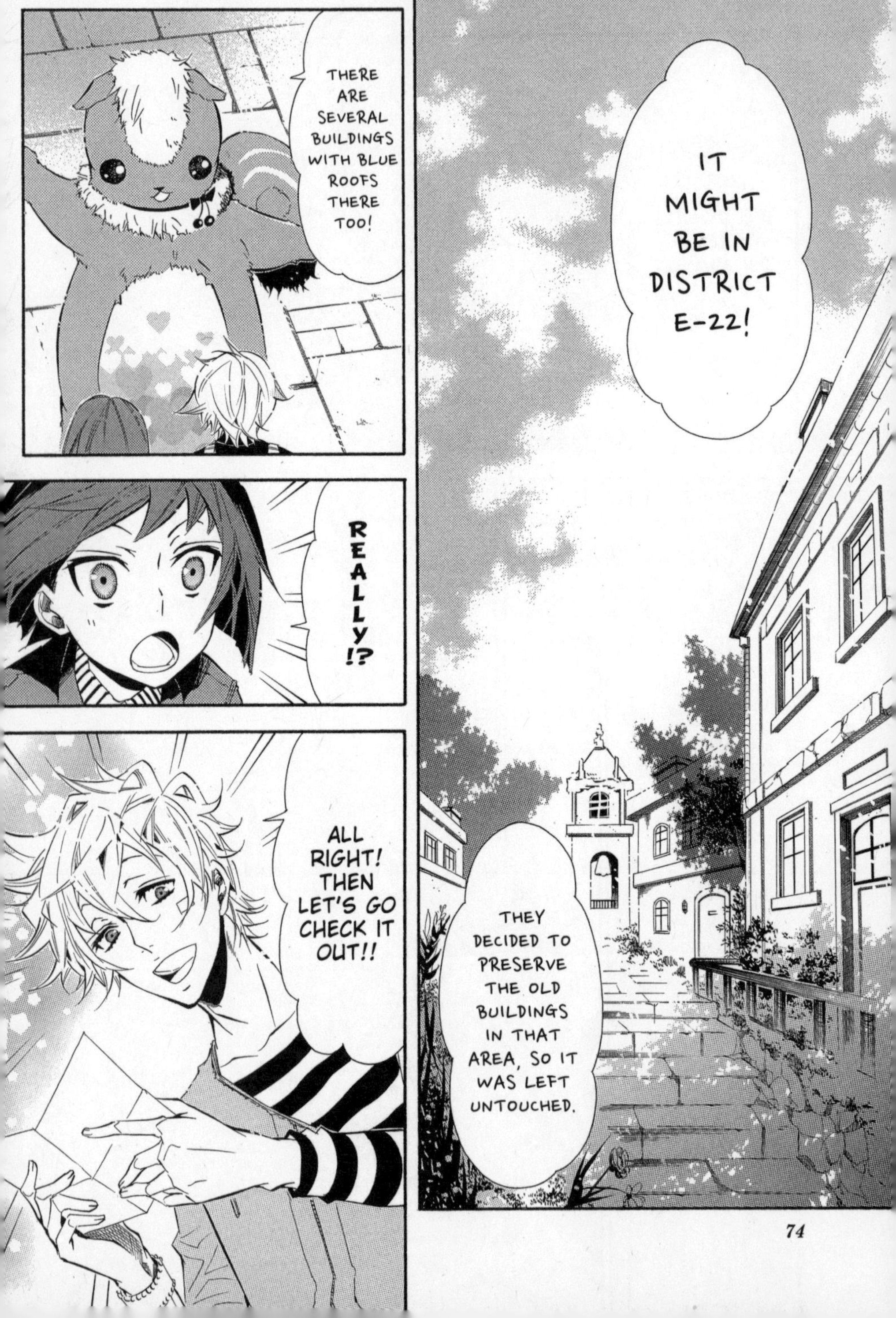
IT MIGHT BE IN DISTRICT E-22!
THEY DECIDED TO PRESERVE THE OLD BUILDINGS IN THAT AREA, SO IT WAS LEFT UNTOUCHED.
THERE ARE SEVERAL BUILDINGS WITH BLUE ROOFS THERE TOO!
REALLY!?
ALL RIGHT! THEN LET'S GO CHECK IT OUT!!

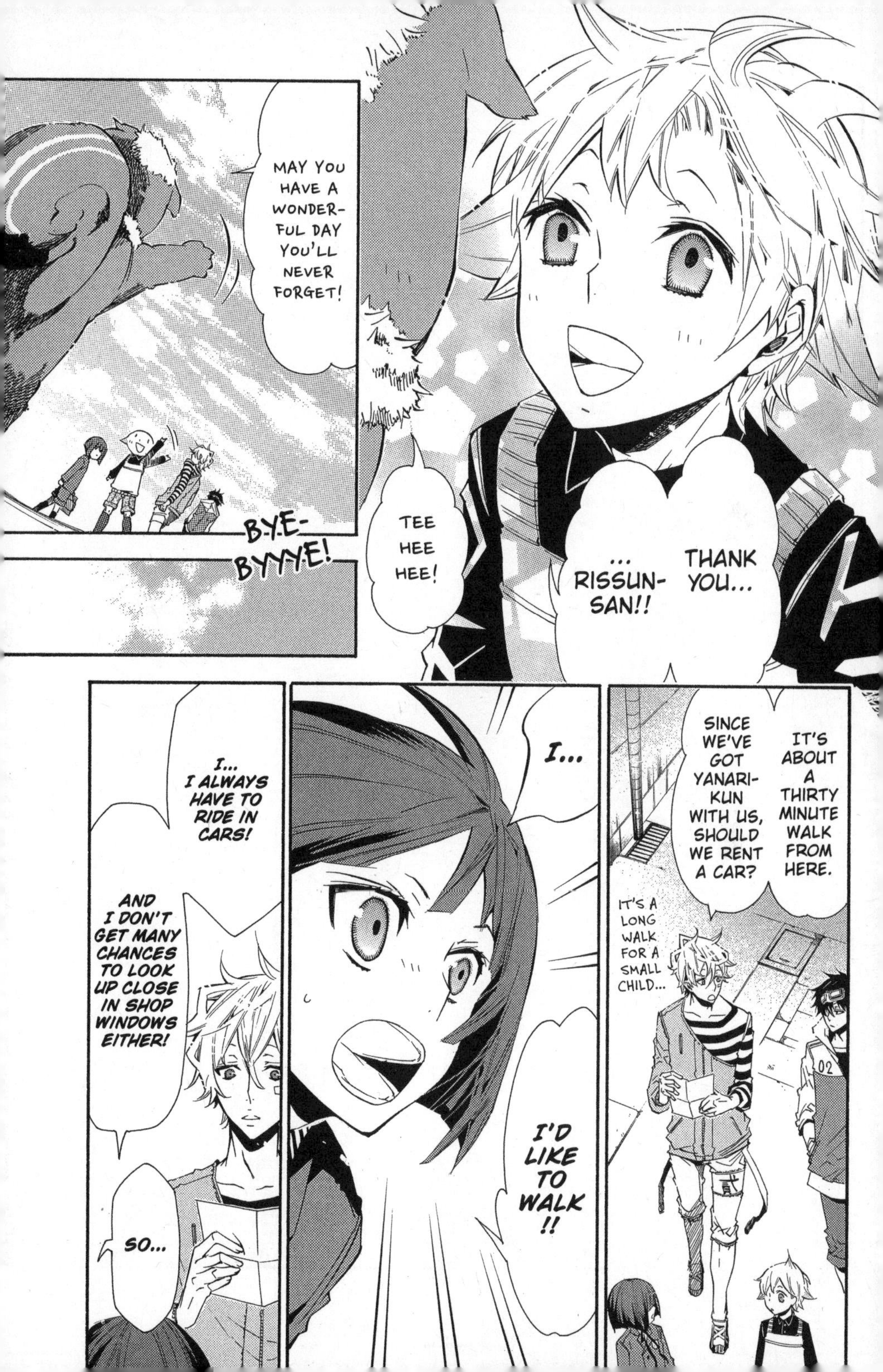
THANK YOU... ...RISSUN-SAN!!
TEE HEE HEE!
MAY YOU HAVE A WONDERFUL DAY YOU'LL NEVER FORGET!
BYE-BYYYE!
IT'S ABOUT A THIRTY MINUTE WALK FROM HERE.
SINCE WE'VE GOT YANARI-KUN WITH US, SHOULD WE RENT A CAR?
IT'S A LONG WALK FOR A SMALL CHILD...
I...
I'D LIKE TO WALK!!
I... I ALWAYS HAVE TO RIDE IN CARS!
AND I DON'T GET MANY CHANCES TO LOOK UP CLOSE IN SHOP WINDOWS EITHER!
SO...

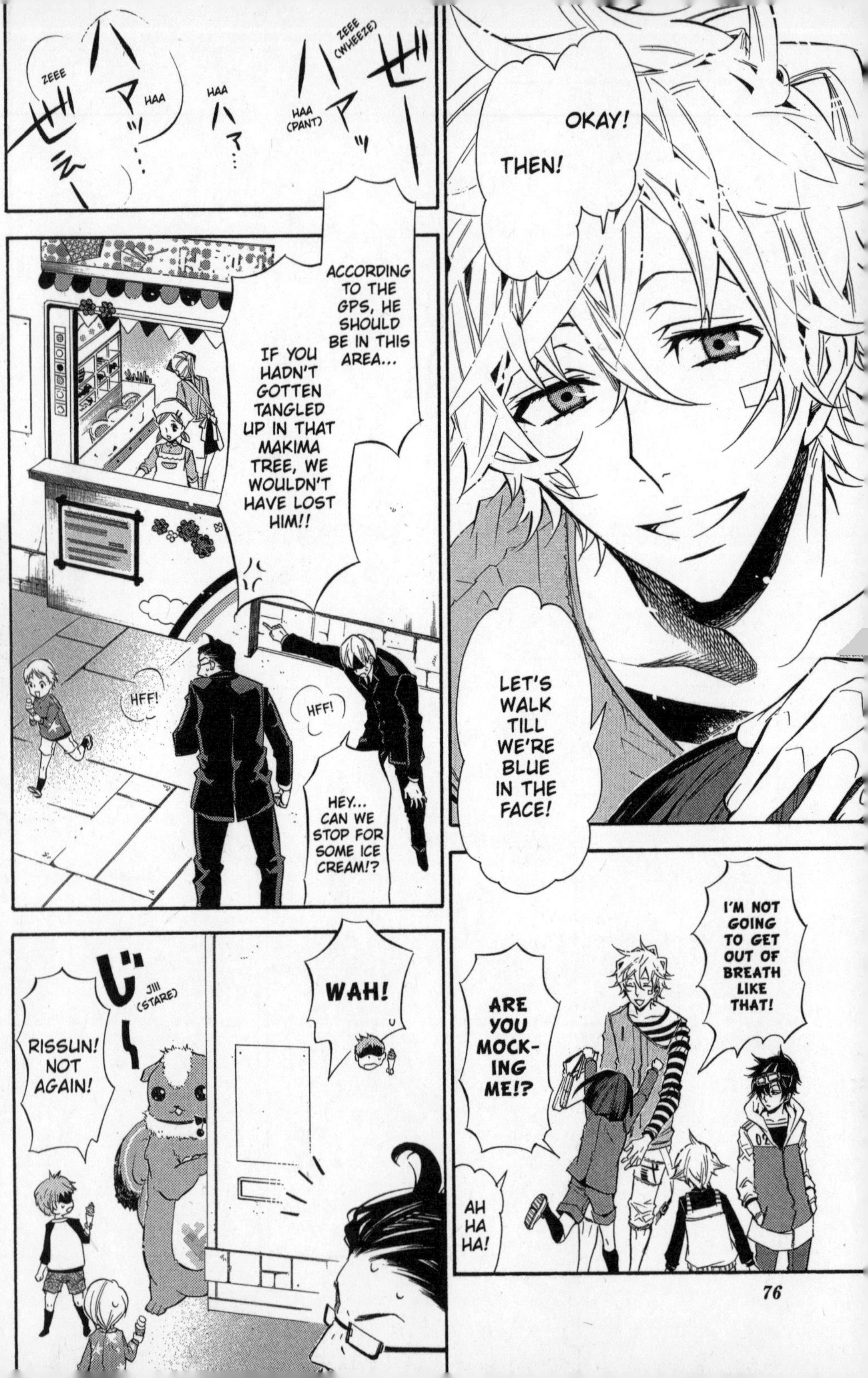
OKAY!
THEN!
LET'S WALK TILL WE'RE BLUE IN THE FACE!
ZEEE (WHEEZE)
HAA (PANT)
HAA
HAA
ZEEE
ACCORDING TO THE GPS, HE SHOULD BE IN THIS AREA...
IF YOU HADN'T GOTTEN TANGLED UP IN THAT MAKIMA TREE, WE WOULDN'T HAVE LOST HIM!!
HFF!
HFF!
HEY... CAN WE STOP FOR SOME ICE CREAM!?
I'M NOT GOING TO GET OUT OF BREATH LIKE THAT!
ARE YOU MOCK-ING ME!?
AH HA HA!
WAH!
JIII (STARE)
RISSUN! NOT AGAIN!

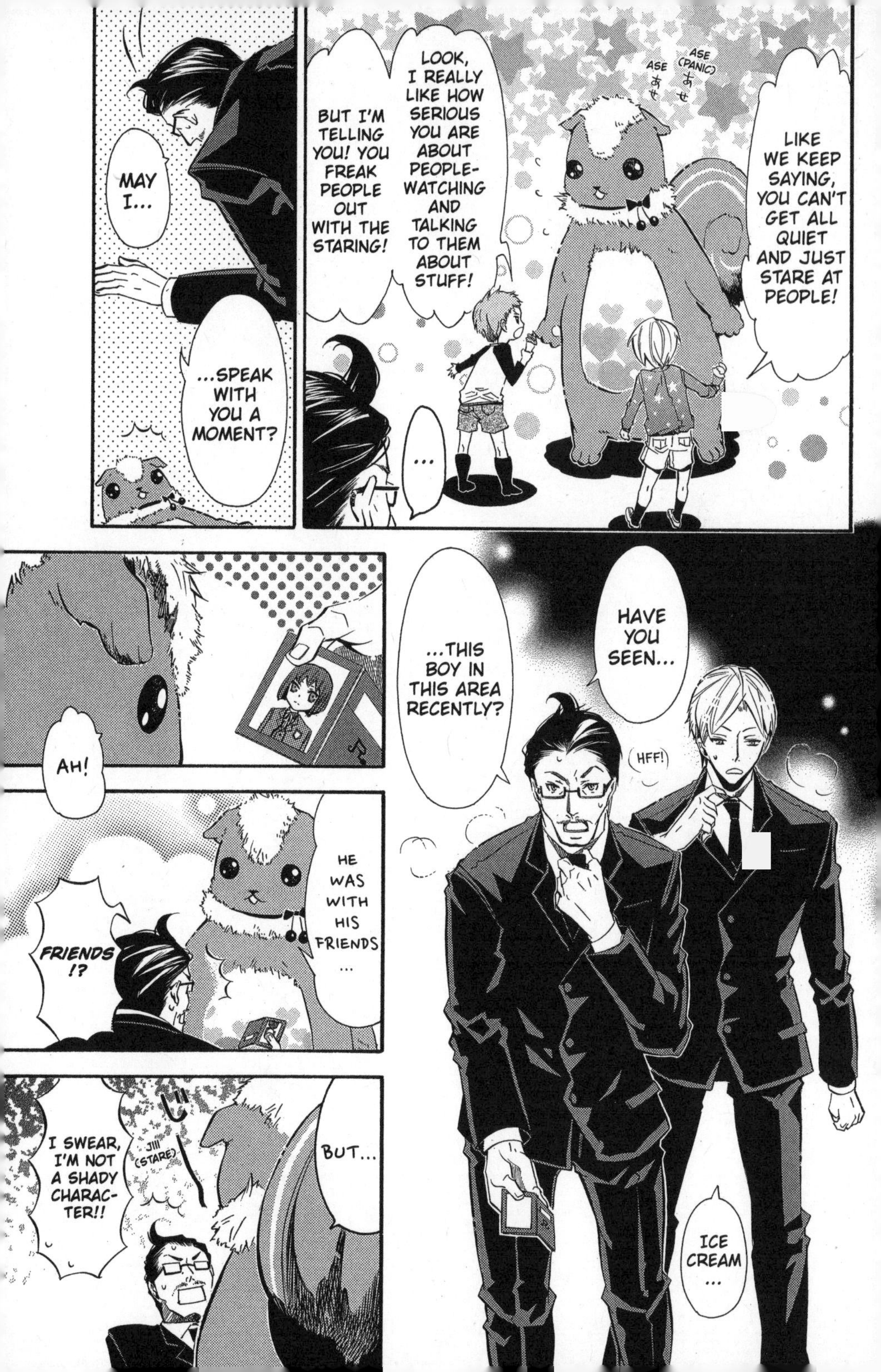
LIKE WE KEEP SAYING, YOU CAN'T GET ALL QUIET AND JUST STARE AT PEOPLE!
ASE (PANIC) あせ
ASE あせ
LOOK, I REALLY LIKE HOW SERIOUS YOU ARE ABOUT PEOPLE-WATCHING AND TALKING TO THEM ABOUT STUFF!
BUT I'M TELLING YOU! YOU FREAK PEOPLE OUT WITH THE STARING!
...
MAY I...
...SPEAK WITH YOU A MOMENT?
HAVE YOU SEEN...
...THIS BOY IN THIS AREA RECENTLY?
(HFF!)
ICE CREAM ...
AH!
HE WAS WITH HIS FRIENDS ...
FRIENDS !?
BUT...
JIII (STARE)
I SWEAR, I'M NOT A SHADY CHARAC-TER!!

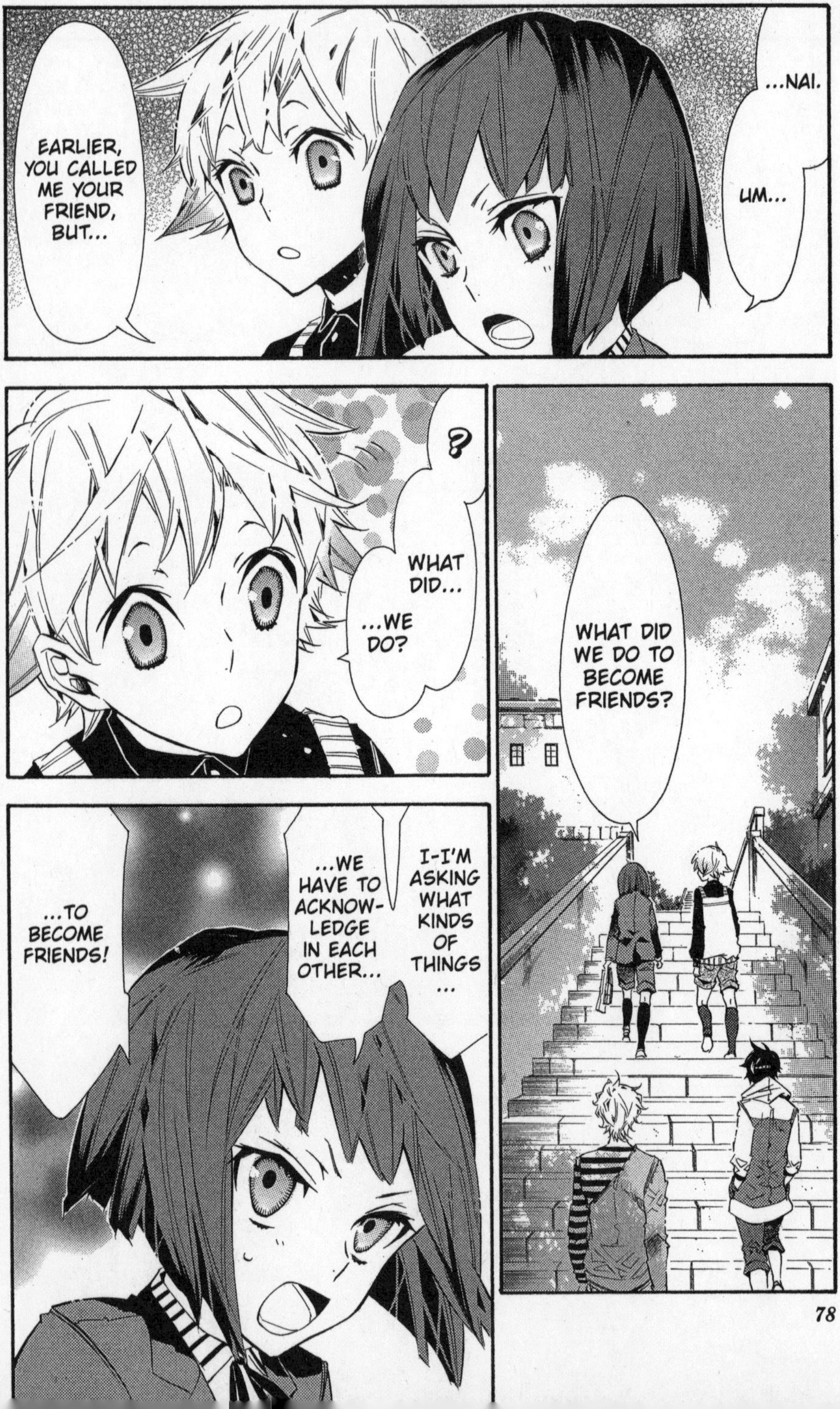
...NAI.
UM...
EARLIER, YOU CALLED ME YOUR FRIEND, BUT...
WHAT DID WE DO TO BECOME FRIENDS?
?
WHAT DID...
...WE DO?
I-I'M ASKING WHAT KINDS OF THINGS...
...WE HAVE TO ACKNOW-LEDGE IN EACH OTHER...
...TO BECOME FRIENDS!

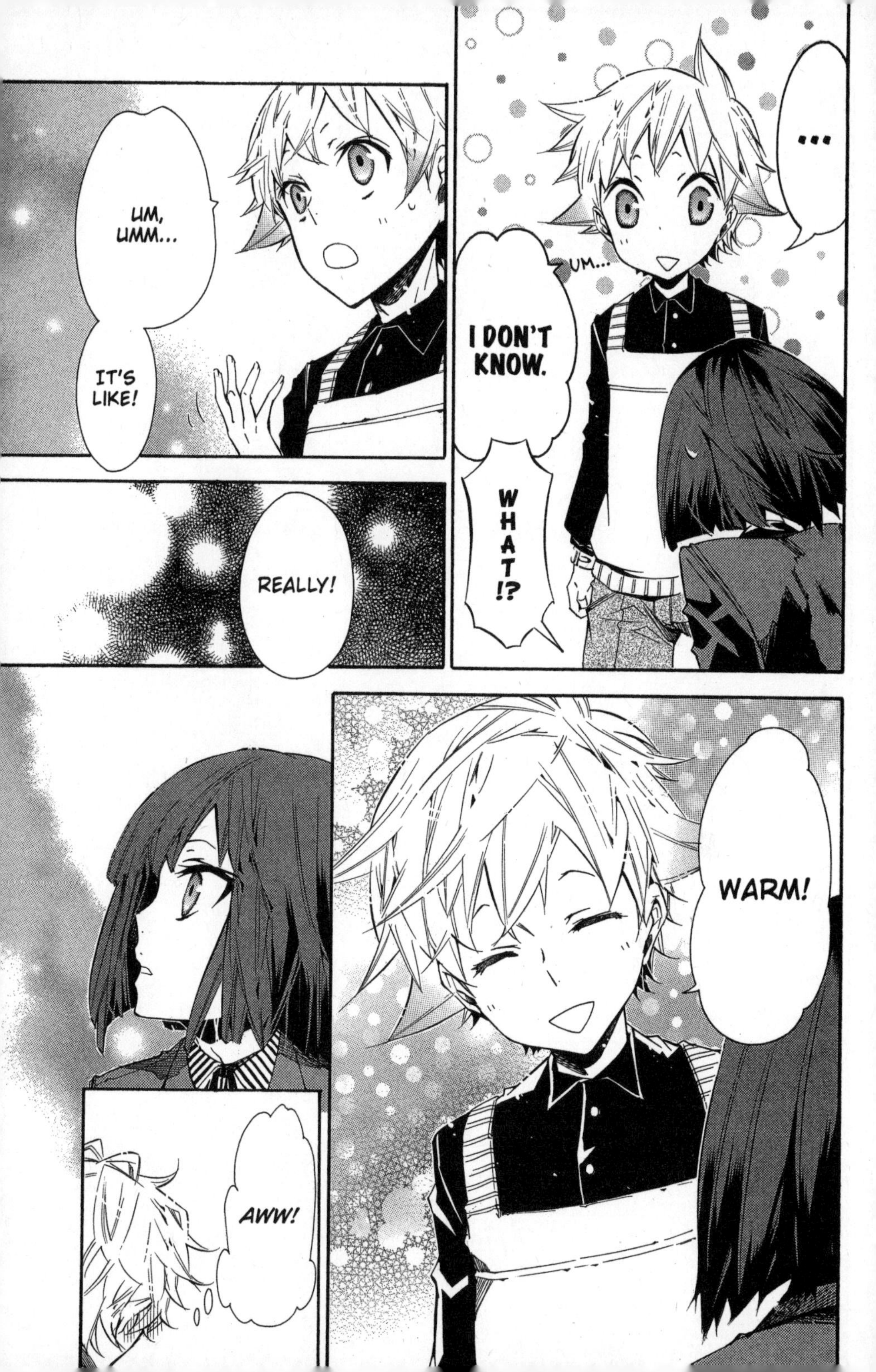
...
UM...
I DON'T KNOW.
WHAT!?
UM, UMM...
IT'S LIKE!
REALLY!
WARM!
AWW!

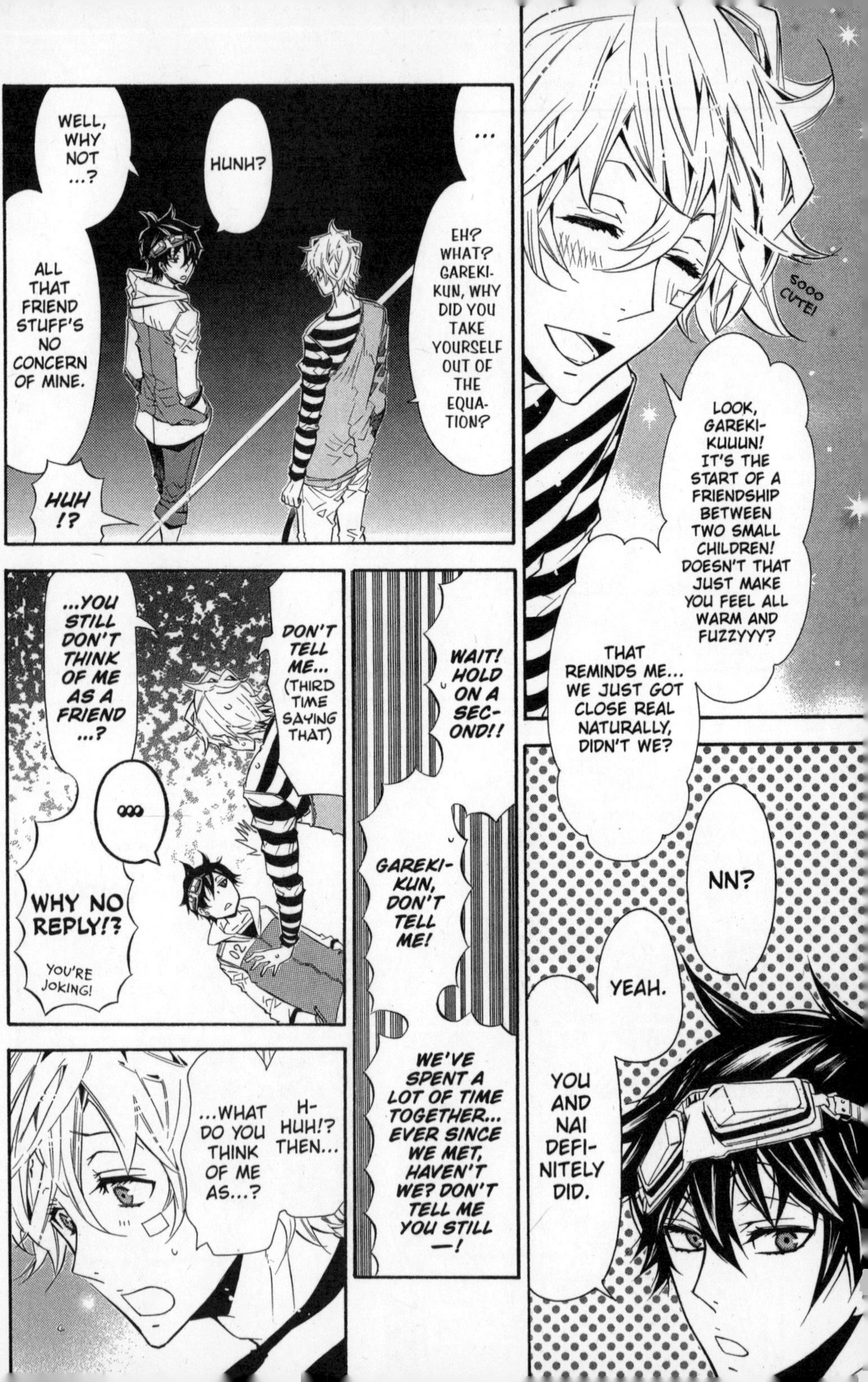
SOOO CUTE!
LOOK, GAREKI-KUUUN! IT'S THE START OF A FRIENDSHIP BETWEEN TWO SMALL CHILDREN! DOESN'T THAT JUST MAKE YOU FEEL ALL WARM AND FUZZYYY?
THAT REMINDS ME... WE JUST GOT CLOSE REAL NATURALLY, DIDN'T WE?
NN?
YEAH.
YOU AND NAI DEFINITELY DID.
...
EH? WHAT? GAREKI-KUN, WHY DID YOU TAKE YOURSELF OUT OF THE EQUATION?
HUNH?
WELL, WHY NOT ...?
ALL THAT FRIEND STUFF'S NO CONCERN OF MINE.
HUH!?
WAIT! HOLD ON A SEC-OND!!
GAREKI-KUN, DON'T TELL ME!
WE'VE SPENT A LOT OF TIME TOGETHER... EVER SINCE WE MET, HAVEN'T WE? DON'T TELL ME YOU STILL—!
DON'T TELL ME... (THIRD TIME SAYING THAT)
...YOU STILL DON'T THINK OF ME AS A FRIEND ...?
...
WHY NO REPLY!?
YOU'RE JOKING!
H-HUH!? THEN...
...WHAT DO YOU THINK OF ME AS...?

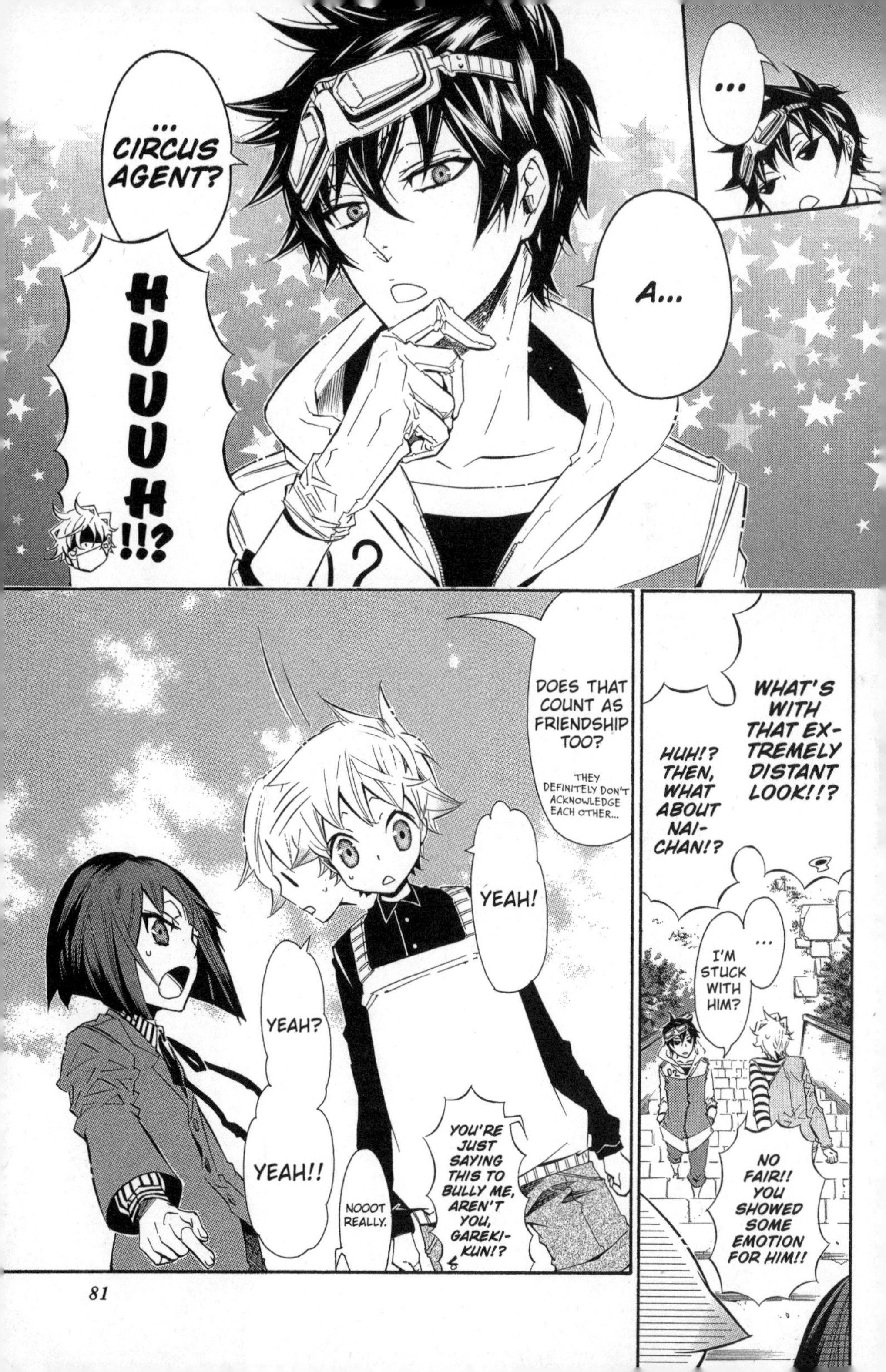
...
A...
... CIRCUS AGENT?
... HUUUUH!!?
WHAT'S WITH THAT EX-TREMELY DISTANT LOOK!!?
HUH!? THEN, WHAT ABOUT NAI-CHAN!?
... I'M STUCK WITH HIM?
NO FAIR!! YOU SHOWED SOME EMOTION FOR HIM!!
DOES THAT COUNT AS FRIENDSHIP TOO?
THEY DEFINITELY DON'T ACKNOWLEDGE EACH OTHER...
YEAH!
YEAH?
YOU'RE JUST SAYING THIS TO BULLY ME, AREN'T YOU, GAREKI-KUN!?
YEAH!!
NOOOT REALLY.

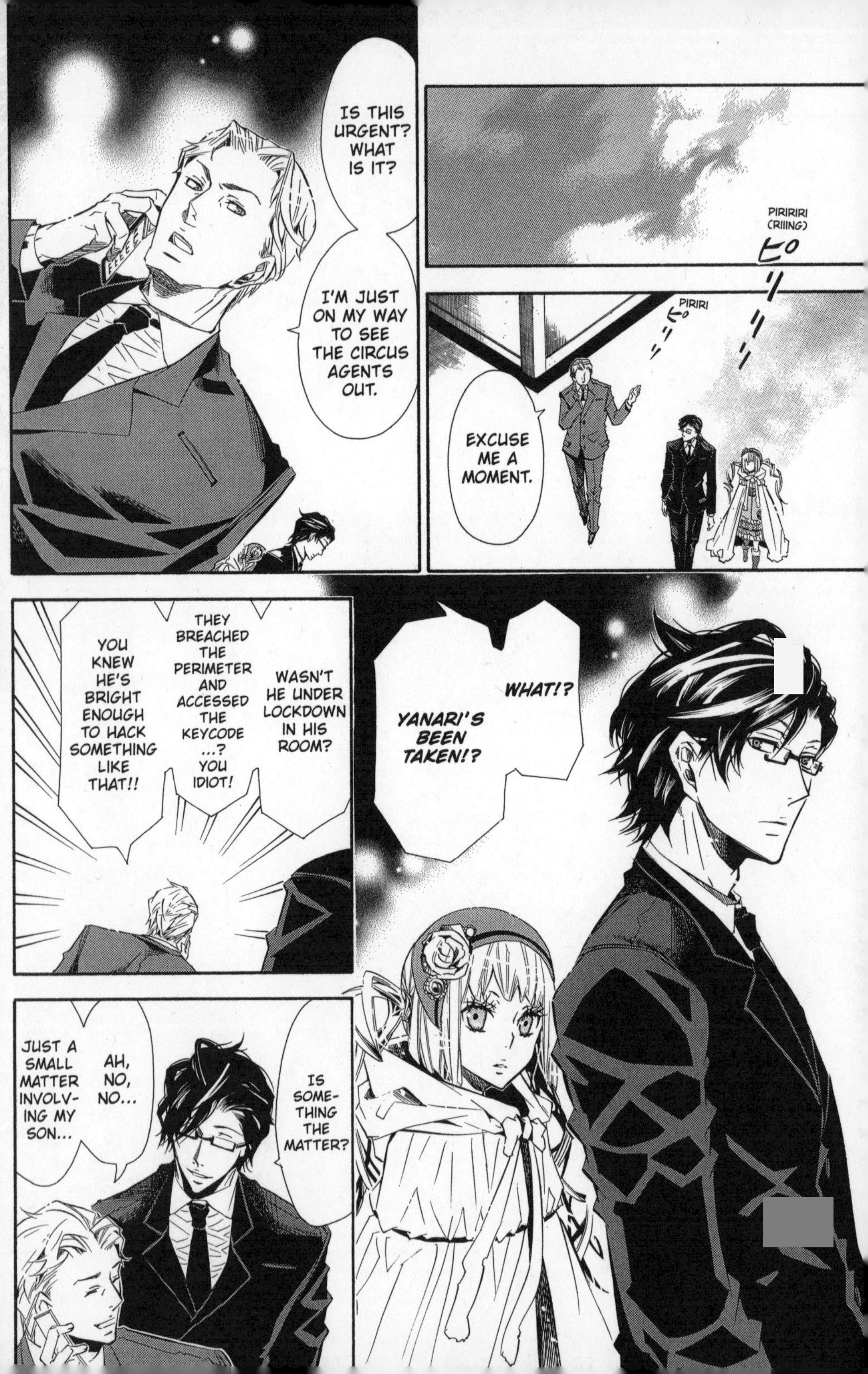
PIRIRIRI (RIIING)
PIRIRI
EXCUSE ME A MOMENT.
IS THIS URGENT? WHAT IS IT?
I'M JUST ON MY WAY TO SEE THE CIRCUS AGENTS OUT.
WHAT!?
YANARI'S BEEN TAKEN!?
WASN'T HE UNDER LOCKDOWN IN HIS ROOM?
THEY BREACHED THE PERIMETER AND ACCESSED THE KEYCODE ...? YOU IDIOT!
YOU KNEW HE'S BRIGHT ENOUGH TO HACK SOMETHING LIKE THAT!!
IS SOME-THING THE MATTER?
AH, NO, NO...
JUST A SMALL MATTER INVOLV-ING MY SON...

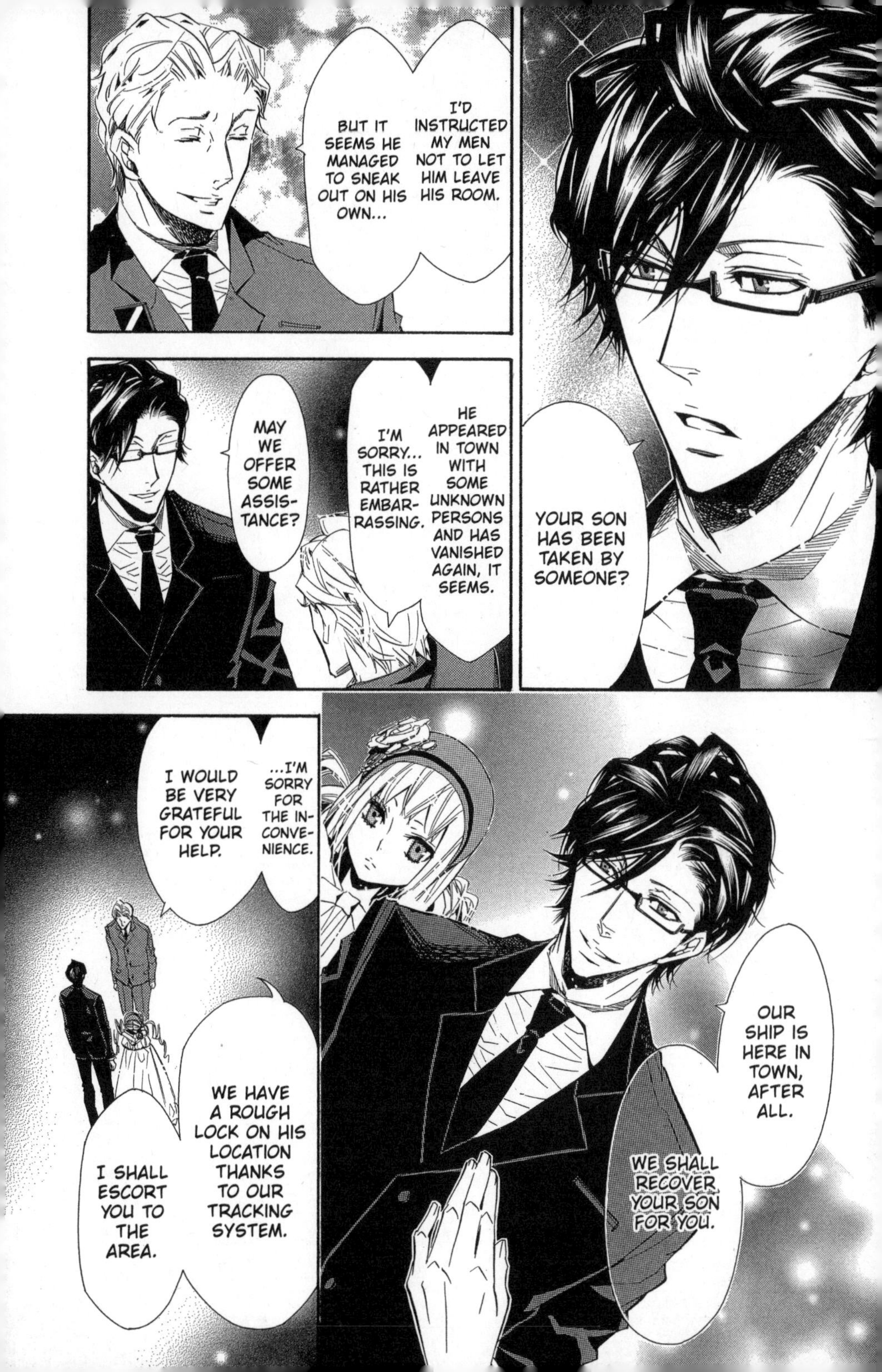
YOUR SON HAS BEEN TAKEN BY SOMEONE?
I'D INSTRUCTED MY MEN NOT TO LET HIM LEAVE HIS ROOM.
BUT IT SEEMS HE MANAGED TO SNEAK OUT ON HIS OWN...
HE APPEARED IN TOWN WITH SOME UNKNOWN PERSONS AND HAS VANISHED AGAIN, IT SEEMS.
I'M SORRY... THIS IS RATHER EMBARRASSING.
MAY WE OFFER SOME ASSISTANCE?
OUR SHIP IS HERE IN TOWN, AFTER ALL.
WE SHALL RECOVER YOUR SON FOR YOU.
...I'M SORRY FOR THE INCONVENIENCE.
I WOULD BE VERY GRATEFUL FOR YOUR HELP.
WE HAVE A ROUGH LOCK ON HIS LOCATION THANKS TO OUR TRACKING SYSTEM.
I SHALL ESCORT YOU TO THE AREA.

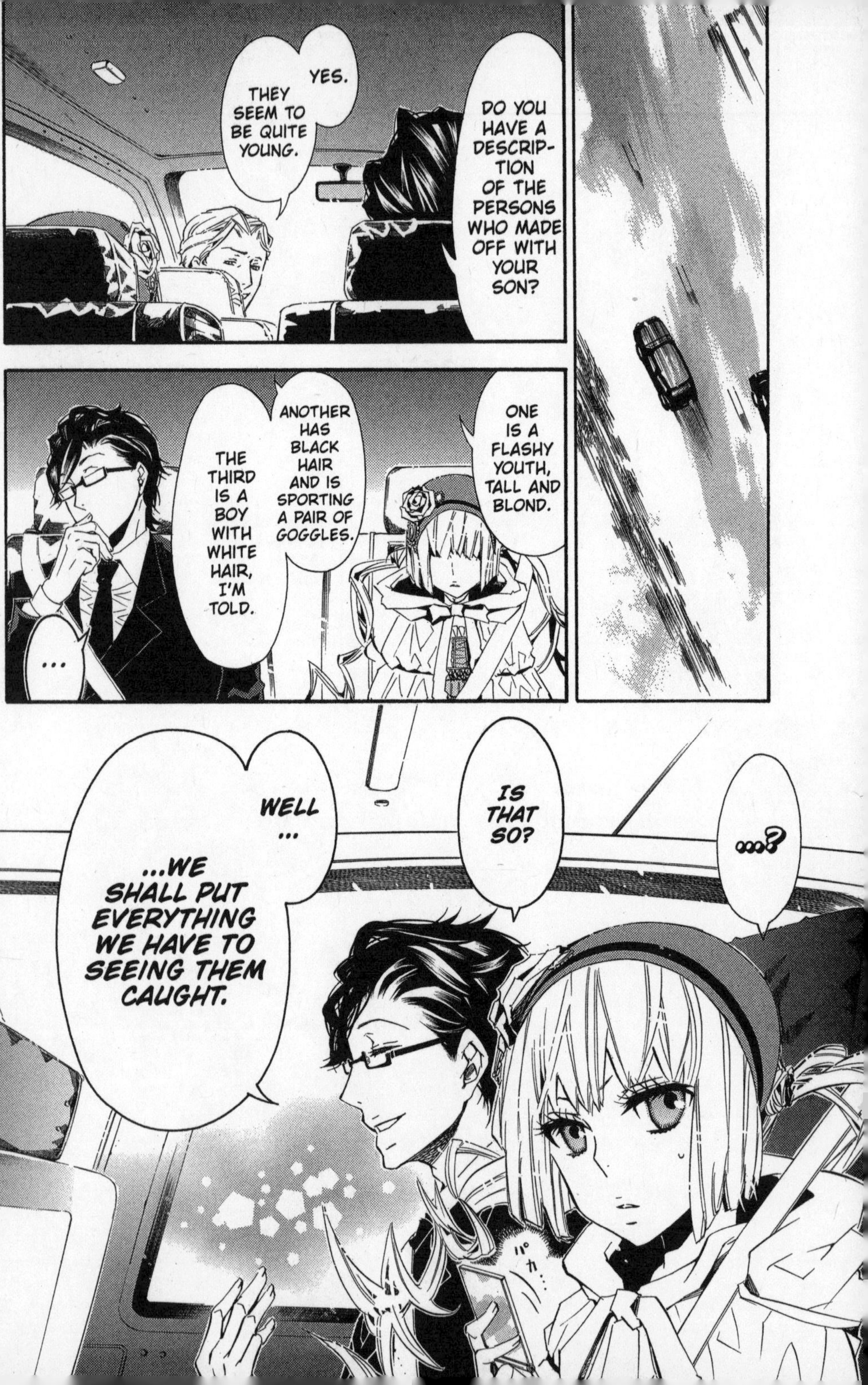
DO YOU HAVE A DESCRIPTION OF THE PERSONS WHO MADE OFF WITH YOUR SON?
YES. THEY SEEM TO BE QUITE YOUNG.
ONE IS A FLASHY YOUTH, TALL AND BLOND.
ANOTHER HAS BLACK HAIR AND IS SPORTING A PAIR OF GOGGLES.
THE THIRD IS A BOY WITH WHITE HAIR, I'M TOLD.
...
...?
IS THAT SO?
WELL...
...WE SHALL PUT EVERYTHING WE HAVE TO SEEING THEM CAUGHT.
パカ…

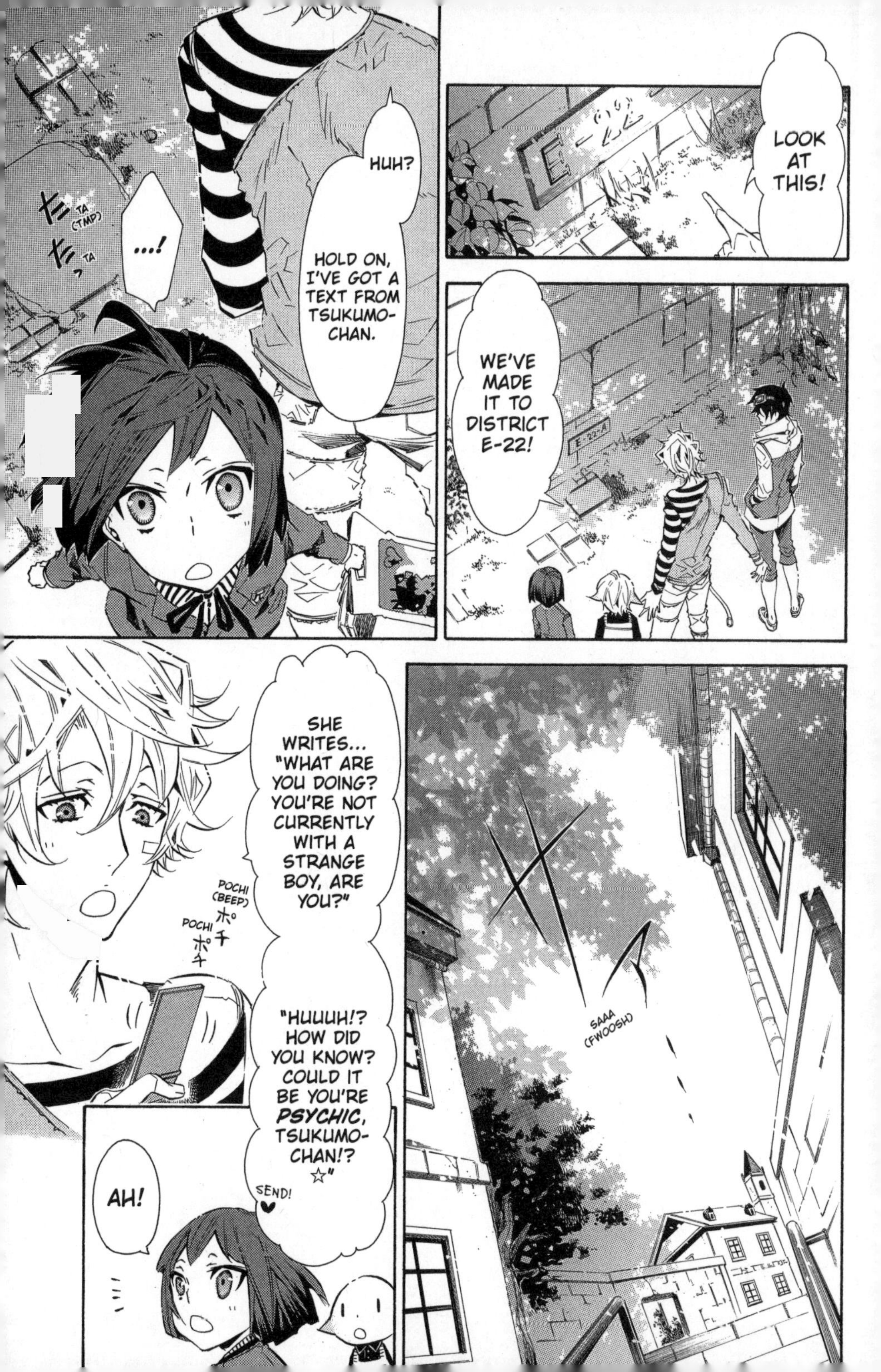
LOOK AT THIS!
WE'VE MADE IT TO DISTRICT E-22!
HUH?
HOLD ON, I'VE GOT A TEXT FROM TSUKUMO-CHAN.
...!
TA (TMP)
TA
SAAA (FWOOSH)
SHE WRITES... "WHAT ARE YOU DOING? YOU'RE NOT CURRENTLY WITH A STRANGE BOY, ARE YOU?"
POCHI (BEEP)
POCHI
"HUUUH!? HOW DID YOU KNOW? COULD IT BE YOU'RE *PSYCHIC*, TSUKUMO-CHAN!? ☆"
SEND!
AH!

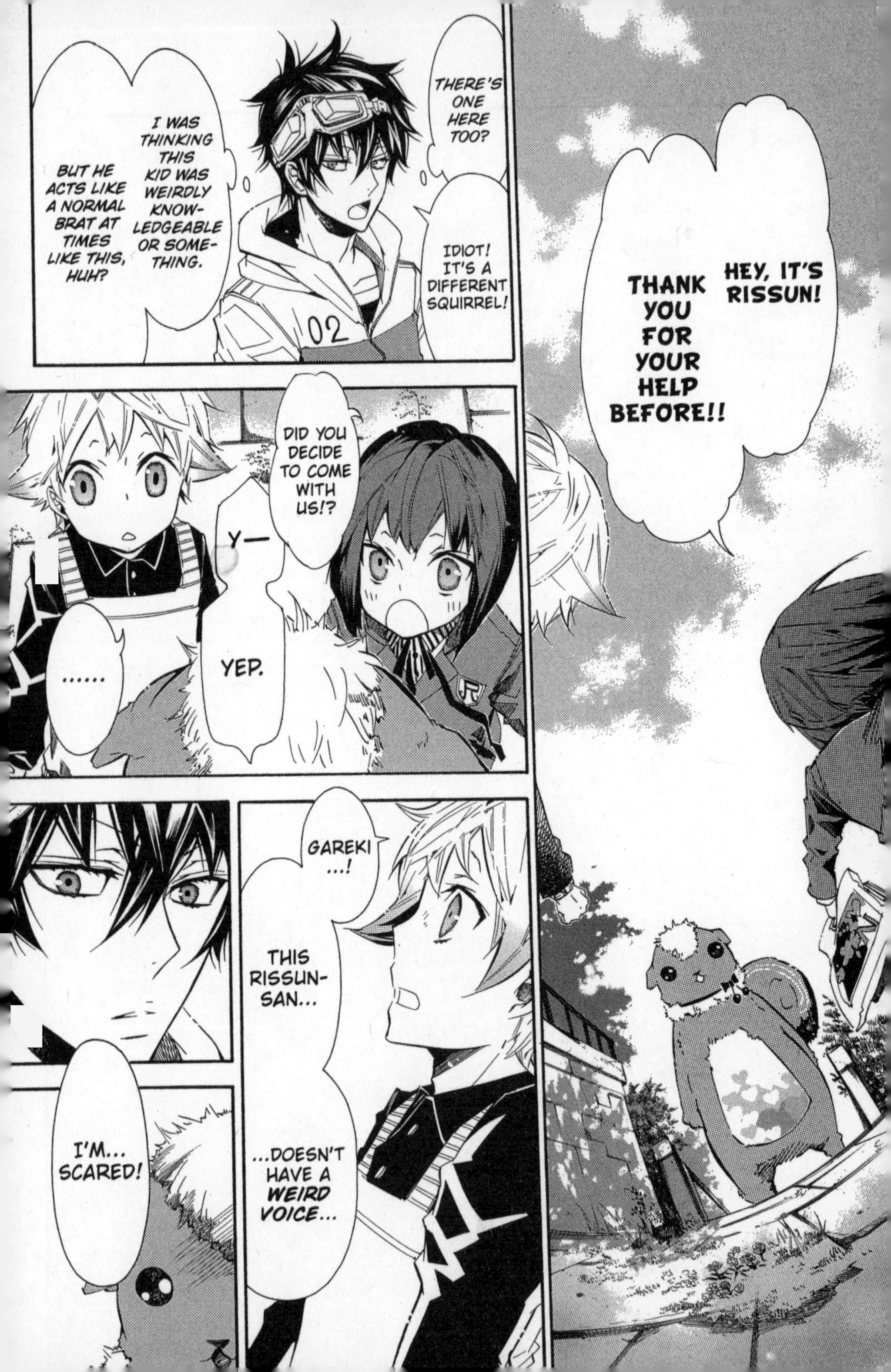
HEY, IT'S RISSUN!
THANK YOU FOR YOUR HELP BEFORE!!
THERE'S ONE HERE TOO?
IDIOT! IT'S A DIFFERENT SQUIRREL!
I WAS THINKING THIS KID WAS WEIRDLY KNOW-LEDGEABLE OR SOME-THING.
BUT HE ACTS LIKE A NORMAL BRAT AT TIMES LIKE THIS, HUH?
DID YOU DECIDE TO COME WITH US!?
Y—
YEP.
......
GAREKI ...!
THIS RISSUN-SAN...
...DOESN'T HAVE A WEIRD VOICE...
I'M... SCARED!

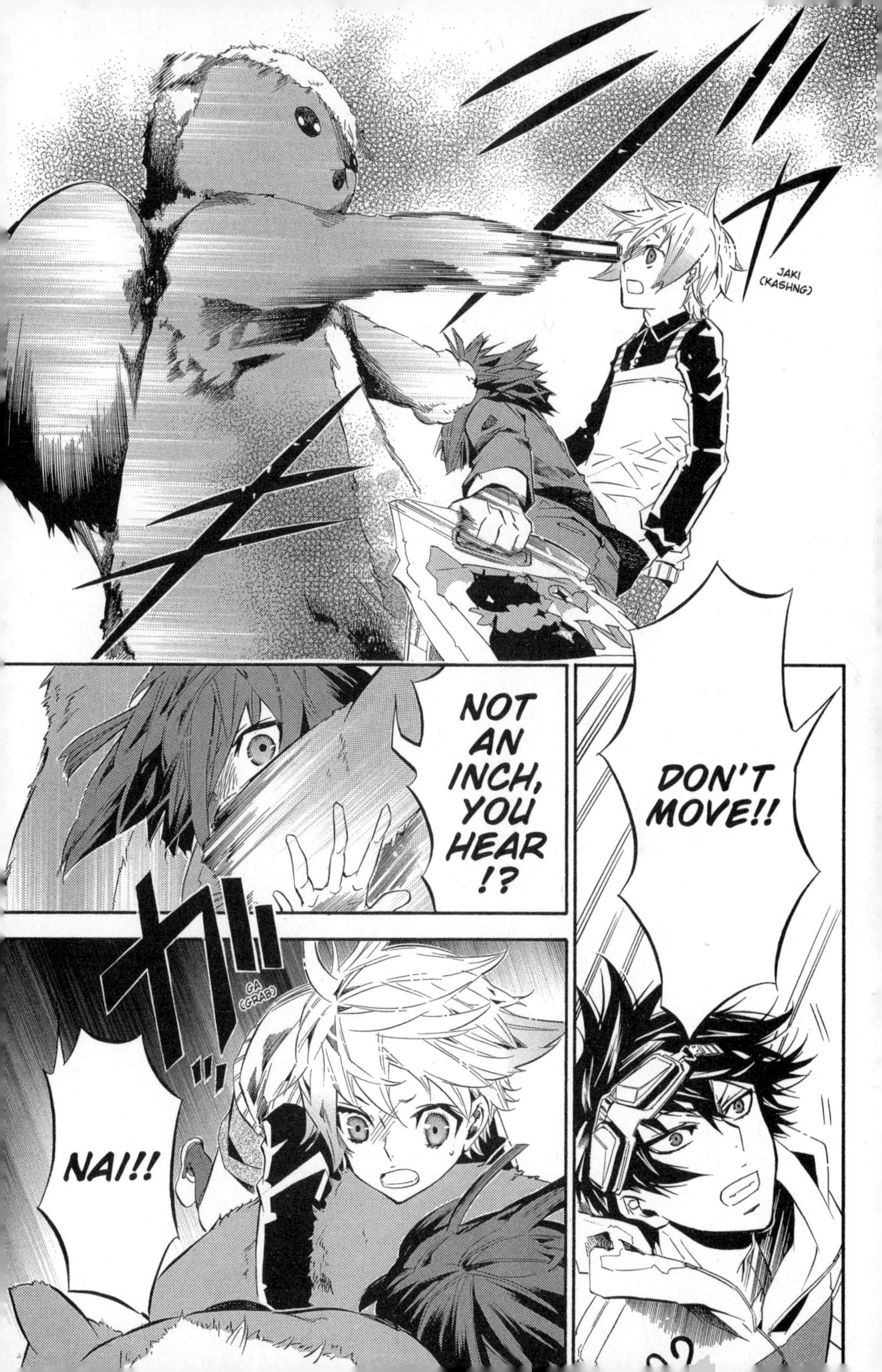
JAKI (KASHNG)
DON'T MOVE!!
NOT AN INCH, YOU HEAR!?
GA (GRAB)
NAI!!

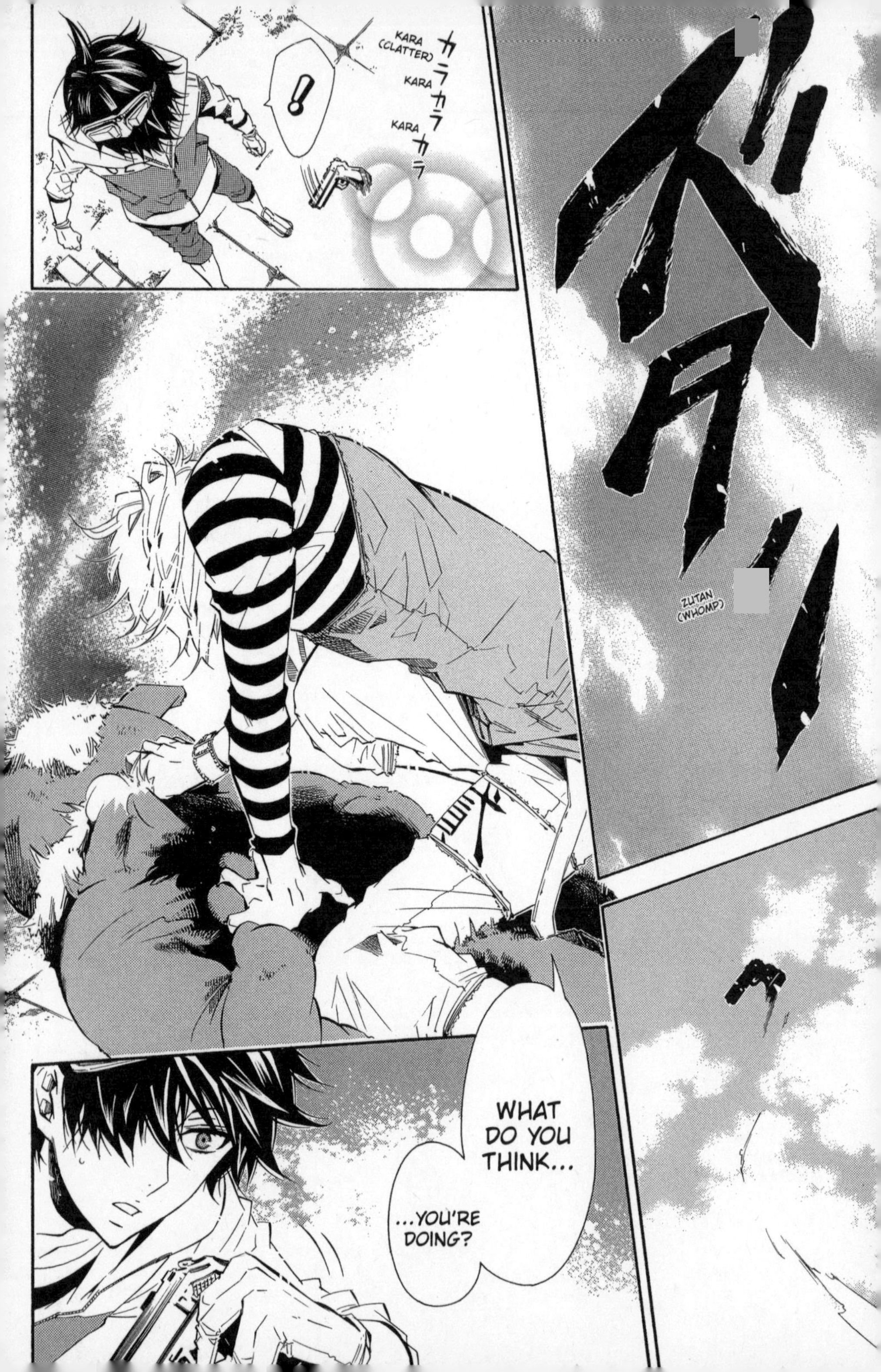
ZUTAN (WHOMP)
KARA (CLATTER)
KARA
KARA
!
WHAT DO YOU THINK...
...YOU'RE DOING?

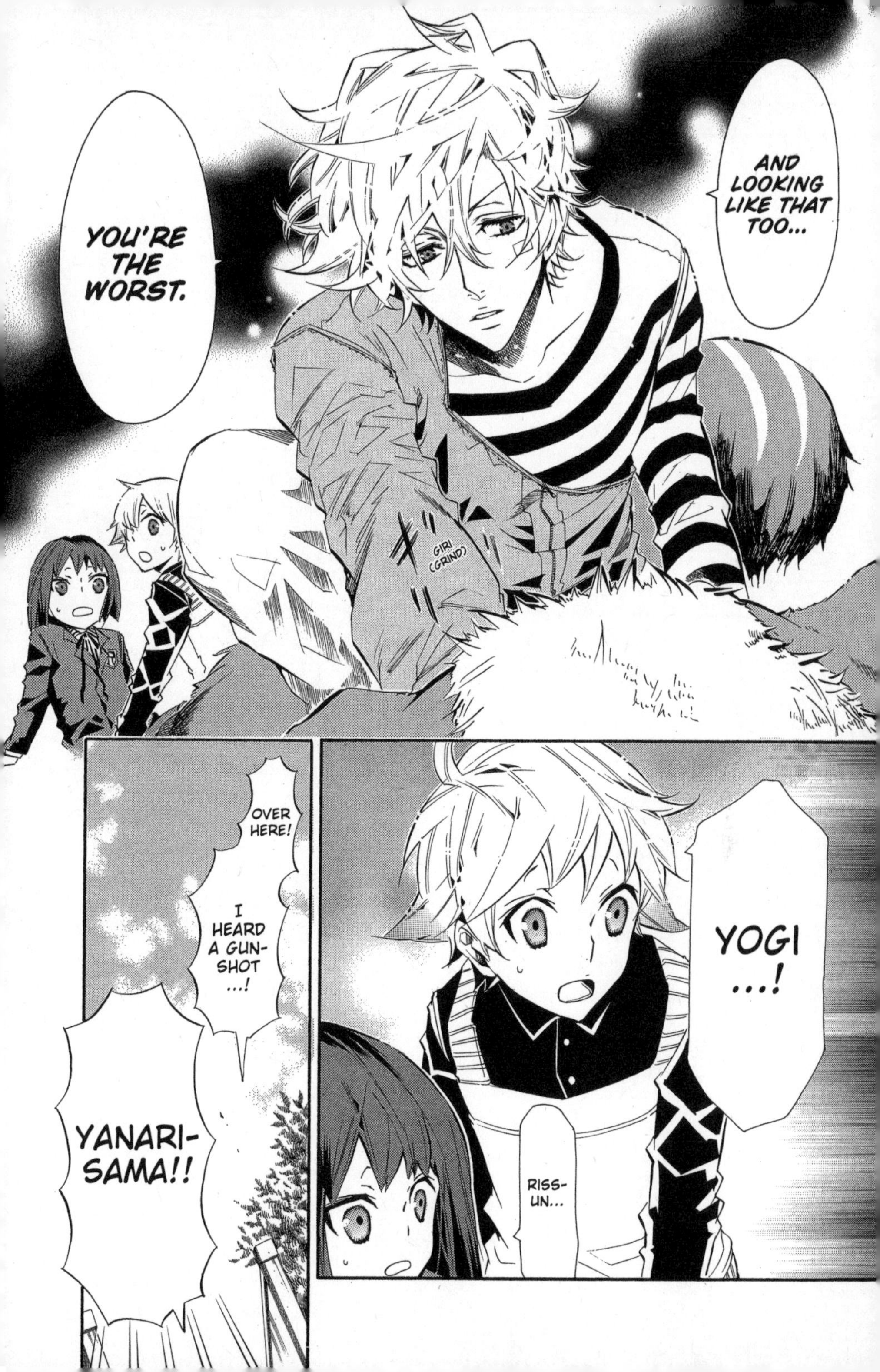
AND LOOKING LIKE THAT TOO...
YOU'RE THE WORST.
GIRI (GRIND)
YOGI ...!
RISS-UN...
OVER HERE!
I HEARD A GUN-SHOT ...!
YANARI-SAMA!!

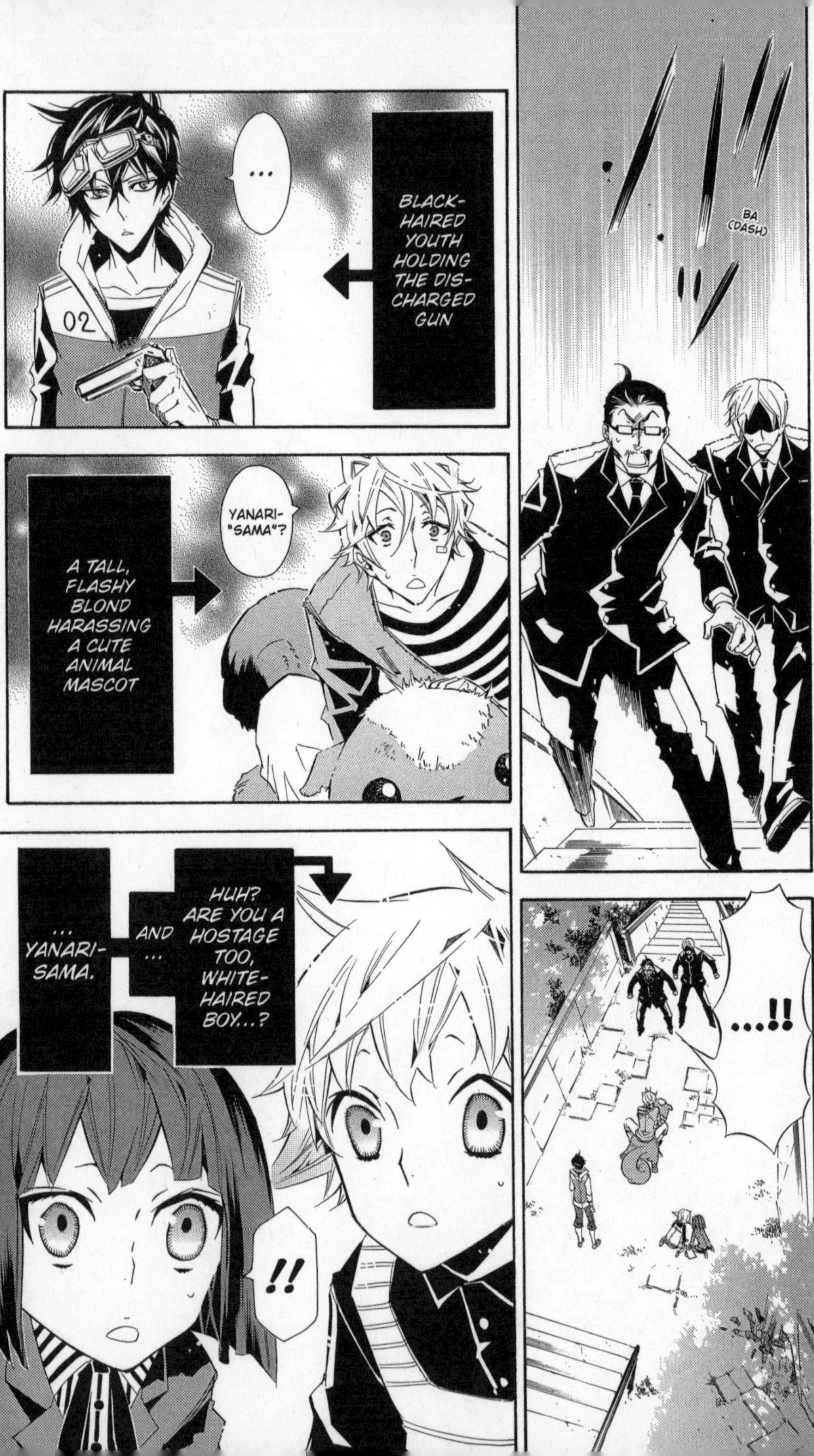
BA (DASH)
BLACK-HAIRED YOUTH HOLDING THE DIS-CHARGED GUN
...
YANARI-"SAMA"?
A TALL, FLASHY BLOND HARASSING A CUTE ANIMAL MASCOT
...!!
HUH? ARE YOU A HOSTAGE TOO, WHITE-HAIRED BOY...?
AND ...
... YANARI-SAMA.
!!

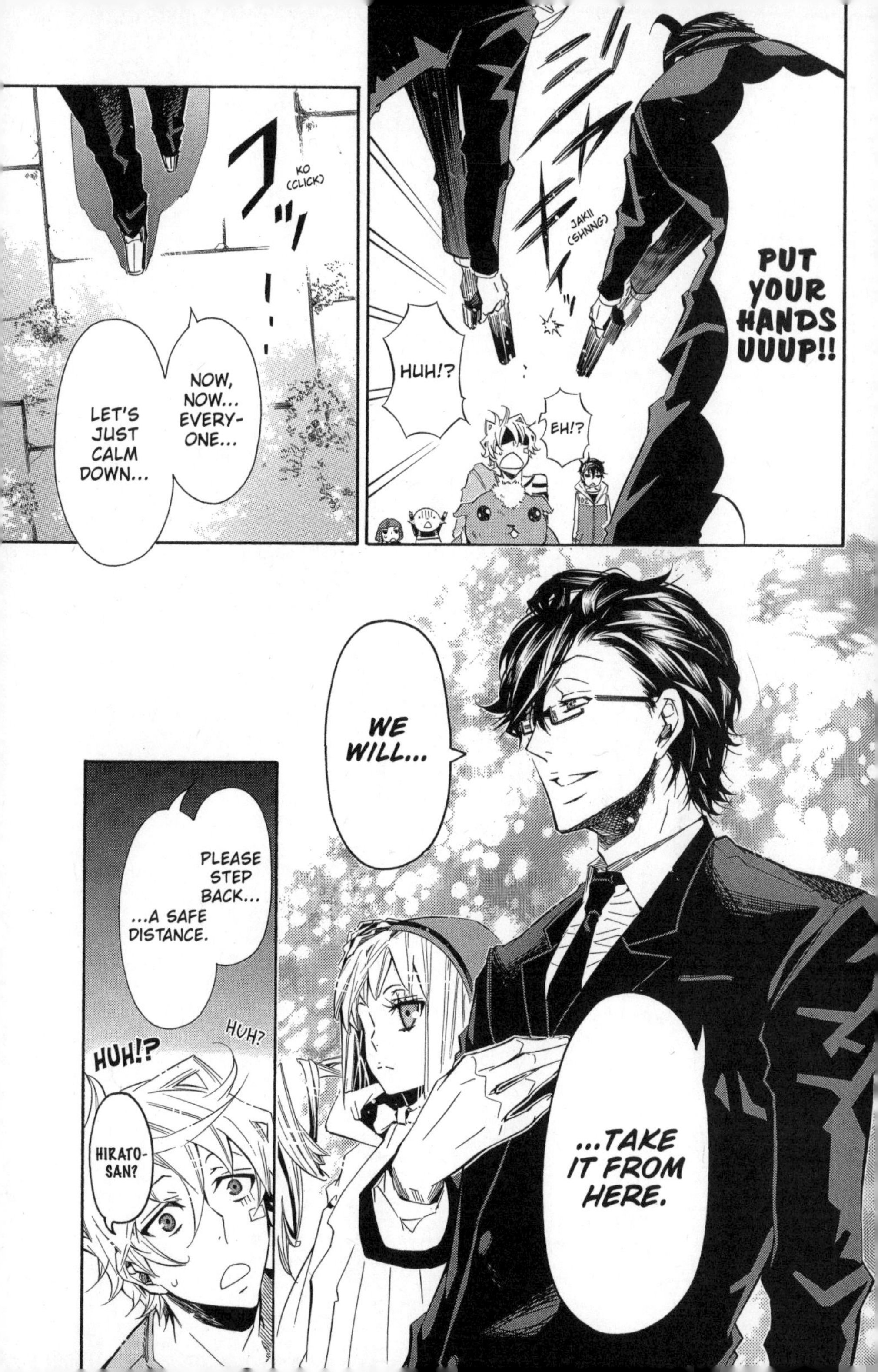
PUT YOUR HANDS UUUP!!
JAKII (SHNNG)
EH!?
HUH!?
KO (CLICK)
NOW, NOW... EVERY-ONE...
LET'S JUST CALM DOWN...
WE WILL...
...TAKE IT FROM HERE.
PLEASE STEP BACK... ...A SAFE DISTANCE.
HUH?
HUH!?
HIRATO-SAN?

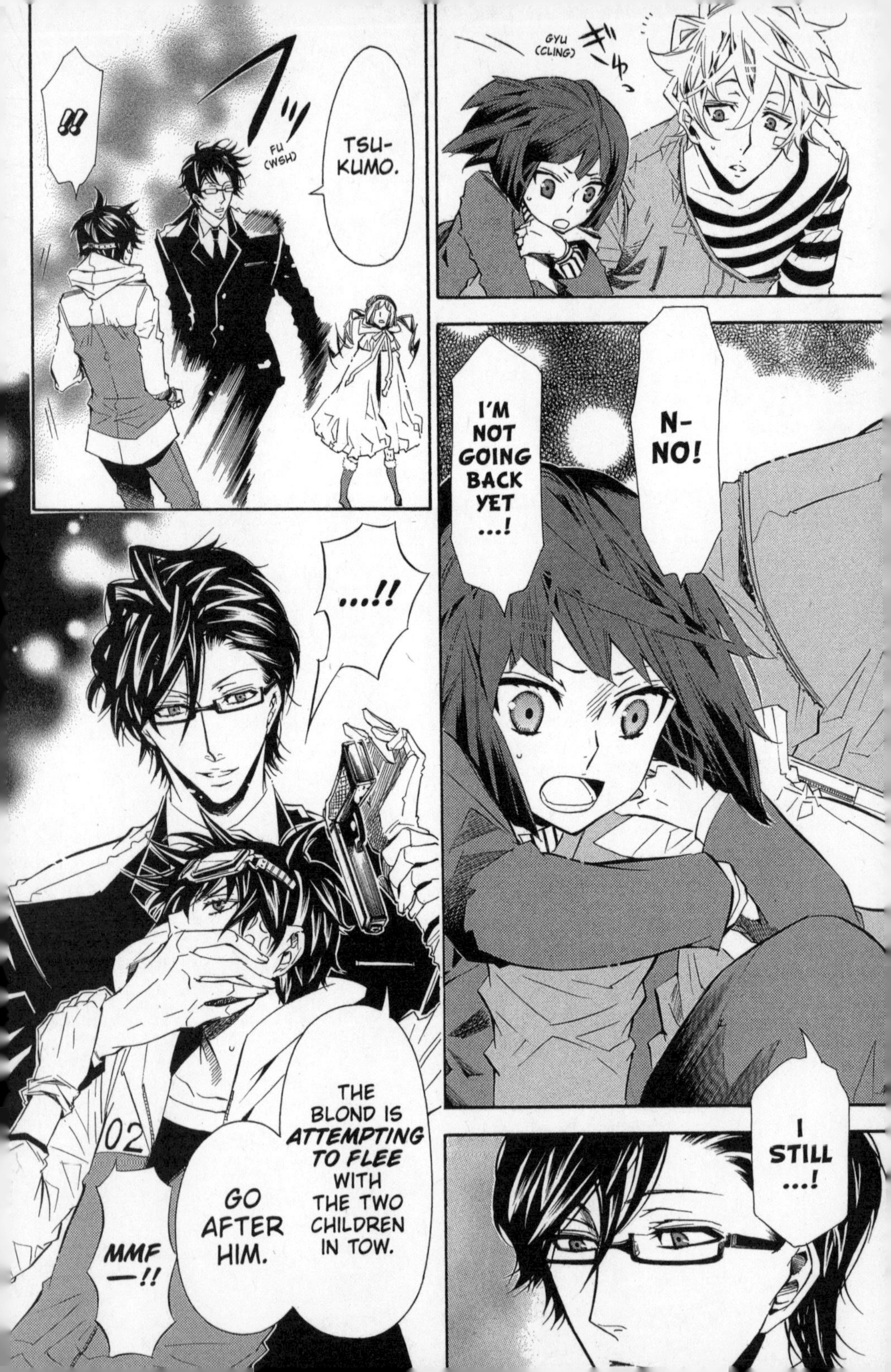
GYU (CLING)
TSU-KUMO.
FU (WSH)
!!
N-NO!
I'M NOT GOING BACK YET ...!
I STILL ...!
...!!
THE BLOND IS *ATTEMPTING TO FLEE* WITH THE TWO CHILDREN IN TOW.
GO AFTER HIM.
MMF—!!

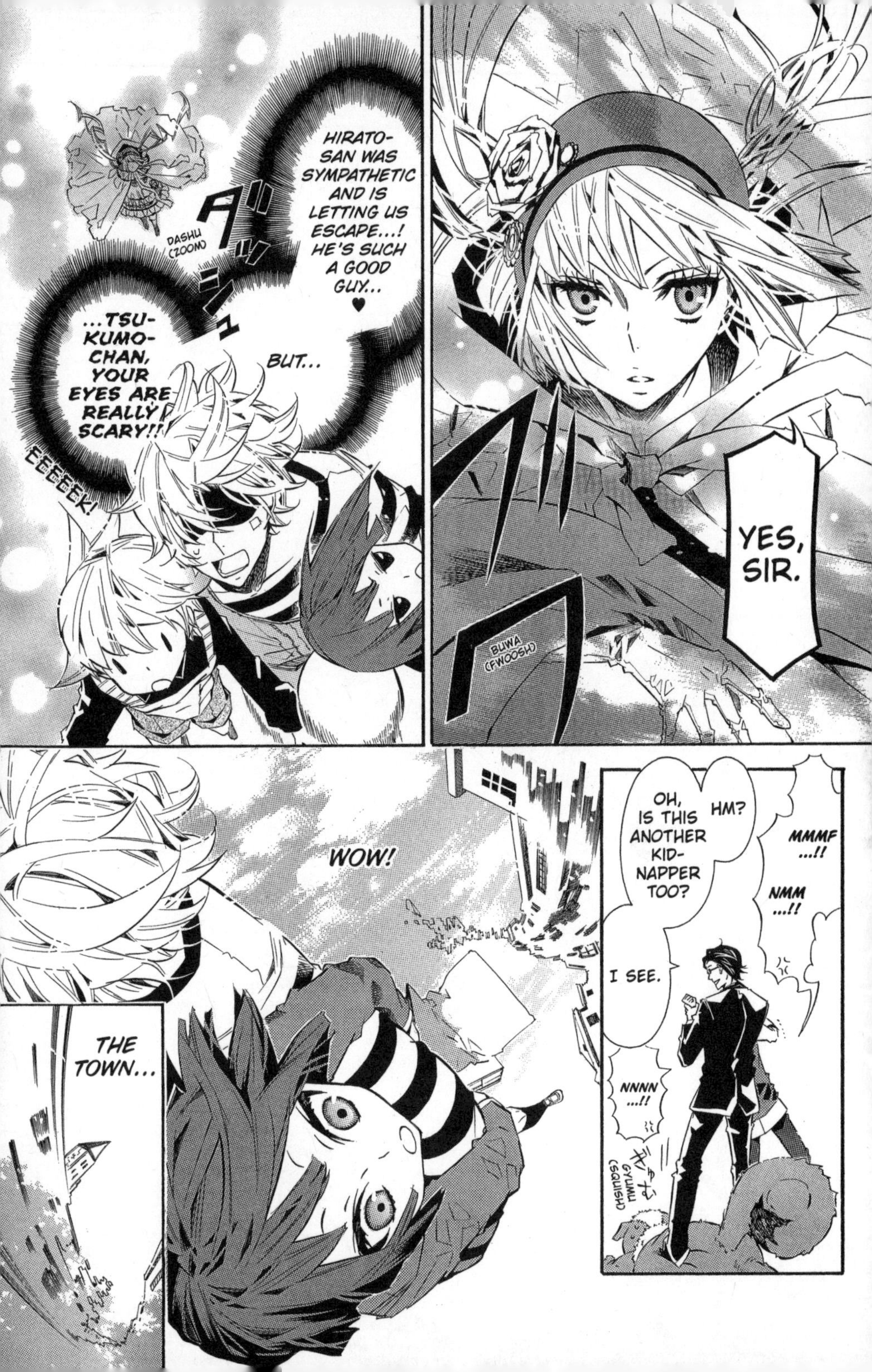
YES, SIR.
BUWA (FWOOSH)
HIRATO-SAN WAS SYMPATHETIC AND IS LETTING US ESCAPE...! HE'S SUCH A GOOD GUY...♥
DASHU (ZOOM)
BUT...
...TSUKUMO-CHAN, YOUR EYES ARE REALLY SCARY!!!
EEEEEEK!
HM?
OH, IS THIS ANOTHER KIDNAPPER TOO?
MMMF ...!!
NMM ...!!
I SEE.
NNNN ...!!
GYUMU (SQUISH)
WOW!
THE TOWN...

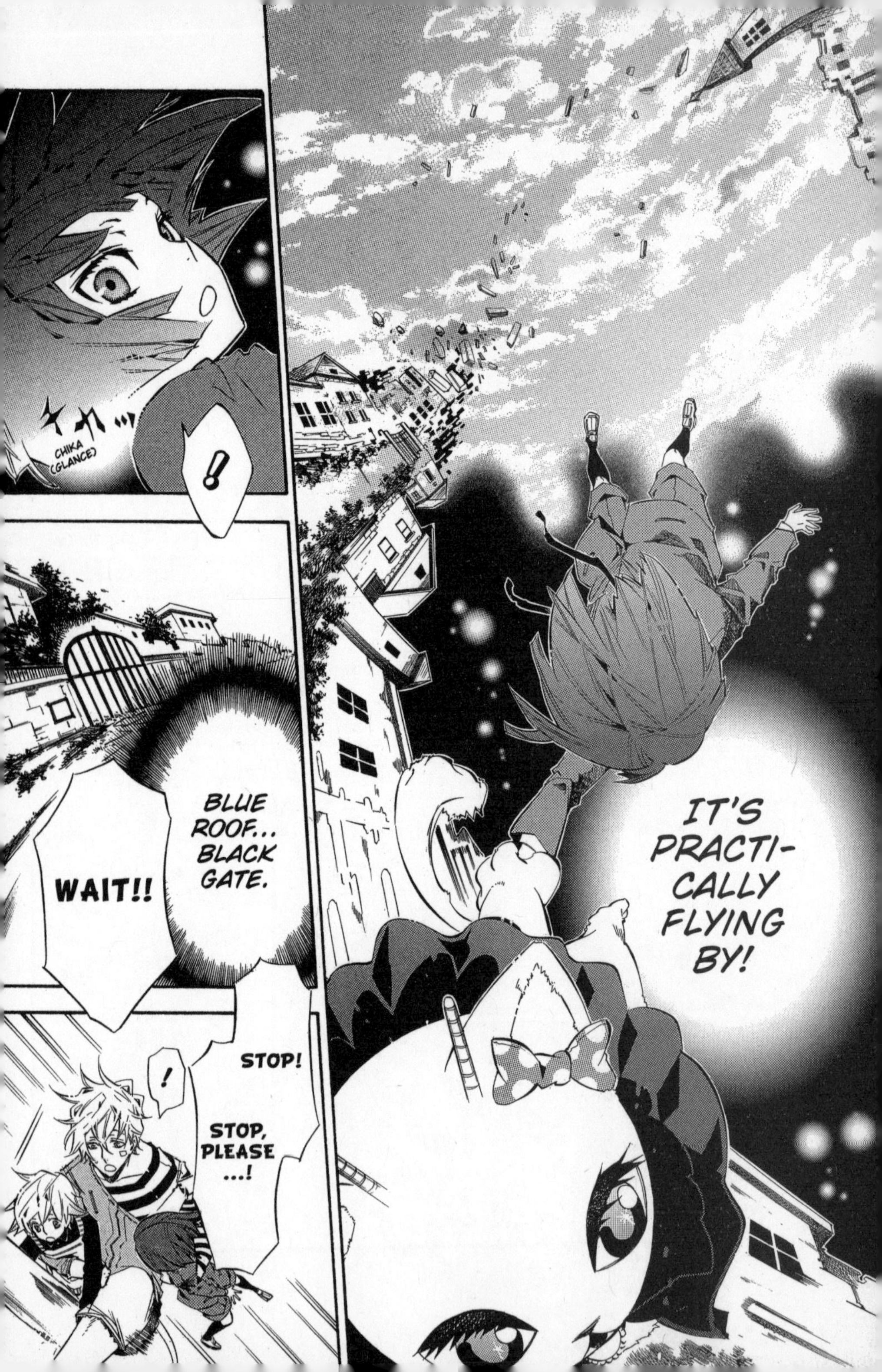
IT'S PRACTI-CALLY FLYING BY!
!
CHIKA (GLANCE)
BLUE ROOF... BLACK GATE.
WAIT!!
STOP!
STOP, PLEASE ...!
!

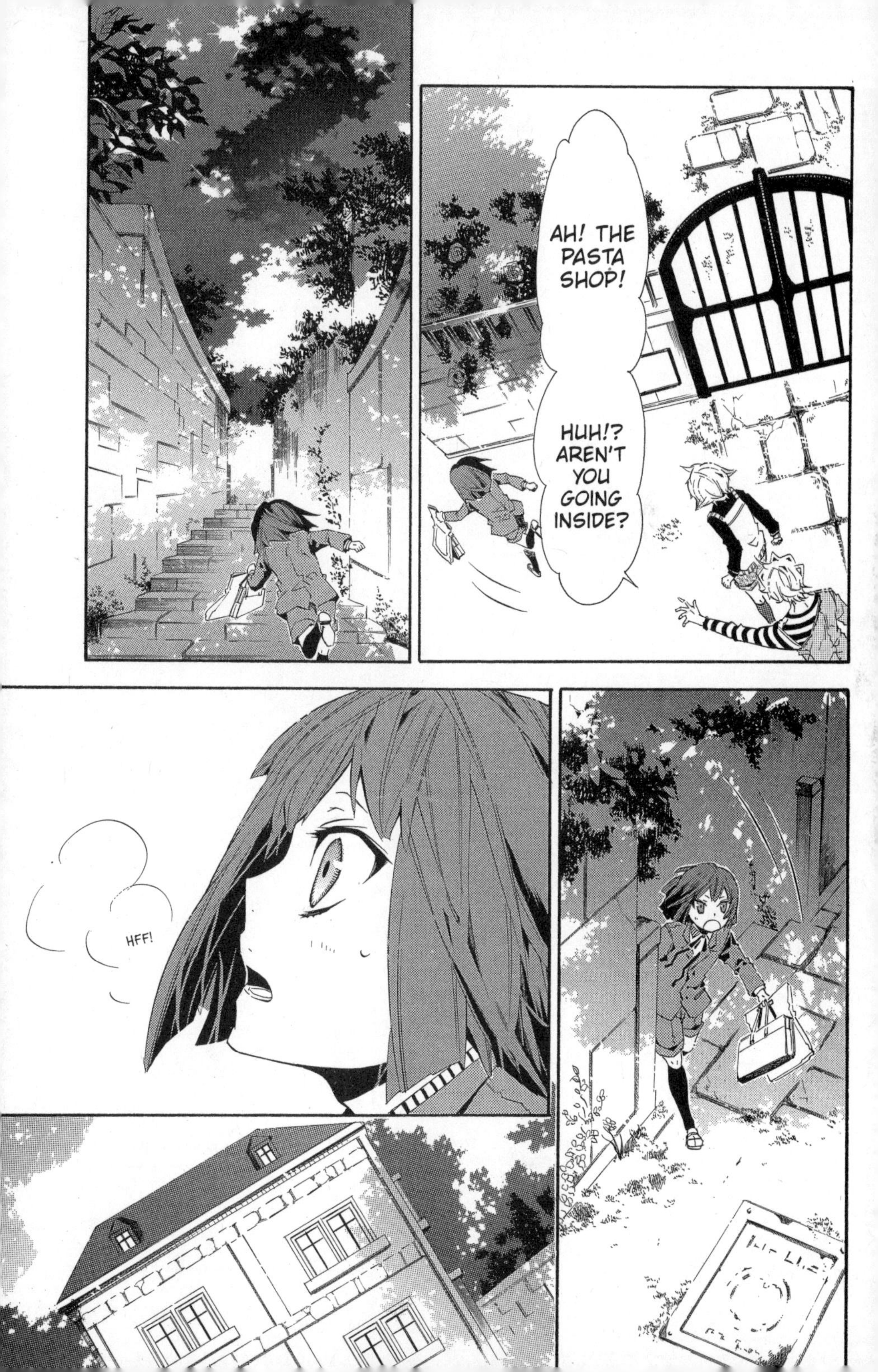
AH! THE PASTA SHOP!
HUH!? AREN'T YOU GOING INSIDE?
HFF!

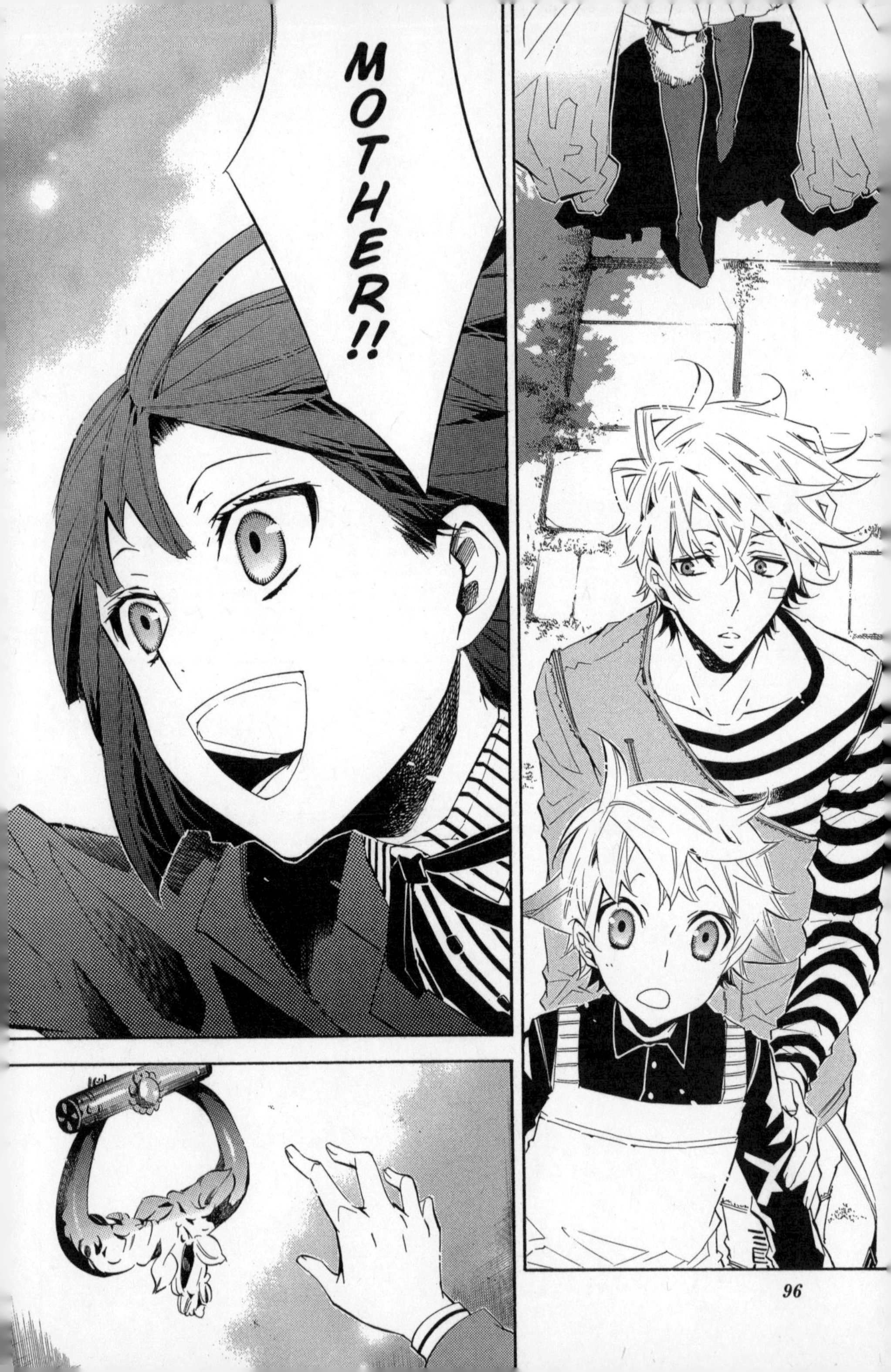
MOTHER!!

Score 28: A Warm Home

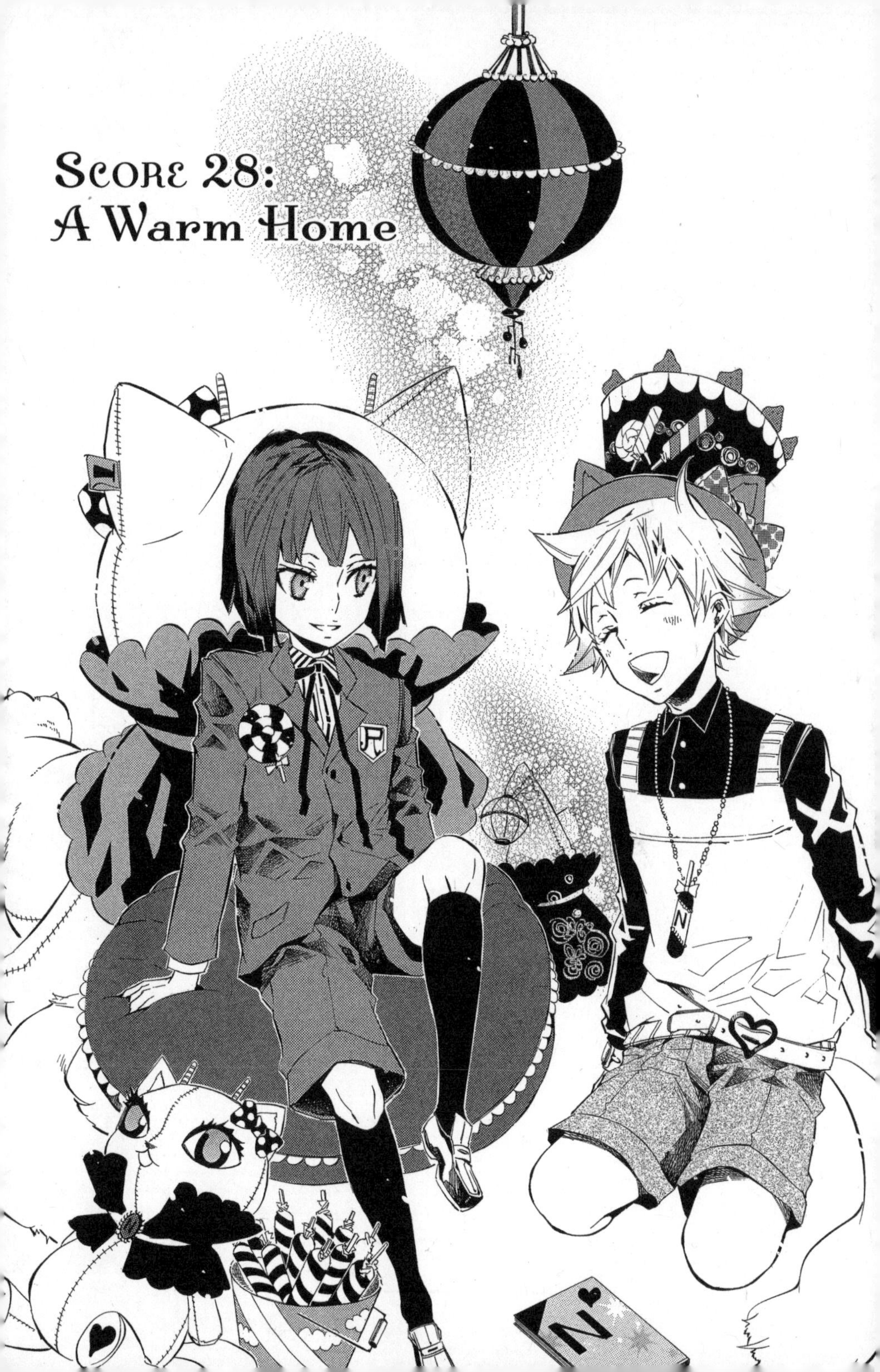

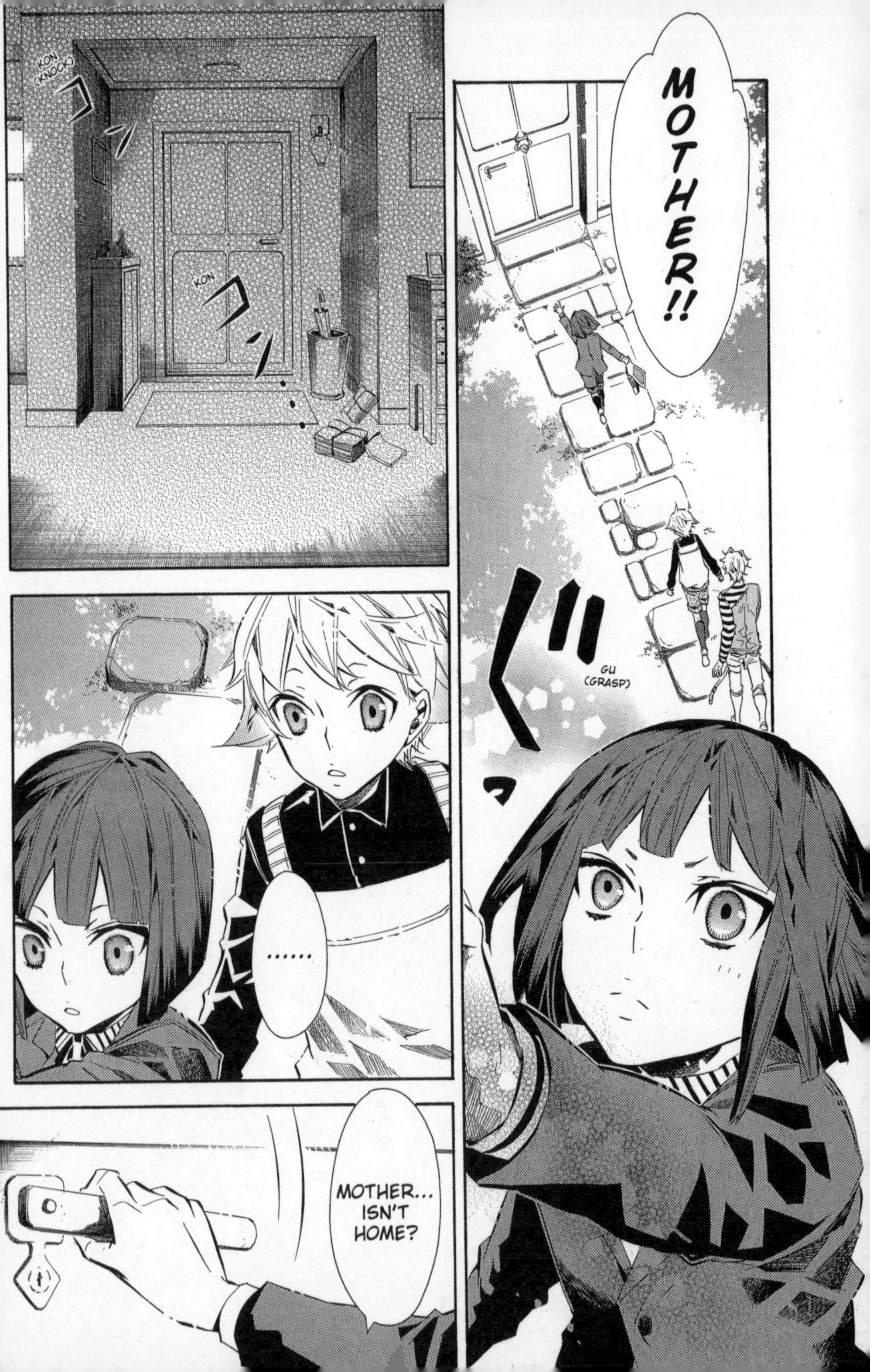
MOTHER!!
GU (GRASP)
KON (KNOCK)
KON
......
MOTHER... ISN'T HOME?

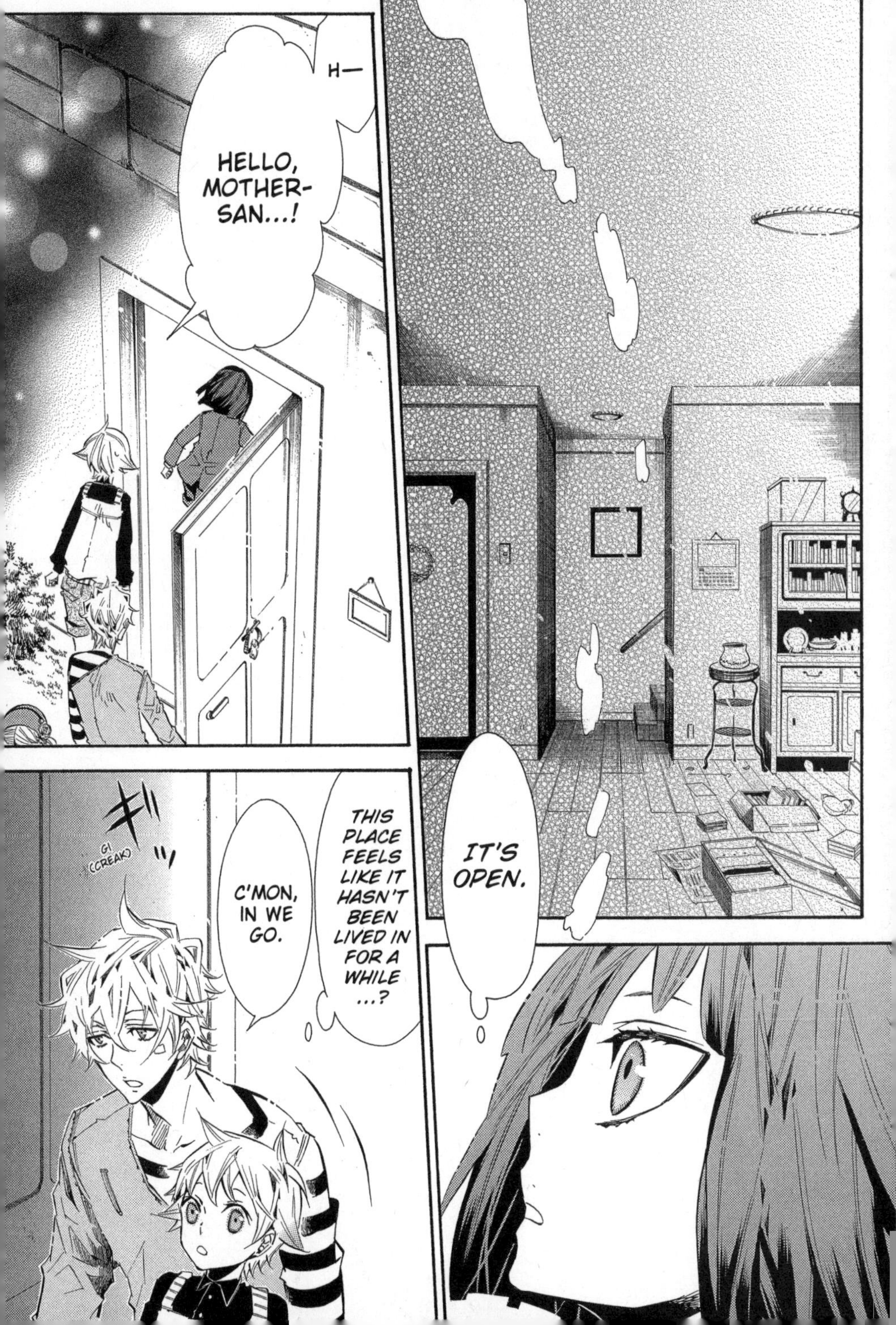

IT'S OPEN.
H—
HELLO, MOTHER-SAN...!
THIS PLACE FEELS LIKE IT HASN'T BEEN LIVED IN FOR A WHILE ...?
GI (CREAK)
C'MON, IN WE GO.

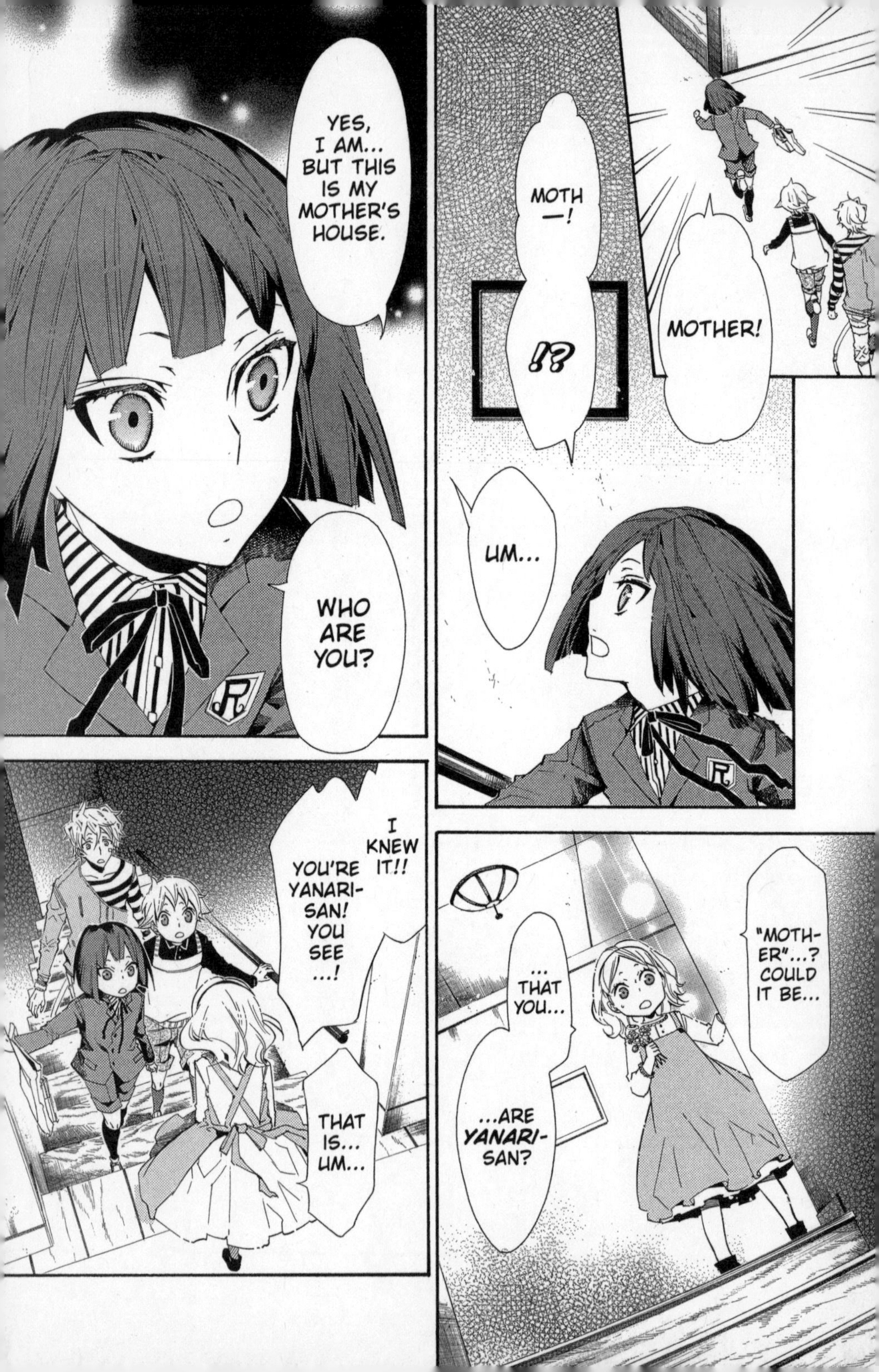
MOTHER!
MOTH—!
!?
UM...
YES, I AM... BUT THIS IS MY MOTHER'S HOUSE.
WHO ARE YOU?
"MOTHER"...? COULD IT BE...
...THAT YOU...
...ARE YANARI-SAN?
I KNEW IT!!
YOU'RE YANARI-SAN! YOU SEE...!
THAT IS... UM...

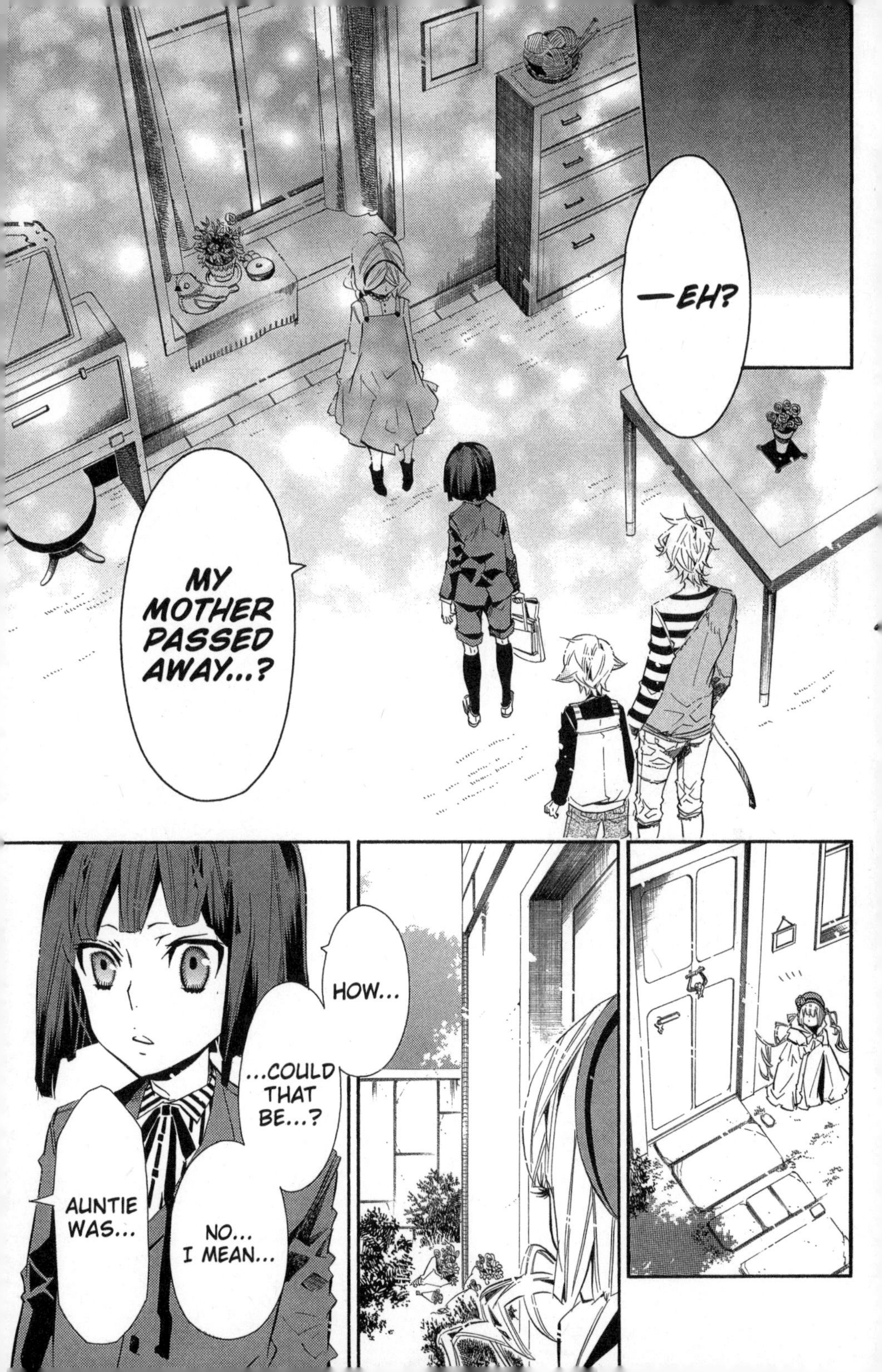
—EH?
MY MOTHER PASSED AWAY...?
HOW...
...COULD THAT BE...?
NO... I MEAN...
AUNTIE WAS...

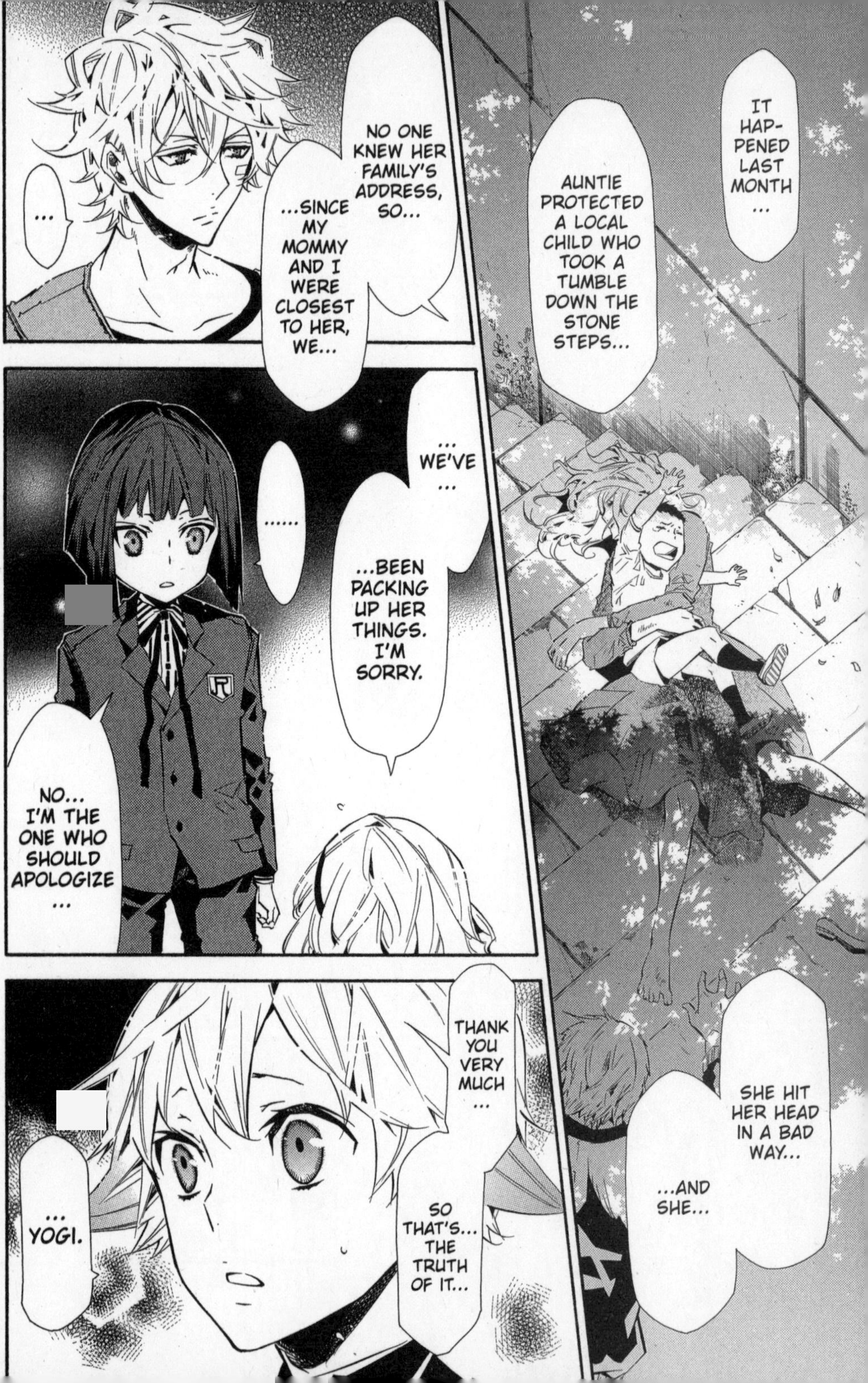

IT HAP-PENED LAST MONTH...
AUNTIE PROTECTED A LOCAL CHILD WHO TOOK A TUMBLE DOWN THE STONE STEPS...
SHE HIT HER HEAD IN A BAD WAY...
...AND SHE...
NO ONE KNEW HER FAMILY'S ADDRESS, SO...
...SINCE MY MOMMY AND I WERE CLOSEST TO HER, WE...
...
... WE'VE ...
...BEEN PACKING UP HER THINGS. I'M SORRY.
......
NO... I'M THE ONE WHO SHOULD APOLOGIZE...
THANK YOU VERY MUCH...
SO THAT'S... THE TRUTH OF IT...
... YOGI.

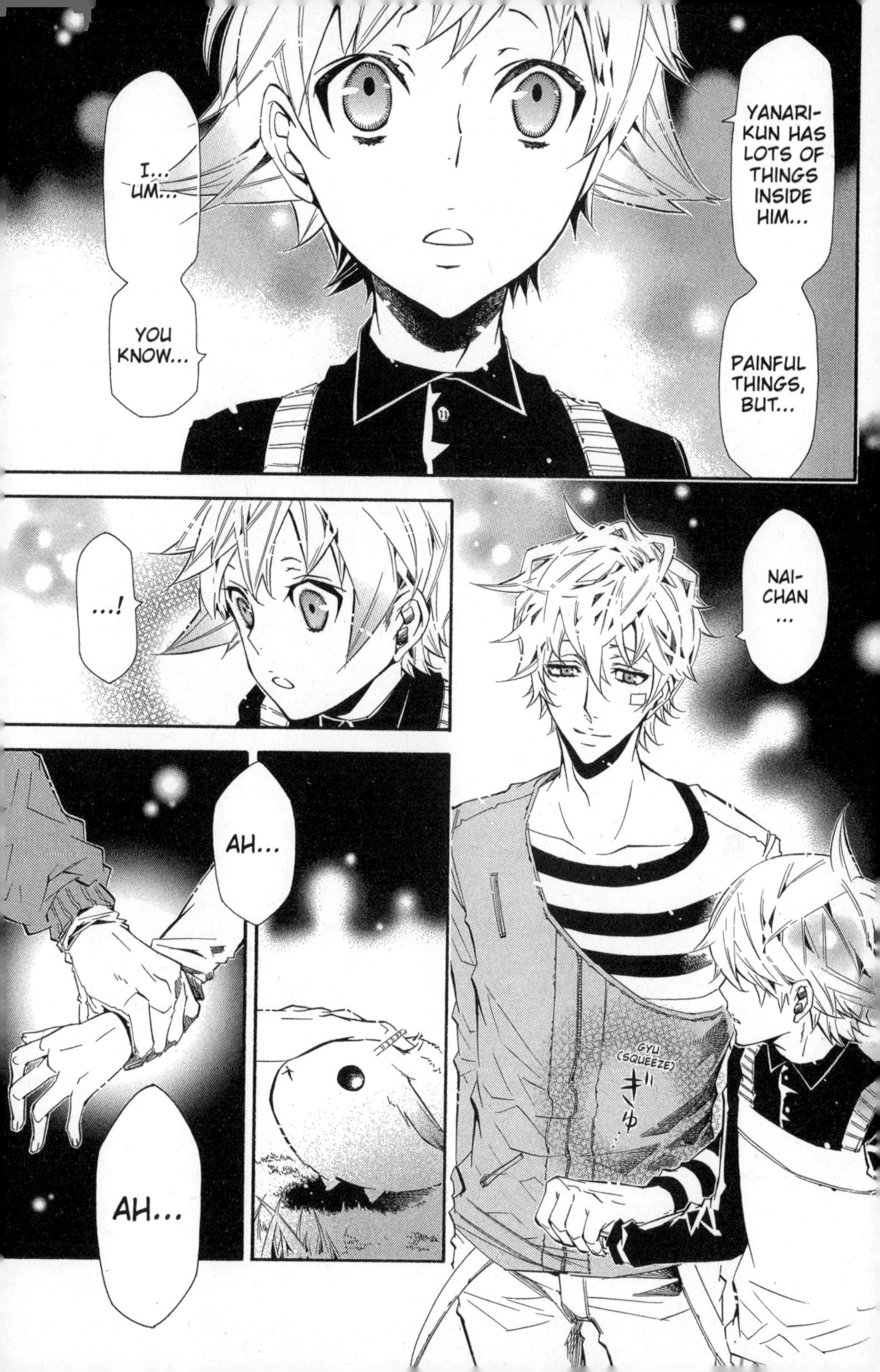
YANARI-KUN HAS LOTS OF THINGS INSIDE HIM...
PAINFUL THINGS, BUT...
I... UM...
YOU KNOW...
NAI-CHAN...
...!
GYU (SQUEEZE)
ぎゅ
AH...
AH...

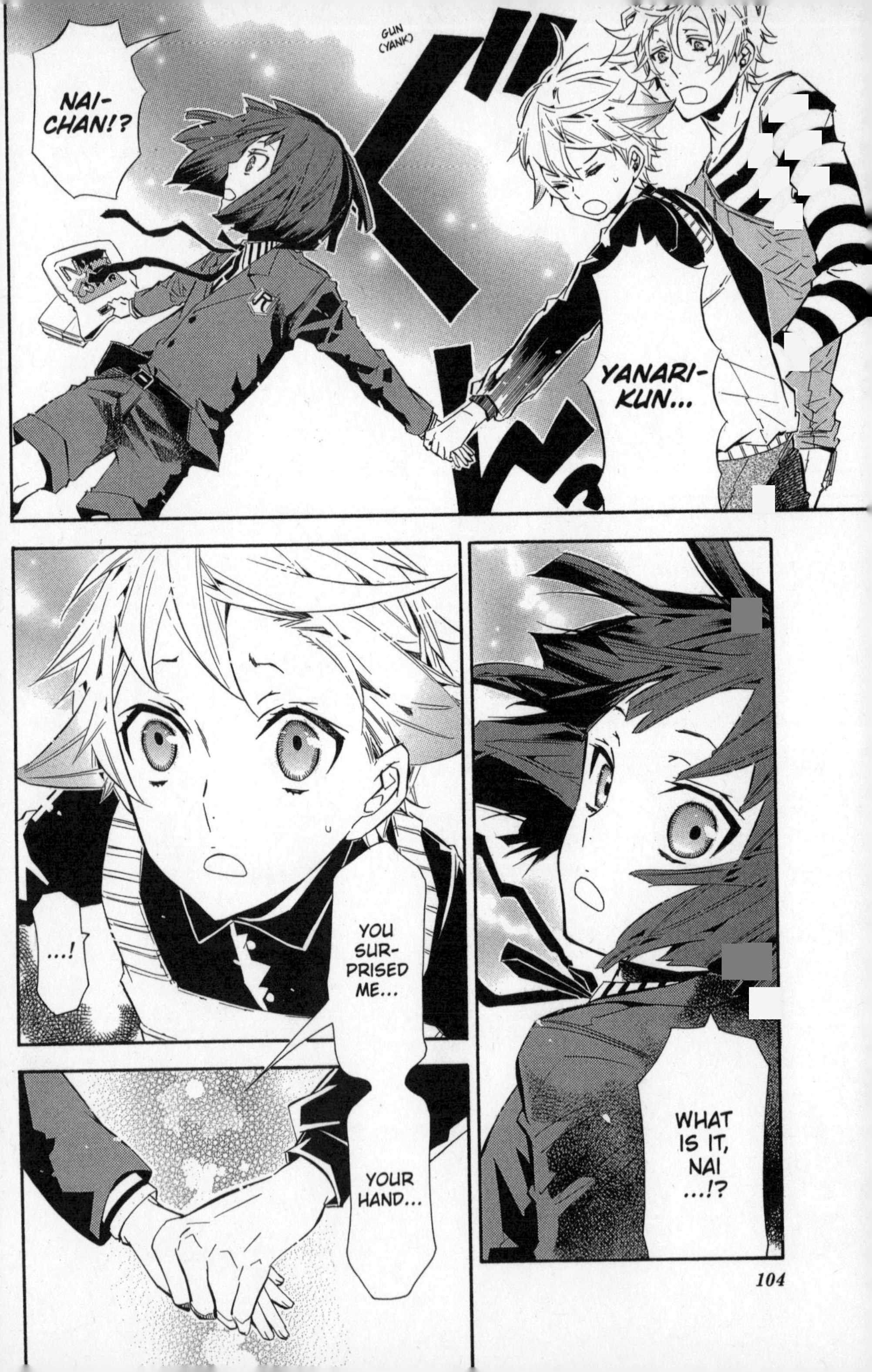
GUN (YANK)
YANARI-KUN...
NAI-CHAN!?
WHAT IS IT, NAI...!?
YOU SURPRISED ME...
...!
YOUR HAND...

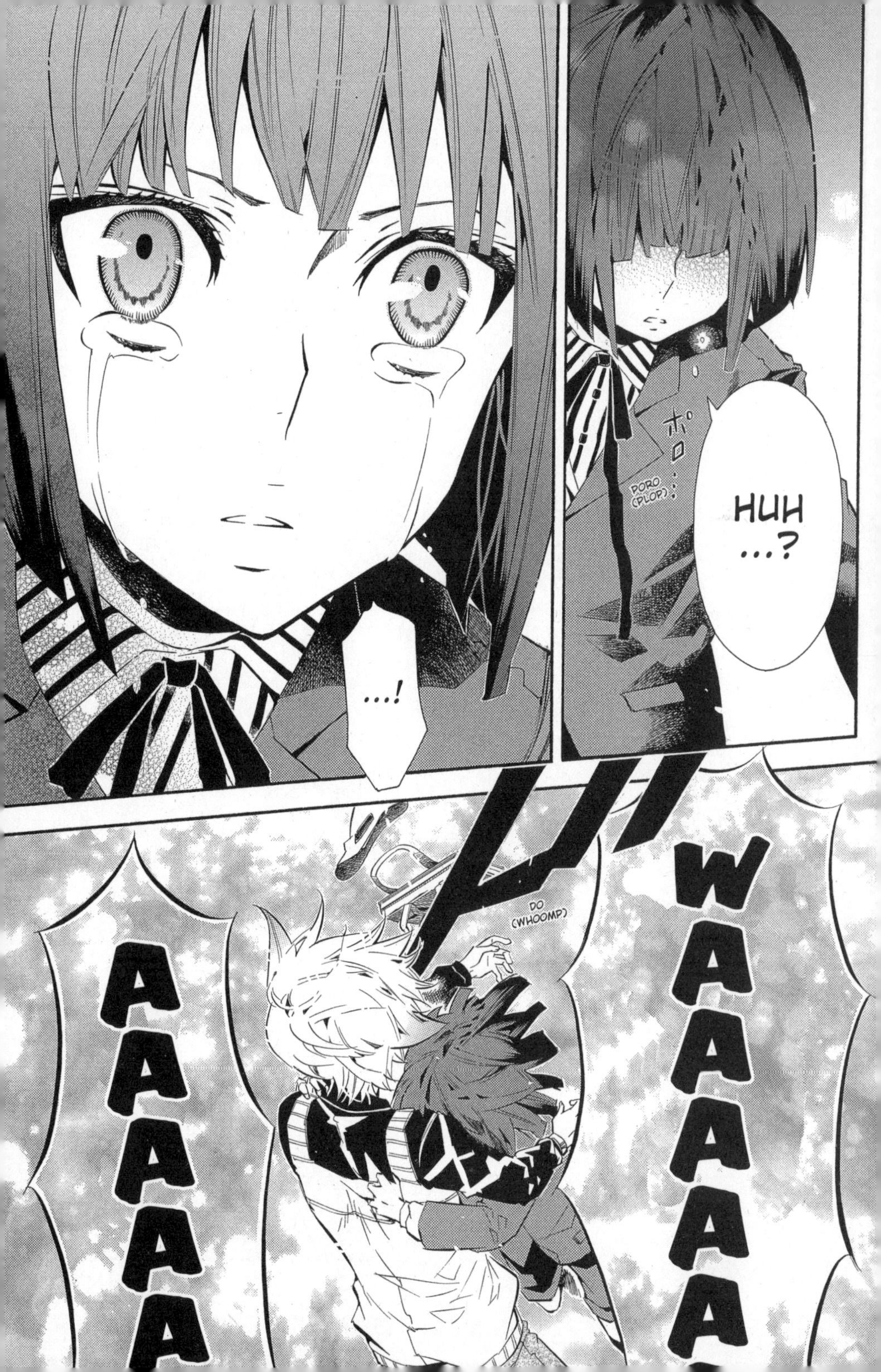
ポロ…
PORO (PLOP)
HUH …?
…!
DO (WHOOMP)
WAAAAAAA
AAAAAA

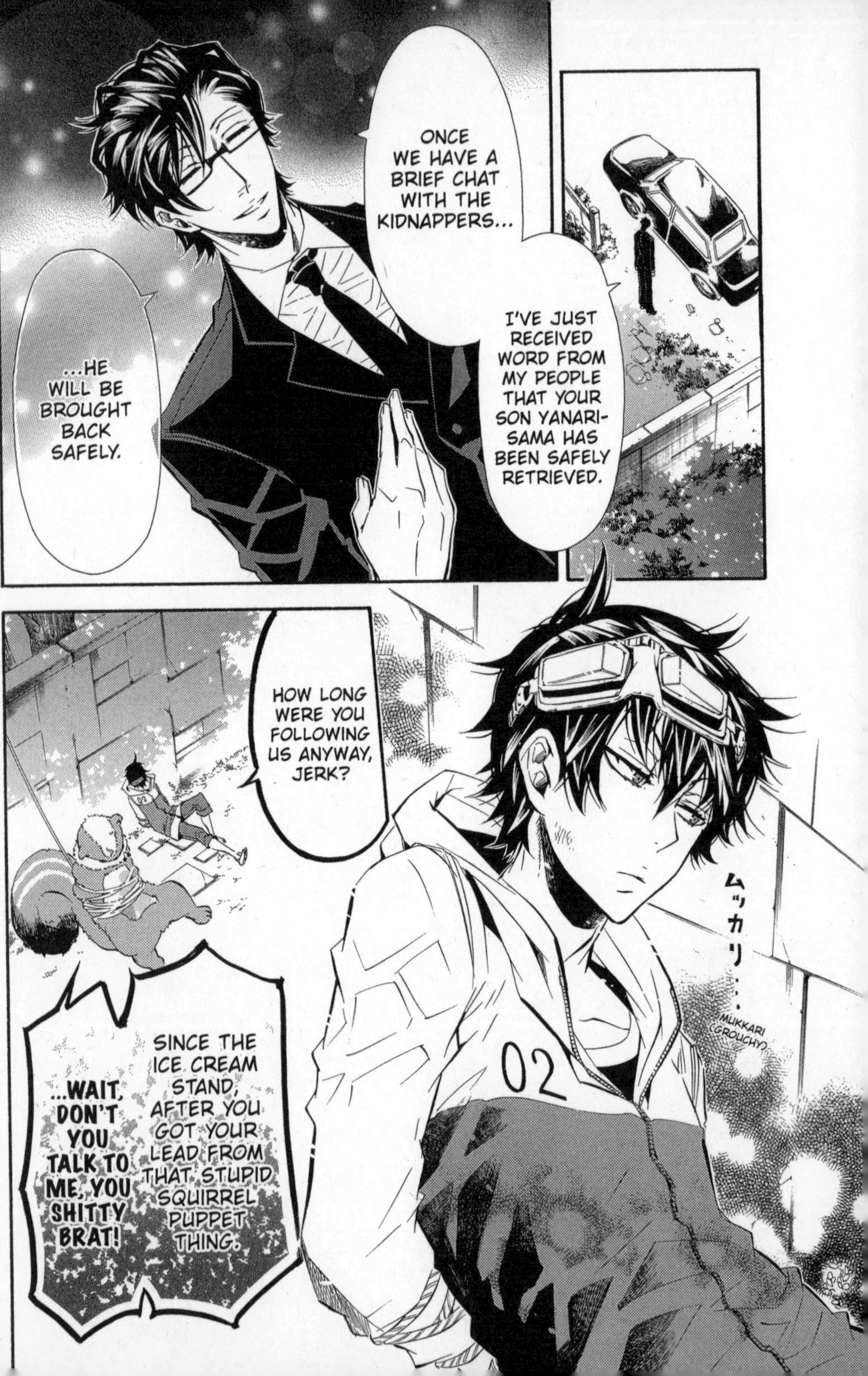
I'VE JUST RECEIVED WORD FROM MY PEOPLE THAT YOUR SON YANARI-SAMA HAS BEEN SAFELY RETRIEVED.
ONCE WE HAVE A BRIEF CHAT WITH THE KIDNAPPERS...
...HE WILL BE BROUGHT BACK SAFELY.
HOW LONG WERE YOU FOLLOWING US ANYWAY, JERK?
ムッカリ…
MUKKARI (GROUCHY)
SINCE THE ICE CREAM STAND, AFTER YOU GOT YOUR LEAD FROM THAT STUPID SQUIRREL PUPPET THING.
...WAIT, DON'T YOU TALK TO ME, YOU SHITTY BRAT!

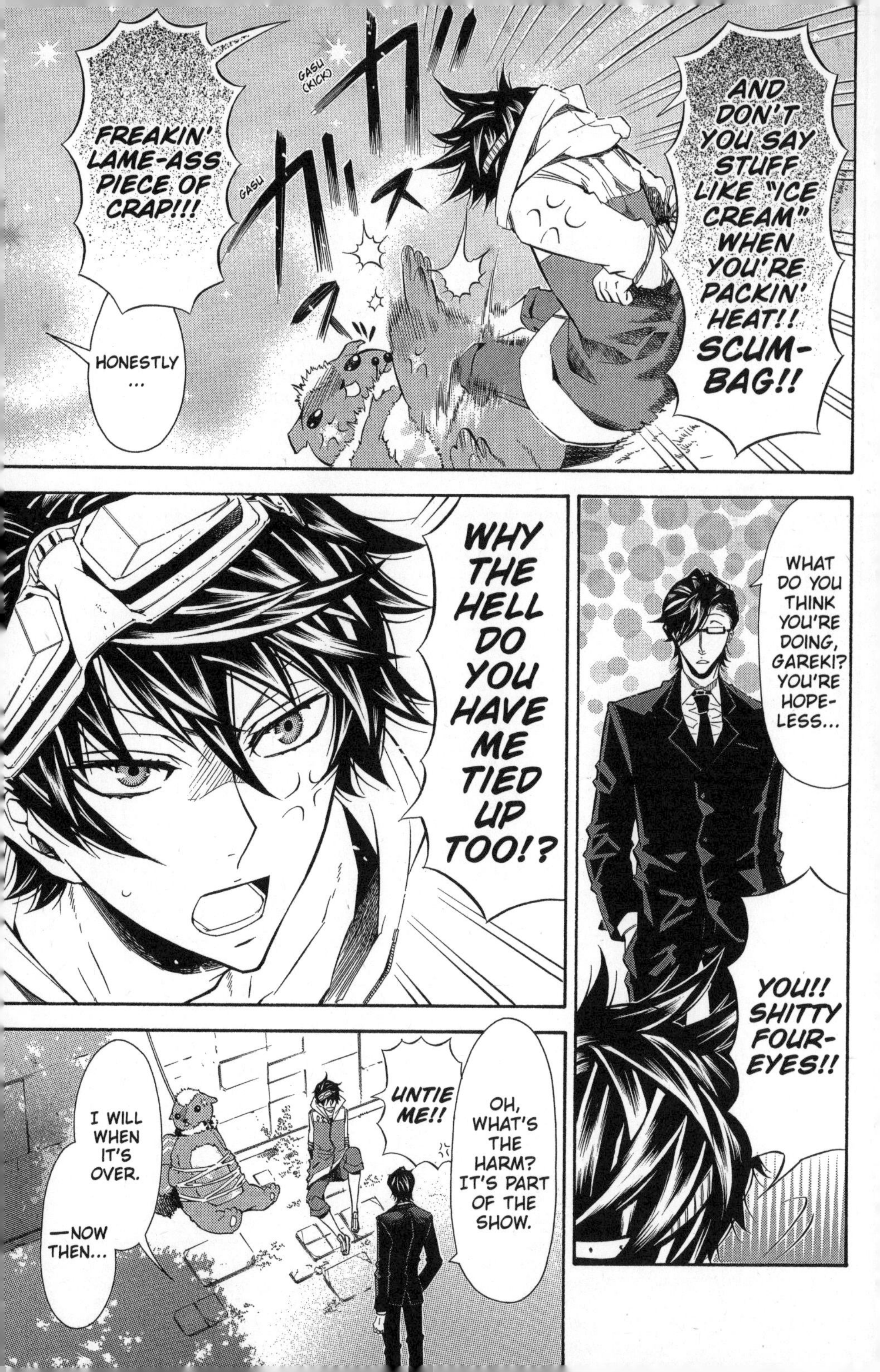
AND DON'T YOU SAY STUFF LIKE "ICE CREAM" WHEN YOU'RE PACKIN' HEAT!! SCUMBAG!!
GASU (KICK)
GASU
FREAKIN' LAME-ASS PIECE OF CRAP!!!
HONESTLY...
WHAT DO YOU THINK YOU'RE DOING, GAREKI? YOU'RE HOPELESS...
YOU!! SHITTY FOUR-EYES!!
WHY THE HELL DO YOU HAVE ME TIED UP TOO!?
OH, WHAT'S THE HARM? IT'S PART OF THE SHOW.
UNTIE ME!!
I WILL WHEN IT'S OVER.
—NOW THEN...

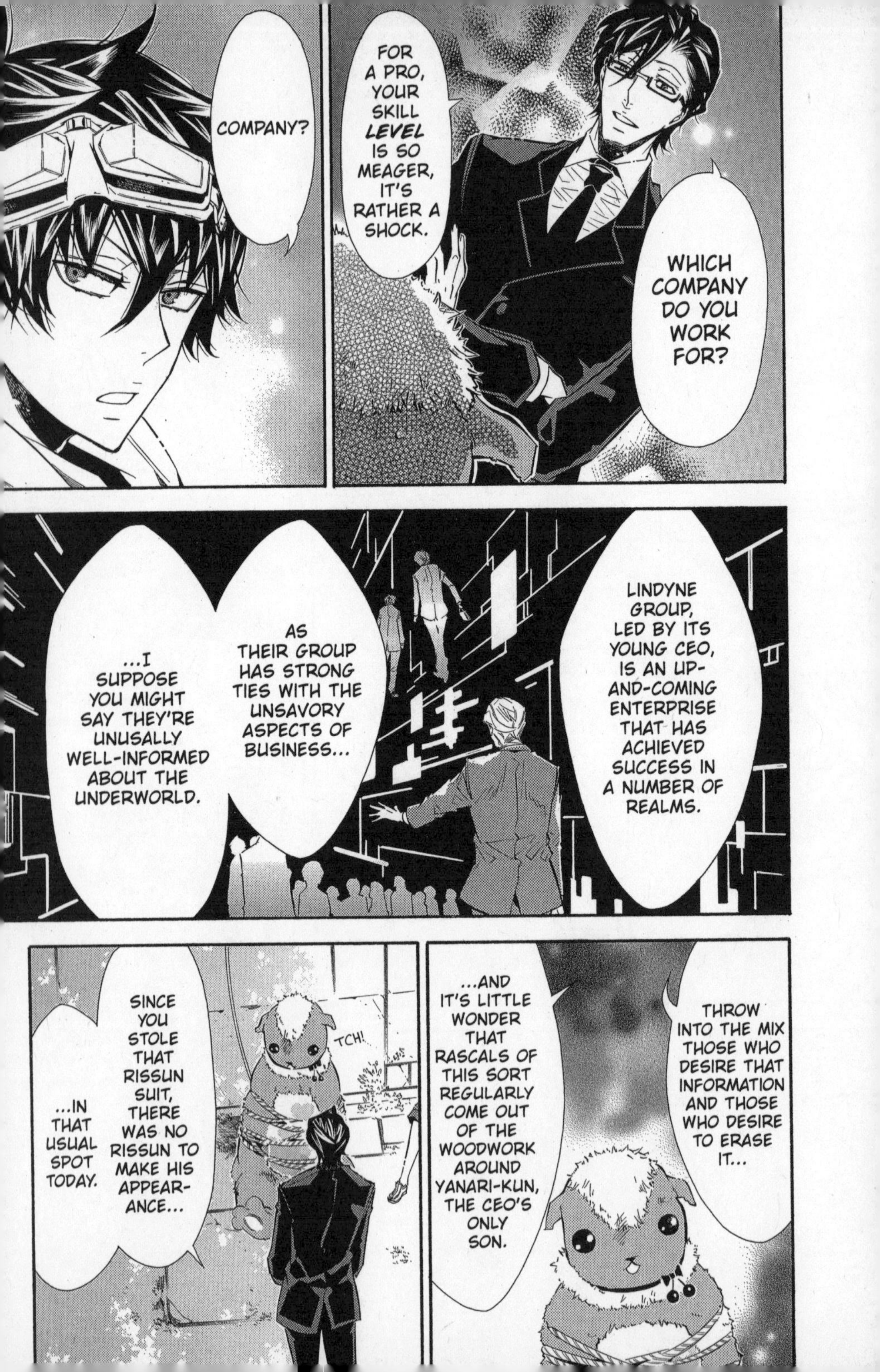
FOR A PRO, YOUR SKILL ***LEVEL*** IS SO MEAGER, IT'S RATHER A SHOCK.
WHICH COMPANY DO YOU WORK FOR?
COMPANY?
LINDYNE GROUP, LED BY ITS YOUNG CEO, IS AN UP-AND-COMING ENTERPRISE THAT HAS ACHIEVED SUCCESS IN A NUMBER OF REALMS.
AS THEIR GROUP HAS STRONG TIES WITH THE UNSAVORY ASPECTS OF BUSINESS...
...I SUPPOSE YOU MIGHT SAY THEY'RE UNUSALLY WELL-INFORMED ABOUT THE UNDERWORLD.
THROW INTO THE MIX THOSE WHO DESIRE THAT INFORMATION AND THOSE WHO DESIRE TO ERASE IT...
...AND IT'S LITTLE WONDER THAT RASCALS OF THIS SORT REGULARLY COME OUT OF THE WOODWORK AROUND YANARI-KUN, THE CEO'S ONLY SON.
SINCE YOU STOLE THAT RISSUN SUIT, THERE WAS NO RISSUN TO MAKE HIS APPEARANCE...
...IN THAT USUAL SPOT TODAY.
TCH!

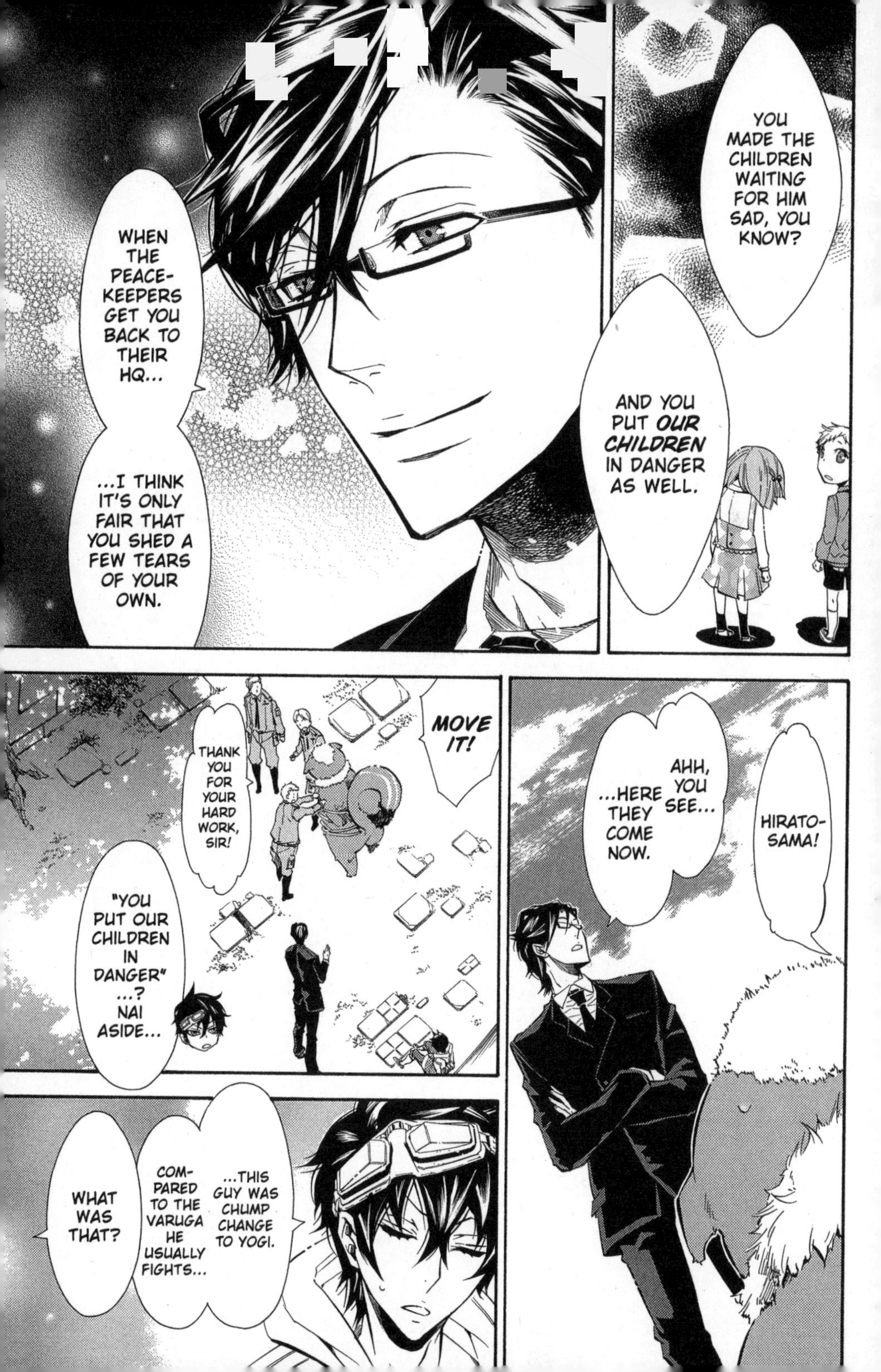
YOU MADE THE CHILDREN WAITING FOR HIM SAD, YOU KNOW?
AND YOU PUT **OUR CHILDREN** IN DANGER AS WELL.
WHEN THE PEACE-KEEPERS GET YOU BACK TO THEIR HQ...
...I THINK IT'S ONLY FAIR THAT YOU SHED A FEW TEARS OF YOUR OWN.
HIRATO-SAMA!
AHH, YOU SEE...
...HERE THEY COME NOW.
MOVE IT!
THANK YOU FOR YOUR HARD WORK, SIR!
"YOU PUT OUR CHILDREN IN DANGER" ...? NAI ASIDE...
...THIS GUY WAS CHUMP CHANGE TO YOGI.
COM-PARED TO THE VARUGA HE USUALLY FIGHTS...
WHAT WAS THAT?

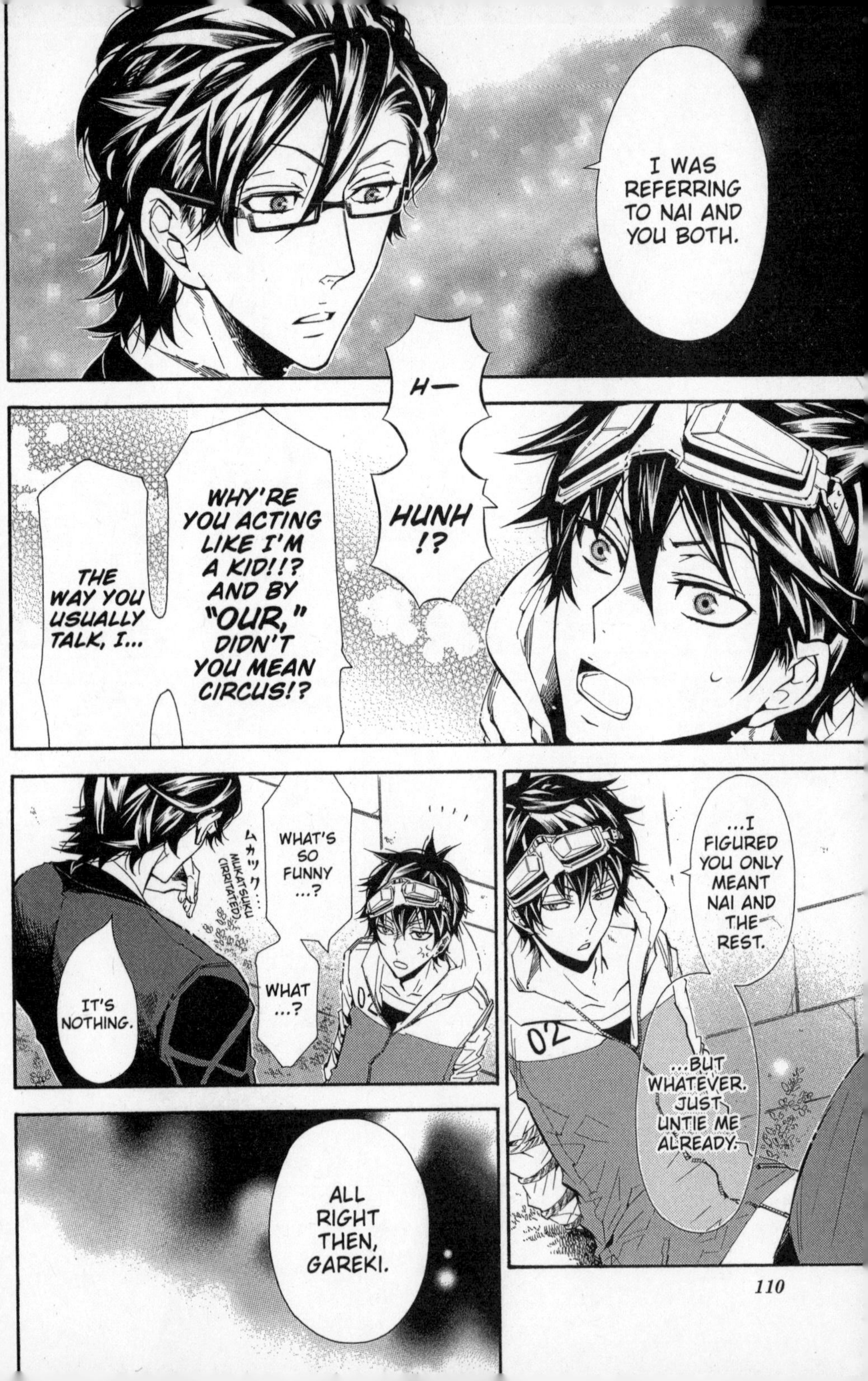
I WAS REFERRING TO NAI AND YOU BOTH.
H—
HUNH!?
WHY'RE YOU ACTING LIKE I'M A KID!!? AND BY "OUR," DIDN'T YOU MEAN CIRCUS!?
THE WAY YOU USUALLY TALK, I...
...I FIGURED YOU ONLY MEANT NAI AND THE REST.
...BUT WHATEVER. JUST UNTIE ME ALREADY.
WHAT'S SO FUNNY ...?
ムカツク… MUKATSUKU (IRRITATED)
WHAT ...?
IT'S NOTHING.
ALL RIGHT THEN, GAREKI.

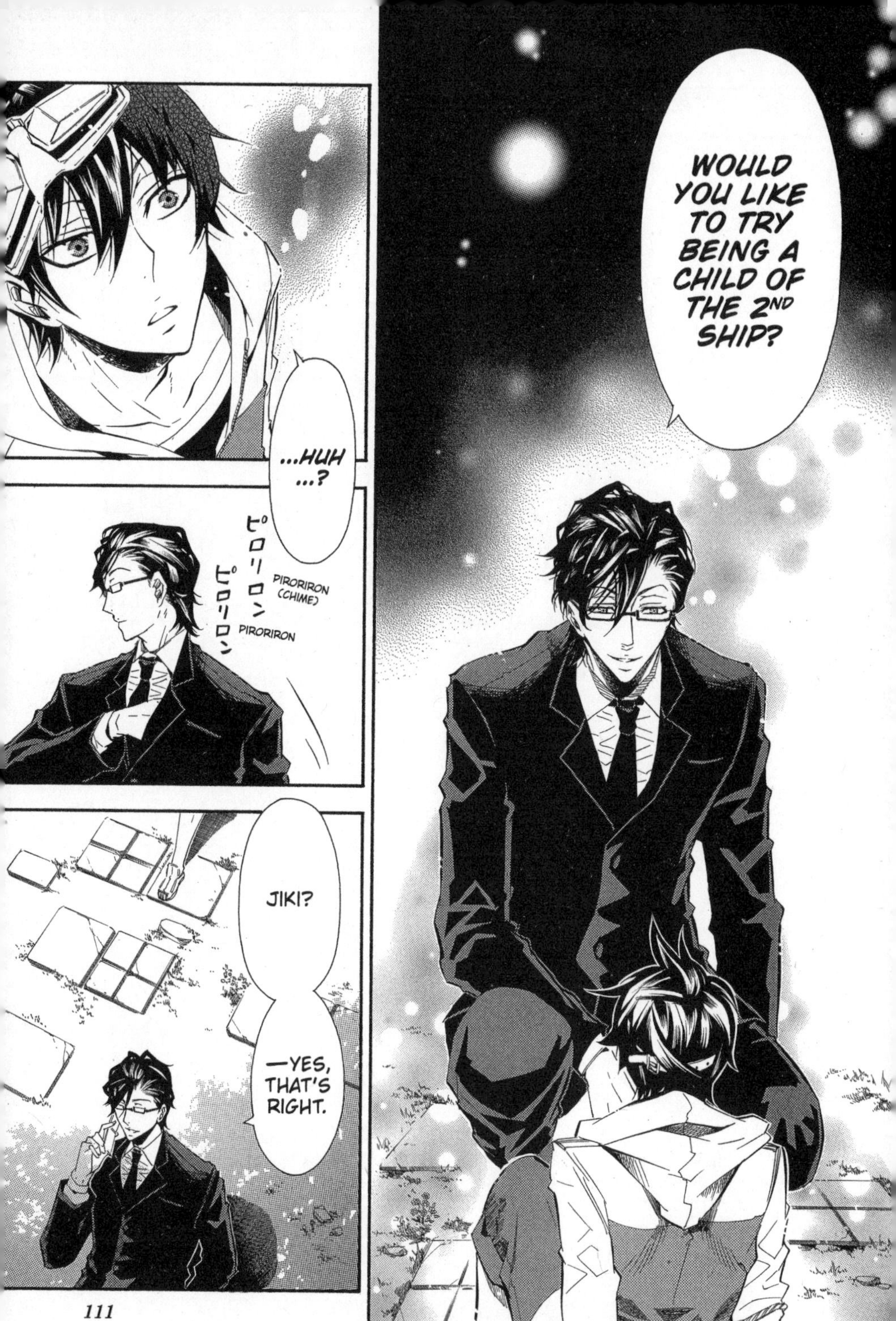
WOULD YOU LIKE TO TRY BEING A CHILD OF THE 2ND SHIP?
...HUH ...?
ピロリロン
PIRORIRON (CHIME)
ピロリロン
PIRORIRON
JIKI?
—YES, THAT'S RIGHT.

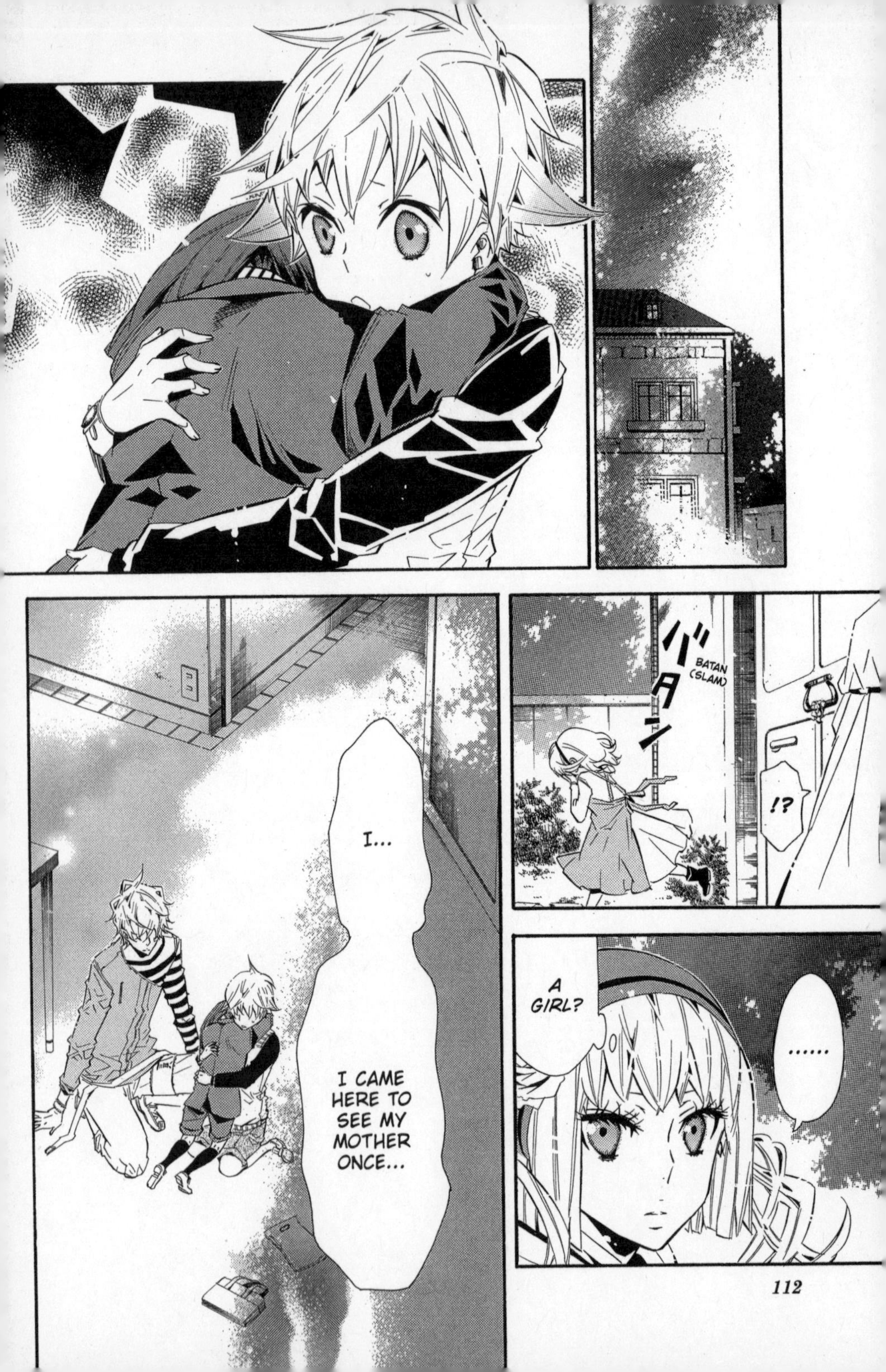
BATAN (SLAM)
!?
......
A GIRL?
I...
I CAME HERE TO SEE MY MOTHER ONCE...

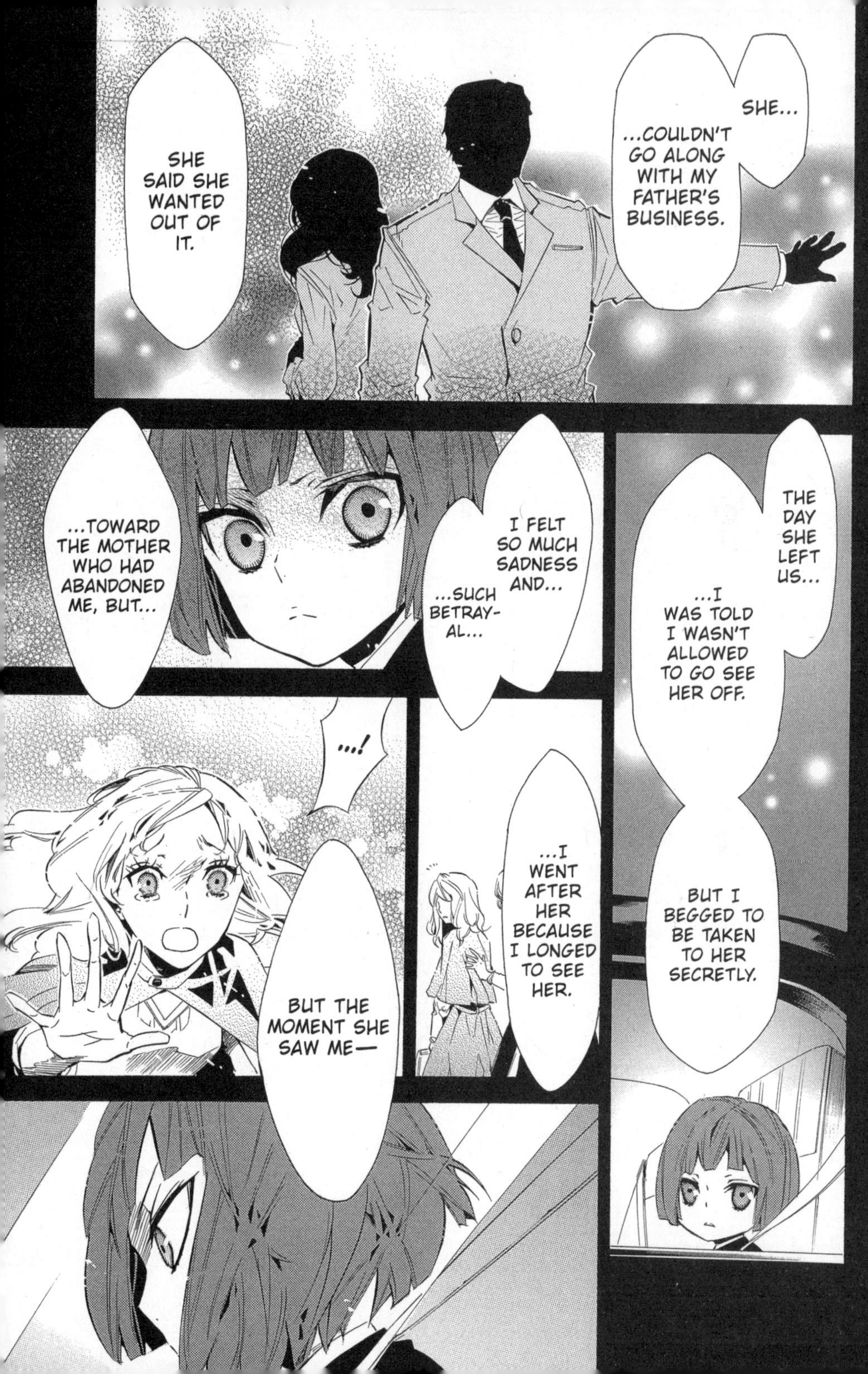
SHE... ...COULDN'T GO ALONG WITH MY FATHER'S BUSINESS.
SHE SAID SHE WANTED OUT OF IT.
THE DAY SHE LEFT US...
...I WAS TOLD I WASN'T ALLOWED TO GO SEE HER OFF.
BUT I BEGGED TO BE TAKEN TO HER SECRETLY.
I FELT SO MUCH SADNESS AND...
...SUCH BETRAYAL...
...TOWARD THE MOTHER WHO HAD ABANDONED ME, BUT...
...I WENT AFTER HER BECAUSE I LONGED TO SEE HER.
...!
BUT THE MOMENT SHE SAW ME—

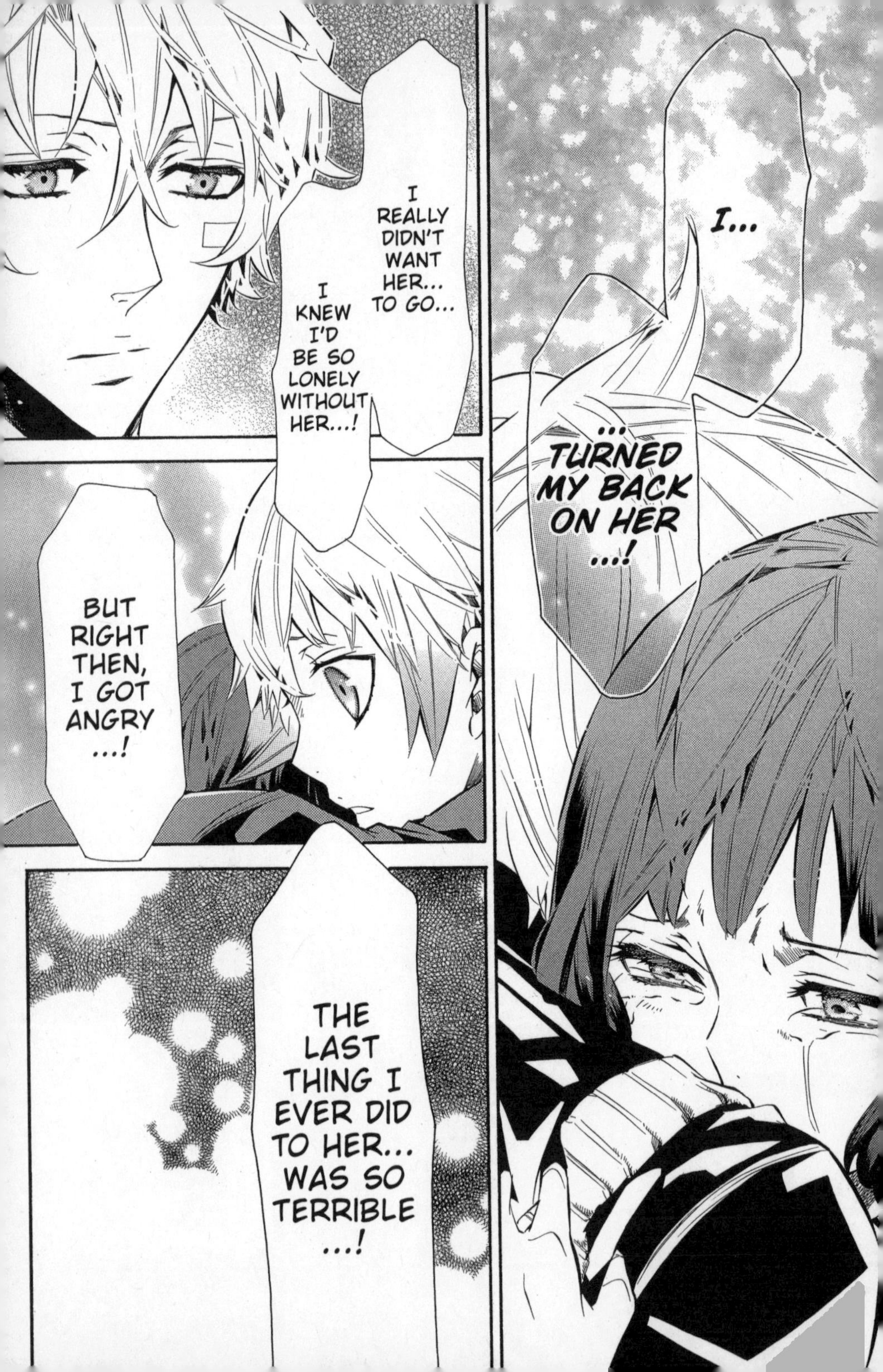
I...
...TURNED MY BACK ON HER ...!
I REALLY DIDN'T WANT HER... TO GO...
I KNEW I'D BE SO LONELY WITHOUT HER...!
BUT RIGHT THEN, I GOT ANGRY ...!
THE LAST THING I EVER DID TO HER... WAS SO TERRIBLE ...!

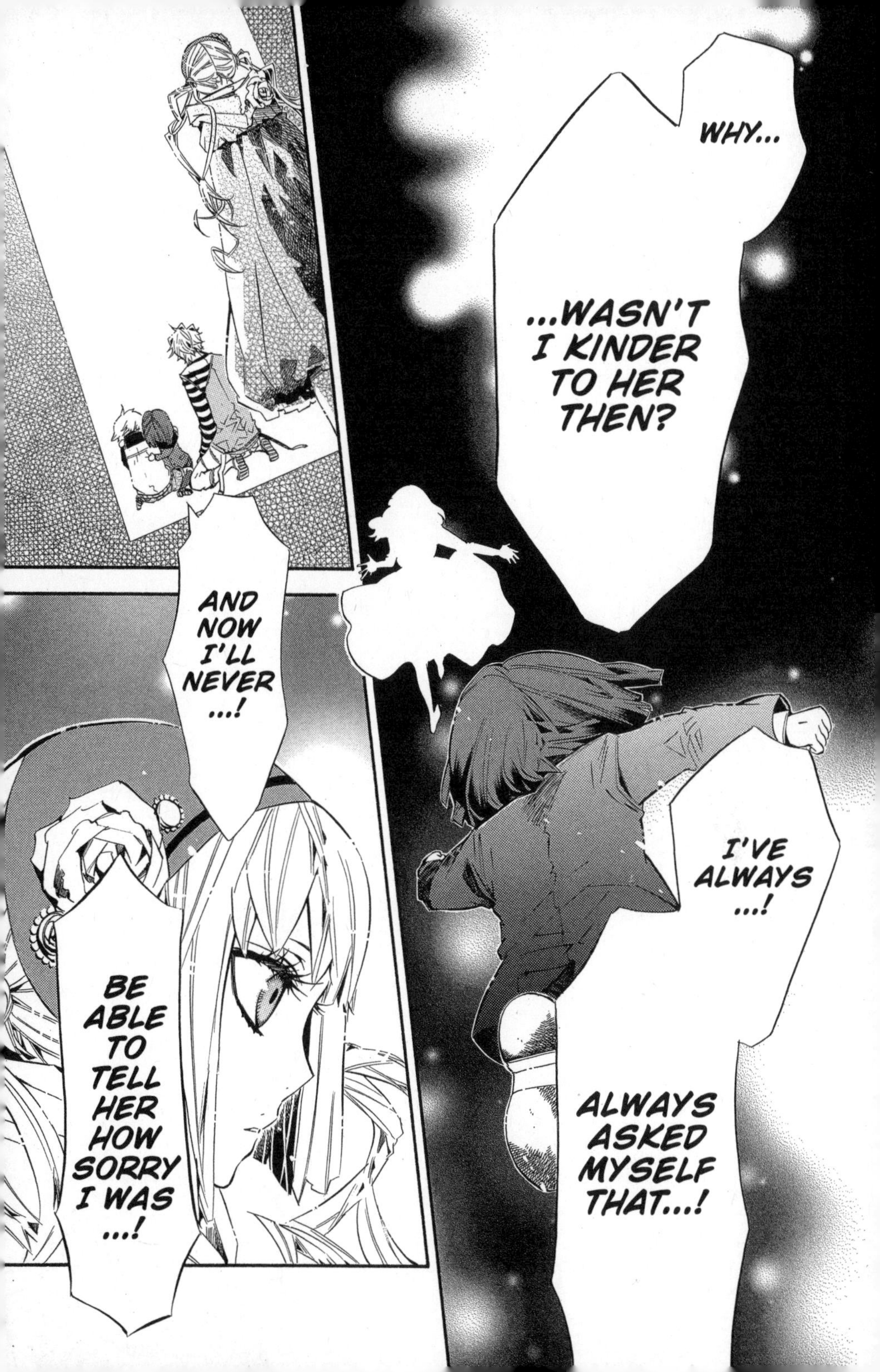
WHY...
...WASN'T I KINDER TO HER THEN?
I'VE ALWAYS ...!
ALWAYS ASKED MYSELF THAT...!
AND NOW I'LL NEVER ...!
BE ABLE TO TELL HER HOW SORRY I WAS ...!

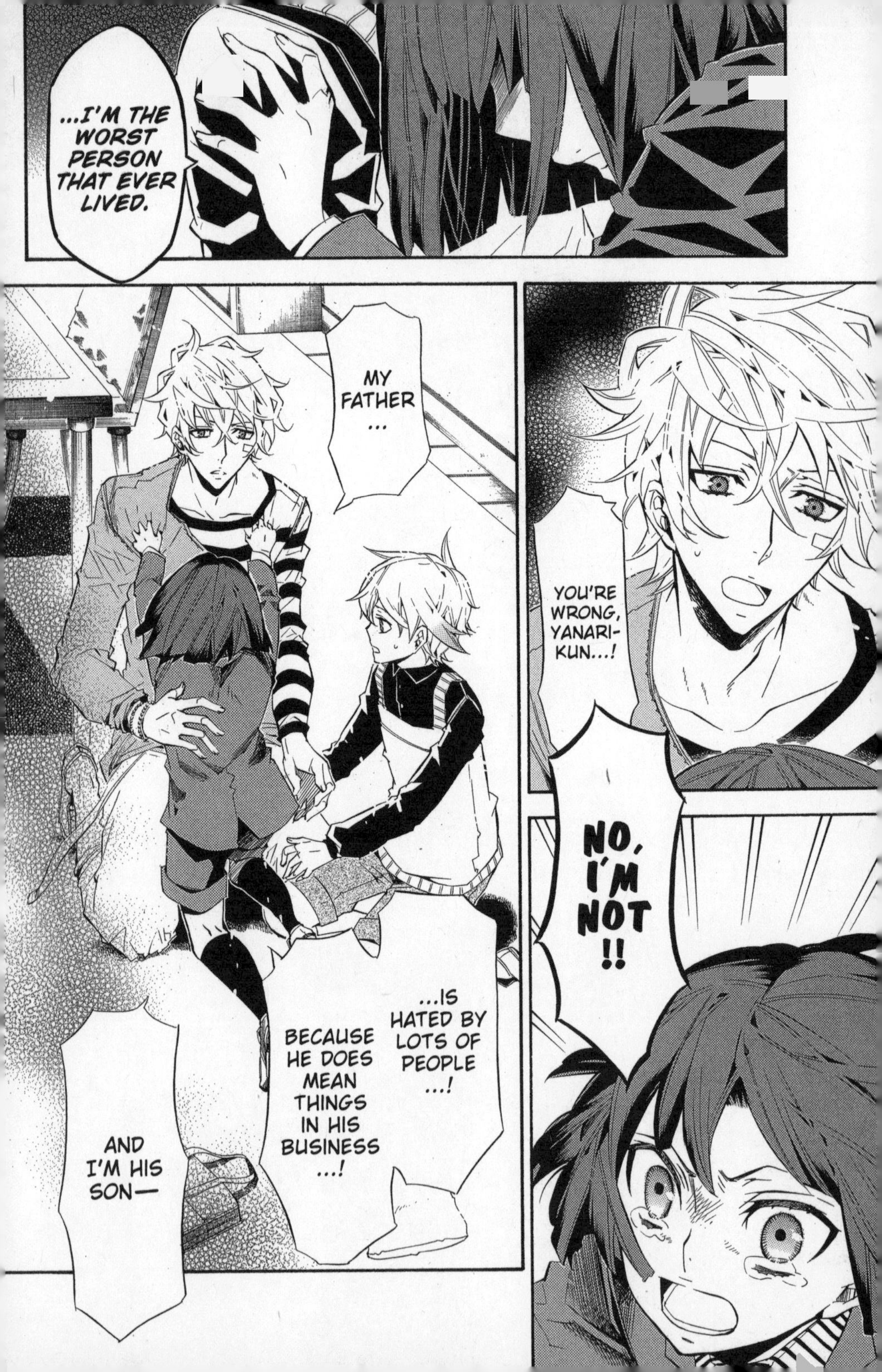
...I'M THE WORST PERSON THAT EVER LIVED.
YOU'RE WRONG, YANARI-KUN...!
NO, I'M NOT!!
MY FATHER...
...IS HATED BY LOTS OF PEOPLE...!
BECAUSE HE DOES MEAN THINGS IN HIS BUSINESS...!
AND I'M HIS SON—

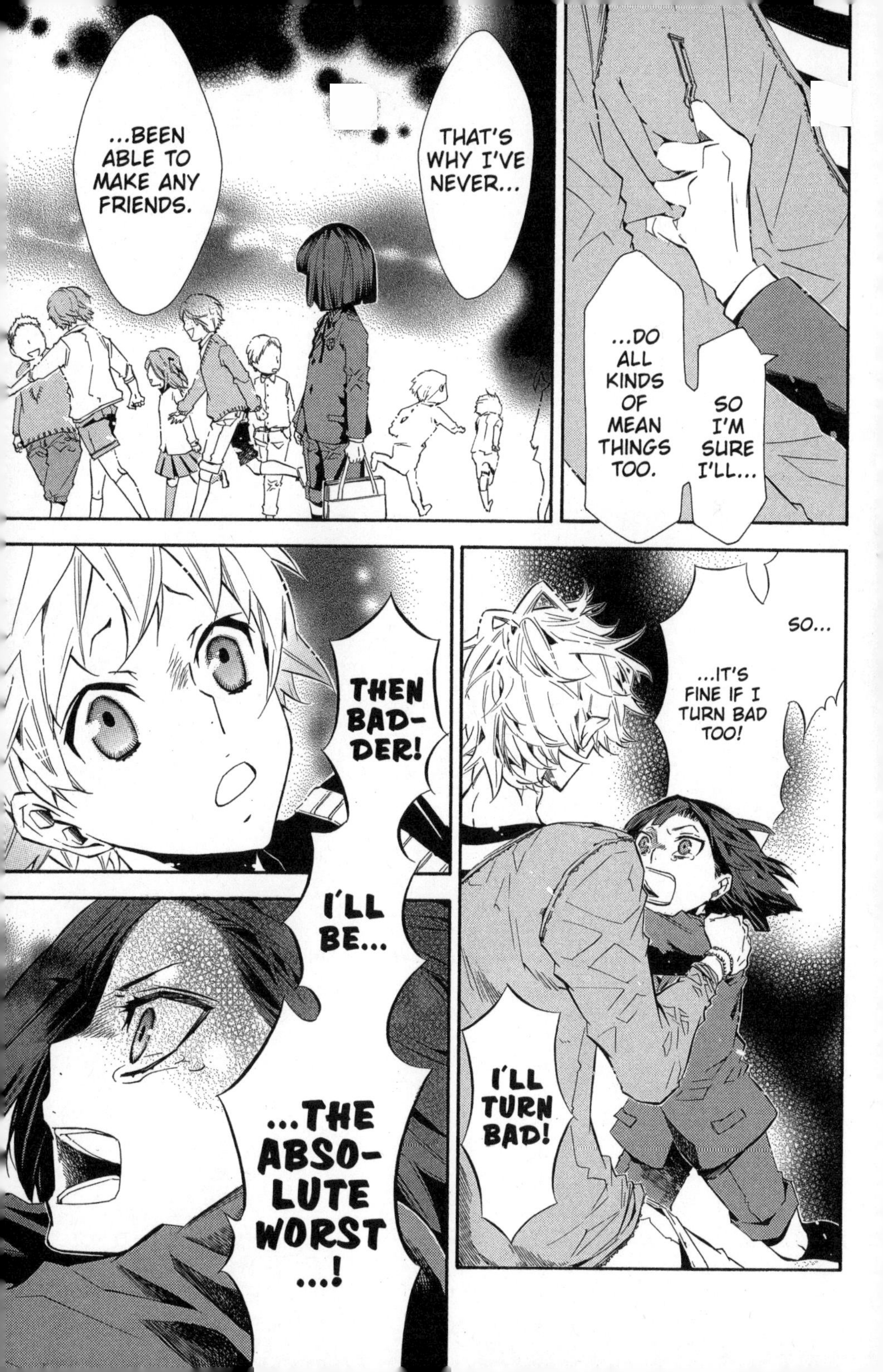
SO I'M SURE I'LL...
...DO ALL KINDS OF MEAN THINGS TOO.
THAT'S WHY I'VE NEVER...
...BEEN ABLE TO MAKE ANY FRIENDS.
SO...
...IT'S FINE IF I TURN BAD TOO!
I'LL TURN BAD!
THEN BAD-DER!
I'LL BE...
...THE ABSO-LUTE WORST ...!

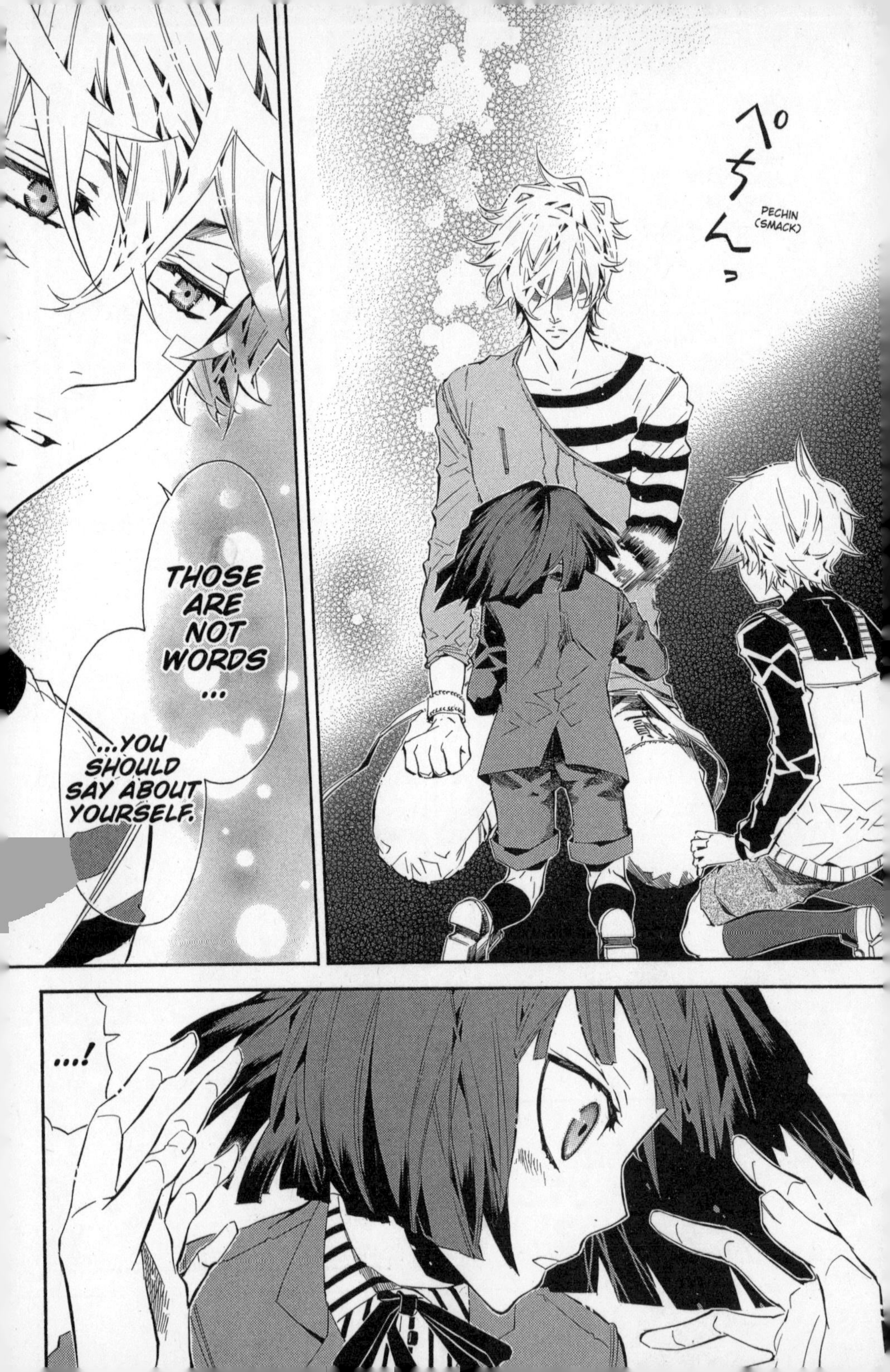
ぺちんっ
PECHIN (SMACK)
THOSE ARE NOT WORDS...
...YOU SHOULD SAY ABOUT YOURSELF.
...!

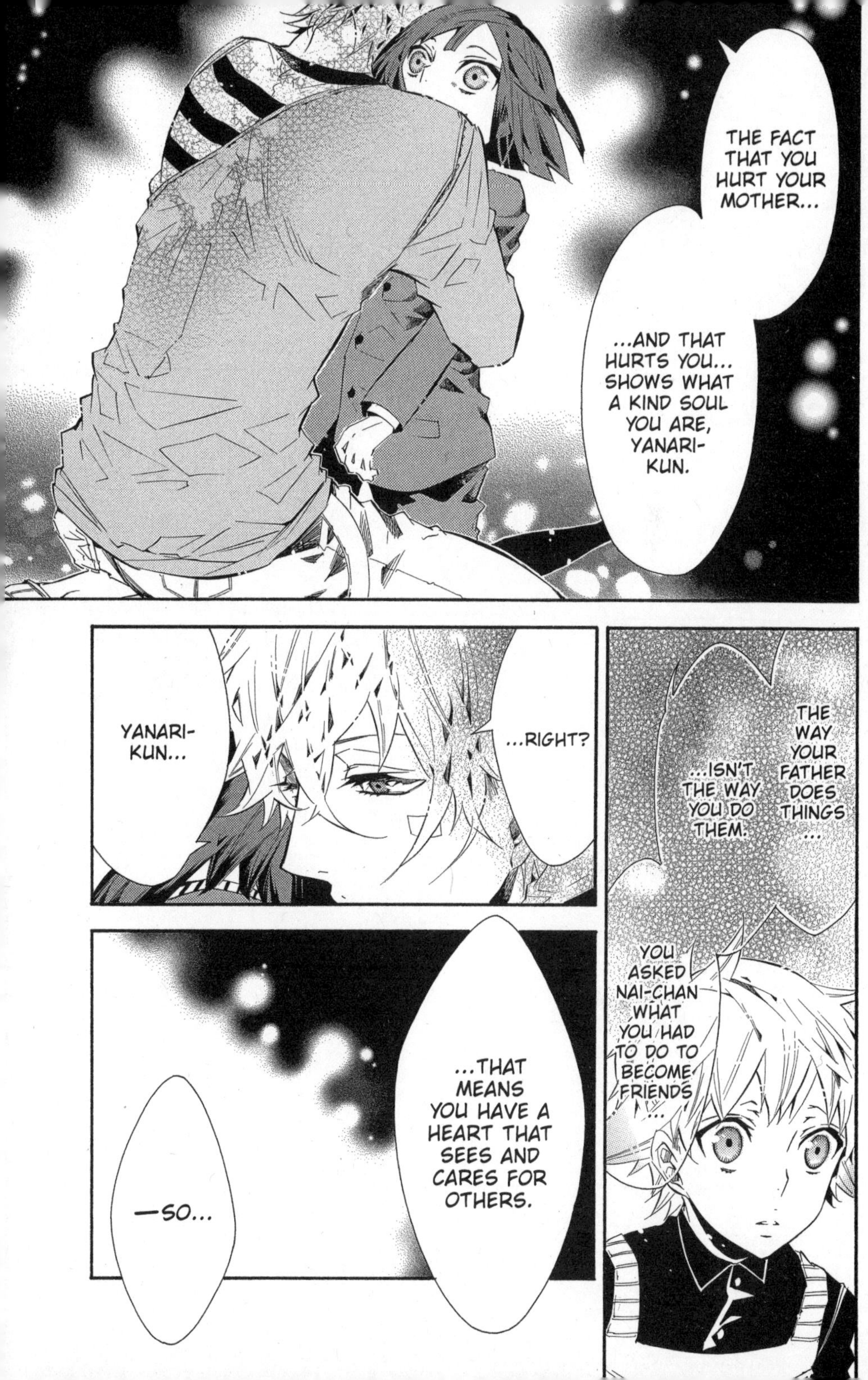
THE FACT THAT YOU HURT YOUR MOTHER...
...AND THAT HURTS YOU... SHOWS WHAT A KIND SOUL YOU ARE, YANARI-KUN.
THE WAY YOUR FATHER DOES THINGS...
...ISN'T THE WAY YOU DO THEM.
YOU ASKED NAI-CHAN WHAT YOU HAD TO DO TO BECOME FRIENDS...
...RIGHT?
YANARI-KUN...
...THAT MEANS YOU HAVE A HEART THAT SEES AND CARES FOR OTHERS.
—SO...

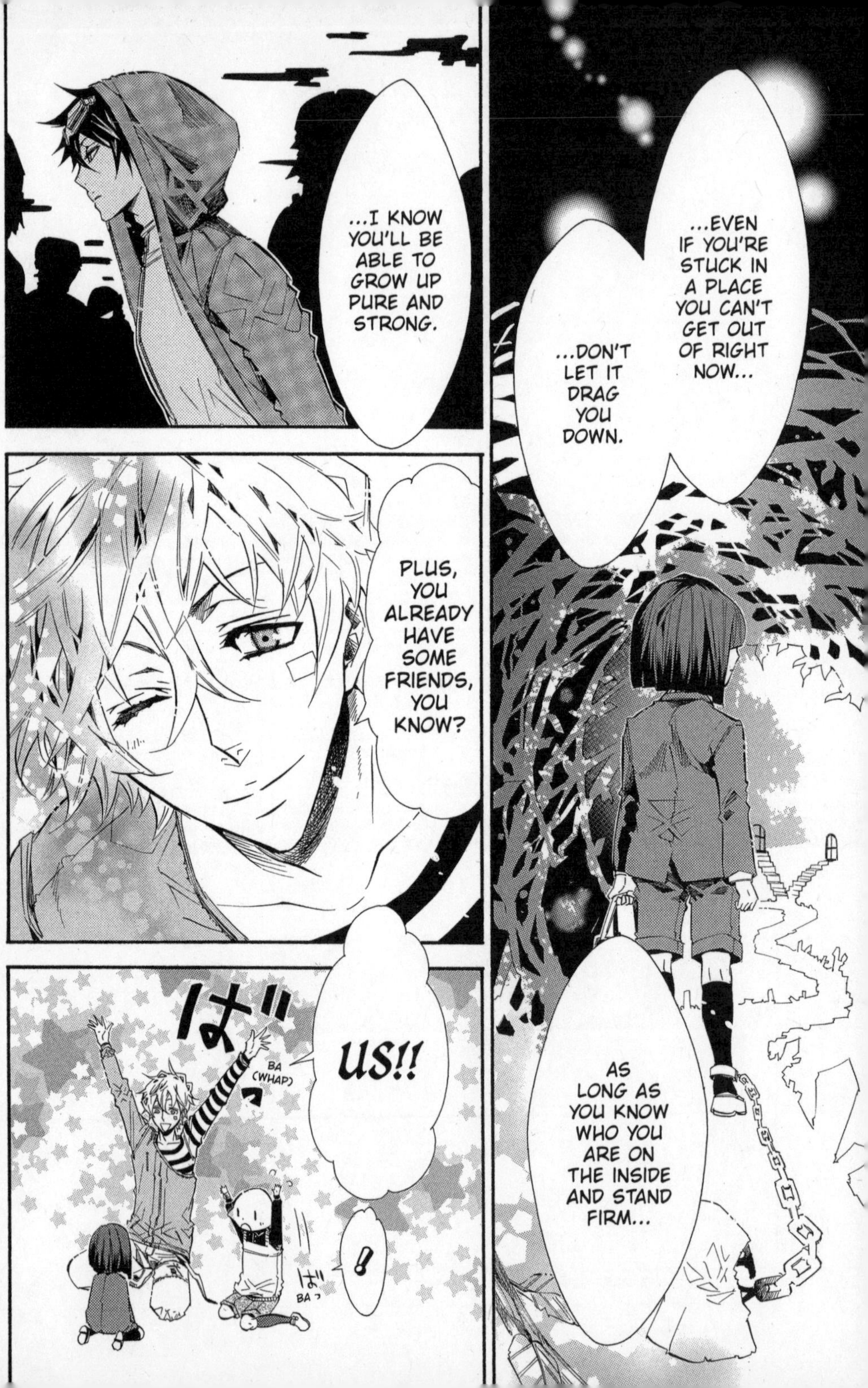
...EVEN IF YOU'RE STUCK IN A PLACE YOU CAN'T GET OUT OF RIGHT NOW...
...DON'T LET IT DRAG YOU DOWN.
AS LONG AS YOU KNOW WHO YOU ARE ON THE INSIDE AND STAND FIRM...
...I KNOW YOU'LL BE ABLE TO GROW UP PURE AND STRONG.
PLUS, YOU ALREADY HAVE SOME FRIENDS, YOU KNOW?
US!!
ば
BA (WHAP)
!
ばっ
BA

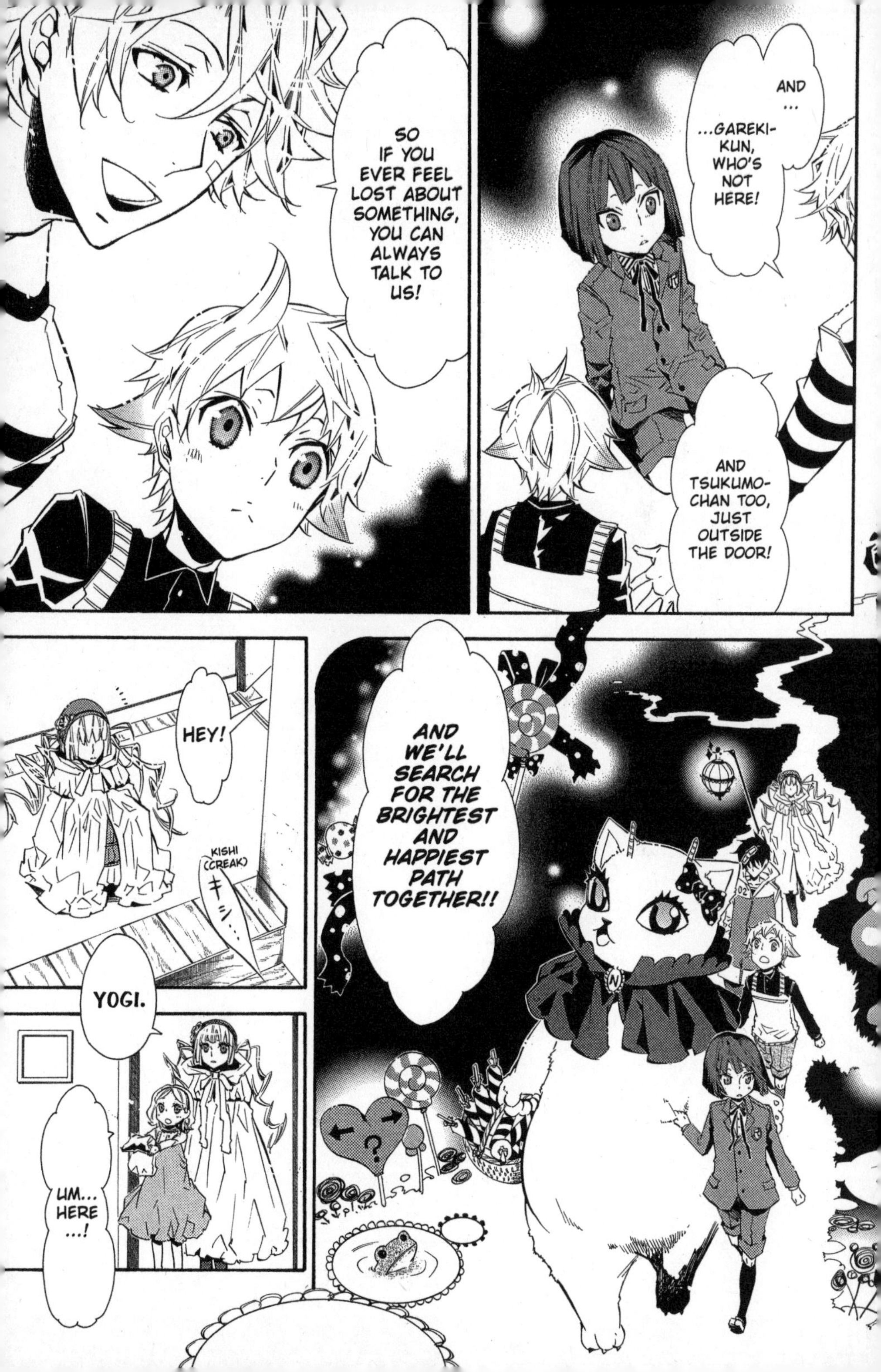
AND ...
...GAREKI-KUN, WHO'S NOT HERE!
AND TSUKUMO-CHAN TOO, JUST OUTSIDE THE DOOR!
SO IF YOU EVER FEEL LOST ABOUT SOMETHING, YOU CAN ALWAYS TALK TO US!
AND WE'LL SEARCH FOR THE BRIGHTEST AND HAPPIEST PATH TOGETHER!!
HEY!
KISHI (CREAK)
キシ…
YOGI.
UM... HERE ...!

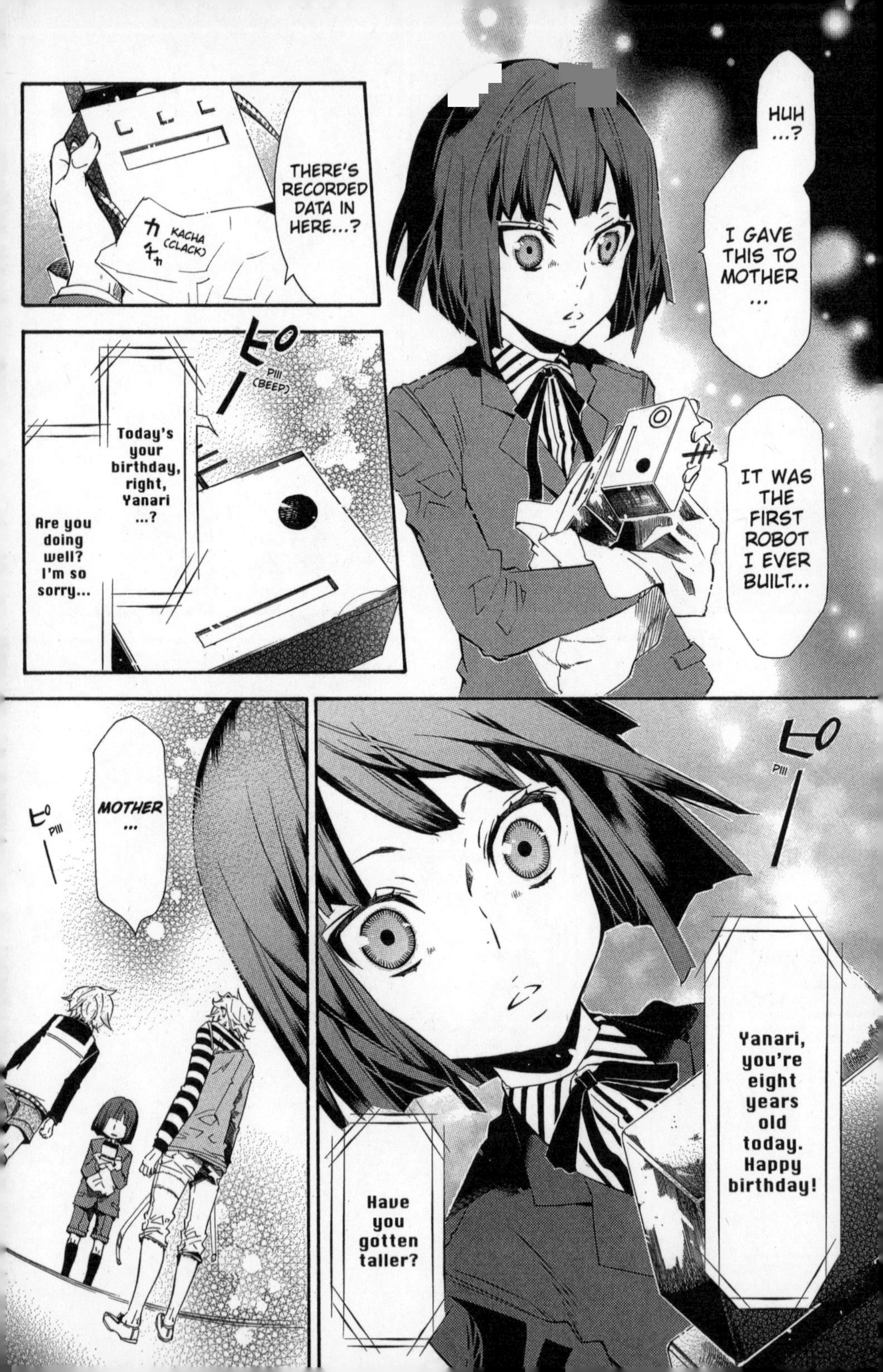
HUH ...?
I GAVE THIS TO MOTHER ...
IT WAS THE FIRST ROBOT I EVER BUILT...
THERE'S RECORDED DATA IN HERE...?
KACHA (CLACK)
PIII (BEEP)
Today's your birthday, right, Yanari ...?
Are you doing well? I'm so sorry...
PIII
Yanari, you're eight years old today. Happy birthday!
Have you gotten taller?
MOTHER ...
PIII

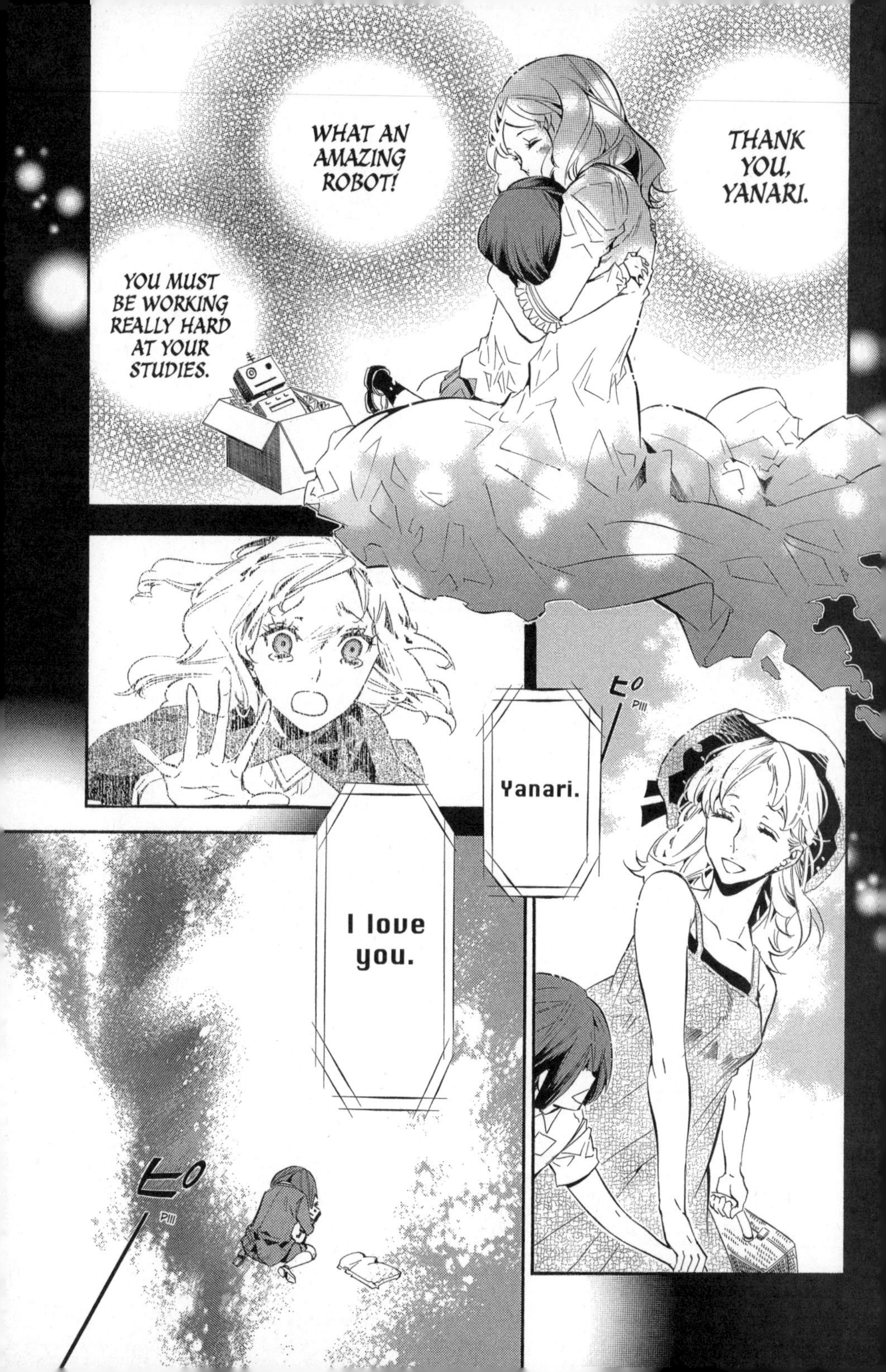
THANK YOU, YANARI.
WHAT AN AMAZING ROBOT!
YOU MUST BE WORKING REALLY HARD AT YOUR STUDIES.
ピ PIII
Yanari.
I love you.
ピ PIII

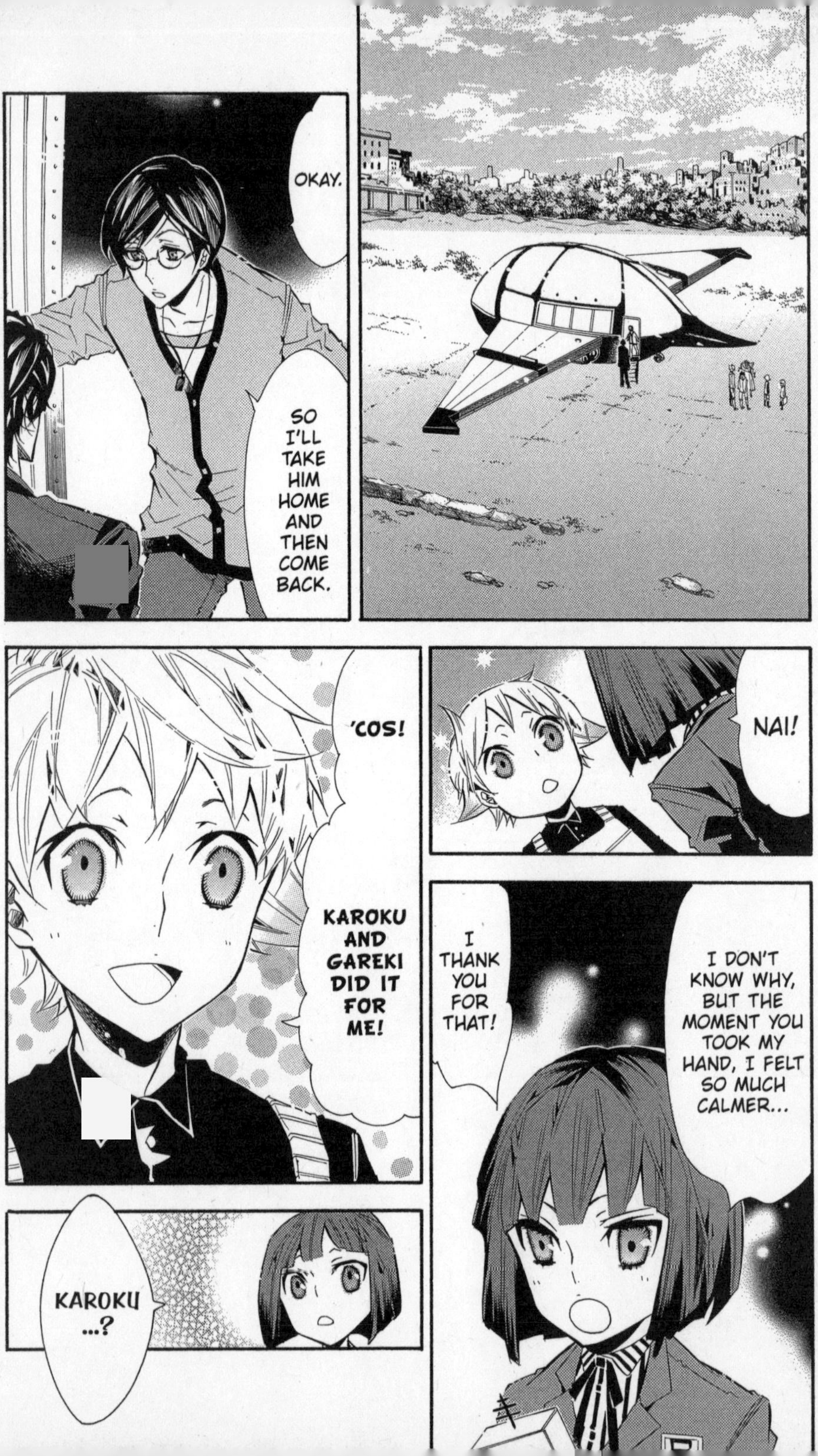
OKAY.
SO I'LL TAKE HIM HOME AND THEN COME BACK.
NAI!
I DON'T KNOW WHY, BUT THE MOMENT YOU TOOK MY HAND, I FELT SO MUCH CALMER...
I THANK YOU FOR THAT!
'COS!
KAROKU AND GAREKI DID IT FOR ME!
KAROKU ...?

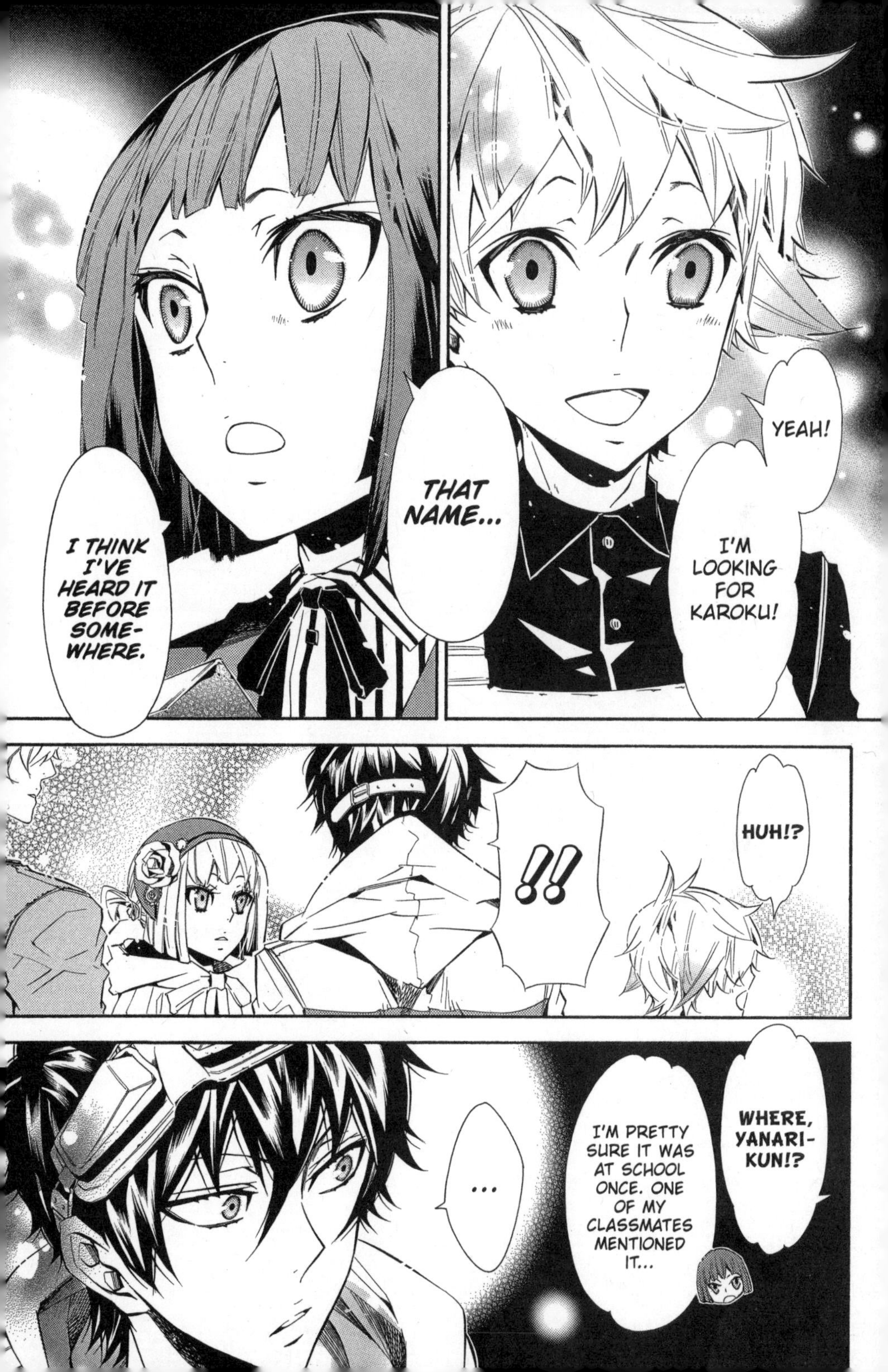
YEAH!
I'M LOOKING FOR KAROKU!
THAT NAME...
I THINK I'VE HEARD IT BEFORE SOME-WHERE.
HUH!?
!!
WHERE, YANARI-KUN!?
I'M PRETTY SURE IT WAS AT SCHOOL ONCE. ONE OF MY CLASSMATES MENTIONED IT...
...

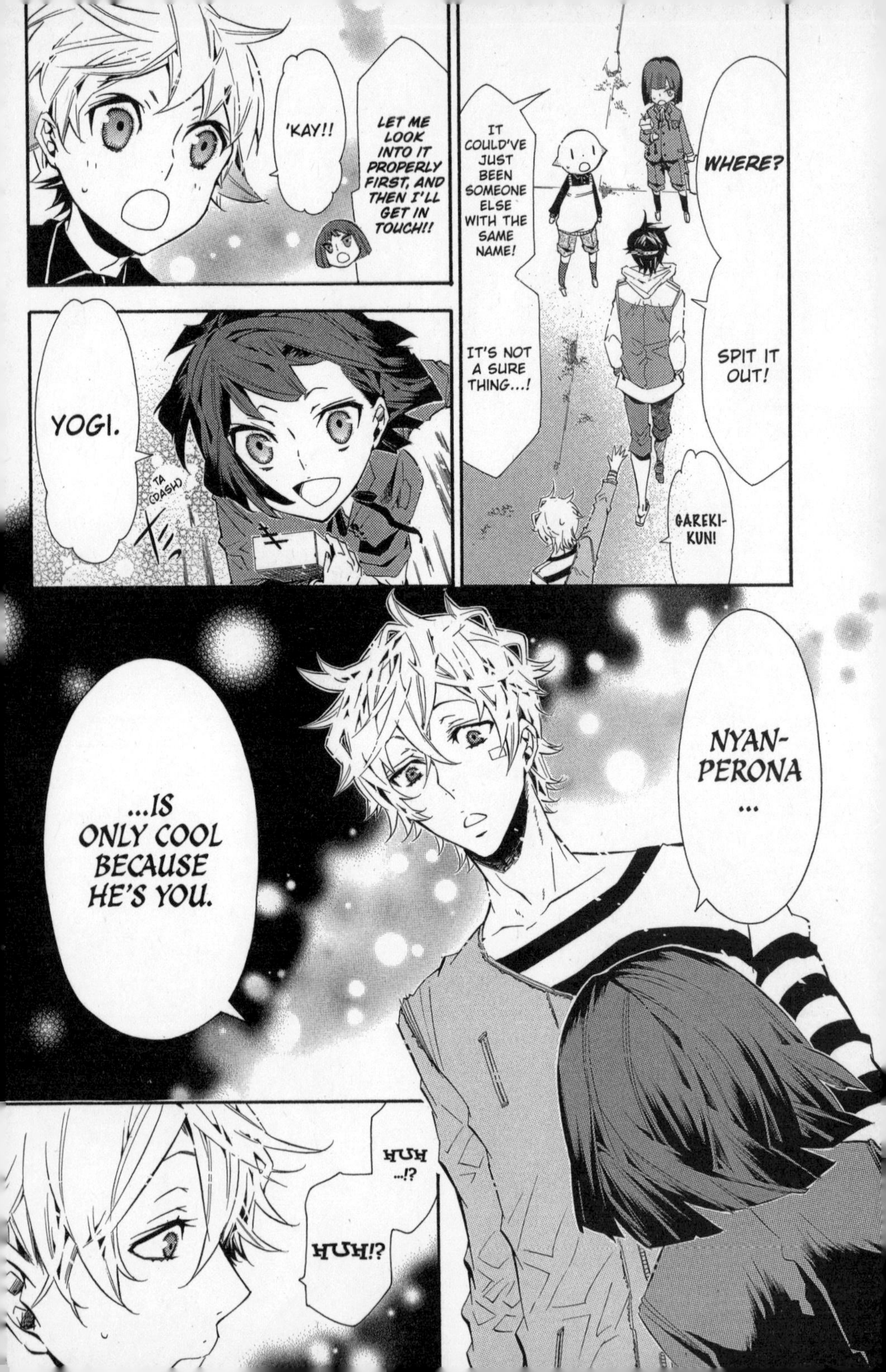
WHERE?
IT COULD'VE JUST BEEN SOMEONE ELSE WITH THE SAME NAME!
SPIT IT OUT!
IT'S NOT A SURE THING...!
GAREKI-KUN!
LET ME LOOK INTO IT PROPERLY FIRST, AND THEN I'LL GET IN TOUCH!!
'KAY!!
YOGI.
TA (DASH)
NYAN-PERONA ...
...IS ONLY COOL BECAUSE HE'S YOU.
HUH ...!?
HUH!?

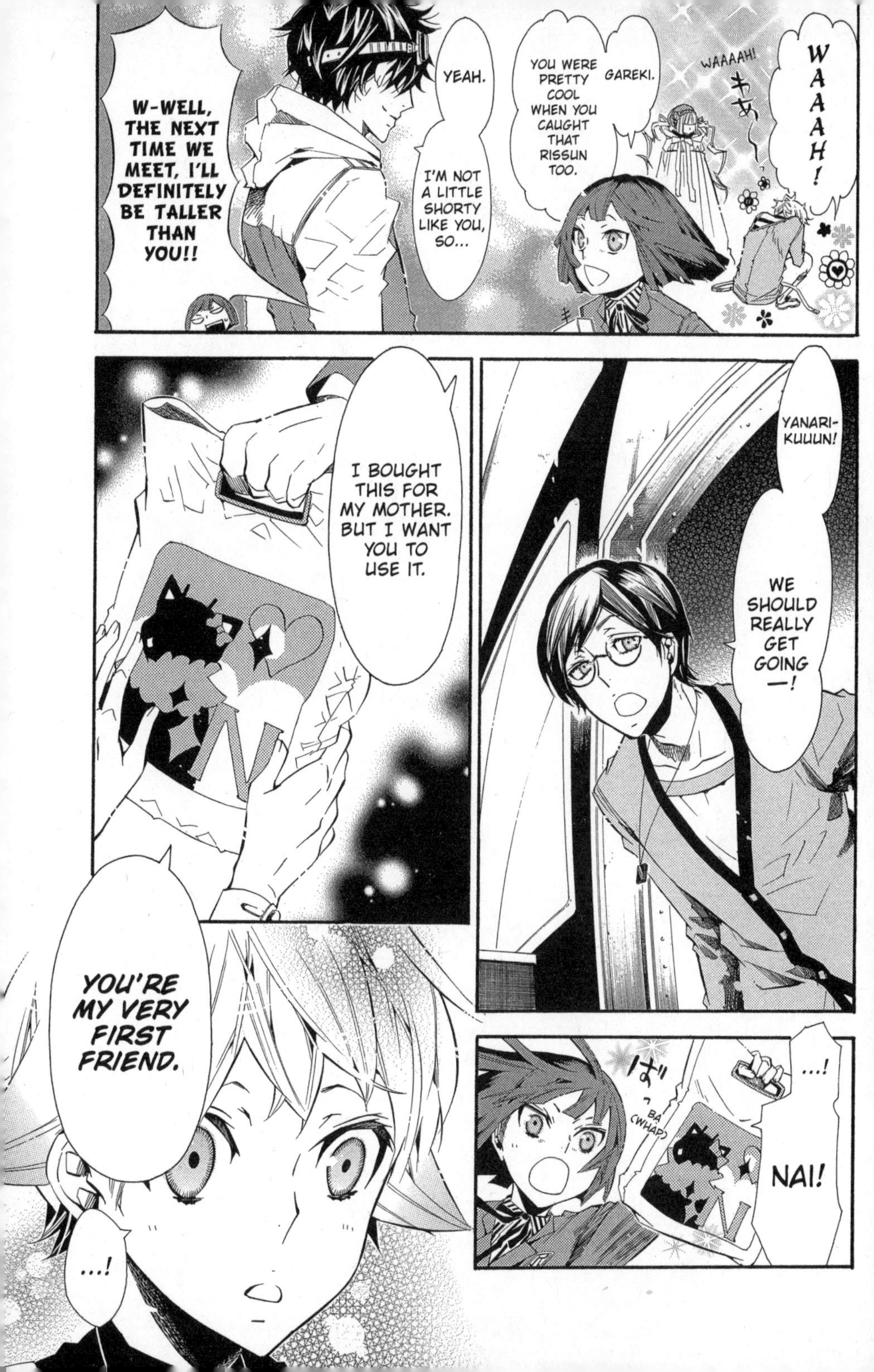
WAAAH!
WAAAAH!
キャ
GAREKI.
YOU WERE PRETTY COOL WHEN YOU CAUGHT THAT RISSUN TOO.
YEAH.
I'M NOT A LITTLE SHORTY LIKE YOU, SO...
W-WELL, THE NEXT TIME WE MEET, I'LL DEFINITELY BE TALLER THAN YOU!!
YANARI-KUUUN!
WE SHOULD REALLY GET GOING—!
I BOUGHT THIS FOR MY MOTHER. BUT I WANT YOU TO USE IT.
...!
ばっ
BA (WHAP)
NAI!
YOU'RE MY VERY FIRST FRIEND.
...!

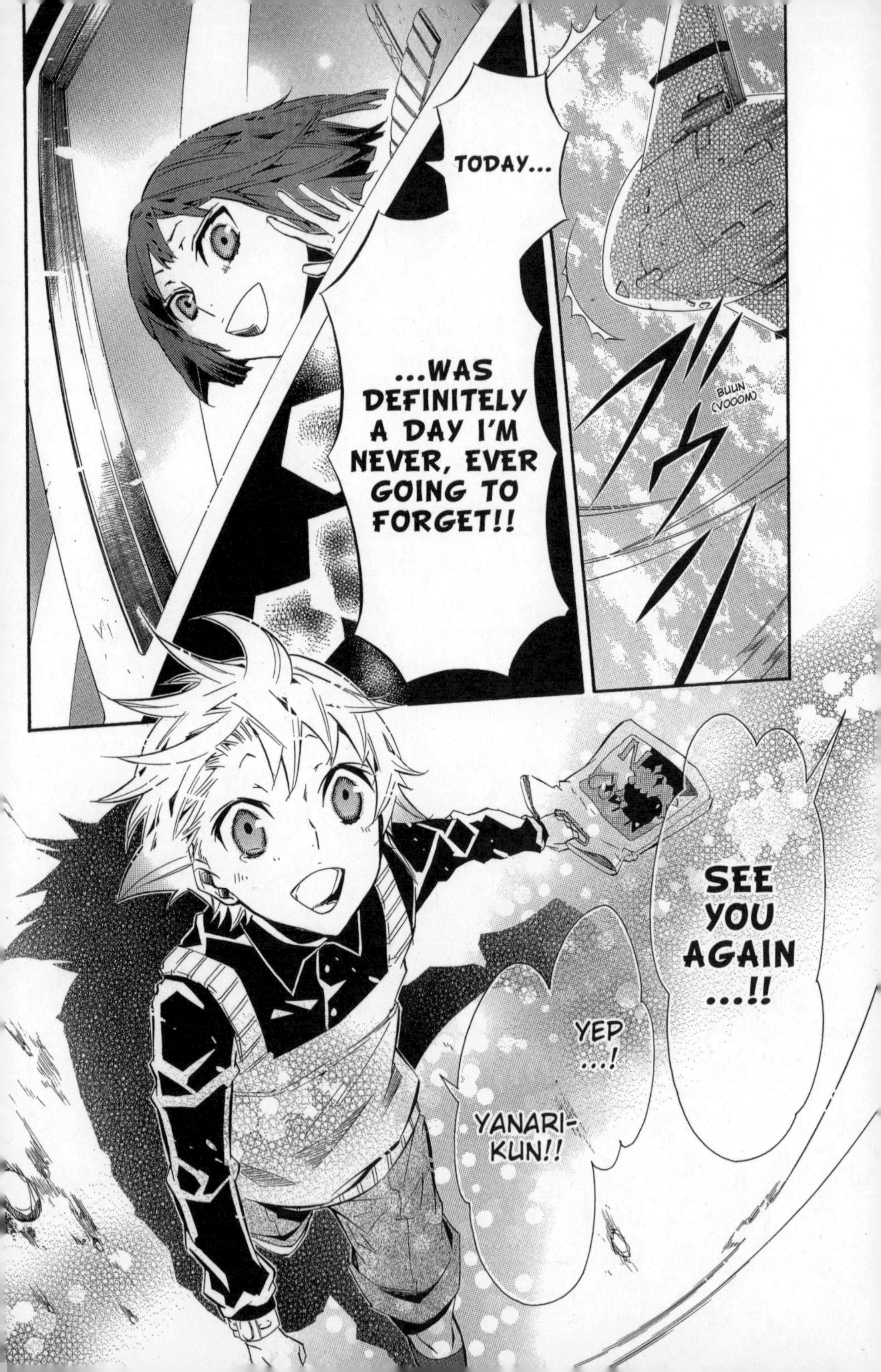
BUUN (VOOOM)
TODAY...
...WAS DEFINITELY A DAY I'M NEVER, EVER GOING TO FORGET!!
SEE YOU AGAIN ...!!
YEP ...!
YANARI-KUN!!

KARNEVAL

BUT I ONLY
DID IT 'COS
YOU SAID
"DO IT! "...

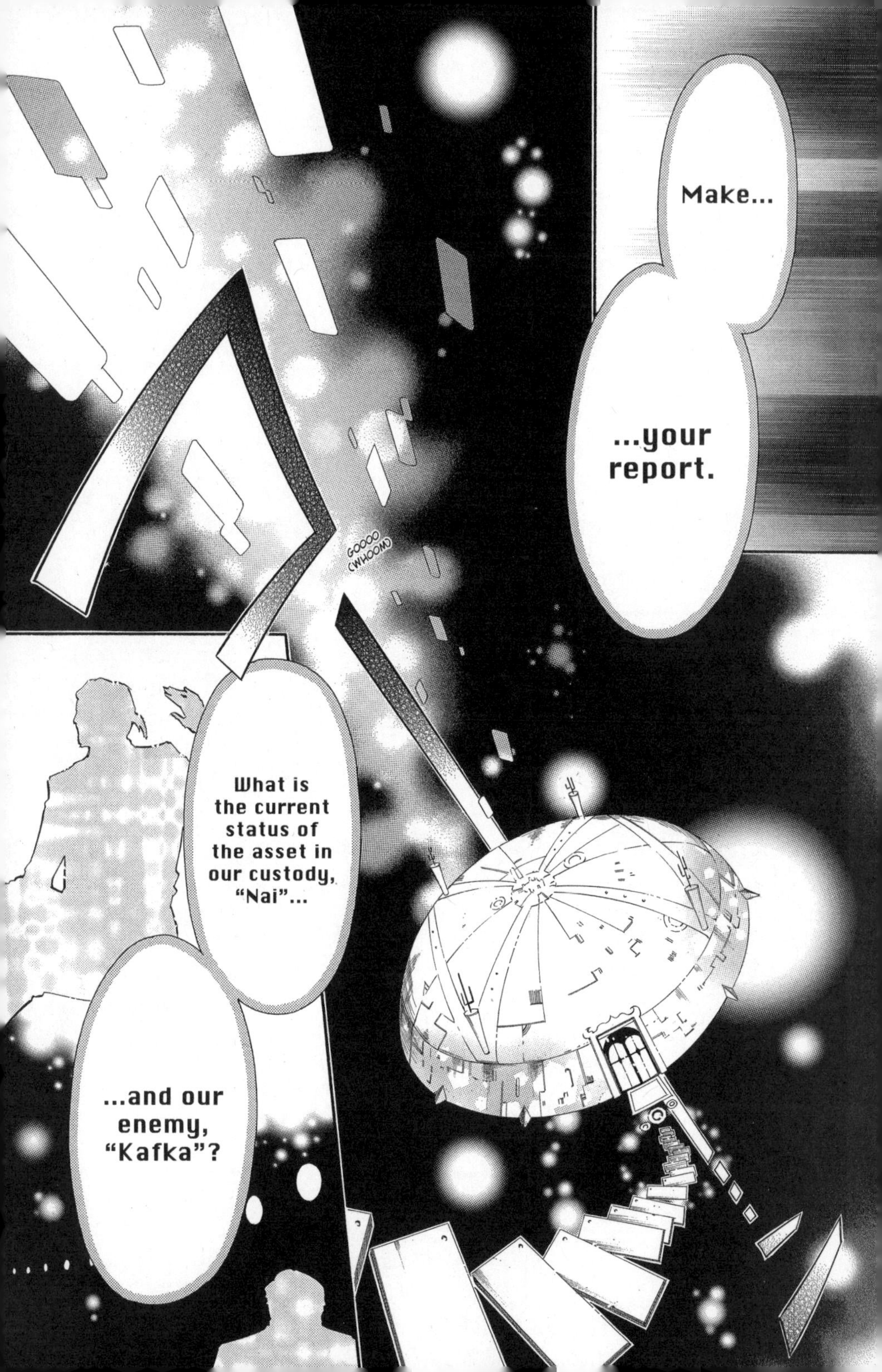
Make...
...your report.
GOOOO (WHOOM)
What is the current status of the asset in our custody, "Nai"...
...and our enemy, "Kafka"?

Score 29: Unsolvable Equation

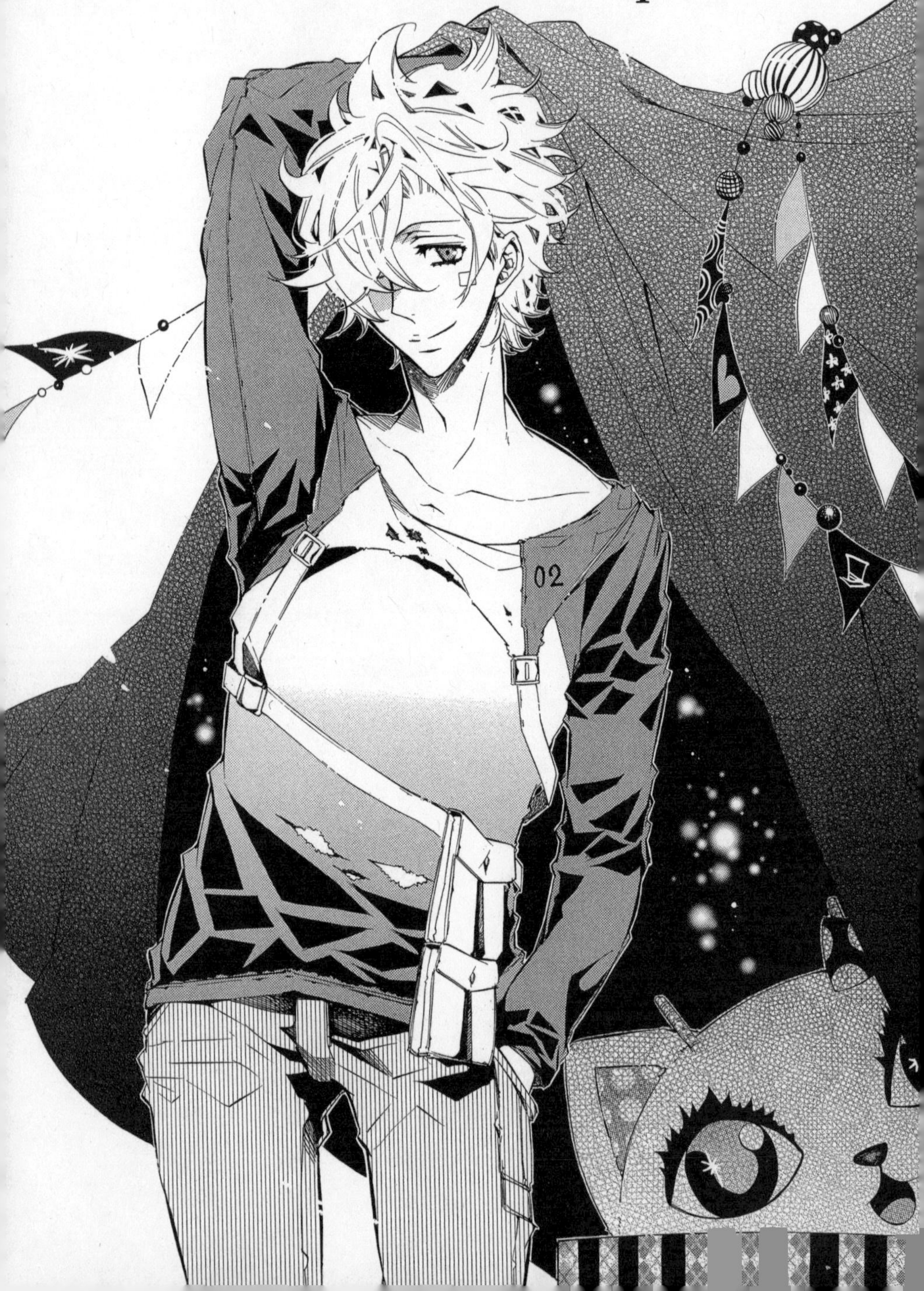
02

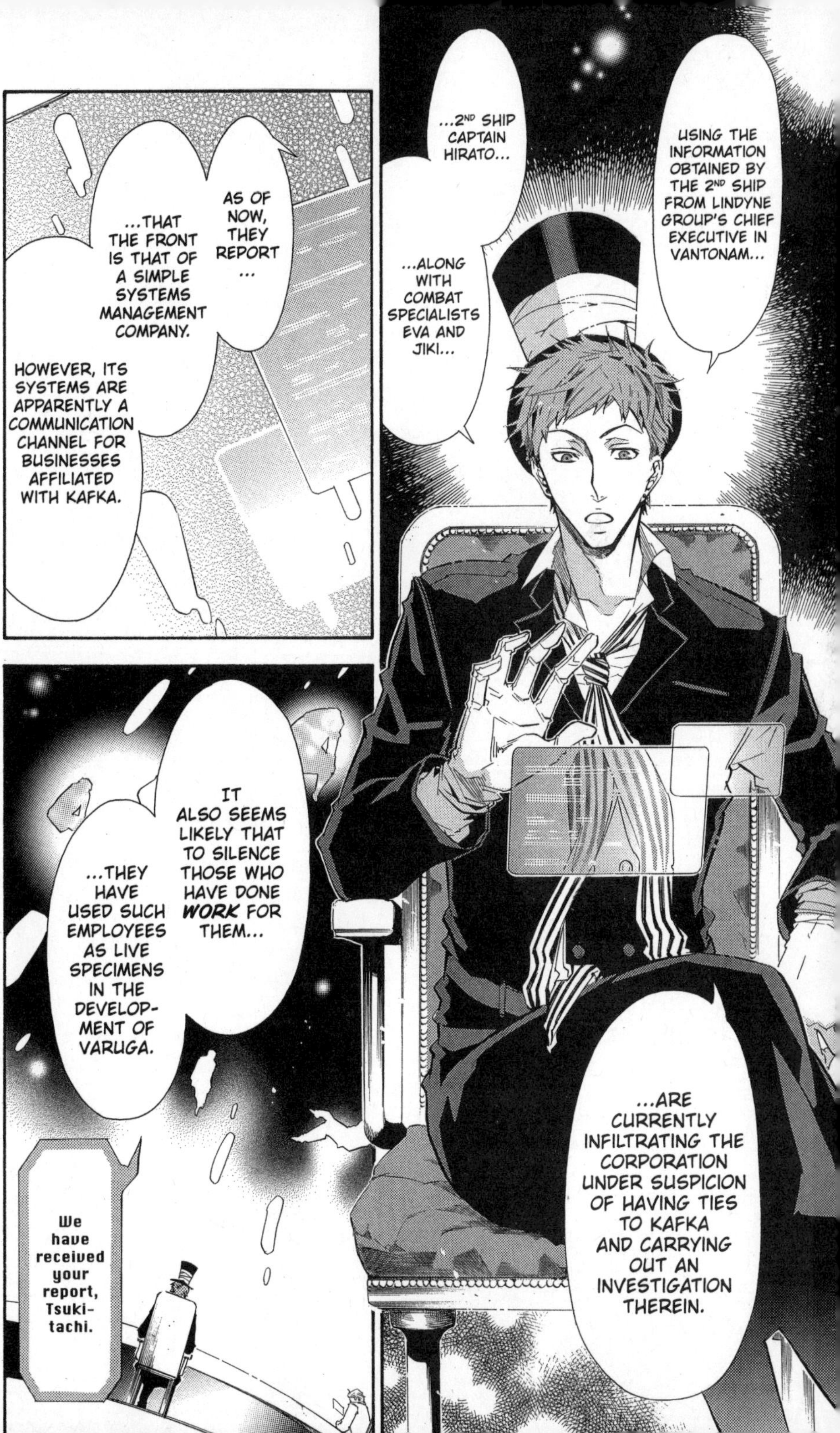
USING THE INFORMATION OBTAINED BY THE 2nd SHIP FROM LINDYNE GROUP'S CHIEF EXECUTIVE IN VANTONAM...
...2nd SHIP CAPTAIN HIRATO...
...ALONG WITH COMBAT SPECIALISTS EVA AND JIKI...
...ARE CURRENTLY INFILTRATING THE CORPORATION UNDER SUSPICION OF HAVING TIES TO KAFKA AND CARRYING OUT AN INVESTIGATION THEREIN.
AS OF NOW, THEY REPORT ...
...THAT THE FRONT IS THAT OF A SIMPLE SYSTEMS MANAGEMENT COMPANY.
HOWEVER, ITS SYSTEMS ARE APPARENTLY A COMMUNICATION CHANNEL FOR BUSINESSES AFFILIATED WITH KAFKA.
IT ALSO SEEMS LIKELY THAT TO SILENCE THOSE WHO HAVE DONE *WORK* FOR THEM...
...THEY HAVE USED SUCH EMPLOYEES AS LIVE SPECIMENS IN THE DEVELOP-MENT OF VARUGA.
We have received your report, Tsuki-tachi.

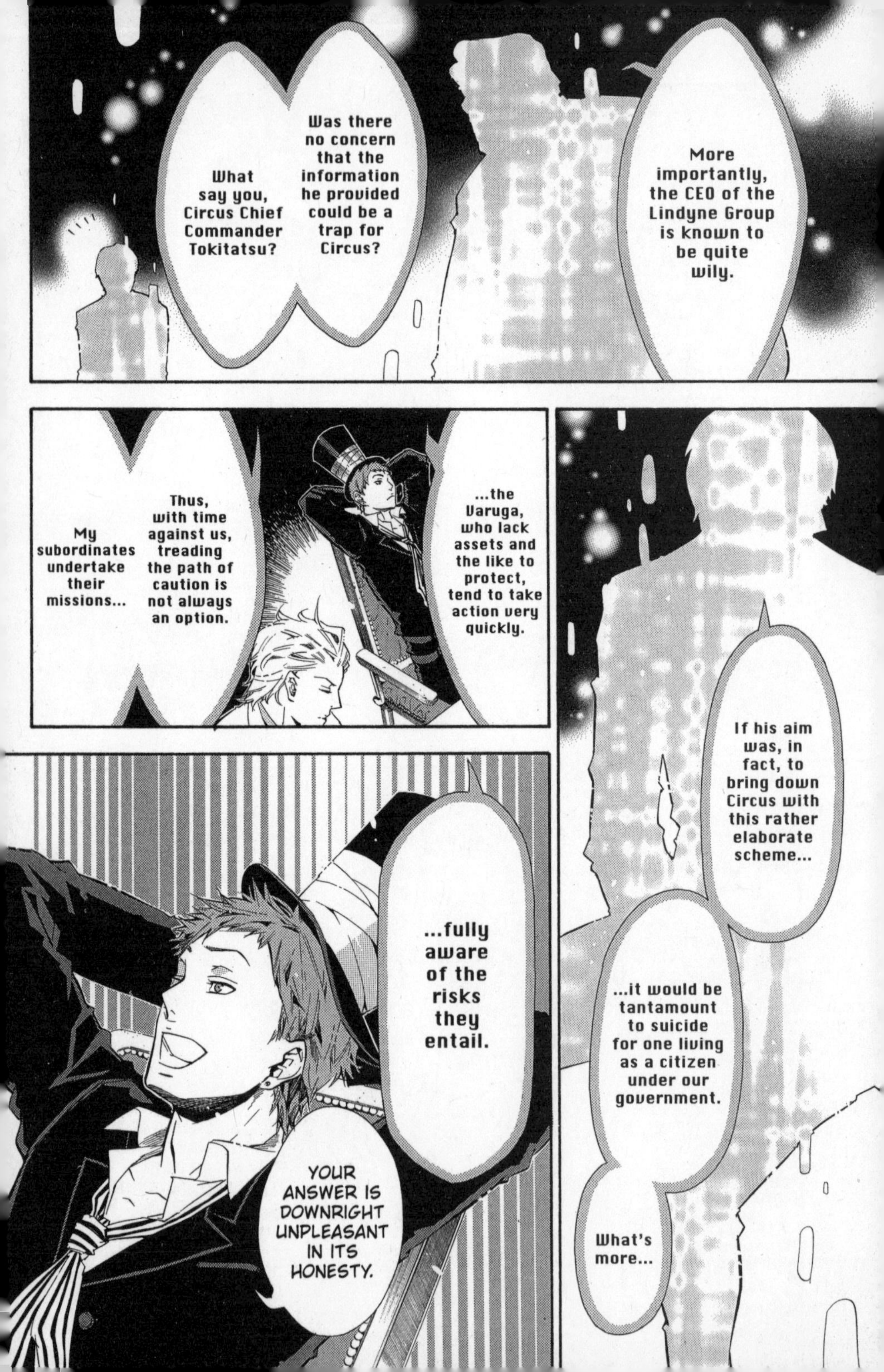
More importantly, the CEO of the Lindyne Group is known to be quite wily.
Was there no concern that the information he provided could be a trap for Circus?
What say you, Circus Chief Commander Tokitatsu?
If his aim was, in fact, to bring down Circus with this rather elaborate scheme...
...it would be tantamount to suicide for one living as a citizen under our government.
What's more...
...the Varuga, who lack assets and the like to protect, tend to take action very quickly.
Thus, with time against us, treading the path of caution is not always an option.
My subordinates undertake their missions...
...fully aware of the risks they entail.
YOUR ANSWER IS DOWNRIGHT UNPLEASANT IN ITS HONESTY.

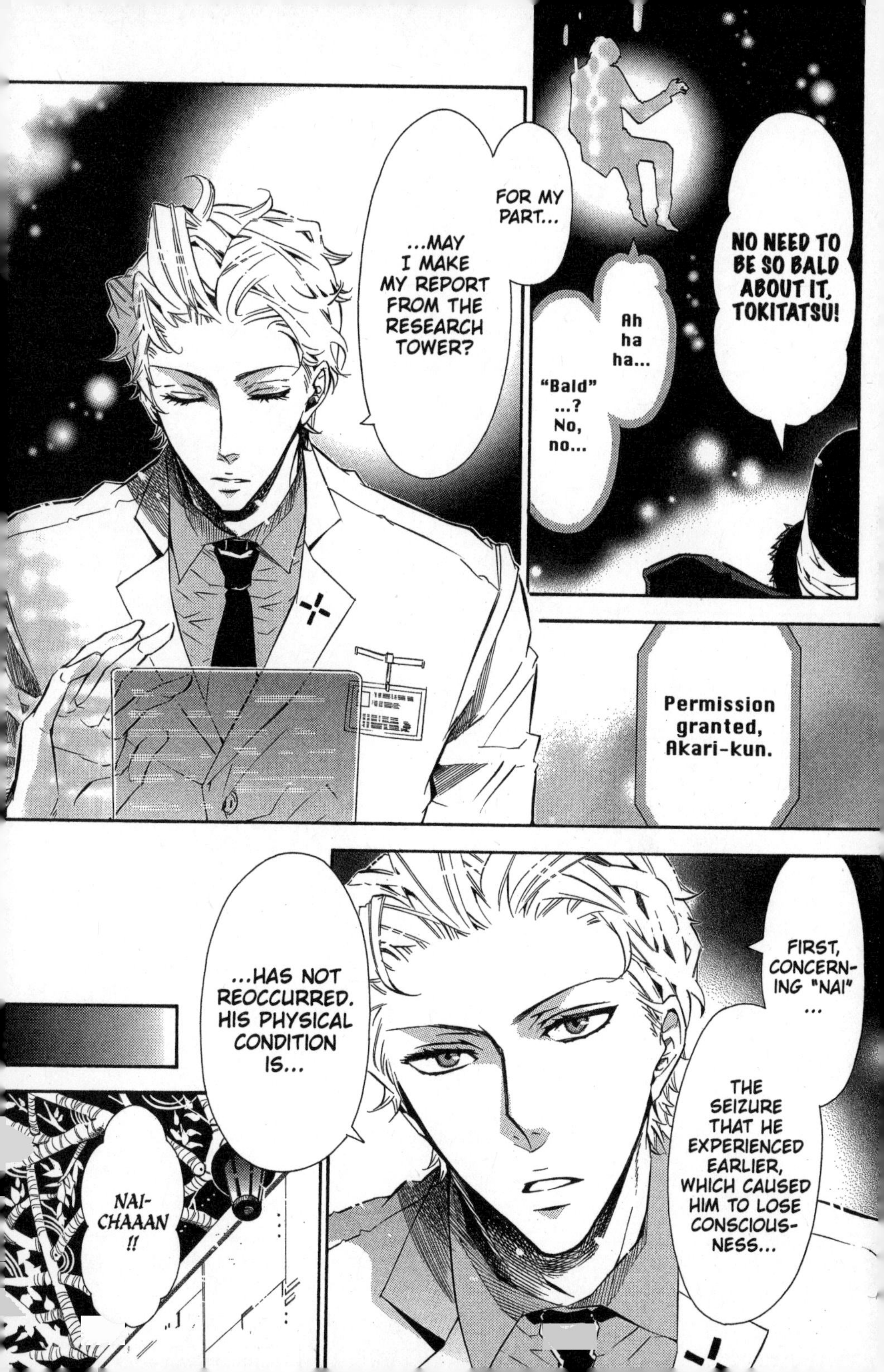
NO NEED TO BE SO BALD ABOUT IT, TOKITATSU!
Ah ha ha... "Bald" ...? No, no...
Permission granted, Akari-kun.
FOR MY PART...
...MAY I MAKE MY REPORT FROM THE RESEARCH TOWER?
FIRST, CONCERNING "NAI" ...
THE SEIZURE THAT HE EXPERIENCED EARLIER, WHICH CAUSED HIM TO LOSE CONSCIOUSNESS...
...HAS NOT REOCCURRED. HIS PHYSICAL CONDITION IS...
NAI-CHAAAN !!

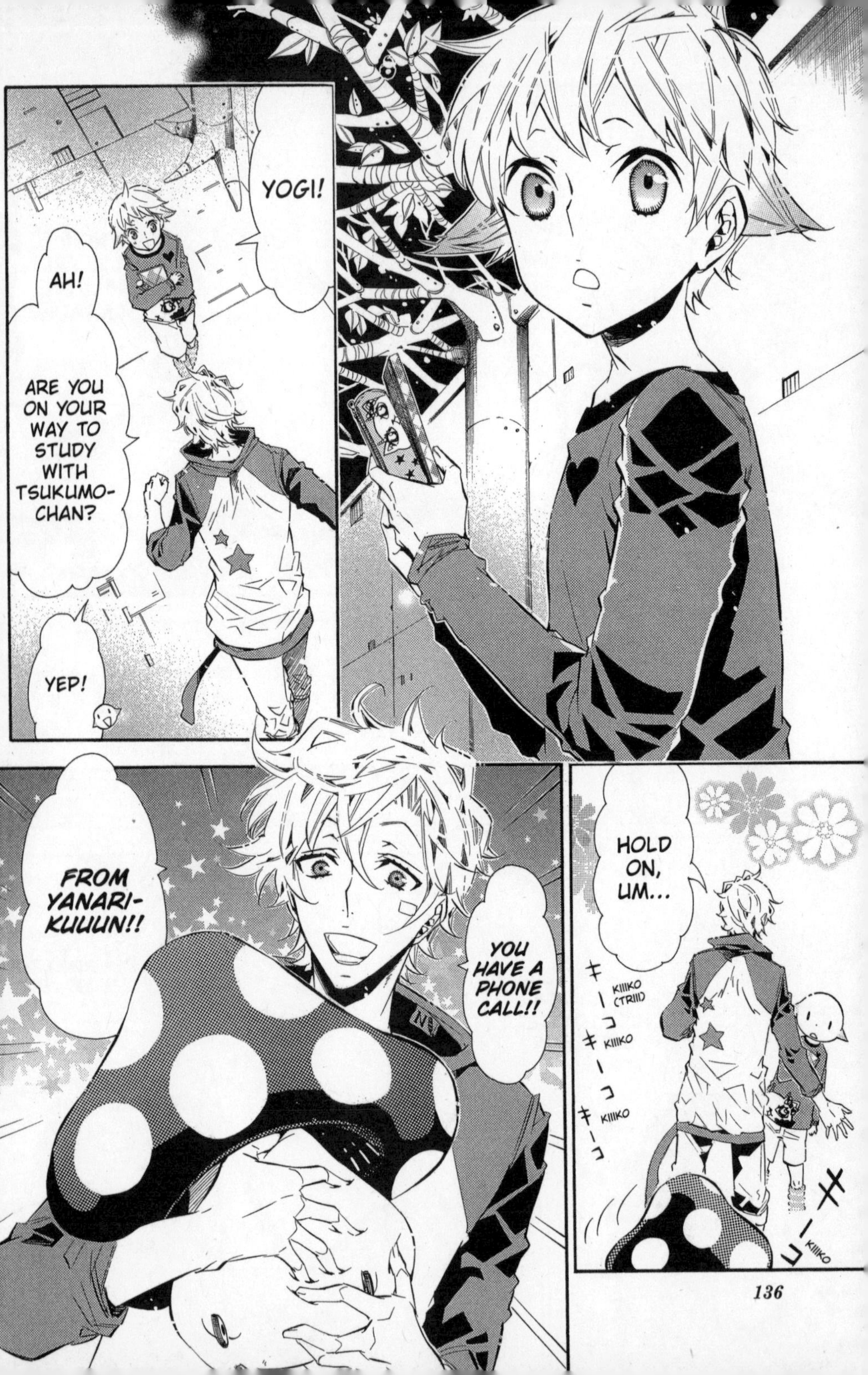
YOGI!
AH!
ARE YOU ON YOUR WAY TO STUDY WITH TSUKUMO-CHAN?
YEP!
HOLD ON, UM...
キーコ KIIIKO (TRIII)
キーコ KIIIKO
キーコ KIIIKO
キーコ KIIIKO
YOU HAVE A PHONE CALL!!
FROM YANARI-KUUUN!!

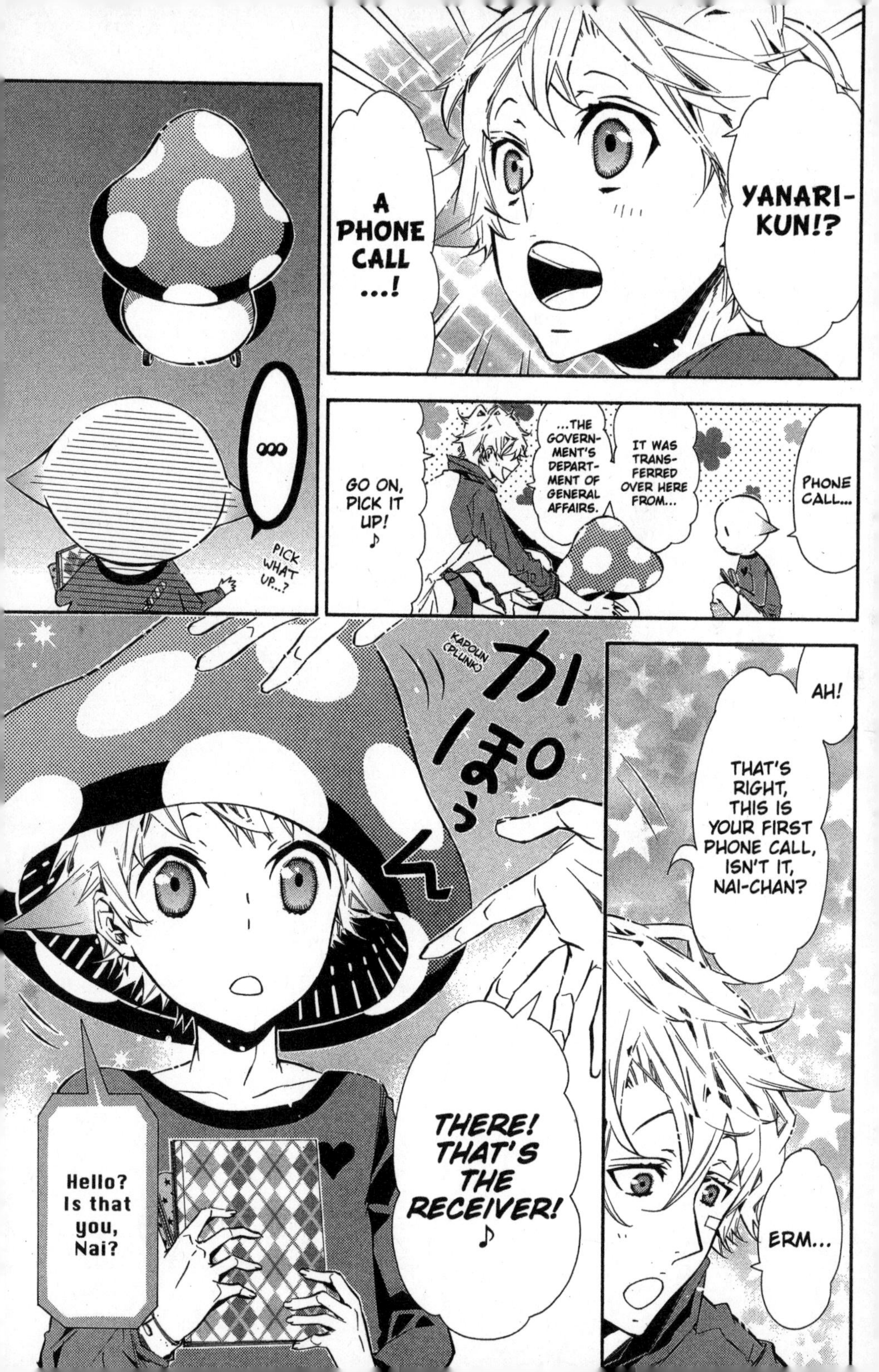
YANARI-KUN!?
A PHONE CALL ...!
PHONE CALL...
IT WAS TRANS-FERRED OVER HERE FROM...
...THE GOVERN-MENT'S DEPART-MENT OF GENERAL AFFAIRS.
GO ON, PICK IT UP! ♪
...
PICK WHAT UP...?
AH!
THAT'S RIGHT, THIS IS YOUR FIRST PHONE CALL, ISN'T IT, NAI-CHAN?
ERM...
KAPOUN (PLUNK)
THERE! THAT'S THE RECEIVER! ♪
Hello? Is that you, Nai?

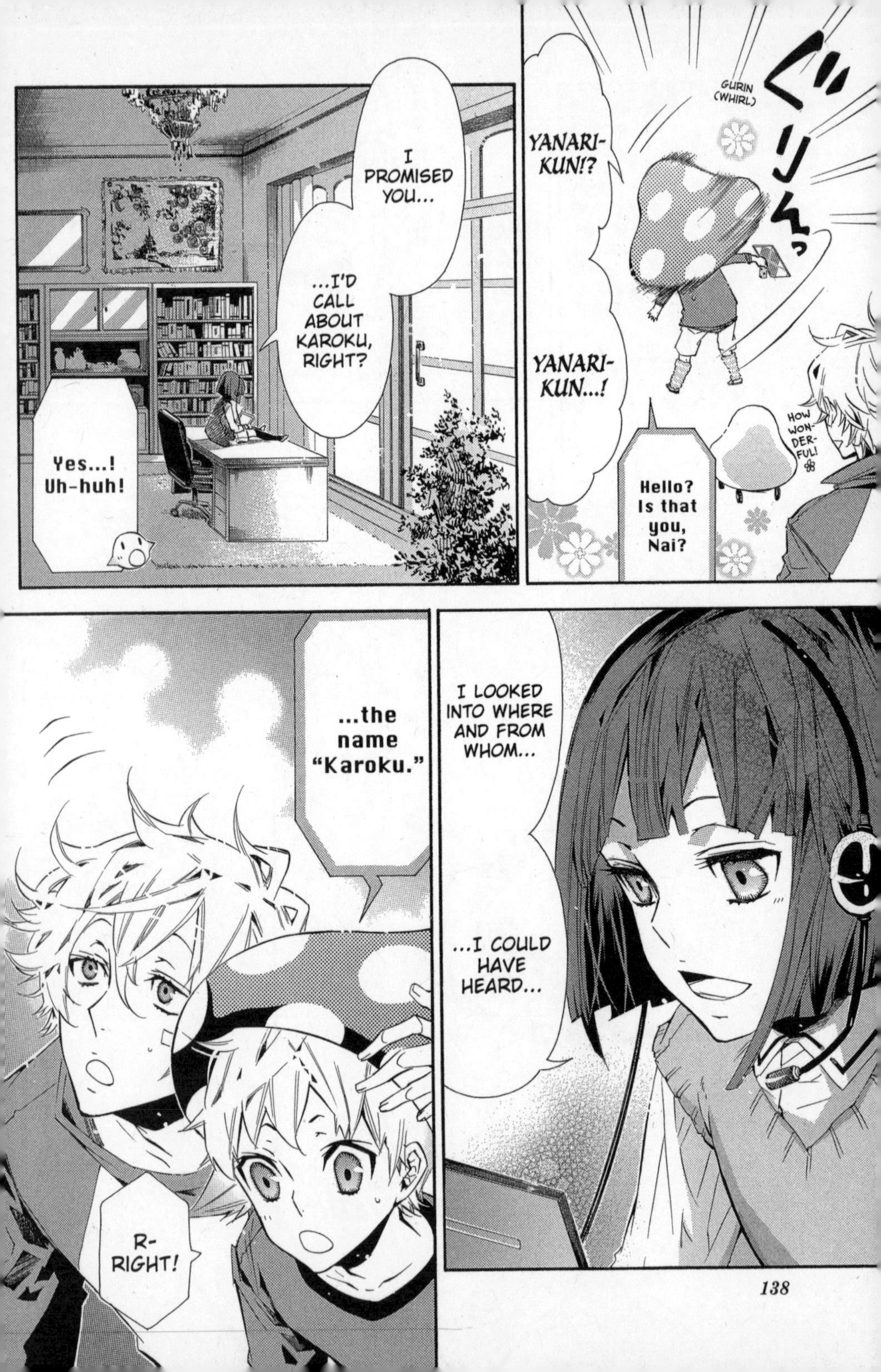
GURIN (WHIRL)
YANARI-KUN!?
HOW WONDERFUL!
YANARI-KUN...!
Hello? Is that you, Nai?
I PROMISED YOU...
...I'D CALL ABOUT KAROKU, RIGHT?
Yes...! Uh-huh!
I LOOKED INTO WHERE AND FROM WHOM...
...I COULD HAVE HEARD...
...the name "Karoku."
R-RIGHT!

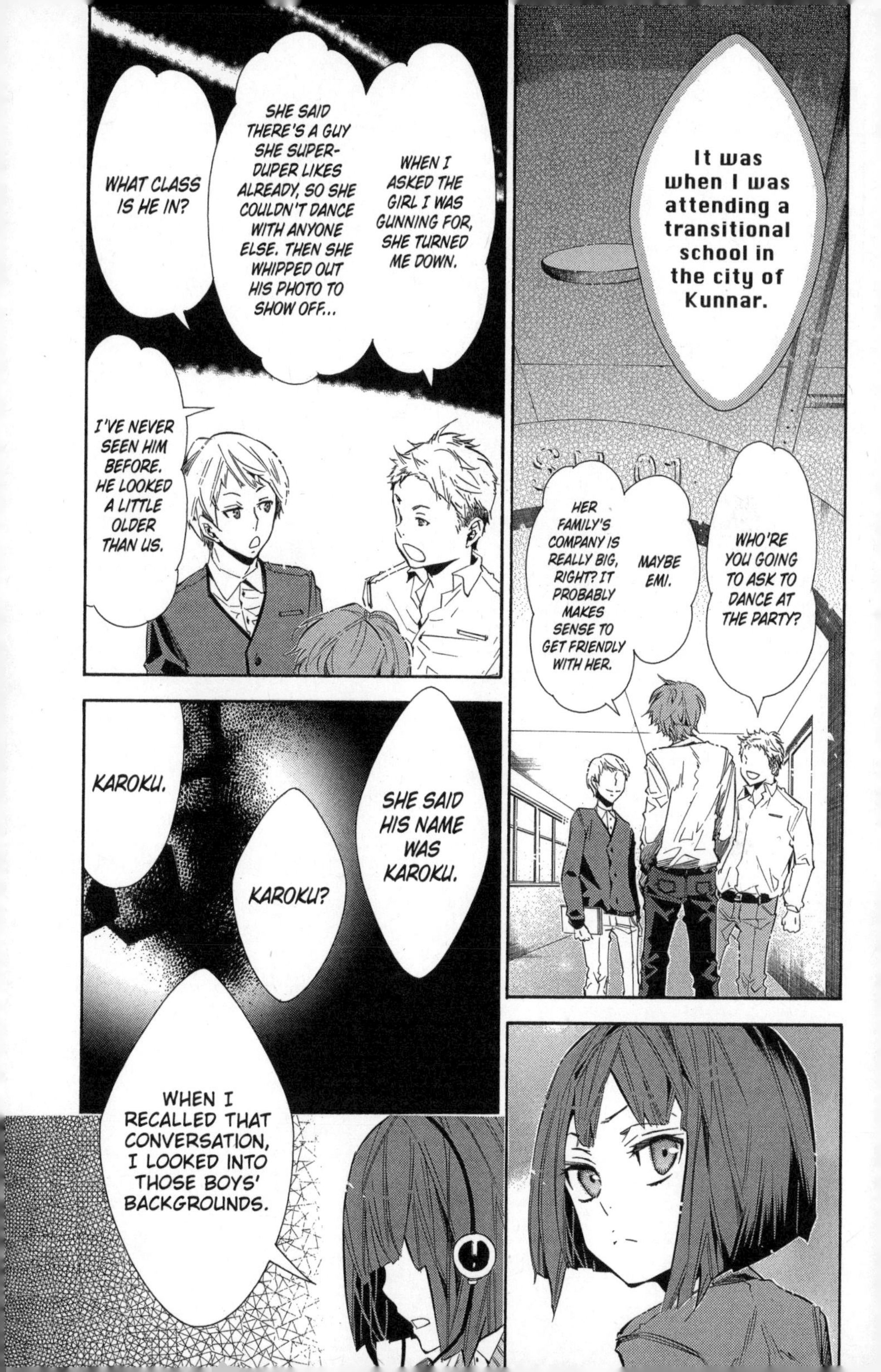
It was when I was attending a transitional school in the city of Kunnar.
WHO'RE YOU GOING TO ASK TO DANCE AT THE PARTY?
MAYBE EMI.
HER FAMILY'S COMPANY IS REALLY BIG, RIGHT? IT PROBABLY MAKES SENSE TO GET FRIENDLY WITH HER.
WHEN I ASKED THE GIRL I WAS GUNNING FOR, SHE TURNED ME DOWN.
SHE SAID THERE'S A GUY SHE SUPER-DUPER LIKES ALREADY, SO SHE COULDN'T DANCE WITH ANYONE ELSE. THEN SHE WHIPPED OUT HIS PHOTO TO SHOW OFF...
WHAT CLASS IS HE IN?
I'VE NEVER SEEN HIM BEFORE. HE LOOKED A LITTLE OLDER THAN US.
SHE SAID HIS NAME WAS KAROKU.
KAROKU?
KAROKU.
WHEN I RECALLED THAT CONVERSATION, I LOOKED INTO THOSE BOYS' BACKGROUNDS.

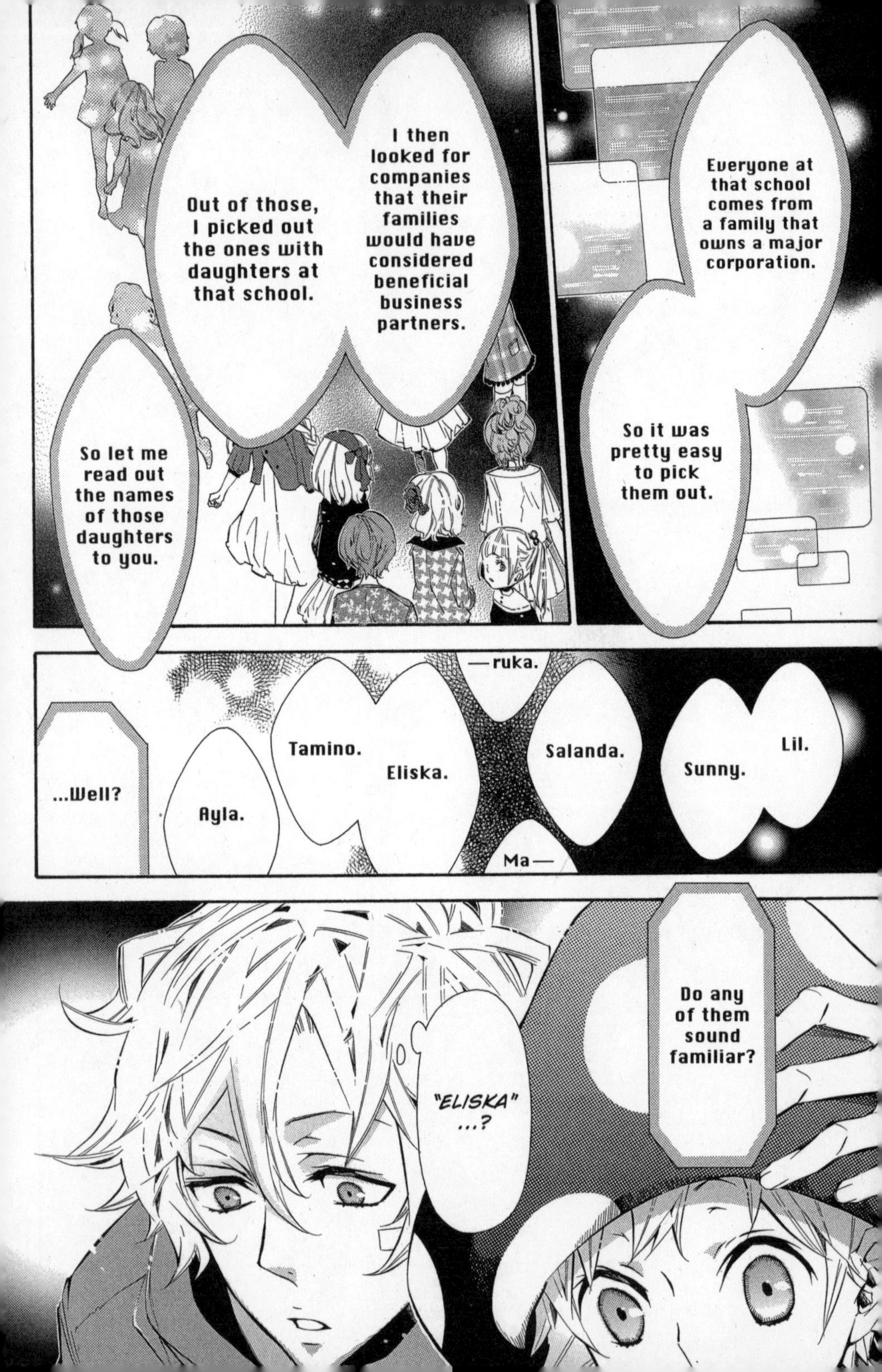
Everyone at that school comes from a family that owns a major corporation.
So it was pretty easy to pick them out.
I then looked for companies that their families would have considered beneficial business partners.
Out of those, I picked out the ones with daughters at that school.
So let me read out the names of those daughters to you.
Lil.
Sunny.
—ruka.
Salanda.
Ma—
Eliska.
Tamino.
Ayla.
...Well?
Do any of them sound familiar?
"ELISKA" ...?

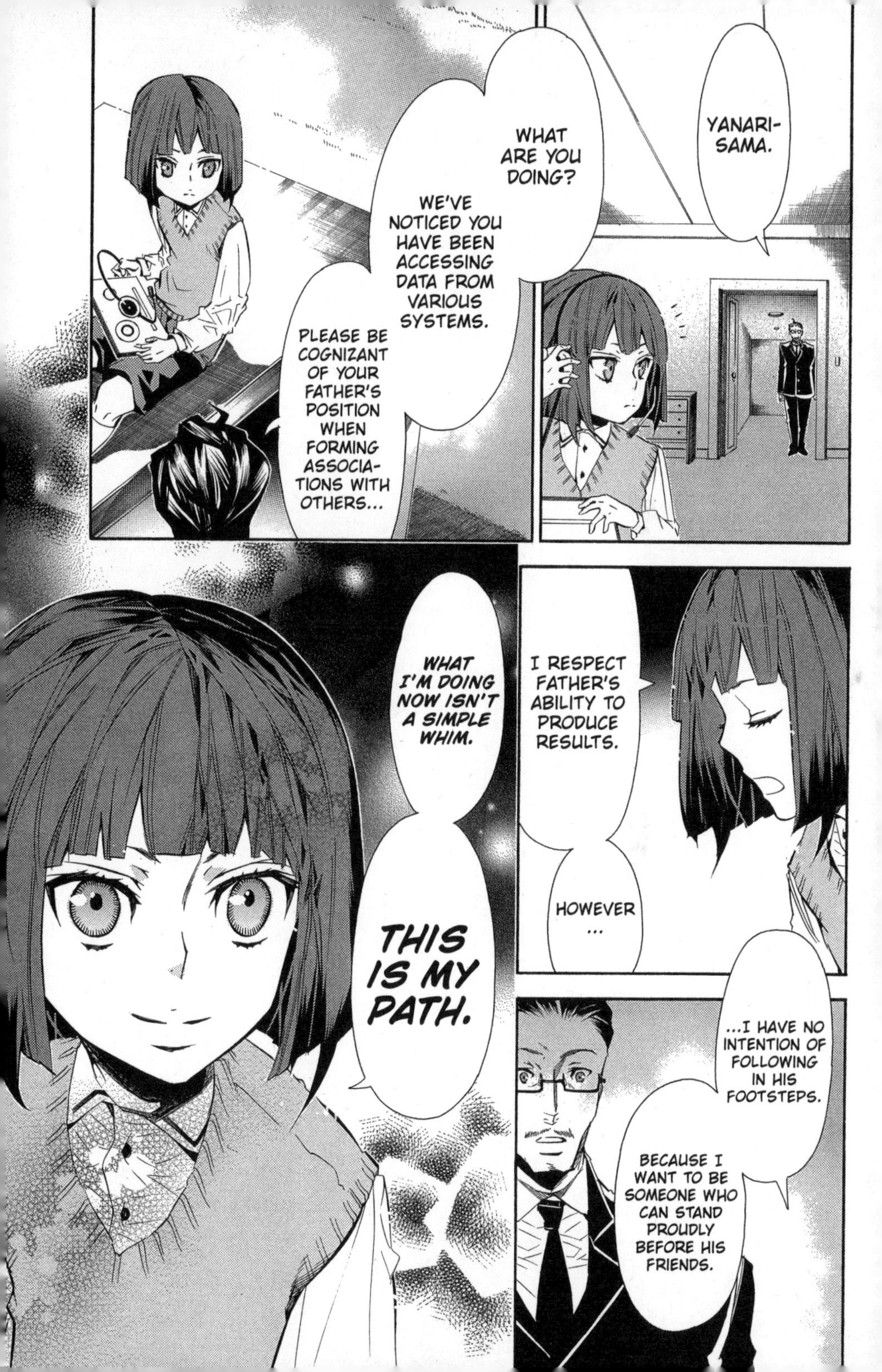
YANARI-SAMA.
WHAT ARE YOU DOING?
WE'VE NOTICED YOU HAVE BEEN ACCESSING DATA FROM VARIOUS SYSTEMS.
PLEASE BE COGNIZANT OF YOUR FATHER'S POSITION WHEN FORMING ASSOCIA-TIONS WITH OTHERS...
I RESPECT FATHER'S ABILITY TO PRODUCE RESULTS.
HOWEVER ...
...I HAVE NO INTENTION OF FOLLOWING IN HIS FOOTSTEPS.
BECAUSE I WANT TO BE SOMEONE WHO CAN STAND PROUDLY BEFORE HIS FRIENDS.
WHAT I'M DOING NOW ISN'T A SIMPLE WHIM.
THIS IS MY PATH.

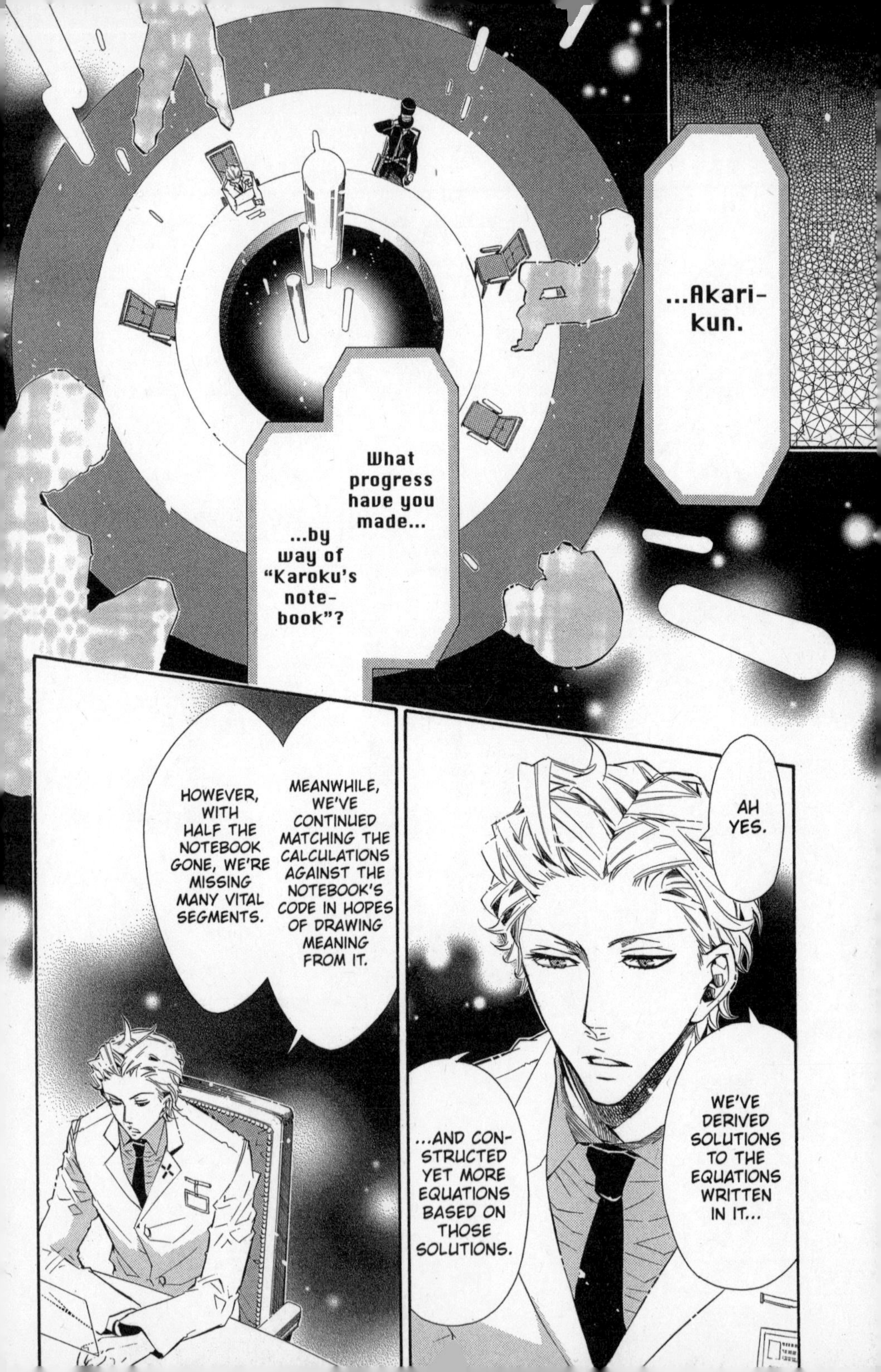
...Akari-kun.
What progress have you made...
...by way of "Karoku's notebook"?
AH YES.
WE'VE DERIVED SOLUTIONS TO THE EQUATIONS WRITTEN IN IT...
...AND CONSTRUCTED YET MORE EQUATIONS BASED ON THOSE SOLUTIONS.
MEANWHILE, WE'VE CONTINUED MATCHING THE CALCULATIONS AGAINST THE NOTEBOOK'S CODE IN HOPES OF DRAWING MEANING FROM IT.
HOWEVER, WITH HALF THE NOTEBOOK GONE, WE'RE MISSING MANY VITAL SEGMENTS.

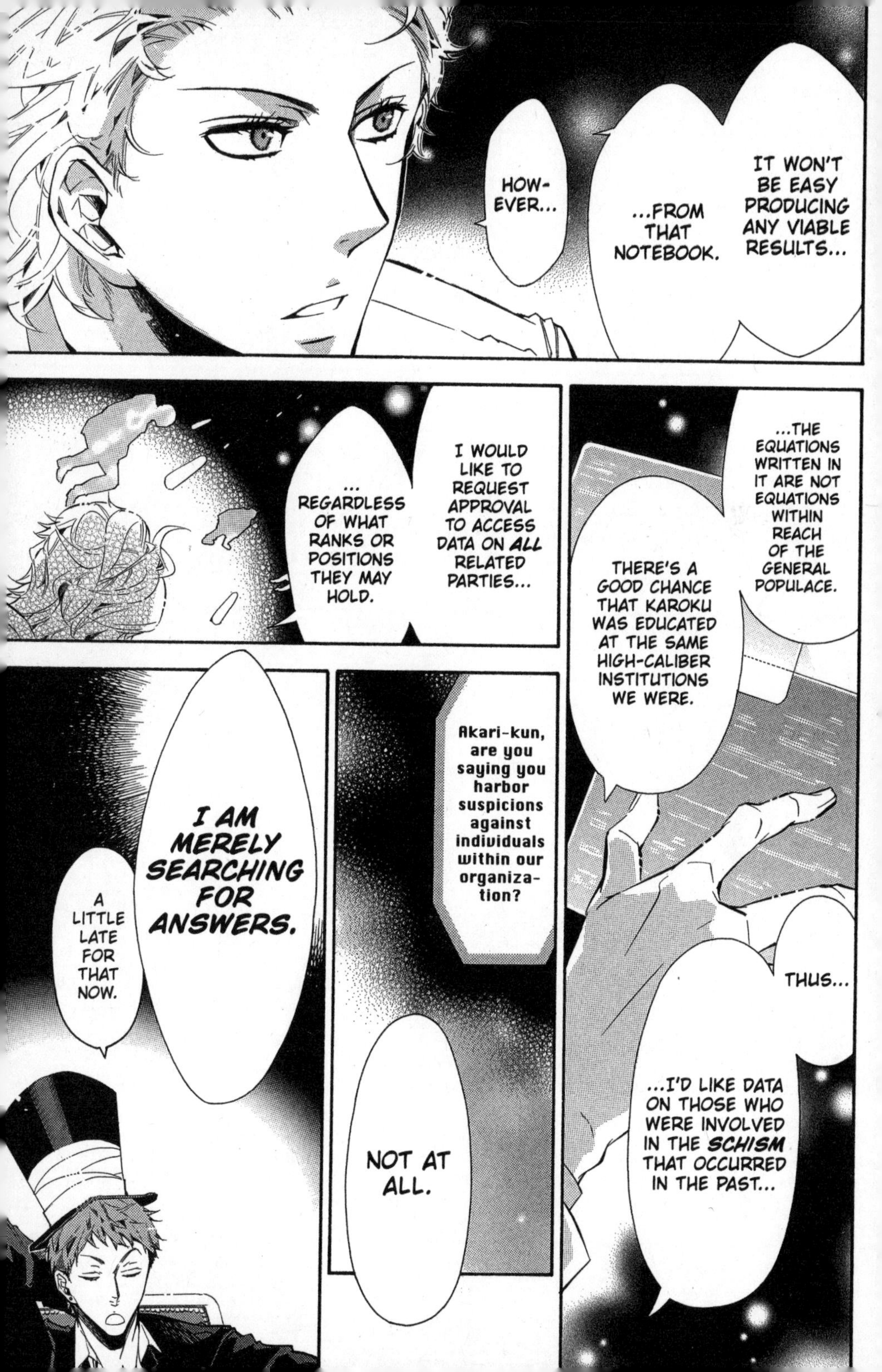
IT WON'T BE EASY PRODUCING ANY VIABLE RESULTS...
...FROM THAT NOTEBOOK.
HOW-EVER...
...THE EQUATIONS WRITTEN IN IT ARE NOT EQUATIONS WITHIN REACH OF THE GENERAL POPULACE.
THERE'S A GOOD CHANCE THAT KAROKU WAS EDUCATED AT THE SAME HIGH-CALIBER INSTITUTIONS WE WERE.
THUS...
...I'D LIKE DATA ON THOSE WHO WERE INVOLVED IN THE SCHISM THAT OCCURRED IN THE PAST...
I WOULD LIKE TO REQUEST APPROVAL TO ACCESS DATA ON ALL RELATED PARTIES...
...REGARDLESS OF WHAT RANKS OR POSITIONS THEY MAY HOLD.
Akari-kun, are you saying you harbor suspicions against individuals within our organiza-tion?
NOT AT ALL.
I AM MERELY SEARCHING FOR ANSWERS.
A LITTLE LATE FOR THAT NOW.

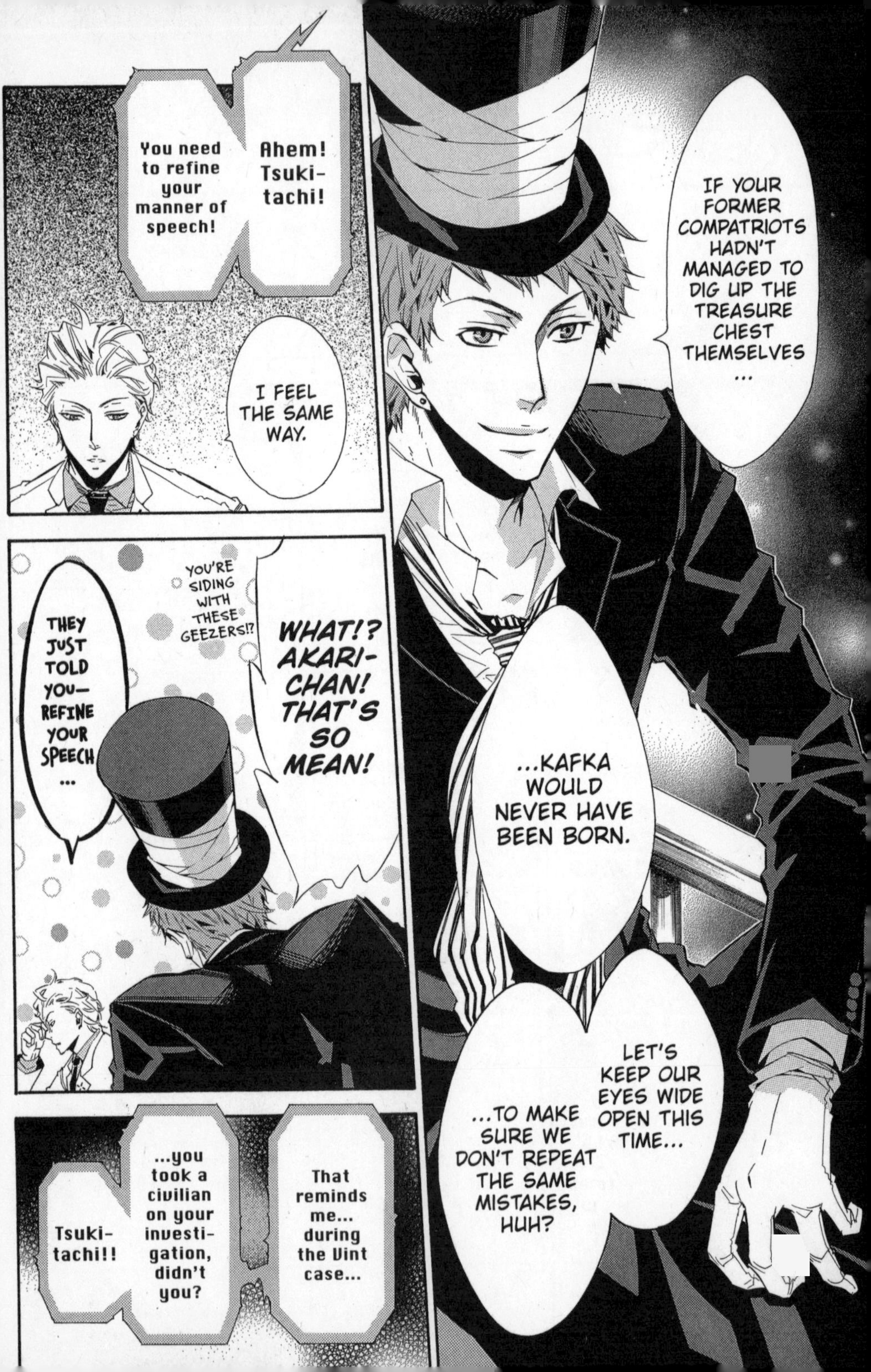
IF YOUR FORMER COMPATRIOTS HADN'T MANAGED TO DIG UP THE TREASURE CHEST THEMSELVES...
...KAFKA WOULD NEVER HAVE BEEN BORN.
LET'S KEEP OUR EYES WIDE OPEN THIS TIME...
...TO MAKE SURE WE DON'T REPEAT THE SAME MISTAKES, HUH?
Ahem! Tsuki-tachi!
You need to refine your manner of speech!
I FEEL THE SAME WAY.
WHAT!? AKARI-CHAN! THAT'S SO MEAN!
YOU'RE SIDING WITH THESE GEEZERS!?
THEY JUST TOLD YOU—REFINE YOUR SPEECH...
That reminds me... during the Vint case...
...you took a civilian on your investigation, didn't you?
Tsuki-tachi!!

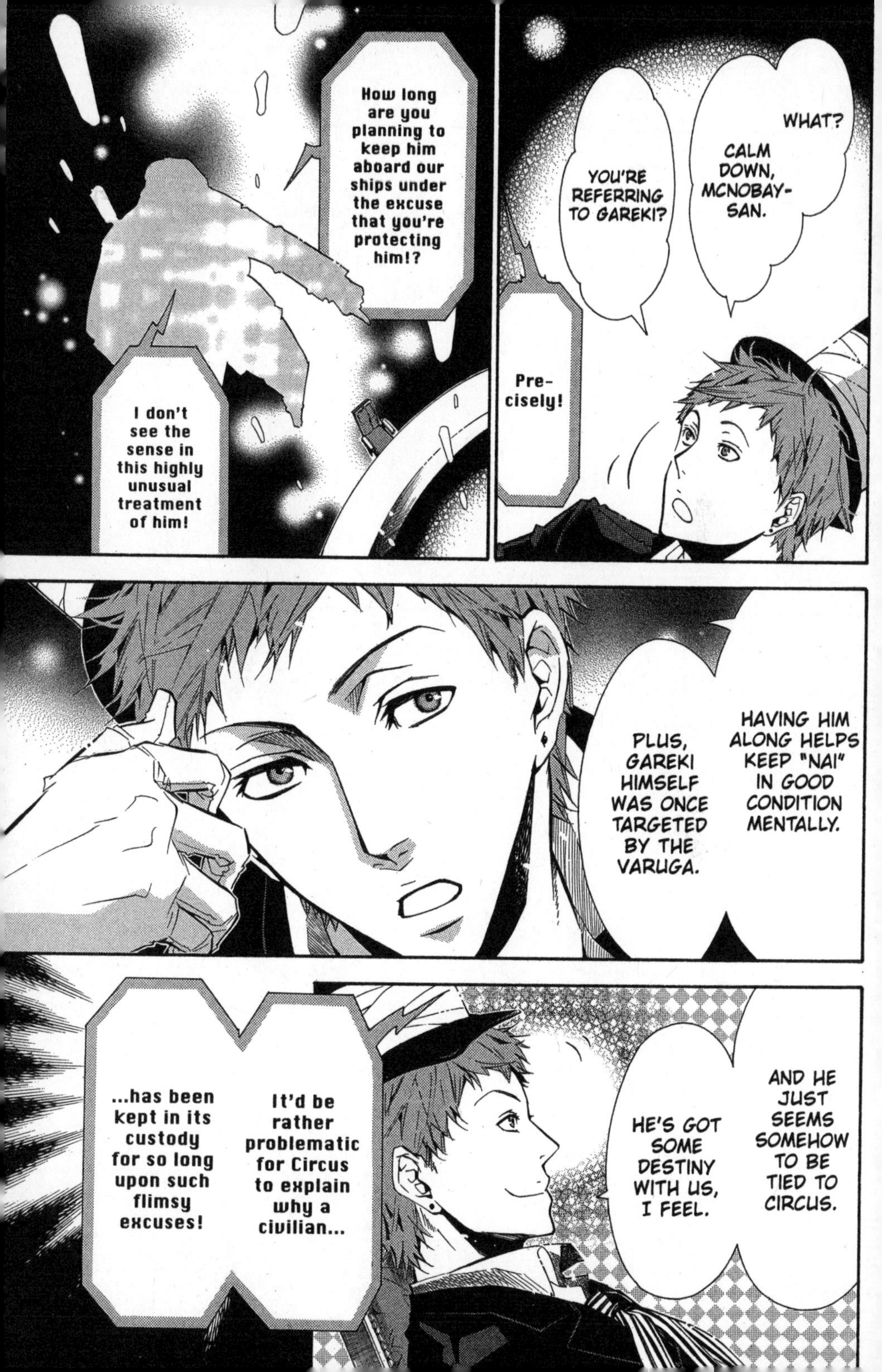
WHAT?
CALM DOWN, MCNOBAY-SAN.
YOU'RE REFERRING TO GAREKI?
Pre-cisely!
How long are you planning to keep him aboard our ships under the excuse that you're protecting him!?
I don't see the sense in this highly unusual treatment of him!
HAVING HIM ALONG HELPS KEEP "NAI" IN GOOD CONDITION MENTALLY.
PLUS, GAREKI HIMSELF WAS ONCE TARGETED BY THE VARUGA.
AND HE JUST SEEMS SOMEHOW TO BE TIED TO CIRCUS.
HE'S GOT SOME DESTINY WITH US, I FEEL.
It'd be rather problematic for Circus to explain why a civilian...
...has been kept in its custody for so long upon such flimsy excuses!

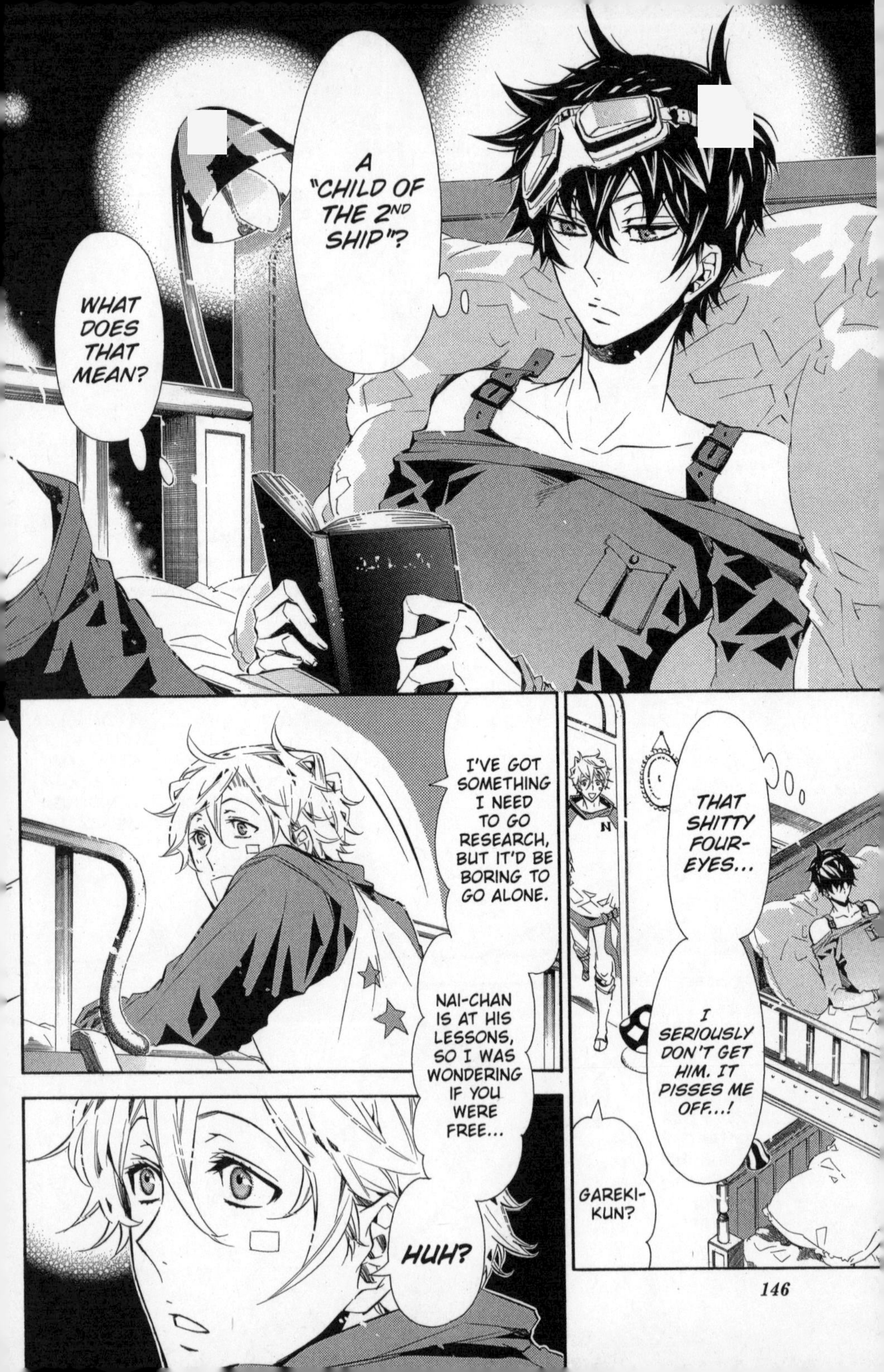
A "CHILD OF THE 2ND SHIP"?
WHAT DOES THAT MEAN?
THAT SHITTY FOUR-EYES...
I SERIOUSLY DON'T GET HIM. IT PISSES ME OFF...!
GAREKI-KUN?
I'VE GOT SOMETHING I NEED TO GO RESEARCH, BUT IT'D BE BORING TO GO ALONE.
NAI-CHAN IS AT HIS LESSONS, SO I WAS WONDERING IF YOU WERE FREE...
HUH?

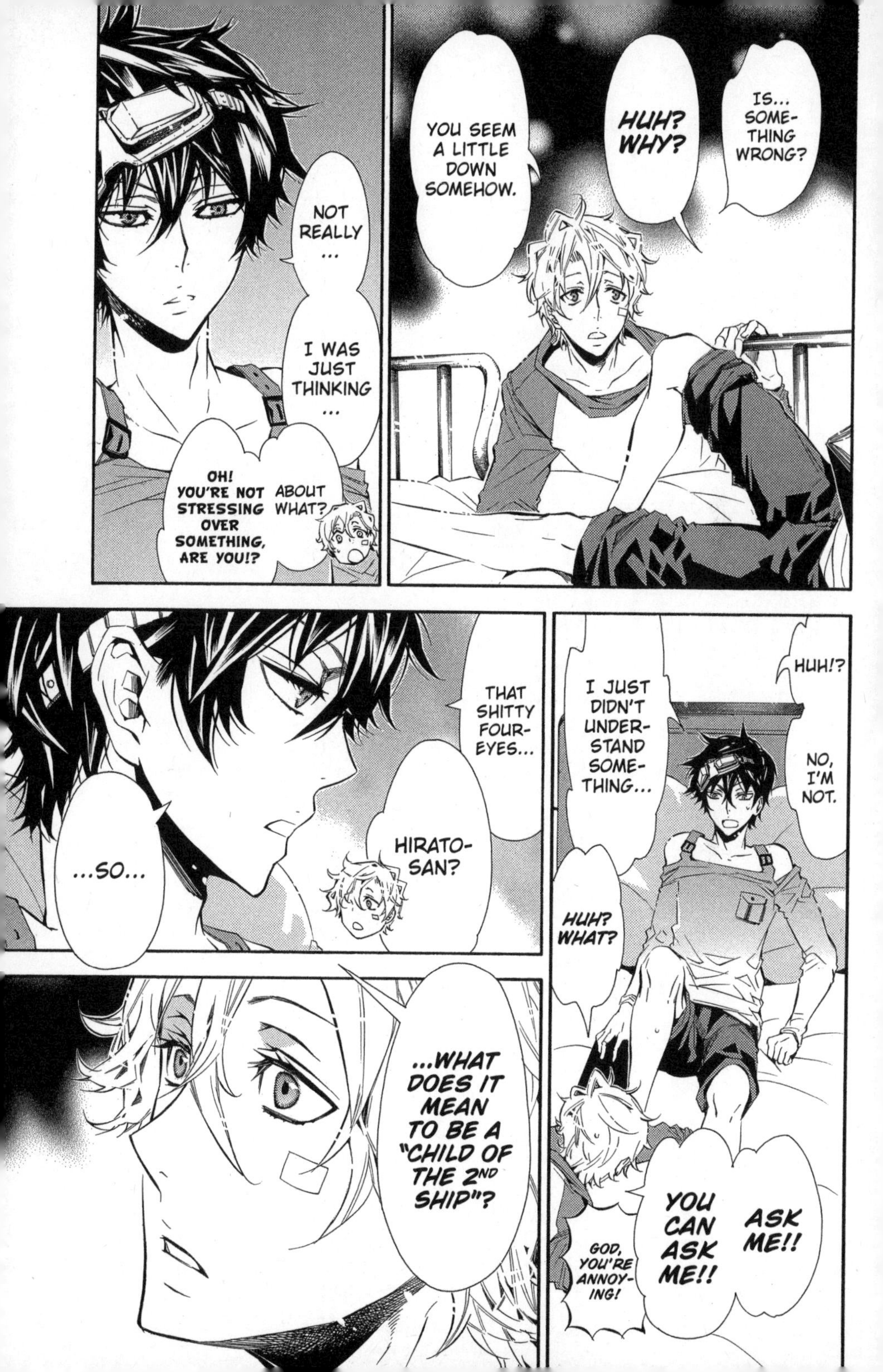
IS... SOME-THING WRONG?
HUH? WHY?
YOU SEEM A LITTLE DOWN SOMEHOW.
NOT REALLY ...
I WAS JUST THINKING ...
ABOUT WHAT?
OH! YOU'RE NOT STRESSING OVER SOMETHING, ARE YOU!?
HUH!?
NO, I'M NOT.
I JUST DIDN'T UNDER-STAND SOME-THING...
HUH? WHAT?
ASK ME!!
YOU CAN ASK ME!!
GOD, YOU'RE ANNOY-ING!
THAT SHITTY FOUR-EYES...
HIRATO-SAN?
...SO...
...WHAT DOES IT MEAN TO BE A "CHILD OF THE 2ND SHIP"?

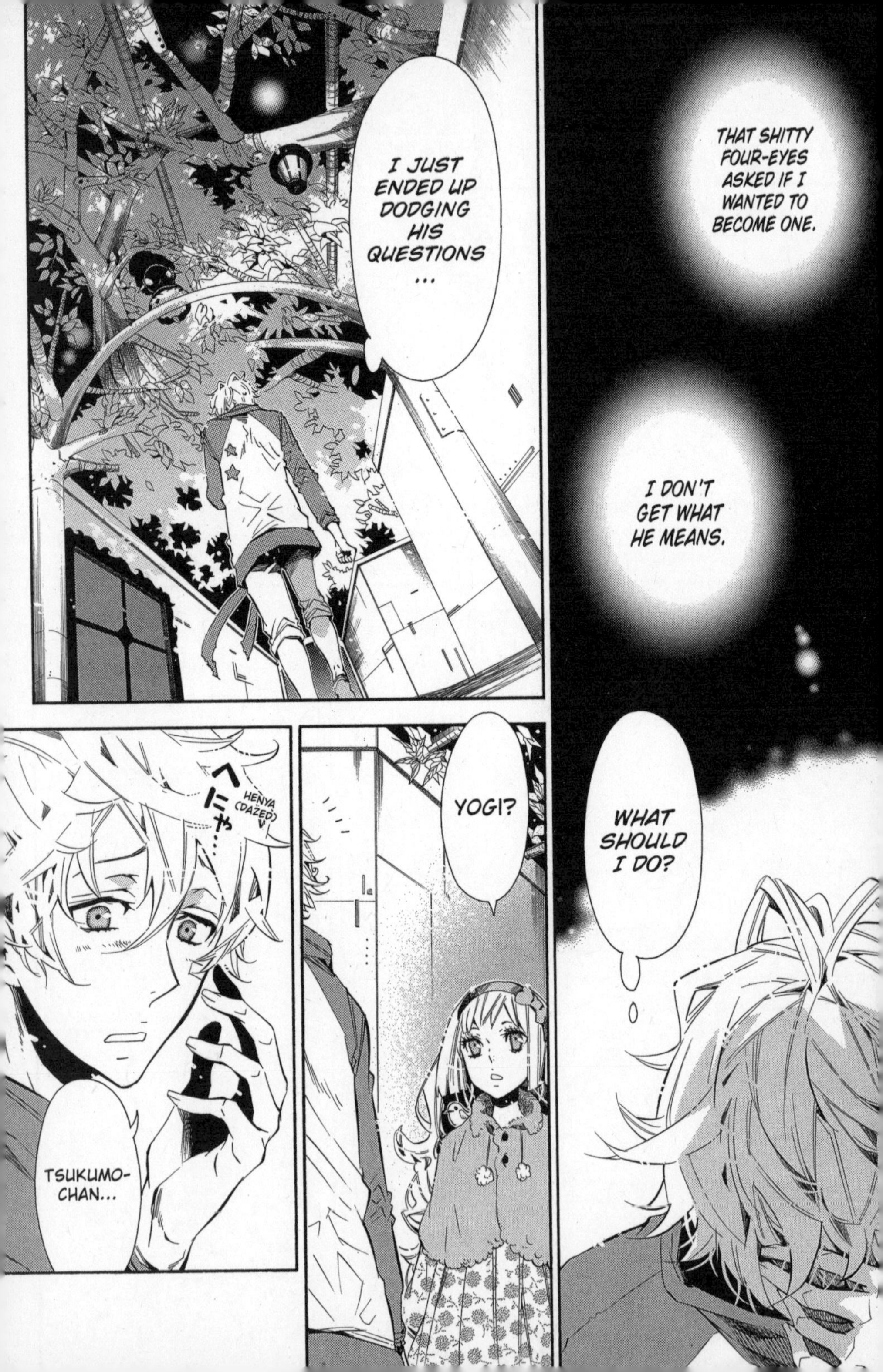
THAT SHITTY FOUR-EYES ASKED IF I WANTED TO BECOME ONE.
I DON'T GET WHAT HE MEANS.
I JUST ENDED UP DODGING HIS QUESTIONS ...
WHAT SHOULD I DO?
YOGI?
へにゃ
HENYA (DAZED)
TSUKUMO-CHAN...

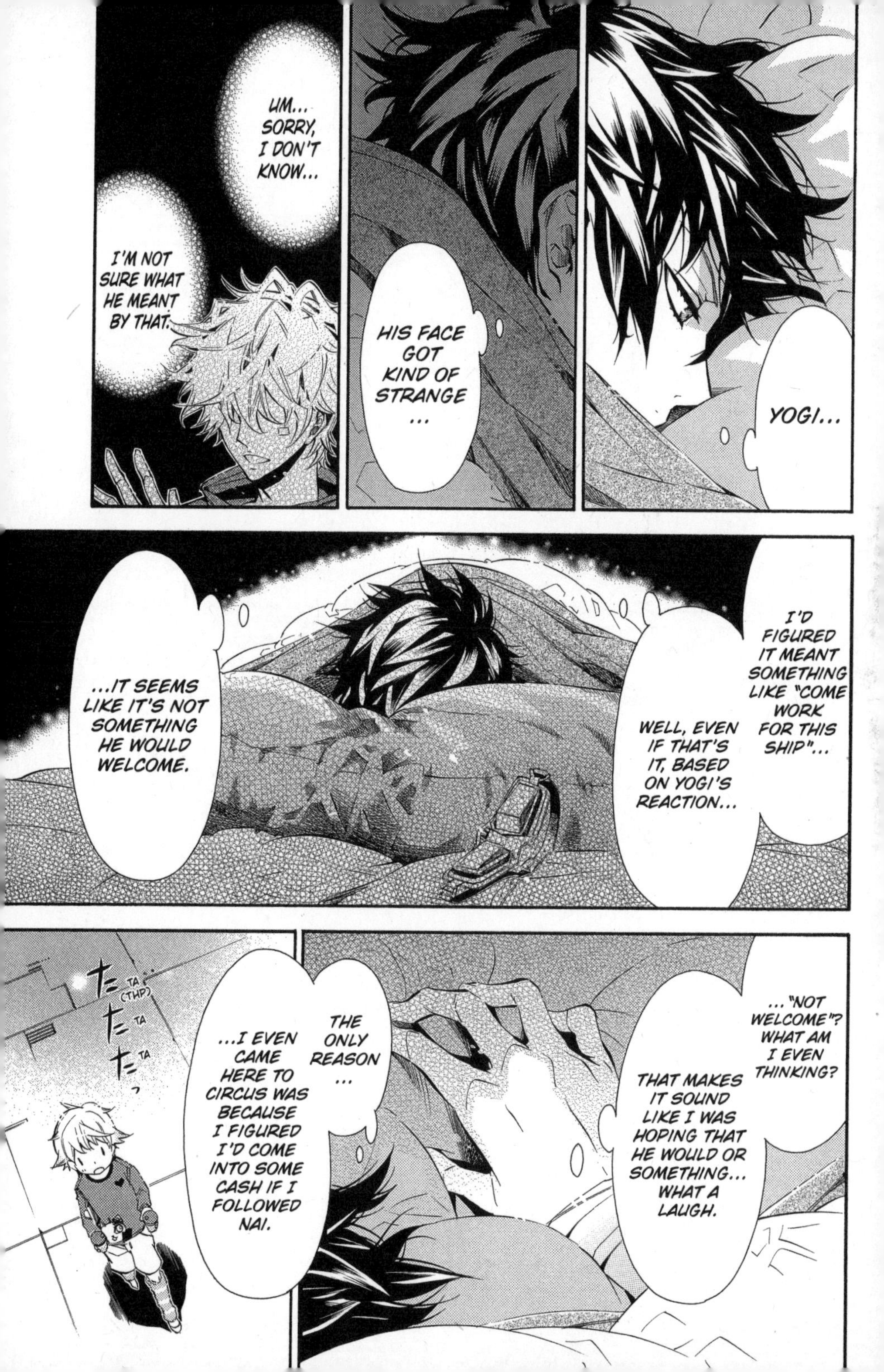
YOGI...
HIS FACE GOT KIND OF STRANGE...
UM... SORRY, I DON'T KNOW...
I'M NOT SURE WHAT HE MEANT BY THAT.
I'D FIGURED IT MEANT SOMETHING LIKE "COME WORK FOR THIS SHIP"...
WELL, EVEN IF THAT'S IT, BASED ON YOGI'S REACTION...
...IT SEEMS LIKE IT'S NOT SOMETHING HE WOULD WELCOME.
..."NOT WELCOME"? WHAT AM I EVEN THINKING?
THAT MAKES IT SOUND LIKE I WAS HOPING THAT HE WOULD OR SOMETHING... WHAT A LAUGH.
THE ONLY REASON...
...I EVEN CAME HERE TO CIRCUS WAS BECAUSE I FIGURED I'D COME INTO SOME CASH IF I FOLLOWED NAI.
TA (THP)
TA
TA

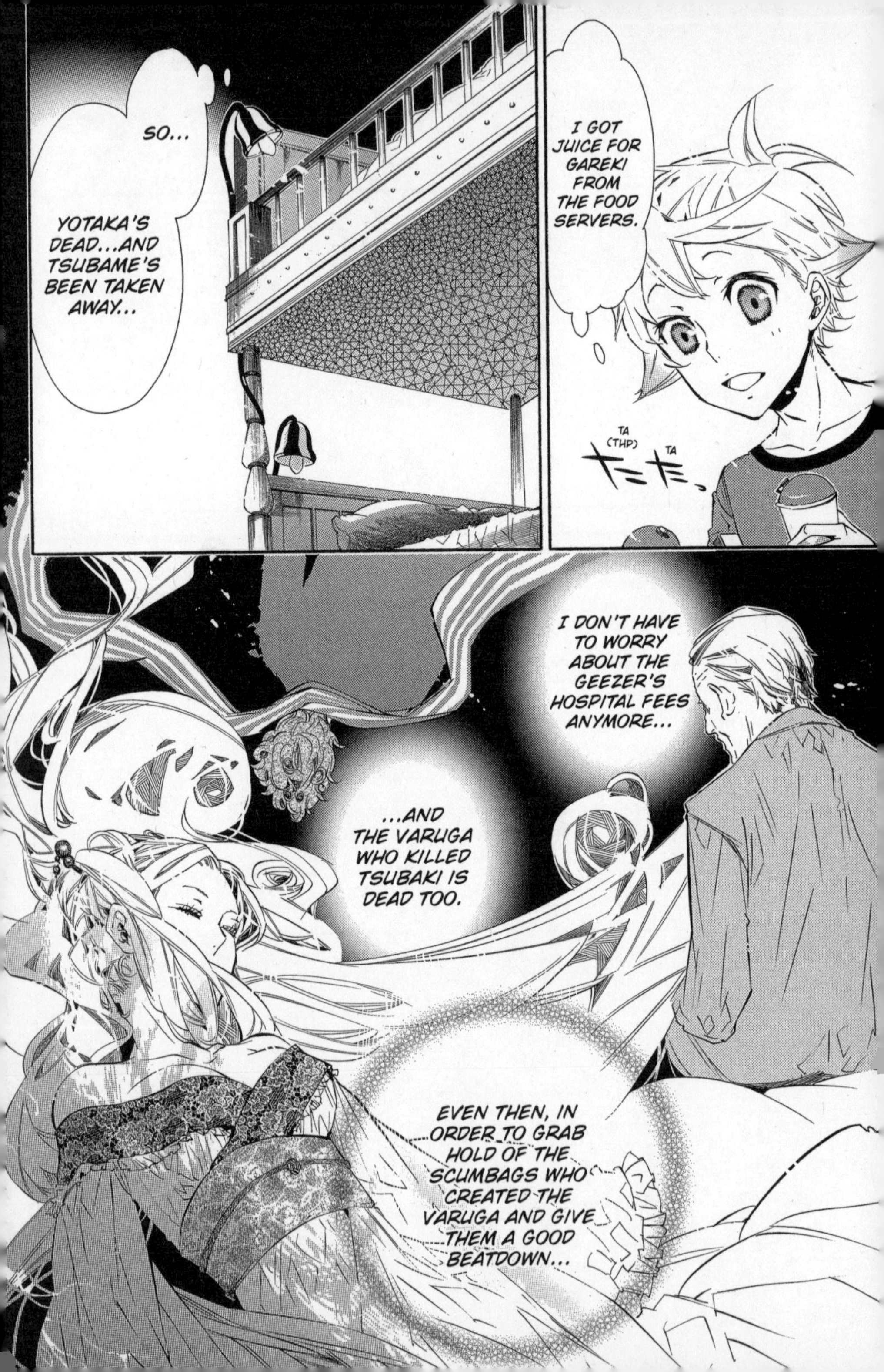
I GOT JUICE FOR GAREKI FROM THE FOOD SERVERS.
TA
(THP)
TA
SO...
YOTAKA'S DEAD...AND TSUBAME'S BEEN TAKEN AWAY...
I DON'T HAVE TO WORRY ABOUT THE GEEZER'S HOSPITAL FEES ANYMORE...
...AND THE VARUGA WHO KILLED TSUBAKI IS DEAD TOO.
EVEN THEN, IN ORDER TO GRAB HOLD OF THE SCUMBAGS WHO CREATED THE VARUGA AND GIVE THEM A GOOD BEATDOWN...

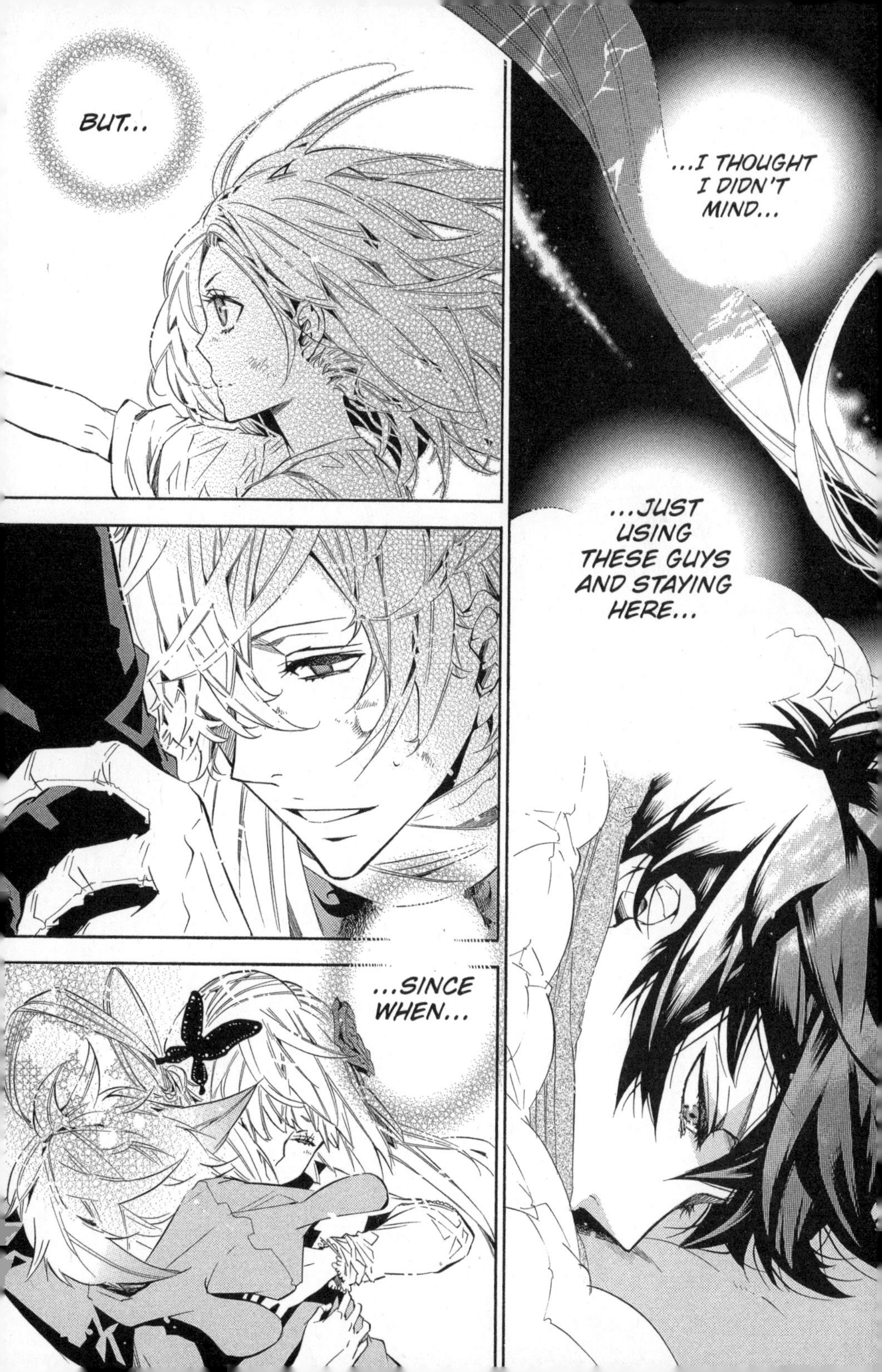
...I THOUGHT I DIDN'T MIND...
...JUST USING THESE GUYS AND STAYING HERE...
BUT...
...SINCE WHEN...

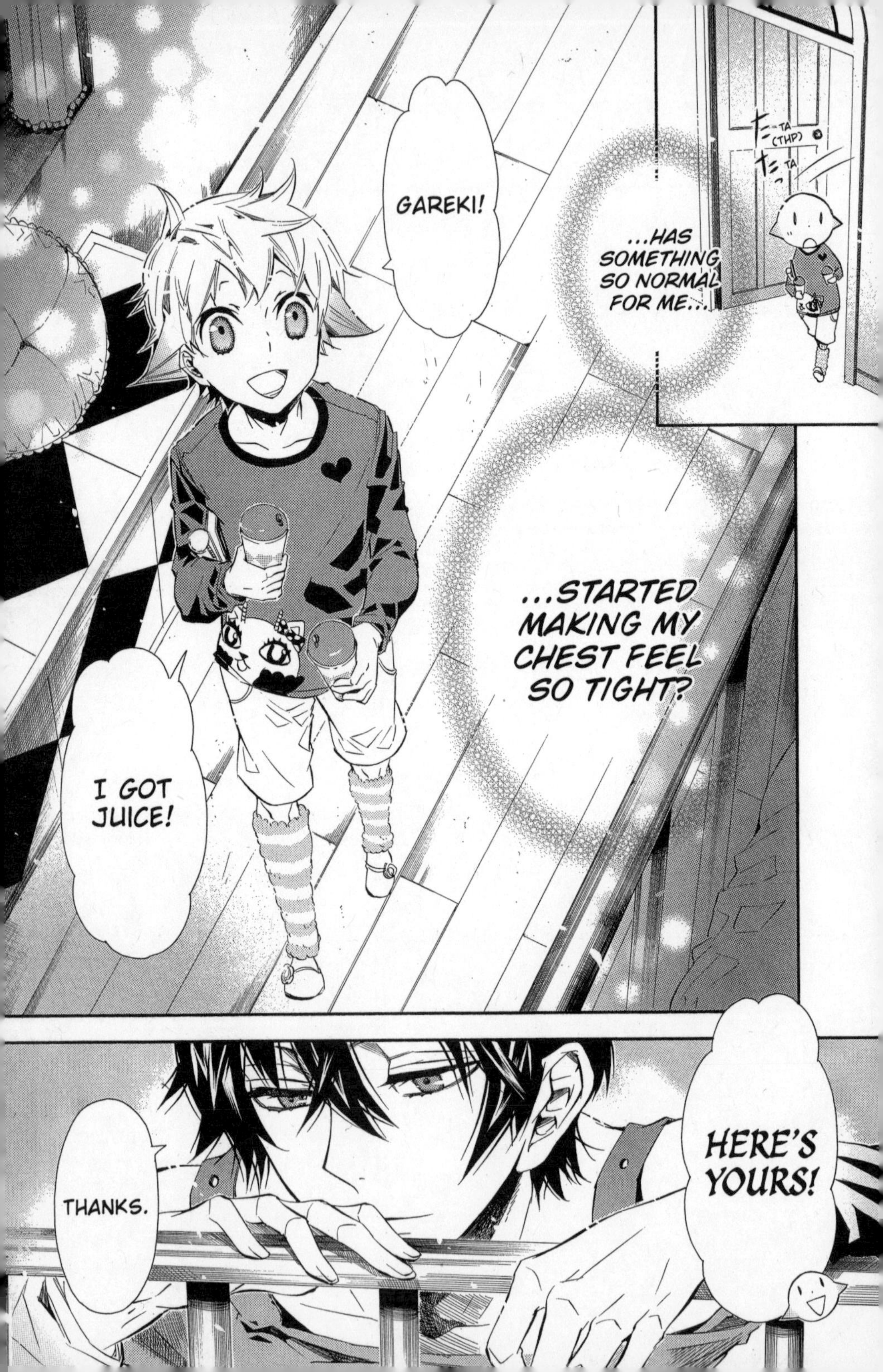
TA (THP)
TA
...HAS SOMETHING SO NORMAL FOR ME...
GAREKI!
...STARTED MAKING MY CHEST FEEL SO TIGHT?
I GOT JUICE!
HERE'S YOURS!
THANKS.

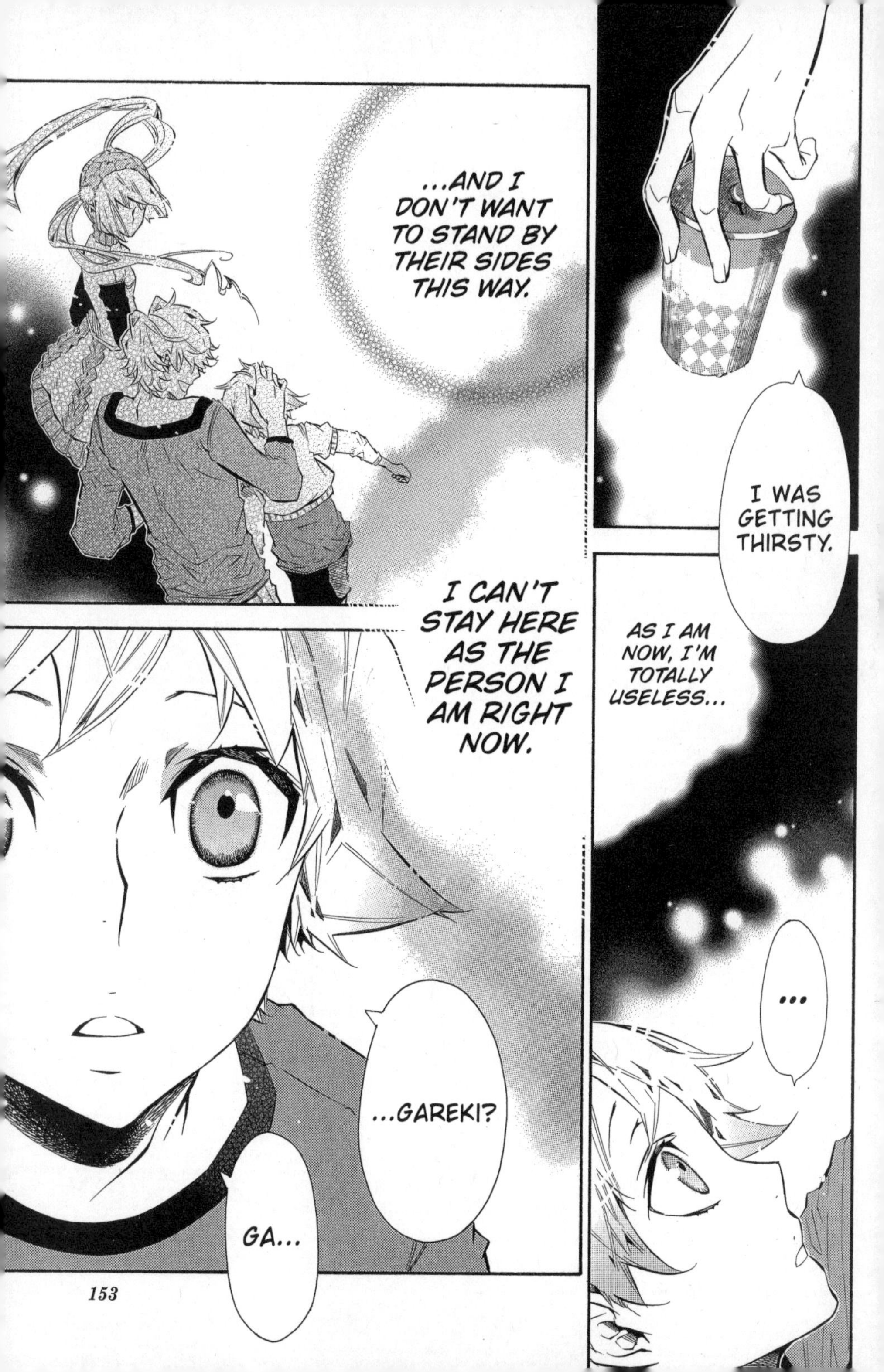
I WAS GETTING THIRSTY.
...AND I DON'T WANT TO STAND BY THEIR SIDES THIS WAY.
AS I AM NOW, I'M TOTALLY USELESS...
...
I CAN'T STAY HERE AS THE PERSON I AM RIGHT NOW.
...GAREKI?
GA...

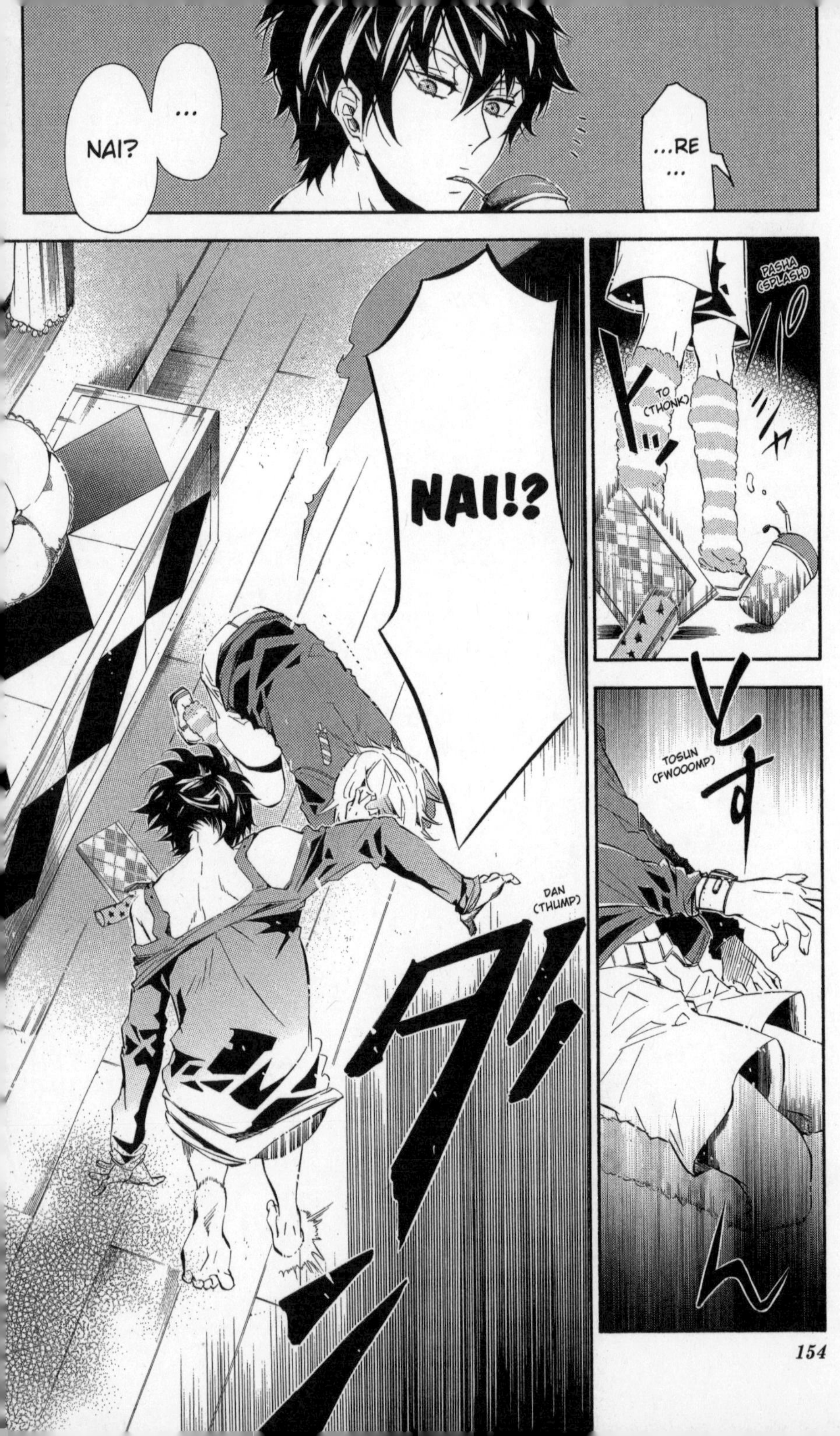
...RE
...
...
NAI?
PASHA (SPLASH)
TO (THONK)
TOSUN (FWOOOMP)
NAI!?
DAN (THUMP)

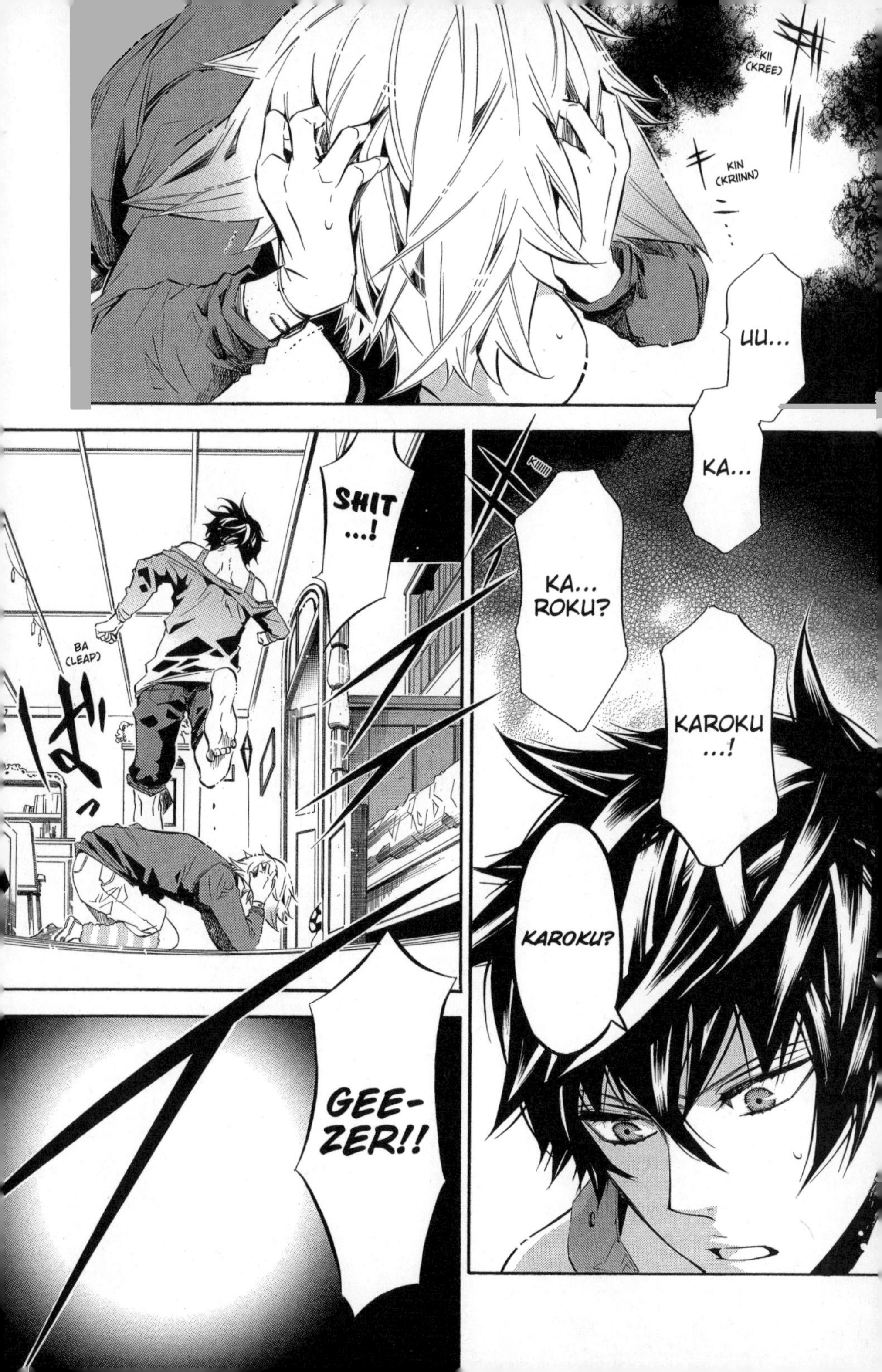
KII (KREE)
KIN (KRIINN)
UU...
KA...
KA... ROKU?
KAROKU ...!
KAROKU?
SHIT ...!
BA (LEAP)
GEE-ZER!!

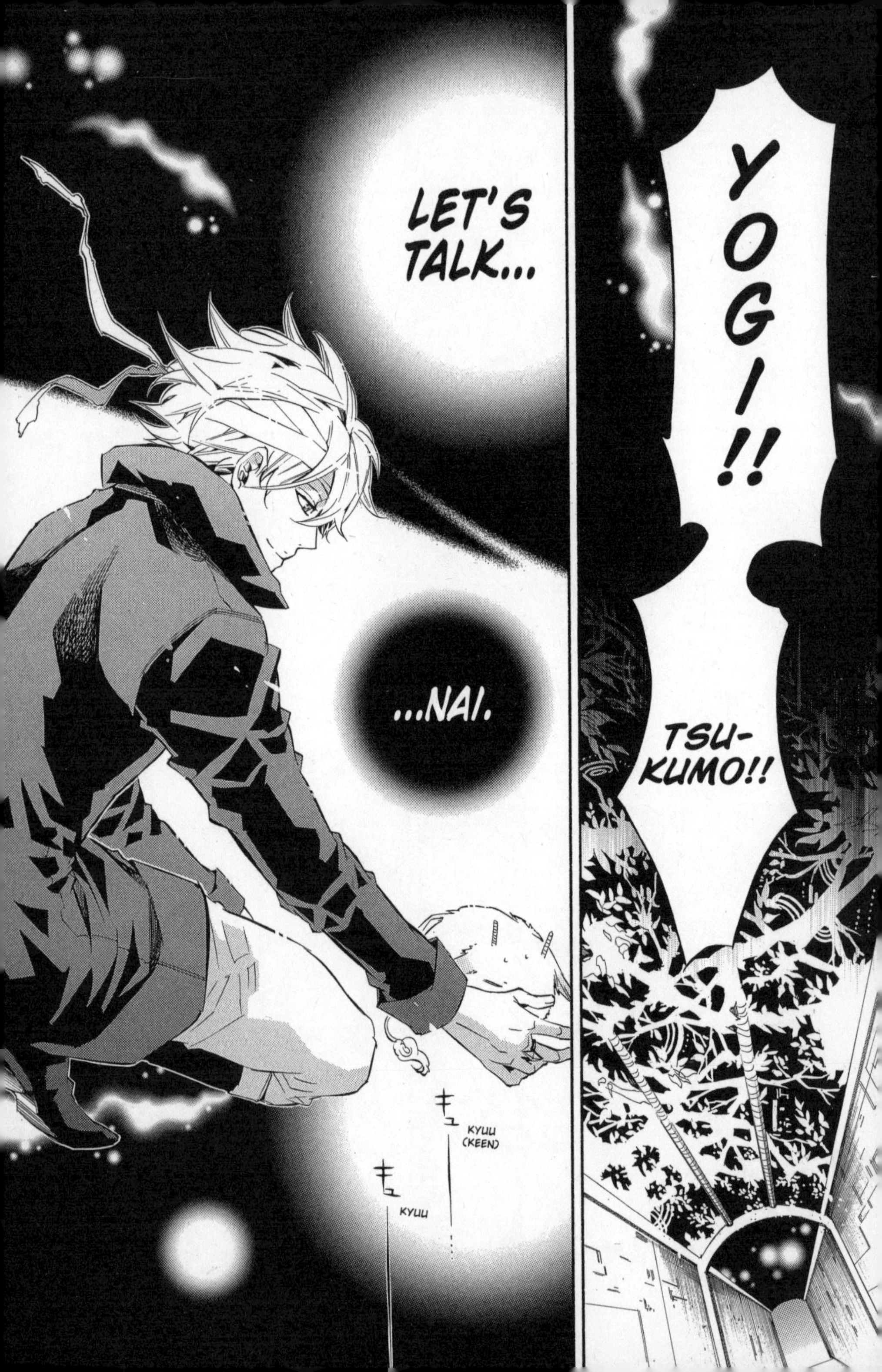
YOGI!!
TSU-KUMO!!
LET'S TALK...
...NAI.
キュ
KYUU (KEEN)
キュ
KYUU

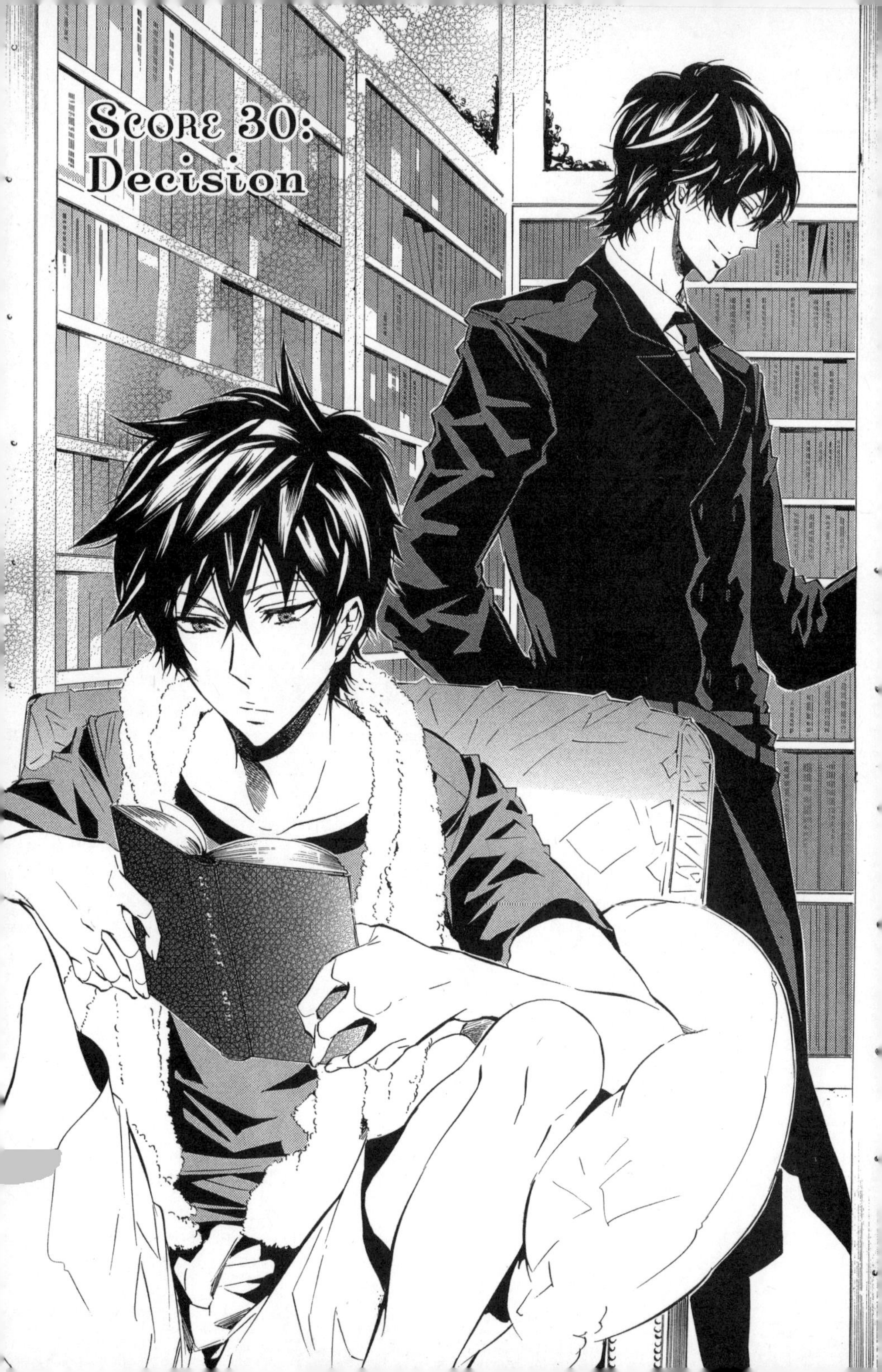
Score 30:
Decision

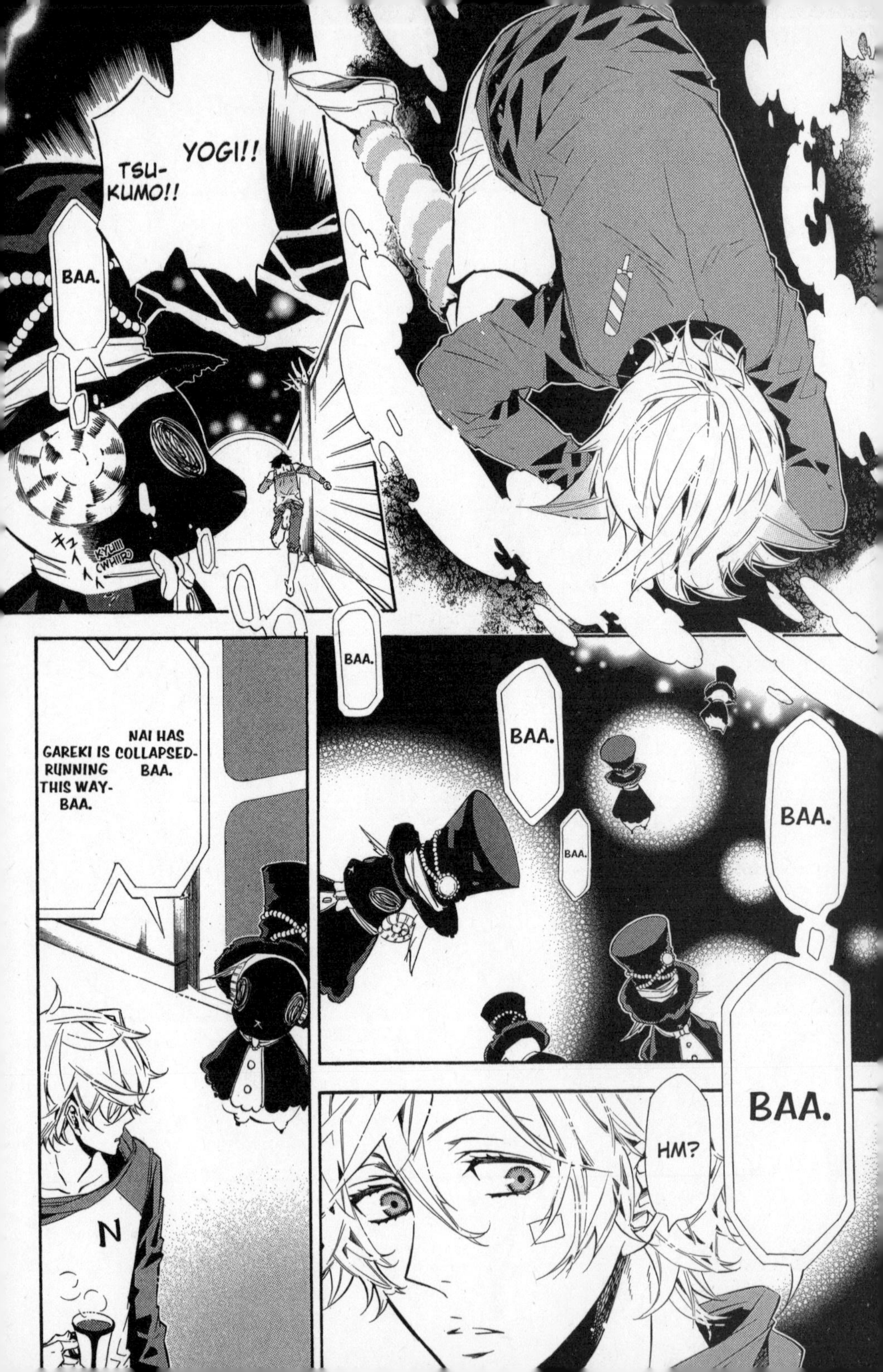
YOGI!!
TSU-KUMO!!
BAA.
キュイィ
KYUIII (WHIR)
BAA.
BAA.
BAA.
BAA.
BAA.
BAA.
HM?
NAI HAS COLLAPSED-BAA.
GAREKI IS RUNNING THIS WAY-BAA.

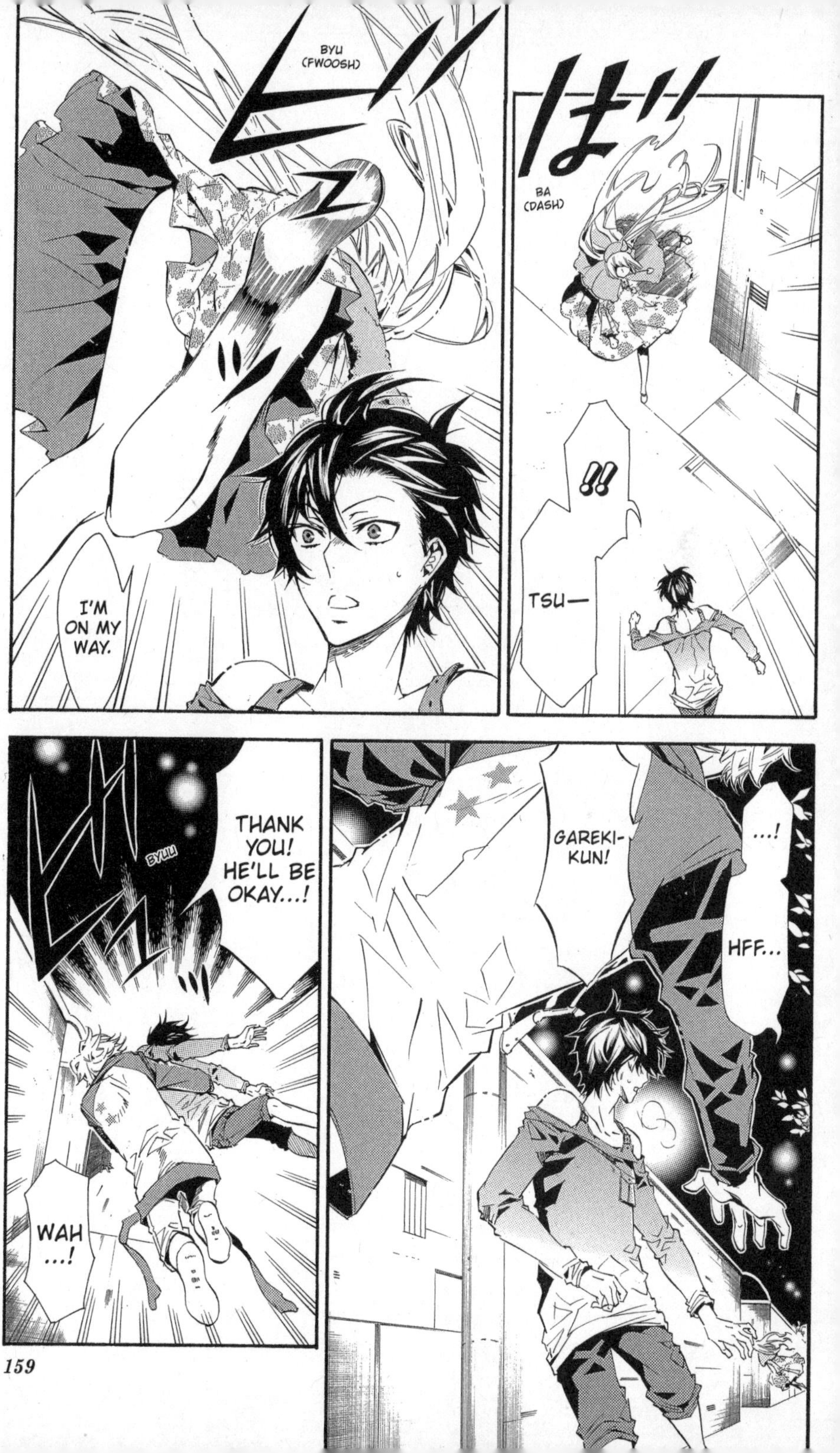
BA
(DASH)
!!
TSU—
BYU
(FWOOSH)
I'M ON MY WAY.
GAREKI-KUN!
...!
HFF...
THANK YOU! HE'LL BE OKAY...!
BYUU
WAH ...!

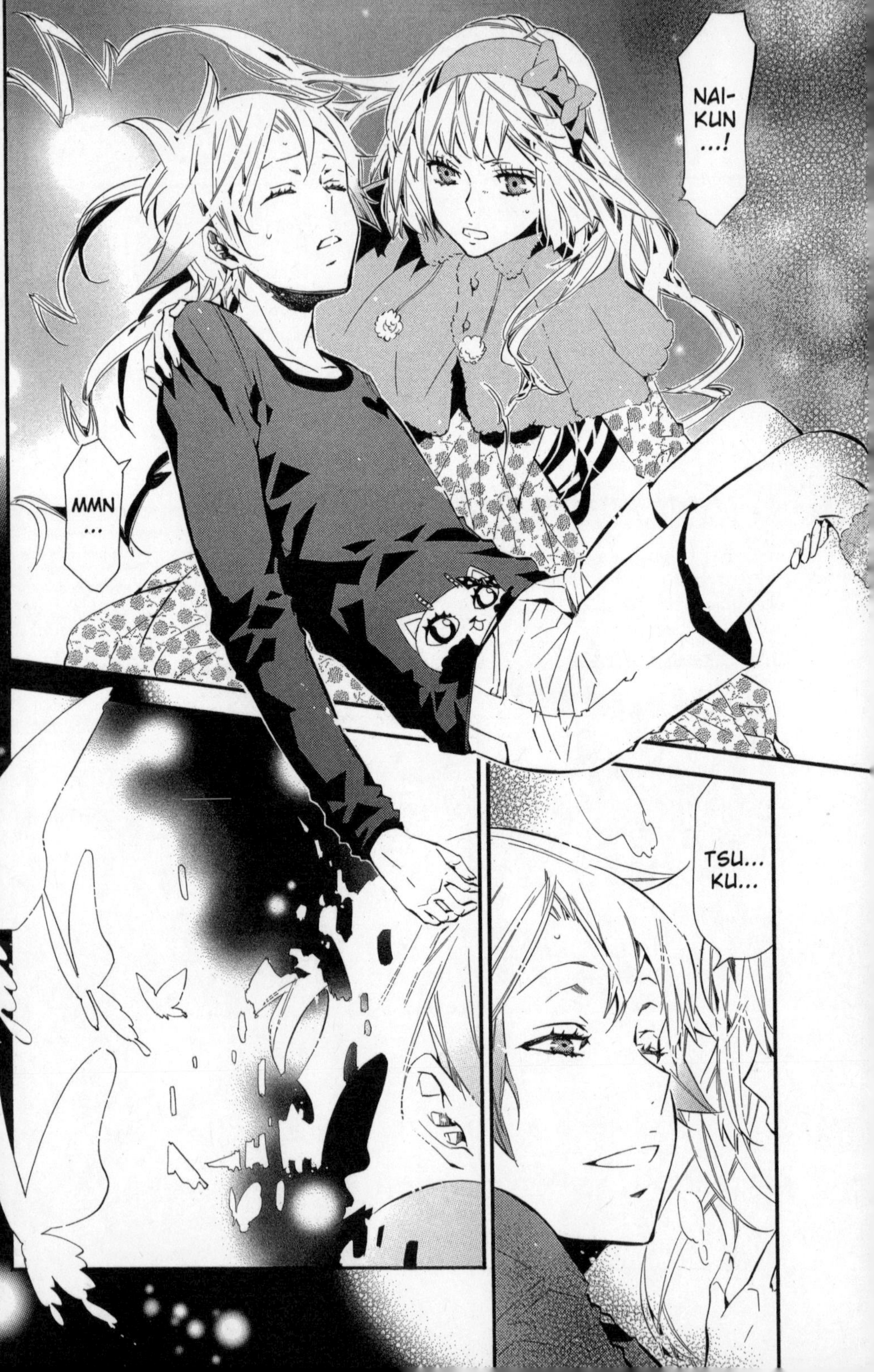
NAI-KUN ...!
MMN ...
TSU... KU...

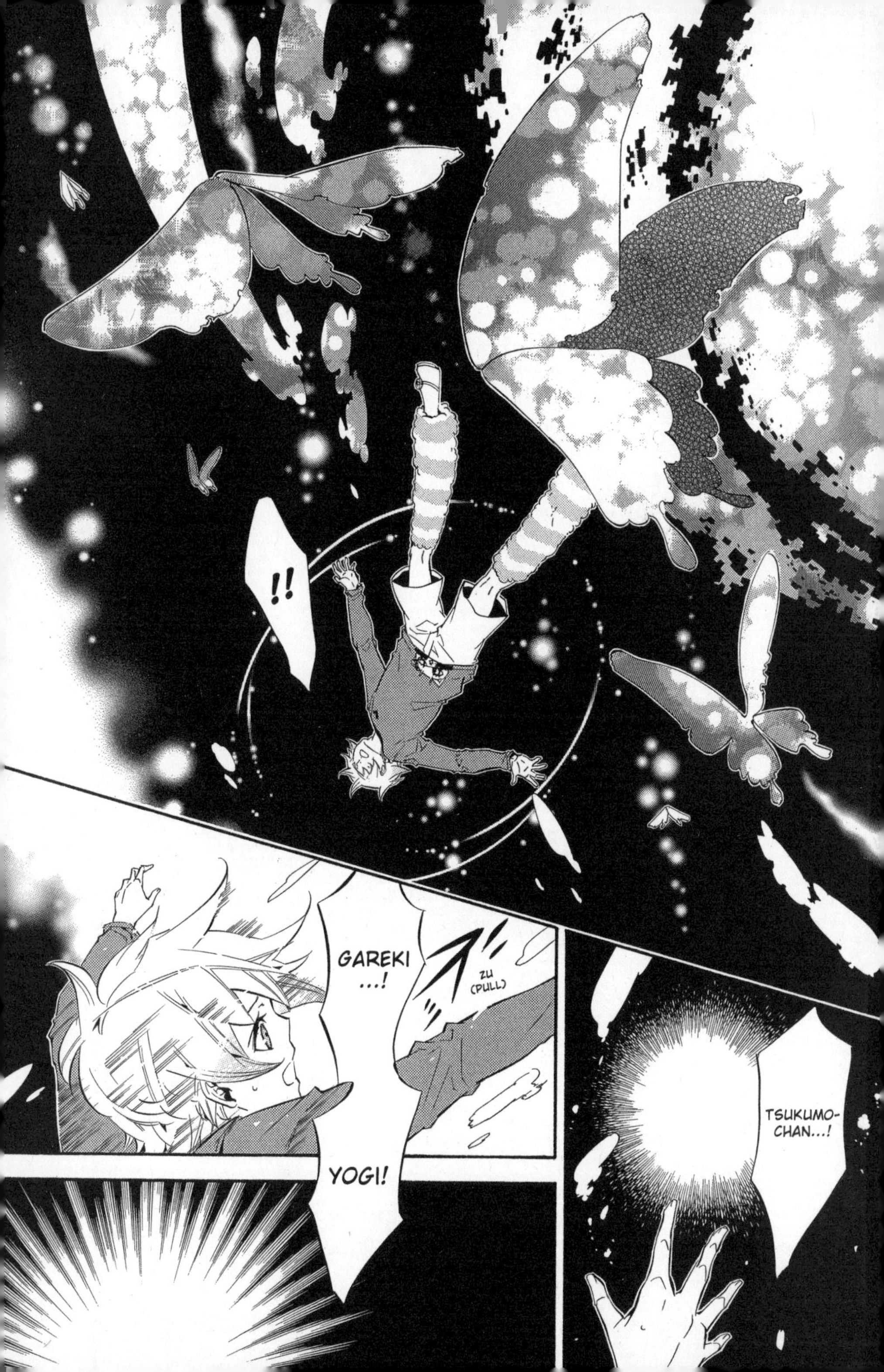
!!
TSUKUMO-CHAN...!
GAREKI ...!
ZU (PULL)
YOGI!

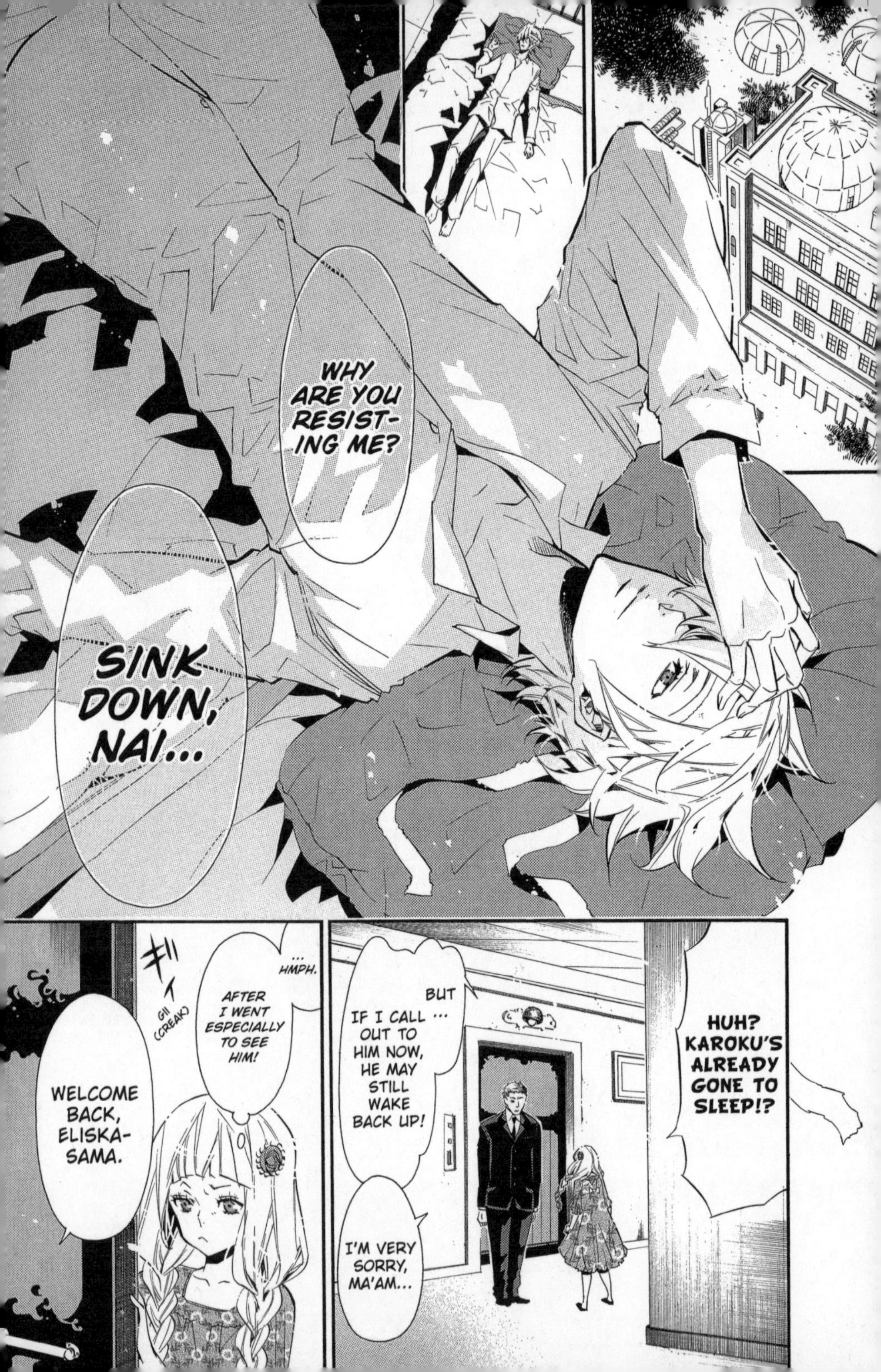
WHY ARE YOU RESIST-ING ME?
SINK DOWN, NAI...
HUH? KAROKU'S ALREADY GONE TO SLEEP!?
BUT ... IF I CALL OUT TO HIM NOW, HE MAY STILL WAKE BACK UP!
I'M VERY SORRY, MA'AM...
... HMPH.
AFTER I WENT ESPECIALLY TO SEE HIM!
GII (CREAK)
WELCOME BACK, ELISKA-SAMA.

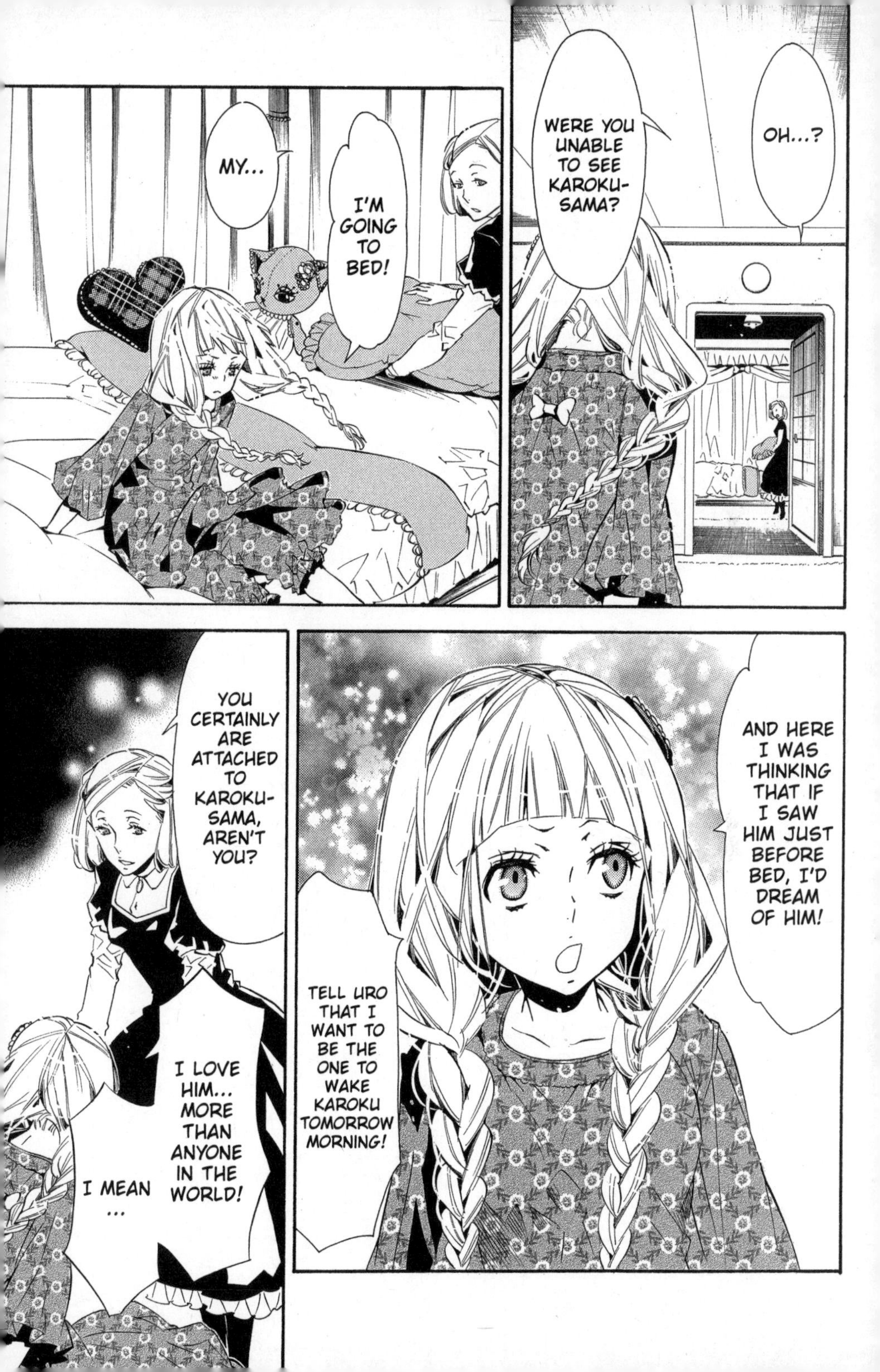
OH...?
WERE YOU UNABLE TO SEE KAROKU-SAMA?
MY...
I'M GOING TO BED!
AND HERE I WAS THINKING THAT IF I SAW HIM JUST BEFORE BED, I'D DREAM OF HIM!
TELL URO THAT I WANT TO BE THE ONE TO WAKE KAROKU TOMORROW MORNING!
YOU CERTAINLY ARE ATTACHED TO KAROKU-SAMA, AREN'T YOU?
I LOVE HIM... MORE THAN ANYONE IN THE WORLD!
I MEAN ...

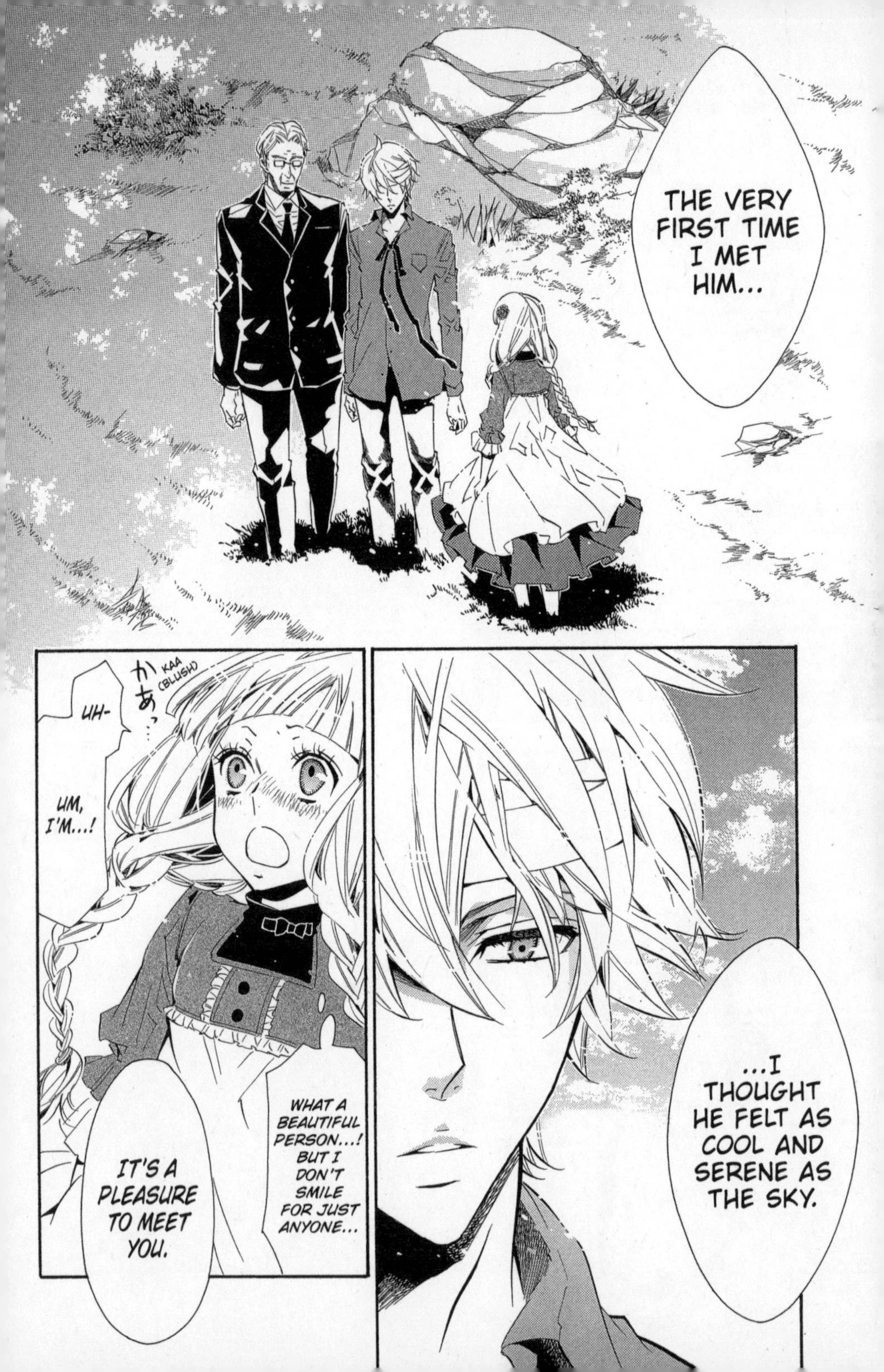
THE VERY FIRST TIME I MET HIM...
...I THOUGHT HE FELT AS COOL AND SERENE AS THE SKY.
かあっ KAA (BLUSH)
UH-
UM, I'M...!
WHAT A BEAUTIFUL PERSON...! BUT I DON'T SMILE FOR JUST ANYONE...
IT'S A PLEASURE TO MEET YOU.

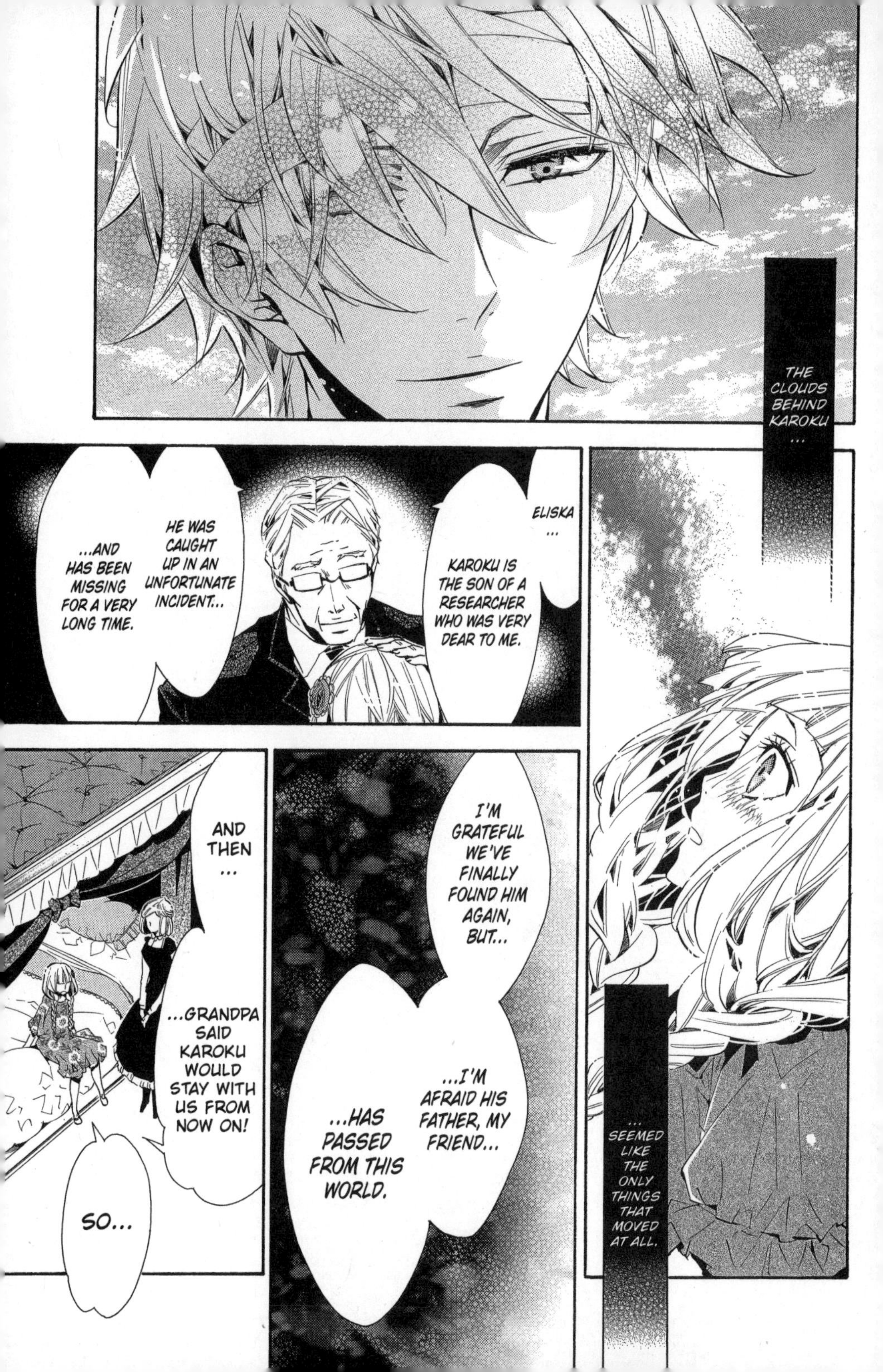
THE CLOUDS BEHIND KAROKU ...
... SEEMED LIKE THE ONLY THINGS THAT MOVED AT ALL.
ELISKA ...
KAROKU IS THE SON OF A RESEARCHER WHO WAS VERY DEAR TO ME.
HE WAS CAUGHT UP IN AN UNFORTUNATE INCIDENT...
...AND HAS BEEN MISSING FOR A VERY LONG TIME.
I'M GRATEFUL WE'VE FINALLY FOUND HIM AGAIN, BUT...
...I'M AFRAID HIS FATHER, MY FRIEND...
...HAS PASSED FROM THIS WORLD.
AND THEN ...
...GRANDPA SAID KAROKU WOULD STAY WITH US FROM NOW ON!
SO...

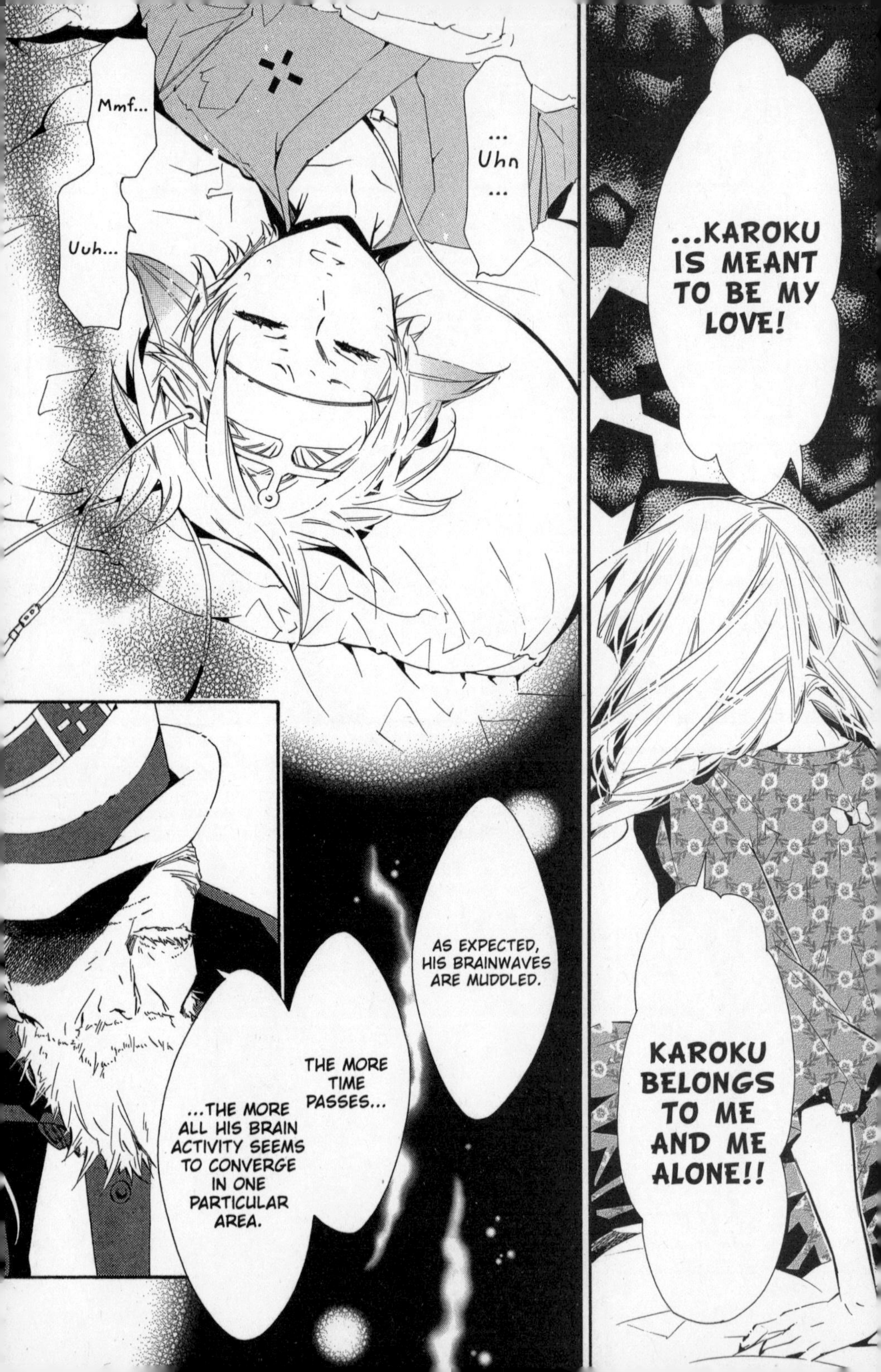
...KAROKU IS MEANT TO BE MY LOVE!
KAROKU BELONGS TO ME AND ME ALONE!!
... Uhn ...
Mmf...
Uuh...
AS EXPECTED, HIS BRAINWAVES ARE MUDDLED.
THE MORE TIME PASSES...
...THE MORE ALL HIS BRAIN ACTIVITY SEEMS TO CONVERGE IN ONE PARTICULAR AREA.

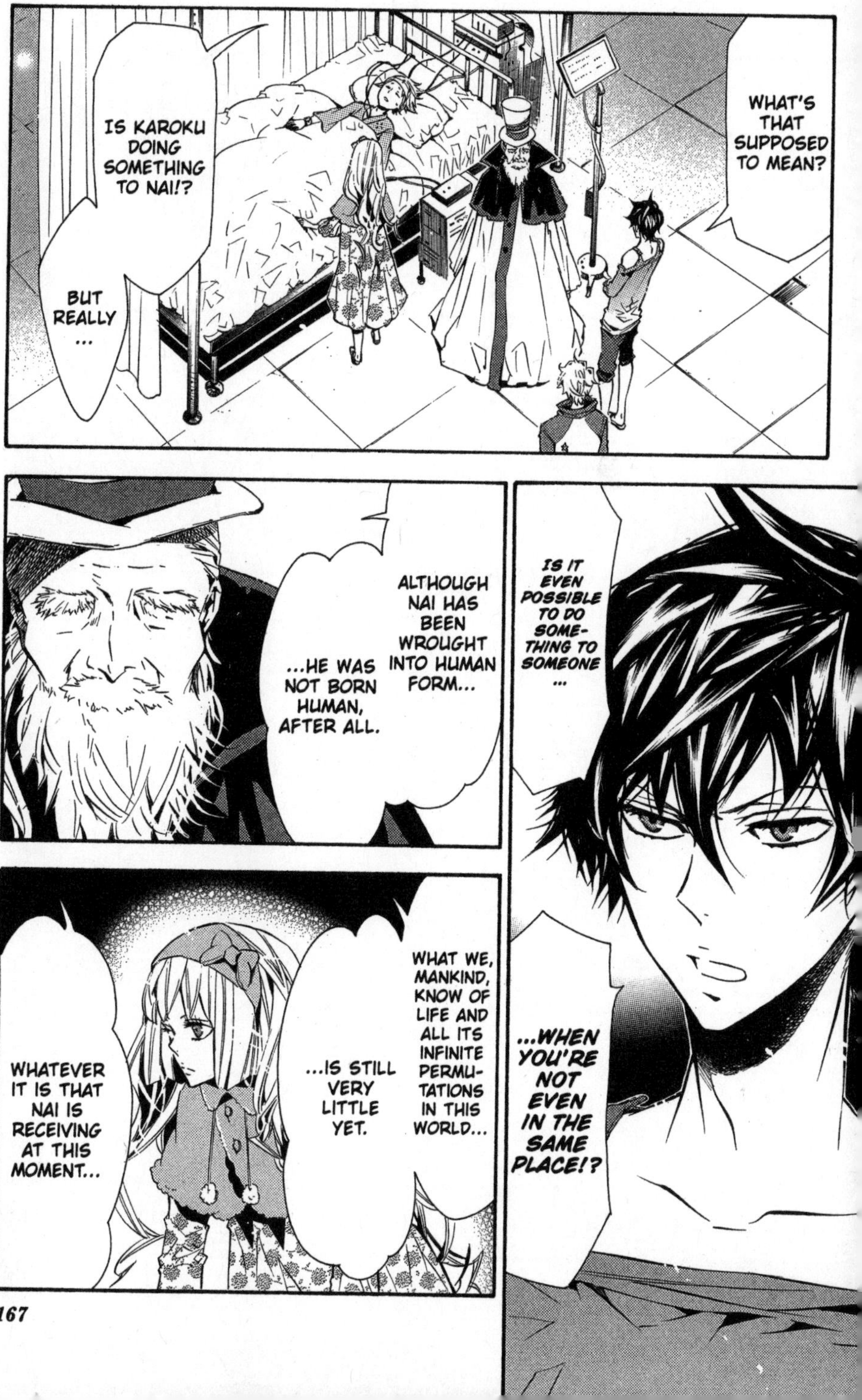
WHAT'S THAT SUPPOSED TO MEAN?
IS KAROKU DOING SOMETHING TO NAI!?
BUT REALLY ...
IS IT EVEN POSSIBLE TO DO SOME-THING TO SOMEONE ...
...WHEN YOU'RE NOT EVEN IN THE SAME PLACE!?
ALTHOUGH NAI HAS BEEN WROUGHT INTO HUMAN FORM...
...HE WAS NOT BORN HUMAN, AFTER ALL.
WHAT WE, MANKIND, KNOW OF LIFE AND ALL ITS INFINITE PERMU-TATIONS IN THIS WORLD...
...IS STILL VERY LITTLE YET.
WHATEVER IT IS THAT NAI IS RECEIVING AT THIS MOMENT...

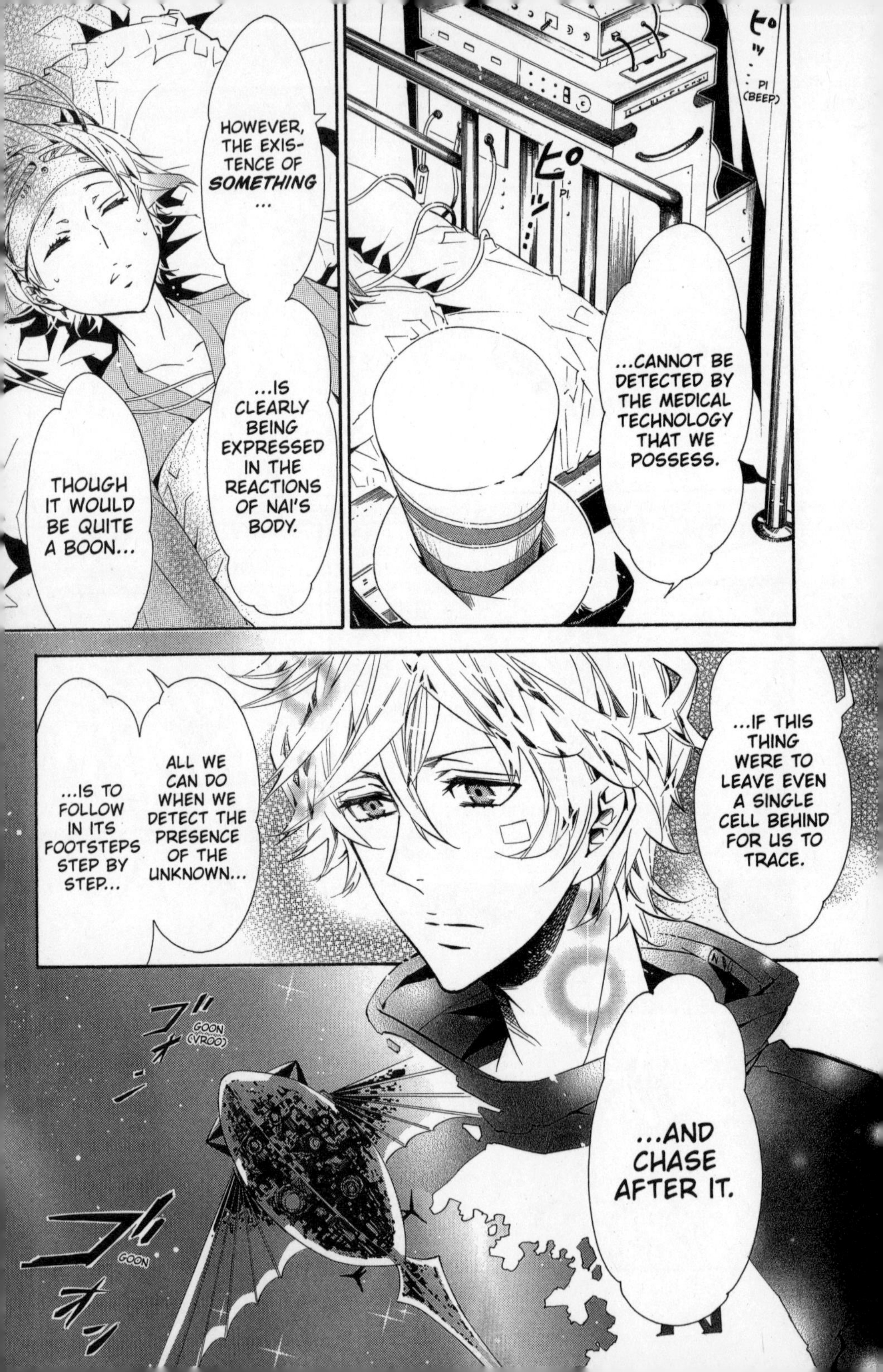
ピ
PI (BEEP)
ピ
PI
...CANNOT BE DETECTED BY THE MEDICAL TECHNOLOGY THAT WE POSSESS.
HOWEVER, THE EXISTENCE OF *SOMETHING* ...
...IS CLEARLY BEING EXPRESSED IN THE REACTIONS OF NAI'S BODY.
THOUGH IT WOULD BE QUITE A BOON...
...IF THIS THING WERE TO LEAVE EVEN A SINGLE CELL BEHIND FOR US TO TRACE.
ALL WE CAN DO WHEN WE DETECT THE PRESENCE OF THE UNKNOWN...
...IS TO FOLLOW IN ITS FOOTSTEPS STEP BY STEP...
GOON (VROO)
GOON
...AND CHASE AFTER IT.

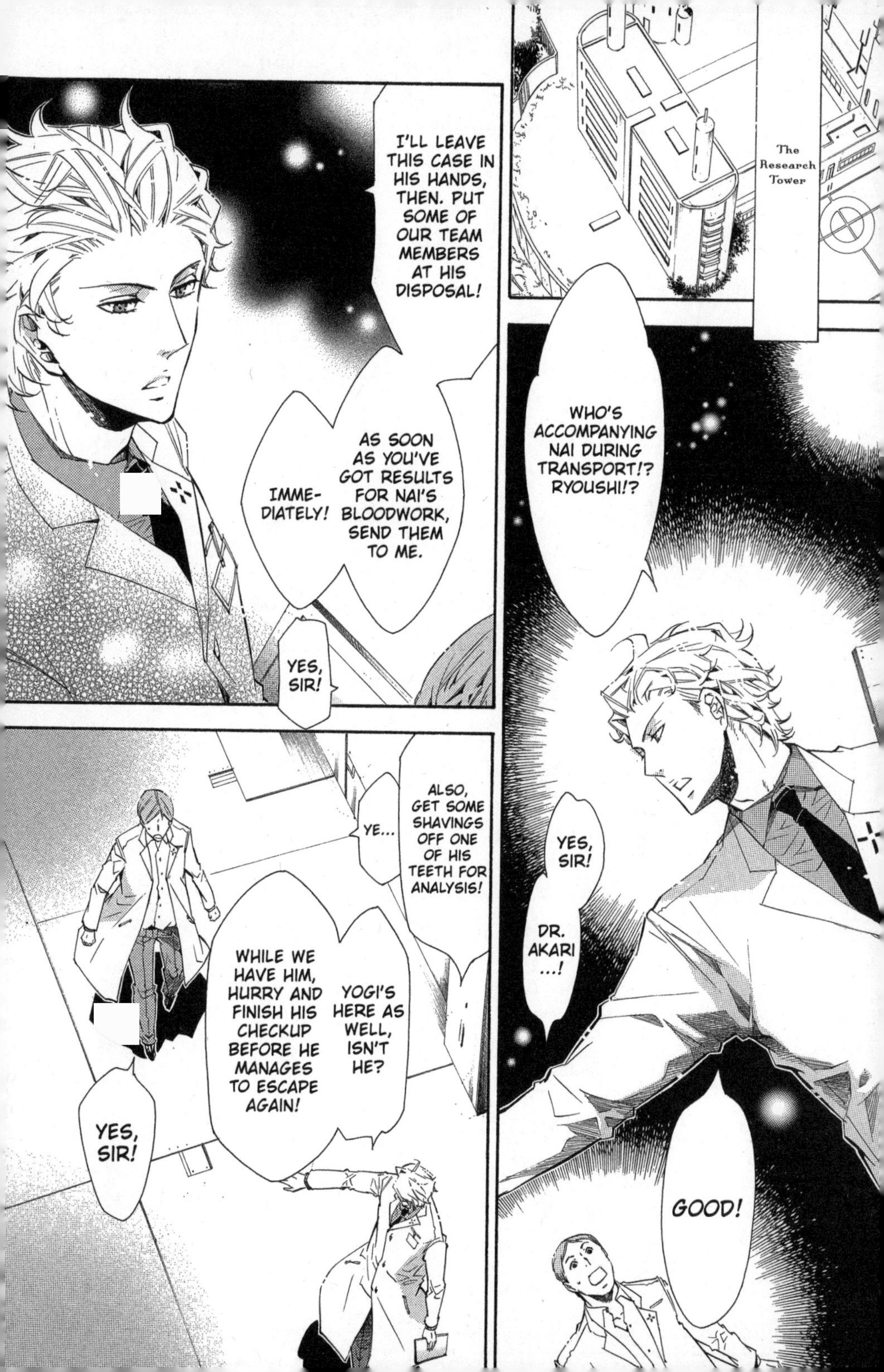
The Research Tower
WHO'S ACCOMPANYING NAI DURING TRANSPORT!? RYOUSHI!?
YES, SIR!
DR. AKARI ...!
GOOD!
I'LL LEAVE THIS CASE IN HIS HANDS, THEN. PUT SOME OF OUR TEAM MEMBERS AT HIS DISPOSAL!
AS SOON AS YOU'VE GOT RESULTS FOR NAI'S BLOODWORK, SEND THEM TO ME.
IMME-DIATELY!
YES, SIR!
ALSO, GET SOME SHAVINGS OFF ONE OF HIS TEETH FOR ANALYSIS!
YE...
YOGI'S HERE AS WELL, ISN'T HE?
WHILE WE HAVE HIM, HURRY AND FINISH HIS CHECKUP BEFORE HE MANAGES TO ESCAPE AGAIN!
YES, SIR!

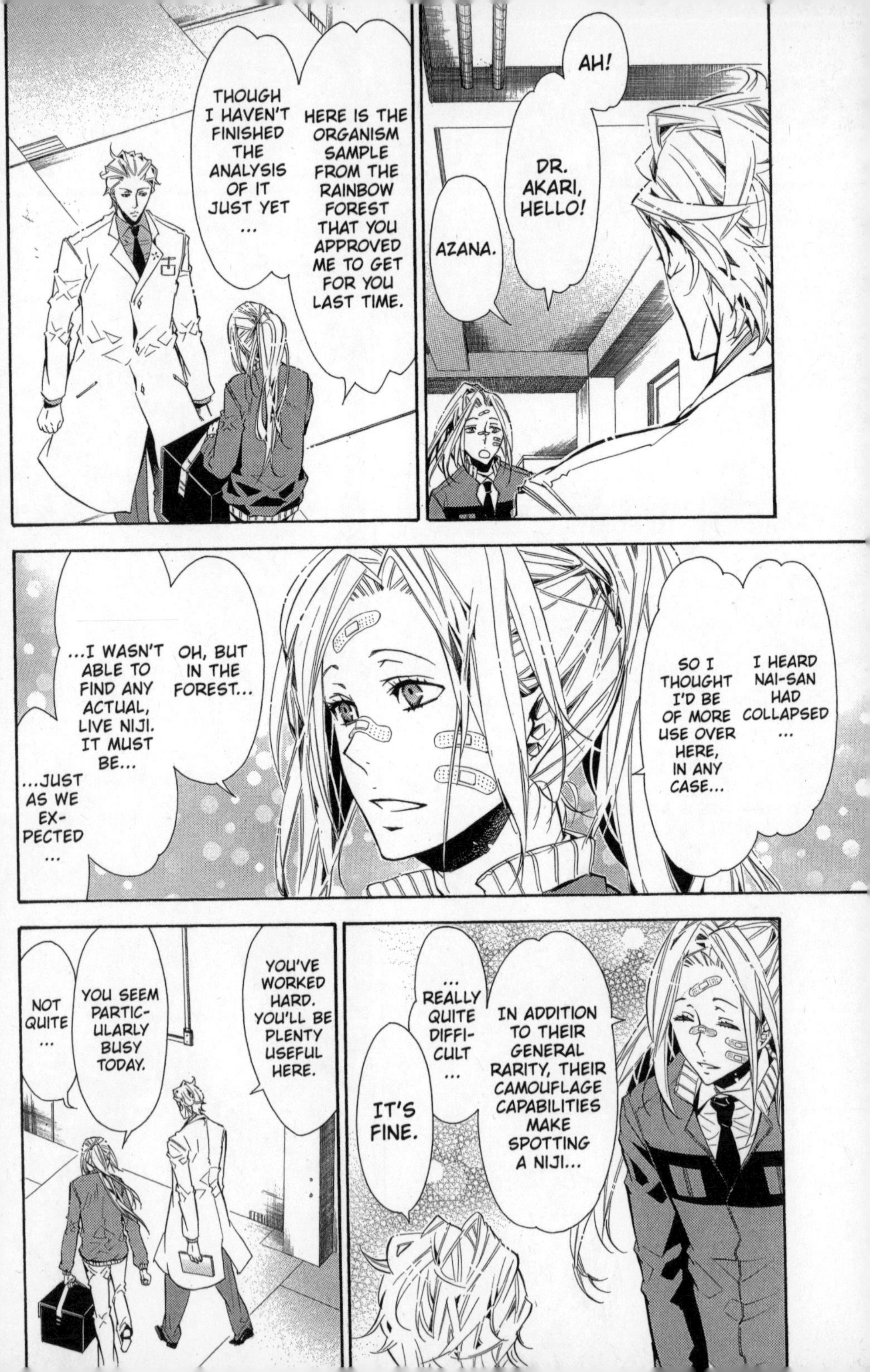
AH!
DR. AKARI, HELLO!
AZANA.
HERE IS THE ORGANISM SAMPLE FROM THE RAINBOW FOREST THAT YOU APPROVED ME TO GET FOR YOU LAST TIME.
THOUGH I HAVEN'T FINISHED THE ANALYSIS OF IT JUST YET ...
I HEARD NAI-SAN HAD COLLAPSED ...
SO I THOUGHT I'D BE OF MORE USE OVER HERE, IN ANY CASE...
OH, BUT IN THE FOREST...
...I WASN'T ABLE TO FIND ANY ACTUAL, LIVE NIJI. IT MUST BE...
...JUST AS WE EX-PECTED ...
IN ADDITION TO THEIR GENERAL RARITY, THEIR CAMOUFLAGE CAPABILITIES MAKE SPOTTING A NIJI...
... REALLY QUITE DIFFI-CULT ...
IT'S FINE.
YOU'VE WORKED HARD. YOU'LL BE PLENTY USEFUL HERE.
YOU SEEM PARTIC-ULARLY BUSY TODAY.
NOT QUITE ...

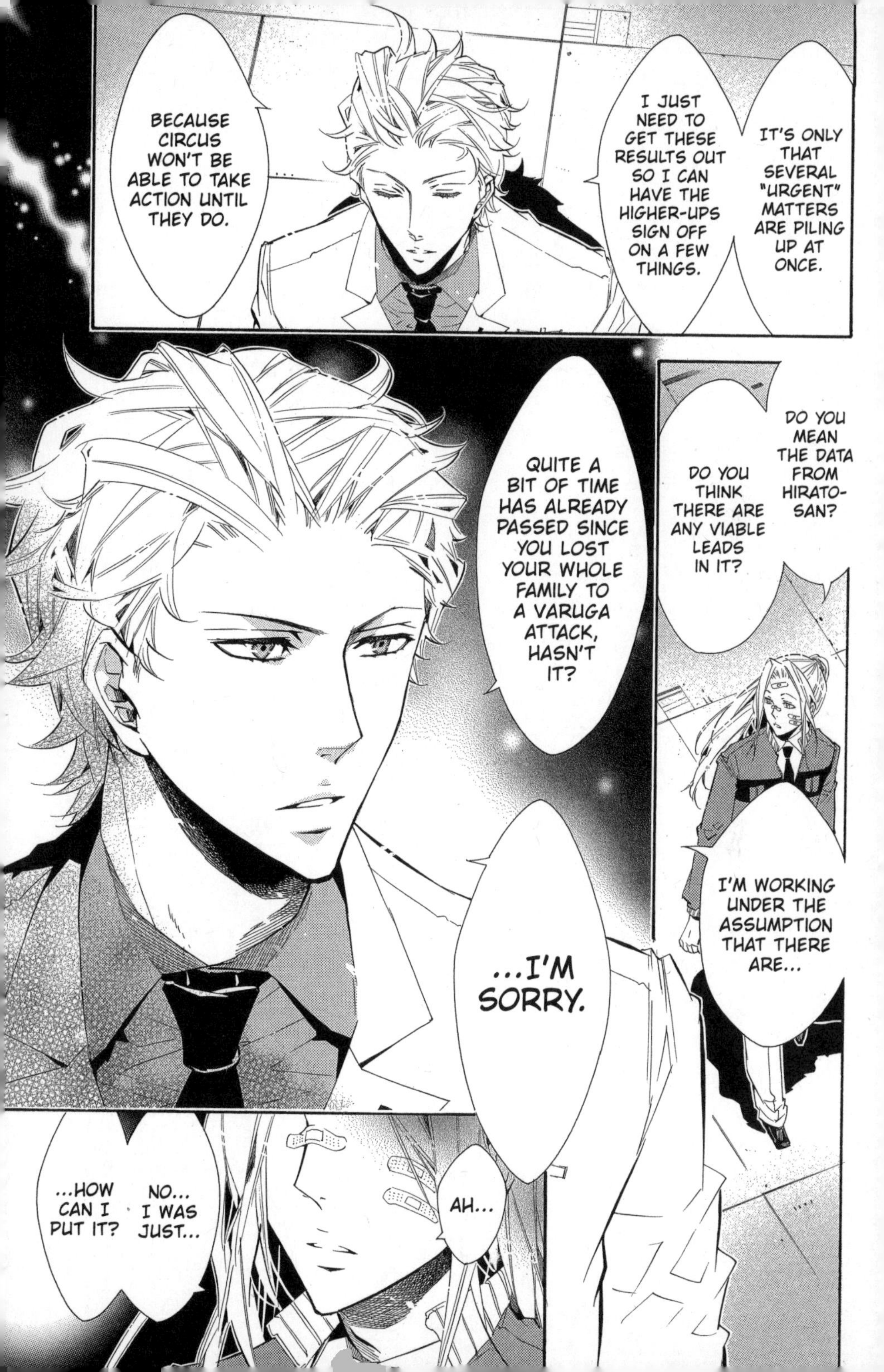
IT'S ONLY THAT SEVERAL "URGENT" MATTERS ARE PILING UP AT ONCE.
I JUST NEED TO GET THESE RESULTS OUT SO I CAN HAVE THE HIGHER-UPS SIGN OFF ON A FEW THINGS.
BECAUSE CIRCUS WON'T BE ABLE TO TAKE ACTION UNTIL THEY DO.
...
DO YOU MEAN THE DATA FROM HIRATO-SAN?
DO YOU THINK THERE ARE ANY VIABLE LEADS IN IT?
I'M WORKING UNDER THE ASSUMPTION THAT THERE ARE...
QUITE A BIT OF TIME HAS ALREADY PASSED SINCE YOU LOST YOUR WHOLE FAMILY TO A VARUGA ATTACK, HASN'T IT?
...I'M SORRY.
AH...
NO... I WAS JUST...
...HOW CAN I PUT IT?

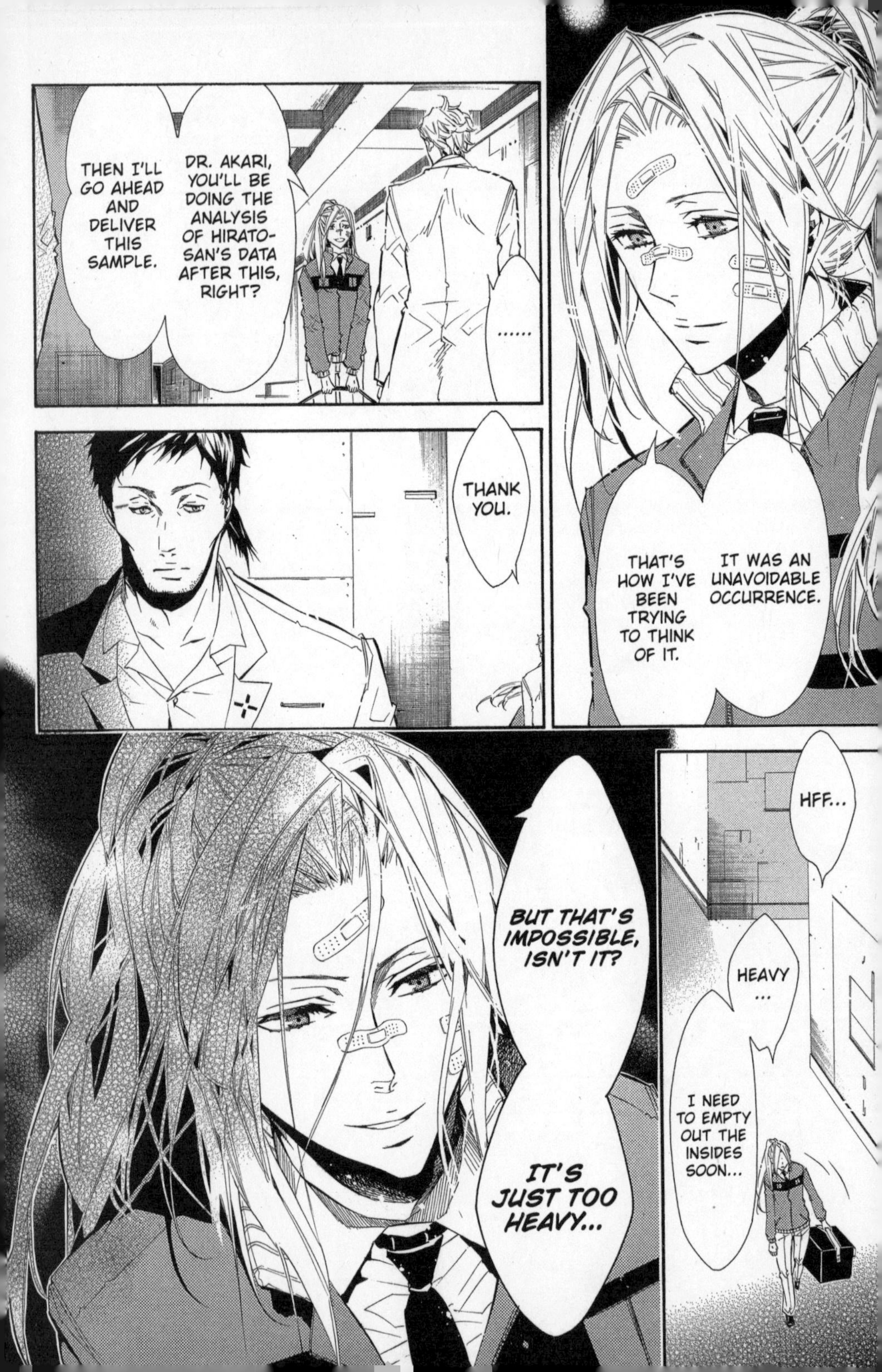
IT WAS AN UNAVOIDABLE OCCURRENCE.
THAT'S HOW I'VE BEEN TRYING TO THINK OF IT.
DR. AKARI, YOU'LL BE DOING THE ANALYSIS OF HIRATO-SAN'S DATA AFTER THIS, RIGHT?
THEN I'LL GO AHEAD AND DELIVER THIS SAMPLE.
......
THANK YOU.
HFF...
HEAVY ...
I NEED TO EMPTY OUT THE INSIDES SOON...
BUT THAT'S IMPOSSIBLE, ISN'T IT?
IT'S JUST TOO HEAVY...

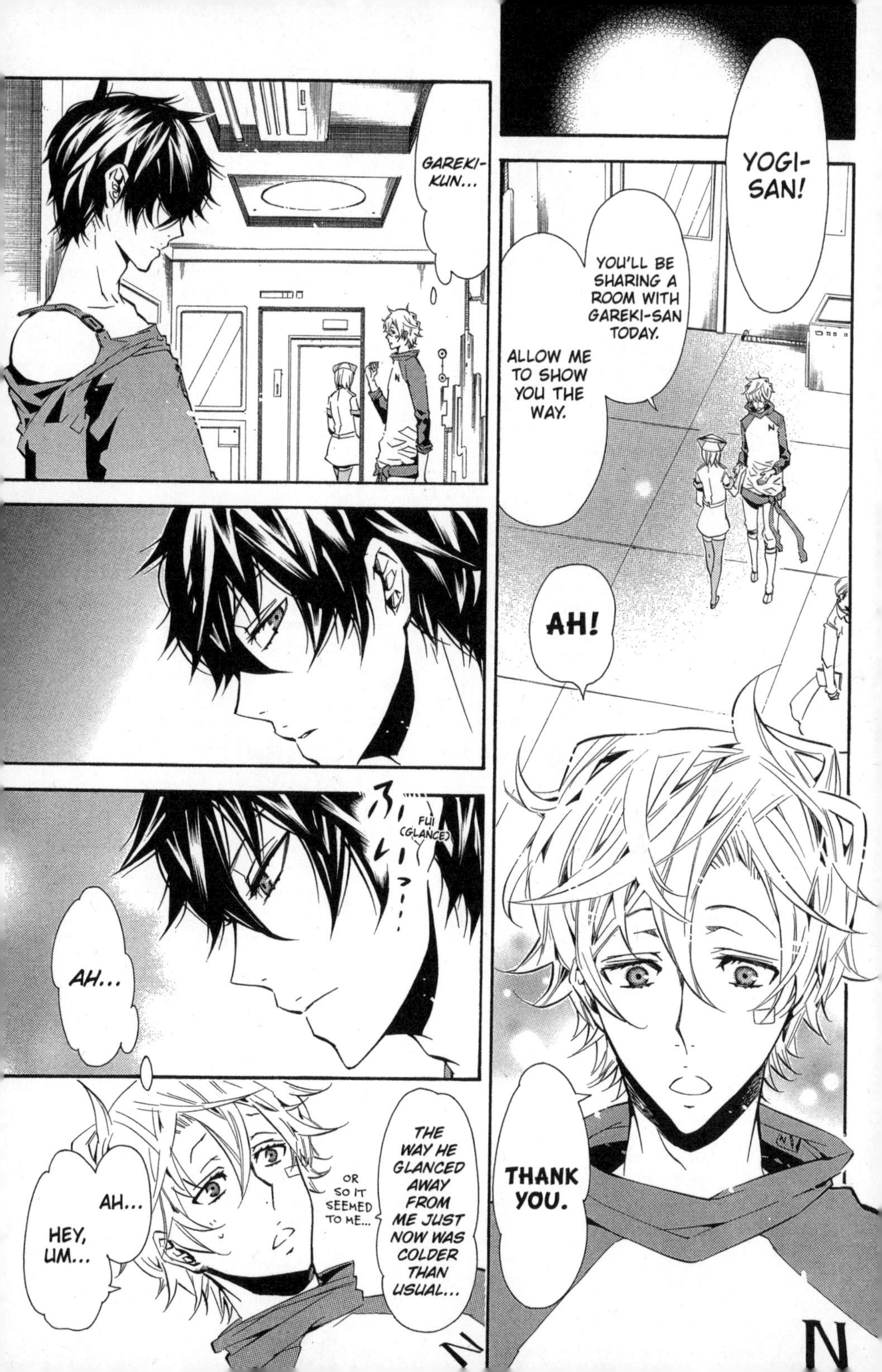
YOGI-SAN!
YOU'LL BE SHARING A ROOM WITH GAREKI-SAN TODAY.
ALLOW ME TO SHOW YOU THE WAY.
AH!
THANK YOU.
GAREKI-KUN...
FUI (GLANCE)
AH...
THE WAY HE GLANCED AWAY FROM ME JUST NOW WAS COLDER THAN USUAL...
OR SO IT SEEMED TO ME...
AH...
HEY, UM...

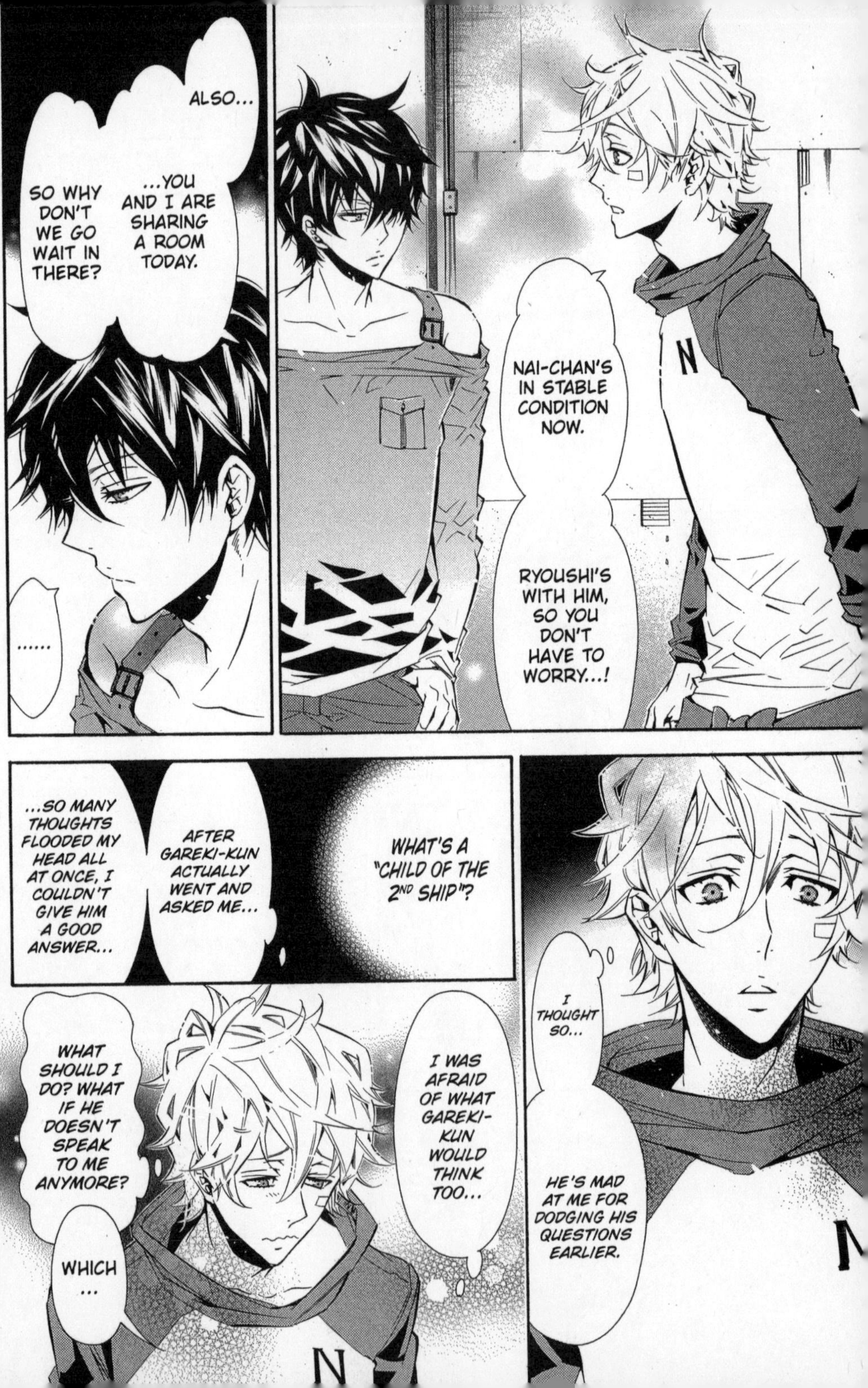
NAI-CHAN'S IN STABLE CONDITION NOW.
RYOUSHI'S WITH HIM, SO YOU DON'T HAVE TO WORRY...!
ALSO...
...YOU AND I ARE SHARING A ROOM TODAY.
SO WHY DON'T WE GO WAIT IN THERE?
......
I THOUGHT SO...
HE'S MAD AT ME FOR DODGING HIS QUESTIONS EARLIER.
WHAT'S A "CHILD OF THE 2ND SHIP"?
AFTER GAREKI-KUN ACTUALLY WENT AND ASKED ME...
...SO MANY THOUGHTS FLOODED MY HEAD ALL AT ONCE, I COULDN'T GIVE HIM A GOOD ANSWER...
I WAS AFRAID OF WHAT GAREKI-KUN WOULD THINK TOO...
WHAT SHOULD I DO? WHAT IF HE DOESN'T SPEAK TO ME ANYMORE?
WHICH ...

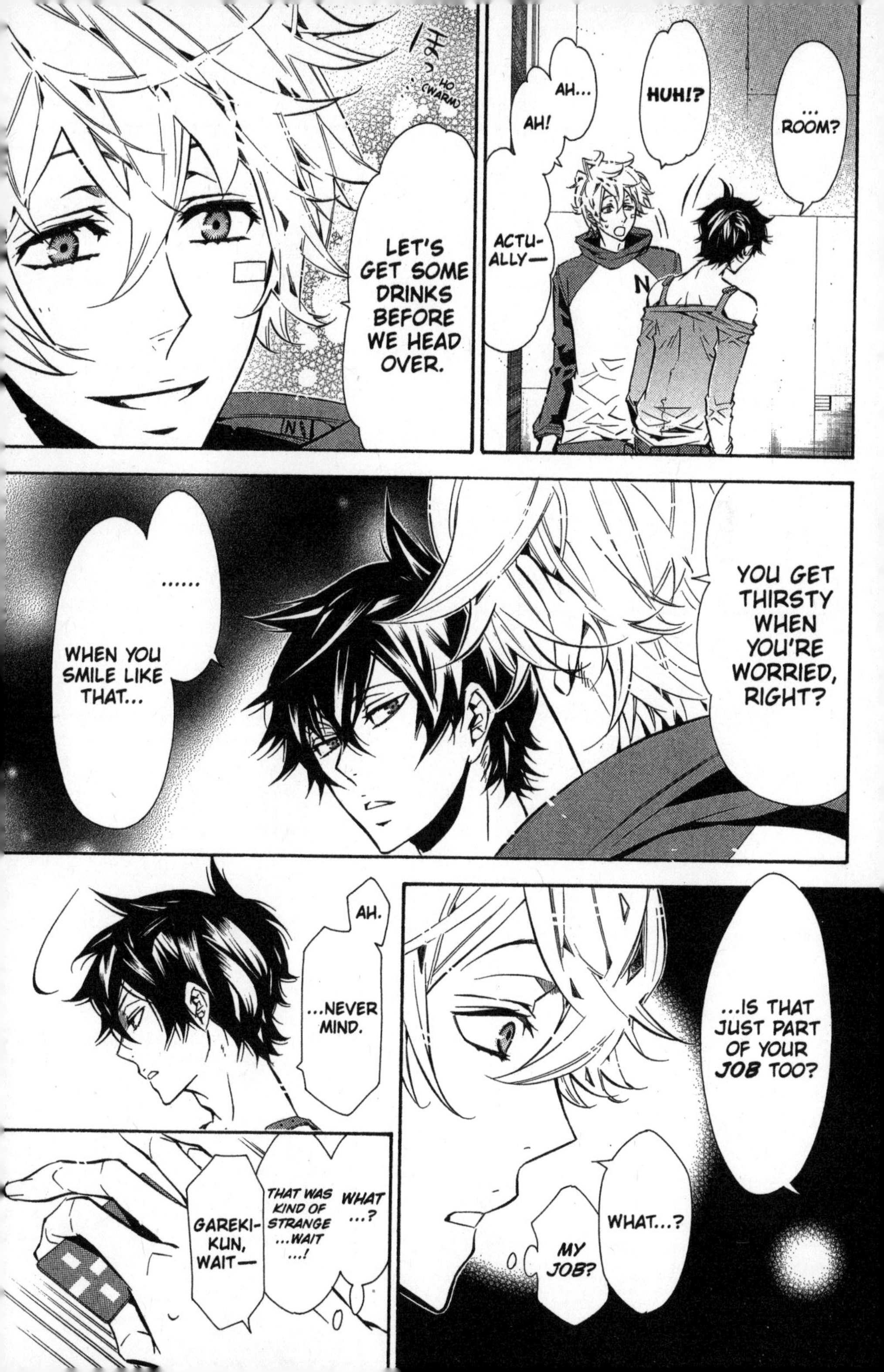
...ROOM?
HUH!?
AH...
AH!
ACTU-ALLY—
ほっ
HO (WARM)
LET'S GET SOME DRINKS BEFORE WE HEAD OVER.
YOU GET THIRSTY WHEN YOU'RE WORRIED, RIGHT?
......
WHEN YOU SMILE LIKE THAT...
...IS THAT JUST PART OF YOUR JOB TOO?
WHAT...?
MY JOB?
AH.
...NEVER MIND.
WHAT ...?
THAT WAS KIND OF STRANGE ...WAIT ...!
GAREKI-KUN, WAIT—

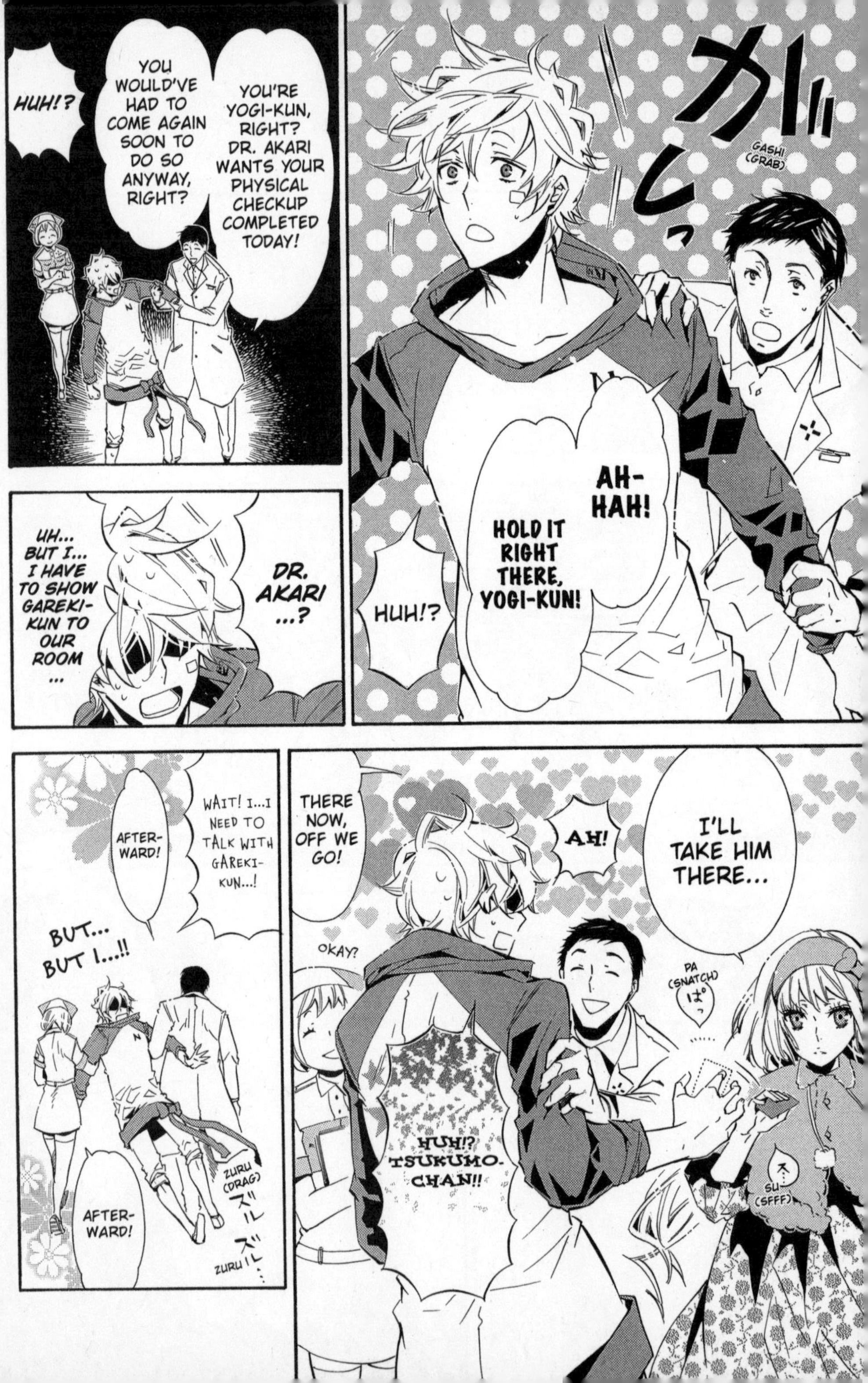
GASHI (GRAB)
AH-HAH!
HOLD IT RIGHT THERE, YOGI-KUN!
HUH!?
YOU'RE YOGI-KUN, RIGHT? DR. AKARI WANTS YOUR PHYSICAL CHECKUP COMPLETED TODAY!
YOU WOULD'VE HAD TO COME AGAIN SOON TO DO SO ANYWAY, RIGHT?
HUH!?
DR. AKARI ...?
UH... BUT I... I HAVE TO SHOW GAREKI-KUN TO OUR ROOM ...
I'LL TAKE HIM THERE...
AH!
PA (SNATCH)
SU (SFFF)
THERE NOW, OFF WE GO!
OKAY?
HUH!? TSUKUMO-CHAN!!
WAIT! I...I NEED TO TALK WITH GAREKI-KUN...!
AFTER-WARD!
BUT... BUT I...!!
ZURU (DRAG)
ZURU
AFTER-WARD!

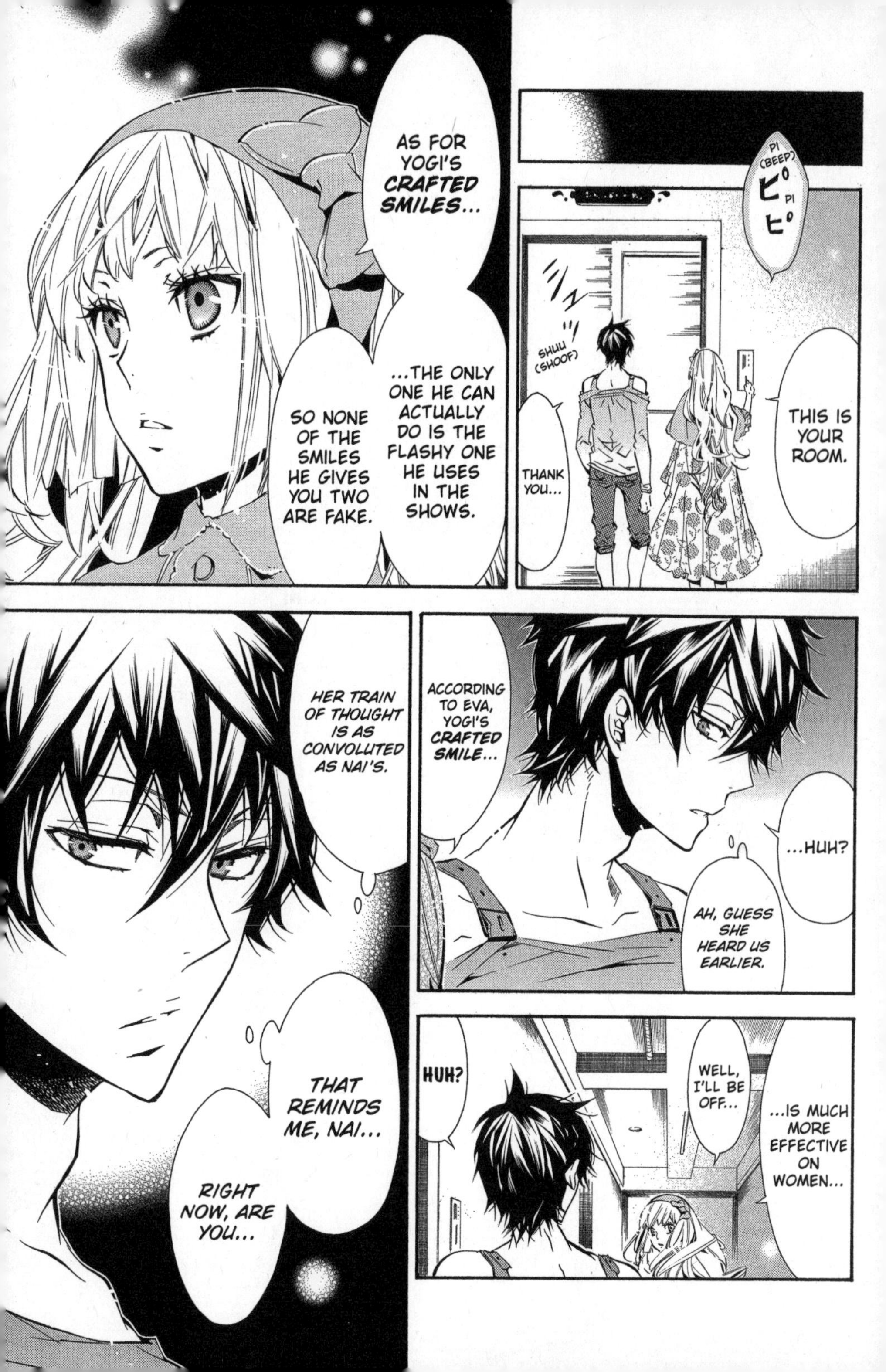
PI (BEEP) PI
THIS IS YOUR ROOM.
SHUU (SHOOF)
THANK YOU...
AS FOR YOGI'S CRAFTED SMILES...
...THE ONLY ONE HE CAN ACTUALLY DO IS THE FLASHY ONE HE USES IN THE SHOWS.
SO NONE OF THE SMILES HE GIVES YOU TWO ARE FAKE.
...HUH?
AH, GUESS SHE HEARD US EARLIER.
ACCORDING TO EVA, YOGI'S CRAFTED SMILE...
...IS MUCH MORE EFFECTIVE ON WOMEN...
WELL, I'LL BE OFF...
HUH?
HER TRAIN OF THOUGHT IS AS CONVOLUTED AS NAI'S.
THAT REMINDS ME, NAI...
RIGHT NOW, ARE YOU...

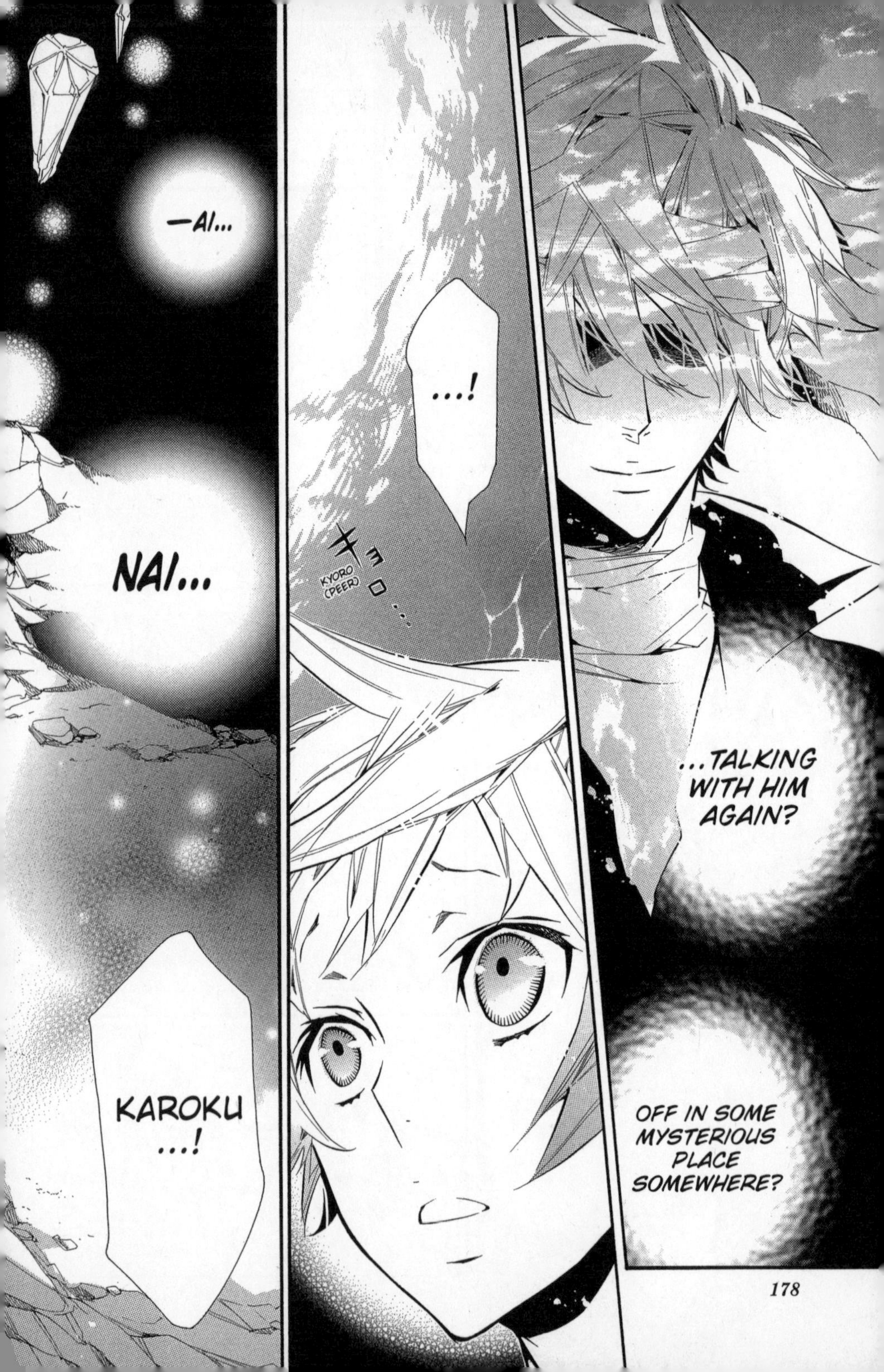
...TALKING WITH HIM AGAIN?
OFF IN SOME MYSTERIOUS PLACE SOMEWHERE?
...!
KYORO (PEER)
—AI...
NAI...
KAROKU ...!

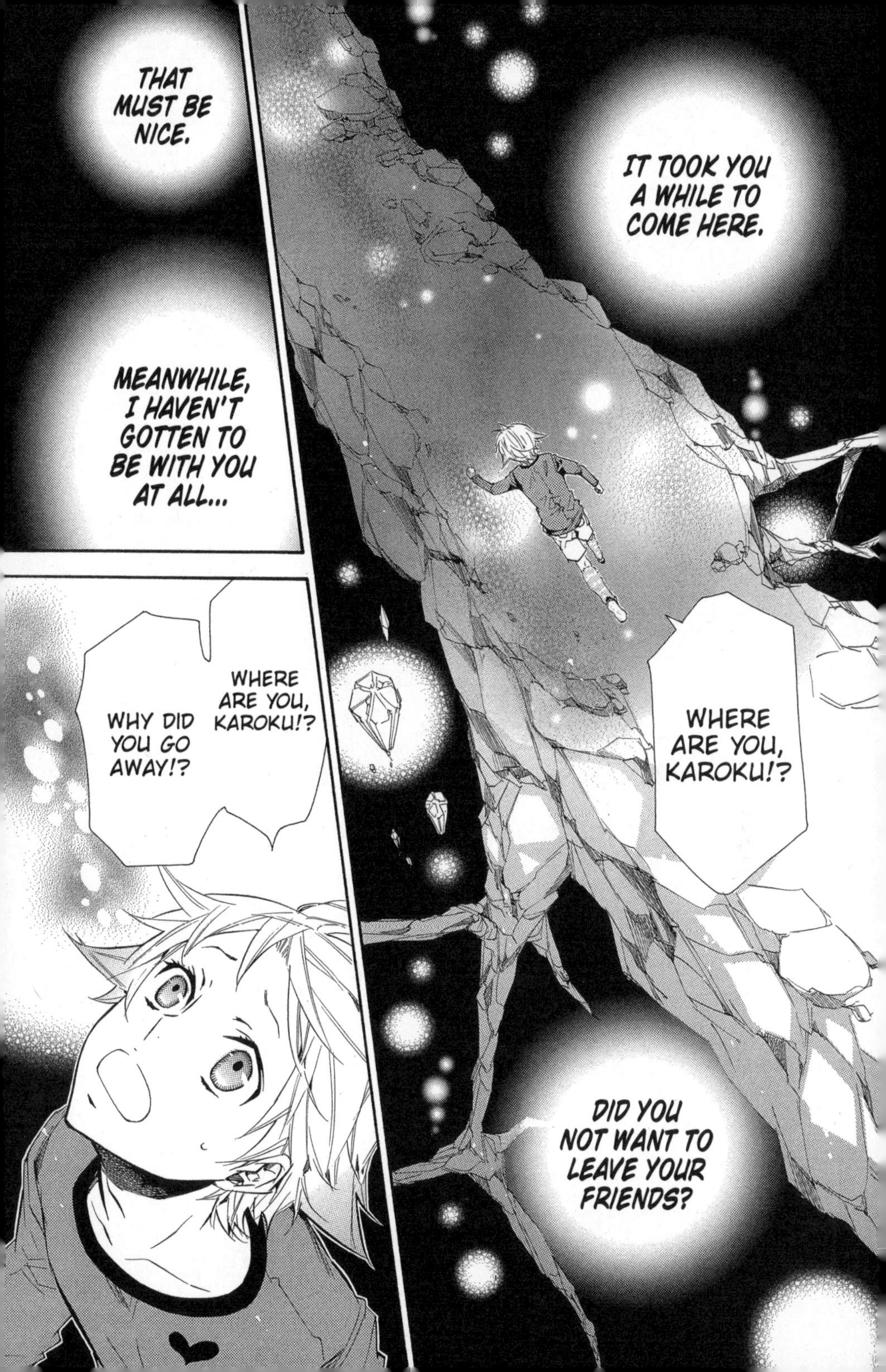
IT TOOK YOU A WHILE TO COME HERE.
WHERE ARE YOU, KAROKU!?
DID YOU NOT WANT TO LEAVE YOUR FRIENDS?
THAT MUST BE NICE.
MEANWHILE, I HAVEN'T GOTTEN TO BE WITH YOU AT ALL...
WHERE ARE YOU, KAROKU!?
WHY DID YOU GO AWAY!?

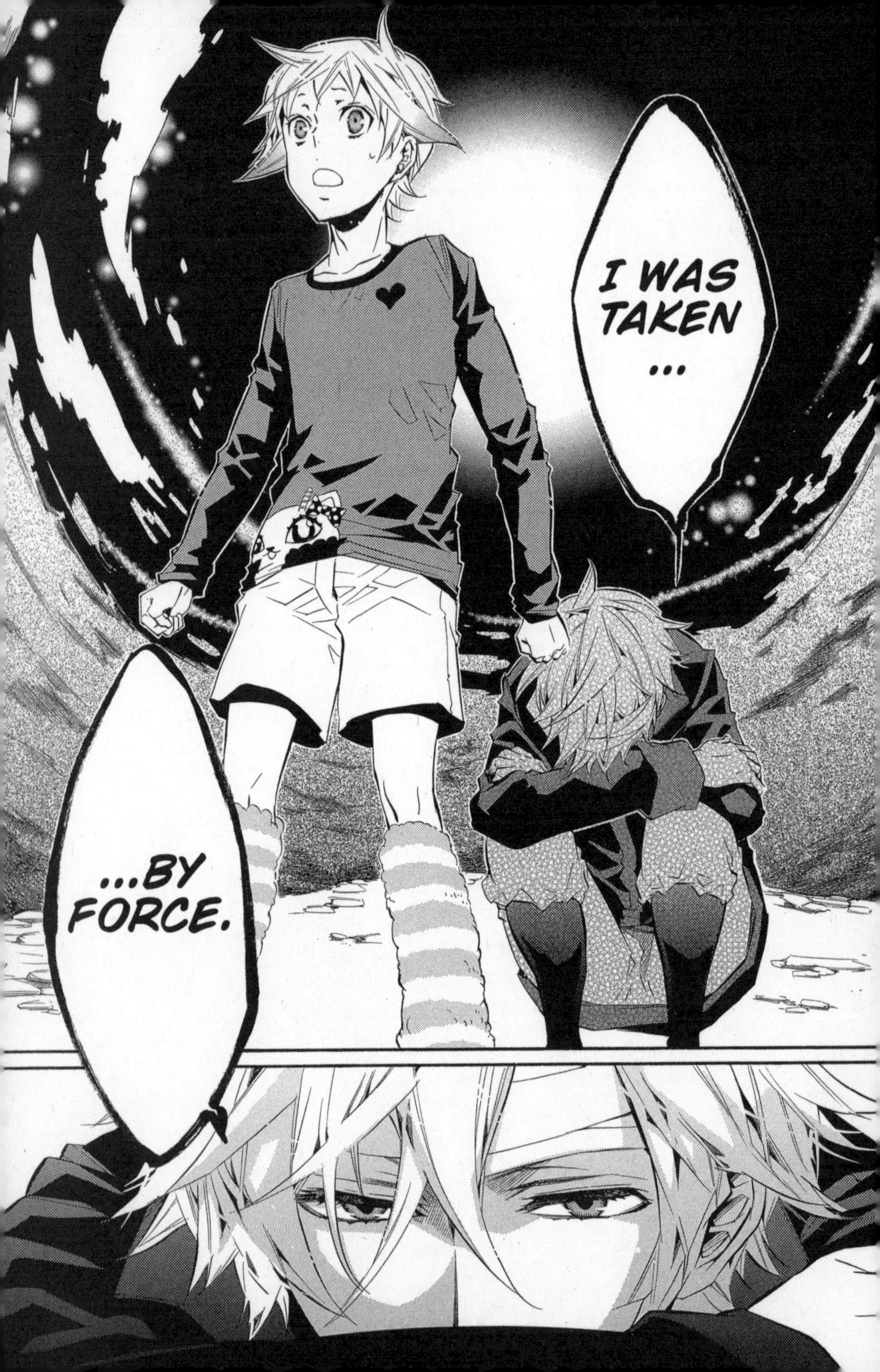
I WAS TAKEN ...
...BY FORCE.

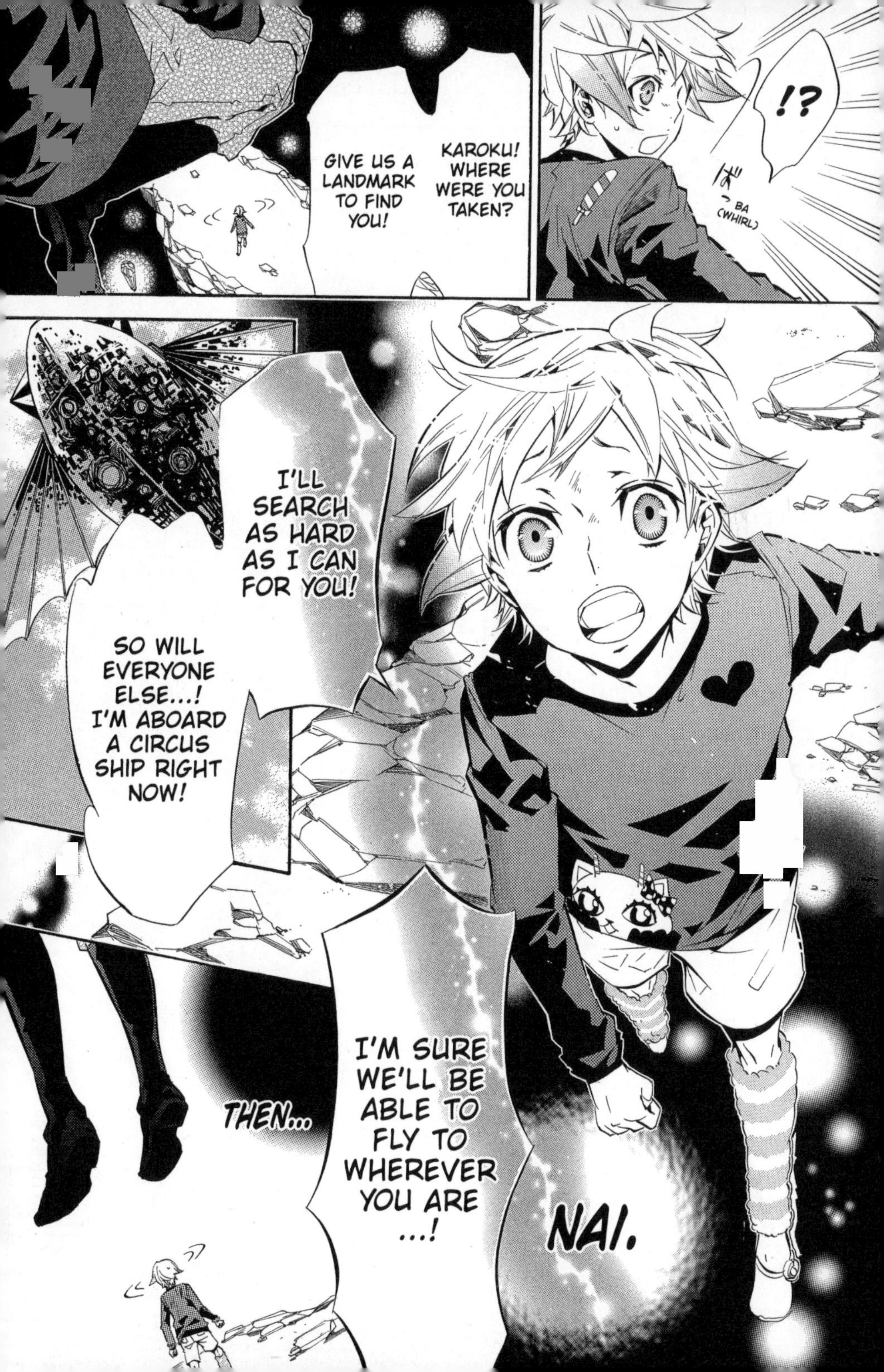
!?
ぱ
BA (WHIRL)
KAROKU! WHERE WERE YOU TAKEN?
GIVE US A LANDMARK TO FIND YOU!
I'LL SEARCH AS HARD AS I CAN FOR YOU!
SO WILL EVERYONE ELSE...! I'M ABOARD A CIRCUS SHIP RIGHT NOW!
I'M SURE WE'LL BE ABLE TO FLY TO WHEREVER YOU ARE ...!
THEN...
NAI.

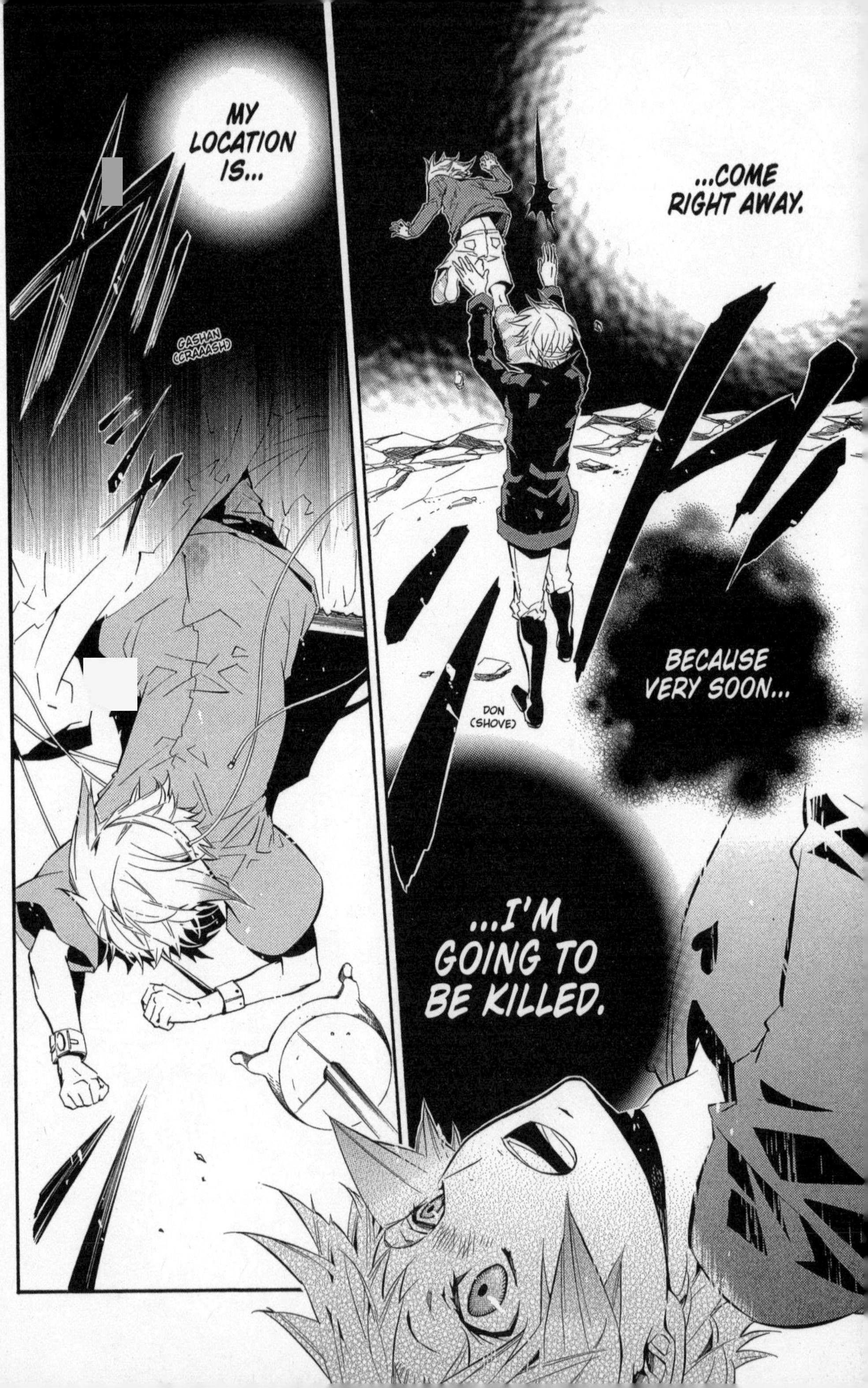
...COME RIGHT AWAY.
DON (SHOVE)
BECAUSE VERY SOON...
...I'M GOING TO BE KILLED.
MY LOCATION IS...
GASHAN (CRAAASH)

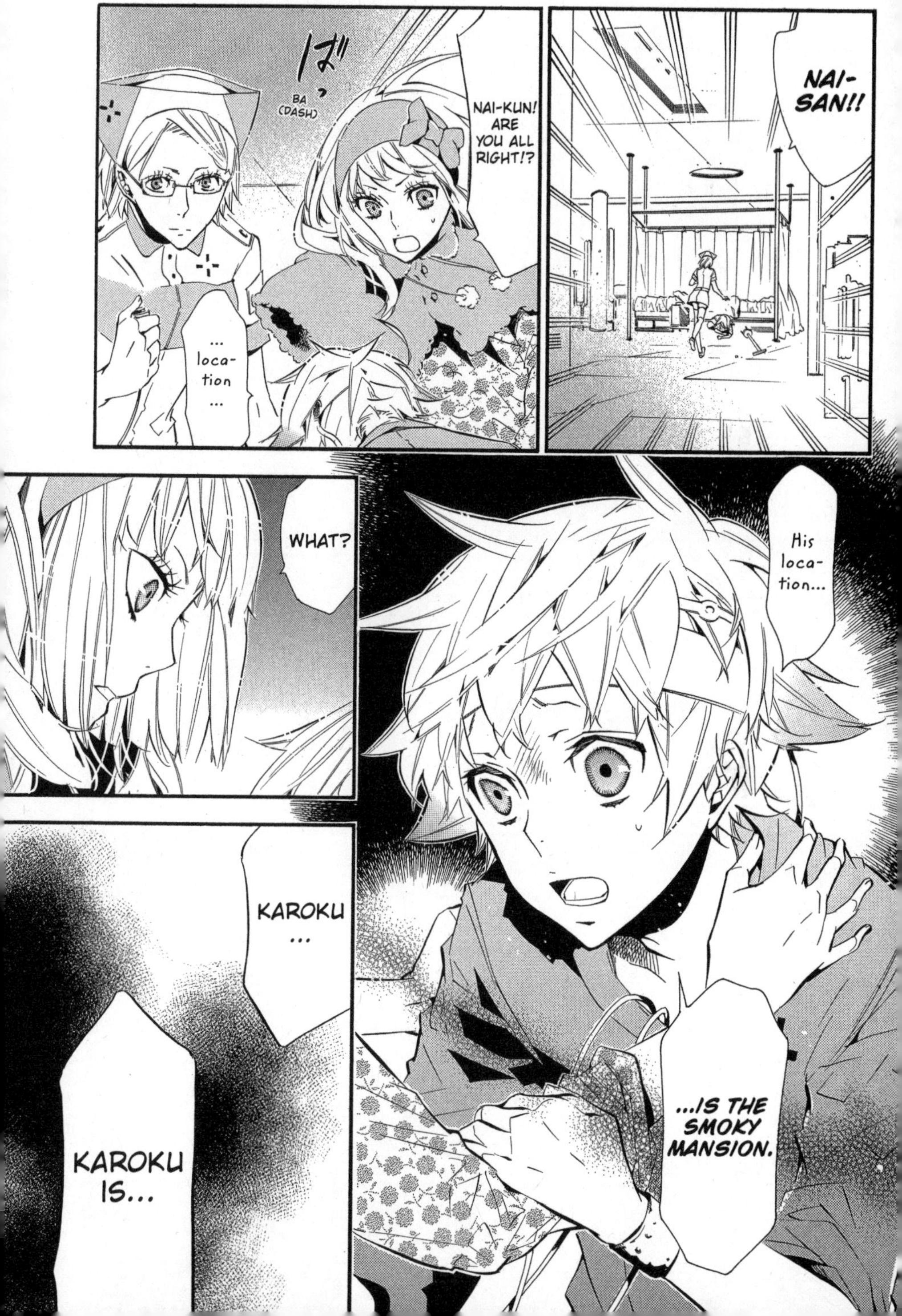
NAI-SAN!!
NAI-KUN! ARE YOU ALL RIGHT!?
ばっ
BA (DASH)
...location...
His location...
WHAT?
KAROKU...
KAROKU IS...
...IS THE SMOKY MANSION.

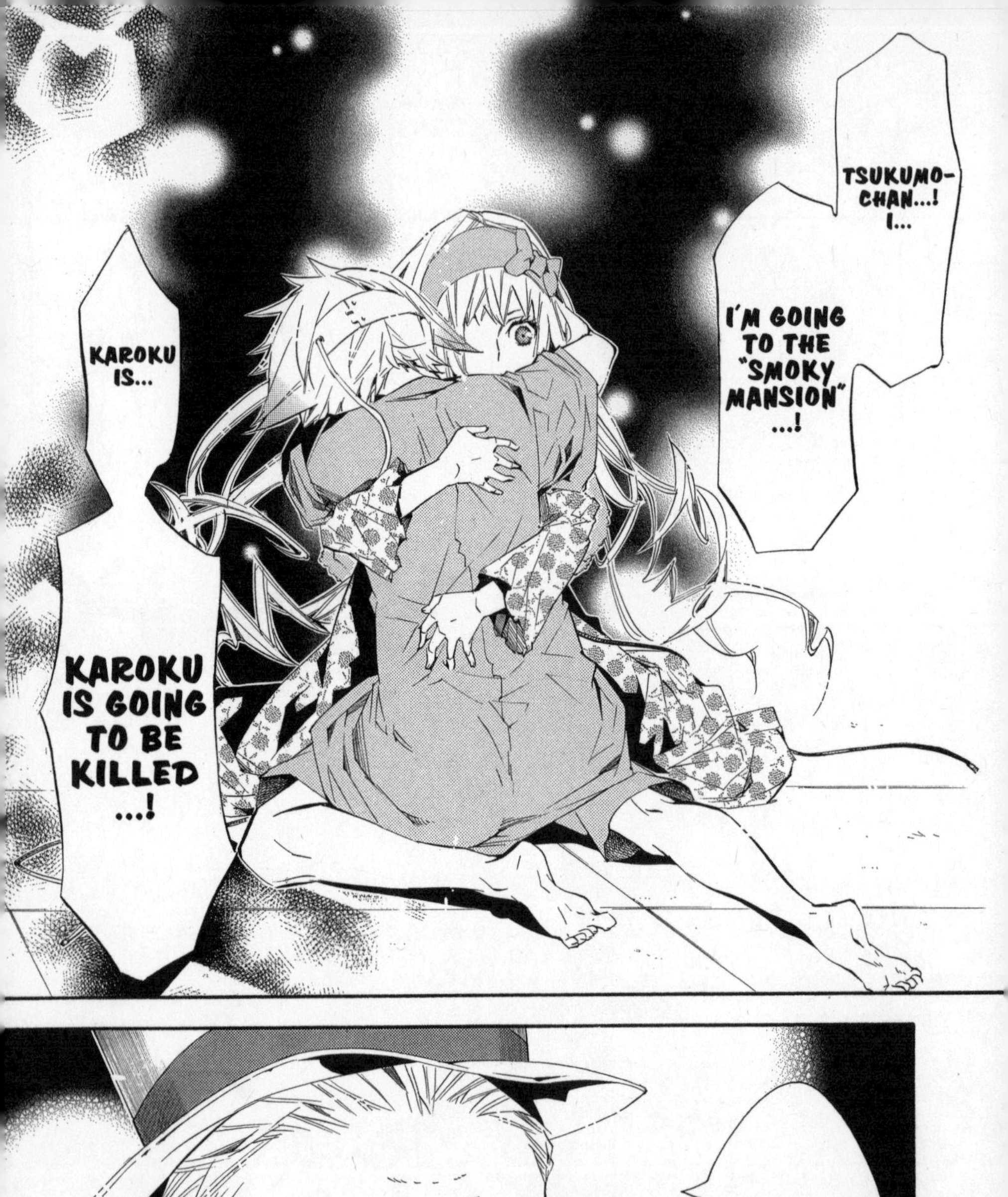
TSUKUMO-CHAN...! I...
I'M GOING TO THE "SMOKY MANSION" ...!
KAROKU IS...
KAROKU IS GOING TO BE KILLED ...!

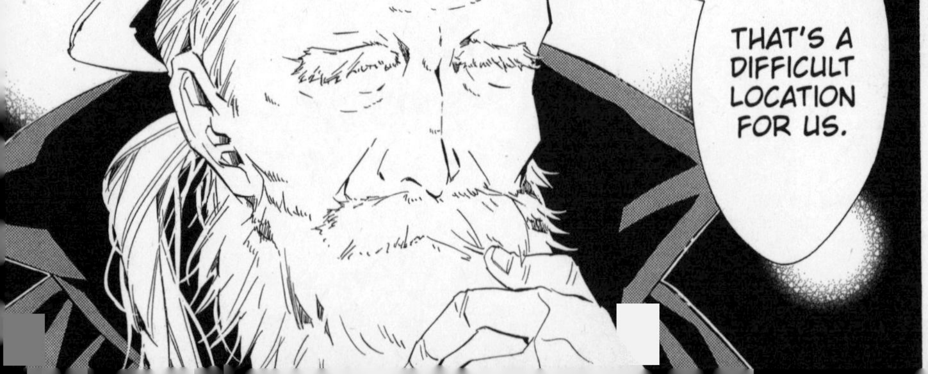
THAT'S A DIFFICULT LOCATION FOR US.

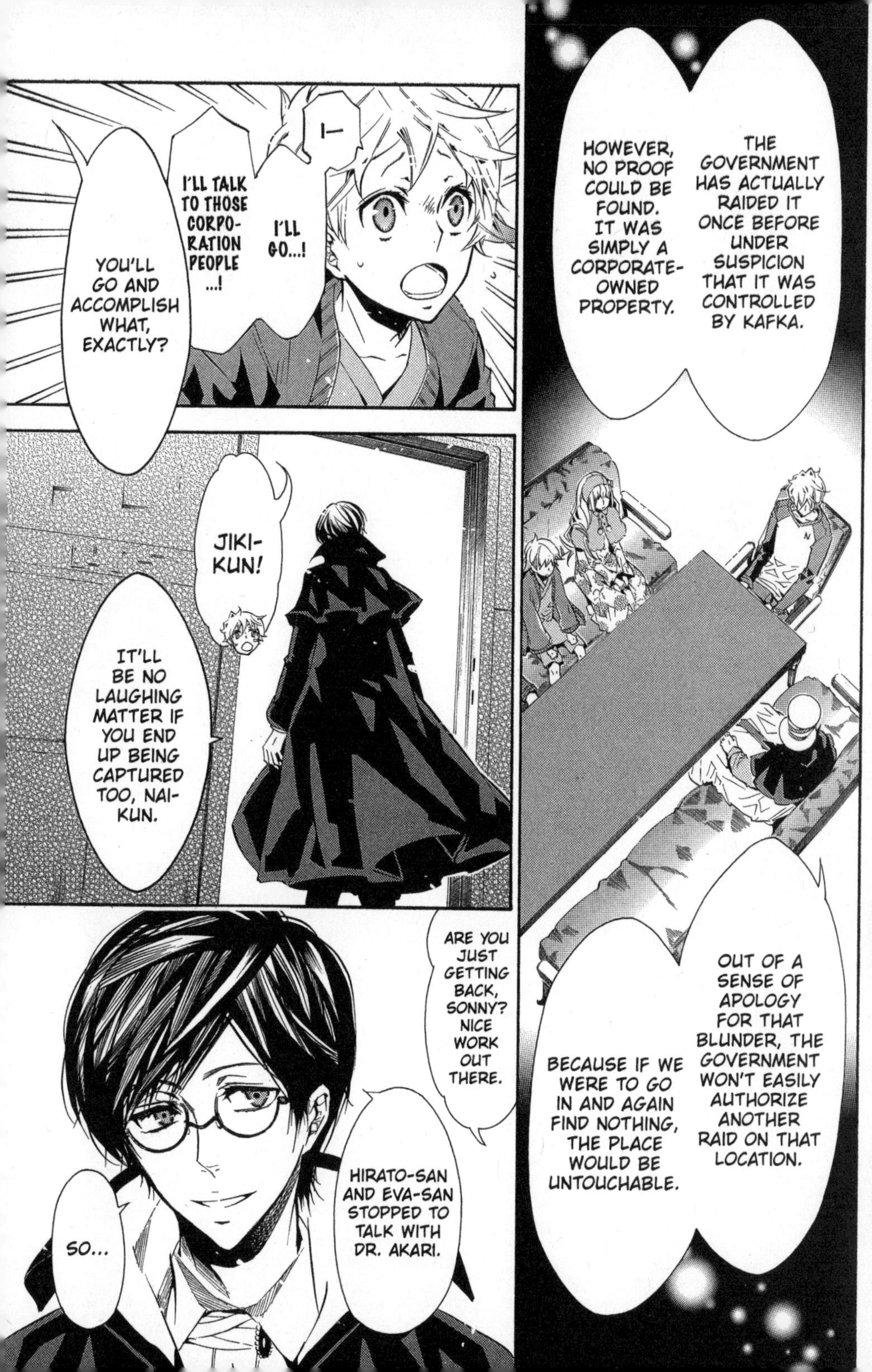
THE GOVERNMENT HAS ACTUALLY RAIDED IT ONCE BEFORE UNDER SUSPICION THAT IT WAS CONTROLLED BY KAFKA.
HOWEVER, NO PROOF COULD BE FOUND. IT WAS SIMPLY A CORPORATE-OWNED PROPERTY.
OUT OF A SENSE OF APOLOGY FOR THAT BLUNDER, THE GOVERNMENT WON'T EASILY AUTHORIZE ANOTHER RAID ON THAT LOCATION.
BECAUSE IF WE WERE TO GO IN AND AGAIN FIND NOTHING, THE PLACE WOULD BE UNTOUCHABLE.
I—
I'LL GO...!
I'LL TALK TO THOSE CORPO-RATION PEOPLE ...!
YOU'LL GO AND ACCOMPLISH WHAT, EXACTLY?
JIKI-KUN!
IT'LL BE NO LAUGHING MATTER IF YOU END UP BEING CAPTURED TOO, NAI-KUN.
ARE YOU JUST GETTING BACK, SONNY? NICE WORK OUT THERE.
HIRATO-SAN AND EVA-SAN STOPPED TO TALK WITH DR. AKARI.
SO...

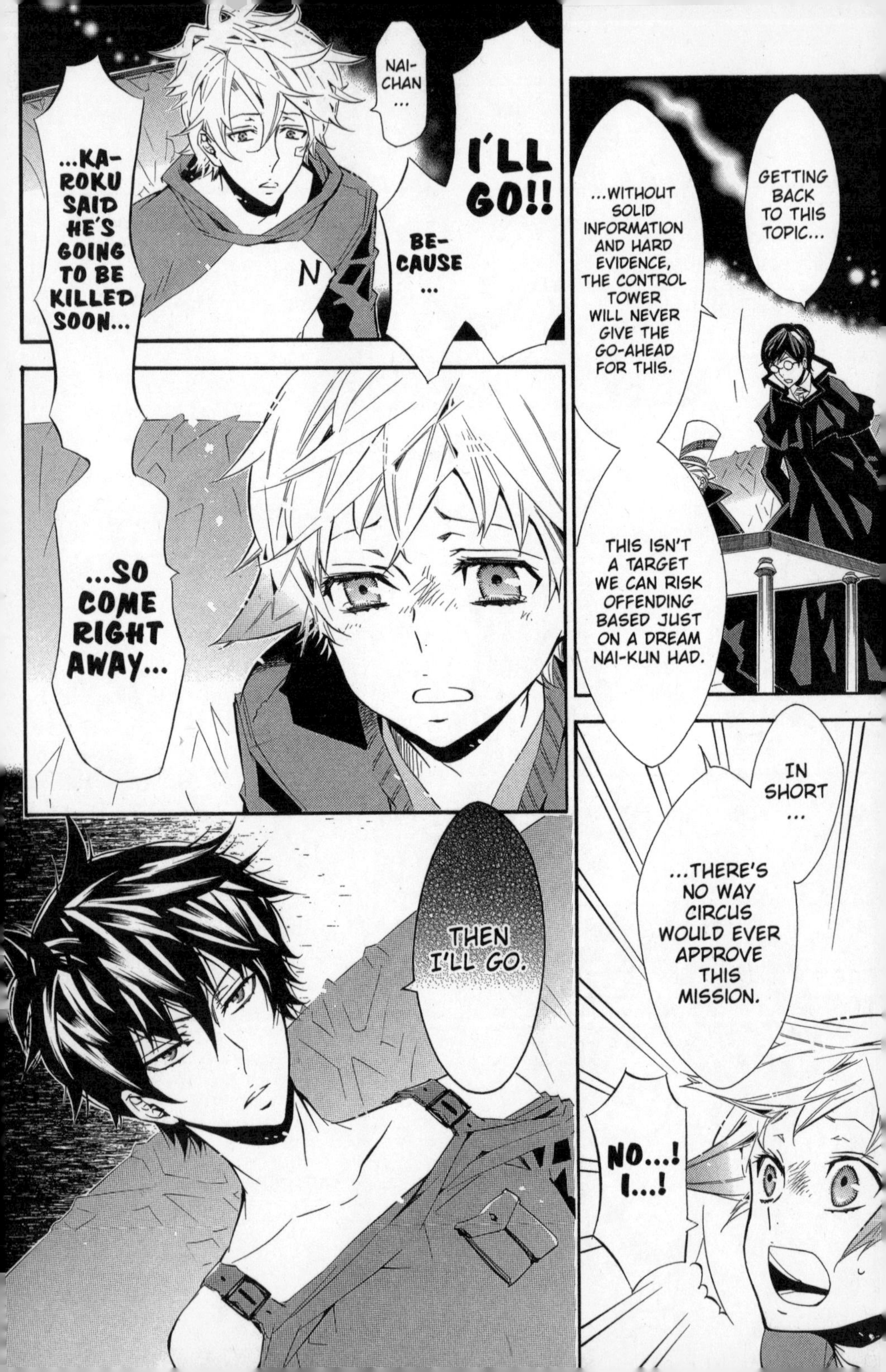
GETTING BACK TO THIS TOPIC...
...WITHOUT SOLID INFORMATION AND HARD EVIDENCE, THE CONTROL TOWER WILL NEVER GIVE THE GO-AHEAD FOR THIS.
THIS ISN'T A TARGET WE CAN RISK OFFENDING BASED JUST ON A DREAM NAI-KUN HAD.
IN SHORT...
...THERE'S NO WAY CIRCUS WOULD EVER APPROVE THIS MISSION.
NO...! I...!
NAI-CHAN...
I'LL GO!!
BE-CAUSE...
...KA-ROKU SAID HE'S GOING TO BE KILLED SOON...
...SO COME RIGHT AWAY...
THEN I'LL GO.

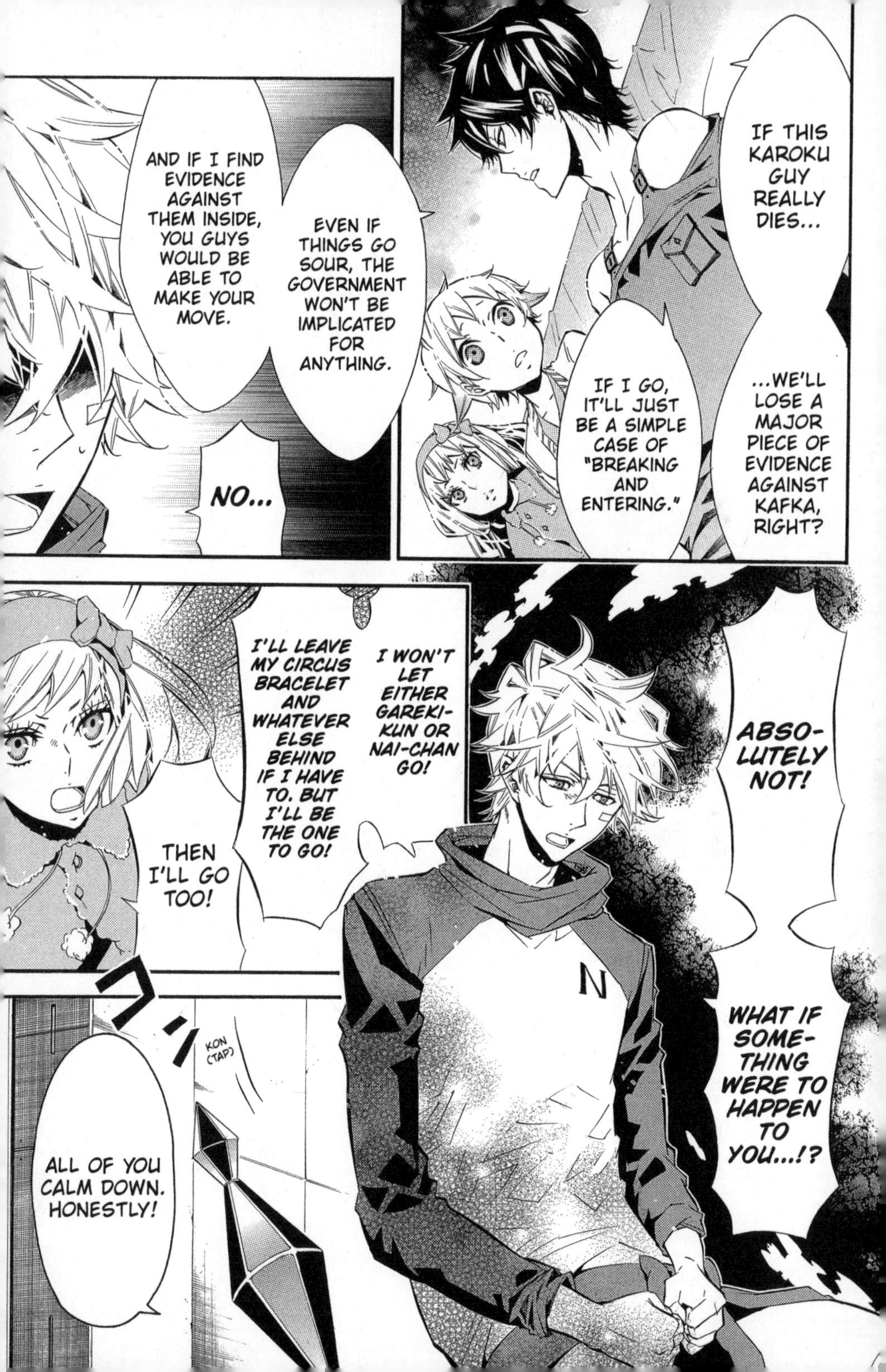
IF THIS KAROKU GUY REALLY DIES...
...WE'LL LOSE A MAJOR PIECE OF EVIDENCE AGAINST KAFKA, RIGHT?
IF I GO, IT'LL JUST BE A SIMPLE CASE OF "BREAKING AND ENTERING."
EVEN IF THINGS GO SOUR, THE GOVERNMENT WON'T BE IMPLICATED FOR ANYTHING.
AND IF I FIND EVIDENCE AGAINST THEM INSIDE, YOU GUYS WOULD BE ABLE TO MAKE YOUR MOVE.
NO...
ABSO-LUTELY NOT!
WHAT IF SOME-THING WERE TO HAPPEN TO YOU...!?
I WON'T LET EITHER GAREKI-KUN OR NAI-CHAN GO!
I'LL LEAVE MY CIRCUS BRACELET AND WHATEVER ELSE BEHIND IF I HAVE TO. BUT I'LL BE THE ONE TO GO!
THEN I'LL GO TOO!
KON (TAP)
ALL OF YOU CALM DOWN. HONESTLY!

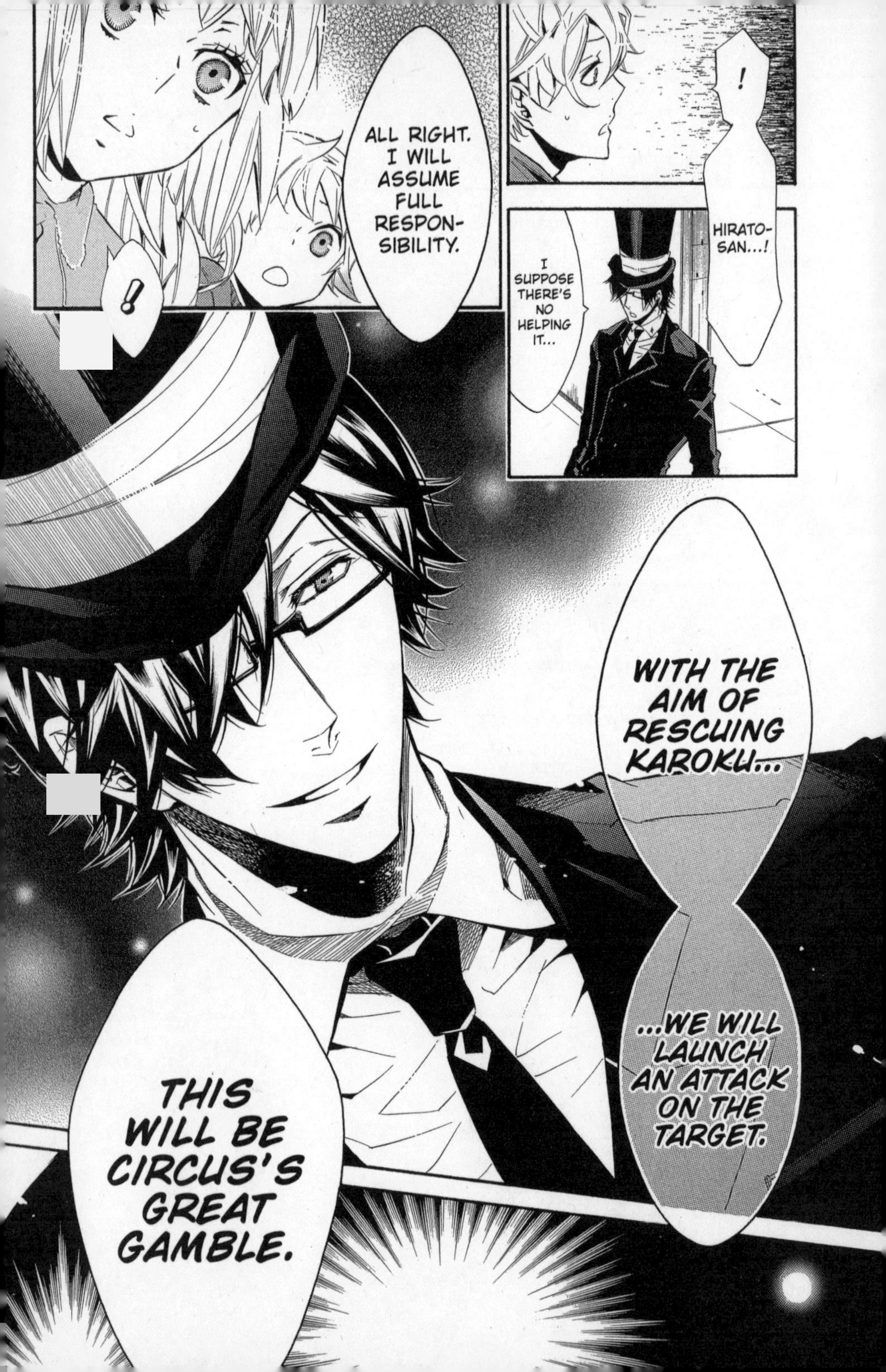
!
HIRATO-SAN...!
I SUPPOSE THERE'S NO HELPING IT...
ALL RIGHT. I WILL ASSUME FULL RESPON-SIBILITY.
!
WITH THE AIM OF RESCUING KAROKU...
...WE WILL LAUNCH AN ATTACK ON THE TARGET.
THIS WILL BE CIRCUS'S GREAT GAMBLE.

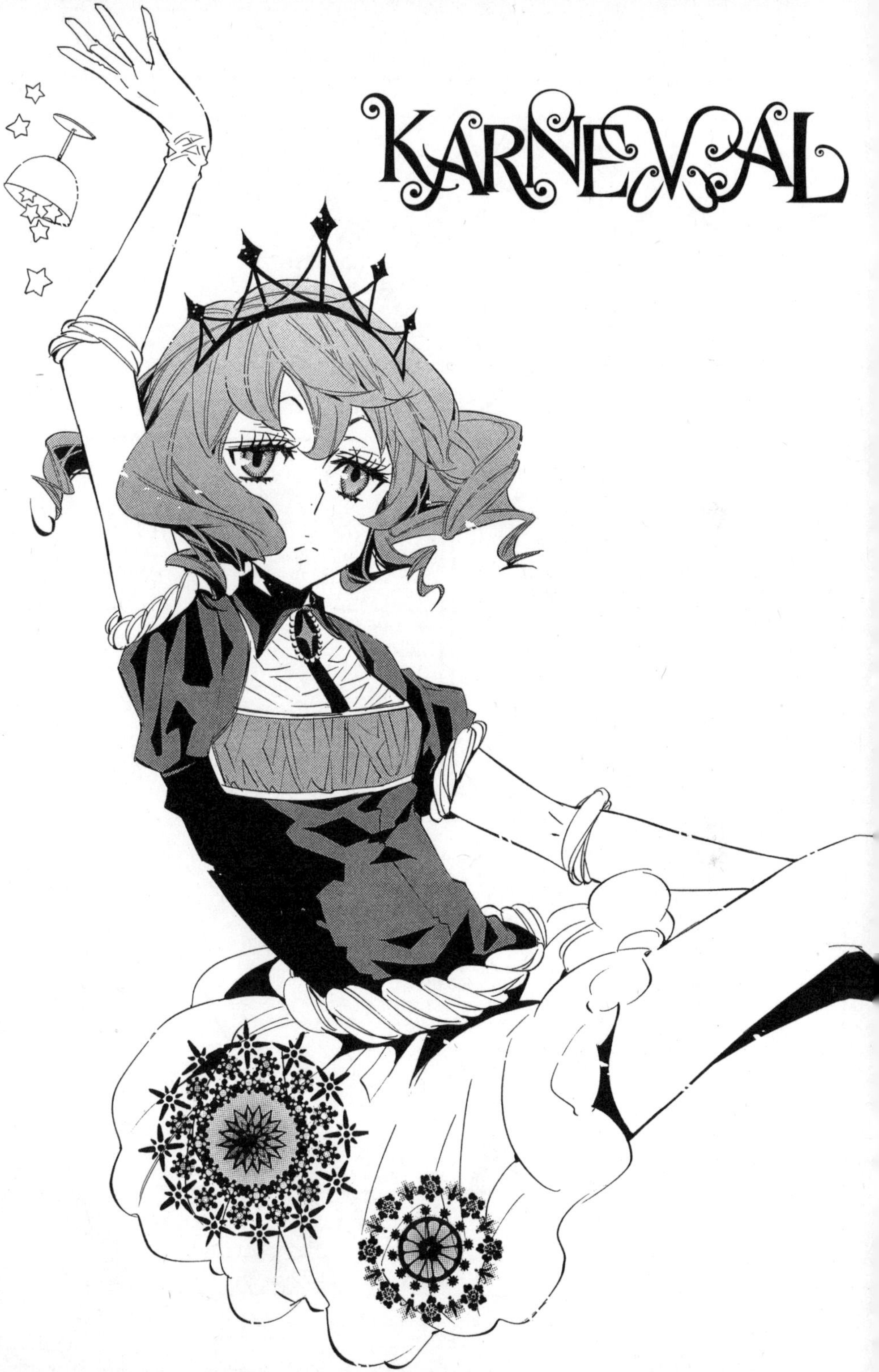
KARNEVAL

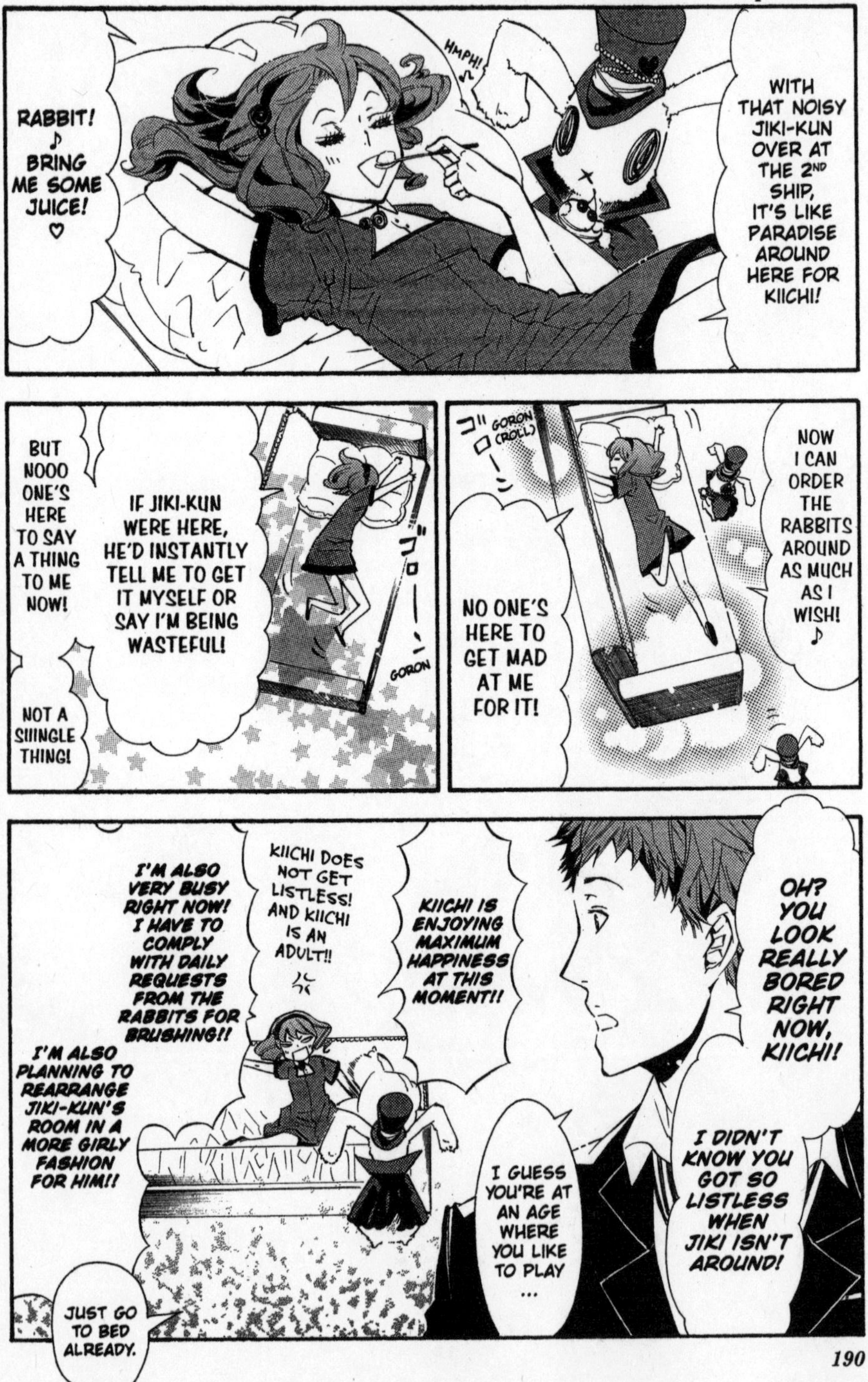
WITH THAT NOISY JIKI-KUN OVER AT THE 2ND SHIP, IT'S LIKE PARADISE AROUND HERE FOR KIICHI!
HMPH! ♪
RABBIT! ♪ BRING ME SOME JUICE! ♡
NOW I CAN ORDER THE RABBITS AROUND AS MUCH AS I WISH! ♪
GORON (ROLL)
NO ONE'S HERE TO GET MAD AT ME FOR IT!
IF JIKI-KUN WERE HERE, HE'D INSTANTLY TELL ME TO GET IT MYSELF OR SAY I'M BEING WASTEFUL!
GORON
BUT NOOO ONE'S HERE TO SAY A THING TO ME NOW!
NOT A SIIINGLE THING!
OH? YOU LOOK REALLY BORED RIGHT NOW, KIICHI!
I DIDN'T KNOW YOU GOT SO LISTLESS WHEN JIKI ISN'T AROUND!
I GUESS YOU'RE AT AN AGE WHERE YOU LIKE TO PLAY ...
KIICHI IS ENJOYING MAXIMUM HAPPINESS AT THIS MOMENT!!
KIICHI DOES NOT GET LISTLESS! AND KIICHI IS AN ADULT!!
I'M ALSO VERY BUSY RIGHT NOW! I HAVE TO COMPLY WITH DAILY REQUESTS FROM THE RABBITS FOR BRUSHING!!
I'M ALSO PLANNING TO REARRANGE JIKI-KUN'S ROOM IN A MORE GIRLY FASHION FOR HIM!!
JUST GO TO BED ALREADY.

Bonus Comic 2 - And Yet, Something Was Conveyed.

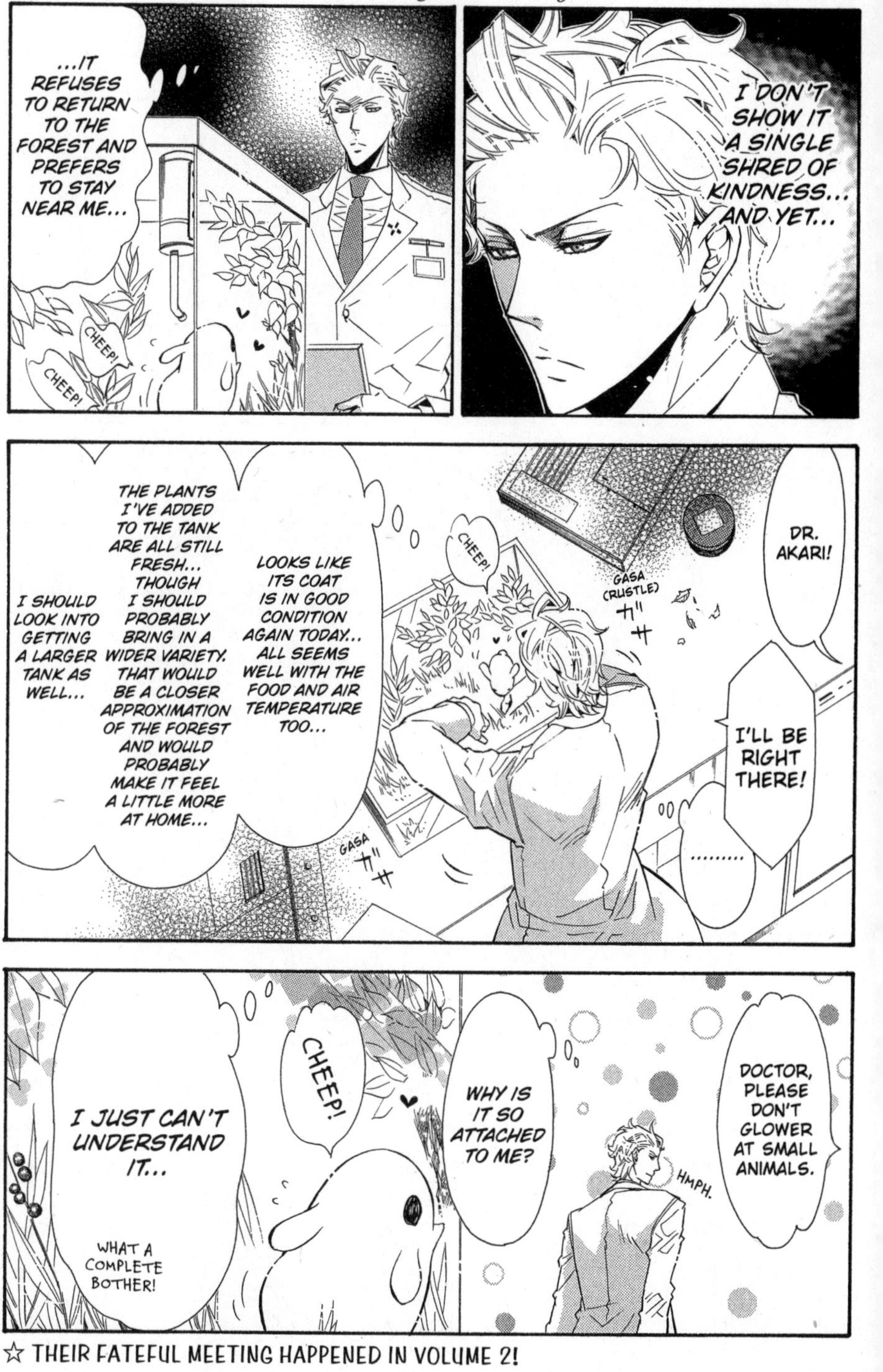
I DON'T SHOW IT A SINGLE SHRED OF KINDNESS... AND YET...
...IT REFUSES TO RETURN TO THE FOREST AND PREFERS TO STAY NEAR ME...
CHEEP!
CHEEP!
DR. AKARI!
I'LL BE RIGHT THERE!
....
GASA (RUSTLE)
CHEEP!
LOOKS LIKE ITS COAT IS IN GOOD CONDITION AGAIN TODAY... ALL SEEMS WELL WITH THE FOOD AND AIR TEMPERATURE TOO...
THE PLANTS I'VE ADDED TO THE TANK ARE ALL STILL FRESH... THOUGH I SHOULD PROBABLY BRING IN A WIDER VARIETY. THAT WOULD BE A CLOSER APPROXIMATION OF THE FOREST AND WOULD PROBABLY MAKE IT FEEL A LITTLE MORE AT HOME...
I SHOULD LOOK INTO GETTING A LARGER TANK AS WELL...
GASA
DOCTOR, PLEASE DON'T GLOWER AT SMALL ANIMALS.
HMPH.
WHY IS IT SO ATTACHED TO ME?
CHEEP!
I JUST CAN'T UNDERSTAND IT...
WHAT A COMPLETE BOTHER!

☆ THEIR FATEFUL MEETING HAPPENED IN VOLUME 2!

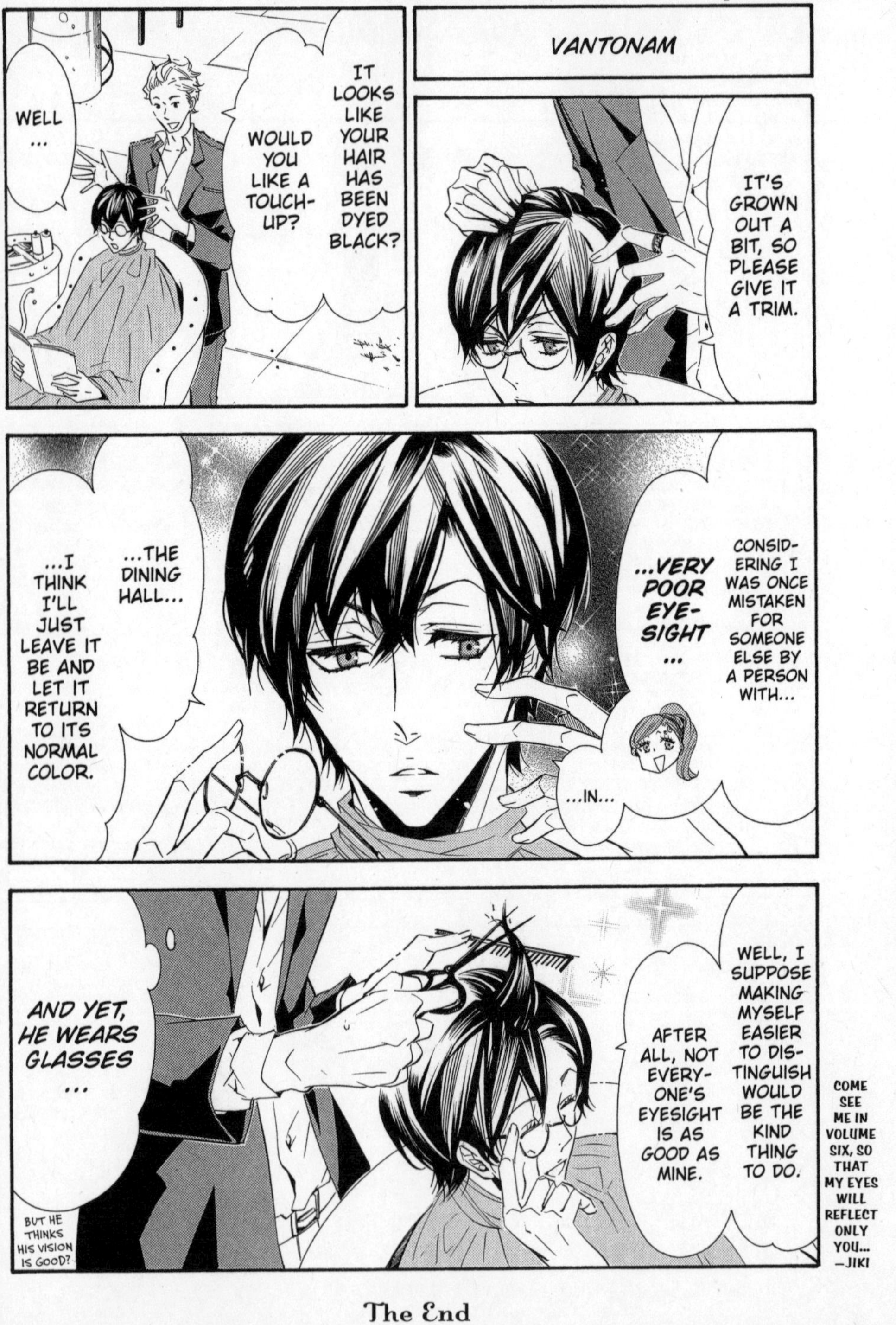
VANTONAM
IT'S GROWN OUT A BIT, SO PLEASE GIVE IT A TRIM.
IT LOOKS LIKE YOUR HAIR HAS BEEN DYED BLACK?
WOULD YOU LIKE A TOUCH-UP?
WELL...
CONSID-ERING I WAS ONCE MISTAKEN FOR SOMEONE ELSE BY A PERSON WITH...
...VERY POOR EYE-SIGHT...
...IN...
...THE DINING HALL...
...I THINK I'LL JUST LEAVE IT BE AND LET IT RETURN TO ITS NORMAL COLOR.
WELL, I SUPPOSE MAKING MYSELF EASIER TO DIS-TINGUISH WOULD BE THE KIND THING TO DO.
AFTER ALL, NOT EVERY-ONE'S EYESIGHT IS AS GOOD AS MINE.
AND YET, HE WEARS GLASSES...
BUT HE THINKS HIS VISION IS GOOD?
COME SEE ME IN VOLUME SIX, SO THAT MY EYES WILL REFLECT ONLY YOU... —JIKI

The End

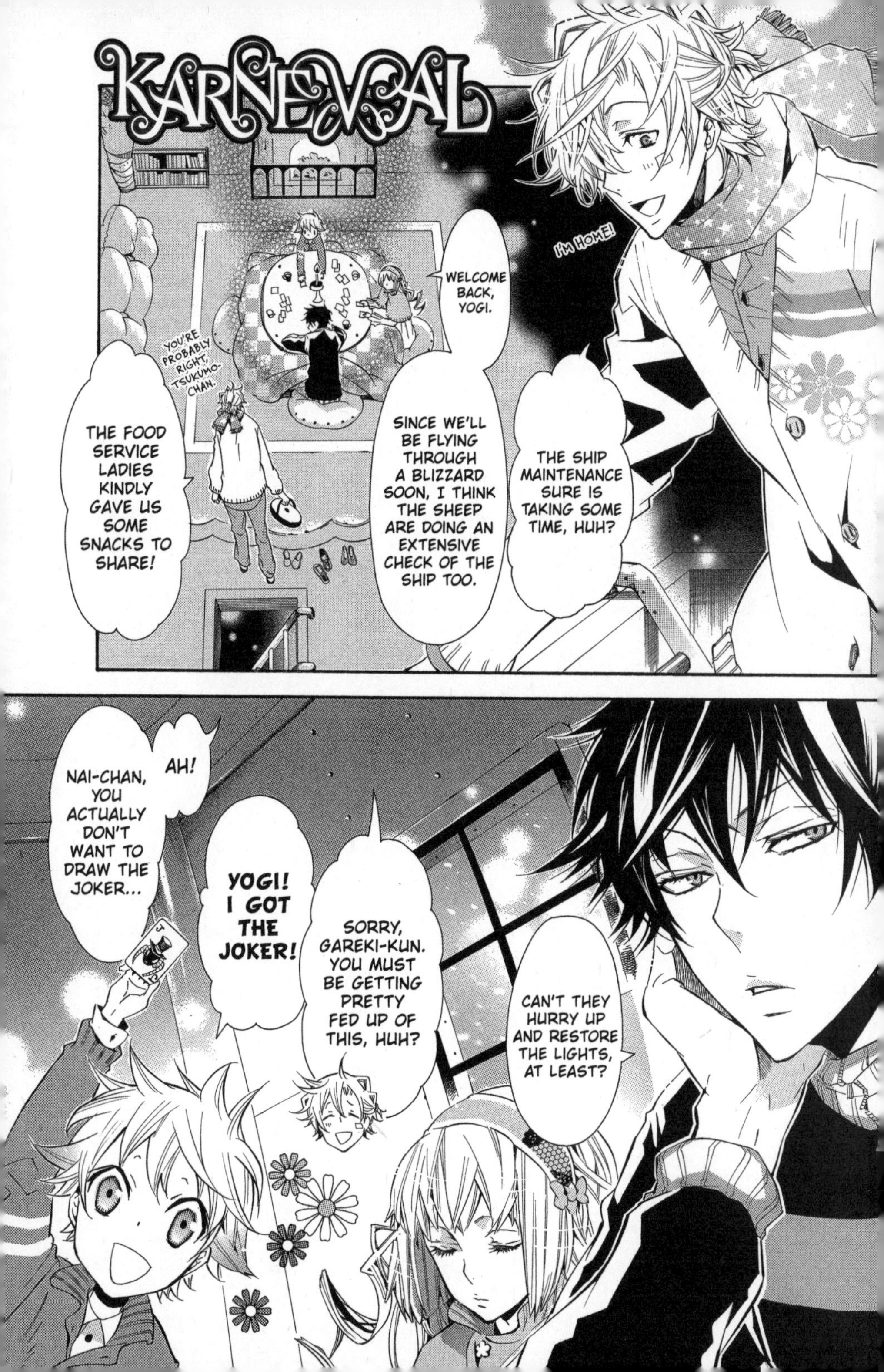
KARNEVAL
I'M HOME!
WELCOME BACK, YOGI.
THE SHIP MAINTENANCE SURE IS TAKING SOME TIME, HUH?
SINCE WE'LL BE FLYING THROUGH A BLIZZARD SOON, I THINK THE SHEEP ARE DOING AN EXTENSIVE CHECK OF THE SHIP TOO.
YOU'RE PROBABLY RIGHT, TSUKUMO-CHAN.
THE FOOD SERVICE LADIES KINDLY GAVE US SOME SNACKS TO SHARE!
CAN'T THEY HURRY UP AND RESTORE THE LIGHTS, AT LEAST?
SORRY, GAREKI-KUN. YOU MUST BE GETTING PRETTY FED UP OF THIS, HUH?
YOGI! I GOT THE JOKER!
AH!
NAI-CHAN, YOU ACTUALLY DON'T WANT TO DRAW THE JOKER...

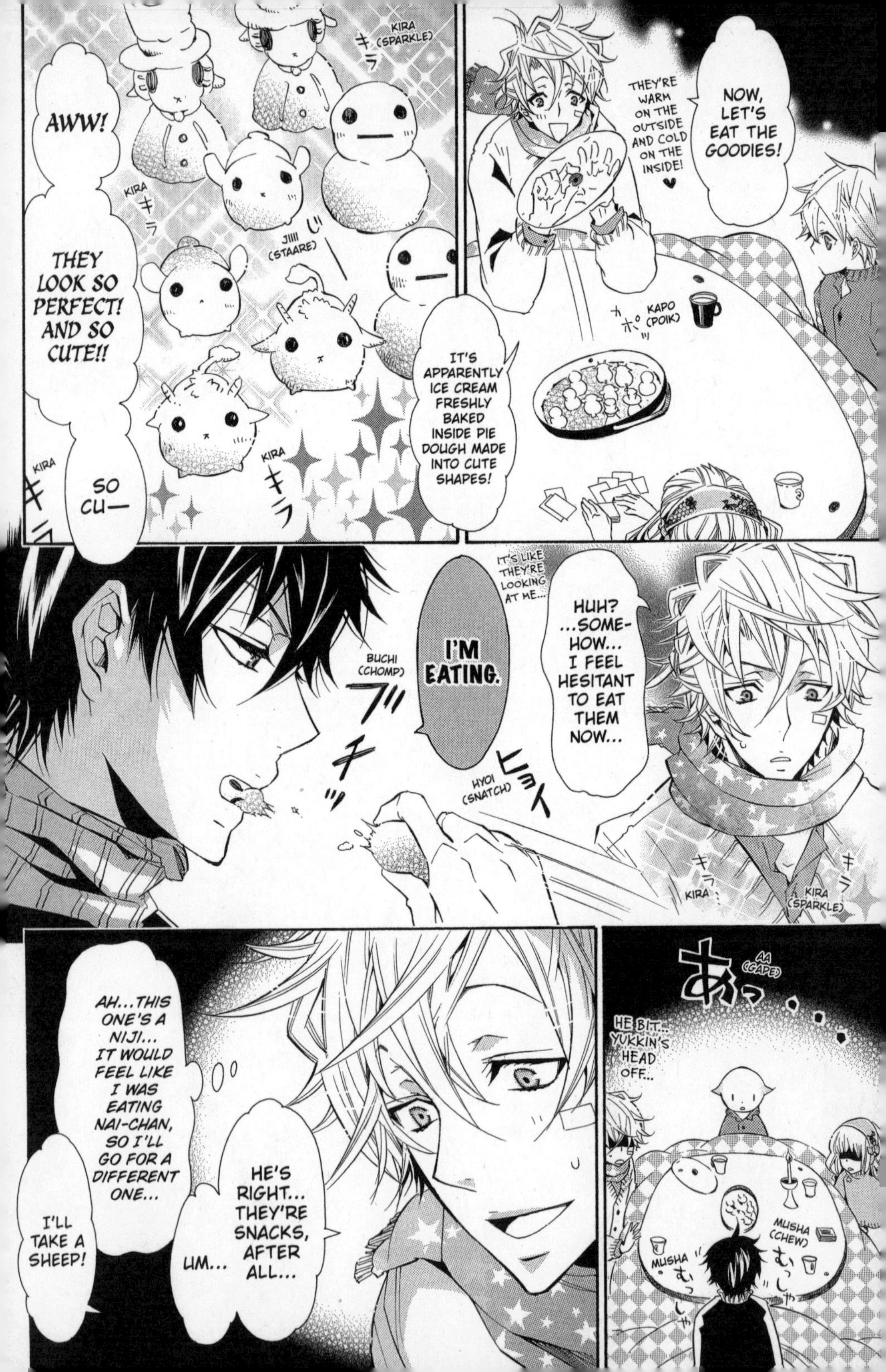
NOW, LET'S EAT THE GOODIES!
THEY'RE WARM ON THE OUTSIDE AND COLD ON THE INSIDE!
KAPO (POIK)
IT'S APPARENTLY ICE CREAM FRESHLY BAKED INSIDE PIE DOUGH MADE INTO CUTE SHAPES!
KIRA (SPARKLE)
AWW!
KIRA
JIIII (STAARE)
THEY LOOK SO PERFECT! AND SO CUTE!!
KIRA
KIRA
SO CU—
IT'S LIKE THEY'RE LOOKING AT ME...
HUH? ...SOMEHOW... I FEEL HESITANT TO EAT THEM NOW...
KIRA (SPARKLE)
KIRA
HYOI (SNATCH)
I'M EATING.
BUCHI (CHOMP)
AA (GAPE)
HE BIT... YUKKIN'S HEAD OFF...
MUSHA (CHEW)
MUSHA
HE'S RIGHT... THEY'RE SNACKS, AFTER ALL...
UM...
AH...THIS ONE'S A NIJI... IT WOULD FEEL LIKE I WAS EATING NAI-CHAN, SO I'LL GO FOR A DIFFERENT ONE...
I'LL TAKE A SHEEP!

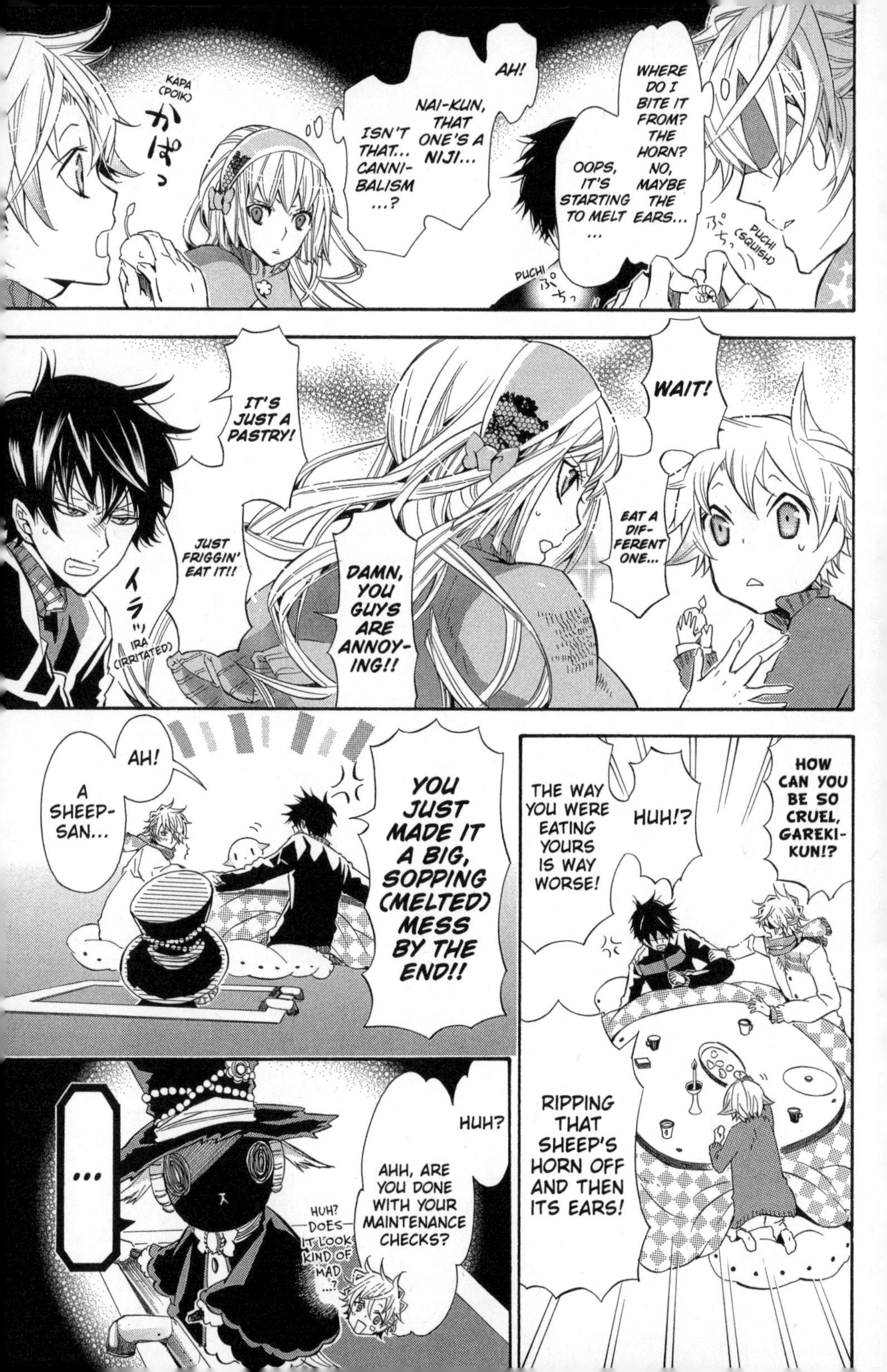
WHERE DO I BITE IT FROM? THE HORN? NO, MAYBE THE EARS...
PUCHI (SQUISH)
ぷちっ
OOPS, IT'S STARTING TO MELT...
PUCHI
ぷちっ
AH!
NAI-KUN, THAT ONE'S A NIJI...
ISN'T THAT... CANNIBALISM...?
KAPA (POIK)
かぽっ
WAIT!
EAT A DIFFERENT ONE...
DAMN, YOU GUYS ARE ANNOYING!!
IT'S JUST A PASTRY!
JUST FRIGGIN' EAT IT!!
イラッ
IRA (IRRITATED)
HOW CAN YOU BE SO CRUEL, GAREKI-KUN!?
HUH!?
THE WAY YOU WERE EATING YOURS IS WAY WORSE!
RIPPING THAT SHEEP'S HORN OFF AND THEN ITS EARS!
YOU JUST MADE IT A BIG, SOPPING (MELTED) MESS BY THE END!!
AH!
A SHEEP-SAN...
HUH?
AHH, ARE YOU DONE WITH YOUR MAINTENANCE CHECKS?
HUH? DOES IT LOOK KIND OF MAD...?
...

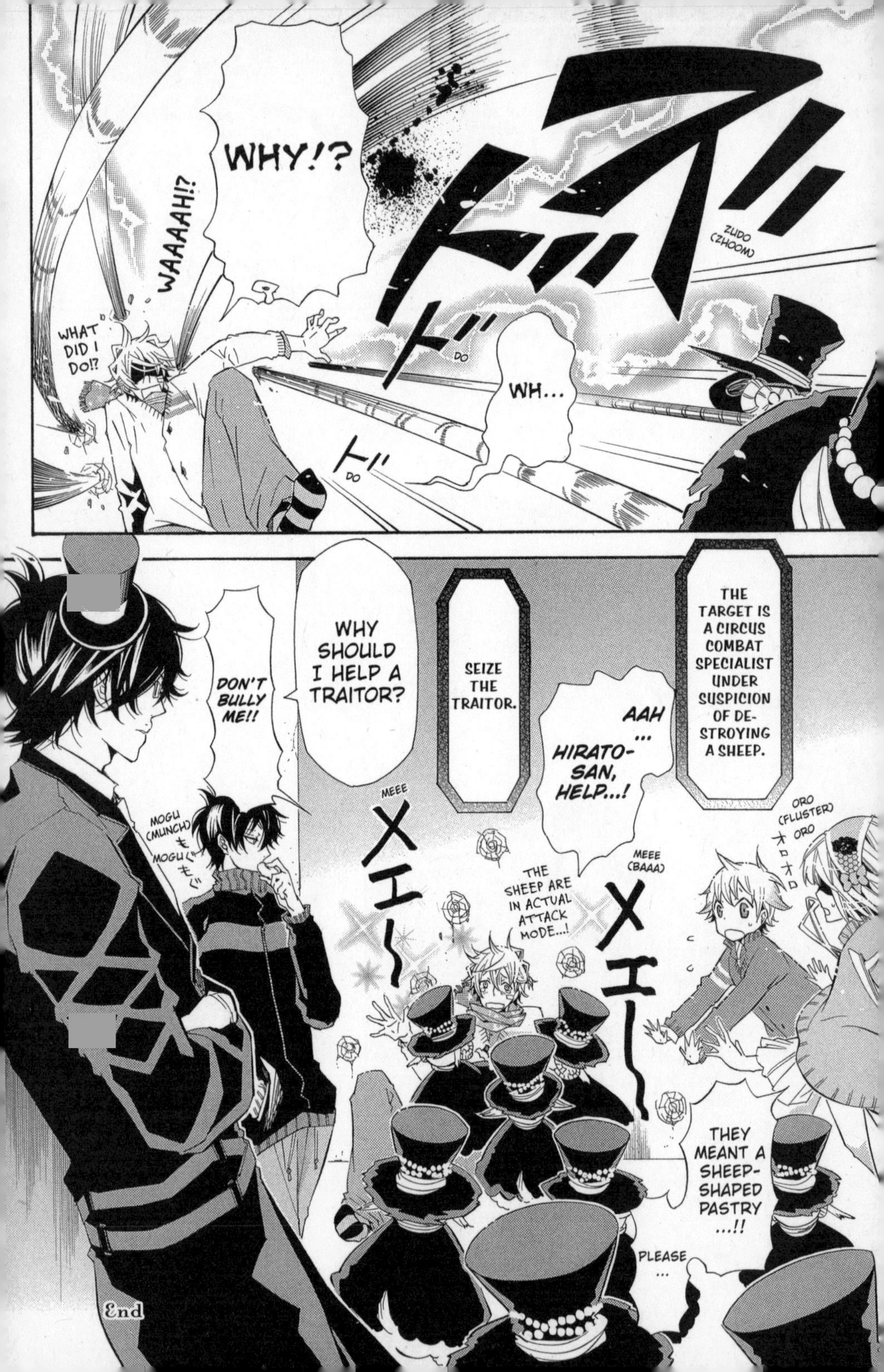
ZUDO (ZHOOM)
DO
DO
WH...
WHY!?
WAAAAH!?
WHAT DID I DO!?
THE TARGET IS A CIRCUS COMBAT SPECIALIST UNDER SUSPICION OF DE-STROYING A SHEEP.
SEIZE THE TRAITOR.
AAH ... HIRATO-SAN, HELP...!
WHY SHOULD I HELP A TRAITOR?
DON'T BULLY ME!!
ORO (FLUSTER) ORO
オロオロ
MEEE (BAAA)
メェ～
THE SHEEP ARE IN ACTUAL ATTACK MODE...!
MEEE
メェ～
MOGU (MUNCH) MOGU
もぐもぐ
THEY MEANT A SHEEP-SHAPED PASTRY ...!!
PLEASE ...
End

THANK YOU VERY MUCH FOR READING *KARNEVAL*! I'M SO HAPPY I WAS ABLE TO MAKE IT ALL THE WAY TO VOLUME 5. I HOPE THAT FROM HERE ON, I CAN POWER UP MY MANGA AND DRAW IT IN A WAY THAT WILL MAKE YOU ALL WANT TO LOVE IT MORE AND MORE! PLEASE CHEER ME ON.

SINCE I INCLUDED CHARACTER PROFILES FOR NAI AND EVERYONE IN VOLUMES 3 AND 4, I'VE STARTED GETTING BIRTHDAY CARDS AND LETTERS FOR THE CHARACTERS FROM FANS. ON VALENTINE'S DAY TOO, I RECEIVED LOVE LETTERS FOR YOGI AND EVERYONE. THANK YOU SO MUCH FOR THOSE! I FELT SO GRATEFUL AS I READ THEM AND THOUGHT, HOW LUCKY THE BOYS ARE TO HAVE ALL YOUR FEELINGS! I ALWAYS GET SO MUCH ENCOURAGEMENT FROM YOU ALL.

SHORTLY BEFORE THIS VOLUME GOES ON SALE IN FEBRUARY, THE 1/28 ISSUE OF ZERO-SUM MAGAZINE WILL GO ON SALE AND FEATURE *KARNEVAL* COVER ART FOR THE FIRST TIME! I WAS SO HAPPY TO GET THAT. I DISCUSSED IT WITH MY EDITOR, AND WE DECIDED TO GO WITH A VERY "THIS IS QUINTESSENTIAL COVER ART!" KIND OF ILLUSTRATION FOR IT. ❀

ALSO, ON THE SAME DAY VOLUME 5 IS GOING ON SALE, WE'RE ALSO RELEASING THE SECOND *KARNEVAL* DRAMA CD, TITLED *KARNEVAL CIRCUS*. THIS TIME, WE'RE RELEASING THROUGH FRONTIER WORKS. I DREW THE COVER ILLUSTRATION AND WROTE THE ORIGINAL SHORT STORY FOR THE DRAMA, SO PLEASE BUY IT AND GIVE IT A LISTEN. THE CAST'S PERFORMANCES WERE SO RICH AND EMOTIONALLY NUANCED THAT I ACTUALLY DISCOVERED A LOT OF NEW FACETS OF FEELING IN NAI, GAREKI, AND THE OTHERS. AND BECAUSE MANY OF YOU WROTE IN AND SAID YOU WANTED TO HEAR IT, WE INCLUDED YOGI'S FAMOUS SPIEL AS WELL!

TOUYA MIKANAGI

Special thanks

- TEN-CHAN & KAZUMI-SAN
- JUN-SAN & MIN-SAN
- MY EDITOR, ABE-SAN

- EVERYONE WHO'S TAKEN CARE OF ME
- MY FAMILY

To You!

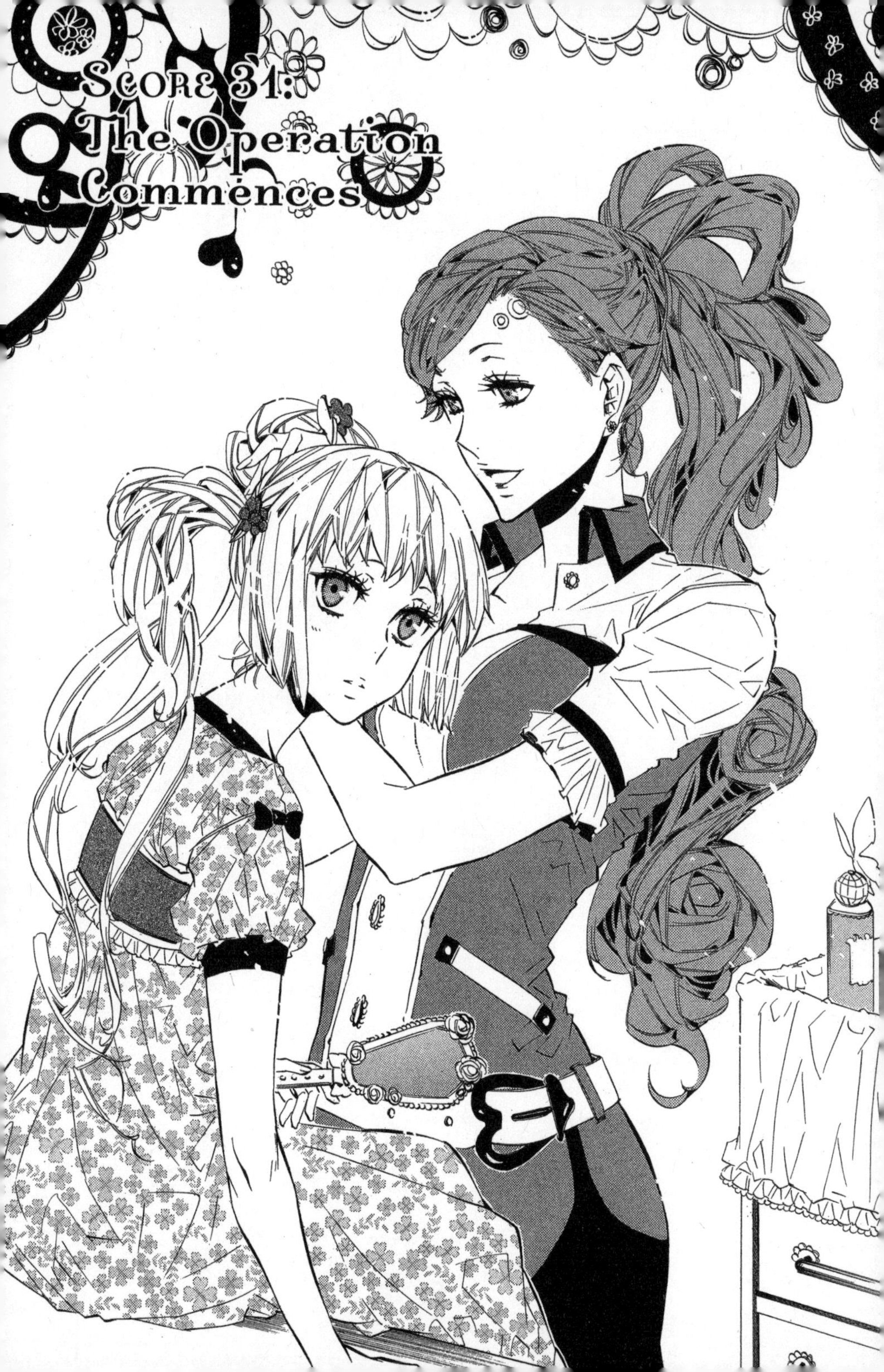
Score 31:
The Operation Commences

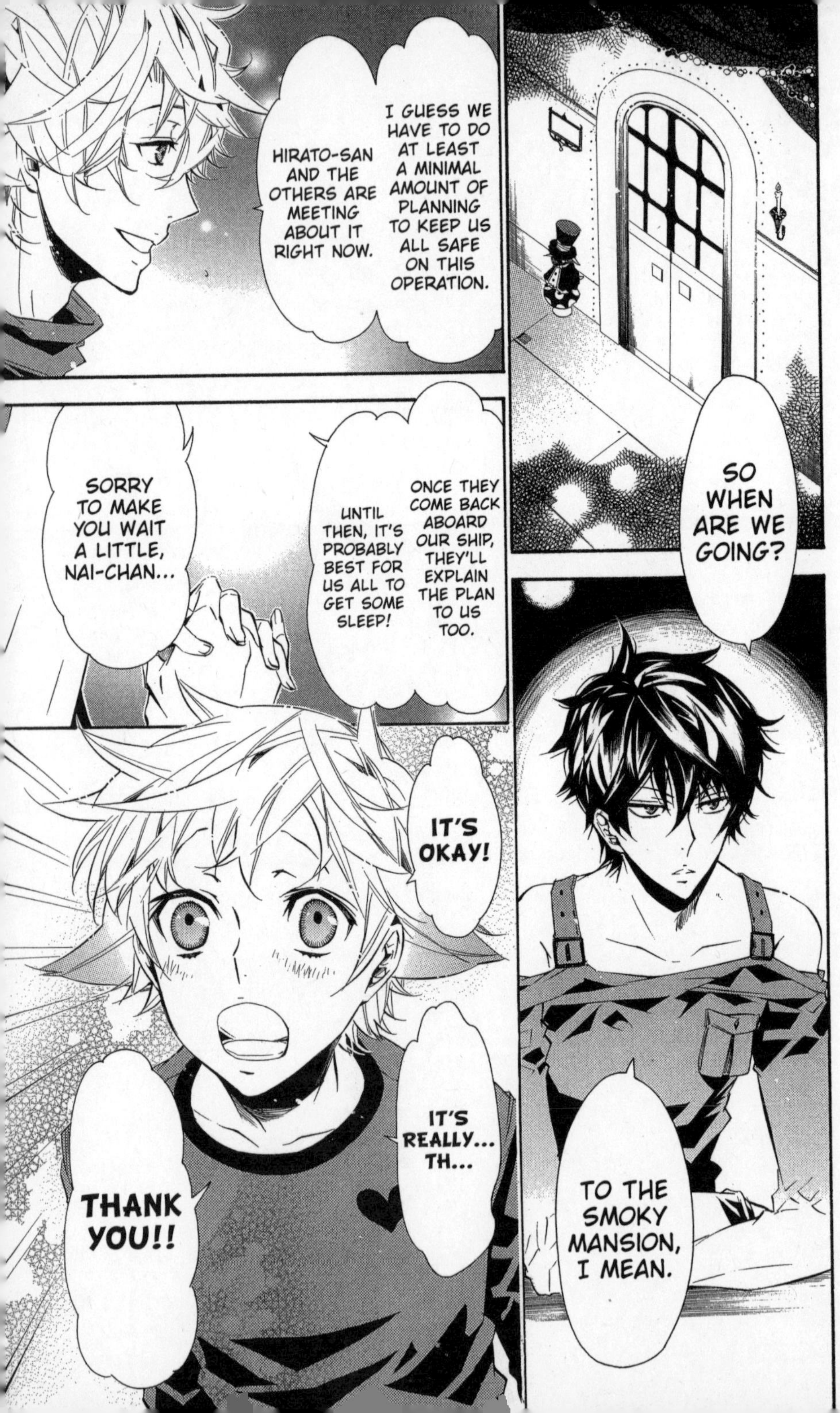
SO WHEN ARE WE GOING?
TO THE SMOKY MANSION, I MEAN.
I GUESS WE HAVE TO DO AT LEAST A MINIMAL AMOUNT OF PLANNING TO KEEP US ALL SAFE ON THIS OPERATION.
HIRATO-SAN AND THE OTHERS ARE MEETING ABOUT IT RIGHT NOW.
ONCE THEY COME BACK ABOARD OUR SHIP, THEY'LL EXPLAIN THE PLAN TO US TOO.
UNTIL THEN, IT'S PROBABLY BEST FOR US ALL TO GET SOME SLEEP!
SORRY TO MAKE YOU WAIT A LITTLE, NAI-CHAN...
IT'S OKAY!
IT'S REALLY... TH...
THANK YOU!!

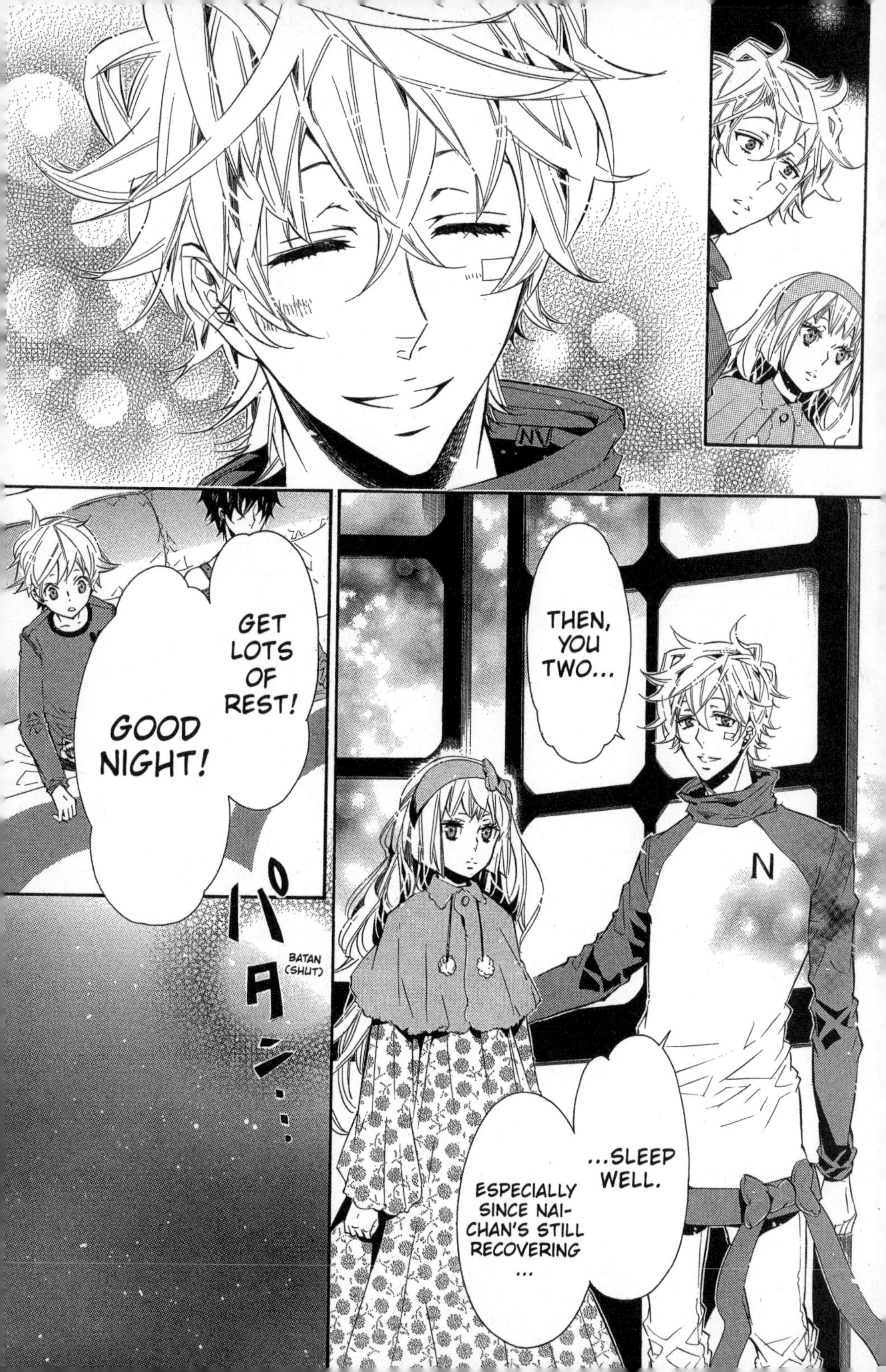
THEN, YOU TWO...
...SLEEP WELL.
ESPECIALLY SINCE NAI-CHAN'S STILL RECOVERING...
GET LOTS OF REST!
GOOD NIGHT!
パタン…
BATAN (SHUT)

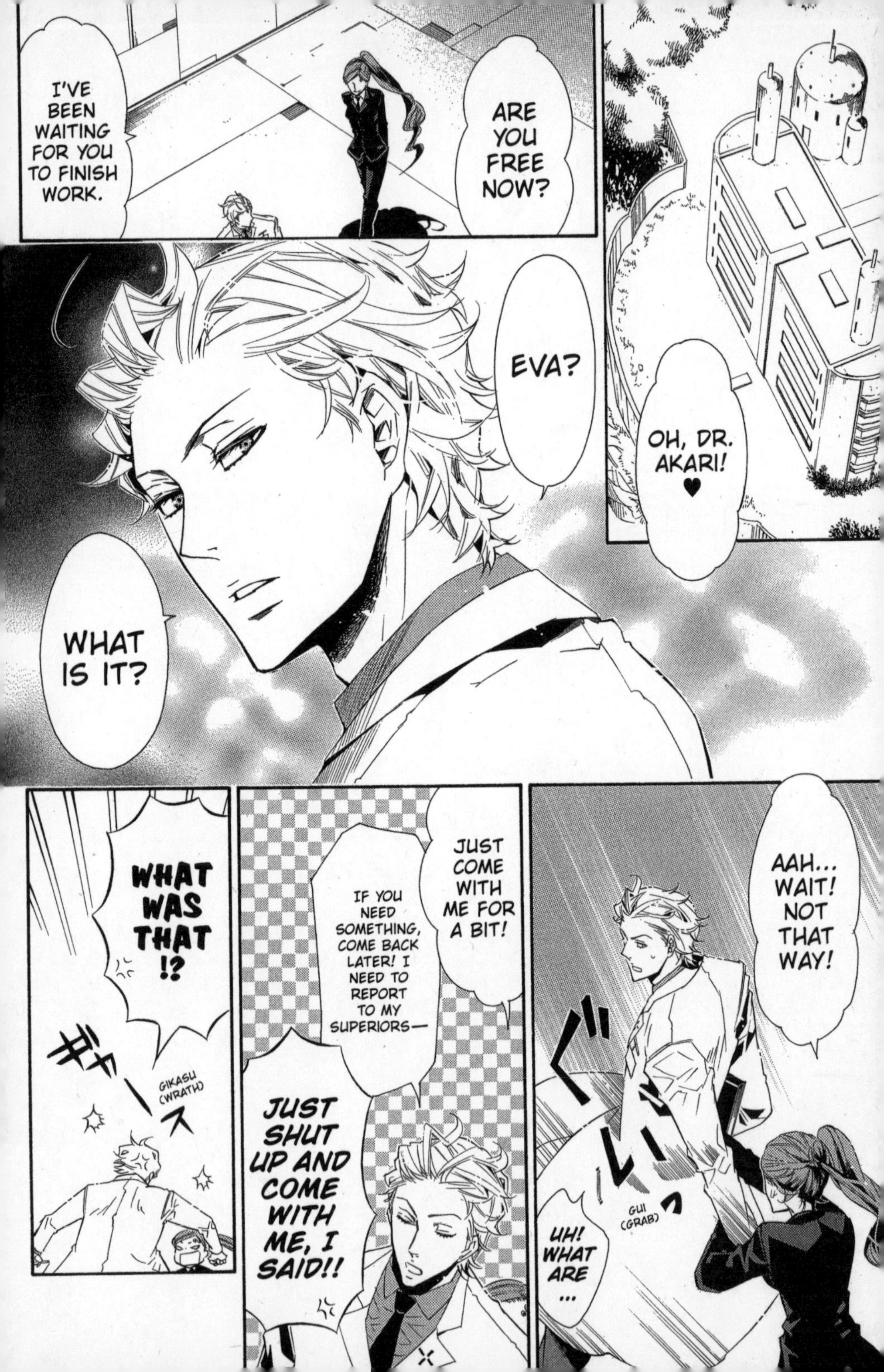
OH, DR. AKARI! ♥
ARE YOU FREE NOW?
I'VE BEEN WAITING FOR YOU TO FINISH WORK.
EVA?
WHAT IS IT?
AAH... WAIT! NOT THAT WAY!
GUI (GRAB)
UH! WHAT ARE ...
JUST COME WITH ME FOR A BIT!
IF YOU NEED SOMETHING, COME BACK LATER! I NEED TO REPORT TO MY SUPERIORS—
JUST SHUT UP AND COME WITH ME, I SAID!!
WHAT WAS THAT!?
GIKASU (WRATH)

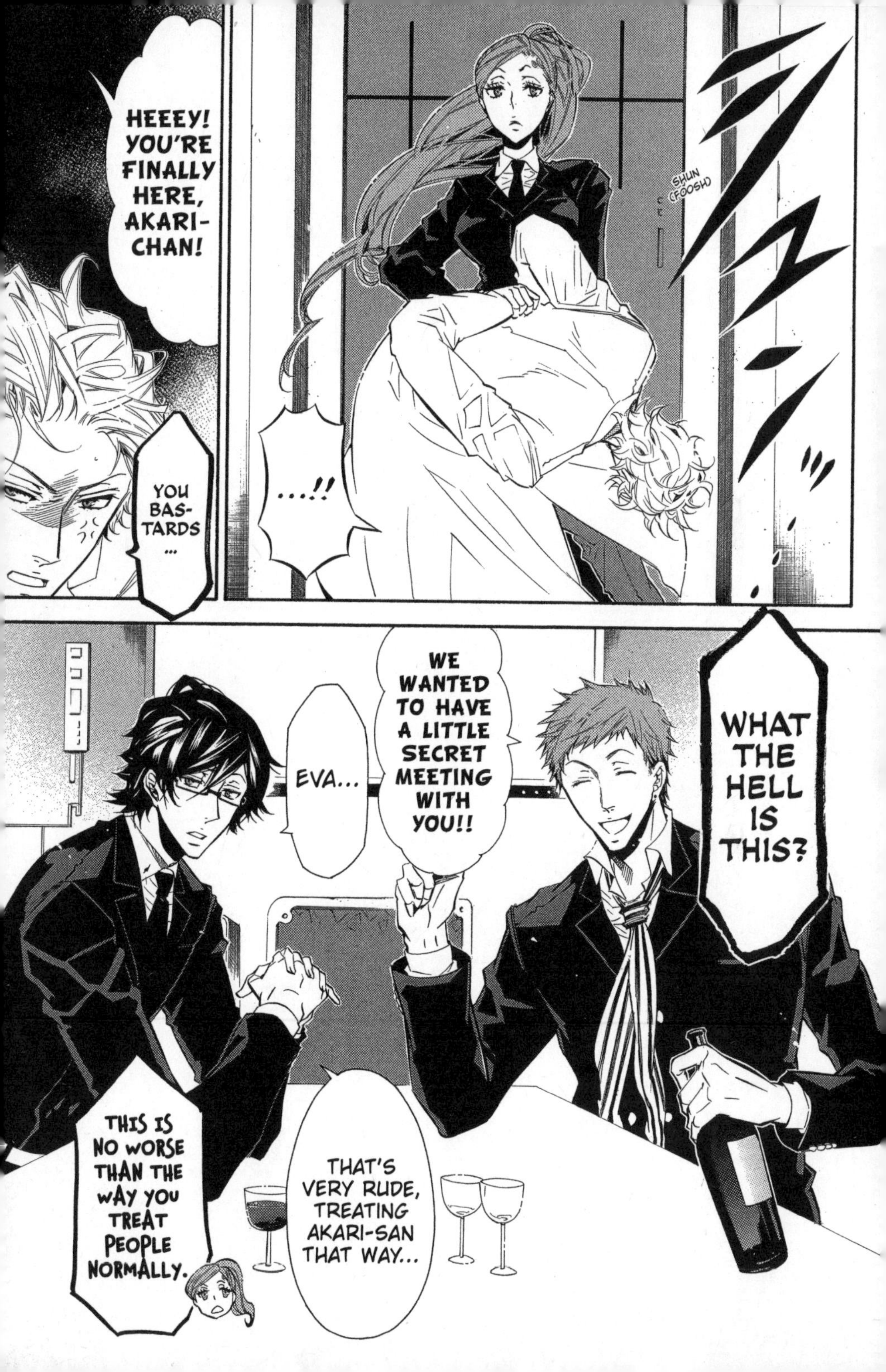
SHUN (FOOSH)
...!!
HEEEY! YOU'RE FINALLY HERE, AKARI-CHAN!
YOU BASTARDS...
WHAT THE HELL IS THIS?
WE WANTED TO HAVE A LITTLE SECRET MEETING WITH YOU!!
EVA...
THAT'S VERY RUDE, TREATING AKARI-SAN THAT WAY...
THIS IS NO WORSE THAN THE WAY YOU TREAT PEOPLE NORMALLY.

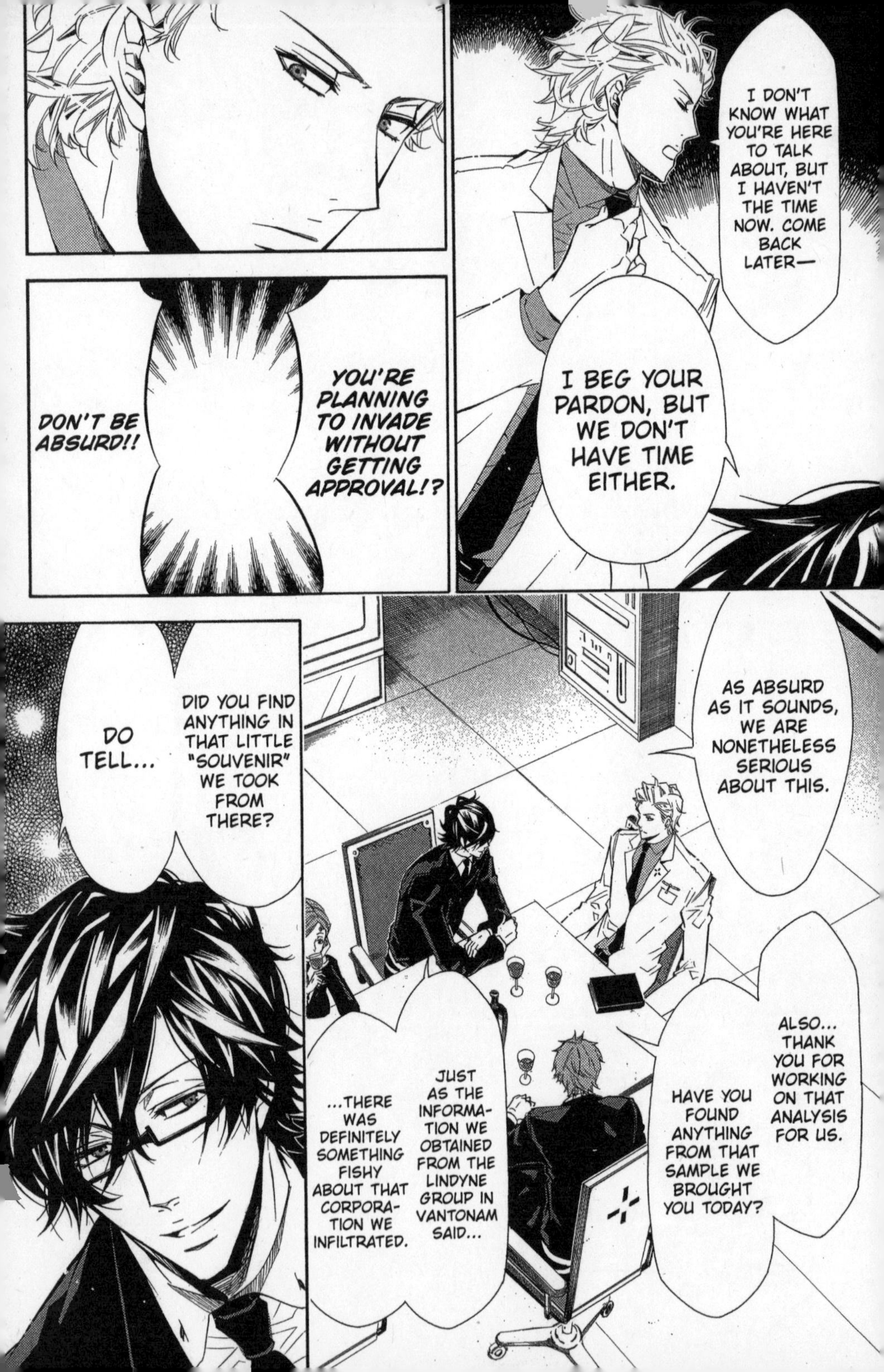
I DON'T KNOW WHAT YOU'RE HERE TO TALK ABOUT, BUT I HAVEN'T THE TIME NOW. COME BACK LATER—
I BEG YOUR PARDON, BUT WE DON'T HAVE TIME EITHER.
YOU'RE PLANNING TO INVADE WITHOUT GETTING APPROVAL!?
DON'T BE ABSURD!!
AS ABSURD AS IT SOUNDS, WE ARE NONETHELESS SERIOUS ABOUT THIS.
ALSO... THANK YOU FOR WORKING ON THAT ANALYSIS FOR US.
HAVE YOU FOUND ANYTHING FROM THAT SAMPLE WE BROUGHT YOU TODAY?
JUST AS THE INFORMATION WE OBTAINED FROM THE LINDYNE GROUP IN VANTONAM SAID...
...THERE WAS DEFINITELY SOMETHING FISHY ABOUT THAT CORPORATION WE INFILTRATED.
DID YOU FIND ANYTHING IN THAT LITTLE "SOUVENIR" WE TOOK FROM THERE?
DO TELL...

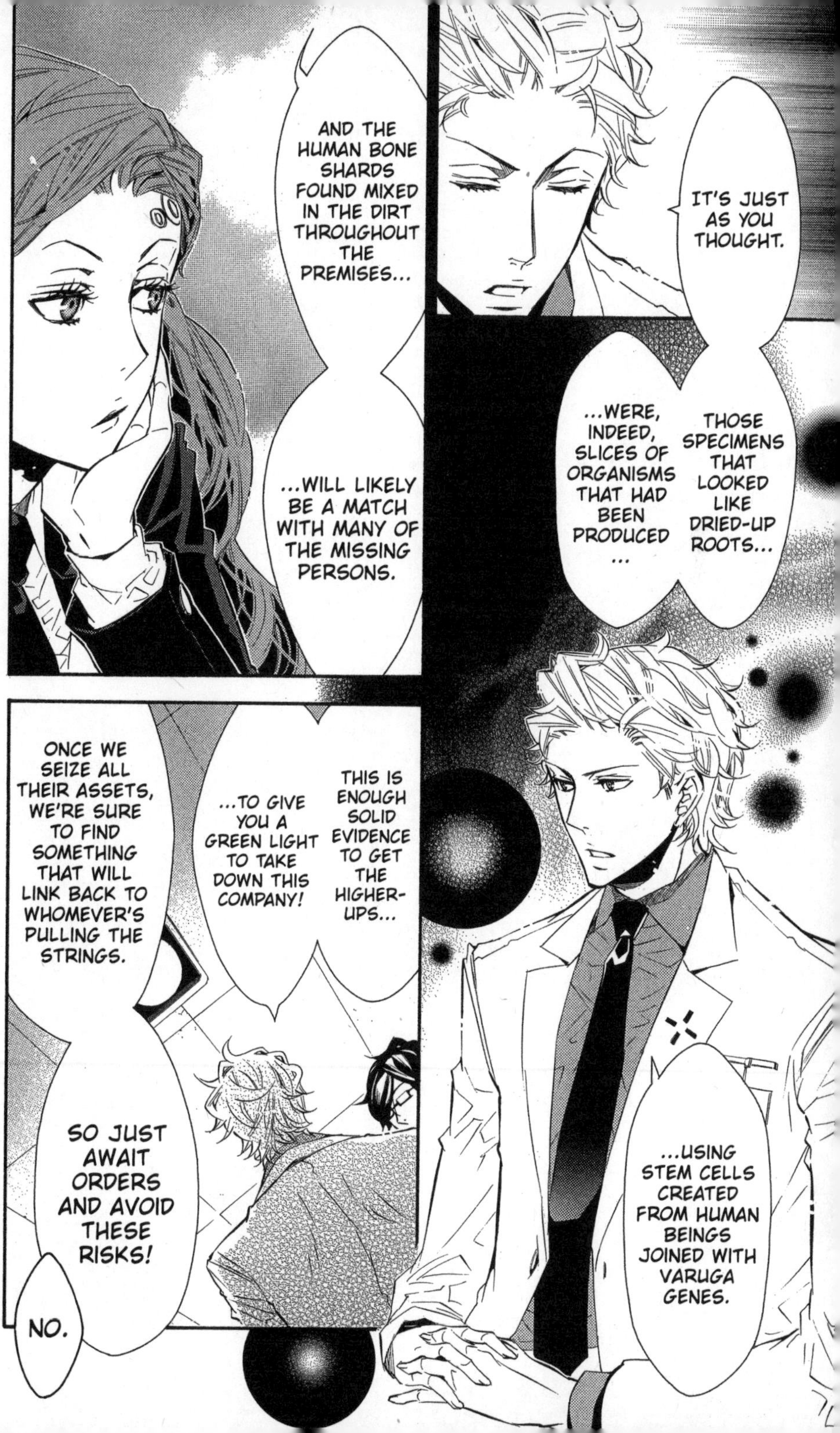
IT'S JUST AS YOU THOUGHT.
THOSE SPECIMENS THAT LOOKED LIKE DRIED-UP ROOTS...
...WERE, INDEED, SLICES OF ORGANISMS THAT HAD BEEN PRODUCED ...
...USING STEM CELLS CREATED FROM HUMAN BEINGS JOINED WITH VARUGA GENES.
AND THE HUMAN BONE SHARDS FOUND MIXED IN THE DIRT THROUGHOUT THE PREMISES...
...WILL LIKELY BE A MATCH WITH MANY OF THE MISSING PERSONS.
THIS IS ENOUGH SOLID EVIDENCE TO GET THE HIGHER-UPS...
...TO GIVE YOU A GREEN LIGHT TO TAKE DOWN THIS COMPANY!
ONCE WE SEIZE ALL THEIR ASSETS, WE'RE SURE TO FIND SOMETHING THAT WILL LINK BACK TO WHOMEVER'S PULLING THE STRINGS.
SO JUST AWAIT ORDERS AND AVOID THESE RISKS!
NO.

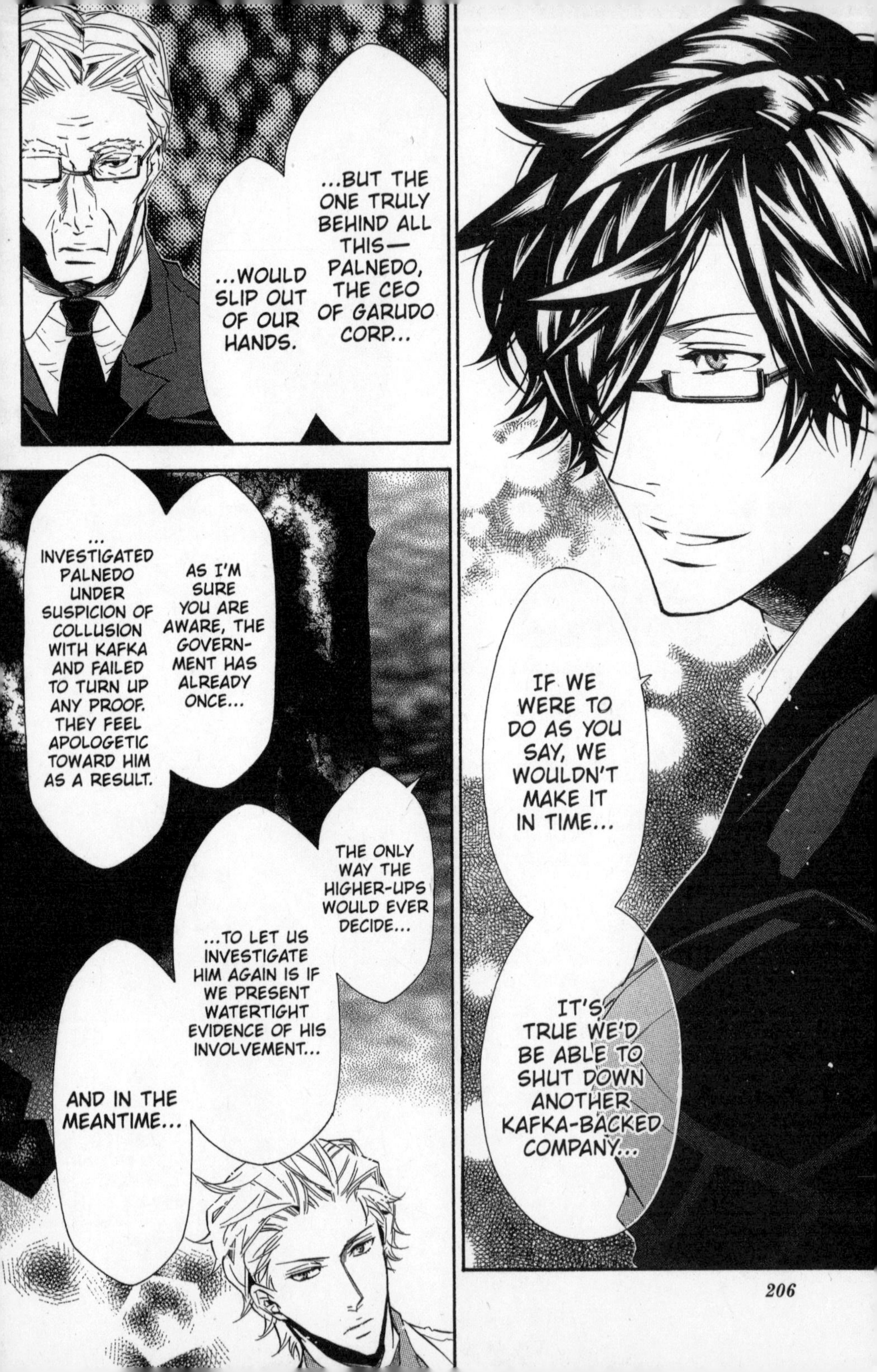
IF WE WERE TO DO AS YOU SAY, WE WOULDN'T MAKE IT IN TIME...
IT'S TRUE WE'D BE ABLE TO SHUT DOWN ANOTHER KAFKA-BACKED COMPANY...
...BUT THE ONE TRULY BEHIND ALL THIS— PALNEDO, THE CEO OF GARUDO CORP...
...WOULD SLIP OUT OF OUR HANDS.
AS I'M SURE YOU ARE AWARE, THE GOVERN-MENT HAS ALREADY ONCE...
...INVESTIGATED PALNEDO UNDER SUSPICION OF COLLUSION WITH KAFKA AND FAILED TO TURN UP ANY PROOF. THEY FEEL APOLOGETIC TOWARD HIM AS A RESULT.
THE ONLY WAY THE HIGHER-UPS WOULD EVER DECIDE...
...TO LET US INVESTIGATE HIM AGAIN IS IF WE PRESENT WATERTIGHT EVIDENCE OF HIS INVOLVEMENT...
AND IN THE MEANTIME...

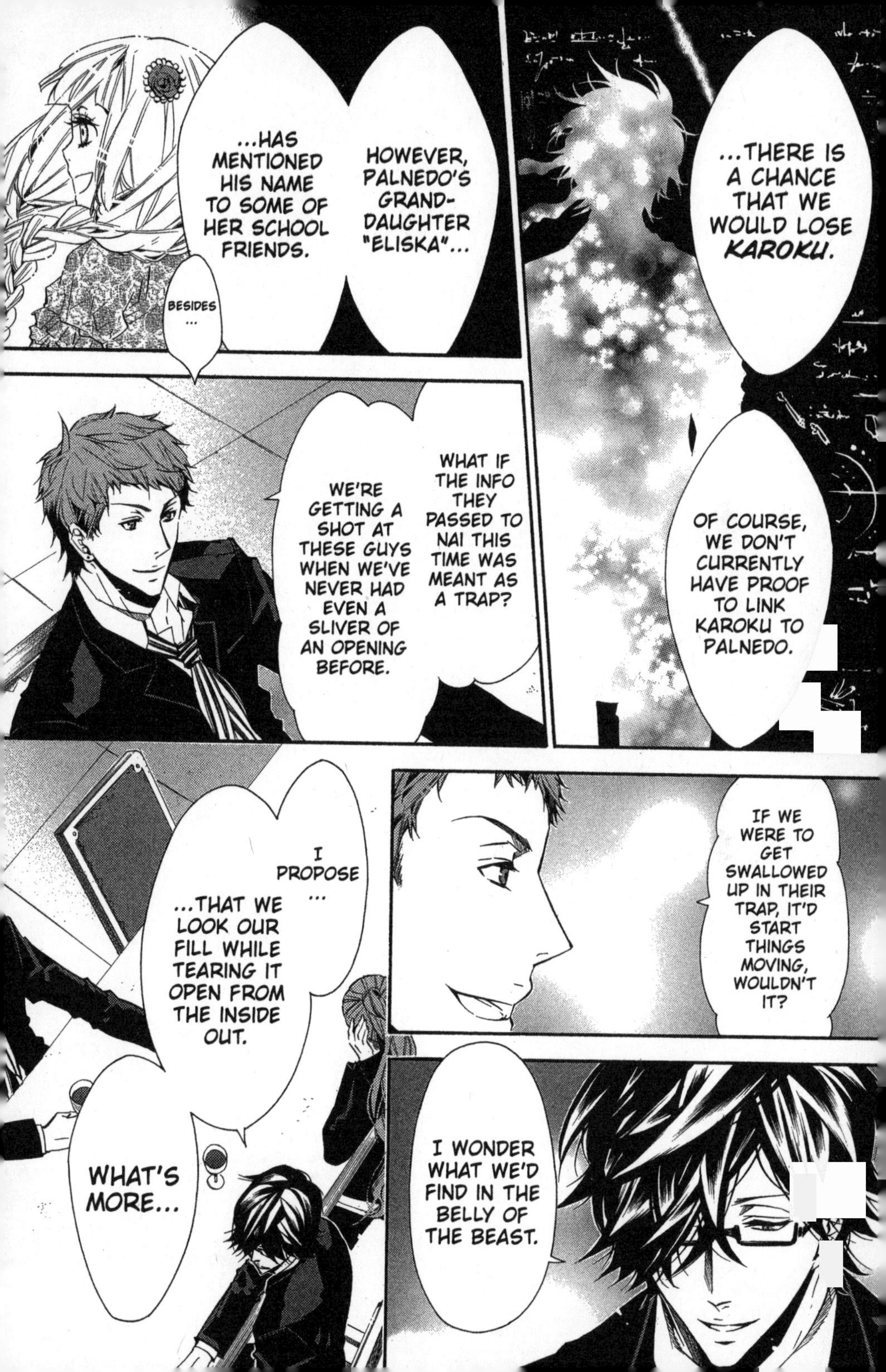
...THERE IS A CHANCE THAT WE WOULD LOSE *KAROKU*.
OF COURSE, WE DON'T CURRENTLY HAVE PROOF TO LINK KAROKU TO PALNEDO.
HOWEVER, PALNEDO'S GRAND-DAUGHTER "ELISKA"...
...HAS MENTIONED HIS NAME TO SOME OF HER SCHOOL FRIENDS.
BESIDES...
WHAT IF THE INFO THEY PASSED TO NAI THIS TIME WAS MEANT AS A TRAP?
WE'RE GETTING A SHOT AT THESE GUYS WHEN WE'VE NEVER HAD EVEN A SLIVER OF AN OPENING BEFORE.
IF WE WERE TO GET SWALLOWED UP IN THEIR TRAP, IT'D START THINGS MOVING, WOULDN'T IT?
I WONDER WHAT WE'D FIND IN THE BELLY OF THE BEAST.
I PROPOSE...
...THAT WE LOOK OUR FILL WHILE TEARING IT OPEN FROM THE INSIDE OUT.
WHAT'S MORE...

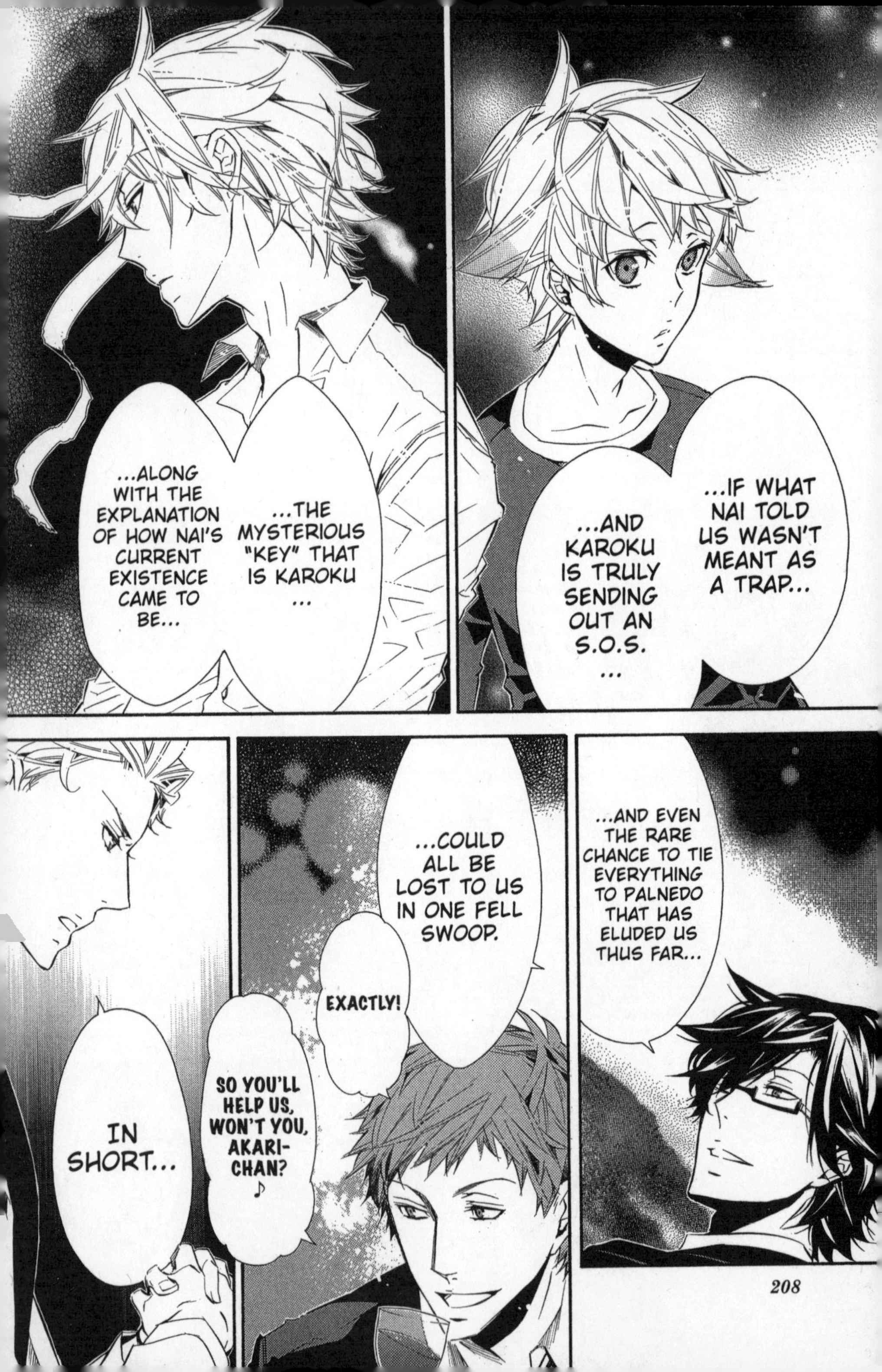
...IF WHAT NAI TOLD US WASN'T MEANT AS A TRAP...
...AND KAROKU IS TRULY SENDING OUT AN S.O.S. ...
...THE MYSTERIOUS "KEY" THAT IS KAROKU ...
...ALONG WITH THE EXPLANATION OF HOW NAI'S CURRENT EXISTENCE CAME TO BE...
...AND EVEN THE RARE CHANCE TO TIE EVERYTHING TO PALNEDO THAT HAS ELUDED US THUS FAR...
...COULD ALL BE LOST TO US IN ONE FELL SWOOP.
EXACTLY!
SO YOU'LL HELP US, WON'T YOU, AKARI-CHAN? ♪
IN SHORT...

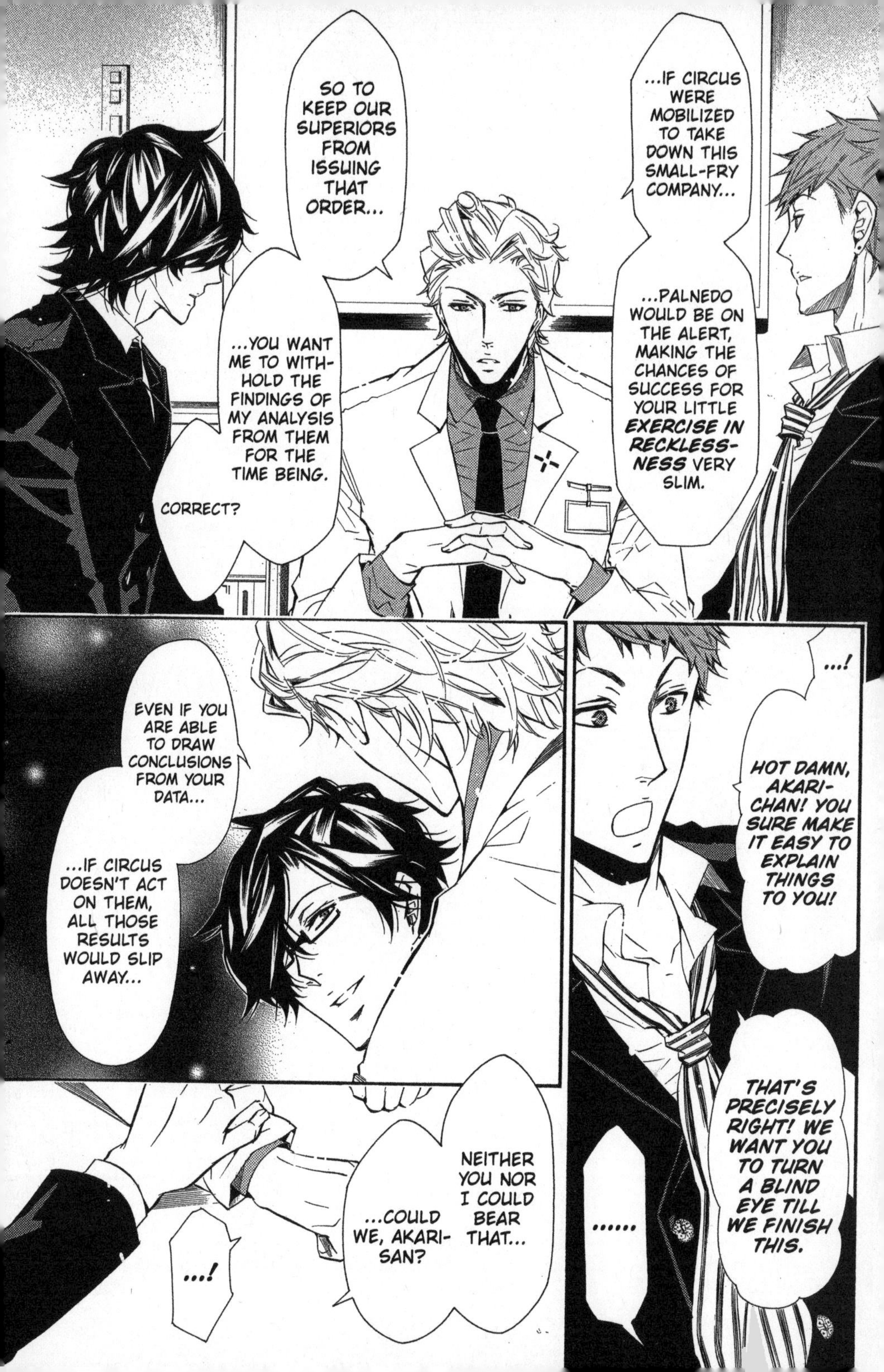

...IF CIRCUS WERE MOBILIZED TO TAKE DOWN THIS SMALL-FRY COMPANY...
...PALNEDO WOULD BE ON THE ALERT, MAKING THE CHANCES OF SUCCESS FOR YOUR LITTLE *EXERCISE IN RECKLESSNESS* VERY SLIM.
SO TO KEEP OUR SUPERIORS FROM ISSUING THAT ORDER...
...YOU WANT ME TO WITHHOLD THE FINDINGS OF MY ANALYSIS FROM THEM FOR THE TIME BEING.
CORRECT?
...!
HOT DAMN, AKARI-CHAN! YOU SURE MAKE IT EASY TO EXPLAIN THINGS TO YOU!
THAT'S PRECISELY RIGHT! WE WANT YOU TO TURN A BLIND EYE TILL WE FINISH THIS.
......
EVEN IF YOU ARE ABLE TO DRAW CONCLUSIONS FROM YOUR DATA...
...IF CIRCUS DOESN'T ACT ON THEM, ALL THOSE RESULTS WOULD SLIP AWAY...
NEITHER YOU NOR I COULD BEAR THAT...
...COULD WE, AKARI-SAN?
...!

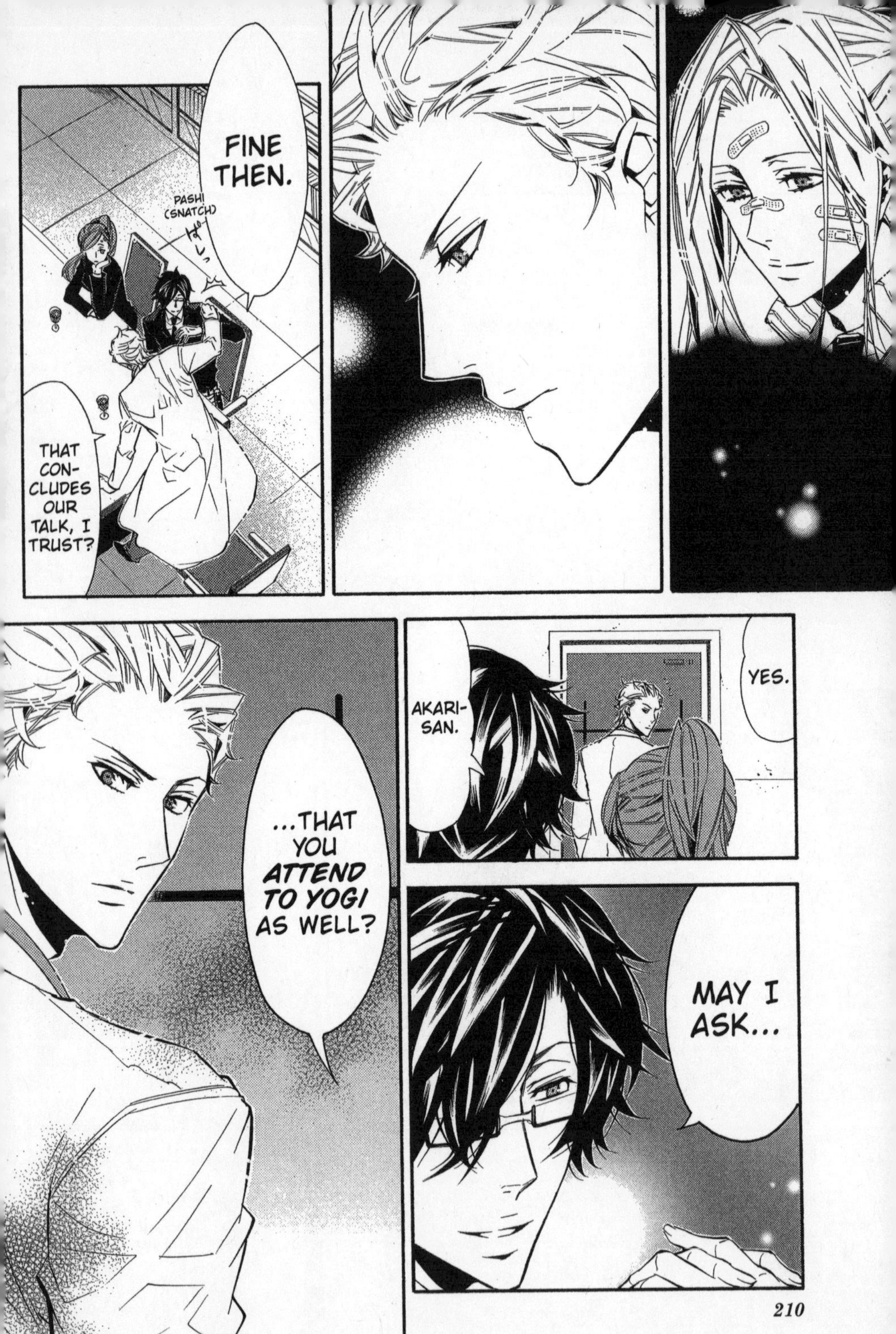
FINE THEN.
PASHI (SNATCH)
ぱしっ
THAT CONCLUDES OUR TALK, I TRUST?
YES.
AKARI-SAN.
MAY I ASK...
...THAT YOU ATTEND TO YOGI AS WELL?

KII
(CREEEAK)

PATAN
(SHUT)

THE HOUR IS LATE-BAA.

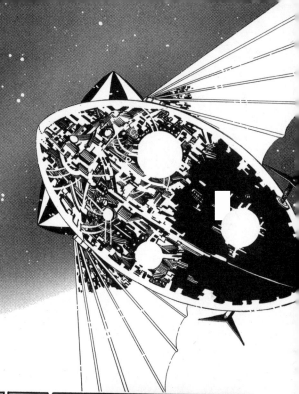

KACHA
(CLACK)

HAS THAT SHITTY FOUR-EYES COME BACK YET?

...

THE TEA'S FOR YOU.

COME IN.

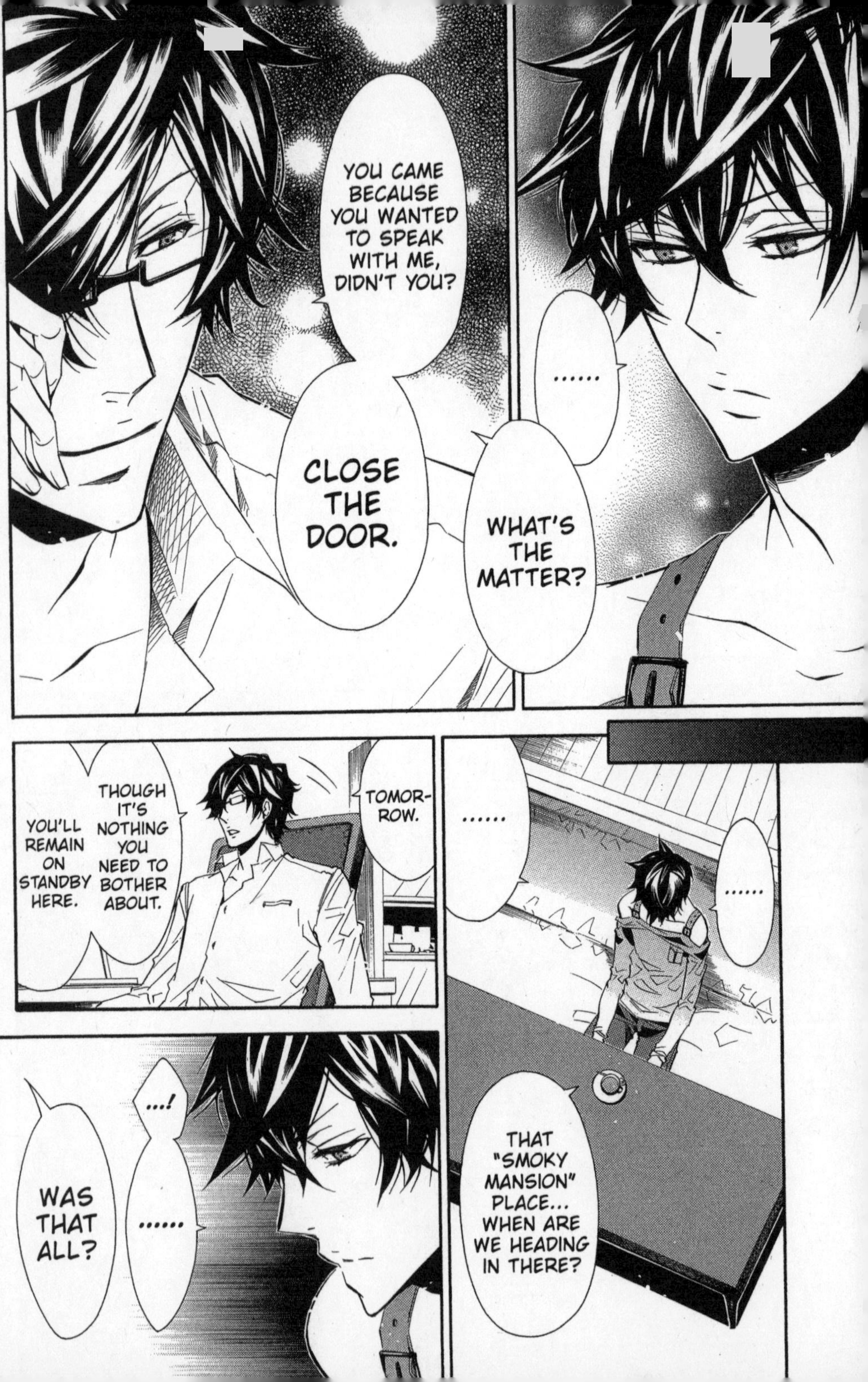
......
WHAT'S THE MATTER?
YOU CAME BECAUSE YOU WANTED TO SPEAK WITH ME, DIDN'T YOU?
CLOSE THE DOOR.
......
......
THAT "SMOKY MANSION" PLACE... WHEN ARE WE HEADING IN THERE?
TOMORROW.
THOUGH IT'S NOTHING YOU NEED TO BOTHER ABOUT.
YOU'LL REMAIN ON STANDBY HERE.
...!
......
WAS THAT ALL?

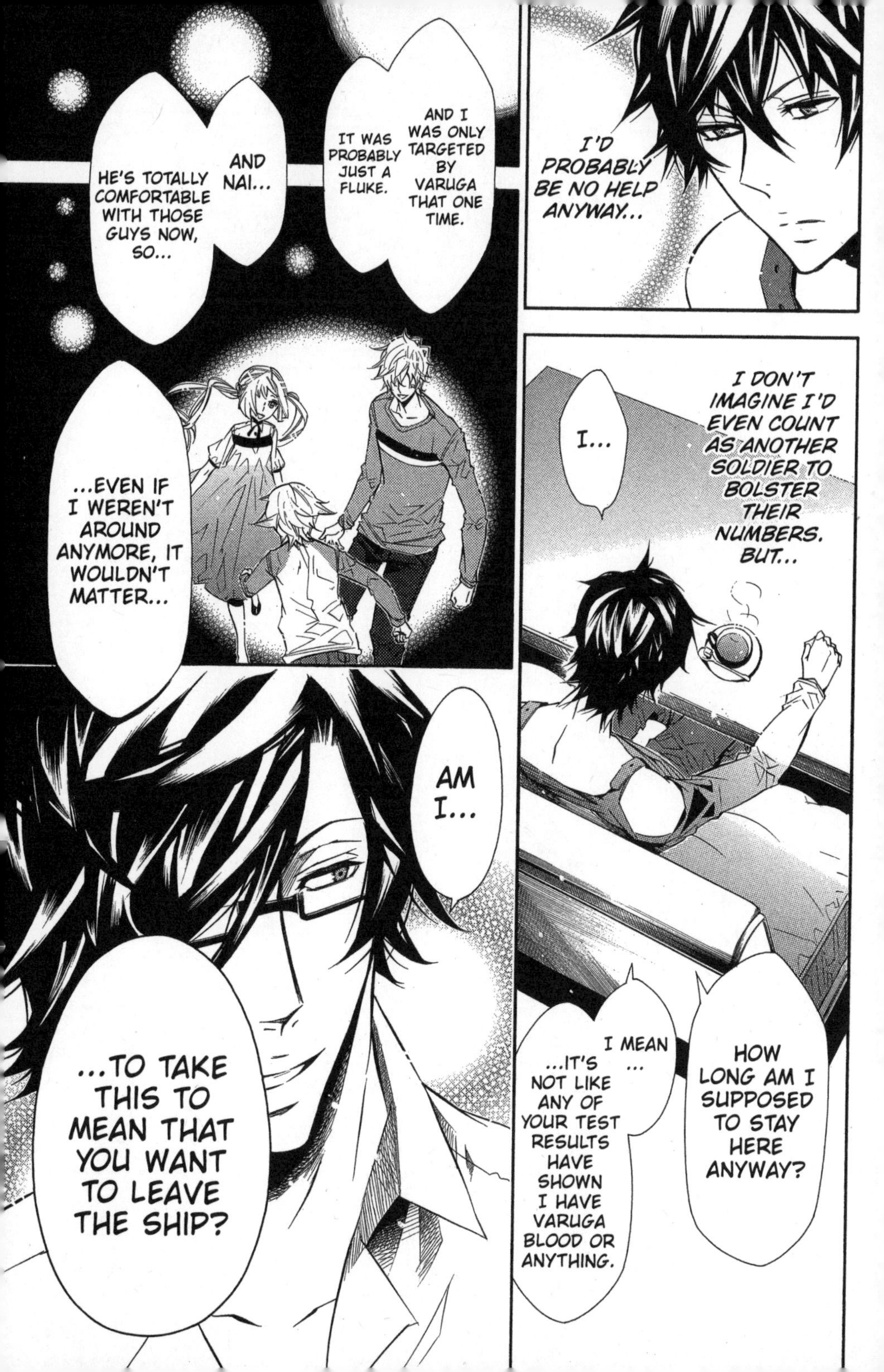
I'D PROBABLY BE NO HELP ANYWAY...
AND I WAS ONLY TARGETED BY VARUGA THAT ONE TIME.
IT WAS PROBABLY JUST A FLUKE.
AND NAI...
HE'S TOTALLY COMFORTABLE WITH THOSE GUYS NOW, SO...
...EVEN IF I WEREN'T AROUND ANYMORE, IT WOULDN'T MATTER...
I DON'T IMAGINE I'D EVEN COUNT AS ANOTHER SOLDIER TO BOLSTER THEIR NUMBERS. BUT...
I...
HOW LONG AM I SUPPOSED TO STAY HERE ANYWAY?
I MEAN...
...IT'S NOT LIKE ANY OF YOUR TEST RESULTS HAVE SHOWN I HAVE VARUGA BLOOD OR ANYTHING.
AM I...
...TO TAKE THIS TO MEAN THAT YOU WANT TO LEAVE THE SHIP?

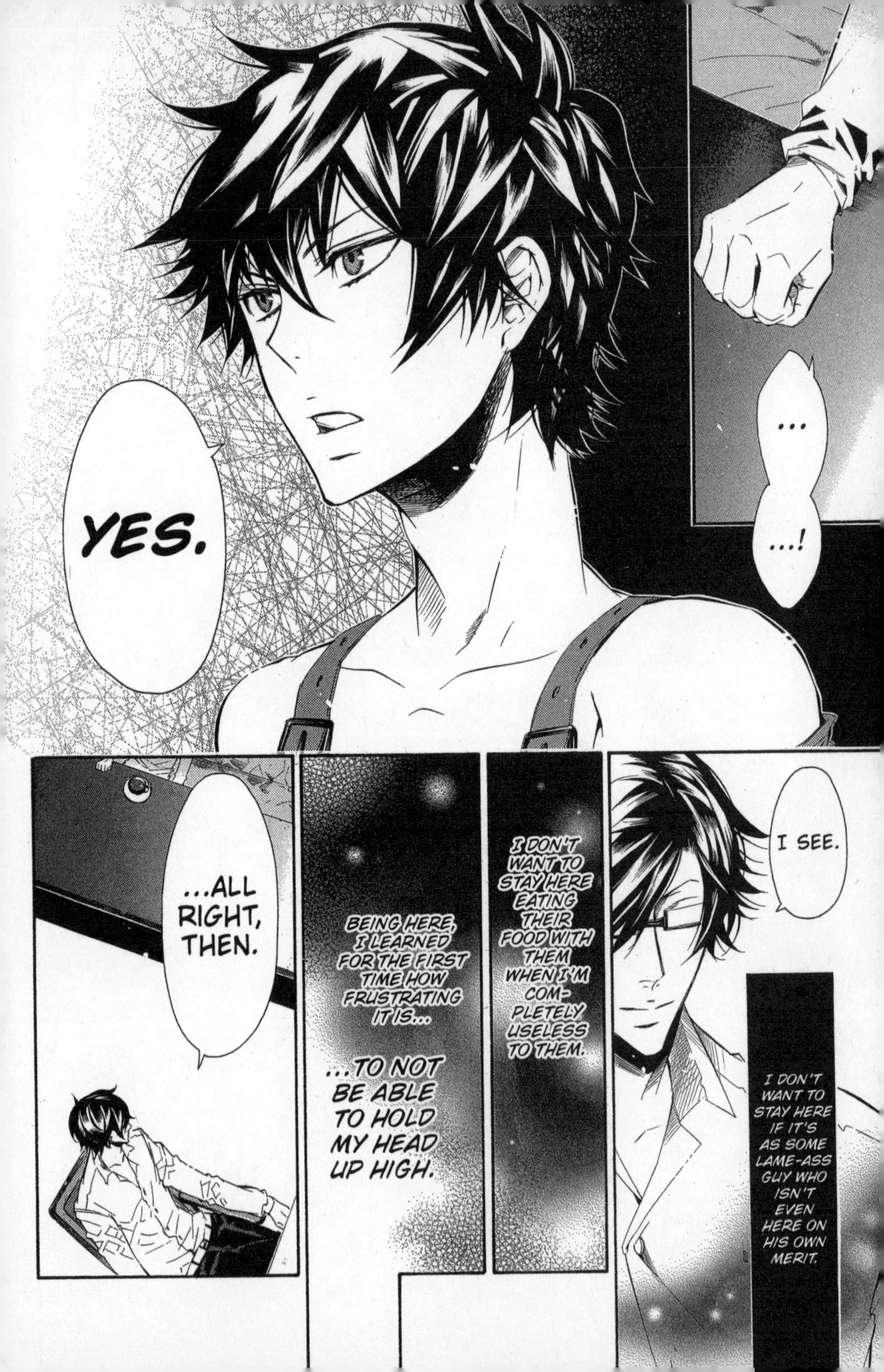
...
...!
YES.
I SEE.
I DON'T WANT TO STAY HERE IF IT'S AS SOME LAME-ASS GUY WHO ISN'T EVEN HERE ON HIS OWN MERIT.
I DON'T WANT TO STAY HERE EATING THEIR FOOD WITH THEM WHEN I'M COM-PLETELY USELESS TO THEM.
BEING HERE, I LEARNED FOR THE FIRST TIME HOW FRUSTRATING IT IS...
...TO NOT BE ABLE TO HOLD MY HEAD UP HIGH.
...ALL RIGHT, THEN.

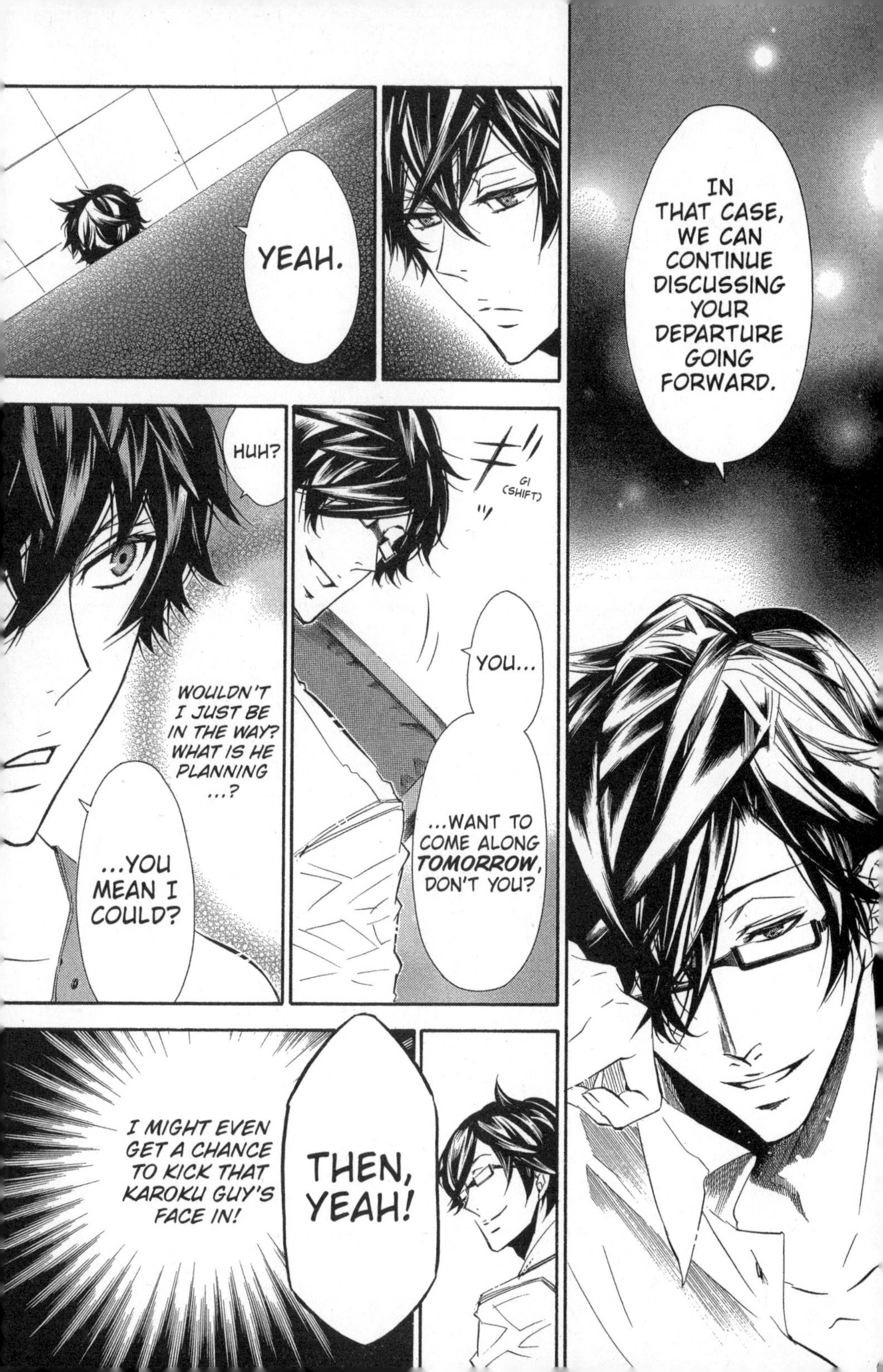
IN THAT CASE, WE CAN CONTINUE DISCUSSING YOUR DEPARTURE GOING FORWARD.
YEAH.
GI (SHIFT)
YOU...
...WANT TO COME ALONG *TOMORROW*, DON'T YOU?
HUH?
WOULDN'T I JUST BE IN THE WAY? WHAT IS HE PLANNING ...?
...YOU MEAN I COULD?
THEN, YEAH!
I MIGHT EVEN GET A CHANCE TO KICK THAT KAROKU GUY'S FACE IN!

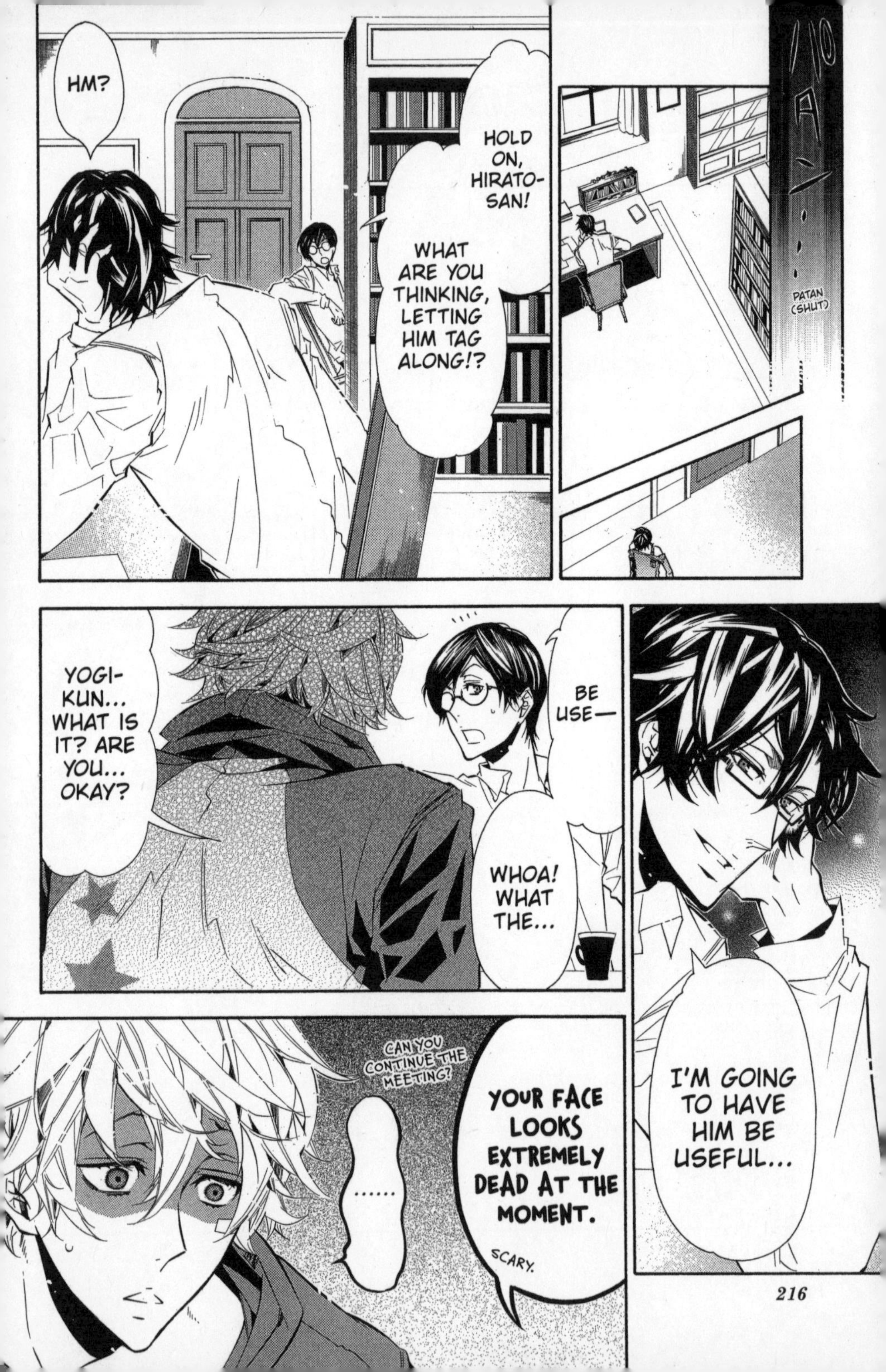
PATAN (SHUT)
HOLD ON, HIRATO-SAN!
WHAT ARE YOU THINKING, LETTING HIM TAG ALONG!?
HM?
I'M GOING TO HAVE HIM BE USEFUL...
BE USE—
WHOA! WHAT THE...
YOGI-KUN... WHAT IS IT? ARE YOU... OKAY?
YOUR FACE LOOKS EXTREMELY DEAD AT THE MOMENT.
SCARY.
CAN YOU CONTINUE THE MEETING?
......

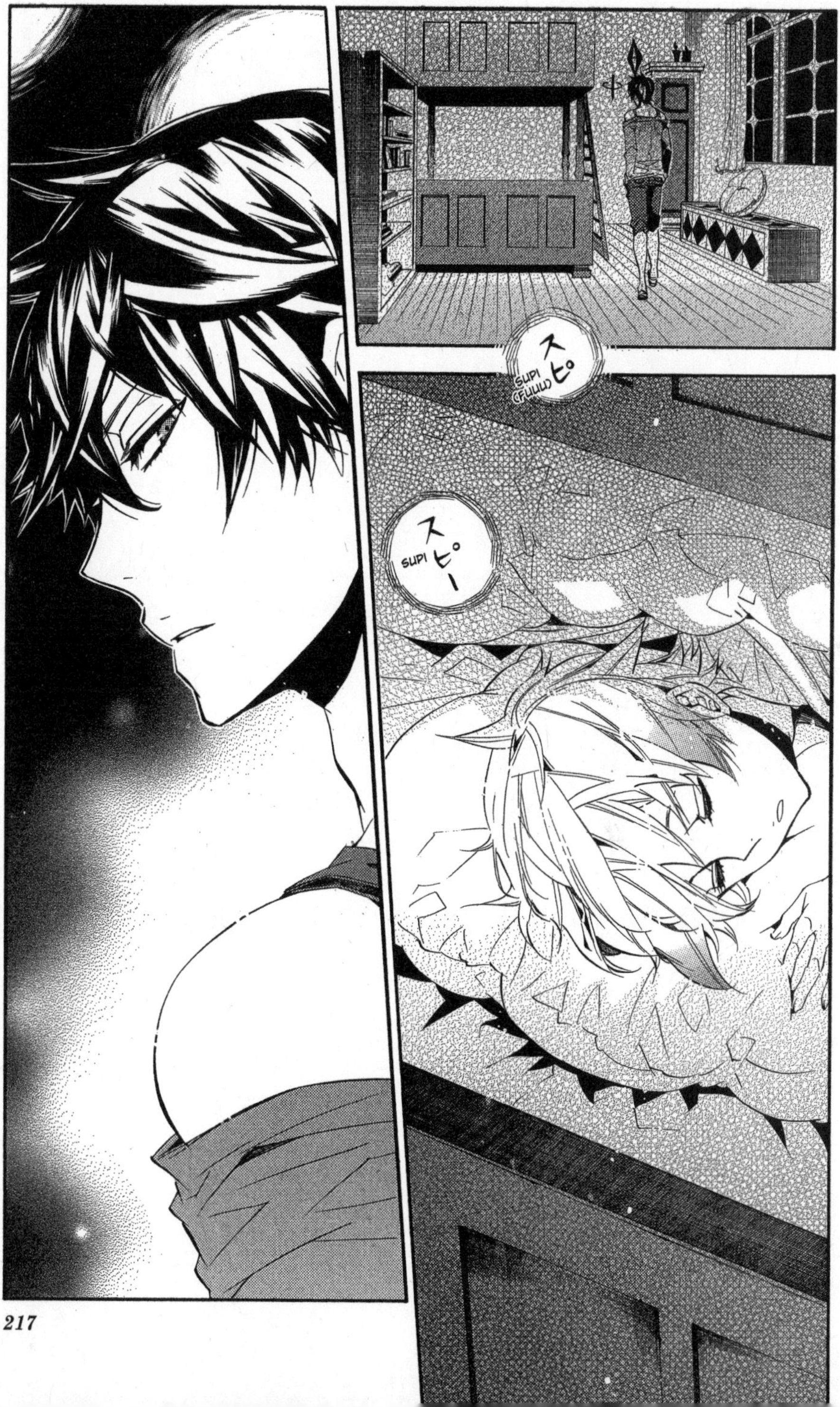
スピ
SUPI (FUUU)
スピー
SUPI

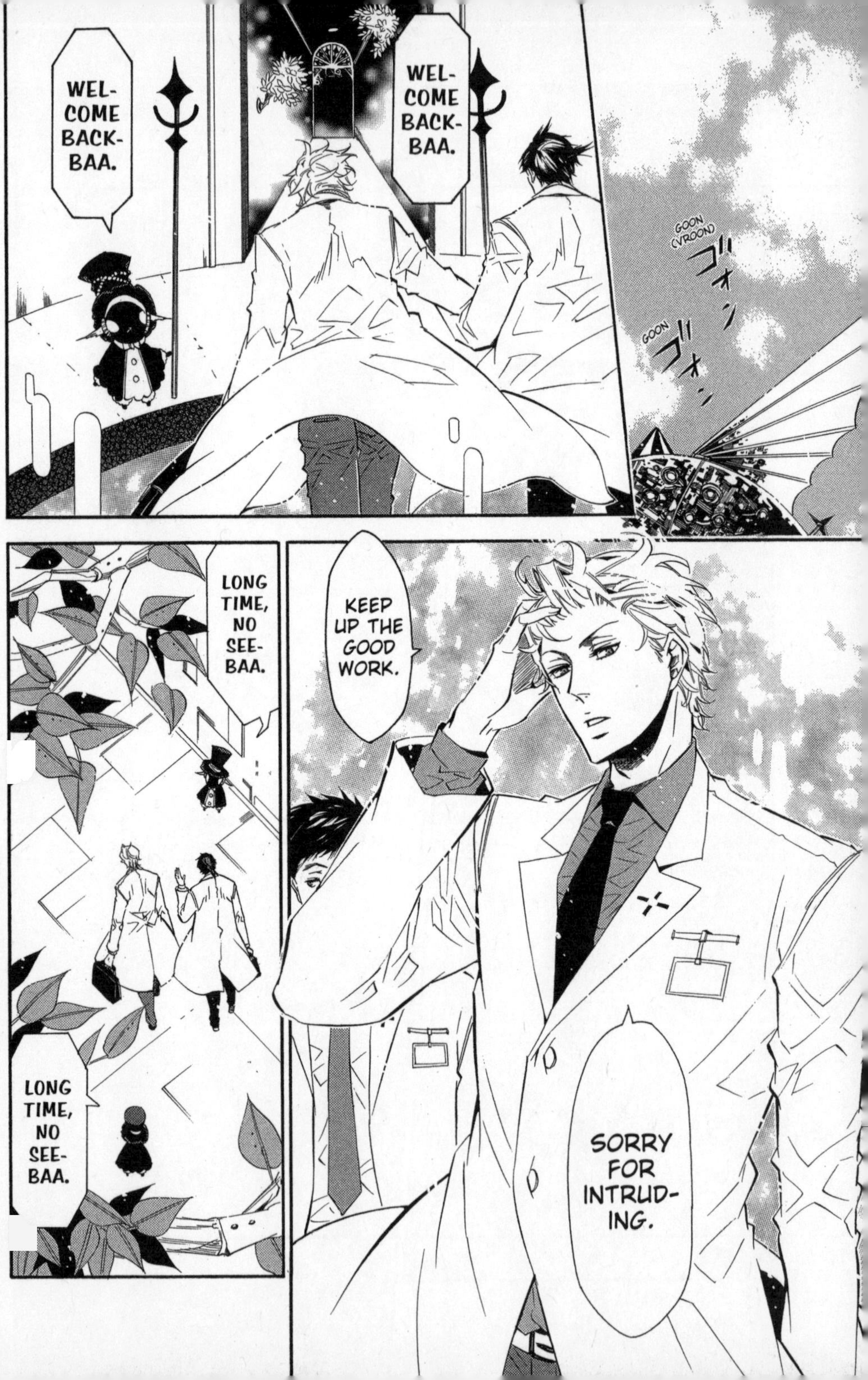
WEL-COME BACK-BAA.
GOON (VROON)
ゴォン
GOON
ゴォ
WEL-COME BACK-BAA.
KEEP UP THE GOOD WORK.
SORRY FOR INTRUD-ING.
LONG TIME, NO SEE-BAA.
LONG TIME, NO SEE-BAA.

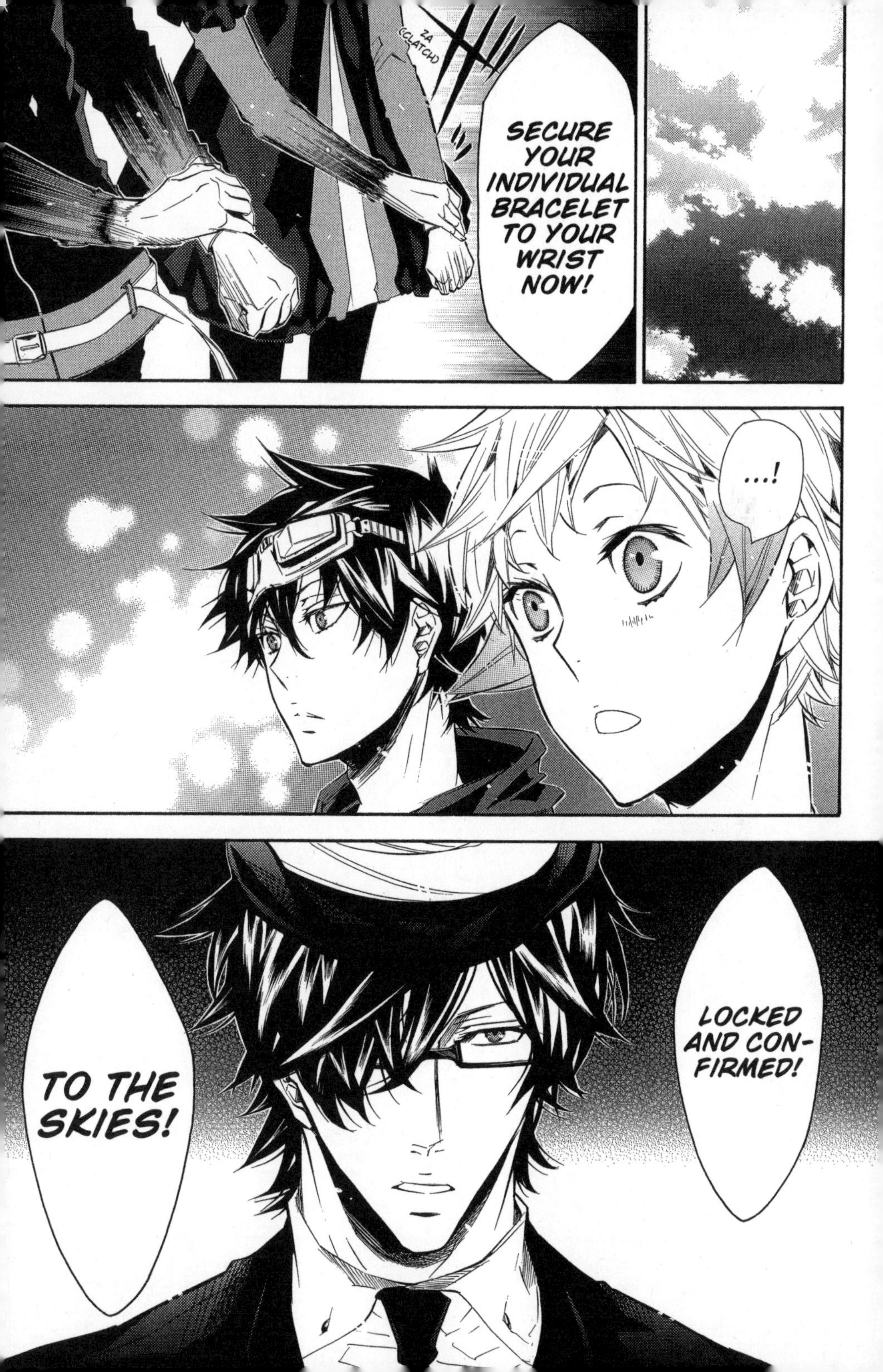
SECURE YOUR INDIVIDUAL BRACELET TO YOUR WRIST NOW!
ZA (CLATCH)
...!
LOCKED AND CON-FIRMED!
TO THE SKIES!

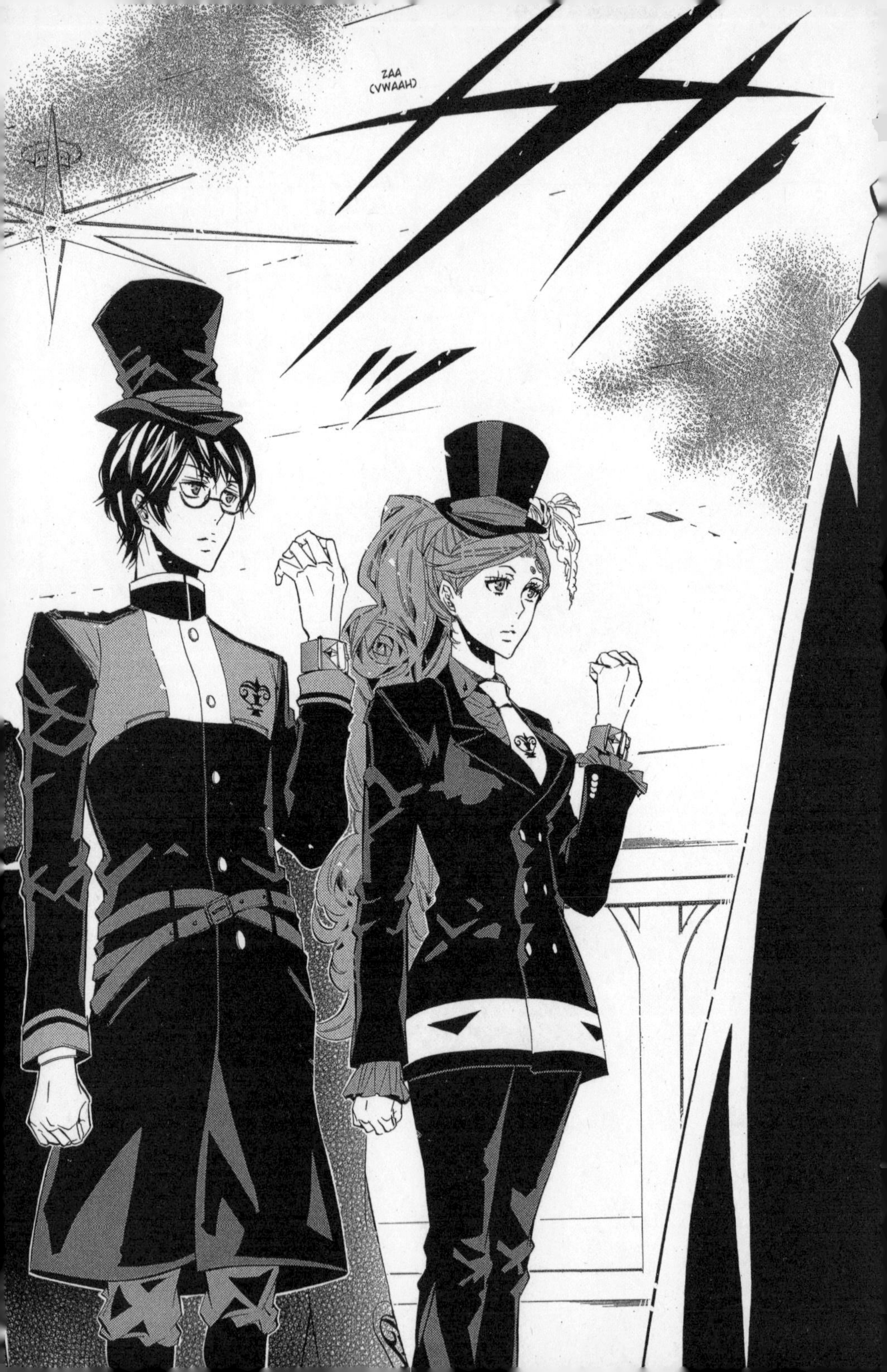
ZAA (VWAAH)

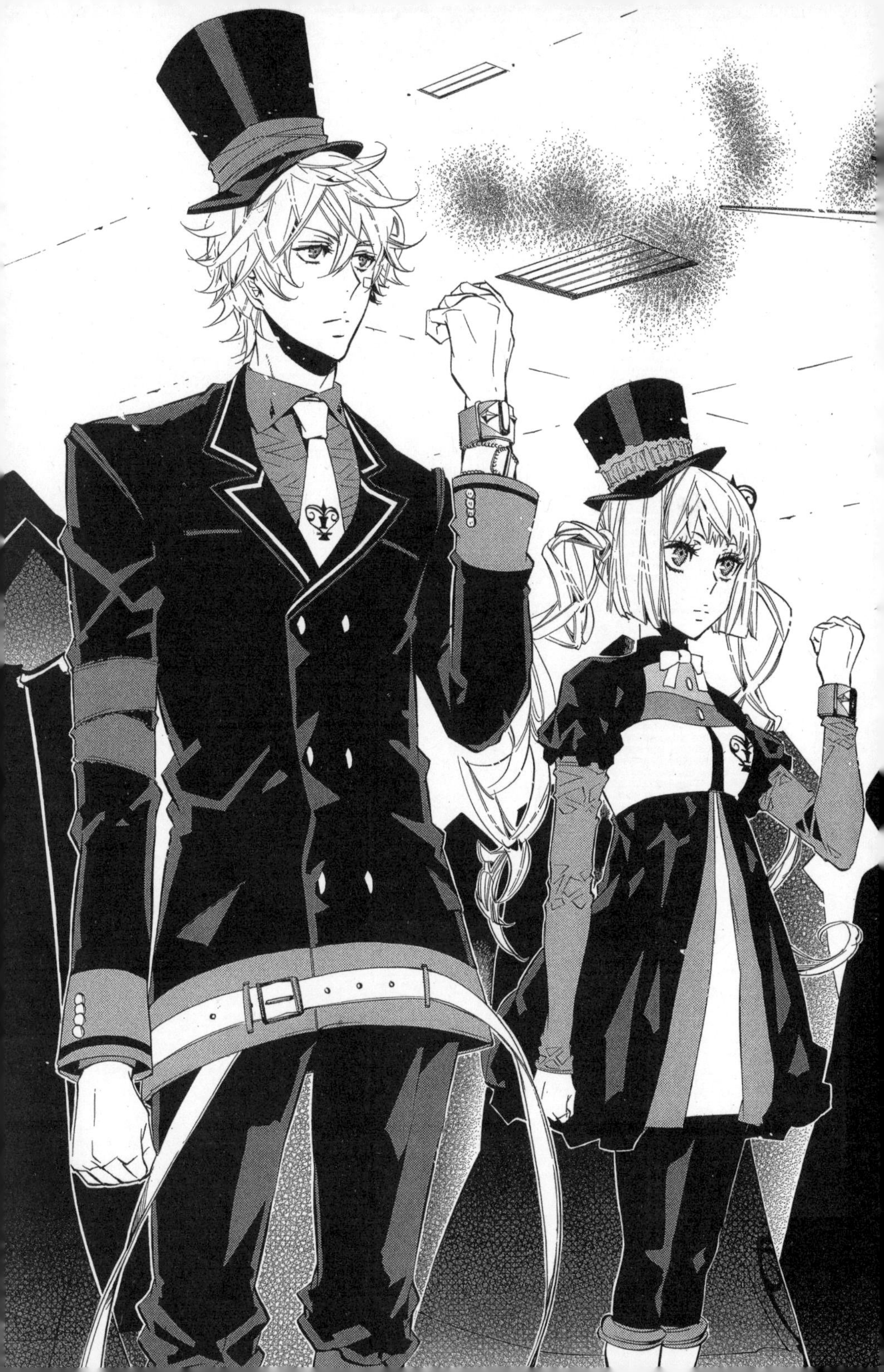

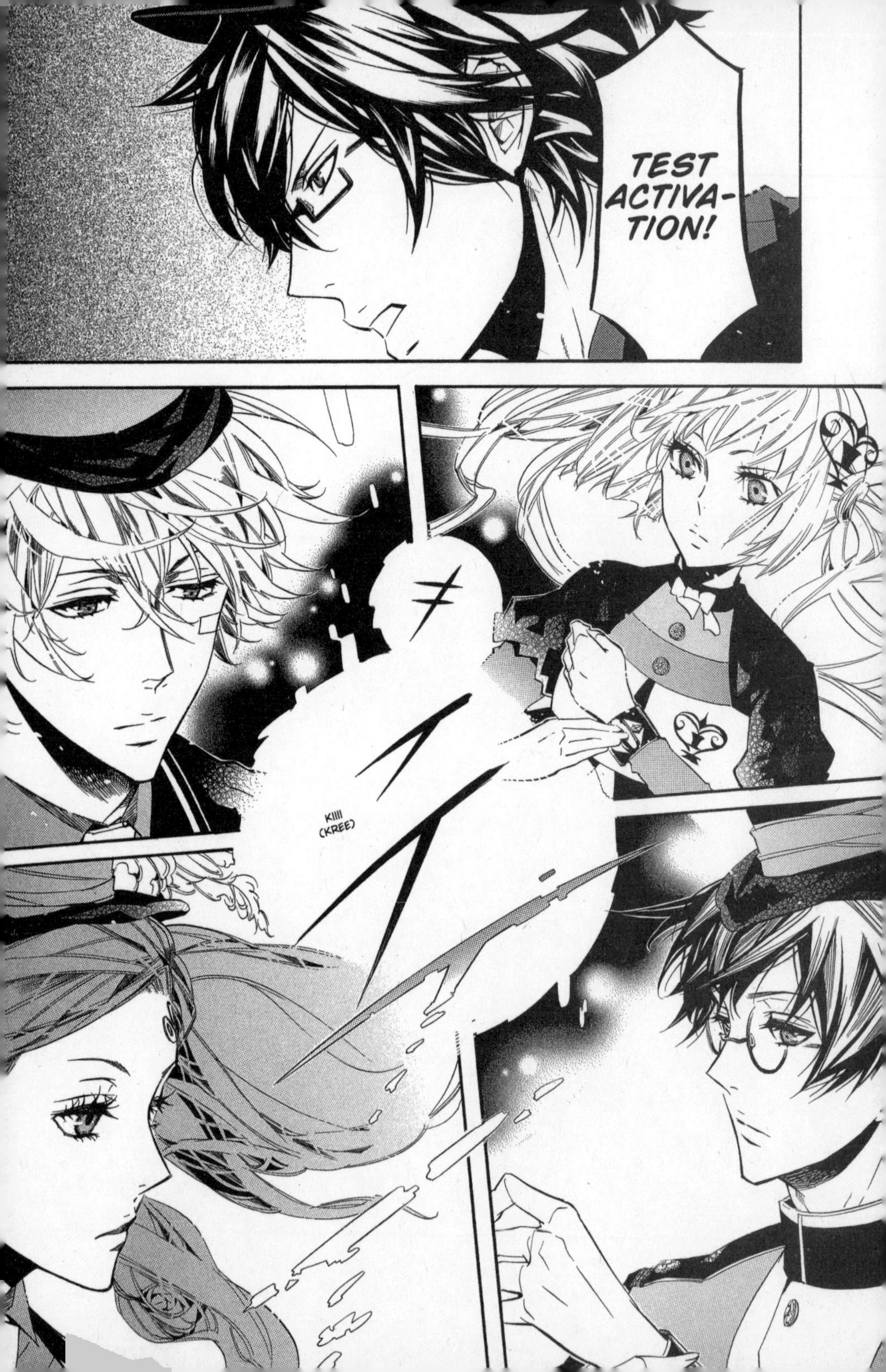
TEST ACTIVATION!
KIIII (KREE)

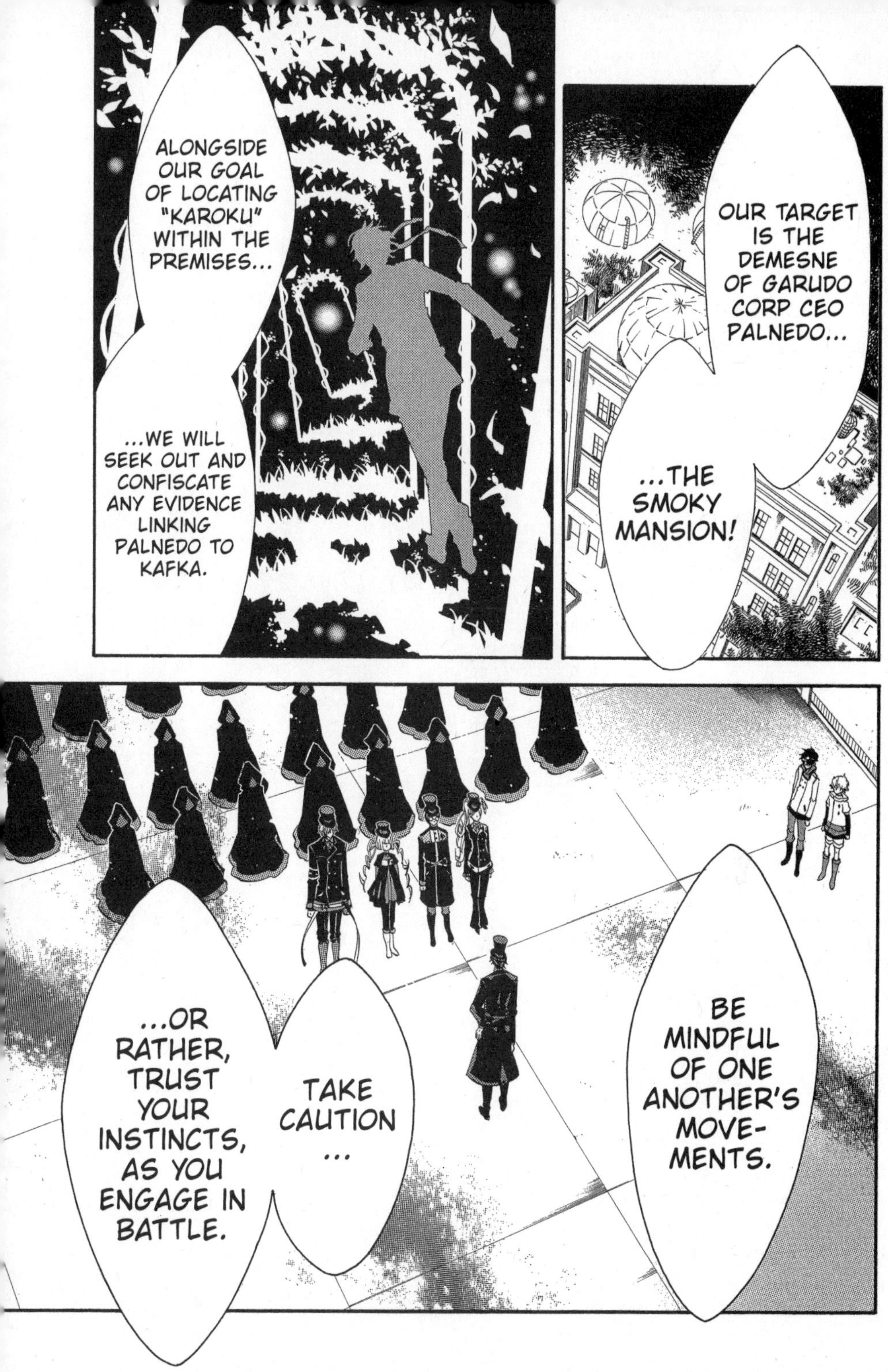
OUR TARGET IS THE DEMESNE OF GARUDO CORP CEO PALNEDO...
...THE SMOKY MANSION!
ALONGSIDE OUR GOAL OF LOCATING "KAROKU" WITHIN THE PREMISES...
...WE WILL SEEK OUT AND CONFISCATE ANY EVIDENCE LINKING PALNEDO TO KAFKA.
BE MINDFUL OF ONE ANOTHER'S MOVE-MENTS.
TAKE CAUTION...
...OR RATHER, TRUST YOUR INSTINCTS, AS YOU ENGAGE IN BATTLE.

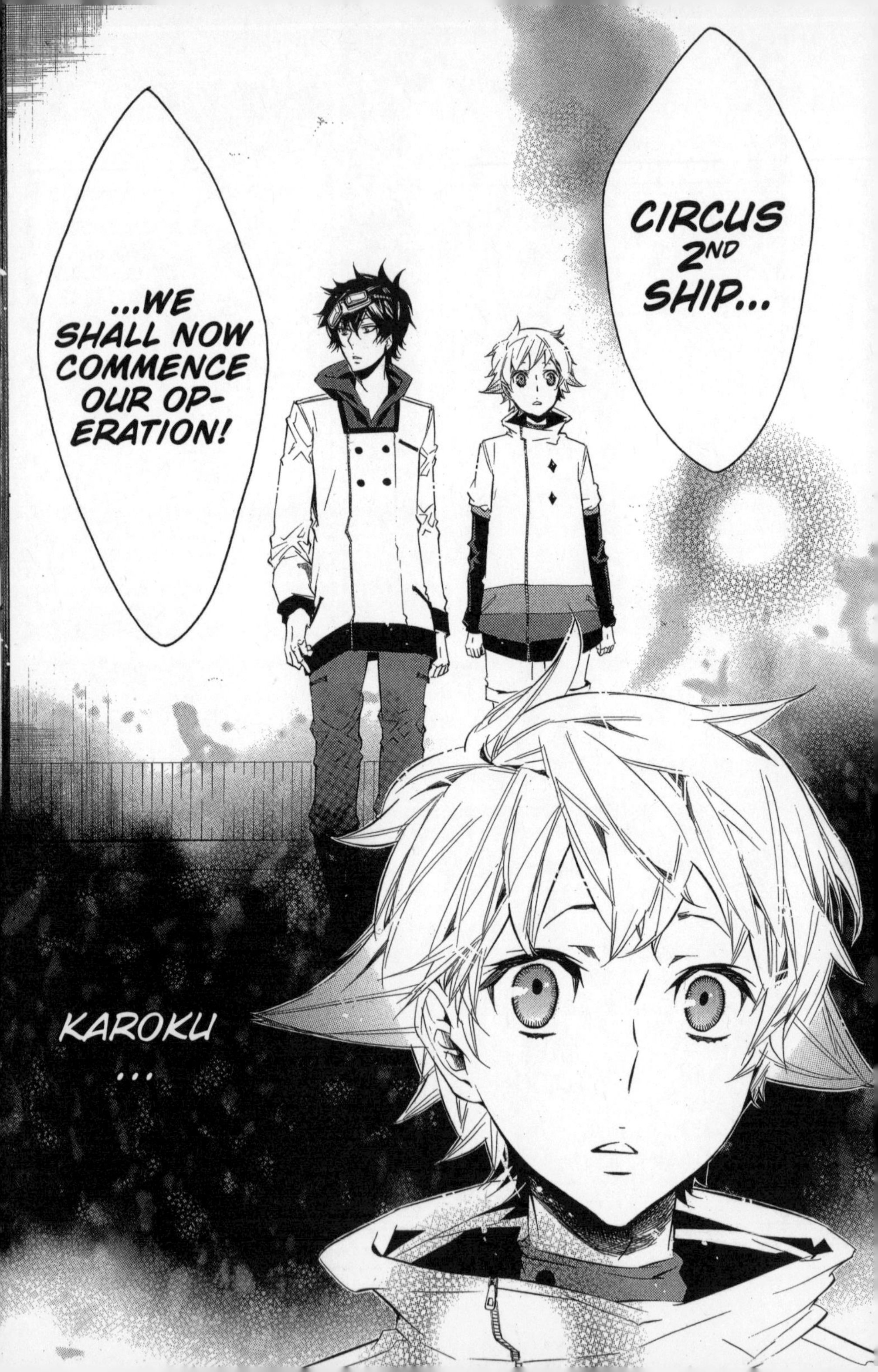
CIRCUS 2ND SHIP...
...WE SHALL NOW COMMENCE OUR OP-ERATION!
KAROKU ...

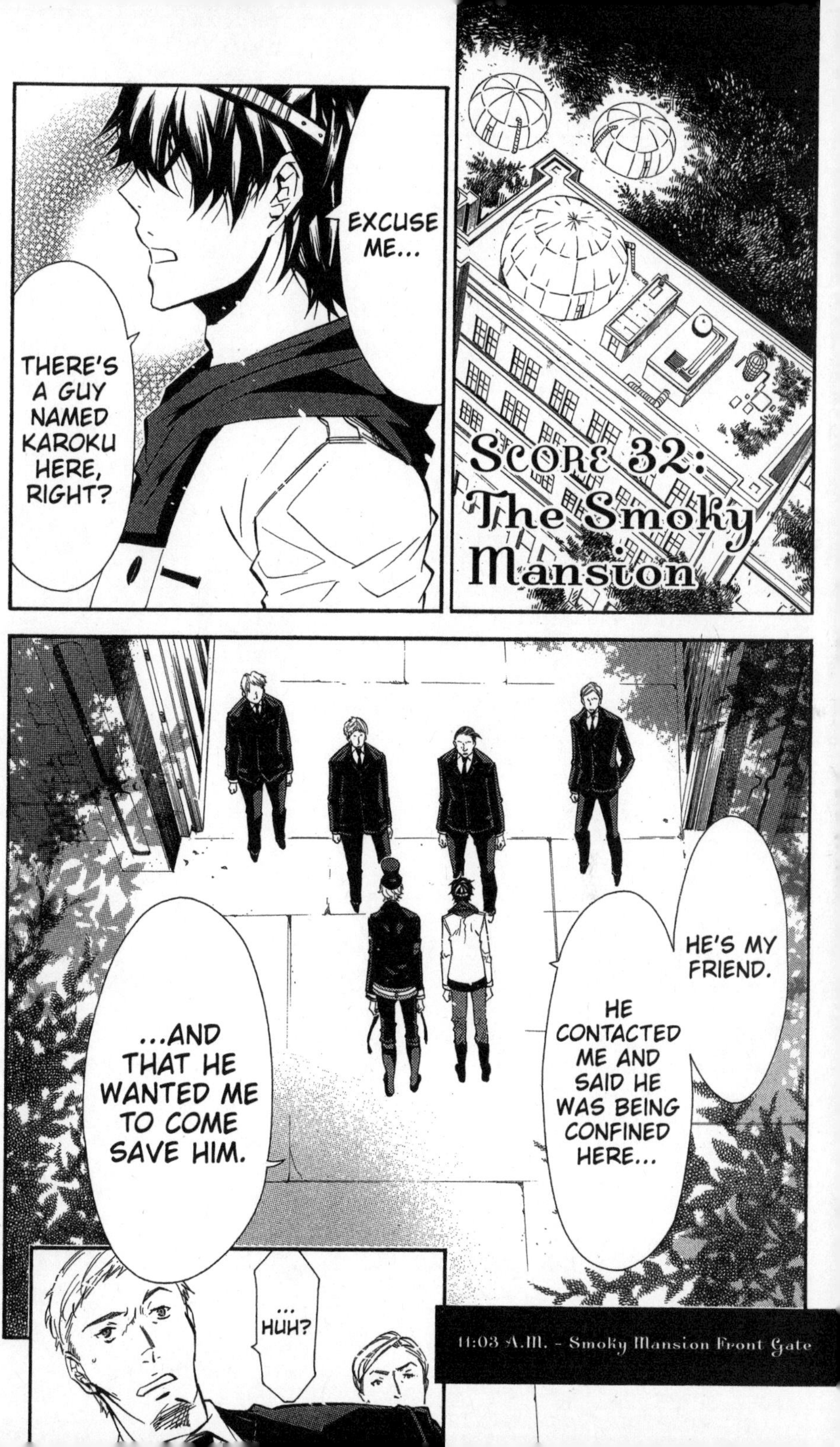
SCORE 32: The Smoky Mansion
EXCUSE ME...
THERE'S A GUY NAMED KAROKU HERE, RIGHT?
HE'S MY FRIEND.
HE CONTACTED ME AND SAID HE WAS BEING CONFINED HERE...
...AND THAT HE WANTED ME TO COME SAVE HIM.
11:03 A.M. - Smoky Mansion Front Gate
... HUH?

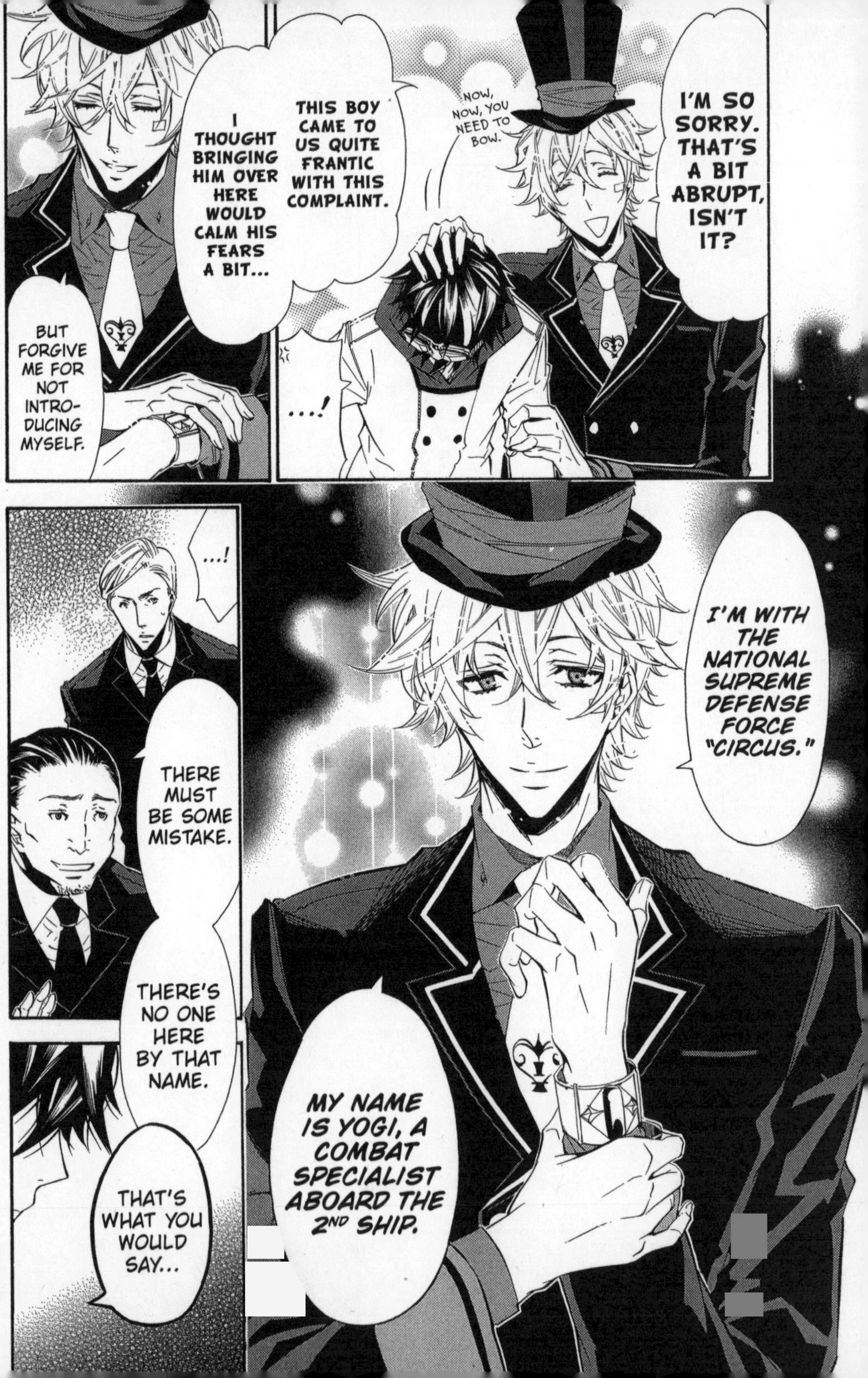
I'M SO SORRY. THAT'S A BIT ABRUPT, ISN'T IT?
NOW, NOW, YOU NEED TO BOW.
...!
THIS BOY CAME TO US QUITE FRANTIC WITH THIS COMPLAINT.
I THOUGHT BRINGING HIM OVER HERE WOULD CALM HIS FEARS A BIT...
BUT FORGIVE ME FOR NOT INTRO-DUCING MYSELF.
I'M WITH THE NATIONAL SUPREME DEFENSE FORCE "CIRCUS."
MY NAME IS YOGI, A COMBAT SPECIALIST ABOARD THE 2ND SHIP.
...!
THERE MUST BE SOME MISTAKE.
THERE'S NO ONE HERE BY THAT NAME.
THAT'S WHAT YOU WOULD SAY...

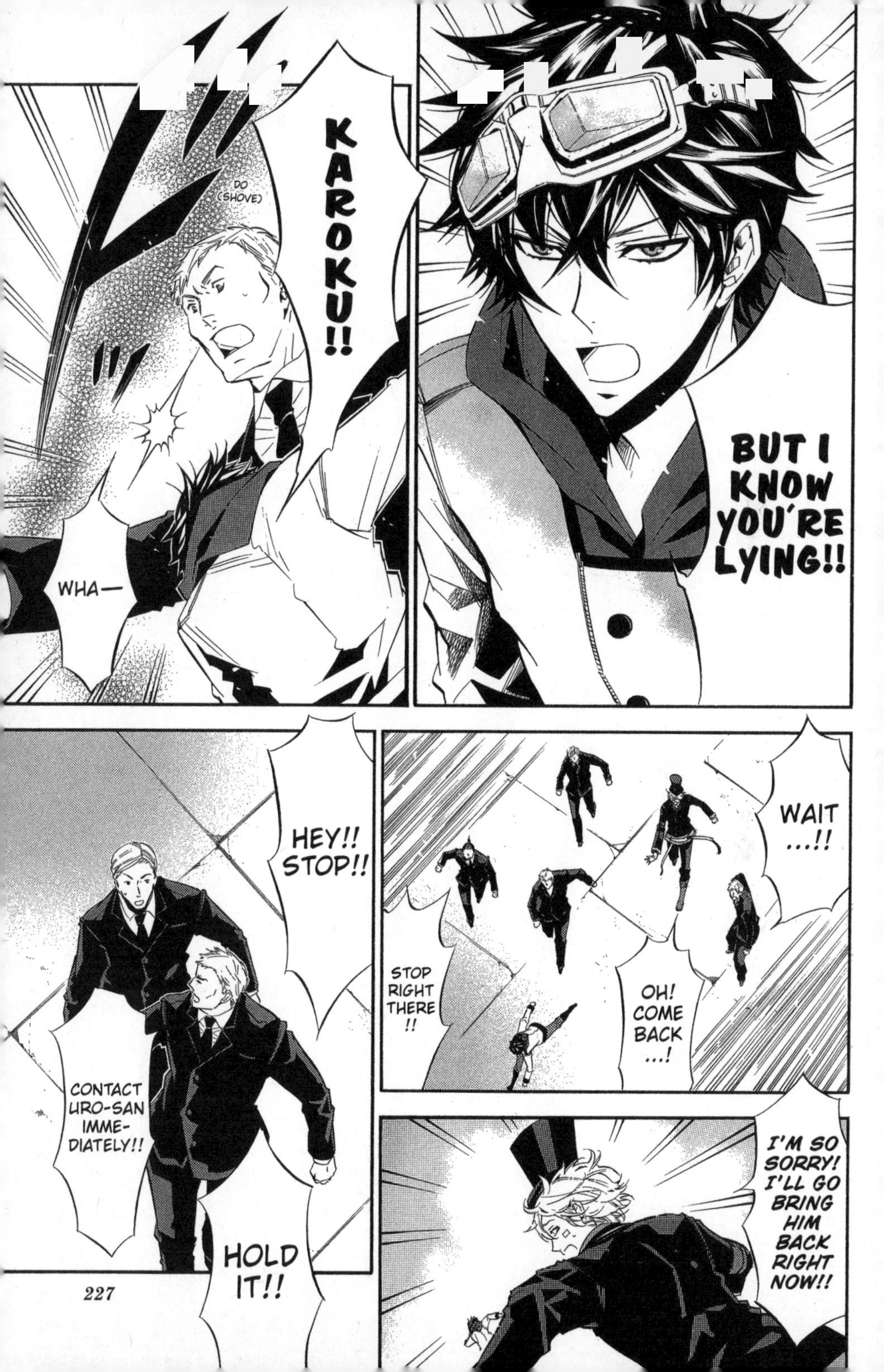
BUT I KNOW YOU'RE LYING!!
KAROKU!!
DO (SHOVE)
WHA—
WAIT ...!!
OH! COME BACK ...!
STOP RIGHT THERE !!
I'M SO SORRY! I'LL GO BRING HIM BACK RIGHT NOW!!
HEY!! STOP!!
CONTACT URO-SAN IMME-DIATELY!!
HOLD IT!!

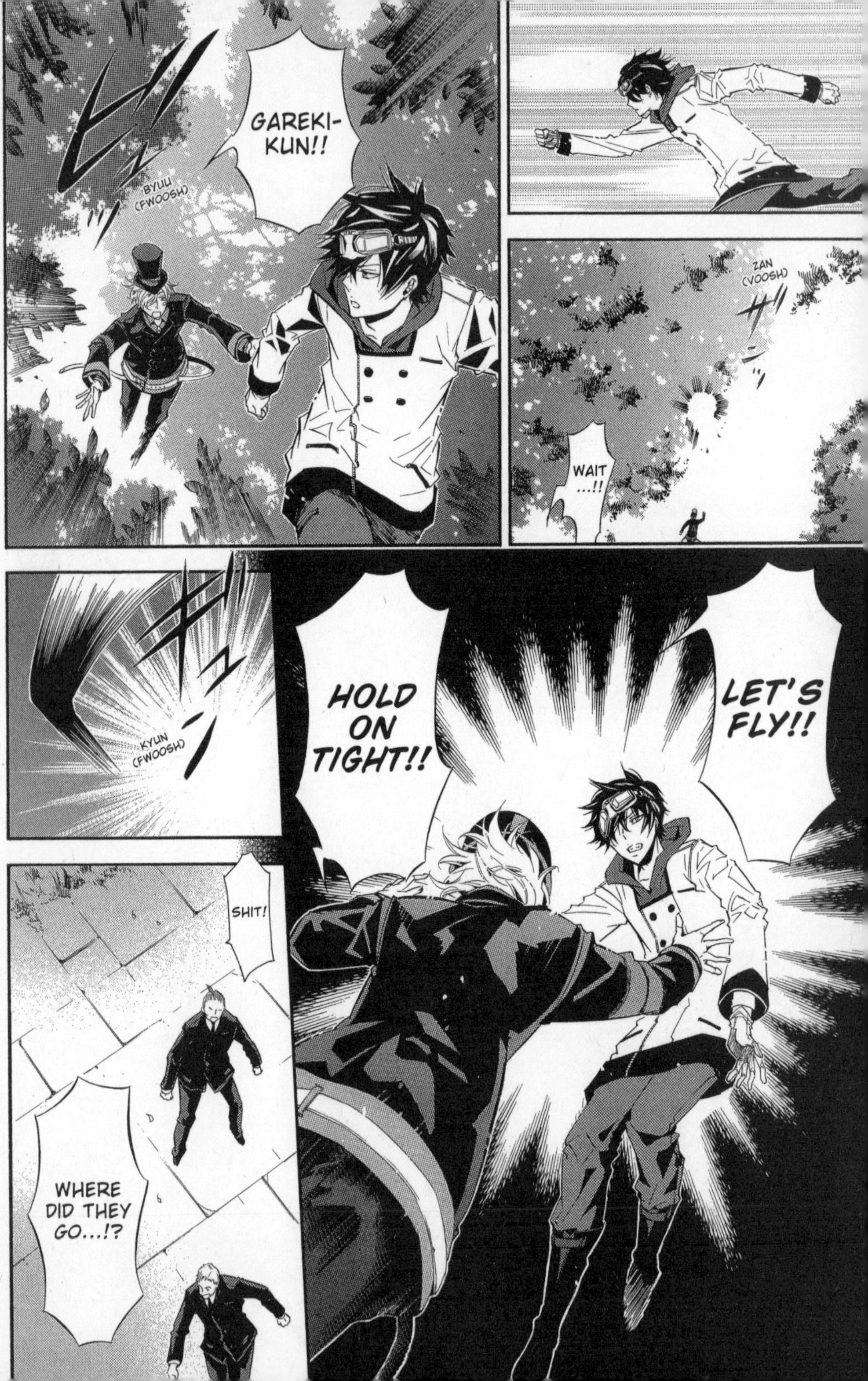
ZAN (VOOSH)
WAIT ...!!
GAREKI-KUN!!
BYUU (FWOOSH)
LET'S FLY!!
HOLD ON TIGHT!!
KYUN (FWOOSH)
SHIT!
WHERE DID THEY GO...!?

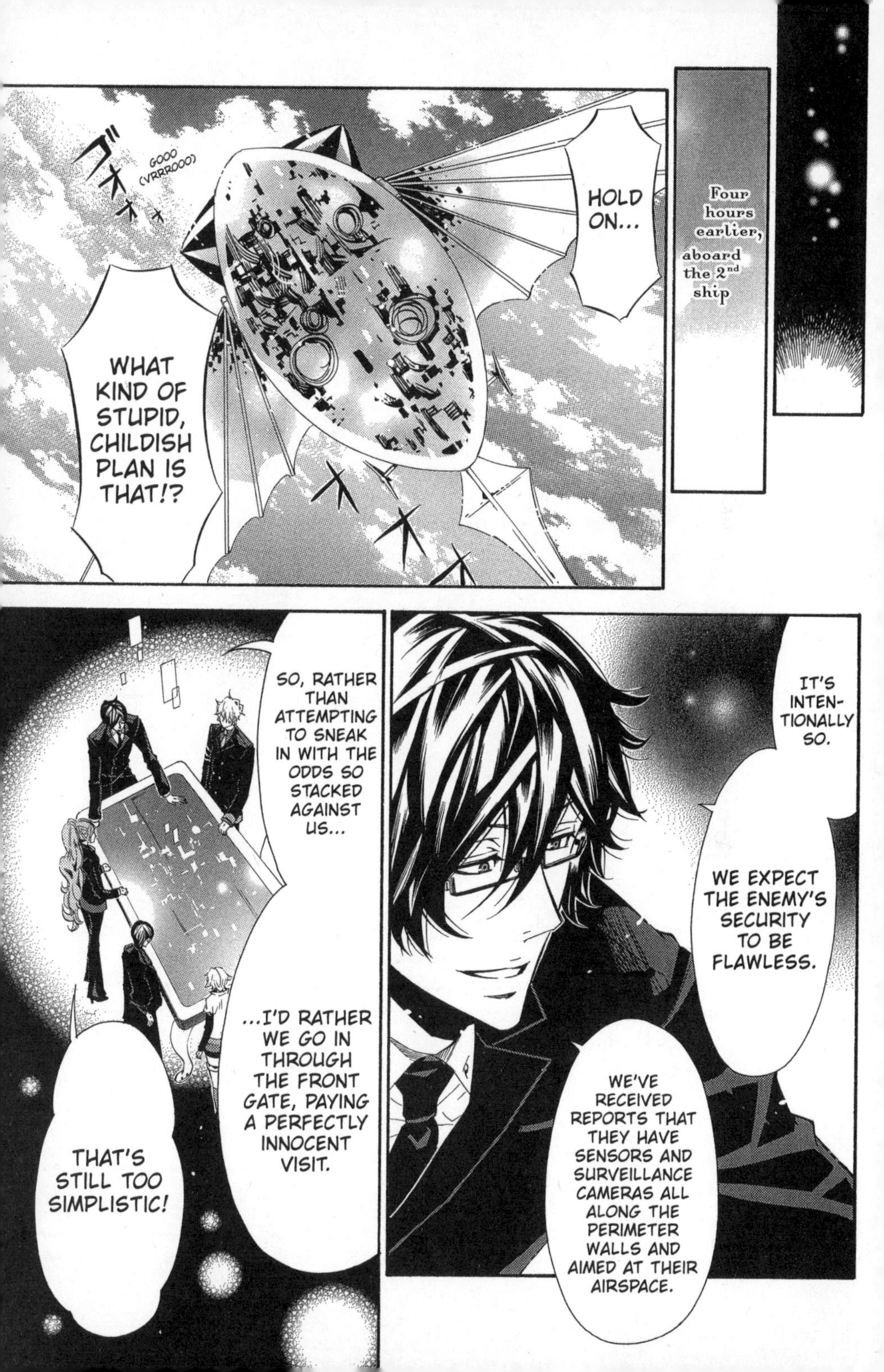
Four hours earlier, aboard the 2nd ship
HOLD ON...
GOOO (VRRROOO)
WHAT KIND OF STUPID, CHILDISH PLAN IS THAT!?
IT'S INTENTIONALLY SO.
WE EXPECT THE ENEMY'S SECURITY TO BE FLAWLESS.
WE'VE RECEIVED REPORTS THAT THEY HAVE SENSORS AND SURVEILLANCE CAMERAS ALL ALONG THE PERIMETER WALLS AND AIMED AT THEIR AIRSPACE.
SO, RATHER THAN ATTEMPTING TO SNEAK IN WITH THE ODDS SO STACKED AGAINST US...
...I'D RATHER WE GO IN THROUGH THE FRONT GATE, PAYING A PERFECTLY INNOCENT VISIT.
THAT'S STILL TOO SIMPLISTIC!

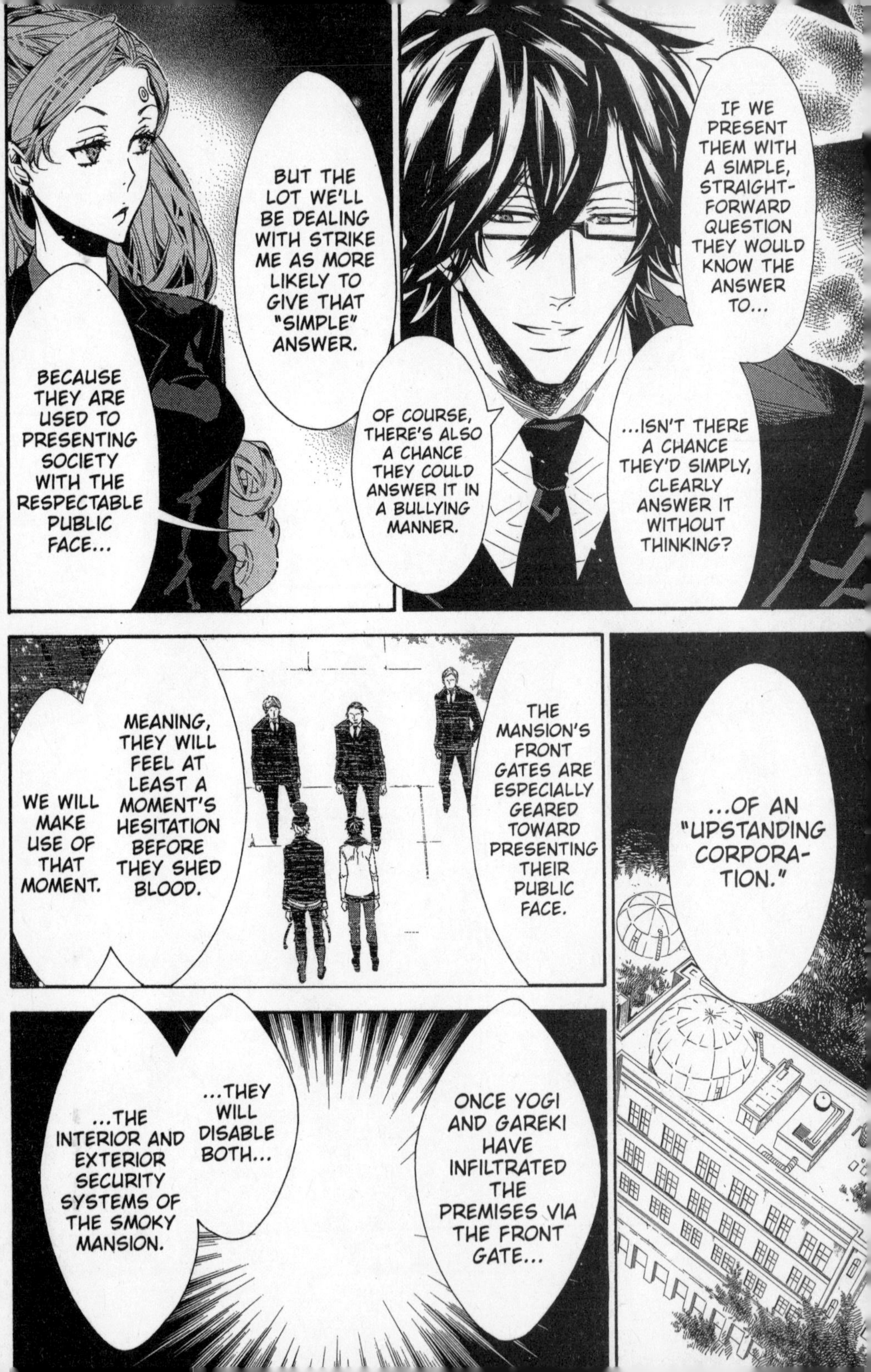
IF WE PRESENT THEM WITH A SIMPLE, STRAIGHT-FORWARD QUESTION THEY WOULD KNOW THE ANSWER TO...
...ISN'T THERE A CHANCE THEY'D SIMPLY, CLEARLY ANSWER IT WITHOUT THINKING?
OF COURSE, THERE'S ALSO A CHANCE THEY COULD ANSWER IT IN A BULLYING MANNER.
BUT THE LOT WE'LL BE DEALING WITH STRIKE ME AS MORE LIKELY TO GIVE THAT "SIMPLE" ANSWER.
BECAUSE THEY ARE USED TO PRESENTING SOCIETY WITH THE RESPECTABLE PUBLIC FACE...
...OF AN "UPSTANDING CORPORA-TION."
THE MANSION'S FRONT GATES ARE ESPECIALLY GEARED TOWARD PRESENTING THEIR PUBLIC FACE.
MEANING, THEY WILL FEEL AT LEAST A MOMENT'S HESITATION BEFORE THEY SHED BLOOD.
WE WILL MAKE USE OF THAT MOMENT.
ONCE YOGI AND GAREKI HAVE INFILTRATED THE PREMISES VIA THE FRONT GATE...
...THEY WILL DISABLE BOTH...
...THE INTERIOR AND EXTERIOR SECURITY SYSTEMS OF THE SMOKY MANSION.

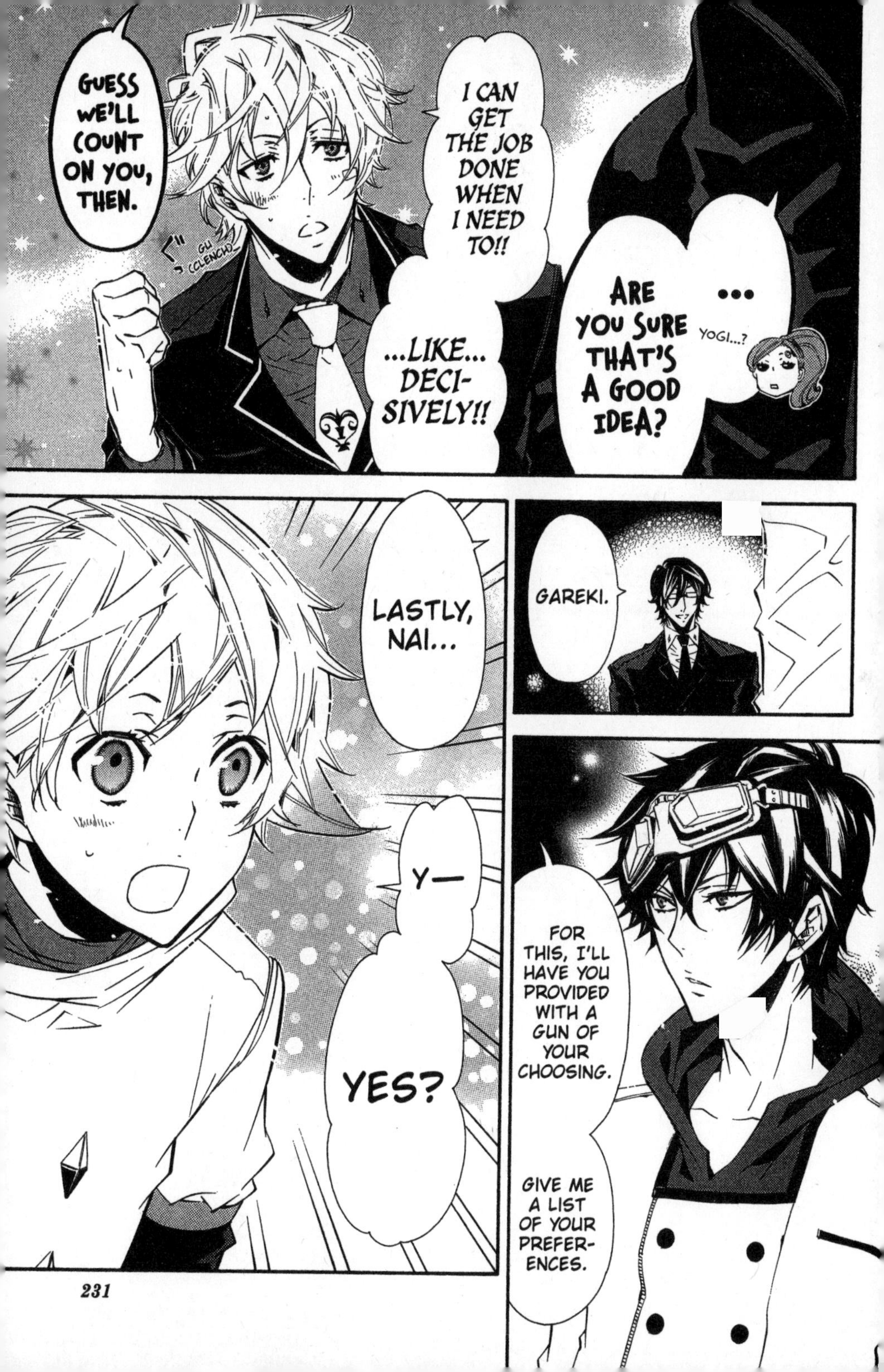
...
ARE YOU SURE THAT'S A GOOD IDEA?
YOGI...?
I CAN GET THE JOB DONE WHEN I NEED TO!!
...LIKE... DECI-SIVELY!!
GUESS WE'LL COUNT ON YOU, THEN.
GU (CLENCH)
GAREKI.
FOR THIS, I'LL HAVE YOU PROVIDED WITH A GUN OF YOUR CHOOSING.
GIVE ME A LIST OF YOUR PREFER-ENCES.
LASTLY, NAI...
Y—
YES?

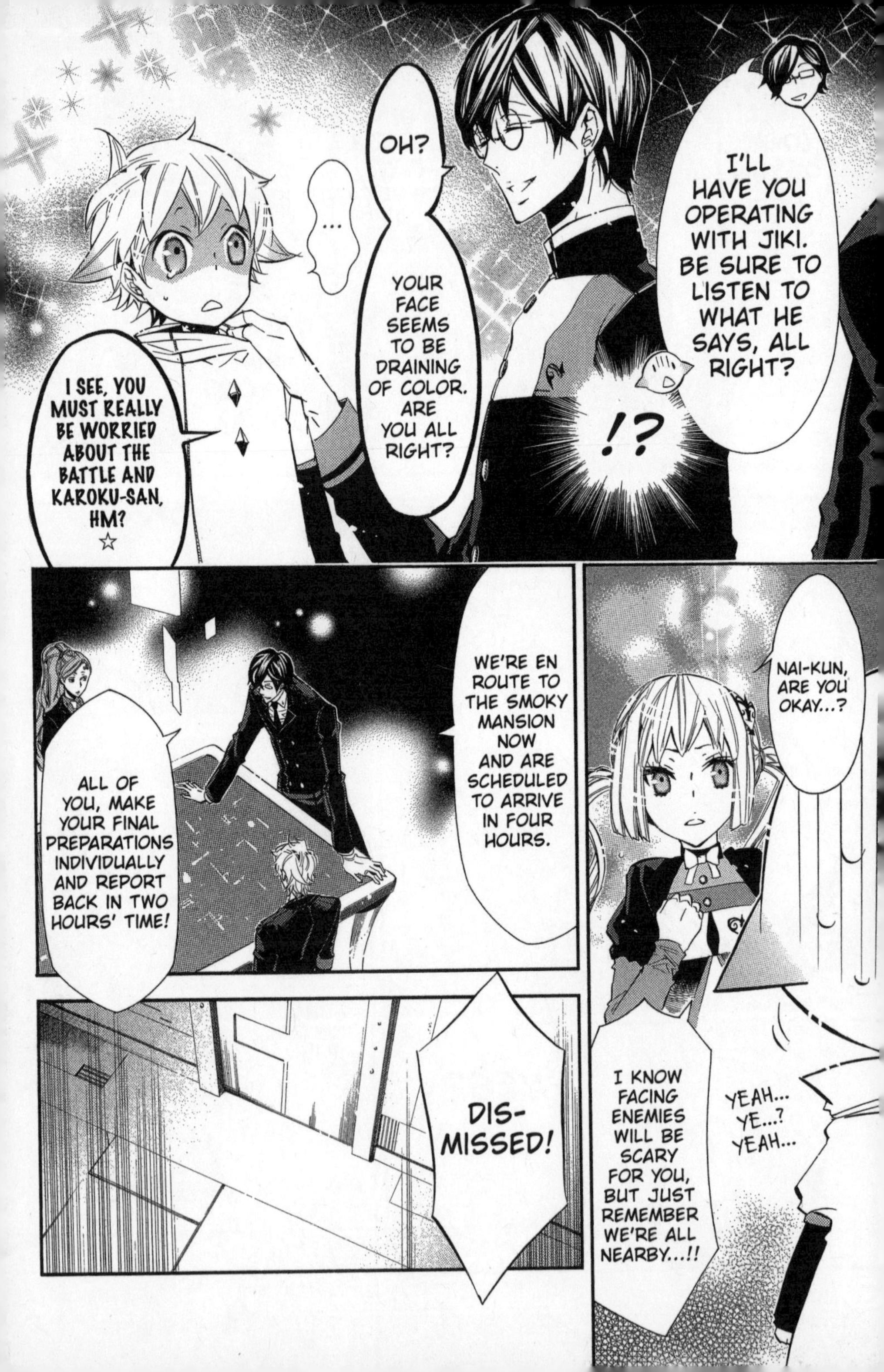
I'LL HAVE YOU OPERATING WITH JIKI. BE SURE TO LISTEN TO WHAT HE SAYS, ALL RIGHT?
!?
OH?
YOUR FACE SEEMS TO BE DRAINING OF COLOR. ARE YOU ALL RIGHT?
...
I SEE, YOU MUST REALLY BE WORRIED ABOUT THE BATTLE AND KAROKU-SAN, HM? ☆
NAI-KUN, ARE YOU OKAY...?
I KNOW FACING ENEMIES WILL BE SCARY FOR YOU, BUT JUST REMEMBER WE'RE ALL NEARBY...!!
YEAH... YE...? YEAH...
WE'RE EN ROUTE TO THE SMOKY MANSION NOW AND ARE SCHEDULED TO ARRIVE IN FOUR HOURS.
ALL OF YOU, MAKE YOUR FINAL PREPARATIONS INDIVIDUALLY AND REPORT BACK IN TWO HOURS' TIME!
DIS-MISSED!

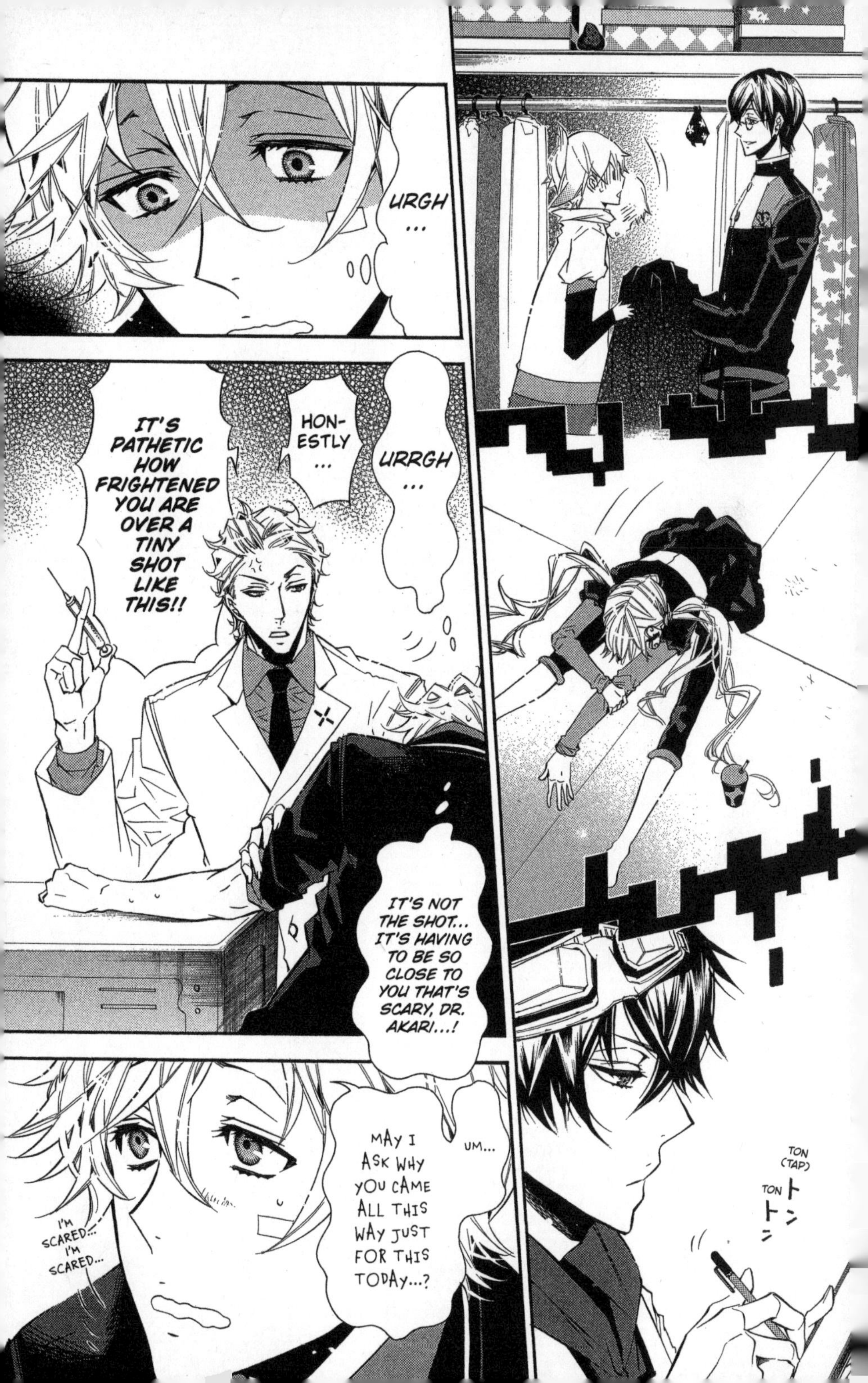
URGH...
HON-ESTLY...
IT'S PATHETIC HOW FRIGHTENED YOU ARE OVER A TINY SHOT LIKE THIS!!
URRGH...
IT'S NOT THE SHOT... IT'S HAVING TO BE SO CLOSE TO YOU THAT'S SCARY, DR. AKARI...!
TON (TAP)
TON トン
トン
UM...
MAY I ASK WHY YOU CAME ALL THIS WAY JUST FOR THIS TODAY...?
I'M SCARED... I'M SCARED...

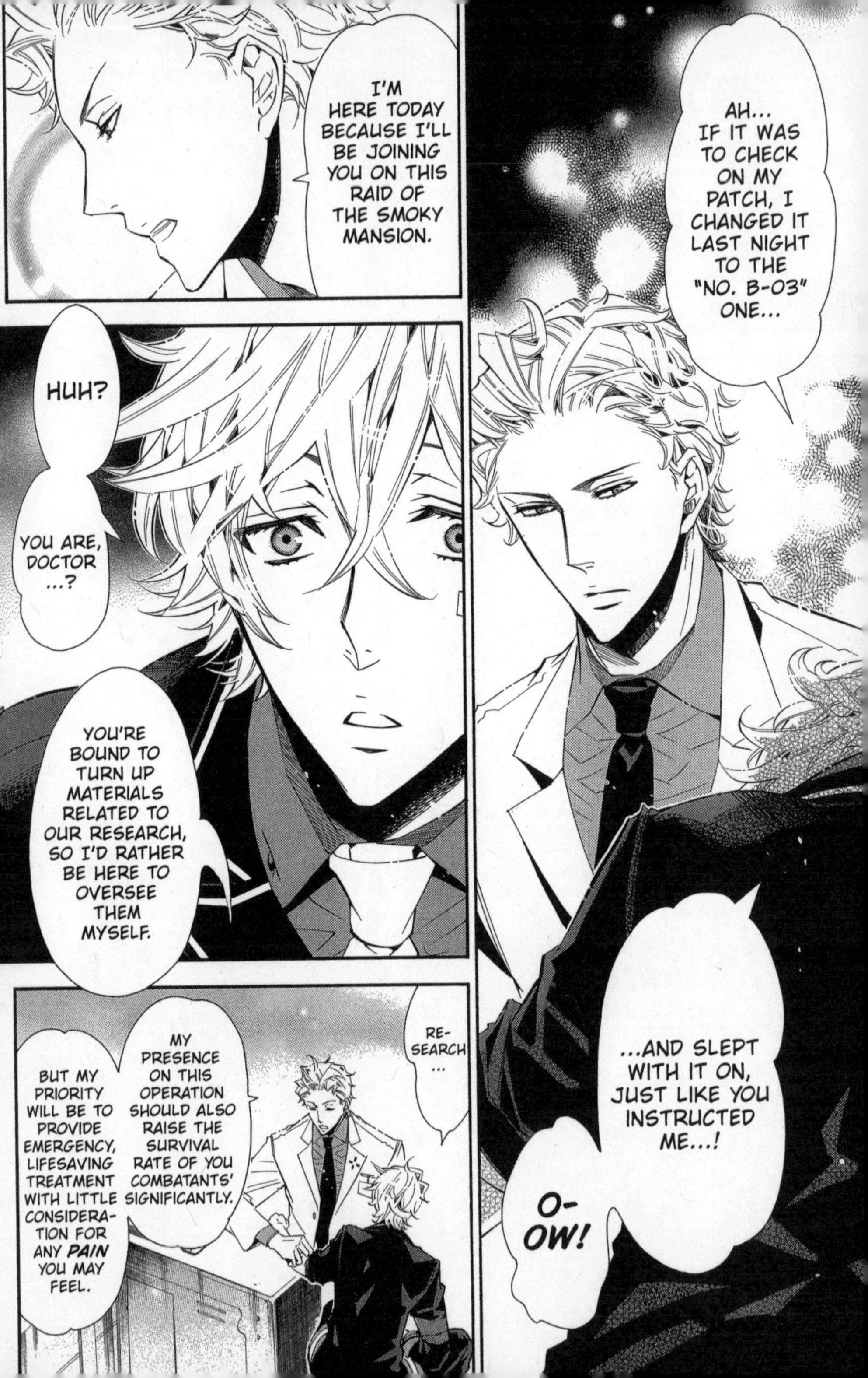
AH... IF IT WAS TO CHECK ON MY PATCH, I CHANGED IT LAST NIGHT TO THE "NO. B-03" ONE...
...AND SLEPT WITH IT ON, JUST LIKE YOU INSTRUCTED ME...!
O-OW!
I'M HERE TODAY BECAUSE I'LL BE JOINING YOU ON THIS RAID OF THE SMOKY MANSION.
HUH?
YOU ARE, DOCTOR ...?
YOU'RE BOUND TO TURN UP MATERIALS RELATED TO OUR RESEARCH, SO I'D RATHER BE HERE TO OVERSEE THEM MYSELF.
RE-SEARCH ...
MY PRESENCE ON THIS OPERATION SHOULD ALSO RAISE THE SURVIVAL RATE OF YOU COMBATANTS' SIGNIFICANTLY.
BUT MY PRIORITY WILL BE TO PROVIDE EMERGENCY, LIFESAVING TREATMENT WITH LITTLE CONSIDERATION FOR ANY PAIN YOU MAY FEEL.

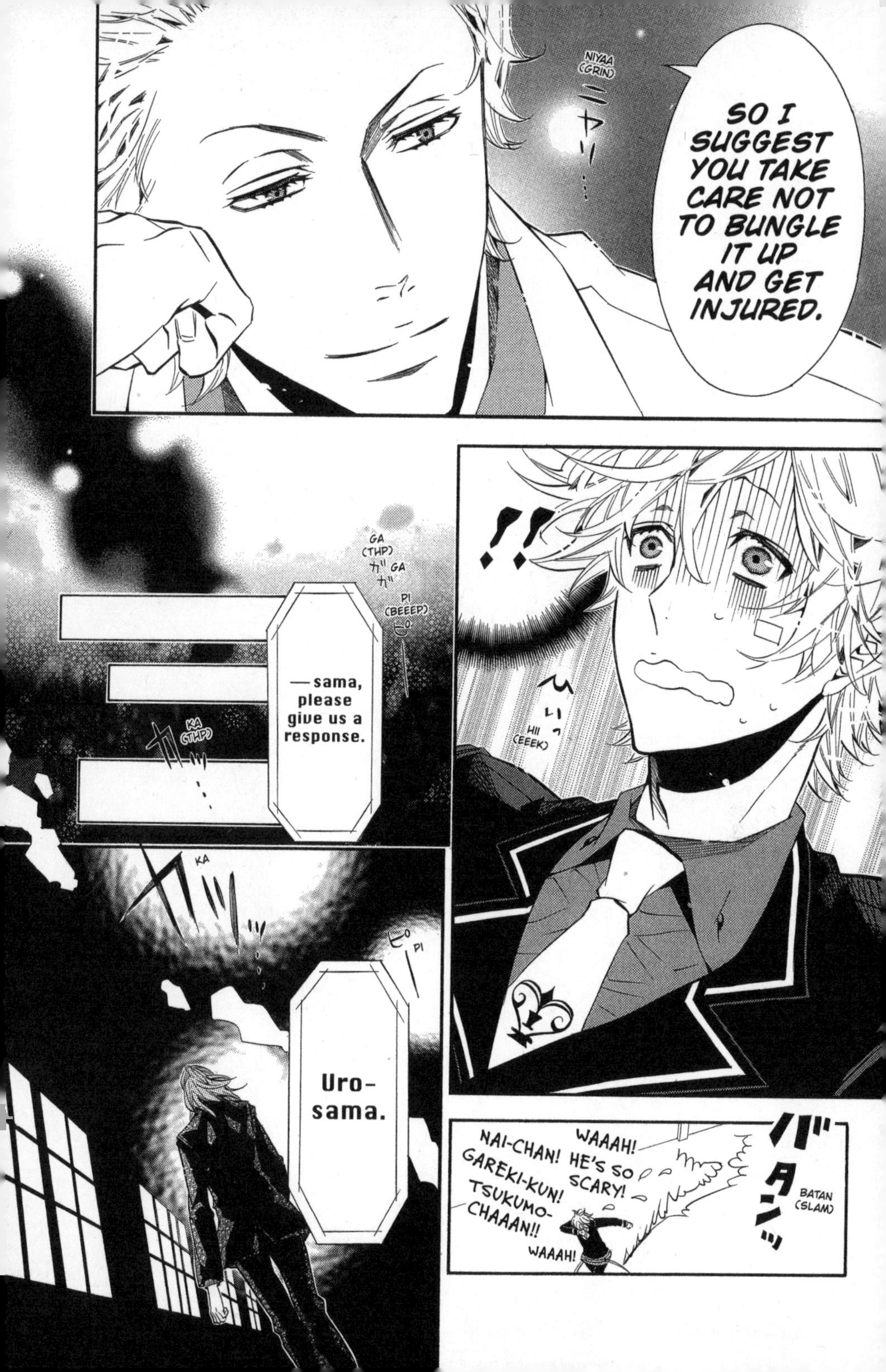NIYAA (GRIN)
SO I SUGGEST YOU TAKE CARE NOT TO BUNGLE IT UP AND GET INJURED.
!!
HII (EEEK)
NAI-CHAN! GAREKI-KUN! TSUKUMO-CHAAAN!!
WAAAH! HE'S SO SCARY!
WAAAH!
BATAN (SLAM)
GA (THP) GA
PI (BEEEP)
KA (THP)
—sama, please give us a response.
KA
PI
Uro-sama.

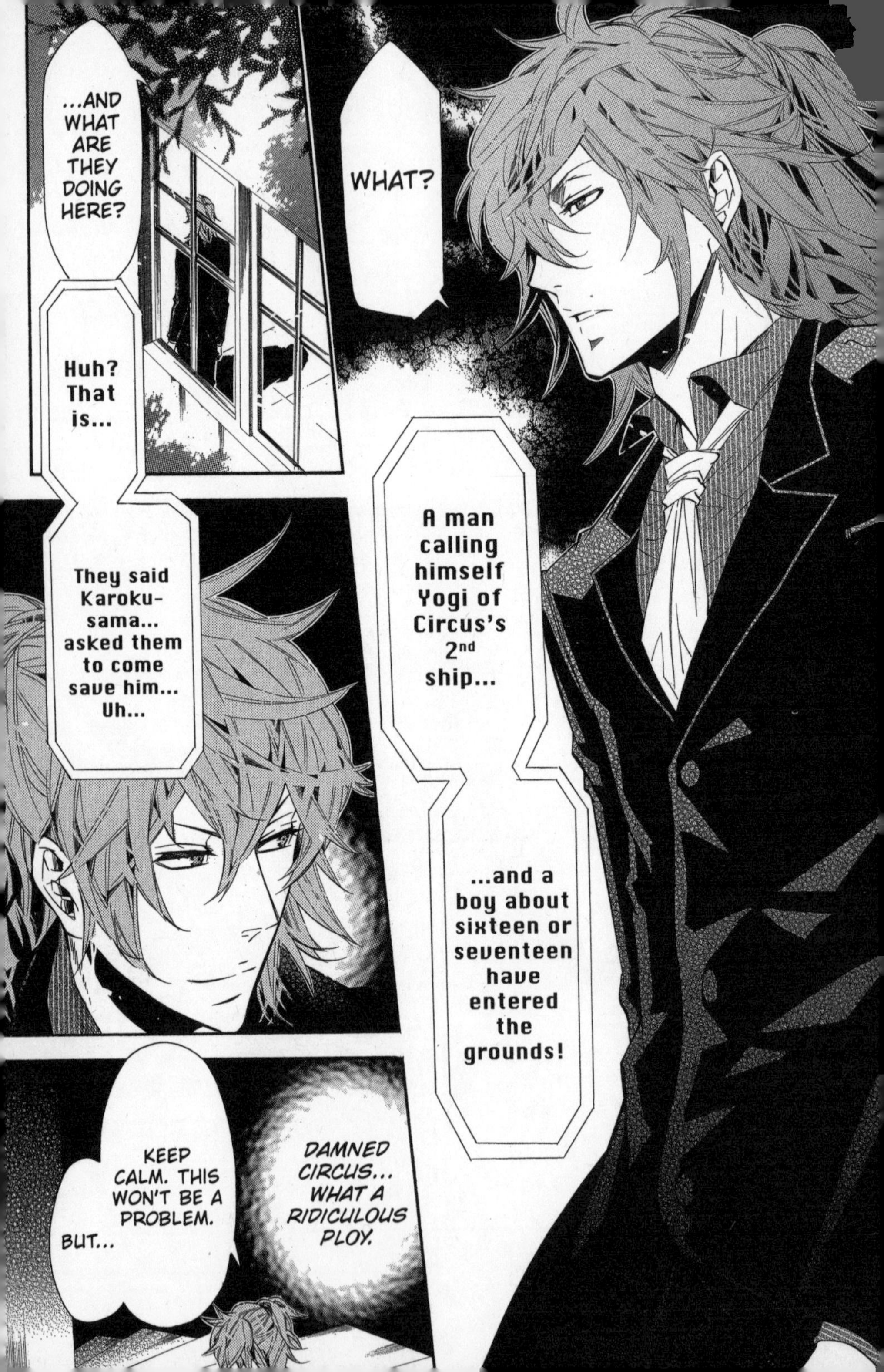

A man calling himself Yogi of Circus's 2nd ship...
...and a boy about sixteen or seventeen have entered the grounds!
WHAT?
...AND WHAT ARE THEY DOING HERE?
Huh? That is...
They said Karoku-sama... asked them to come save him... Uh...
DAMNED CIRCUS... WHAT A RIDICULOUS PLOY.
KEEP CALM. THIS WON'T BE A PROBLEM. BUT...

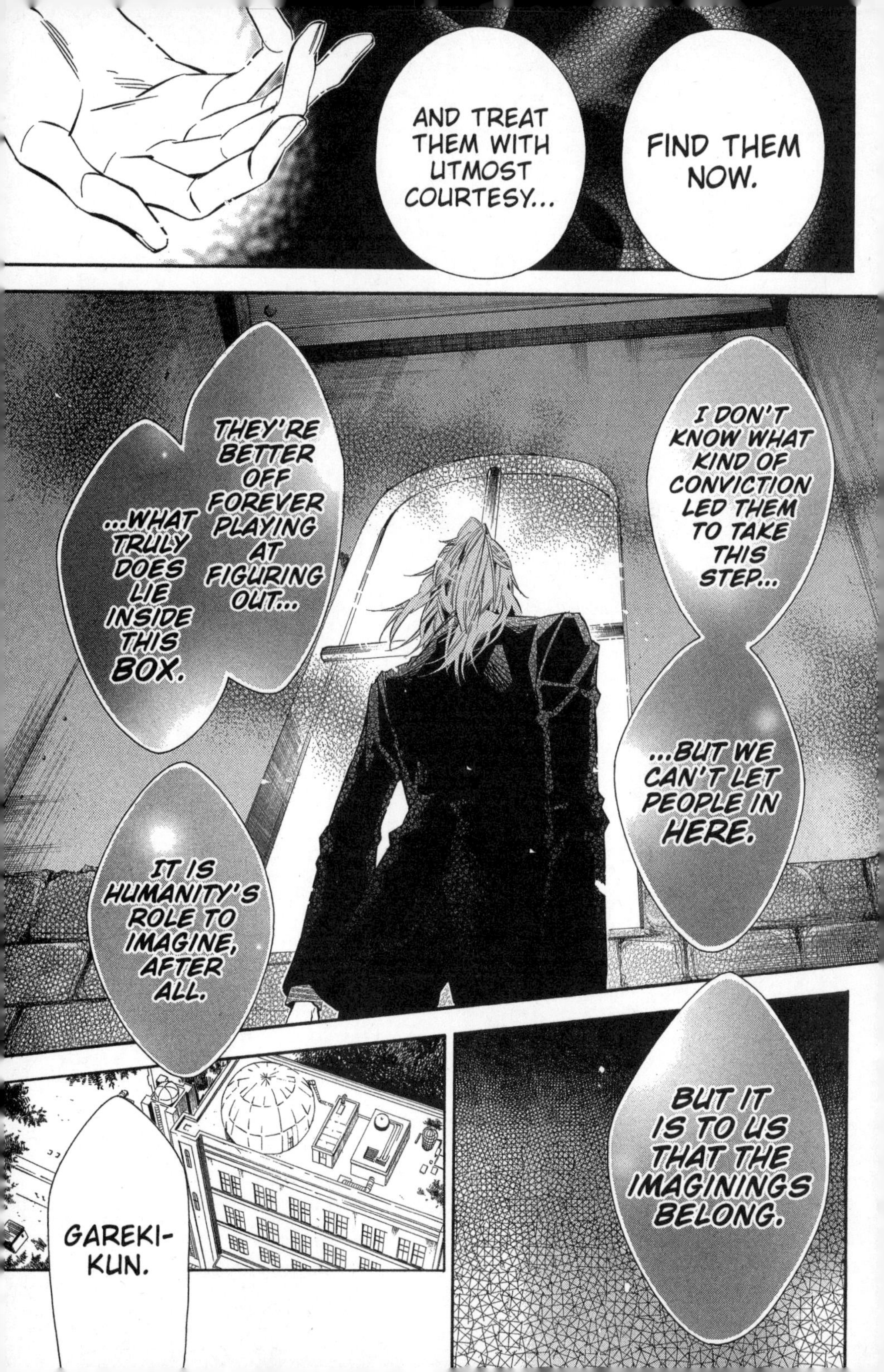
FIND THEM NOW.
AND TREAT THEM WITH UTMOST COURTESY...
I DON'T KNOW WHAT KIND OF CONVICTION LED THEM TO TAKE THIS STEP...
...BUT WE CAN'T LET PEOPLE IN HERE.
THEY'RE BETTER OFF FOREVER PLAYING AT FIGURING OUT...
...WHAT TRULY DOES LIE INSIDE THIS BOX.
IT IS HUMANITY'S ROLE TO IMAGINE, AFTER ALL.
BUT IT IS TO US THAT THE IMAGININGS BELONG.
GAREKI-KUN.

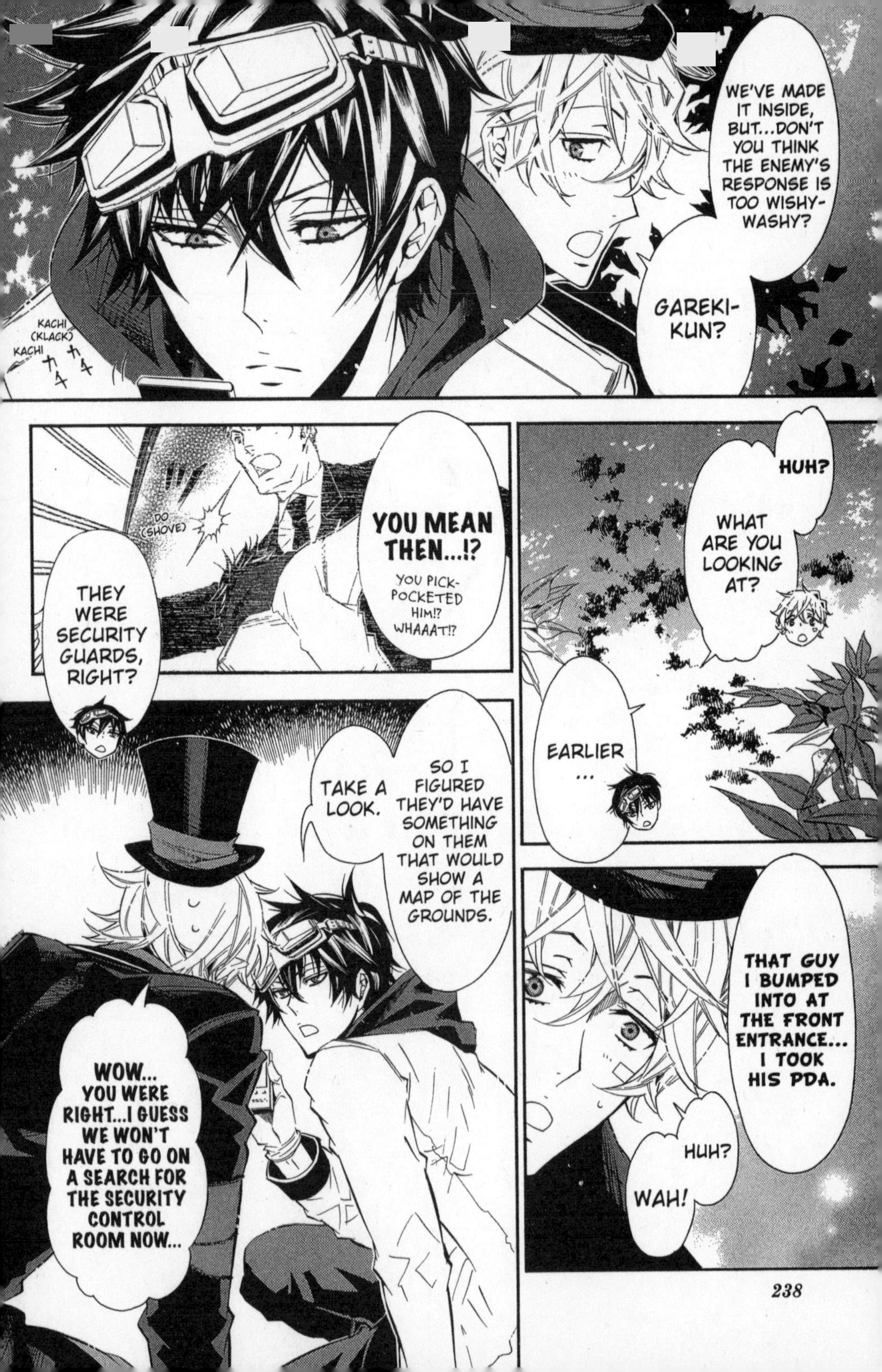
WE'VE MADE IT INSIDE, BUT...DON'T YOU THINK THE ENEMY'S RESPONSE IS TOO WISHY-WASHY?
GAREKI-KUN?
KACHI (KLACK) KACHI
HUH?
WHAT ARE YOU LOOKING AT?
EARLIER...
THAT GUY I BUMPED INTO AT THE FRONT ENTRANCE... I TOOK HIS PDA.
HUH?
WAH!
YOU MEAN THEN...!?
YOU PICK-POCKETED HIM!? WHAAAT!?
DO (SHOVE)
THEY WERE SECURITY GUARDS, RIGHT?
SO I FIGURED THEY'D HAVE SOMETHING ON THEM THAT WOULD SHOW A MAP OF THE GROUNDS.
TAKE A LOOK.
WOW... YOU WERE RIGHT...I GUESS WE WON'T HAVE TO GO ON A SEARCH FOR THE SECURITY CONTROL ROOM NOW...

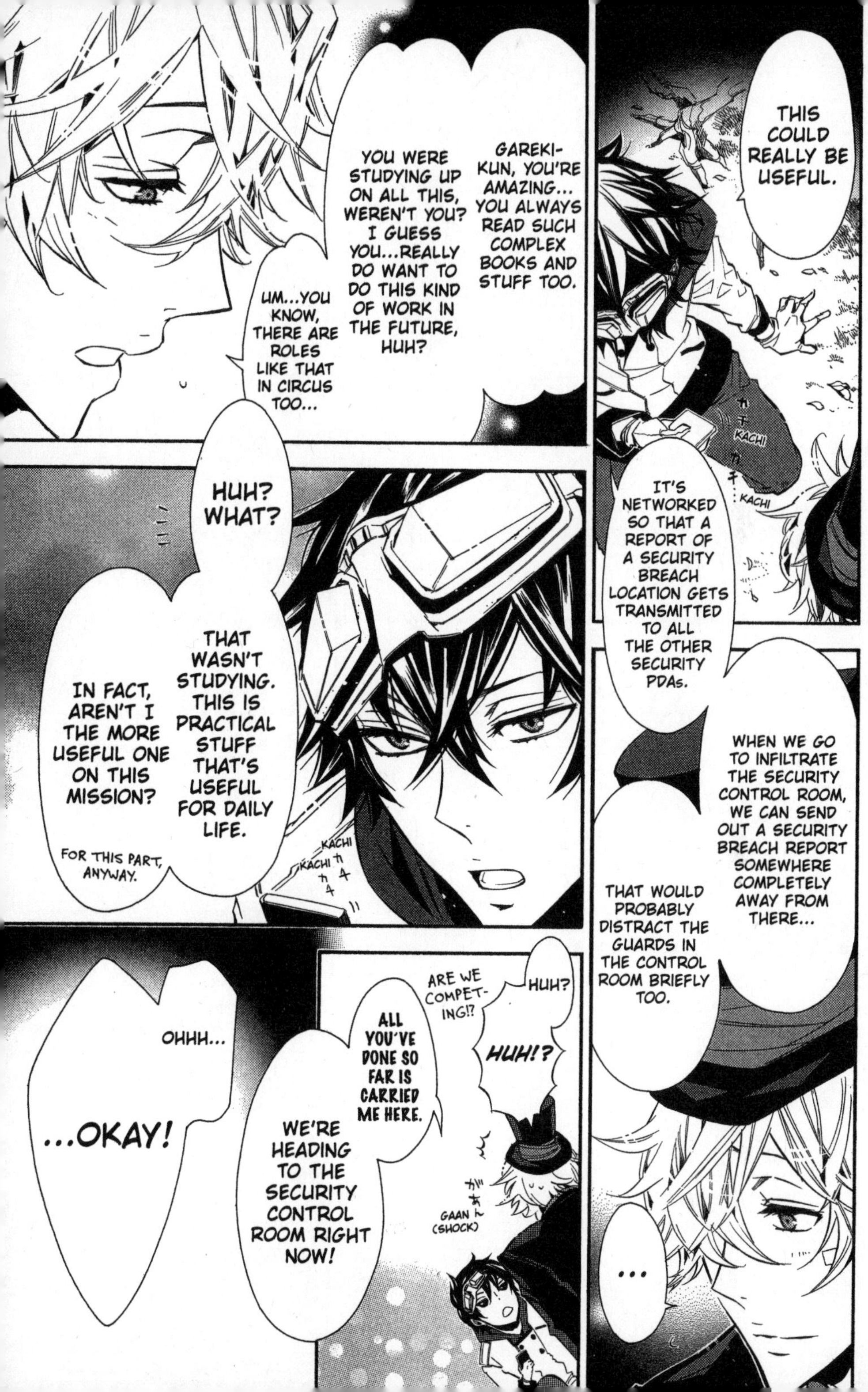
THIS COULD REALLY BE USEFUL.
KACHI
KACHI
IT'S NETWORKED SO THAT A REPORT OF A SECURITY BREACH LOCATION GETS TRANSMITTED TO ALL THE OTHER SECURITY PDAs.
WHEN WE GO TO INFILTRATE THE SECURITY CONTROL ROOM, WE CAN SEND OUT A SECURITY BREACH REPORT SOMEWHERE COMPLETELY AWAY FROM THERE...
THAT WOULD PROBABLY DISTRACT THE GUARDS IN THE CONTROL ROOM BRIEFLY TOO.
...
GAREKI-KUN, YOU'RE AMAZING... YOU ALWAYS READ SUCH COMPLEX BOOKS AND STUFF TOO.
YOU WERE STUDYING UP ON ALL THIS, WEREN'T YOU? I GUESS YOU...REALLY DO WANT TO DO THIS KIND OF WORK IN THE FUTURE, HUH?
UM...YOU KNOW, THERE ARE ROLES LIKE THAT IN CIRCUS TOO...
HUH? WHAT?
THAT WASN'T STUDYING. THIS IS PRACTICAL STUFF THAT'S USEFUL FOR DAILY LIFE.
IN FACT, AREN'T I THE MORE USEFUL ONE ON THIS MISSION?
FOR THIS PART, ANYWAY.
KACHI
KACHI
HUH?
ARE WE COMPET-ING!?
HUH!?
ALL YOU'VE DONE SO FAR IS CARRIED ME HERE.
WE'RE HEADING TO THE SECURITY CONTROL ROOM RIGHT NOW!
GAAN (SHOCK)
OHHH...
...OKAY!

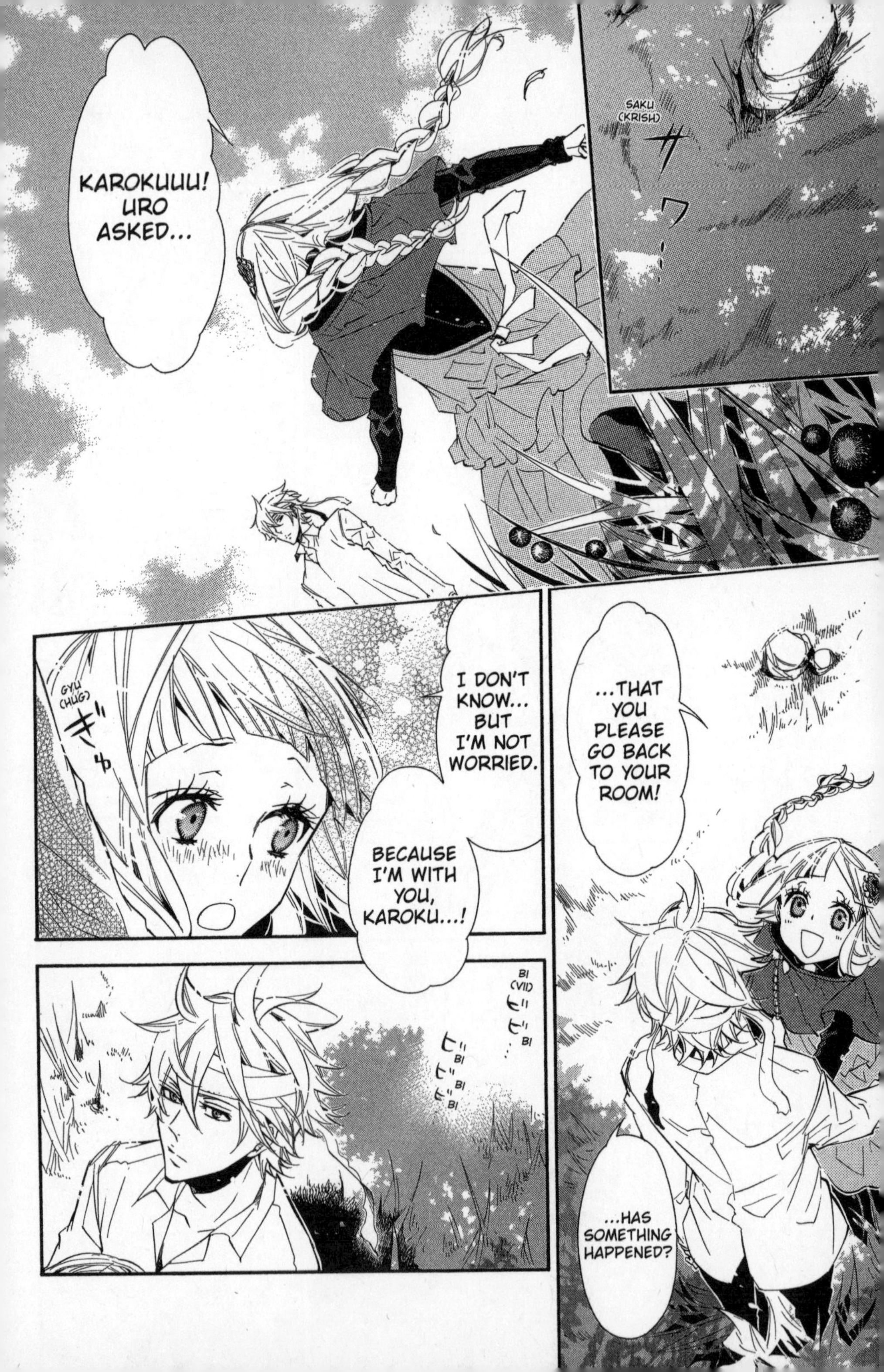
SAKU (KRISH)
KAROKUUU! URO ASKED...
...THAT YOU PLEASE GO BACK TO YOUR ROOM!
...HAS SOMETHING HAPPENED?
I DON'T KNOW... BUT I'M NOT WORRIED.
GYU (HUG)
BECAUSE I'M WITH YOU, KAROKU...!
BI (VII)
BI BI BI BI BI

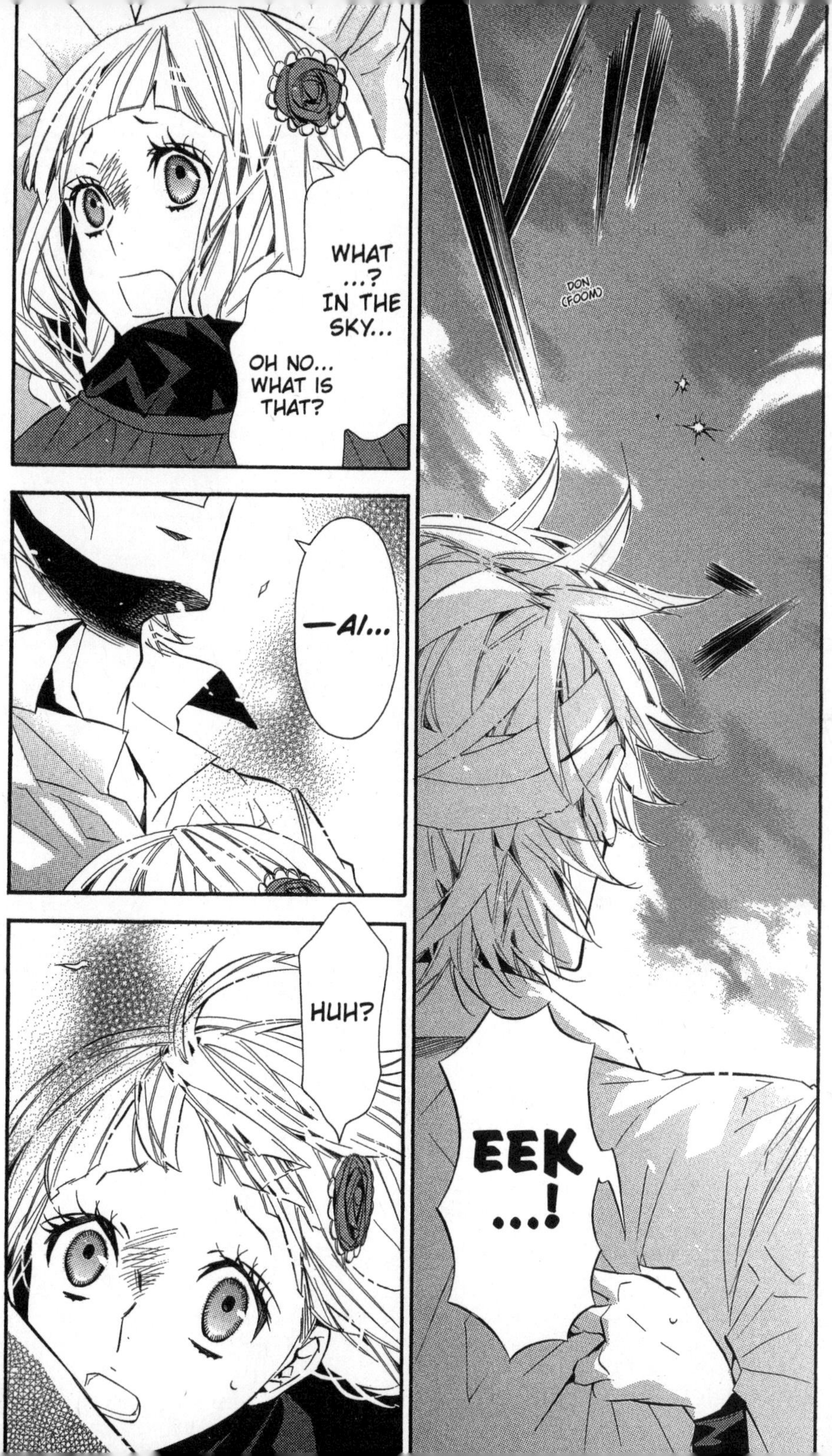
DON (FOOM)
EEK ...!
WHAT ...? IN THE SKY...
OH NO... WHAT IS THAT?
—AI...
HUH?

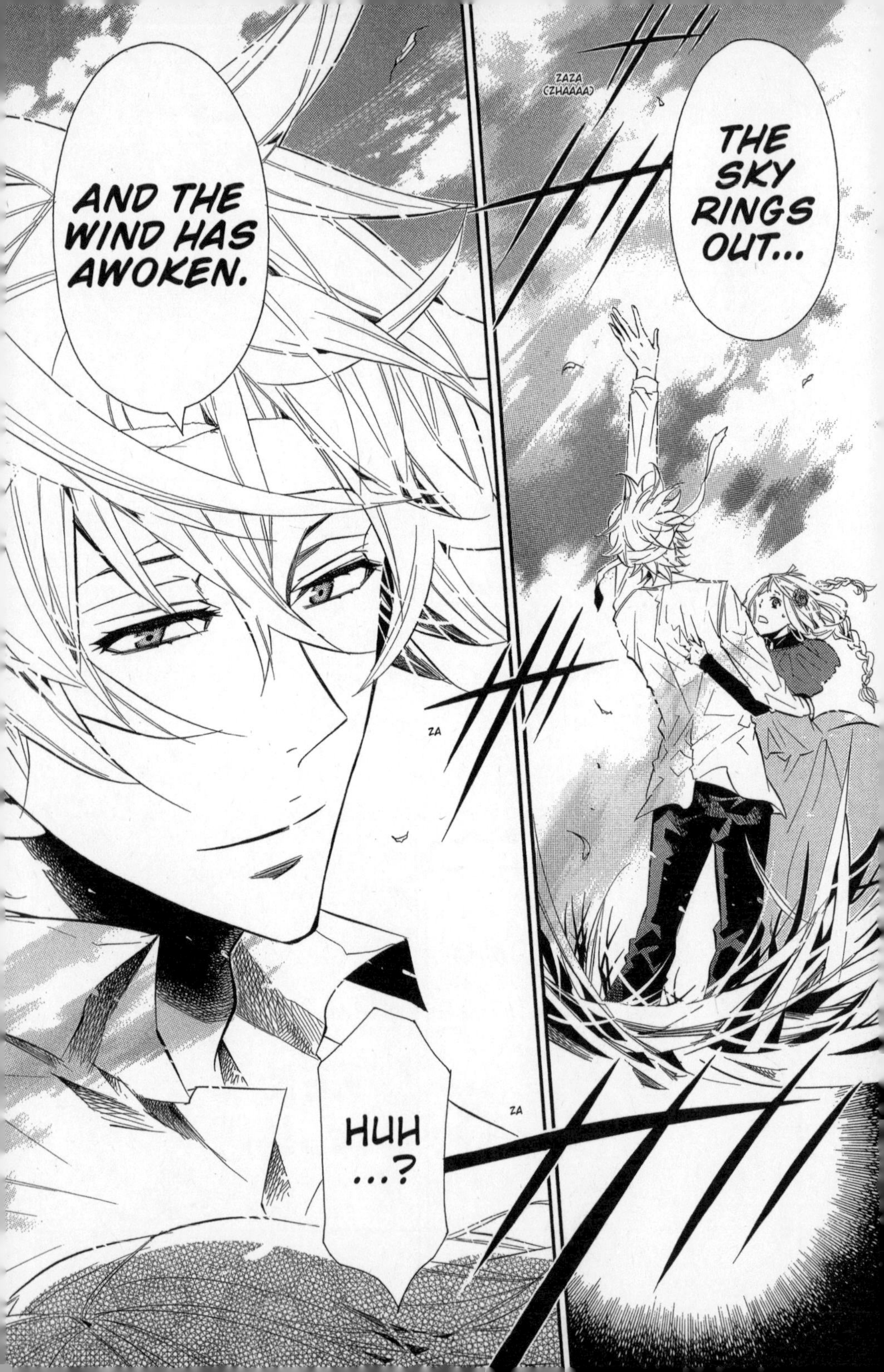
ZAZA (ZHAAAA)
THE SKY RINGS OUT...
AND THE WIND HAS AWOKEN.
ZA
ZA
HUH ...?

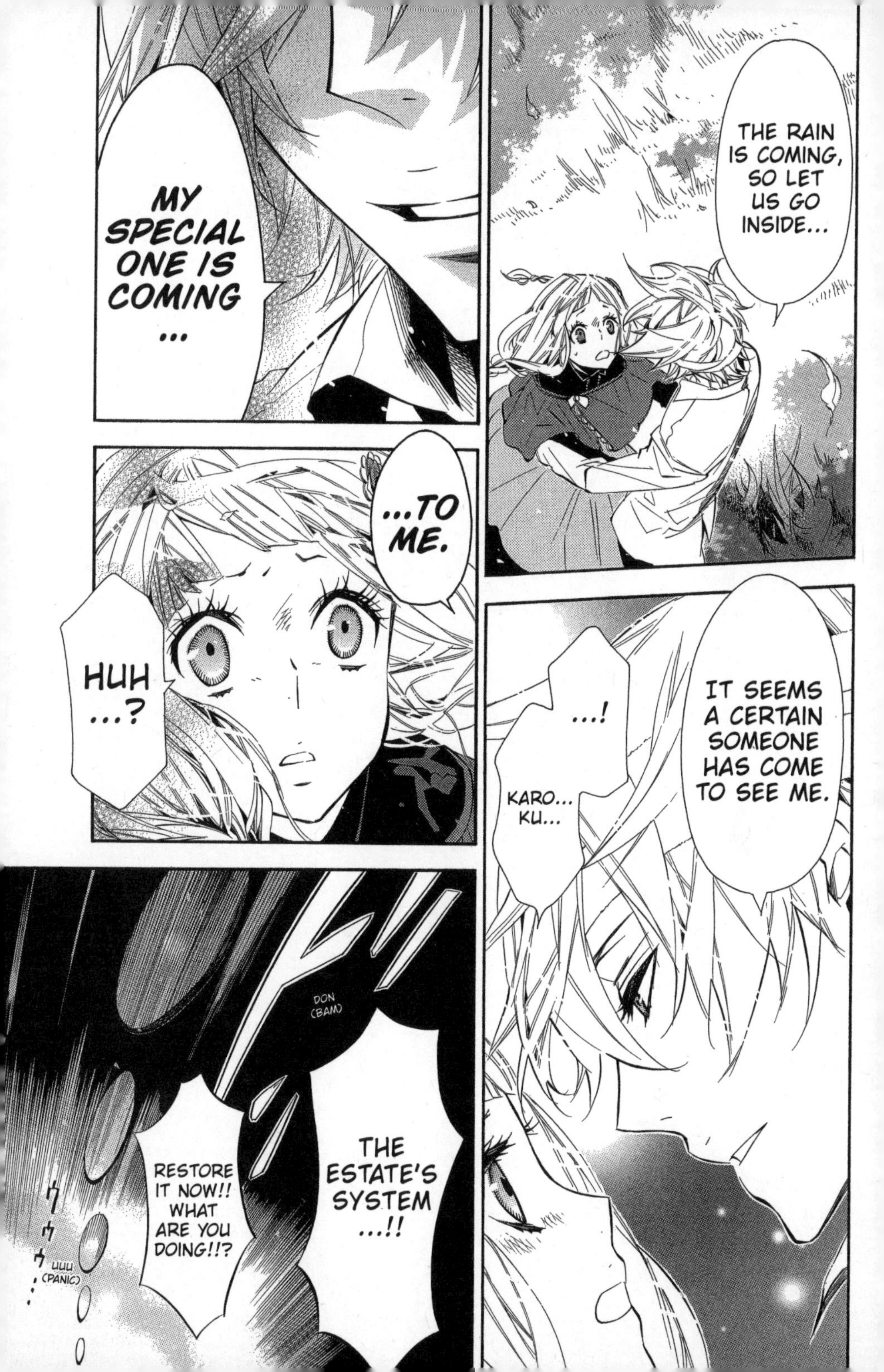
THE RAIN IS COMING, SO LET US GO INSIDE...
MY SPECIAL ONE IS COMING...
...TO ME.
HUH...?
IT SEEMS A CERTAIN SOMEONE HAS COME TO SEE ME.
...!
KARO... KU...
DON (BAM)
THE ESTATE'S SYSTEM...!!
RESTORE IT NOW!! WHAT ARE YOU DOING!!?
ウウウ…
UUU (PANIC)

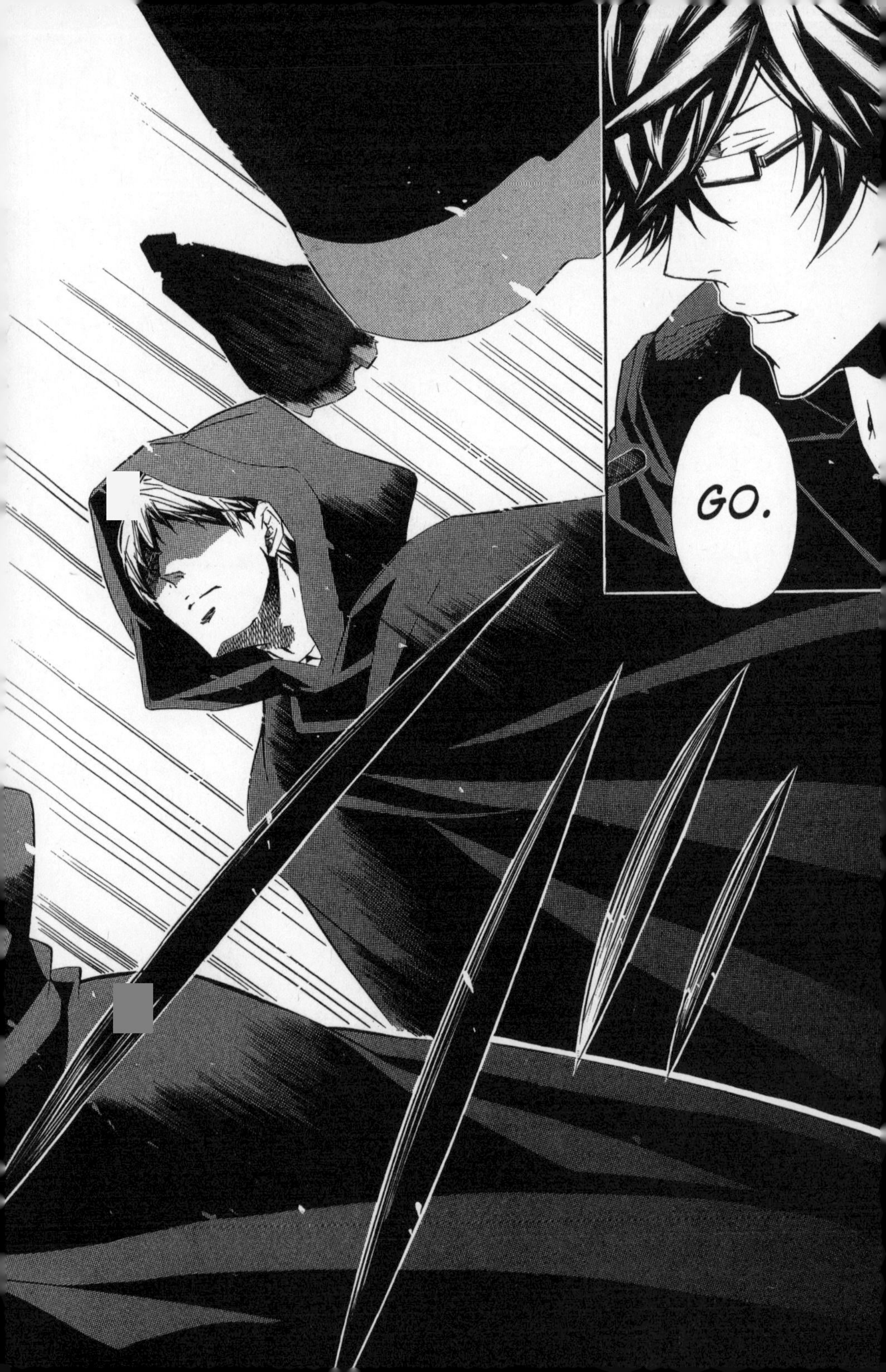
GO.

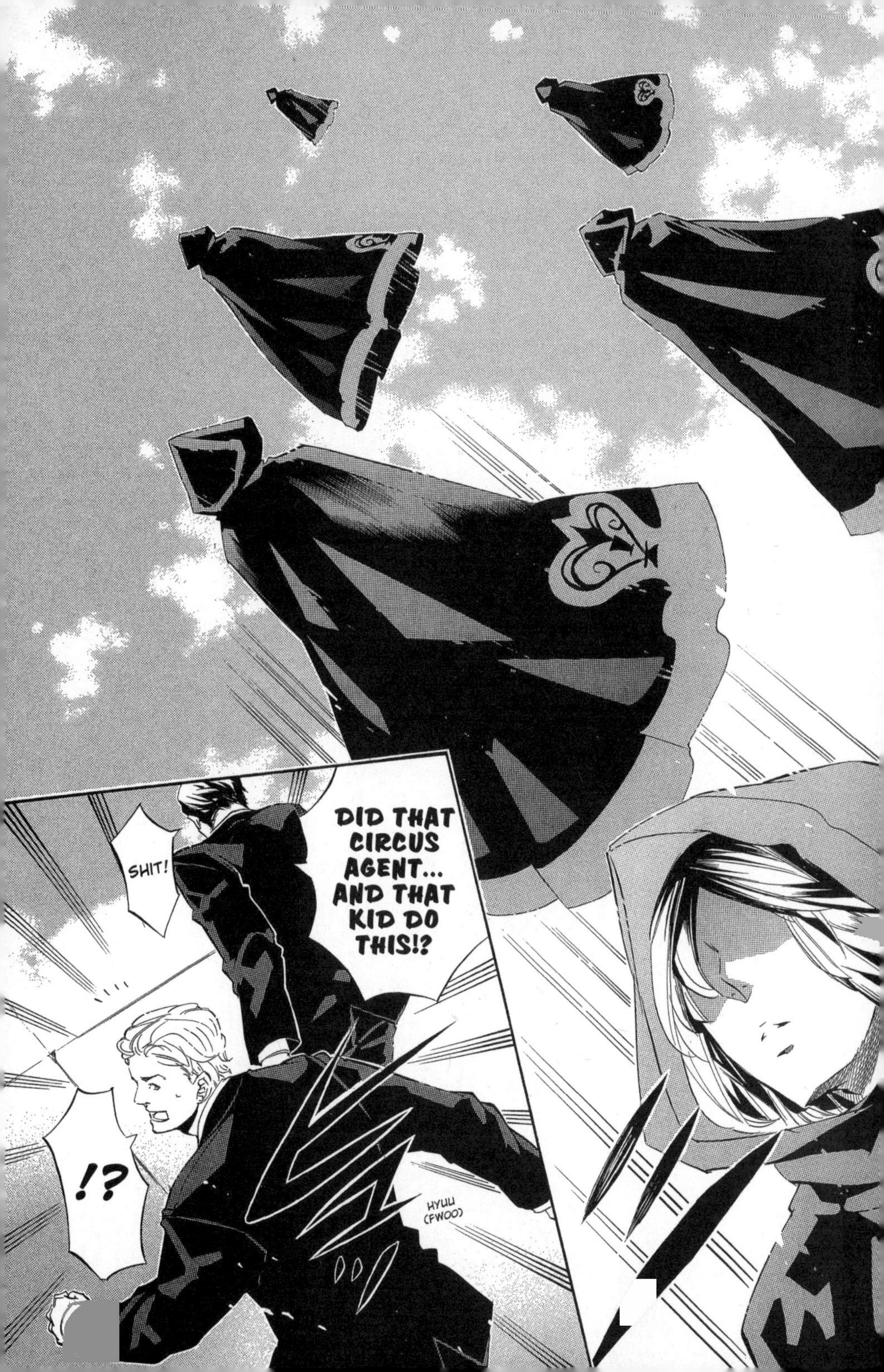
DID THAT CIRCUS AGENT... AND THAT KID DO THIS!?
SHIT!
HYUU (FWOO)
!?

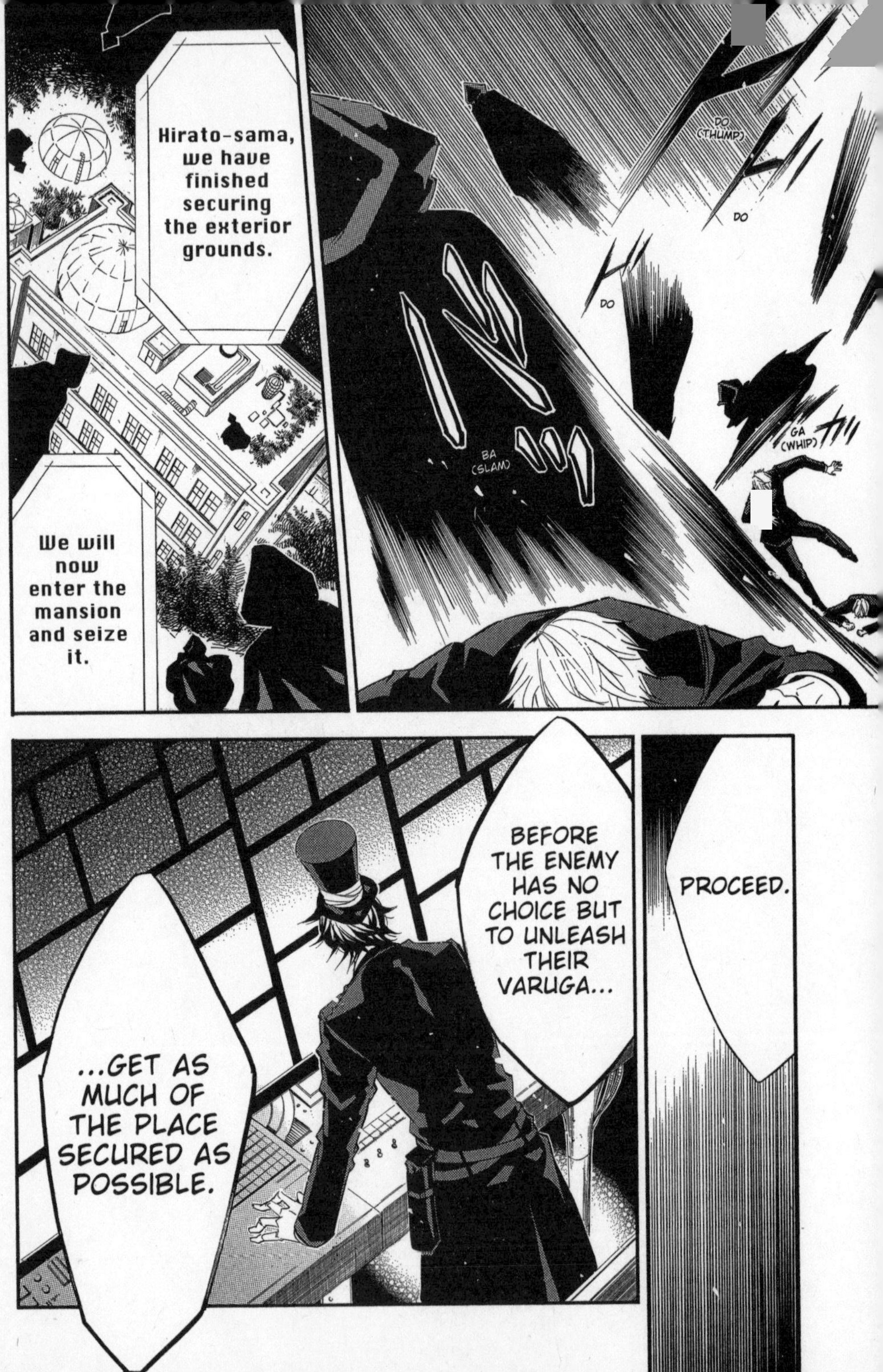
DO (THUMP)
DO
DO
BA (SLAM)
GA (WHIP)
Hirato-sama, we have finished securing the exterior grounds.
We will now enter the mansion and seize it.
PROCEED.
BEFORE THE ENEMY HAS NO CHOICE BUT TO UNLEASH THEIR VARUGA...
...GET AS MUCH OF THE PLACE SECURED AS POSSIBLE.

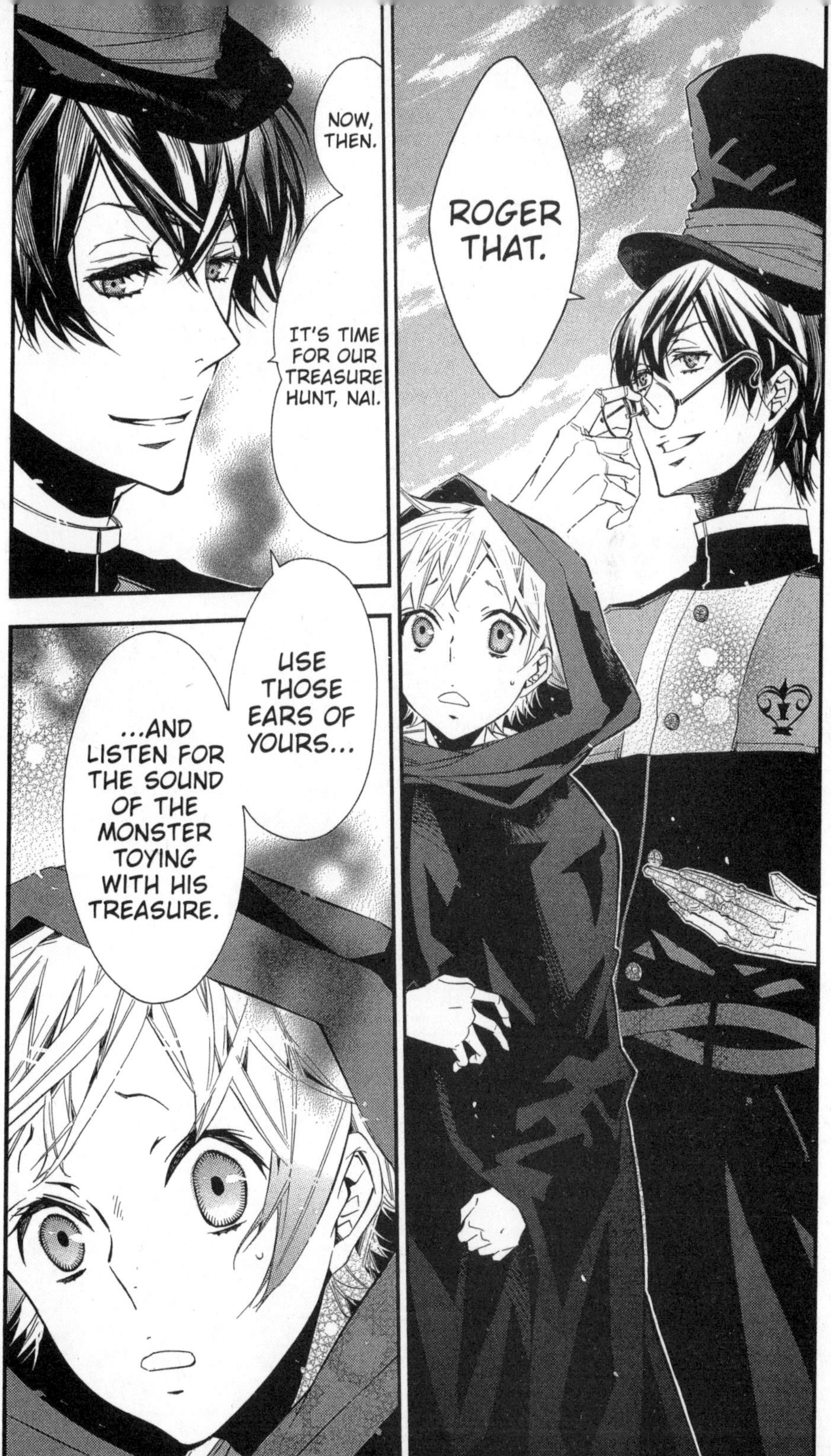
ROGER THAT.
NOW, THEN.
IT'S TIME FOR OUR TREASURE HUNT, NAI.
USE THOSE EARS OF YOURS...
...AND LISTEN FOR THE SOUND OF THE MONSTER TOYING WITH HIS TREASURE.

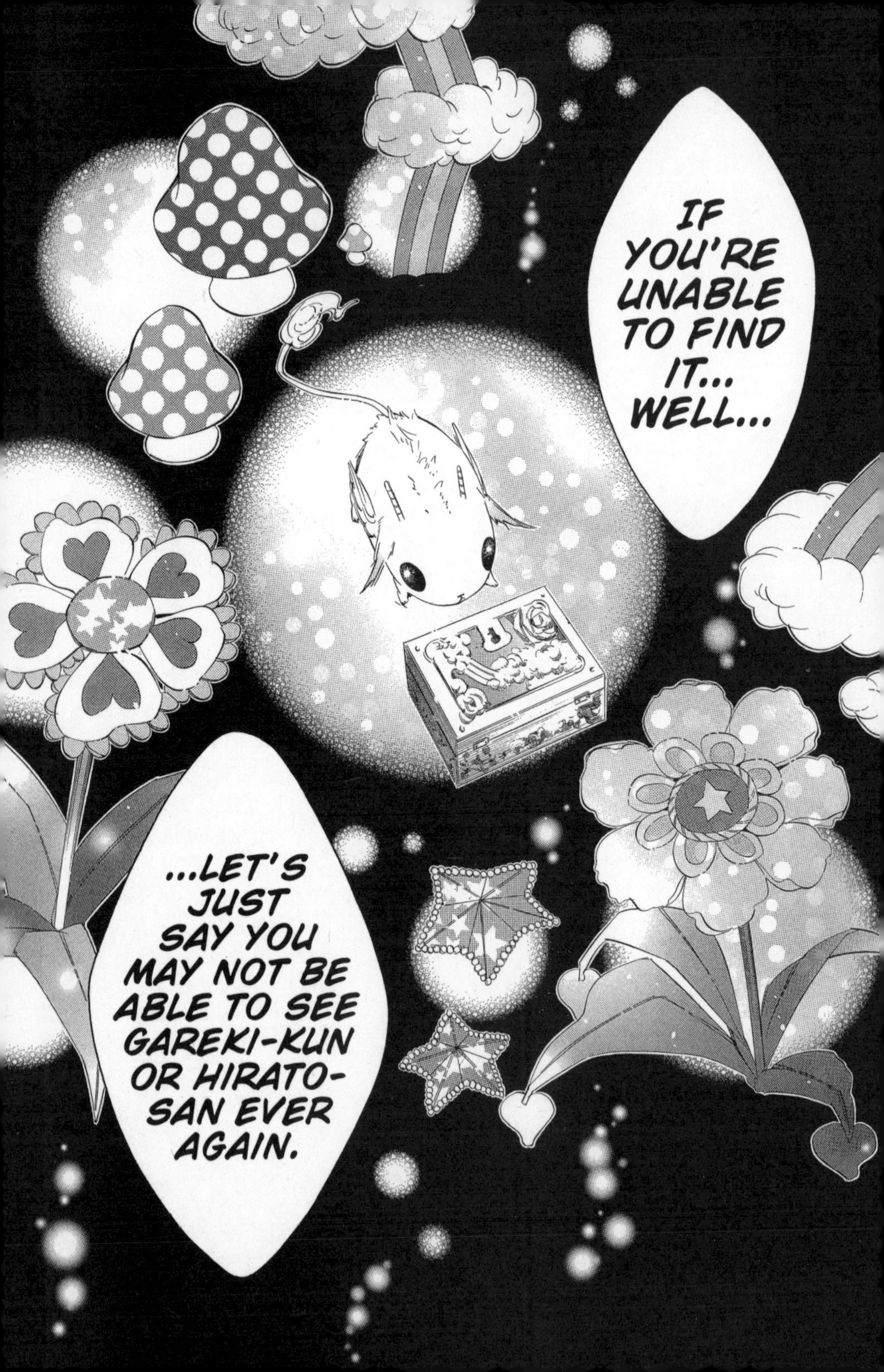
IF YOU'RE UNABLE TO FIND IT... WELL...
...LET'S JUST SAY YOU MAY NOT BE ABLE TO SEE GAREKI-KUN OR HIRATO-SAN EVER AGAIN.

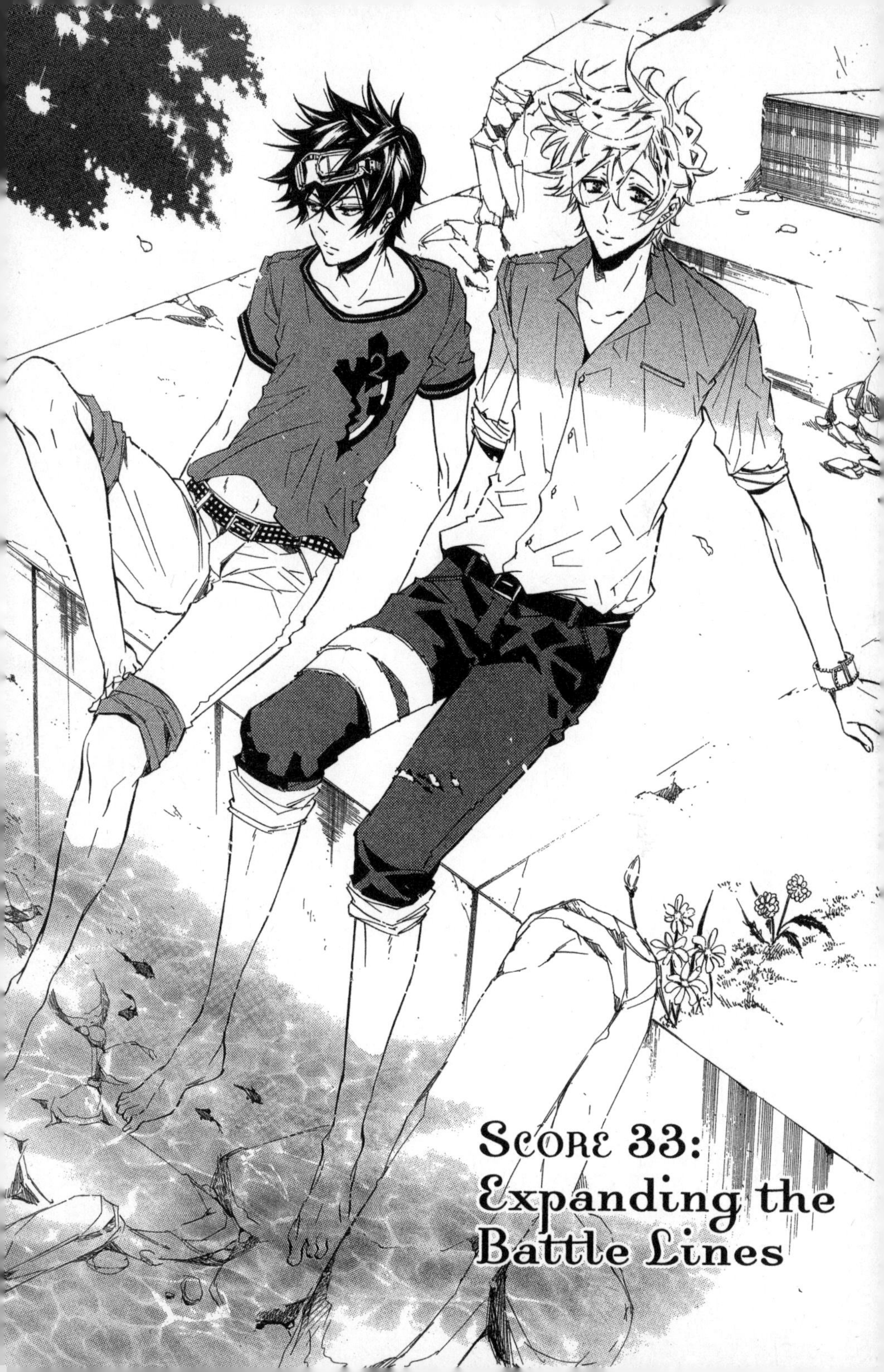
Score 33:
Expanding the
Battle Lines

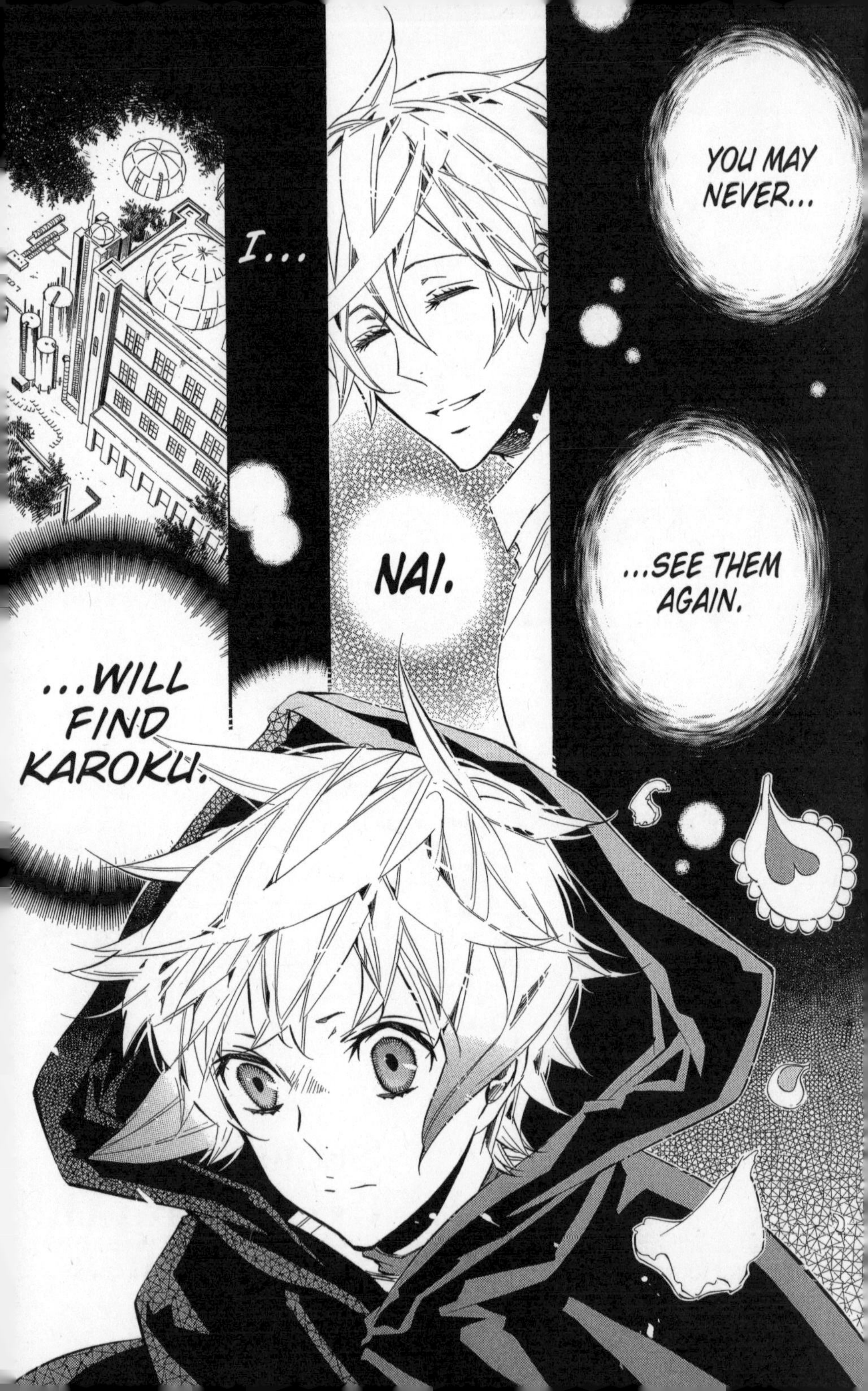
YOU MAY NEVER...
...SEE THEM AGAIN.
NAI.
I...
...WILL FIND KAROKU.

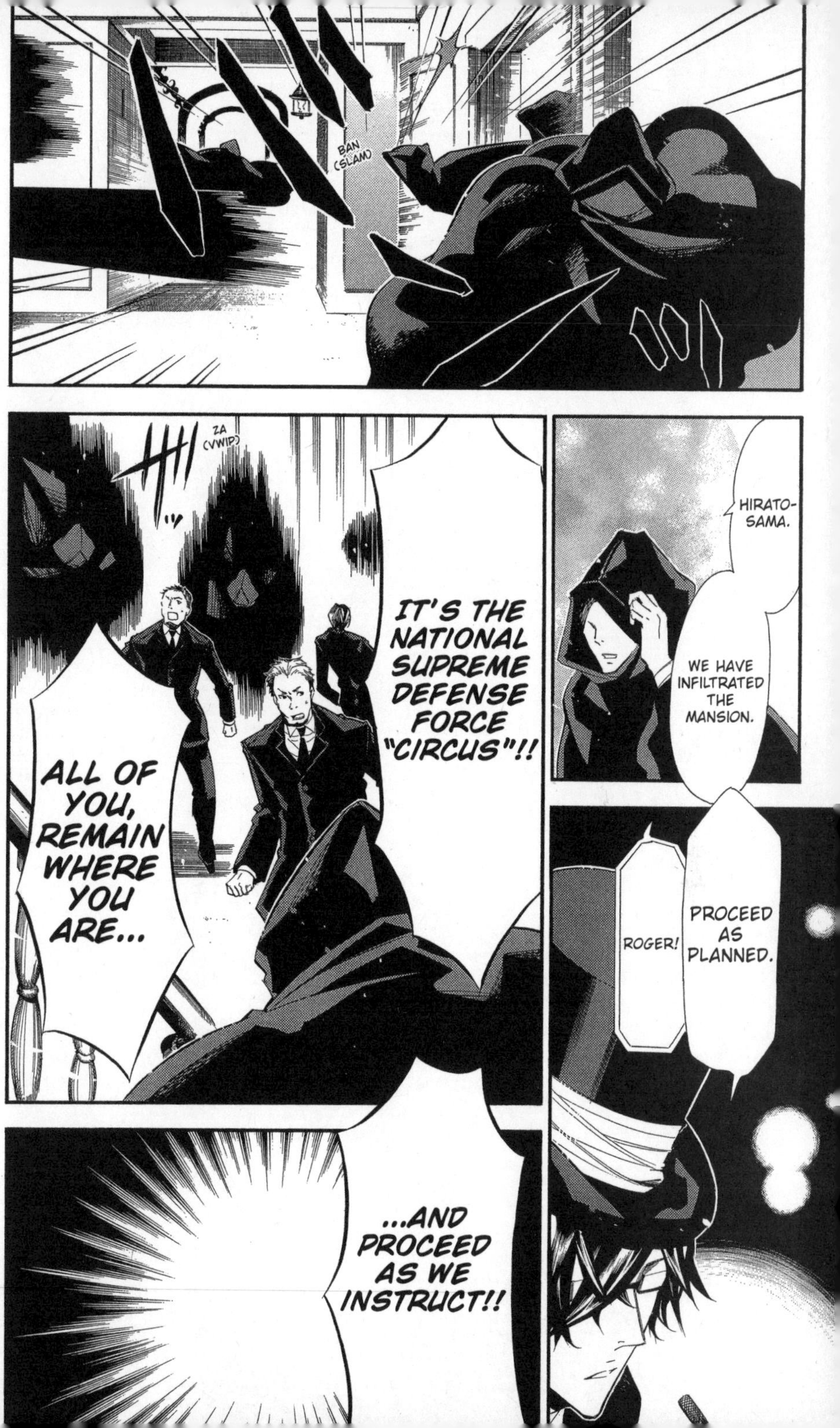
BAN (SLAM)
HIRATO-SAMA.
WE HAVE INFILTRATED THE MANSION.
PROCEED AS PLANNED.
ROGER!
ZA (VWIP)
IT'S THE NATIONAL SUPREME DEFENSE FORCE "CIRCUS"!!
ALL OF YOU, REMAIN WHERE YOU ARE...
...AND PROCEED AS WE INSTRUCT!!

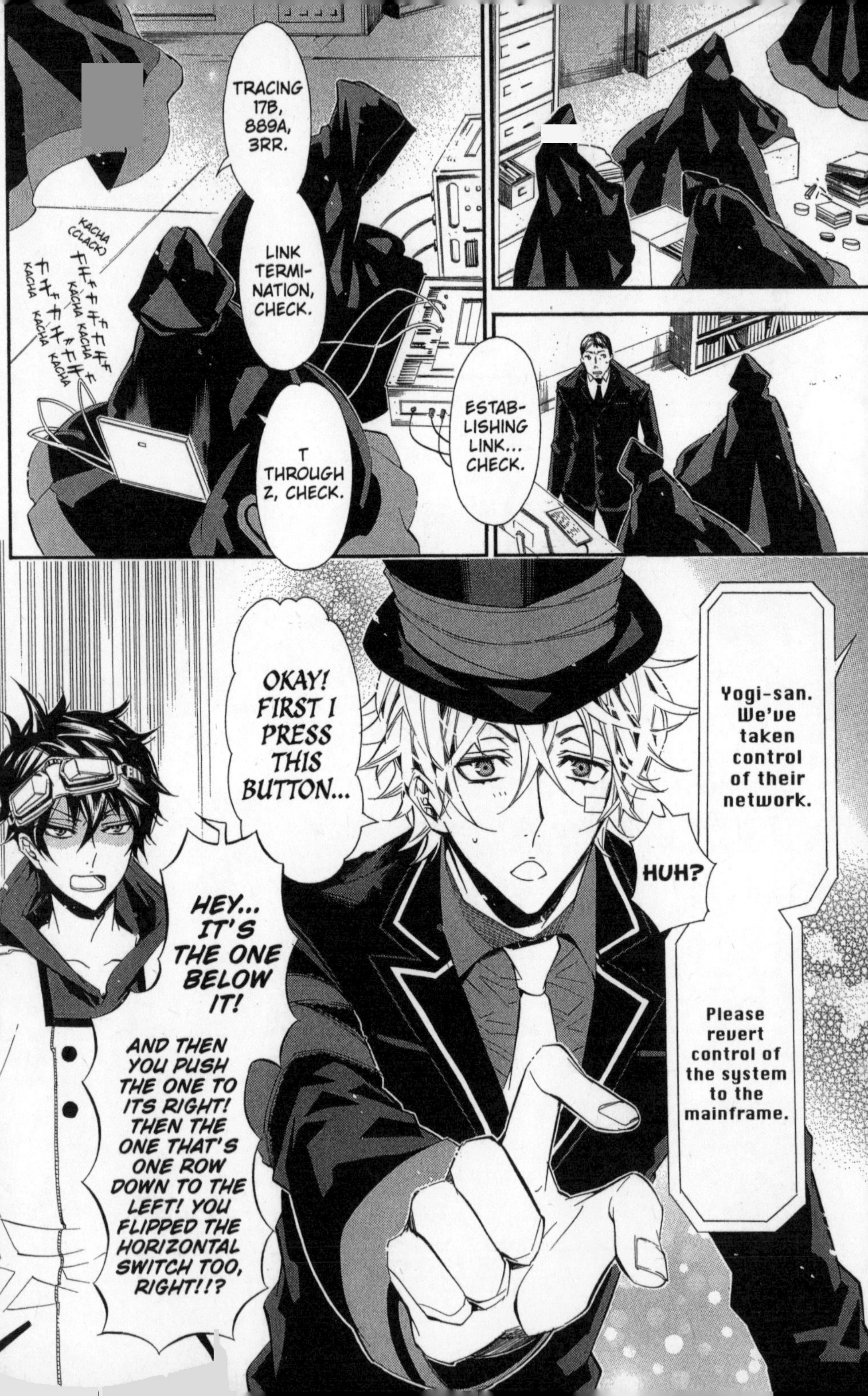
ESTAB-LISHING LINK... CHECK.
TRACING 17B, 889A, 3RR.
LINK TERMI-NATION, CHECK.
T THROUGH Z, CHECK.
KACHA (CLACK)
KACHA KACHA
KACHA KACHA
Yogi-san. We've taken control of their network.
Please revert control of the system to the mainframe.
HUH?
OKAY! FIRST I PRESS THIS BUTTON...
HEY... IT'S THE ONE BELOW IT!
AND THEN YOU PUSH THE ONE TO ITS RIGHT! THEN THE ONE THAT'S ONE ROW DOWN TO THE LEFT! YOU FLIPPED THE HORIZONTAL SWITCH TOO, RIGHT!!?

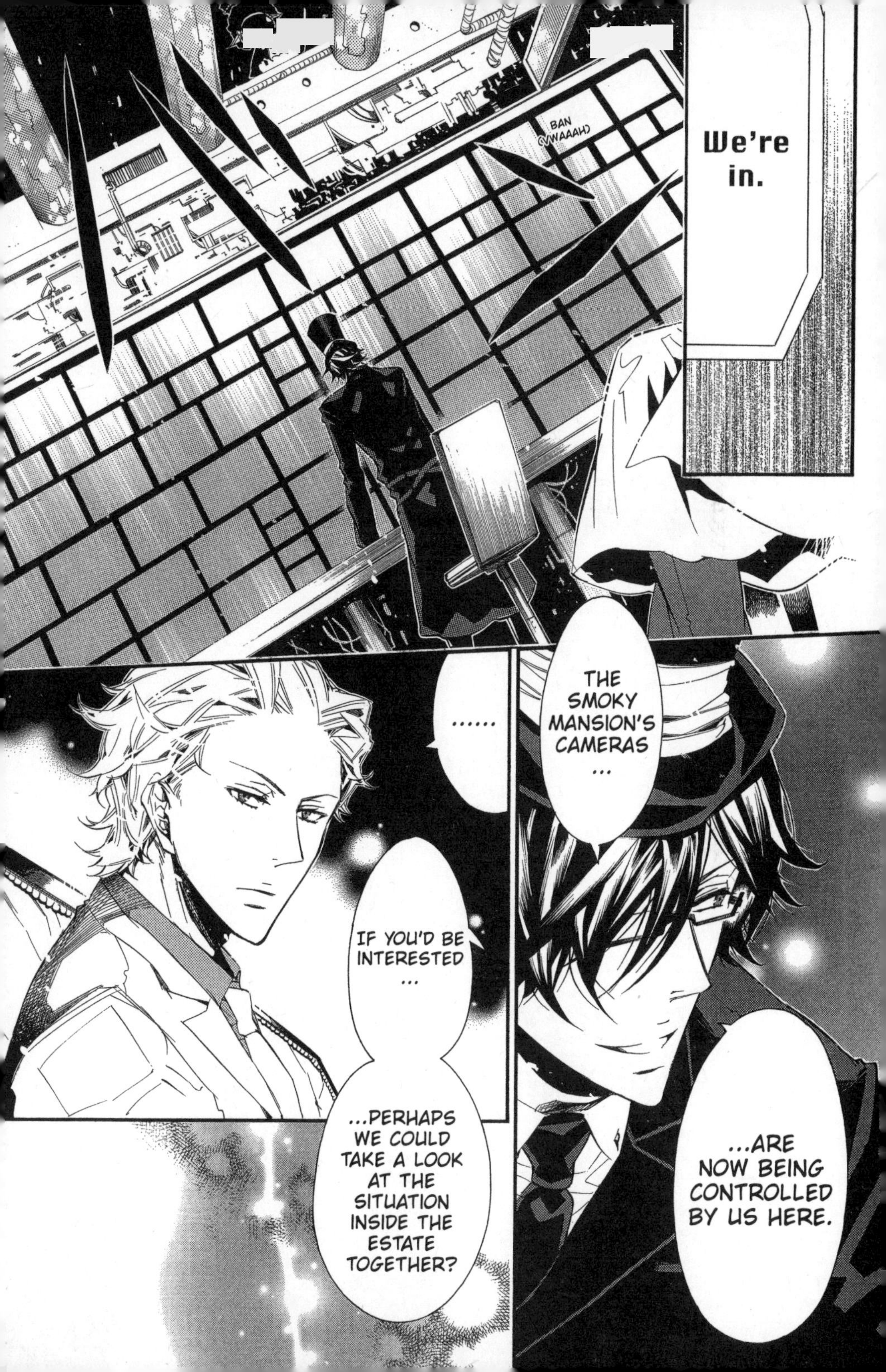
We're in.
BAN (VWAAAH)
THE SMOKY MANSION'S CAMERAS ...
...ARE NOW BEING CONTROLLED BY US HERE.
......
IF YOU'D BE INTERESTED ...
...PERHAPS WE COULD TAKE A LOOK AT THE SITUATION INSIDE THE ESTATE TOGETHER?

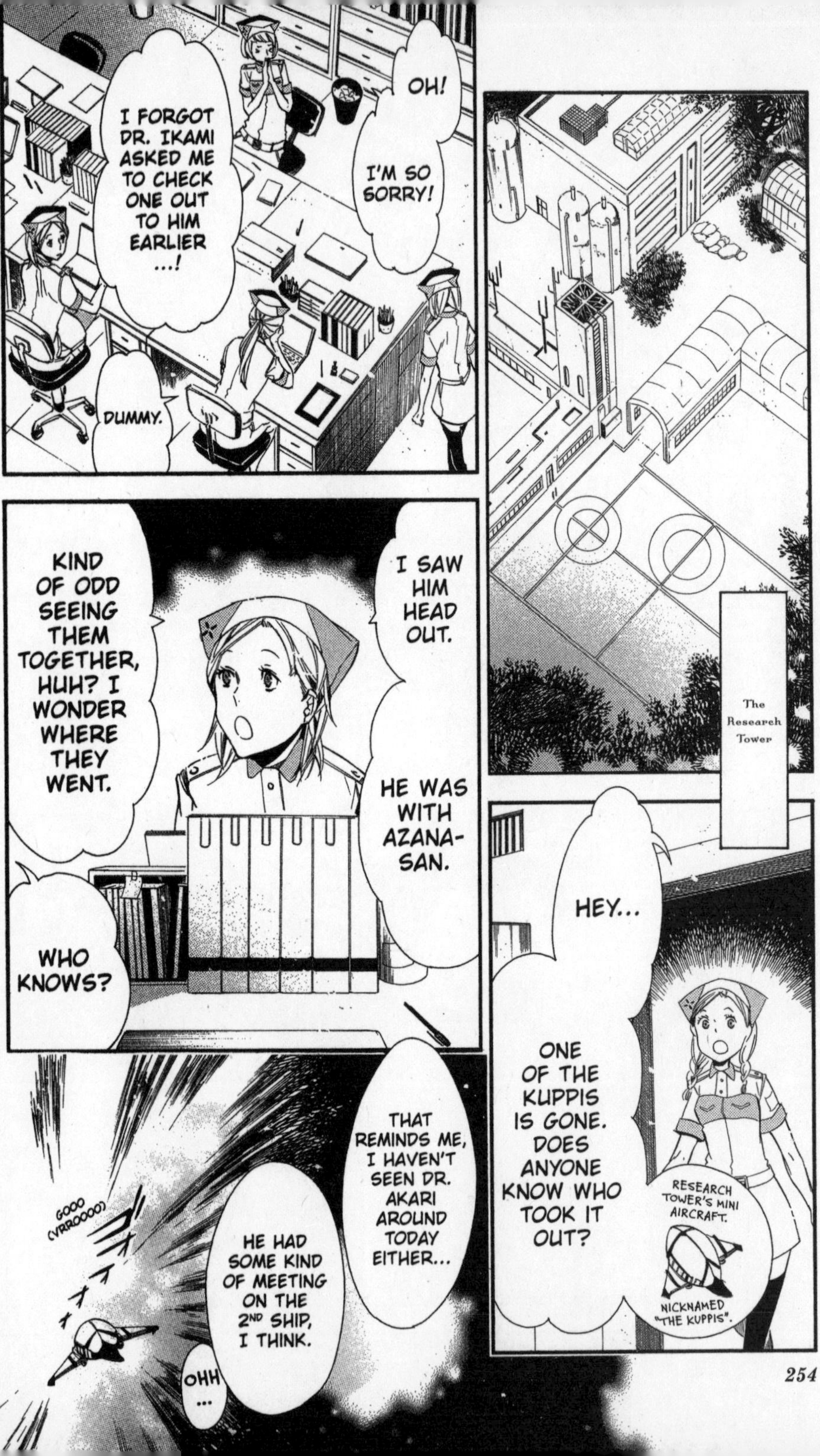
The Research Tower
HEY...
ONE OF THE KUPPIS IS GONE. DOES ANYONE KNOW WHO TOOK IT OUT?
RESEARCH TOWER'S MINI AIRCRAFT.
NICKNAMED "THE KUPPIS".
OH!
I'M SO SORRY!
I FORGOT DR. IKAMI ASKED ME TO CHECK ONE OUT TO HIM EARLIER ...!
DUMMY.
I SAW HIM HEAD OUT.
HE WAS WITH AZANA-SAN.
KIND OF ODD SEEING THEM TOGETHER, HUH? I WONDER WHERE THEY WENT.
WHO KNOWS?
THAT REMINDS ME, I HAVEN'T SEEN DR. AKARI AROUND TODAY EITHER...
HE HAD SOME KIND OF MEETING ON THE 2ND SHIP, I THINK.
OHH ...
GOOO (VRROOOO)

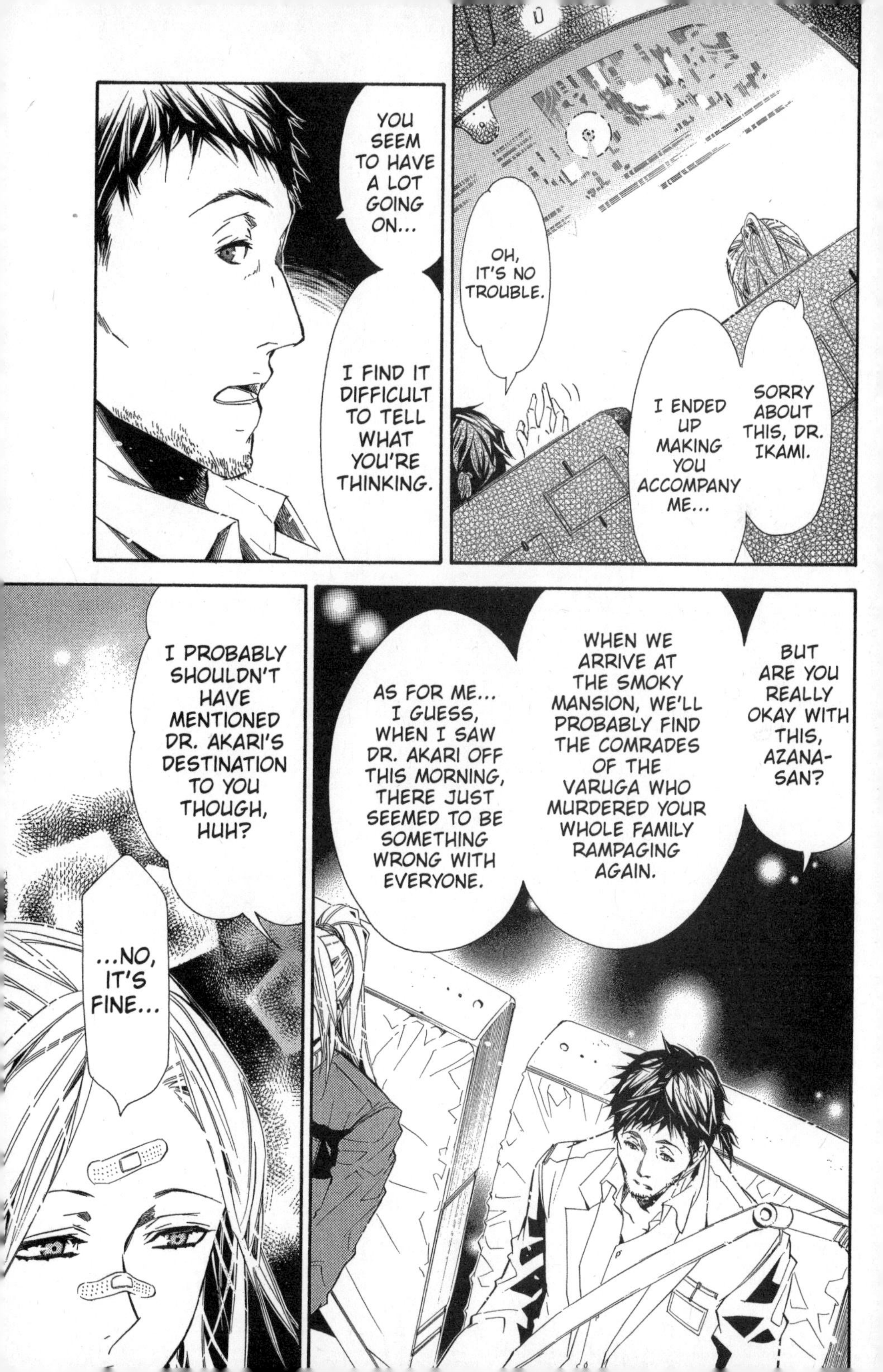
SORRY ABOUT THIS, DR. IKAMI.
I ENDED UP MAKING YOU ACCOMPANY ME...
OH, IT'S NO TROUBLE.
YOU SEEM TO HAVE A LOT GOING ON...
I FIND IT DIFFICULT TO TELL WHAT YOU'RE THINKING.
BUT ARE YOU REALLY OKAY WITH THIS, AZANA-SAN?
WHEN WE ARRIVE AT THE SMOKY MANSION, WE'LL PROBABLY FIND THE COMRADES OF THE VARUGA WHO MURDERED YOUR WHOLE FAMILY RAMPAGING AGAIN.
AS FOR ME... I GUESS, WHEN I SAW DR. AKARI OFF THIS MORNING, THERE JUST SEEMED TO BE SOMETHING WRONG WITH EVERYONE.
I PROBABLY SHOULDN'T HAVE MENTIONED DR. AKARI'S DESTINATION TO YOU THOUGH, HUH?
...NO, IT'S FINE...

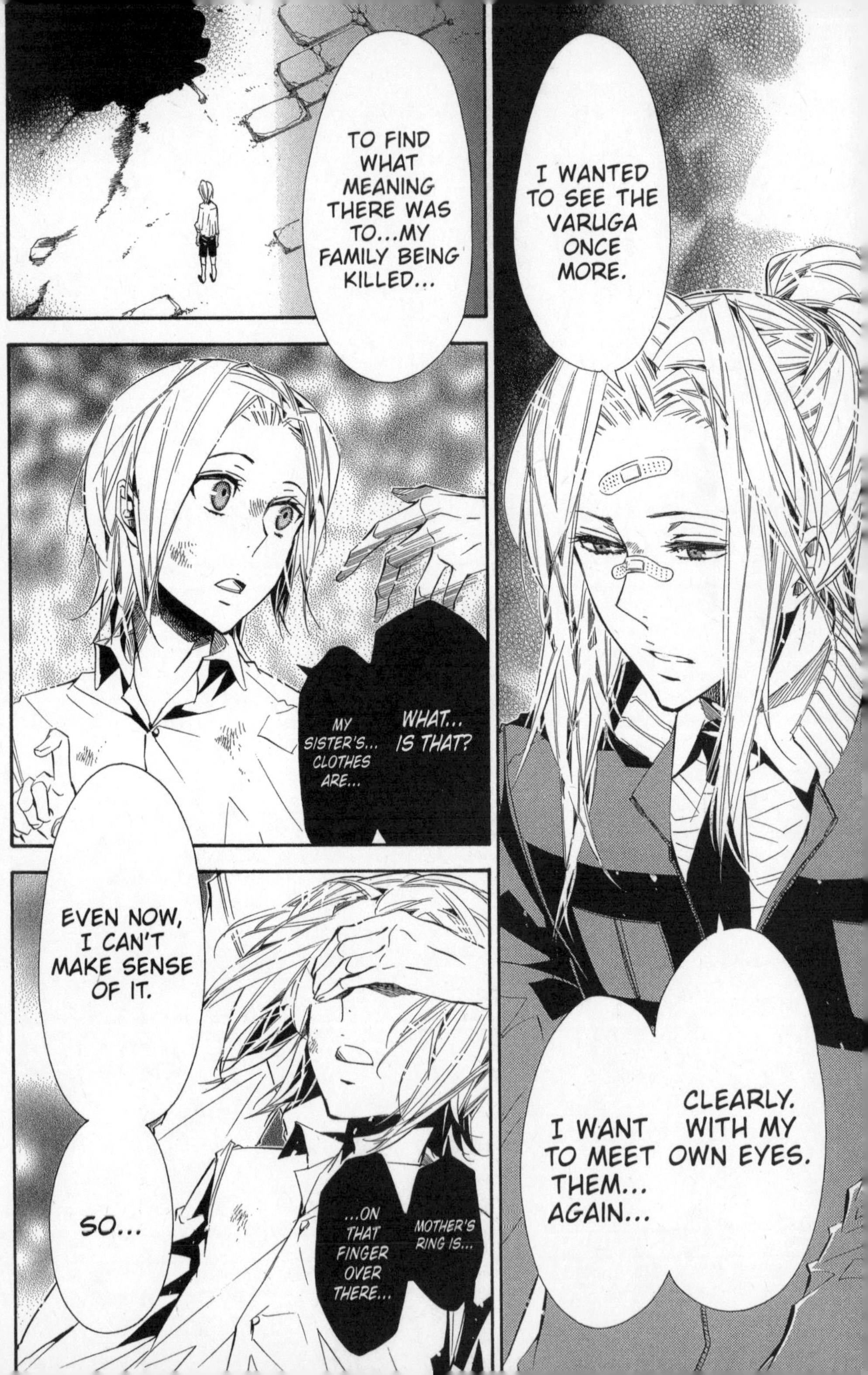
I WANTED TO SEE THE VARUGA ONCE MORE.
CLEARLY. WITH MY OWN EYES.
I WANT TO MEET THEM... AGAIN...
TO FIND WHAT MEANING THERE WAS TO...MY FAMILY BEING KILLED...
WHAT... IS THAT?
MY SISTER'S... CLOTHES ARE...
EVEN NOW, I CAN'T MAKE SENSE OF IT.
MOTHER'S RING IS...
...ON THAT FINGER OVER THERE...
SO...

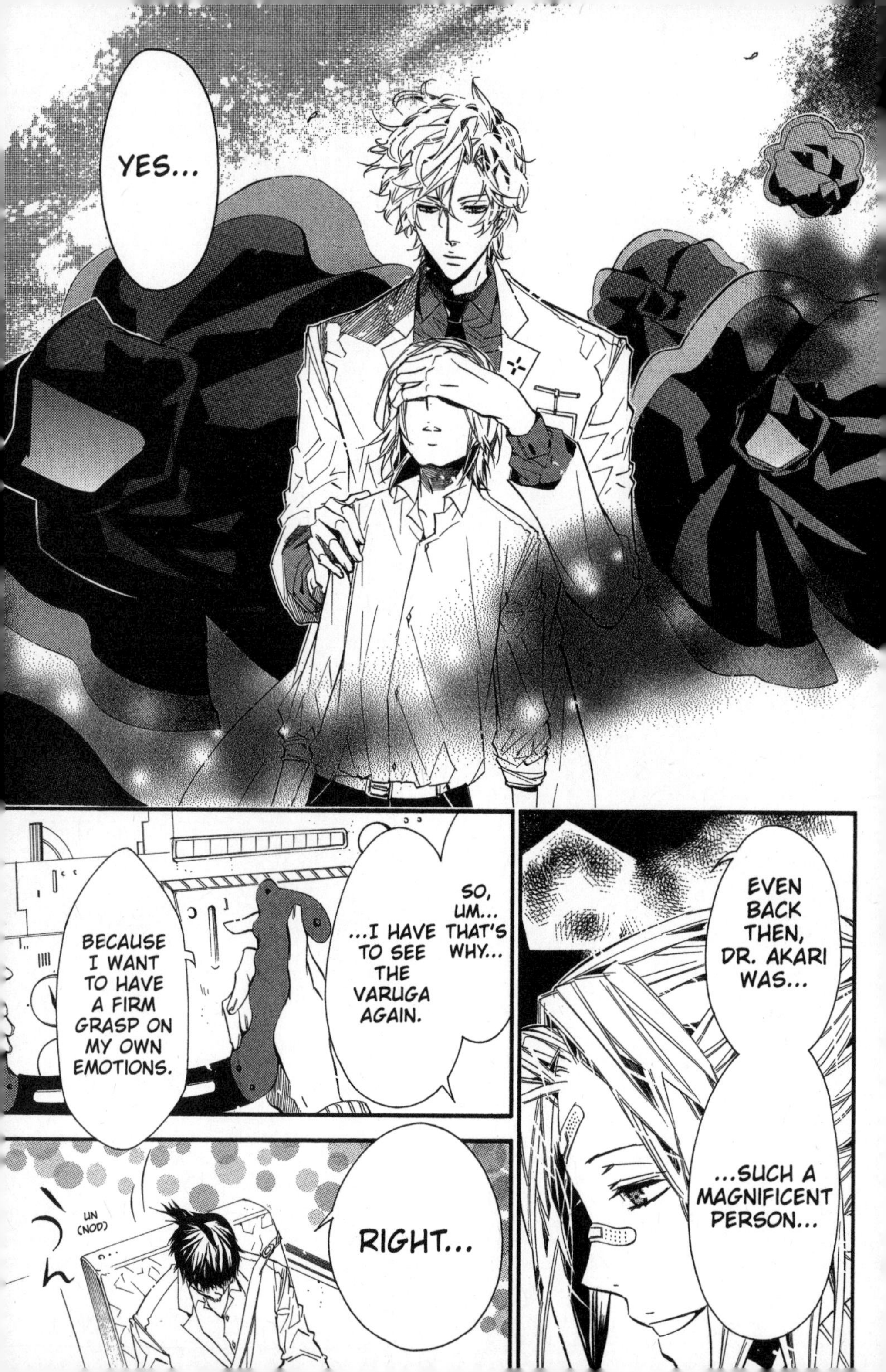
YES...
EVEN BACK THEN, DR. AKARI WAS...
...SUCH A MAGNIFICENT PERSON...
SO, UM... THAT'S WHY...
...I HAVE TO SEE THE VARUGA AGAIN.
BECAUSE I WANT TO HAVE A FIRM GRASP ON MY OWN EMOTIONS.
RIGHT...
UN (NOD)

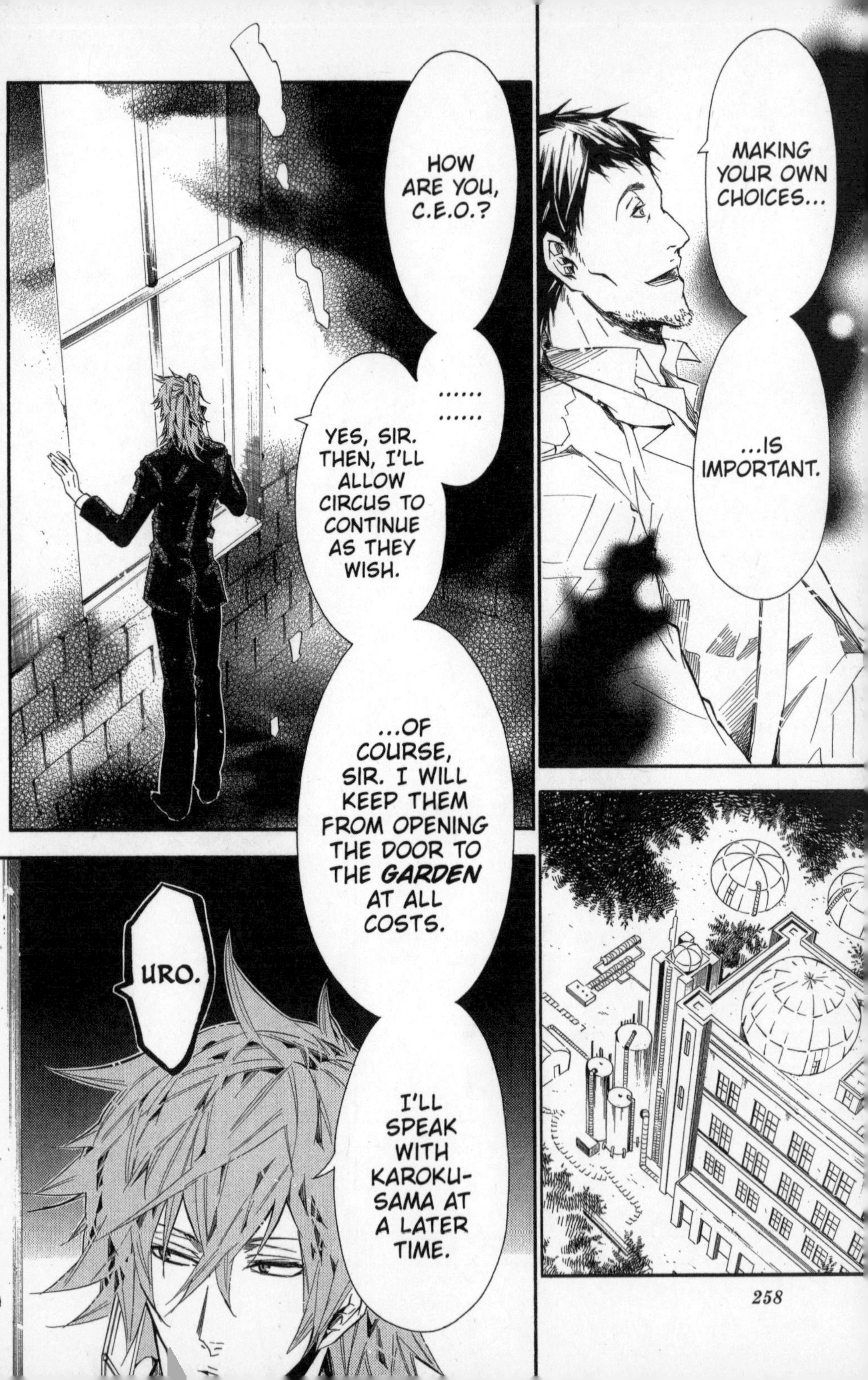
MAKING YOUR OWN CHOICES...
...IS IMPORTANT.
HOW ARE YOU, C.E.O.?
....
YES, SIR. THEN, I'LL ALLOW CIRCUS TO CONTINUE AS THEY WISH.
...OF COURSE, SIR. I WILL KEEP THEM FROM OPENING THE DOOR TO THE ***GARDEN*** AT ALL COSTS.
I'LL SPEAK WITH KAROKU-SAMA AT A LATER TIME.
URO.

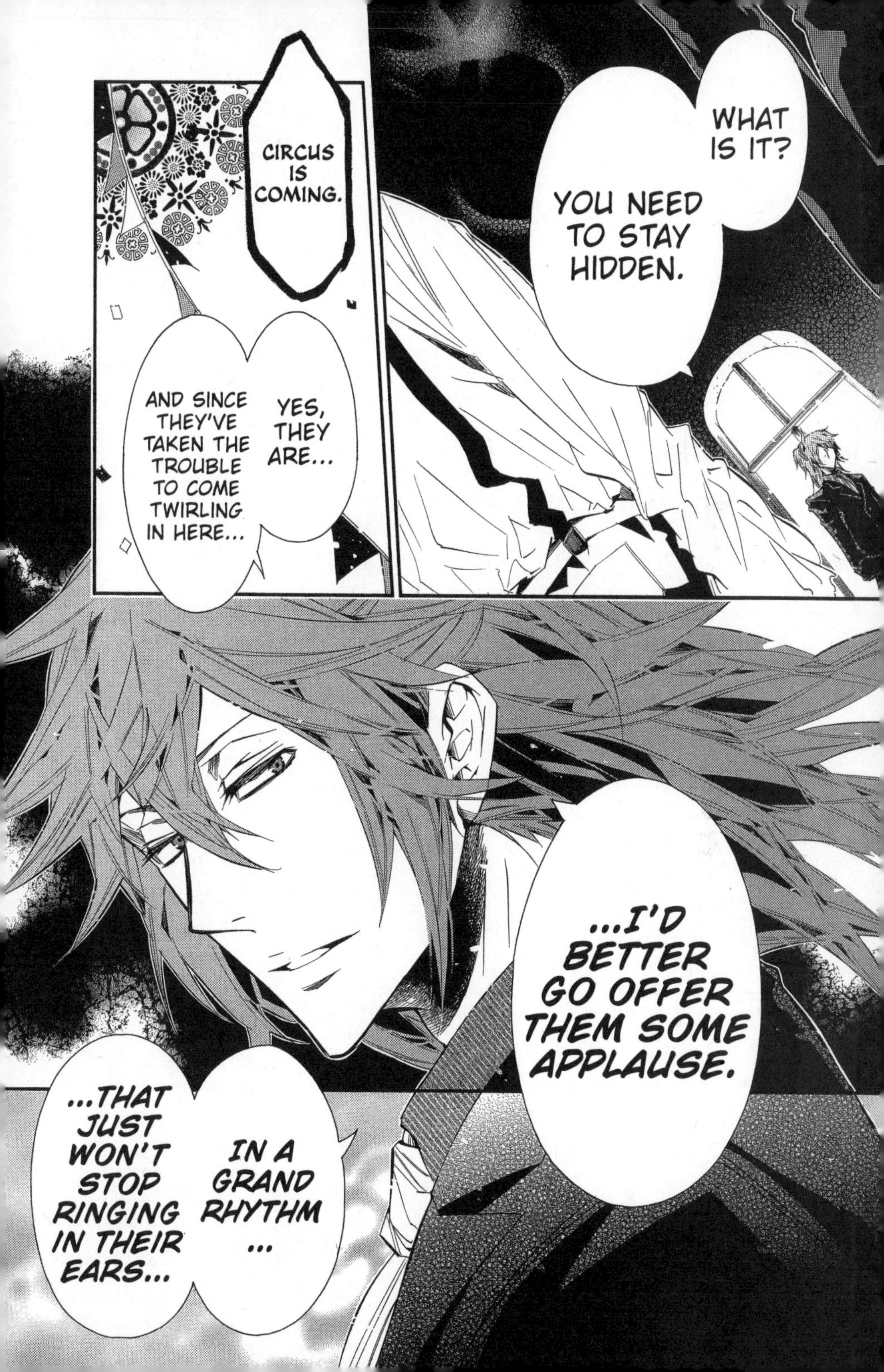
WHAT IS IT?
YOU NEED TO STAY HIDDEN.
CIRCUS IS COMING.
YES, THEY ARE...
AND SINCE THEY'VE TAKEN THE TROUBLE TO COME TWIRLING IN HERE...
...I'D BETTER GO OFFER THEM SOME APPLAUSE.
IN A GRAND RHYTHM...
...THAT JUST WON'T STOP RINGING IN THEIR EARS...

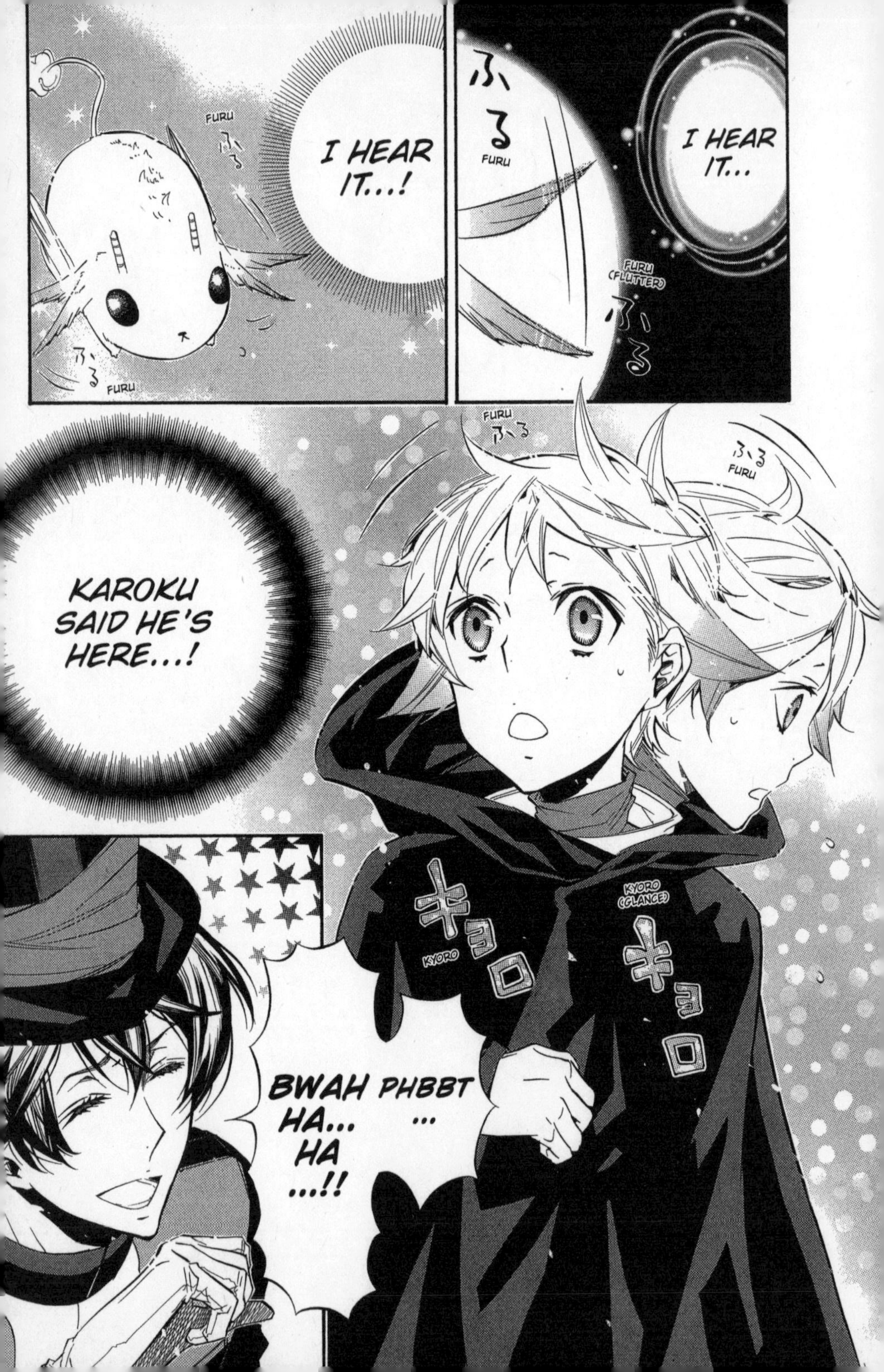
I HEAR IT...
ふる
FURU
FURU (FLUTTER)
ふる
I HEAR IT...!
FURU
ふる
ふる
FURU
ふる
FURU
FURU
ふる
KYORO (GLANCE)
キョロ
キョロ
KYORO
KAROKU SAID HE'S HERE...!
PHBBT ...
BWAH HA... HA ...!!

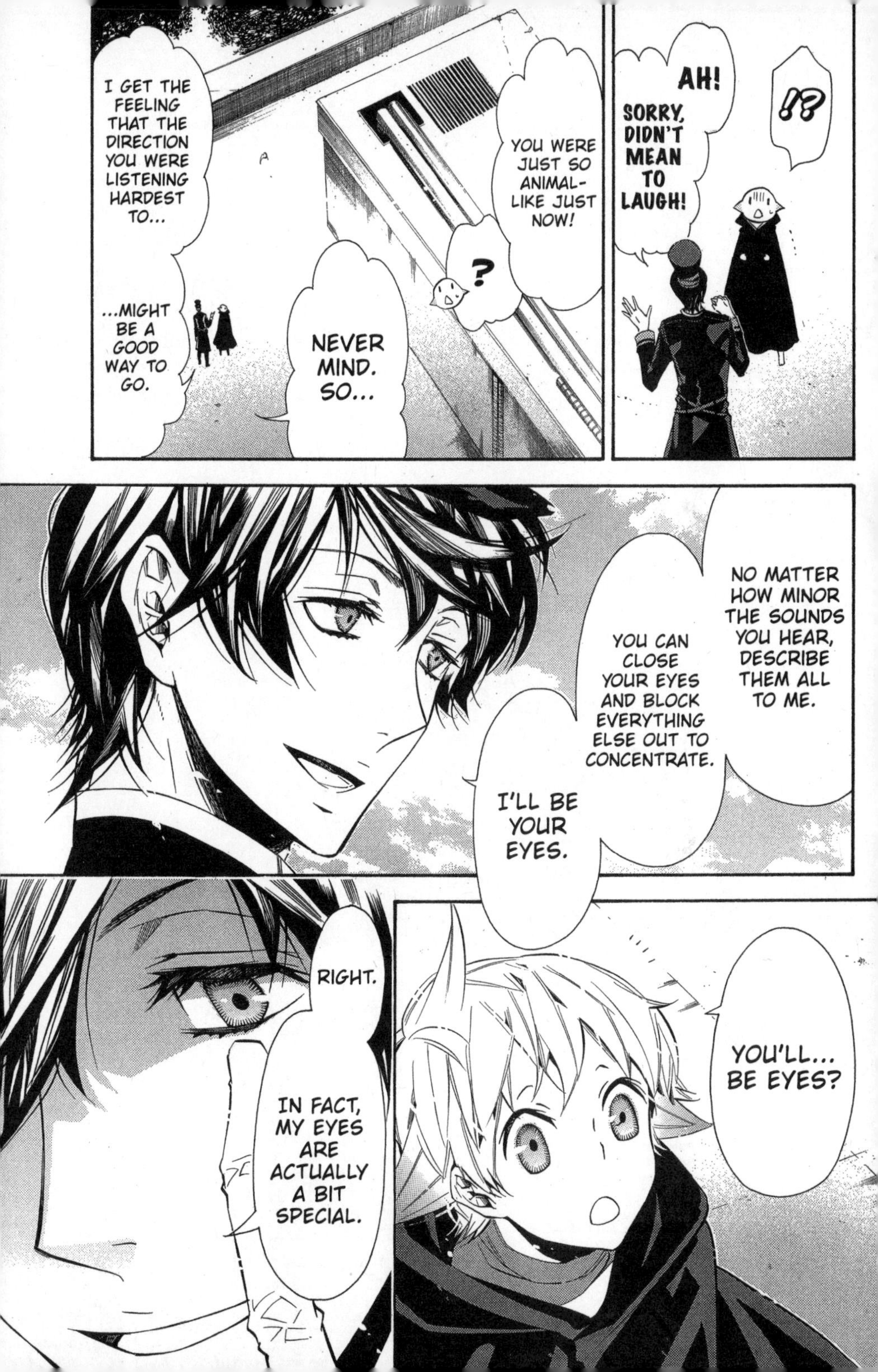
!?
AH! SORRY, DIDN'T MEAN TO LAUGH!
YOU WERE JUST SO ANIMAL-LIKE JUST NOW!
?
NEVER MIND. SO...
I GET THE FEELING THAT THE DIRECTION YOU WERE LISTENING HARDEST TO...
...MIGHT BE A GOOD WAY TO GO.
NO MATTER HOW MINOR THE SOUNDS YOU HEAR, DESCRIBE THEM ALL TO ME.
YOU CAN CLOSE YOUR EYES AND BLOCK EVERYTHING ELSE OUT TO CONCENTRATE.
I'LL BE YOUR EYES.
YOU'LL... BE EYES?
RIGHT.
IN FACT, MY EYES ARE ACTUALLY A BIT SPECIAL.

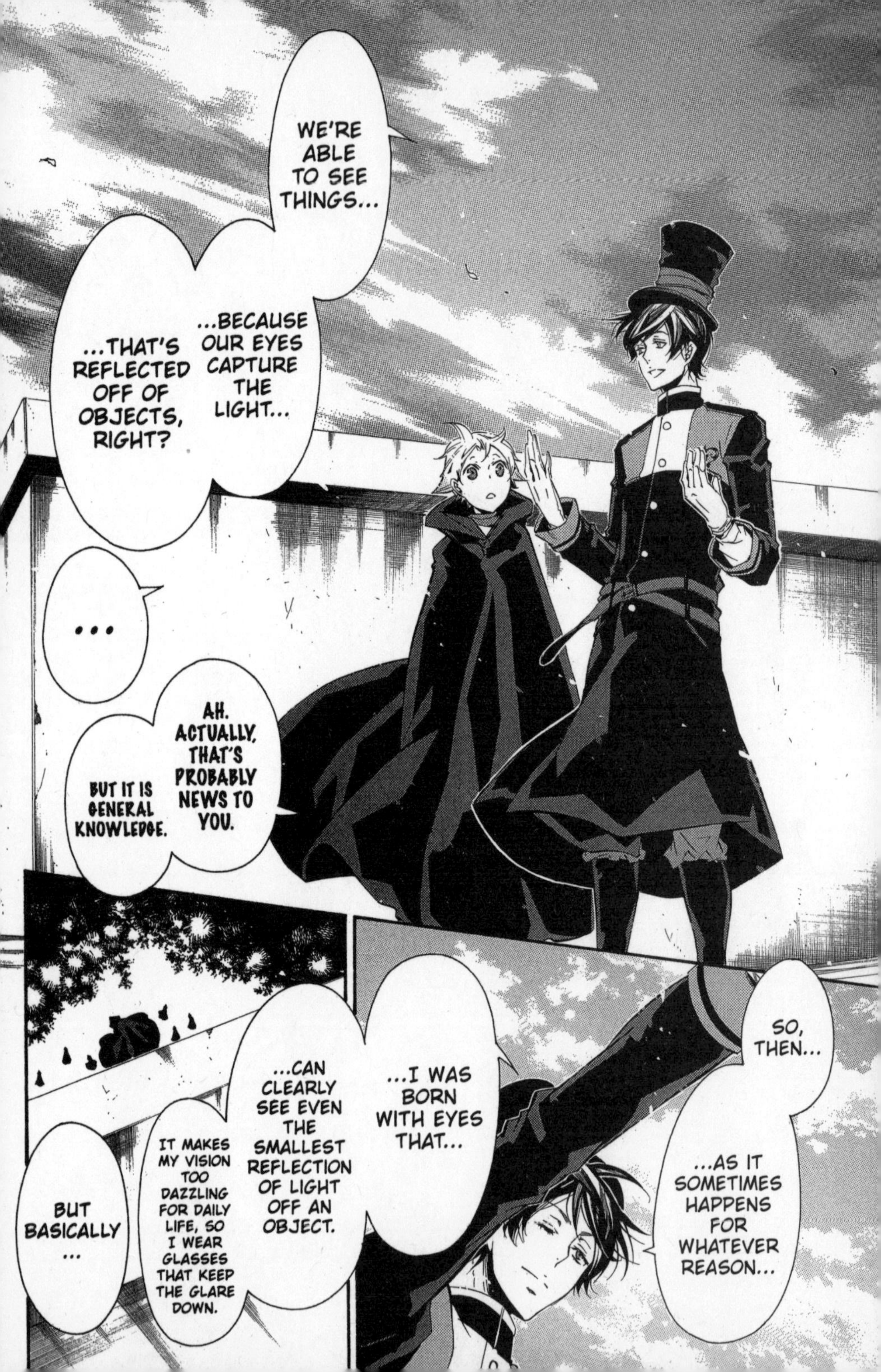
WE'RE ABLE TO SEE THINGS...
...BECAUSE OUR EYES CAPTURE THE LIGHT...
...THAT'S REFLECTED OFF OF OBJECTS, RIGHT?
...
AH. ACTUALLY, THAT'S PROBABLY NEWS TO YOU.
BUT IT IS GENERAL KNOWLEDGE.
SO, THEN...
...AS IT SOMETIMES HAPPENS FOR WHATEVER REASON...
...I WAS BORN WITH EYES THAT...
...CAN CLEARLY SEE EVEN THE SMALLEST REFLECTION OF LIGHT OFF AN OBJECT.
IT MAKES MY VISION TOO DAZZLING FOR DAILY LIFE, SO I WEAR GLASSES THAT KEEP THE GLARE DOWN.
BUT BASICALLY ...

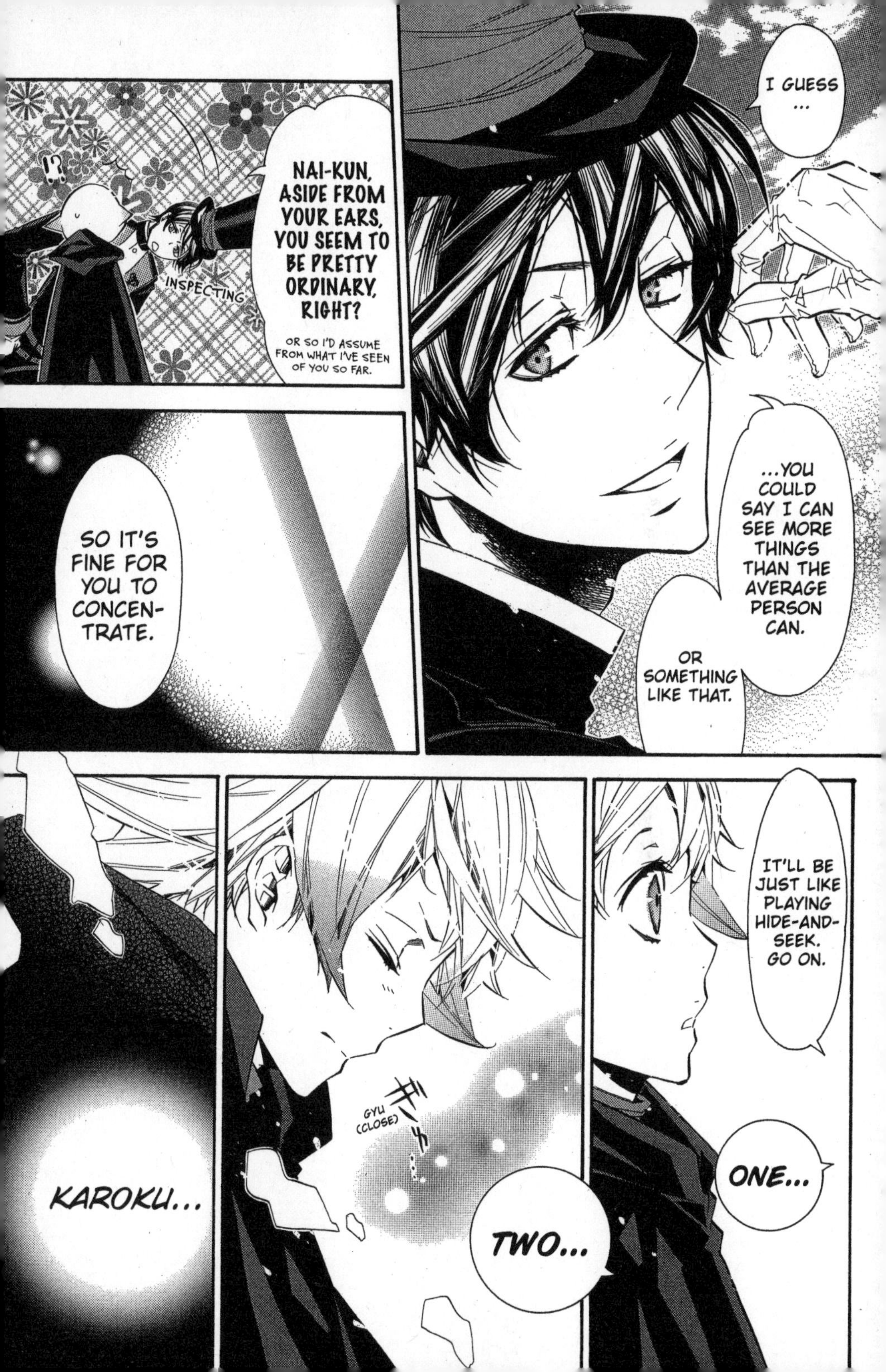

I GUESS ...
...YOU COULD SAY I CAN SEE MORE THINGS THAN THE AVERAGE PERSON CAN.
OR SOMETHING LIKE THAT.
NAI-KUN, ASIDE FROM YOUR EARS, YOU SEEM TO BE PRETTY ORDINARY, RIGHT?
OR SO I'D ASSUME FROM WHAT I'VE SEEN OF YOU SO FAR.
!?
INSPECTING
SO IT'S FINE FOR YOU TO CONCENTRATE.
IT'LL BE JUST LIKE PLAYING HIDE-AND-SEEK. GO ON.
ONE...
TWO...
GYU (CLOSE)
KAROKU...

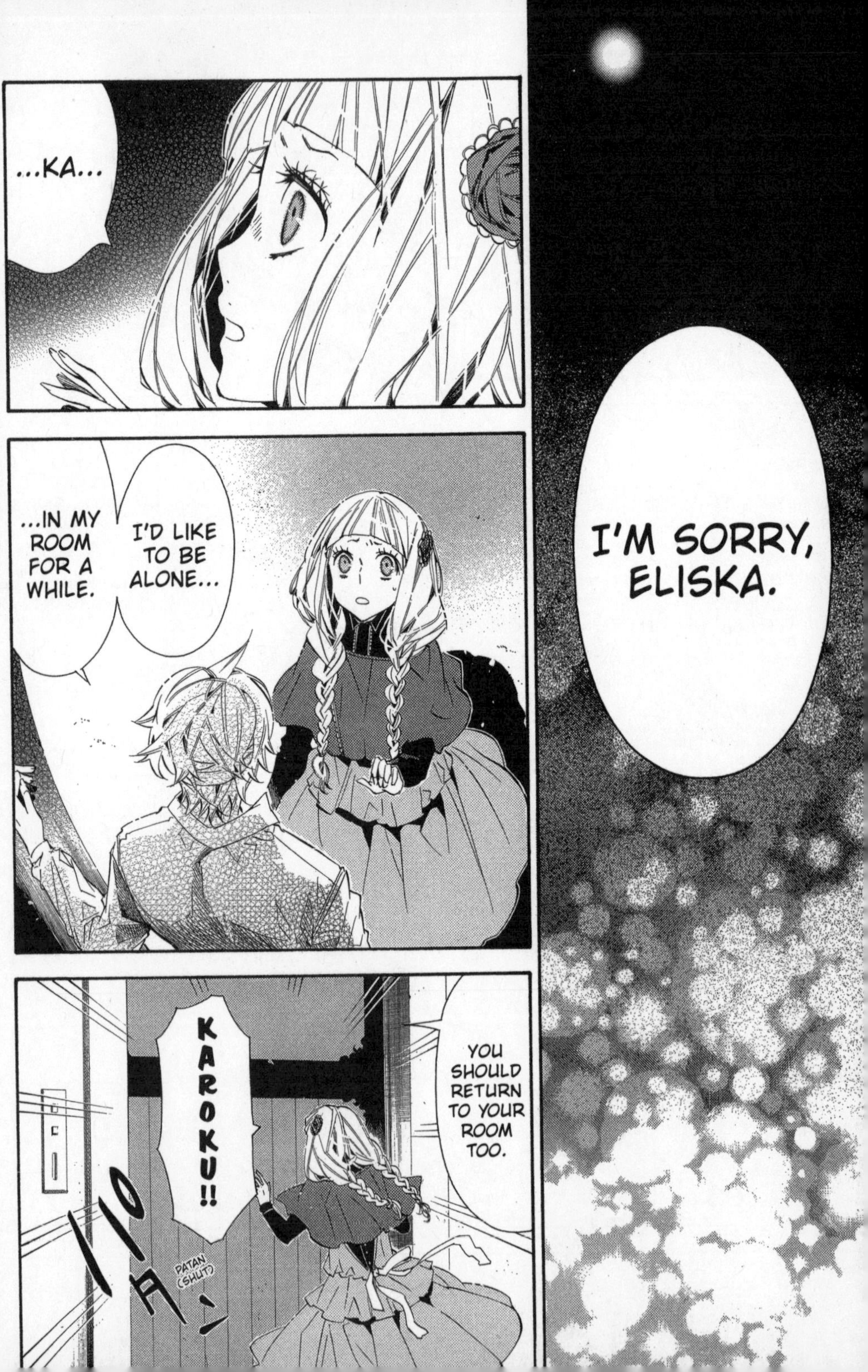
I'M SORRY, ELISKA.
...KA...
I'D LIKE TO BE ALONE...
...IN MY ROOM FOR A WHILE.
YOU SHOULD RETURN TO YOUR ROOM TOO.
KAROKU!!
PATAN (SHUT)

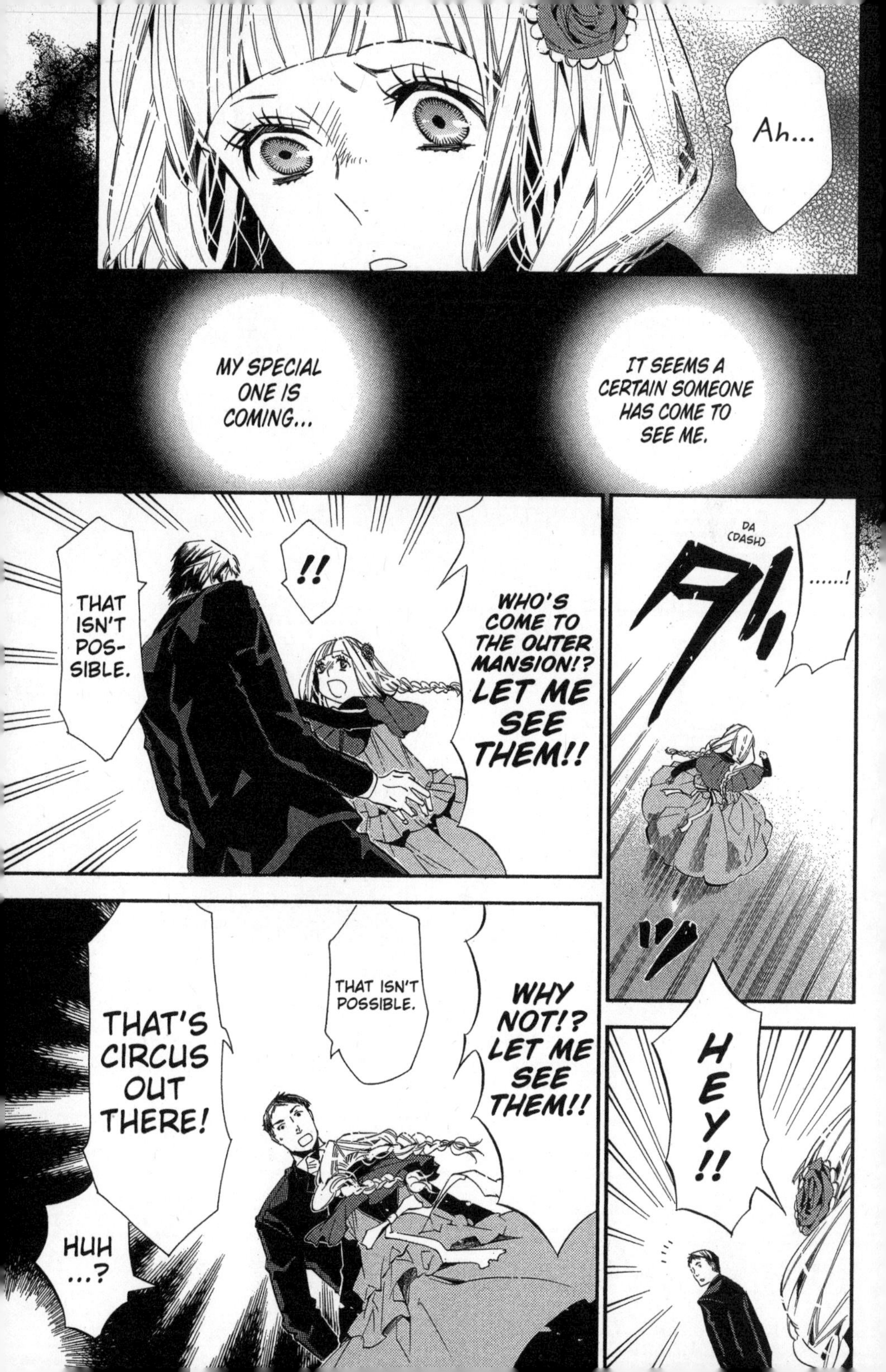
Ah...
IT SEEMS A CERTAIN SOMEONE HAS COME TO SEE ME.
MY SPECIAL ONE IS COMING...
......!
DA (DASH)
HEY!!
WHO'S COME TO THE OUTER MANSION!? LET ME SEE THEM!!
!!
THAT ISN'T POSSIBLE.
WHY NOT!? LET ME SEE THEM!!
THAT ISN'T POSSIBLE.
THAT'S CIRCUS OUT THERE!
HUH ...?

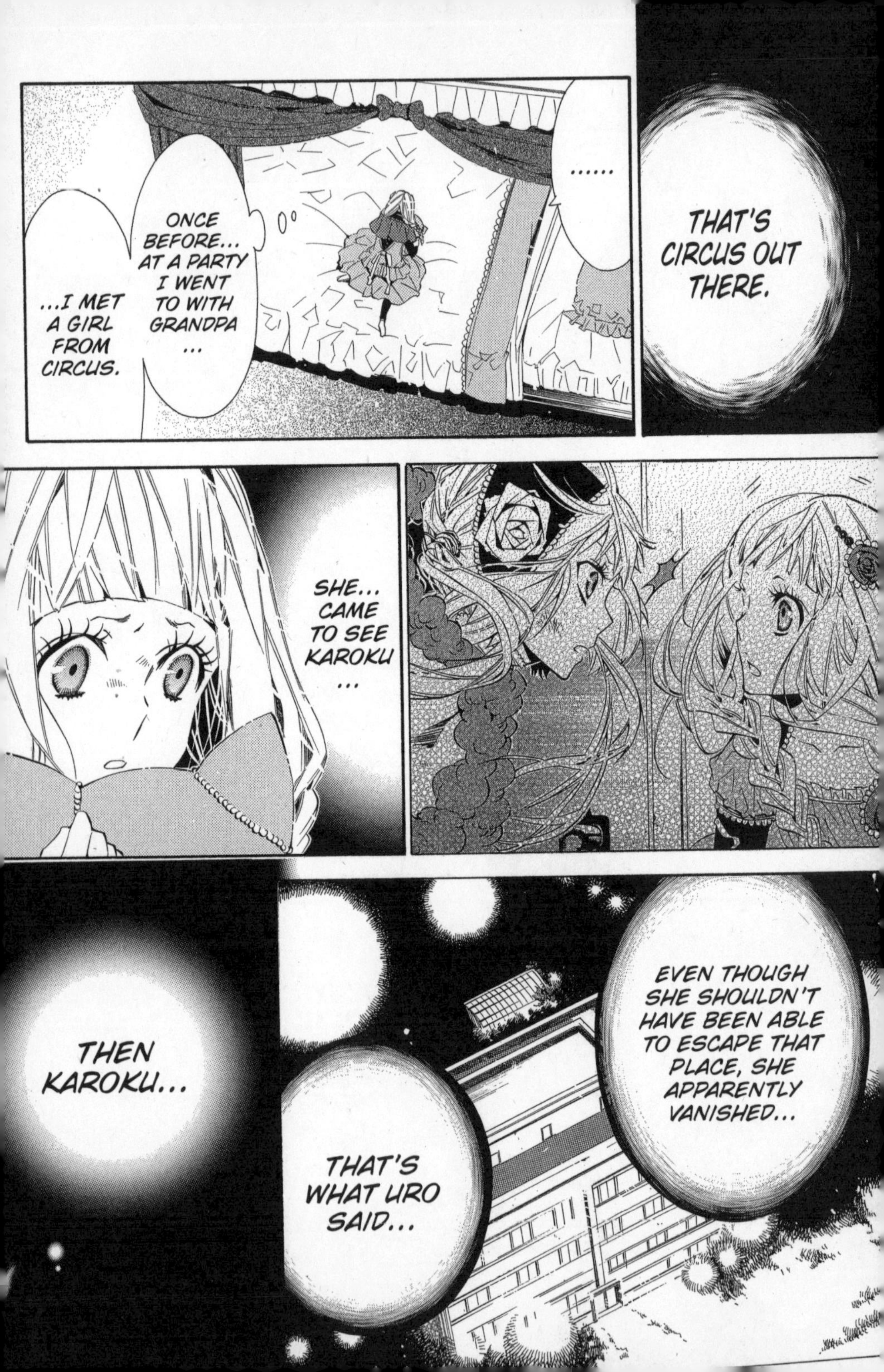
THAT'S CIRCUS OUT THERE.
......
ONCE BEFORE... AT A PARTY I WENT TO WITH GRANDPA ...
...I MET A GIRL FROM CIRCUS.
SHE... CAME TO SEE KAROKU ...
EVEN THOUGH SHE SHOULDN'T HAVE BEEN ABLE TO ESCAPE THAT PLACE, SHE APPARENTLY VANISHED...
THAT'S WHAT URO SAID...
THEN KAROKU...

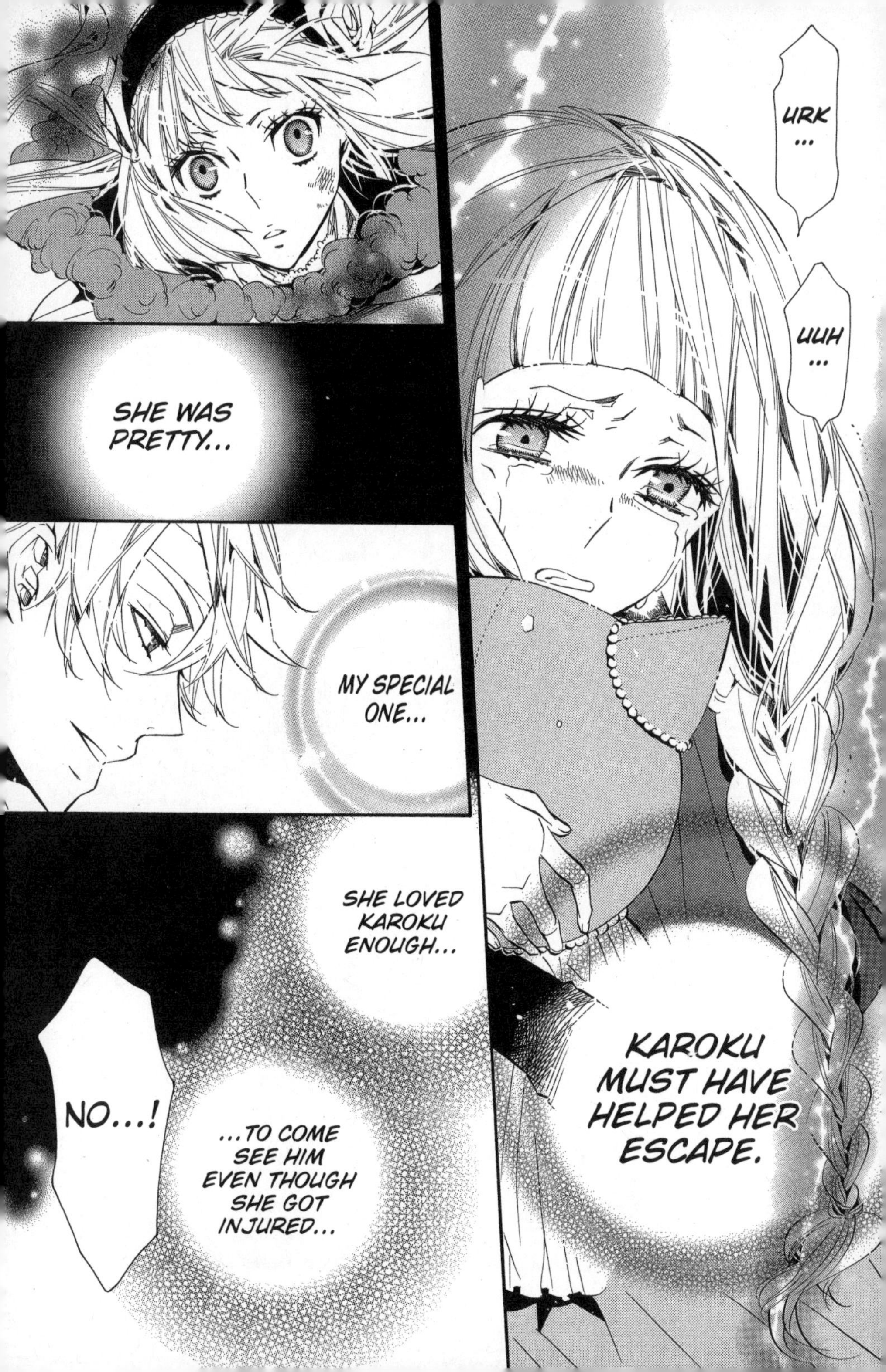
URK...
UUH...
KAROKU MUST HAVE HELPED HER ESCAPE.
SHE WAS PRETTY...
MY SPECIAL ONE...
SHE LOVED KAROKU ENOUGH...
...TO COME SEE HIM EVEN THOUGH SHE GOT INJURED...
NO...!

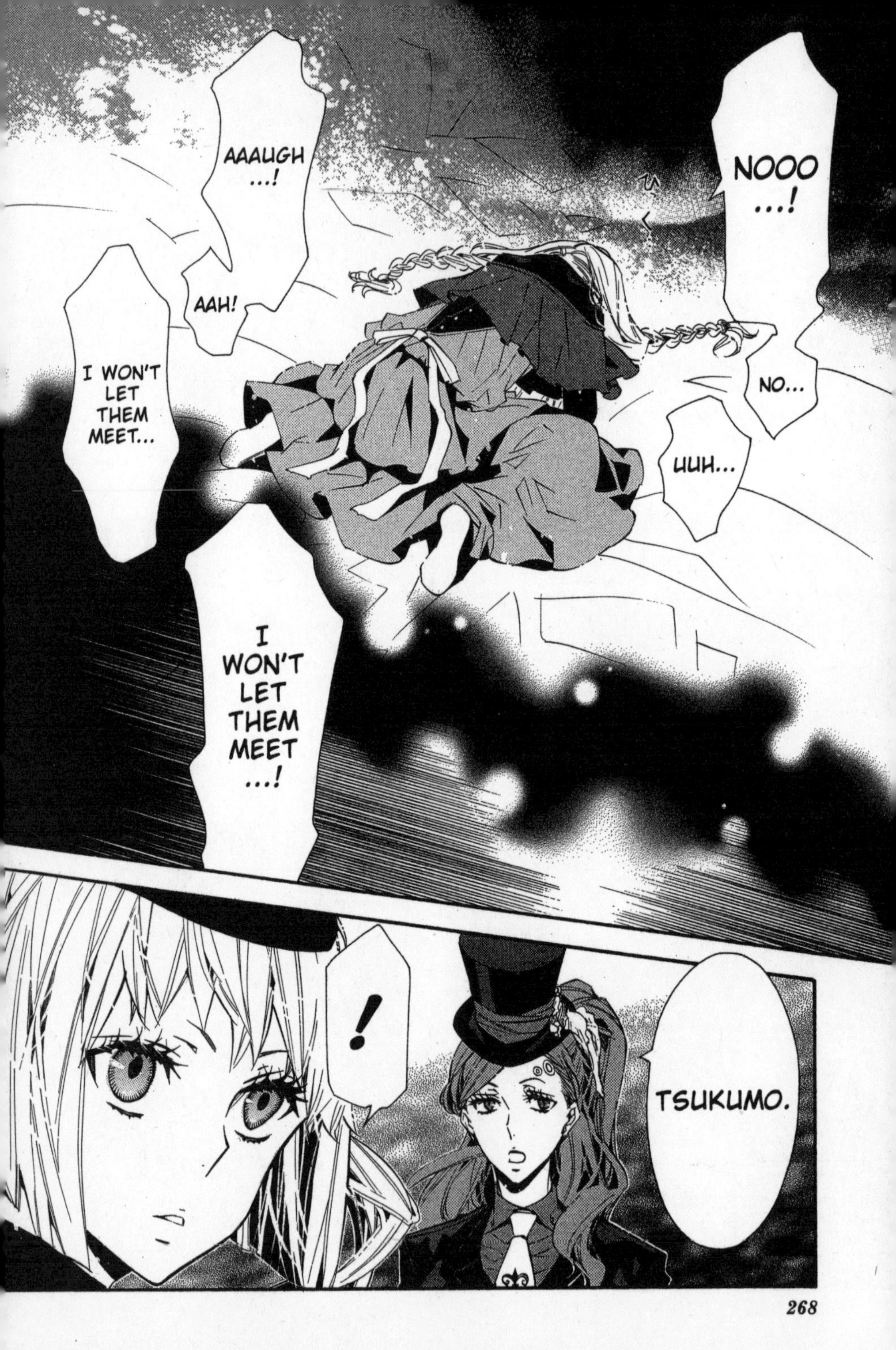
NOOO ...!
NO...
UUH...
AAAUGH ...!
AAH!
I WON'T LET THEM MEET...
I WON'T LET THEM MEET ...!
TSUKUMO.
!

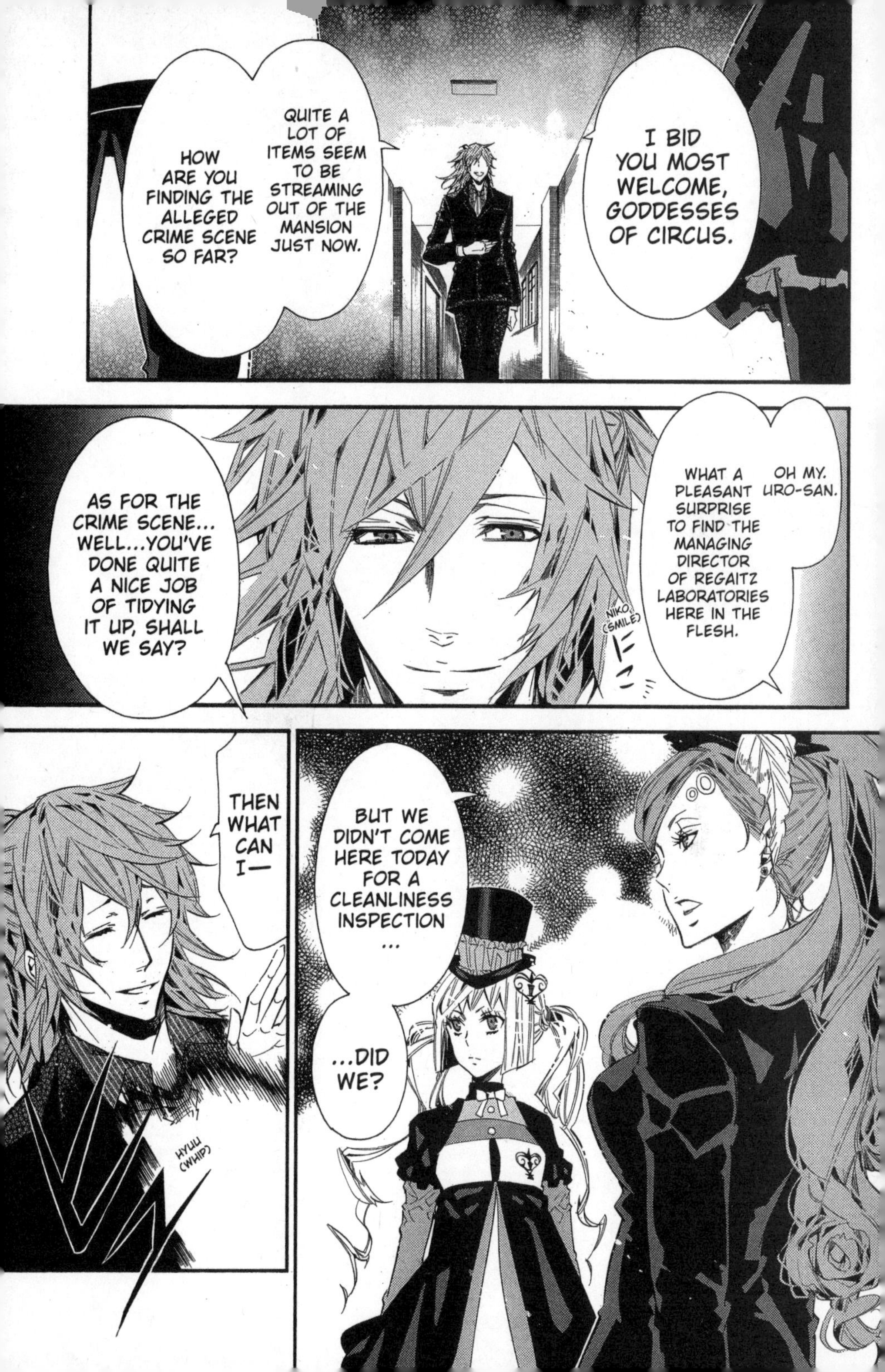
I BID YOU MOST WELCOME, GODDESSES OF CIRCUS.
QUITE A LOT OF ITEMS SEEM TO BE STREAMING OUT OF THE MANSION JUST NOW.
HOW ARE YOU FINDING THE ALLEGED CRIME SCENE SO FAR?
OH MY. URO-SAN.
WHAT A PLEASANT SURPRISE TO FIND THE MANAGING DIRECTOR OF REGAITZ LABORATORIES HERE IN THE FLESH.
NIKO (SMILE)
AS FOR THE CRIME SCENE... WELL...YOU'VE DONE QUITE A NICE JOB OF TIDYING IT UP, SHALL WE SAY?
BUT WE DIDN'T COME HERE TODAY FOR A CLEANLINESS INSPECTION ...
...DID WE?
THEN WHAT CAN I—
HYUU (WHIP)

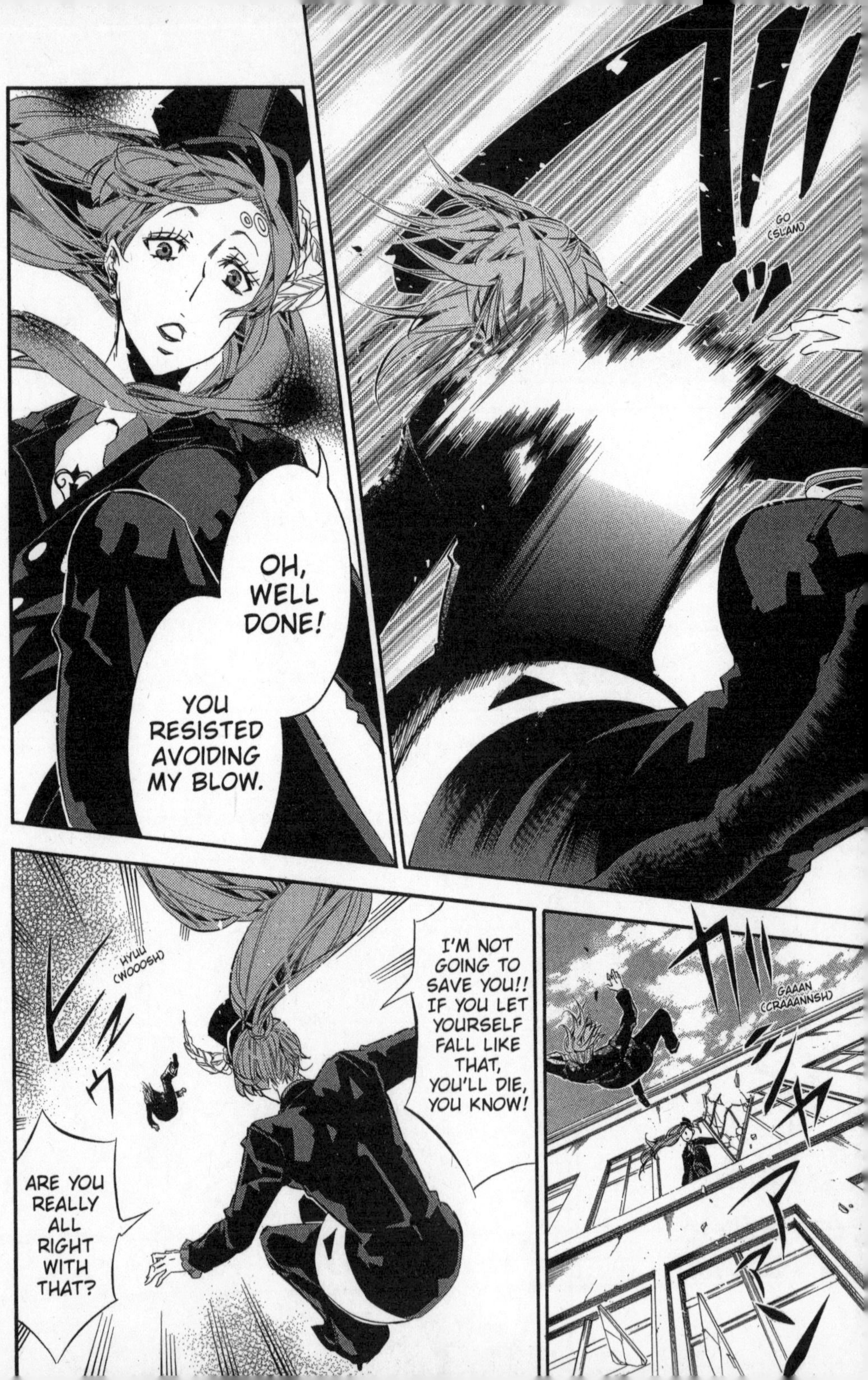
GO
(SLAM)
OH, WELL DONE!
YOU RESISTED AVOIDING MY BLOW.
GAAAN
(CRAAANNSH)
I'M NOT GOING TO SAVE YOU!! IF YOU LET YOURSELF FALL LIKE THAT, YOU'LL DIE, YOU KNOW!
HYUU
(WOOOSH)
ARE YOU REALLY ALL RIGHT WITH THAT?

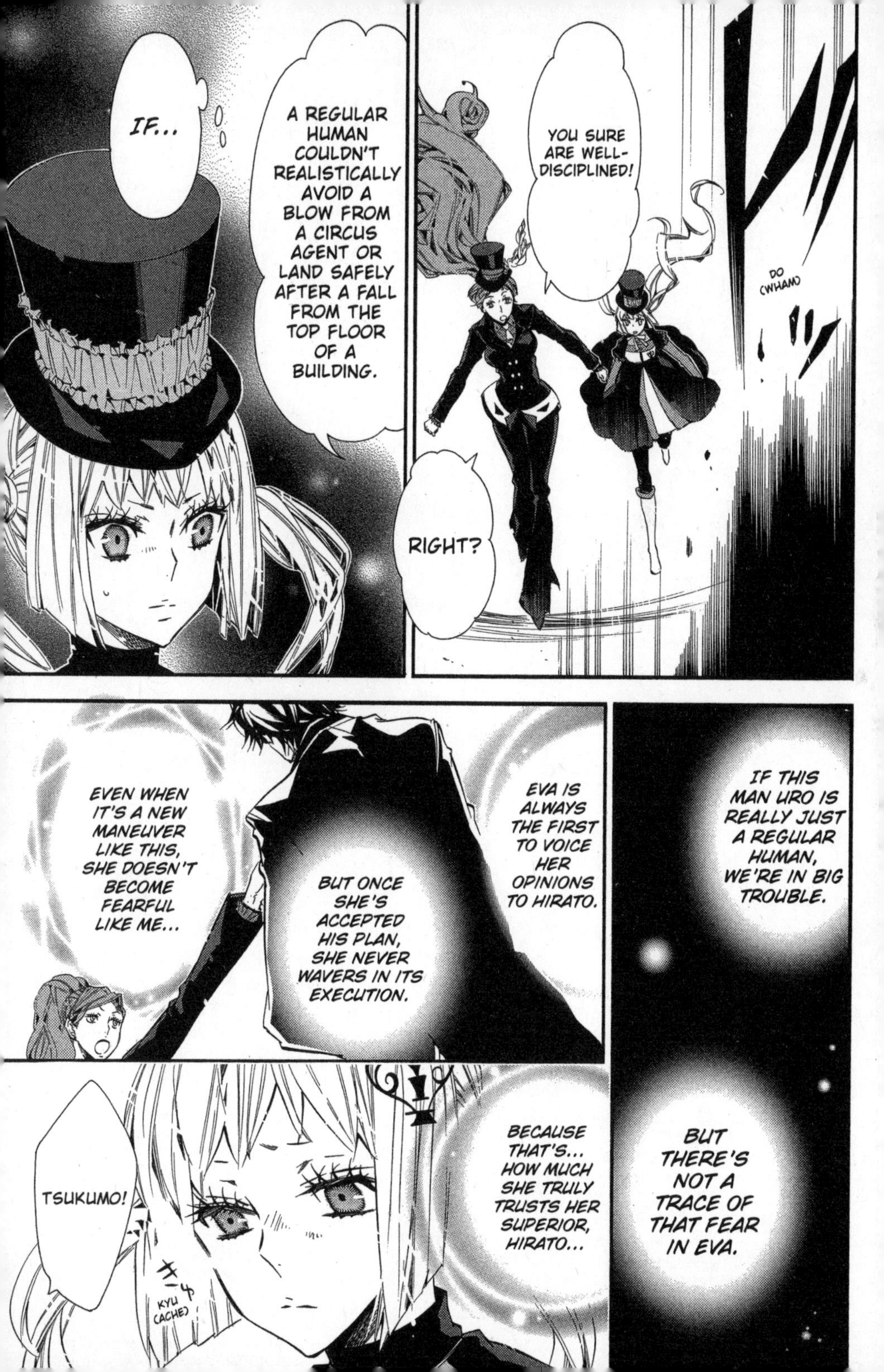
DO (WHAM)
YOU SURE ARE WELL-DISCIPLINED!
RIGHT?
A REGULAR HUMAN COULDN'T REALISTICALLY AVOID A BLOW FROM A CIRCUS AGENT OR LAND SAFELY AFTER A FALL FROM THE TOP FLOOR OF A BUILDING.
IF...
IF THIS MAN URO IS REALLY JUST A REGULAR HUMAN, WE'RE IN BIG TROUBLE.
BUT THERE'S NOT A TRACE OF THAT FEAR IN EVA.
EVA IS ALWAYS THE FIRST TO VOICE HER OPINIONS TO HIRATO.
BUT ONCE SHE'S ACCEPTED HIS PLAN, SHE NEVER WAVERS IN ITS EXECUTION.
EVEN WHEN IT'S A NEW MANEUVER LIKE THIS, SHE DOESN'T BECOME FEARFUL LIKE ME...
BECAUSE THAT'S... HOW MUCH SHE TRULY TRUSTS HER SUPERIOR, HIRATO...
TSUKUMO!
KYU (ACHE)

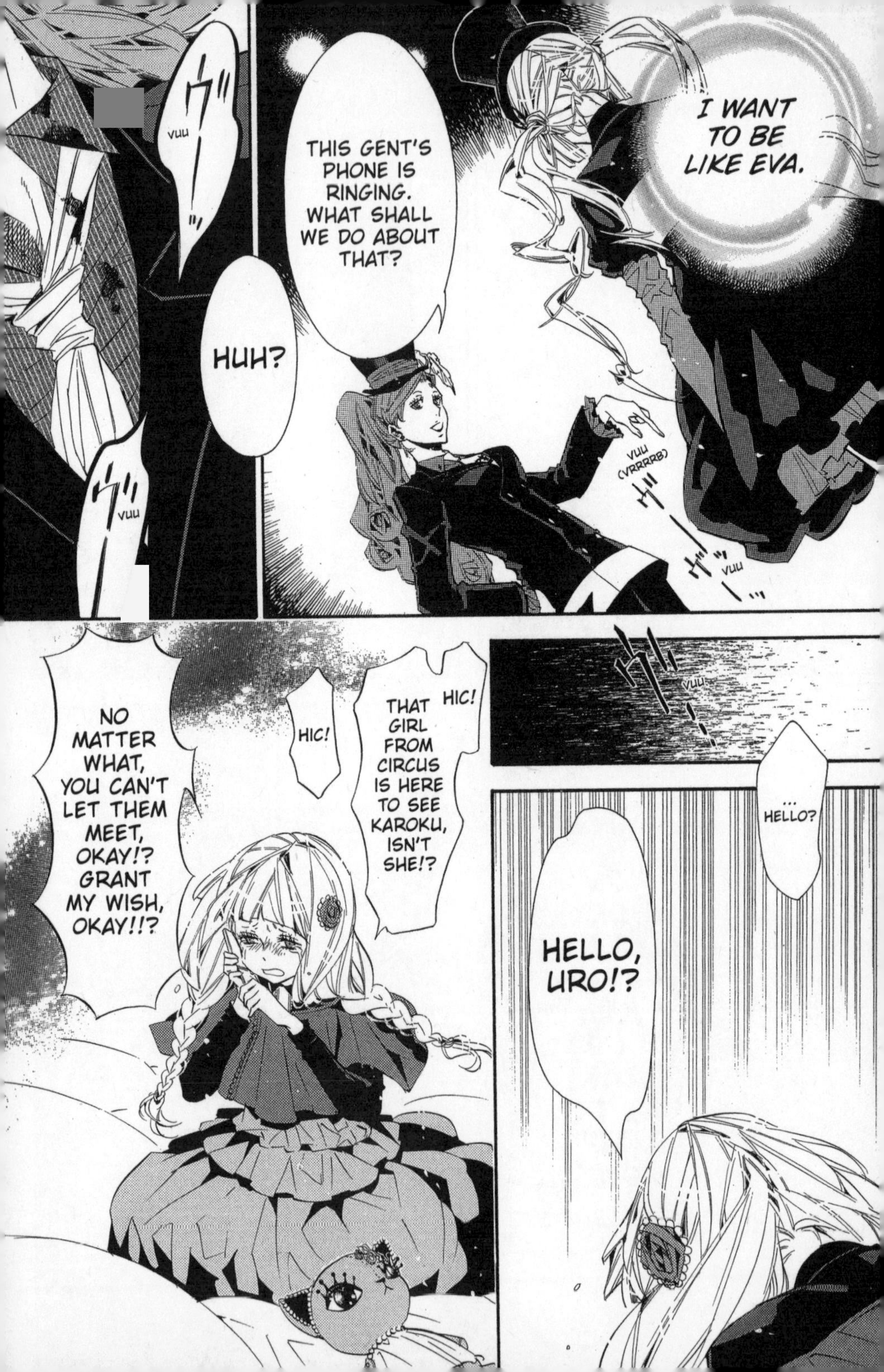
I WANT TO BE LIKE EVA.
THIS GENT'S PHONE IS RINGING. WHAT SHALL WE DO ABOUT THAT?
HUH?
VUU (VRRRRB)
VUU
VUU
VUU
VUU
... HELLO?
HELLO, URO!?
HIC!
THAT GIRL FROM CIRCUS IS HERE TO SEE KAROKU, ISN'T SHE!?
HIC!
NO MATTER WHAT, YOU CAN'T LET THEM MEET, OKAY!? GRANT MY WISH, OKAY!!?

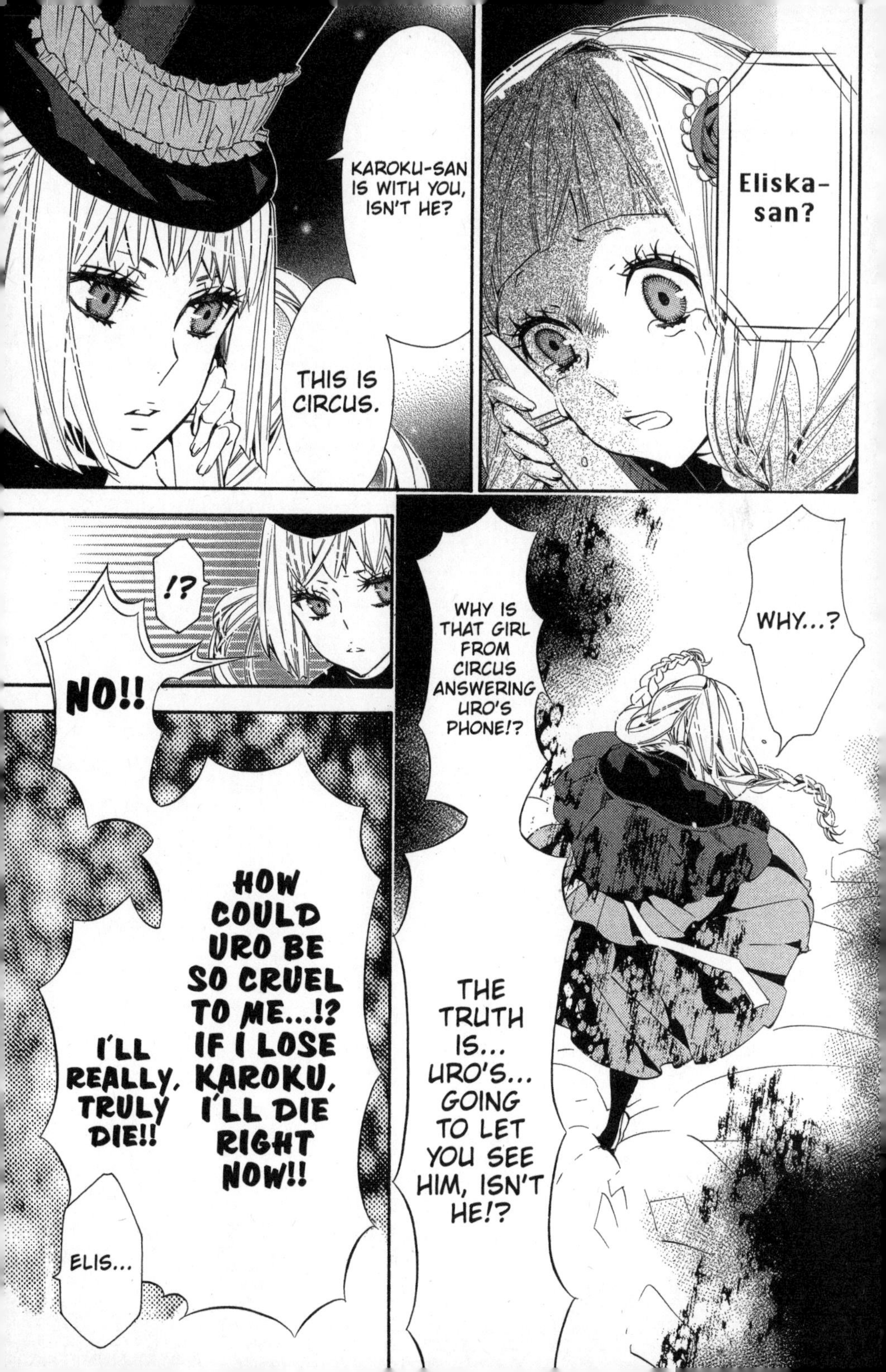
Eliska-san?
KAROKU-SAN IS WITH YOU, ISN'T HE?
THIS IS CIRCUS.
WHY...?
WHY IS THAT GIRL FROM CIRCUS ANSWERING URO'S PHONE!?
THE TRUTH IS... URO'S... GOING TO LET YOU SEE HIM, ISN'T HE!?
!?
NO!!
HOW COULD URO BE SO CRUEL TO ME...!? IF I LOSE KAROKU, I'LL DIE RIGHT NOW!!
I'LL REALLY, TRULY DIE!!
ELIS...

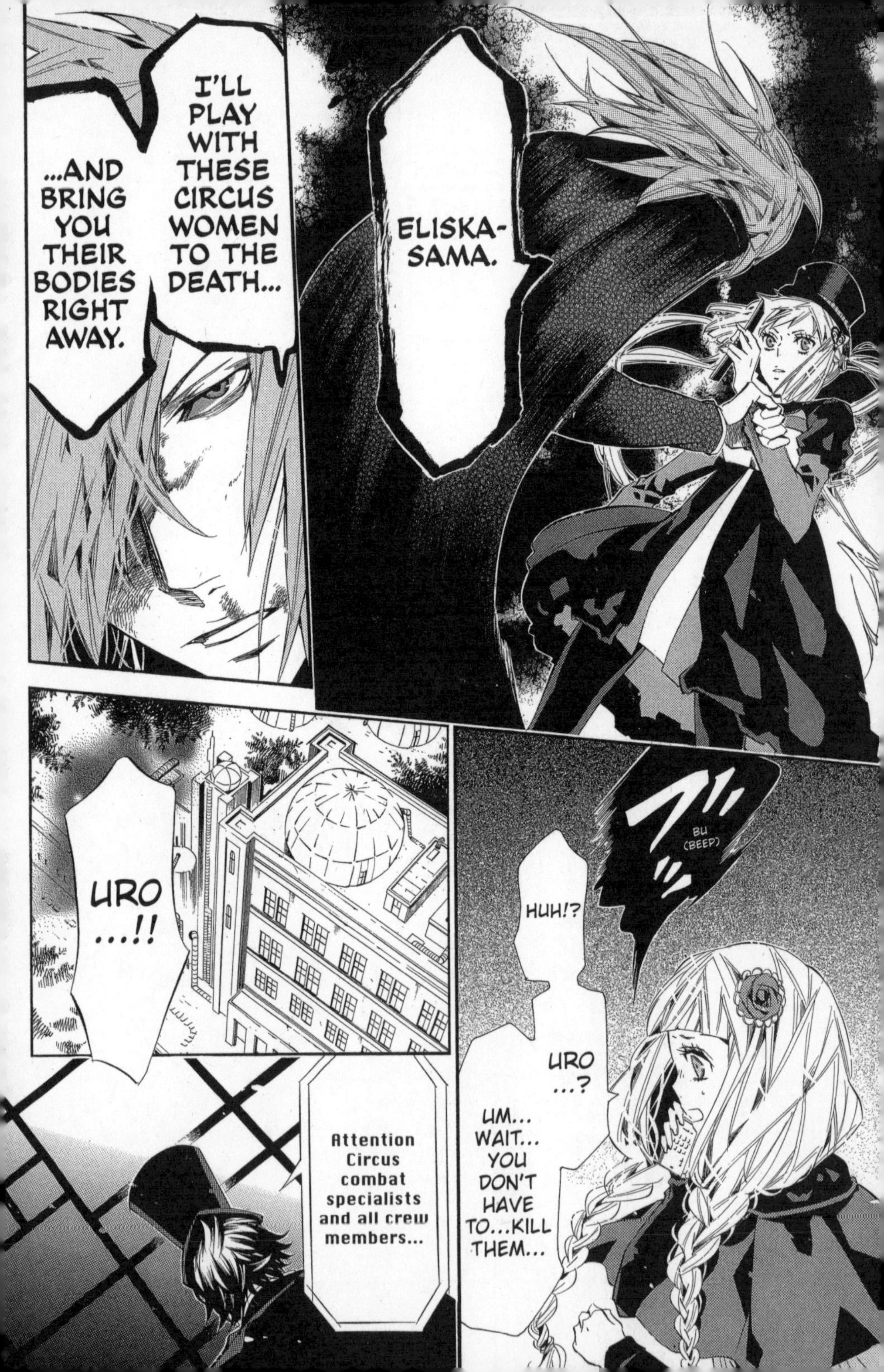
ELISKA-SAMA.
I'LL PLAY WITH THESE CIRCUS WOMEN TO THE DEATH...
...AND BRING YOU THEIR BODIES RIGHT AWAY.
BU (BEEP)
HUH!?
URO ...?
UM... WAIT... YOU DON'T HAVE TO...KILL THEM...
URO ...!!
Attention Circus combat specialists and all crew members...

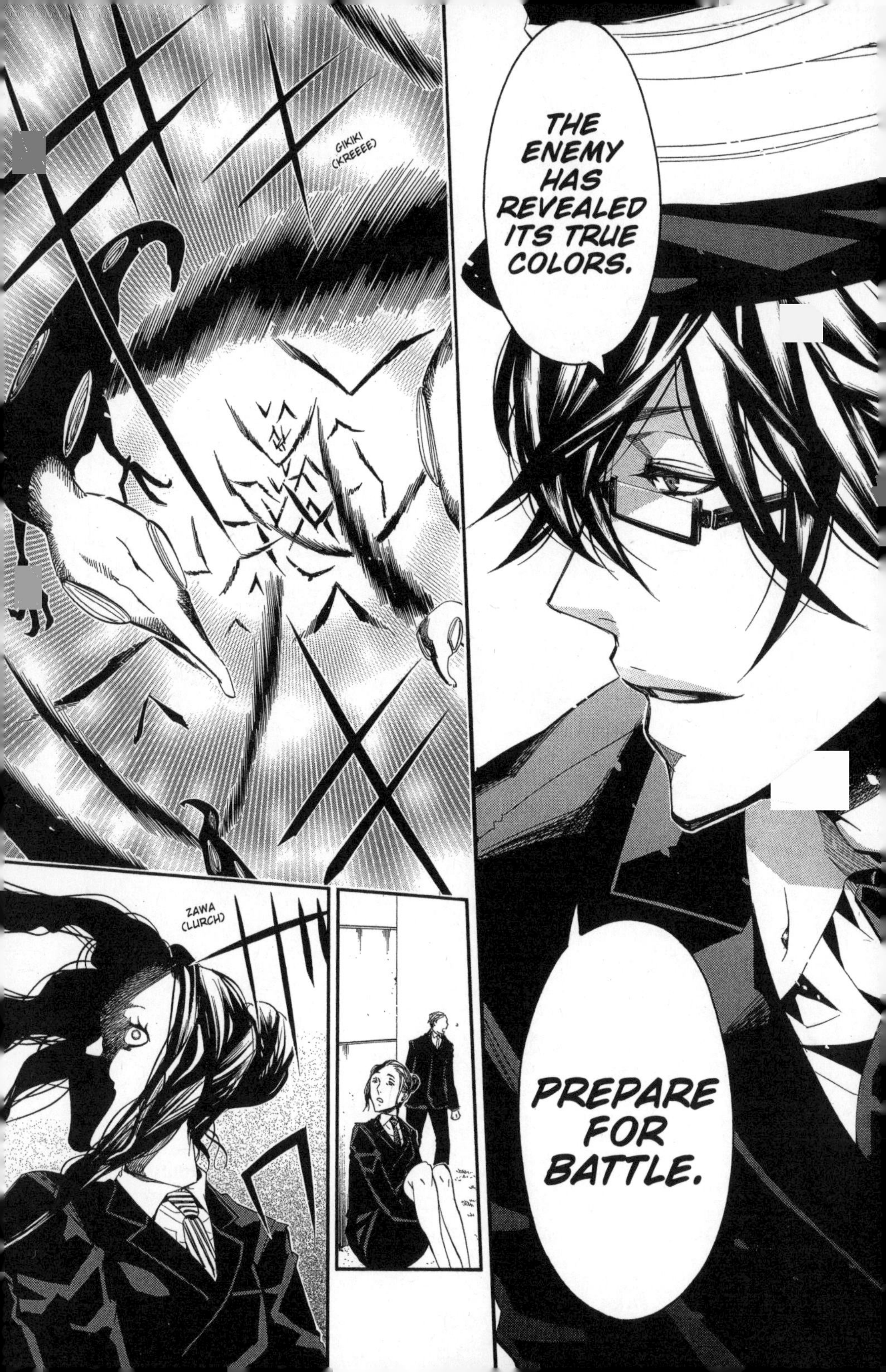
THE ENEMY HAS REVEALED ITS TRUE COLORS.
PREPARE FOR BATTLE.
GIKIKI (KREEEE)
ZAWA (LURCH)

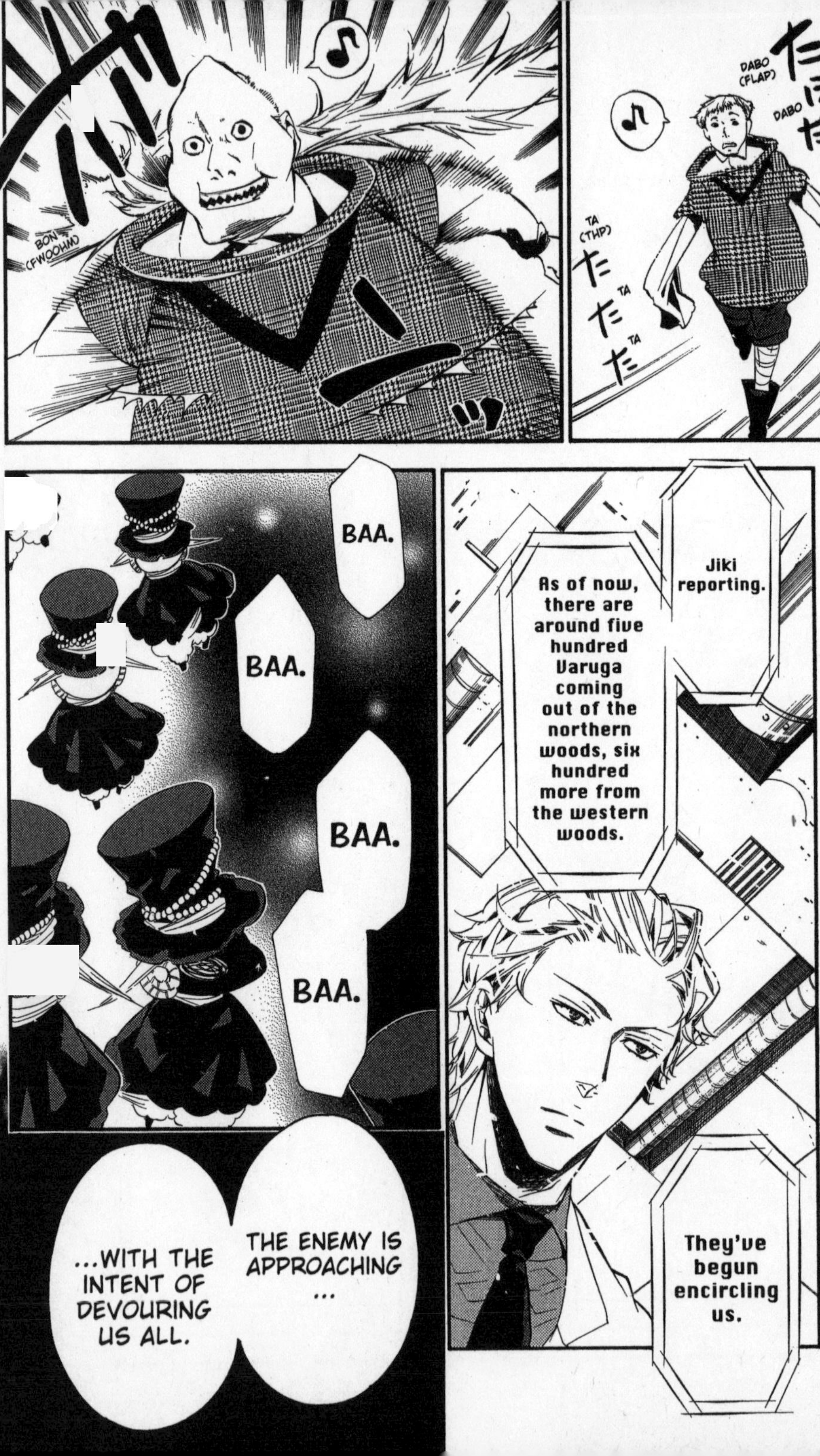
DABO (FLAP)
だぼだぼ
DABO
♪
TA (THP)
たたた
TA
TA
TA
♪
BON (FWOOHM)
Jiki reporting.
As of now, there are around five hundred Varuga coming out of the northern woods, six hundred more from the western woods.
They've begun encircling us.
BAA.
BAA.
BAA.
BAA.
THE ENEMY IS APPROACHING ...
...WITH THE INTENT OF DEVOURING US ALL.

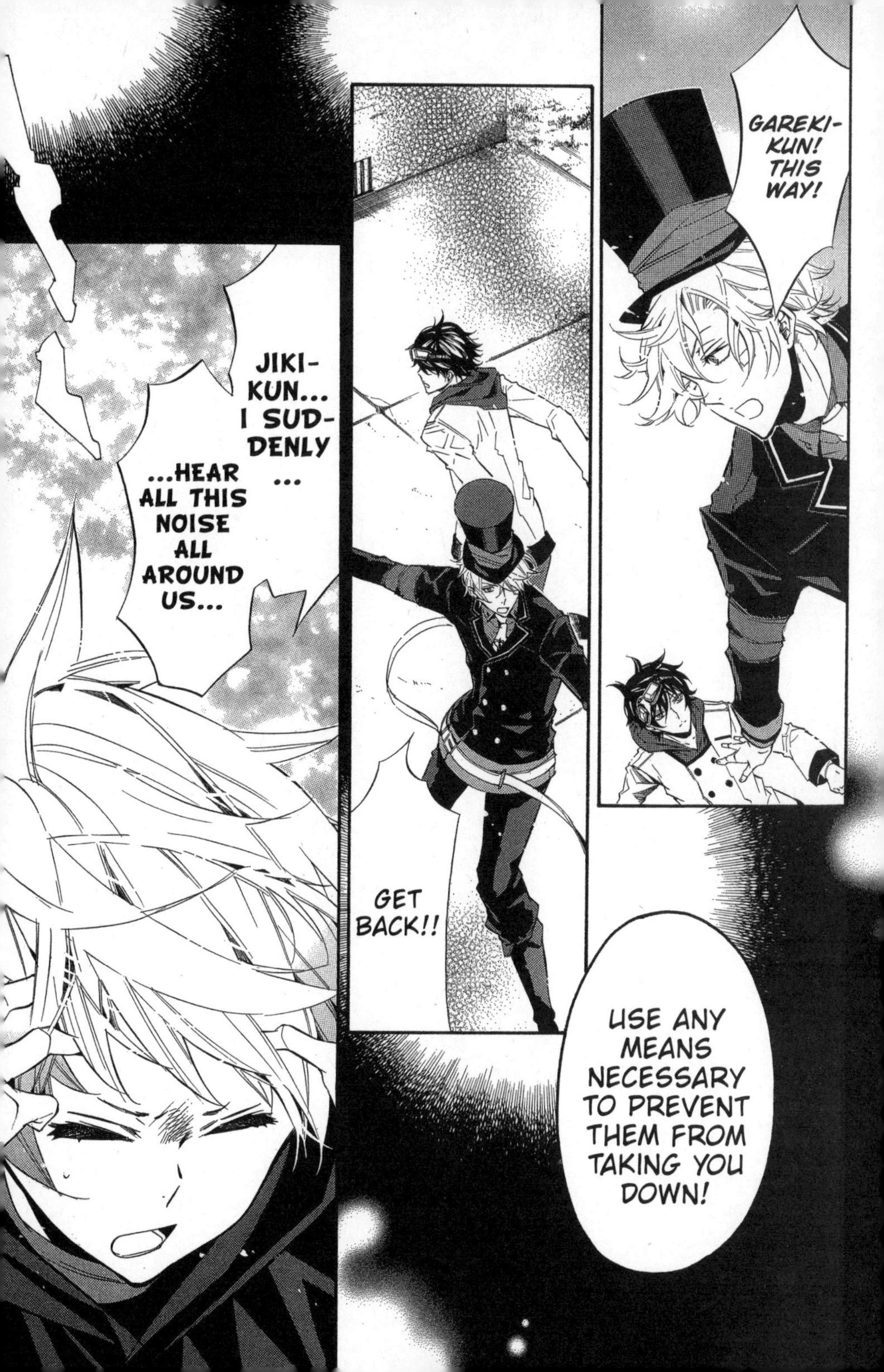
GAREKI-KUN! THIS WAY!
GET BACK!!
USE ANY MEANS NECESSARY TO PREVENT THEM FROM TAKING YOU DOWN!
JIKI-KUN... I SUDDENLY ...
...HEAR ALL THIS NOISE ALL AROUND US...

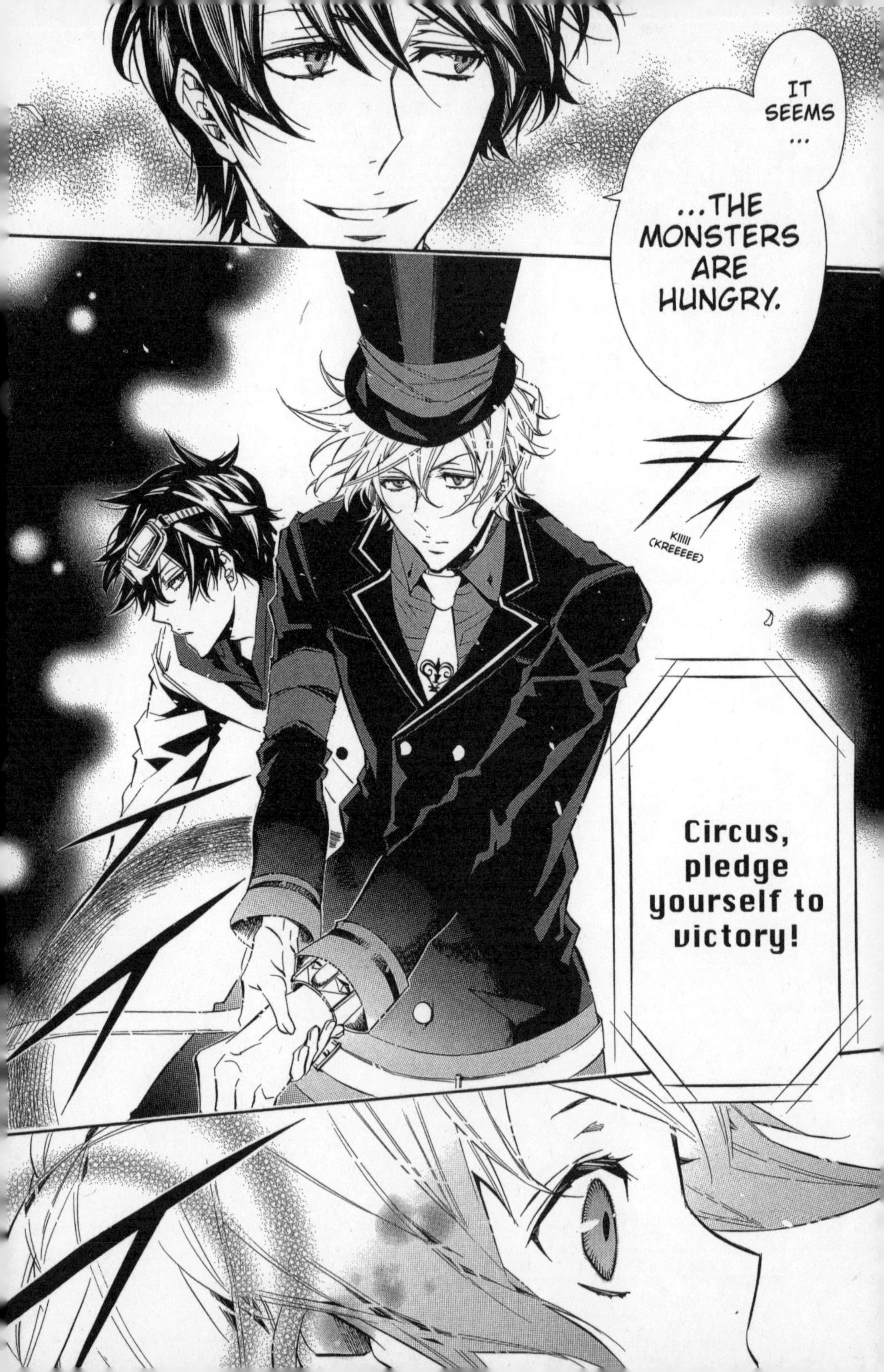
IT SEEMS ...
...THE MONSTERS ARE HUNGRY.
KIIII (KREEEEE)
Circus, pledge yourself to victory!

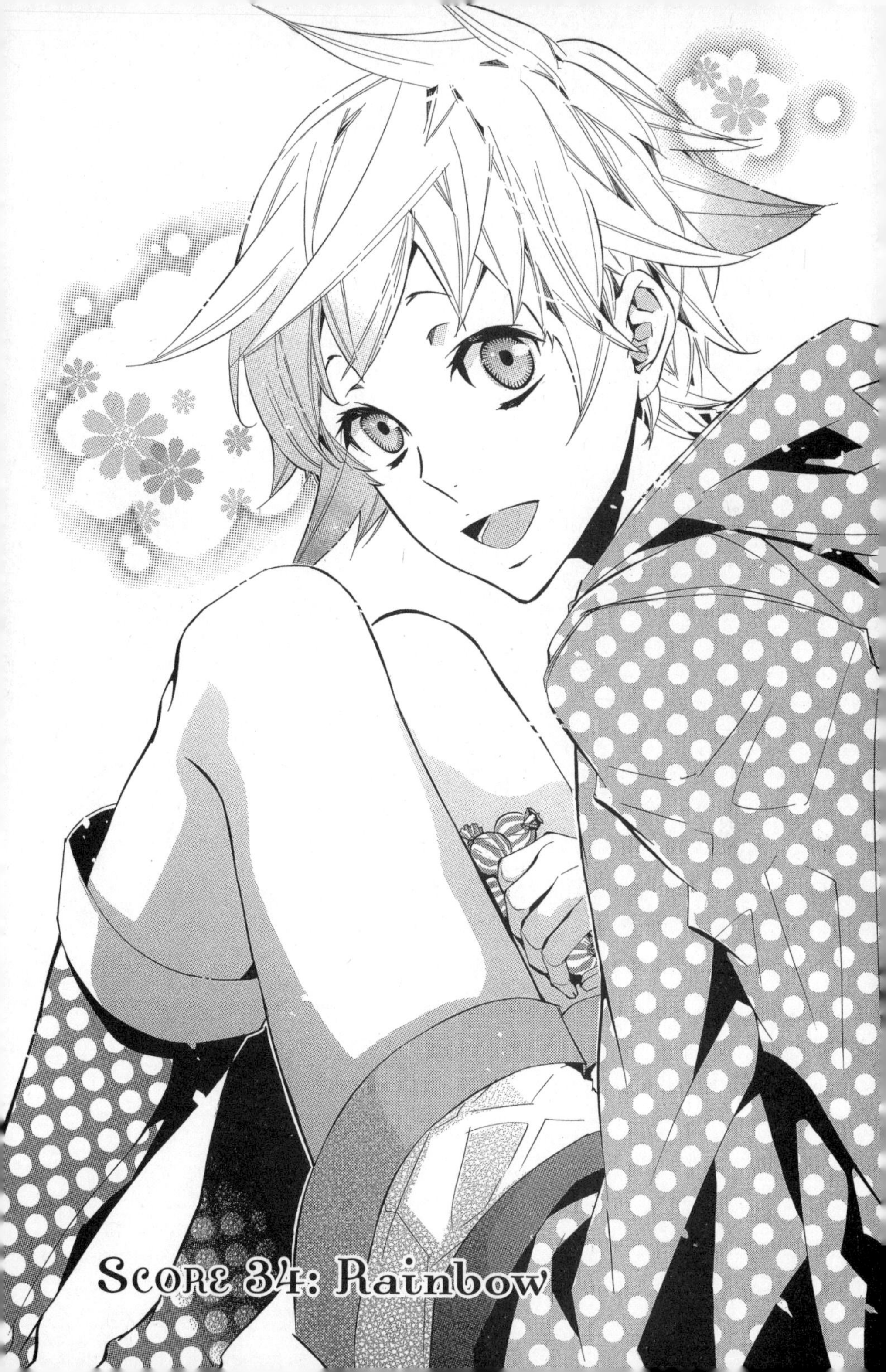
SCORE 34: Rainbow

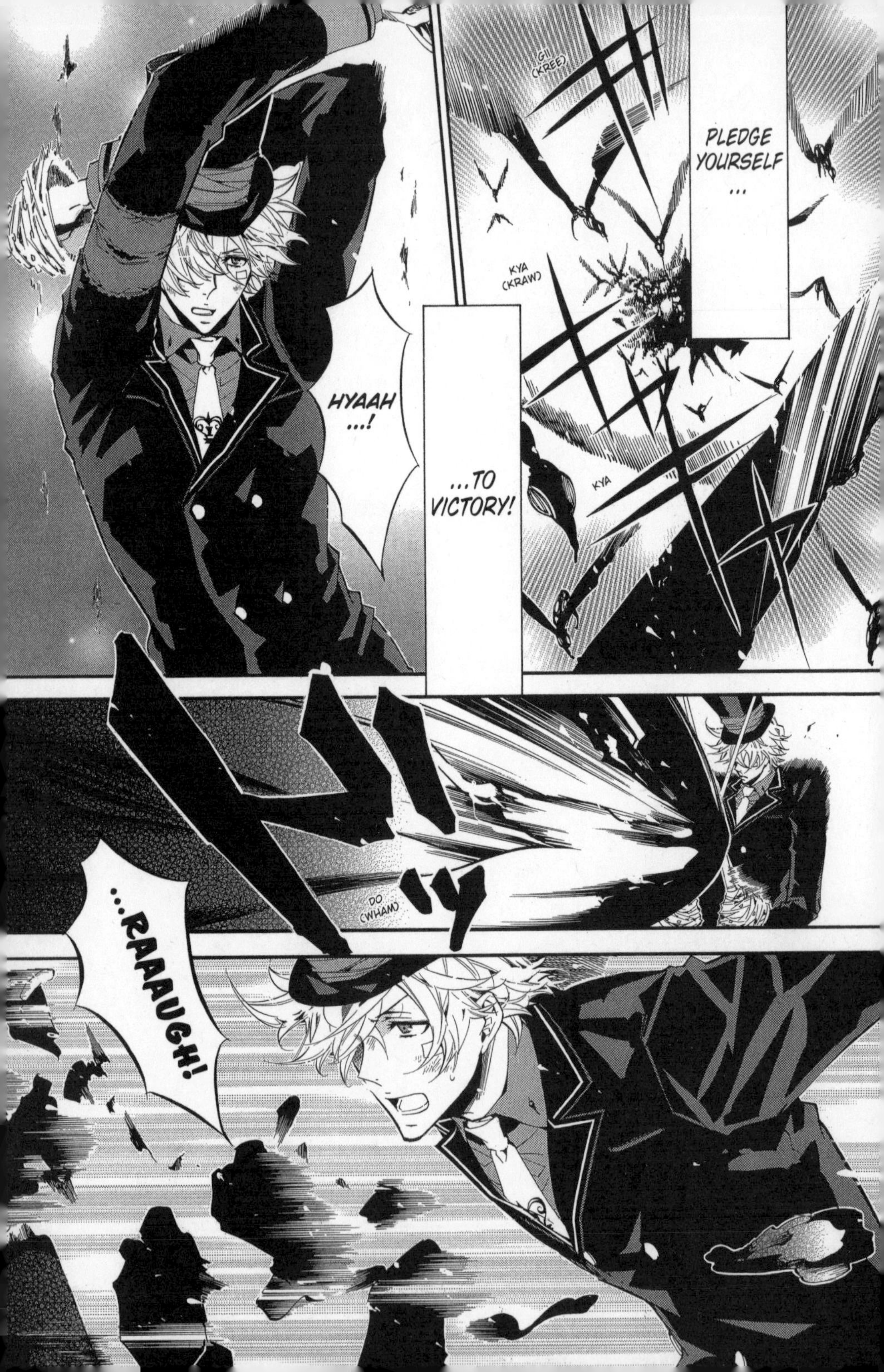
GII (KREE)
PLEDGE YOURSELF ...
KYA (KRAW)
KYA
...TO VICTORY!
HYAAH ...!
DO (WHAM)
...RAAAUGH!

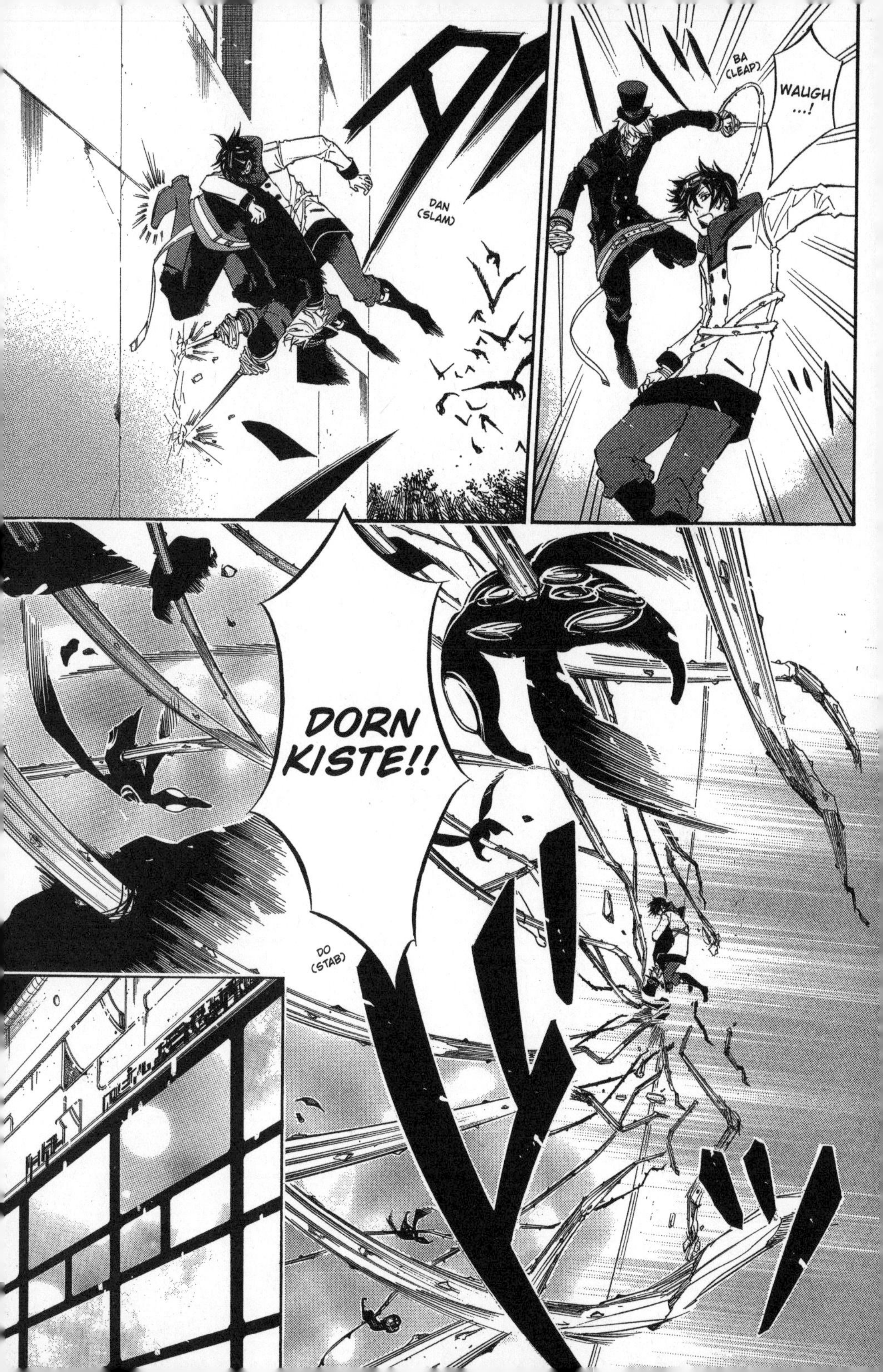
BA (LEAP)
WAUGH ...!
DAN (SLAM)
DORN KISTE!!
DO (STAB)

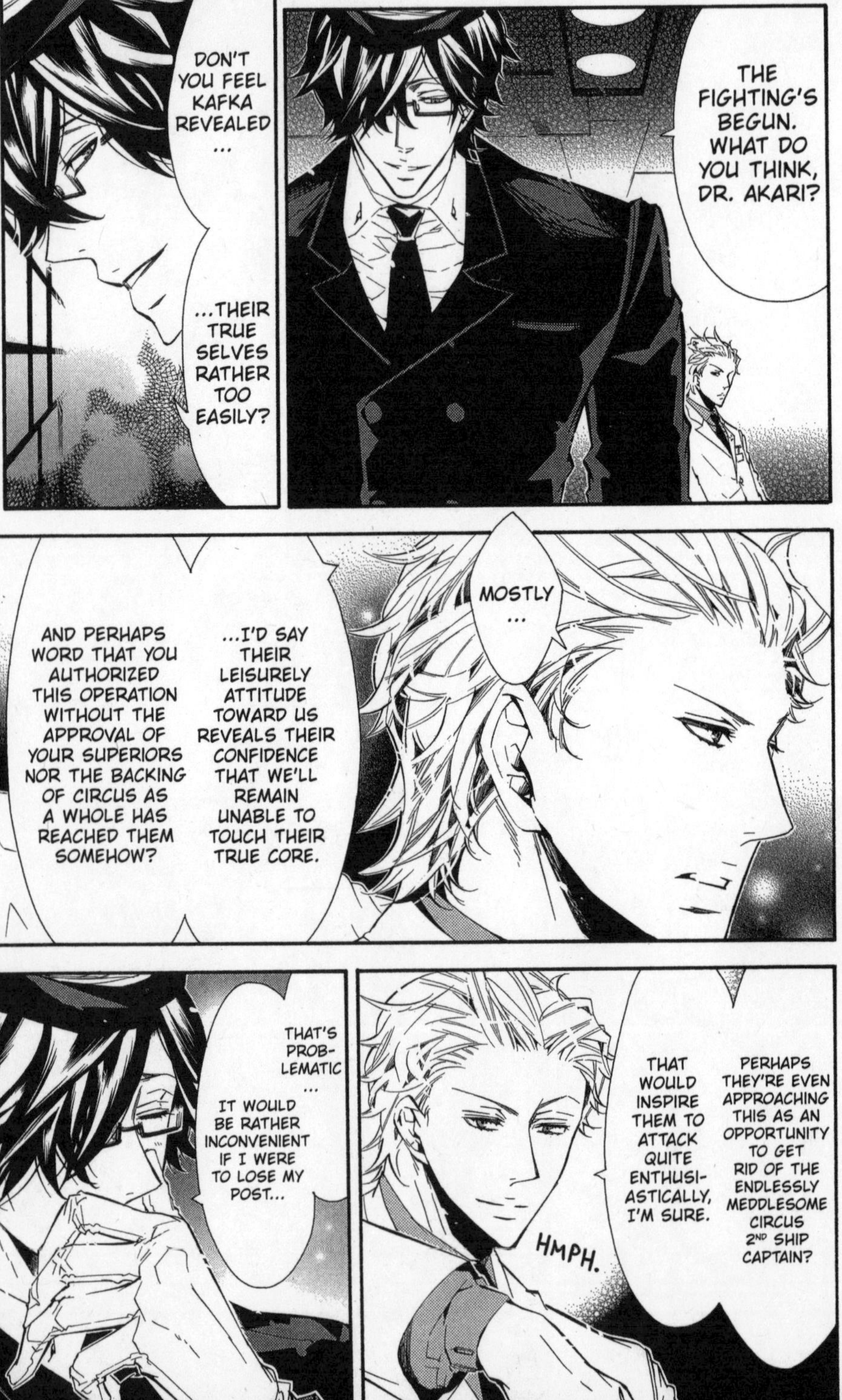
THE FIGHTING'S BEGUN. WHAT DO YOU THINK, DR. AKARI?
DON'T YOU FEEL KAFKA REVEALED...
...THEIR TRUE SELVES RATHER TOO EASILY?
MOSTLY...
...I'D SAY THEIR LEISURELY ATTITUDE TOWARD US REVEALS THEIR CONFIDENCE THAT WE'LL REMAIN UNABLE TO TOUCH THEIR TRUE CORE.
AND PERHAPS WORD THAT YOU AUTHORIZED THIS OPERATION WITHOUT THE APPROVAL OF YOUR SUPERIORS NOR THE BACKING OF CIRCUS AS A WHOLE HAS REACHED THEM SOMEHOW?
PERHAPS THEY'RE EVEN APPROACHING THIS AS AN OPPORTUNITY TO GET RID OF THE ENDLESSLY MEDDLESOME CIRCUS 2ND SHIP CAPTAIN?
THAT WOULD INSPIRE THEM TO ATTACK QUITE ENTHUSI-ASTICALLY, I'M SURE.
HMPH.
THAT'S PROB-LEMATIC...
IT WOULD BE RATHER INCONVENIENT IF I WERE TO LOSE MY POST...

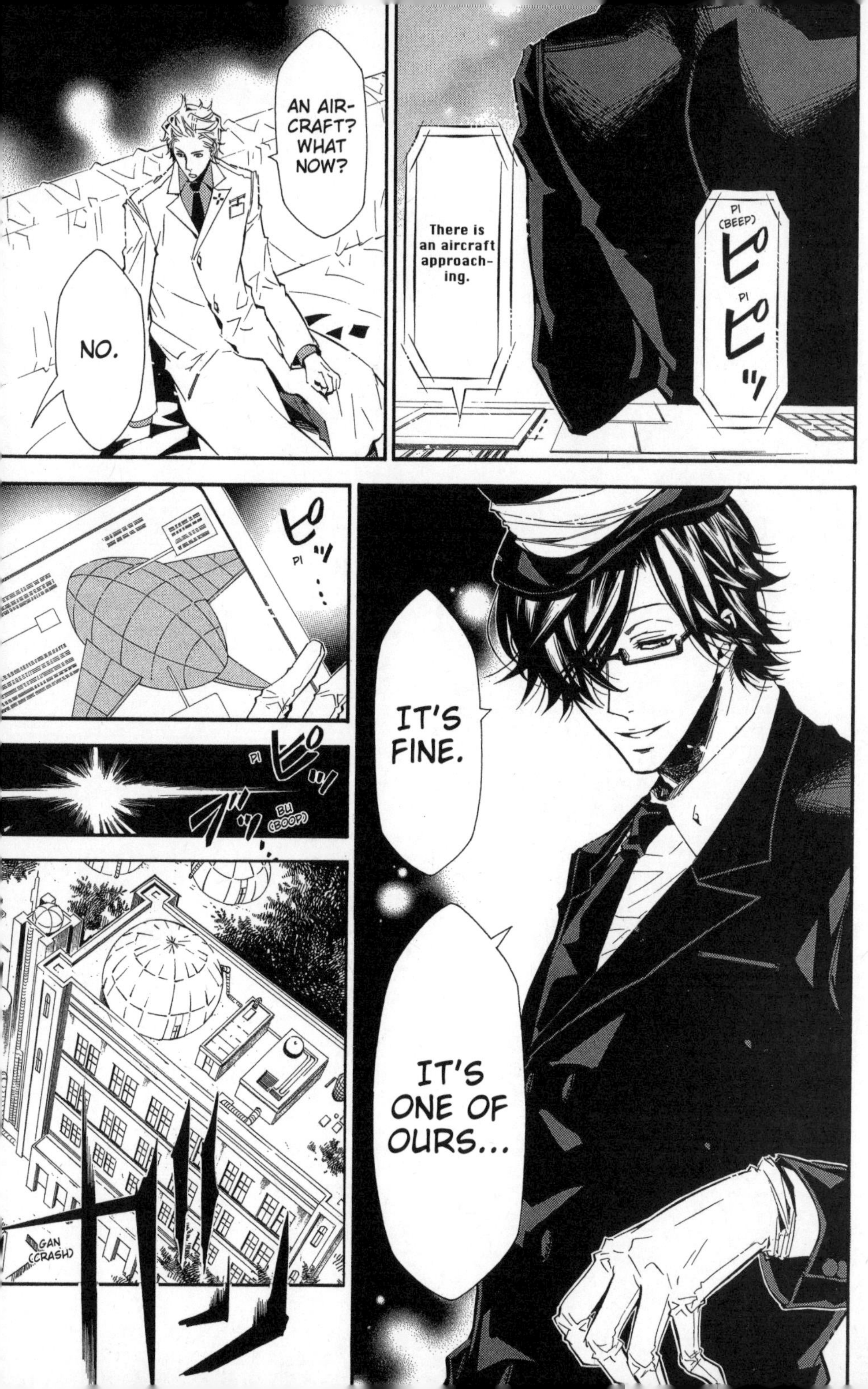
PI (BEEP)
ピ
PI
ピッ
There is an aircraft approaching.
AN AIR-CRAFT? WHAT NOW?
NO.
IT'S FINE.
IT'S ONE OF OURS...
ピッ
PI
...
PI
ピッ
BU (BOOP)
GAN (CRASH)

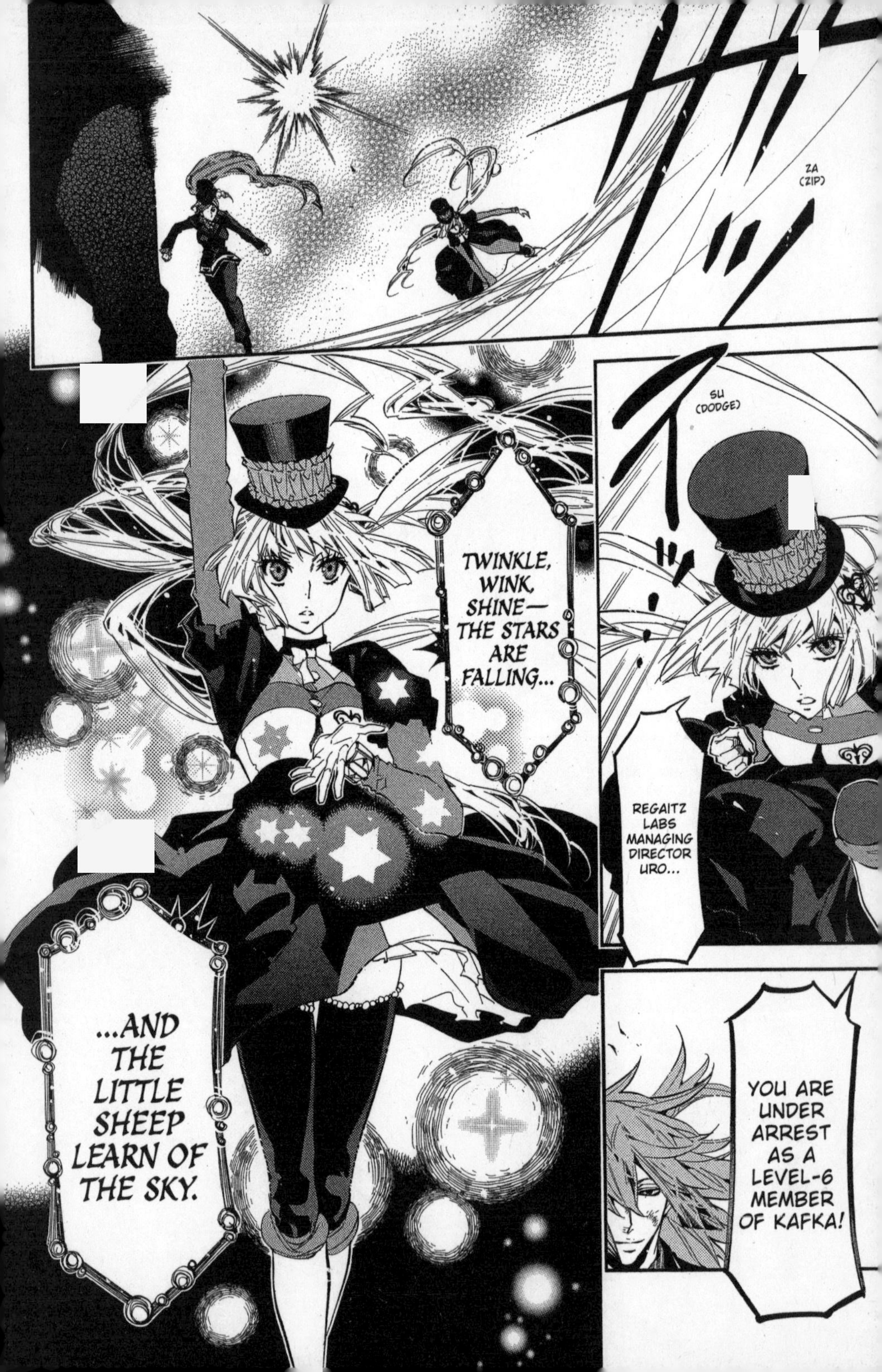
ZA (ZIP)
SU (DODGE)
REGAITZ LABS MANAGING DIRECTOR URO...
YOU ARE UNDER ARREST AS A LEVEL-6 MEMBER OF KAFKA!
TWINKLE, WINK, SHINE—THE STARS ARE FALLING...
...AND THE LITTLE SHEEP LEARN OF THE SKY.

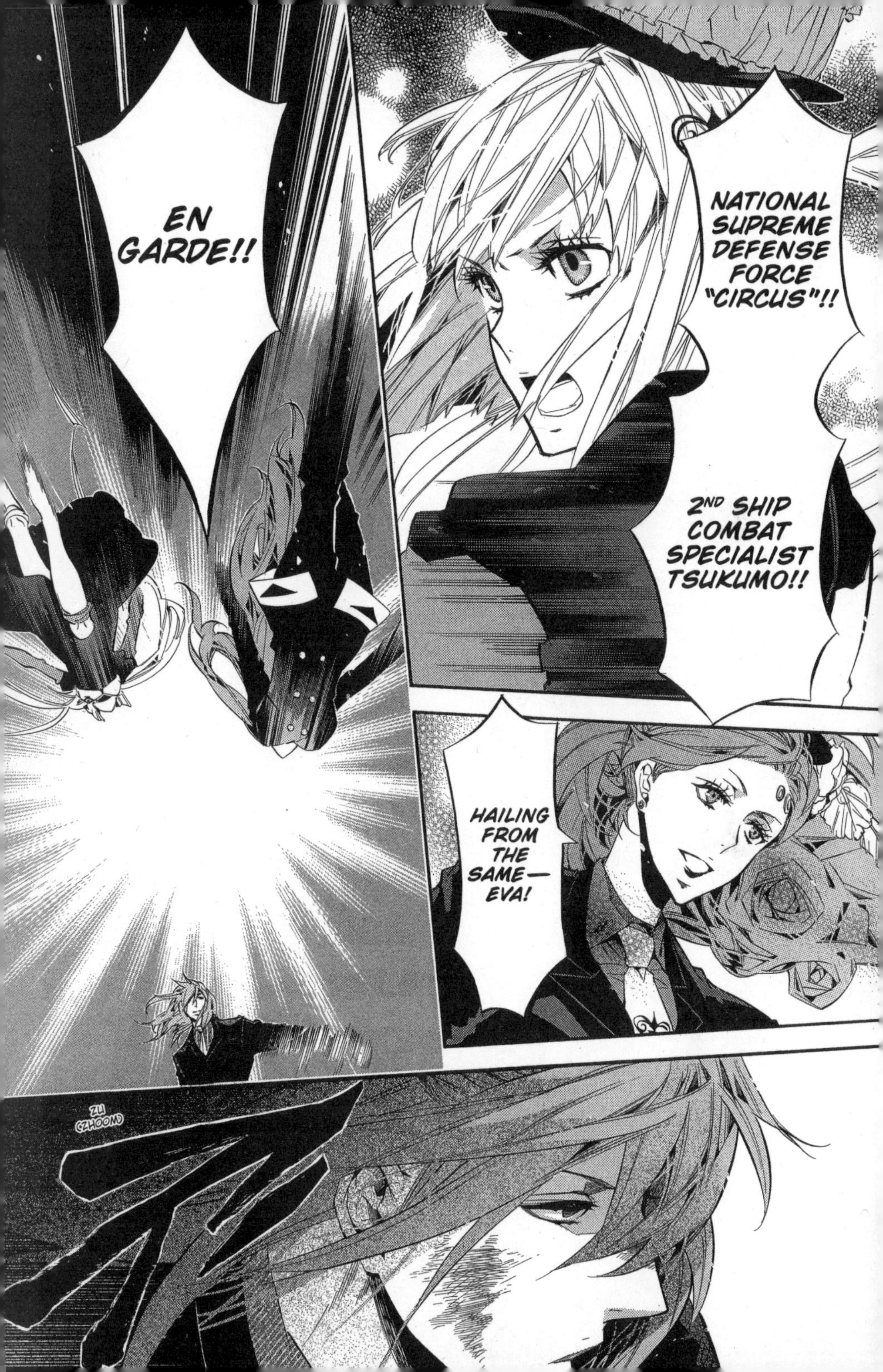
NATIONAL SUPREME DEFENSE FORCE "CIRCUS"!!
2ND SHIP COMBAT SPECIALIST TSUKUMO!!
HAILING FROM THE SAME—EVA!
EN GARDE!!
ZU (ZHOOM)

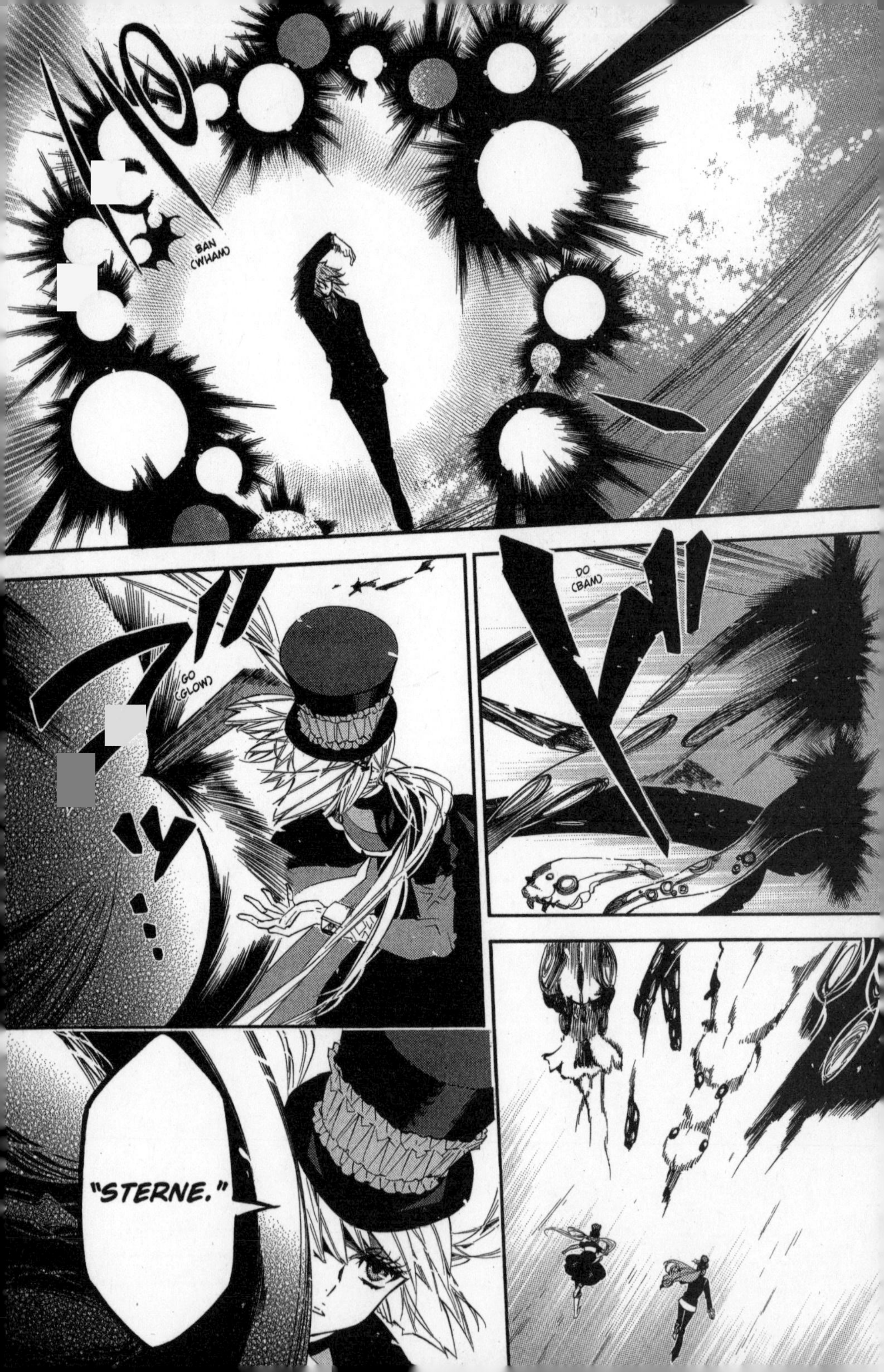
BAN
(WHAM)
DO
(BAM)
GO
(GLOW)
"STERNE."

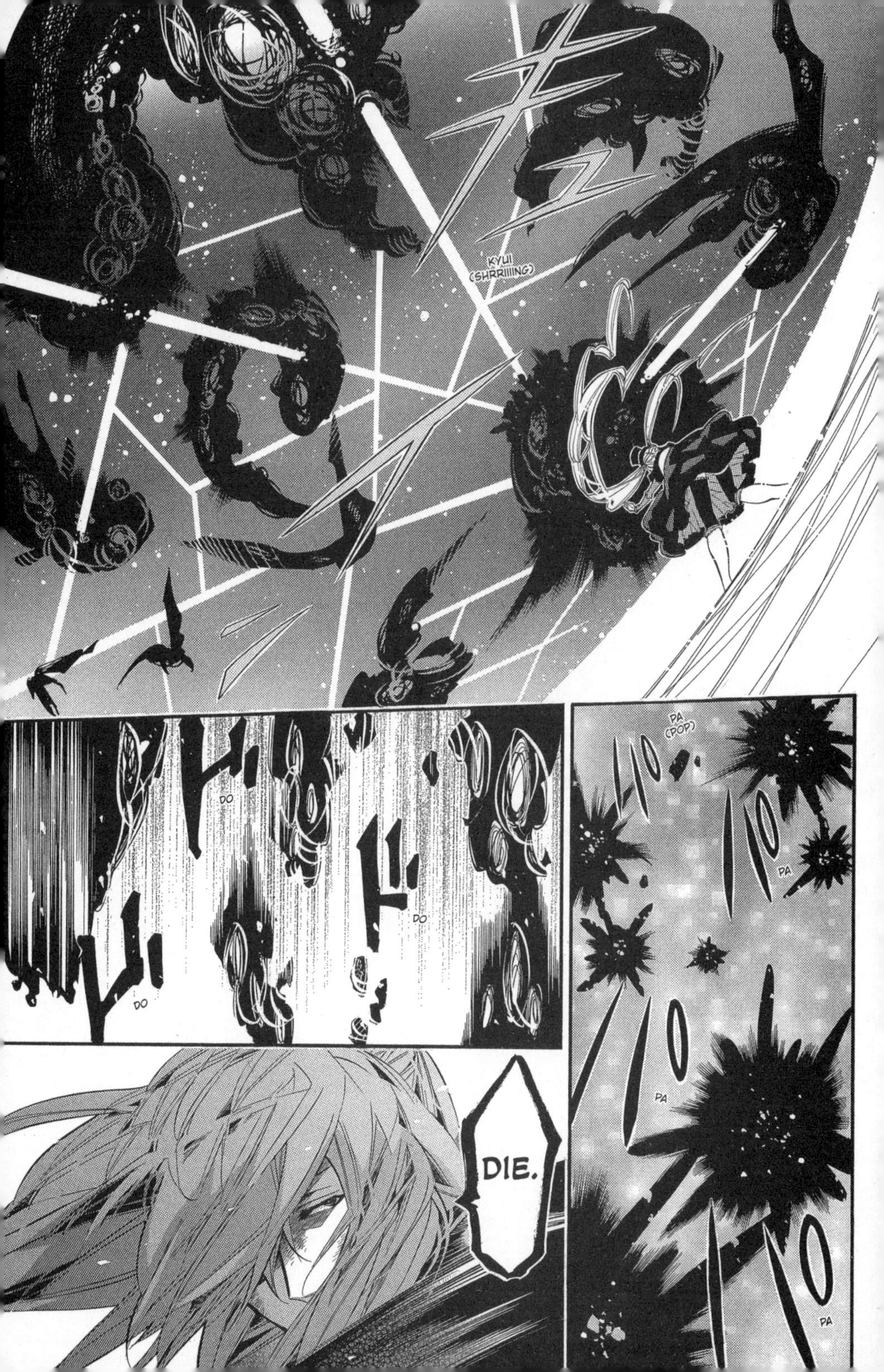
KYUI
(SHRRIIIING)
PA
(POP)
PA
PA
PA
DO
DO
DO
DIE.

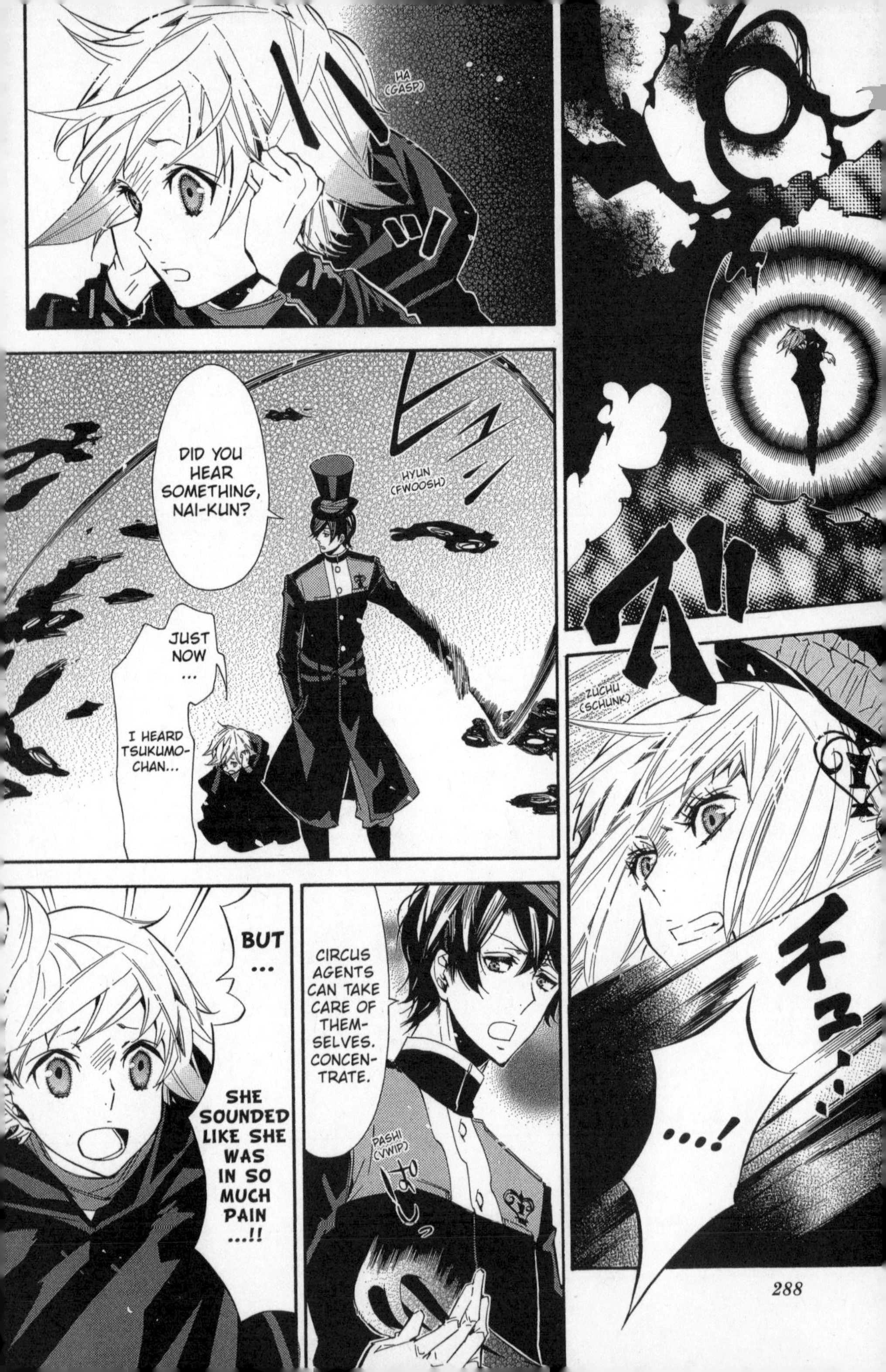
ZUCHU (SCHUNK)
...!
HA (GASP)
DID YOU HEAR SOMETHING, NAI-KUN?
HYUN (FWOOSH)
JUST NOW ...
I HEARD TSUKUMO-CHAN...
CIRCUS AGENTS CAN TAKE CARE OF THEMSELVES. CONCENTRATE.
PASHI (VWIP)
BUT ...
SHE SOUNDED LIKE SHE WAS IN SO MUCH PAIN ...!!

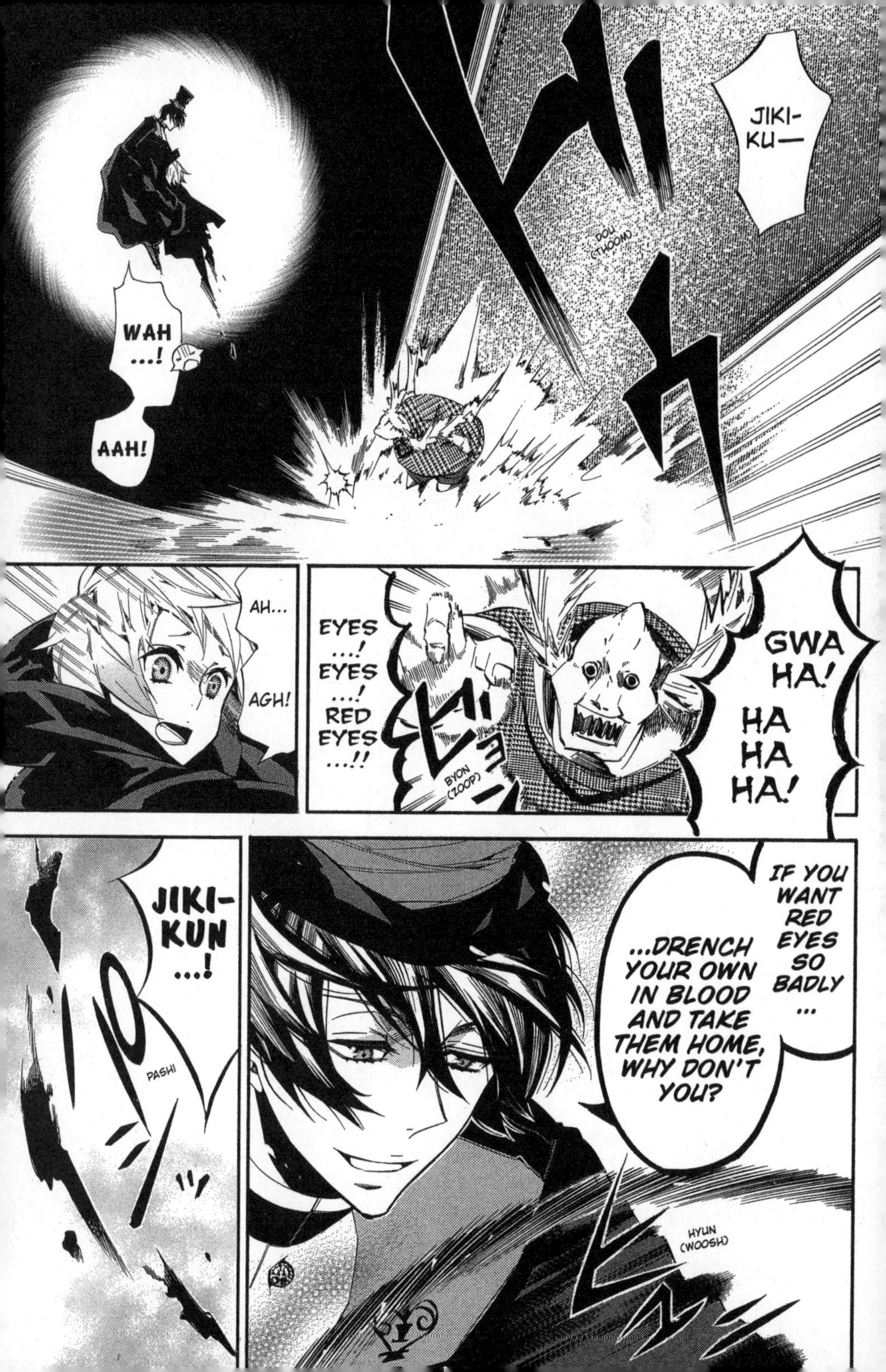
JIKI-KU—
DOU (THOOM)
WAH ...!
AAH!
GWA HA! HA HA HA!
EYES ...! EYES ...! RED EYES ...!!
BYON (ZOOP)
AH...
AGH!
IF YOU WANT RED EYES SO BADLY ...
...DRENCH YOUR OWN IN BLOOD AND TAKE THEM HOME, WHY DON'T YOU?
HYUN (WOOSH)
JIKI-KUN ...!
PASHI

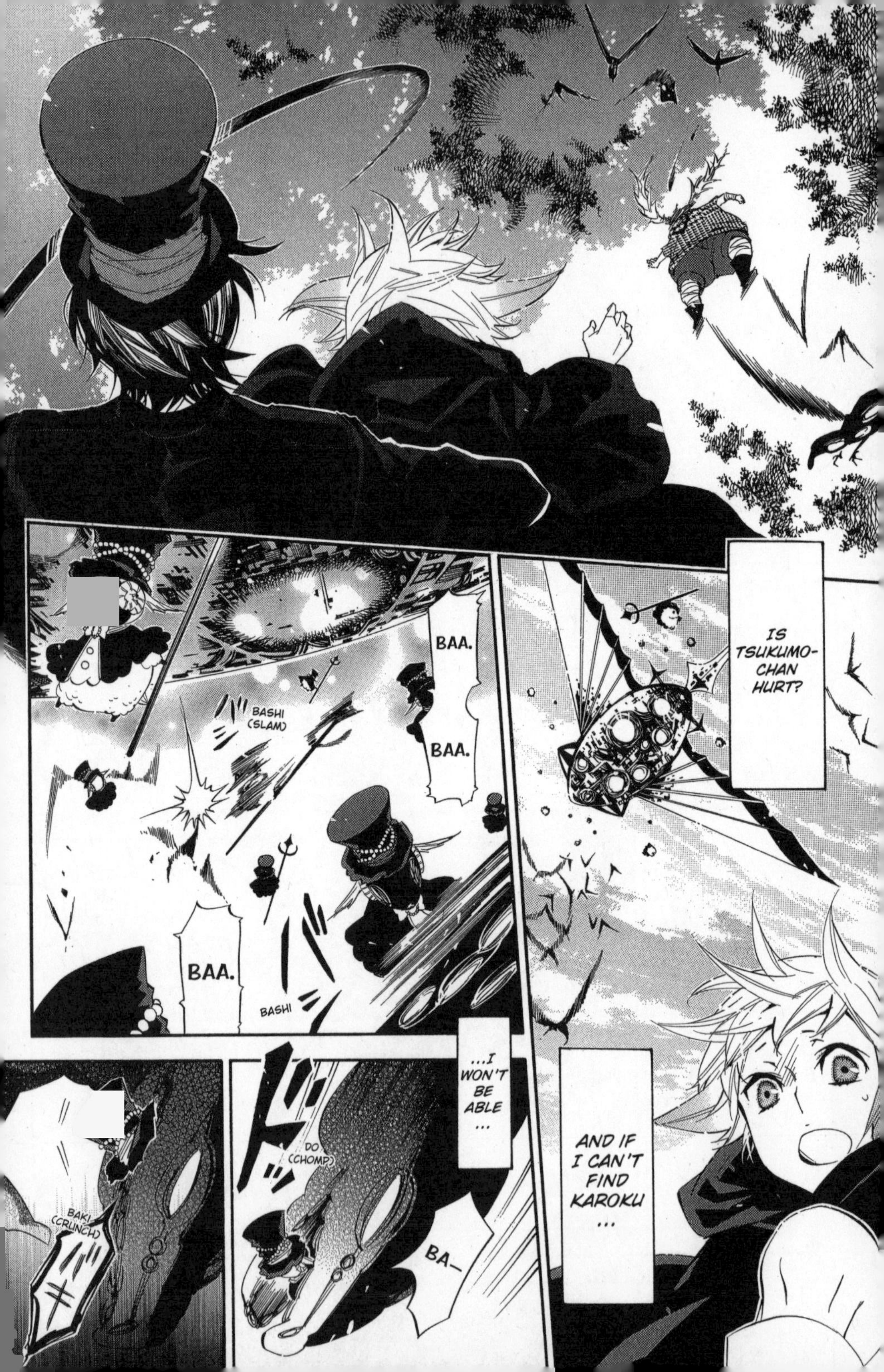
IS TSUKUMO-CHAN HURT?
BAA.
BAA.
BASHI (SLAM)
BAA.
BASHI
AND IF I CAN'T FIND KAROKU ...
...I WON'T BE ABLE ...
DO (CHOMP)
BA—
BAKI (CRUNCH)

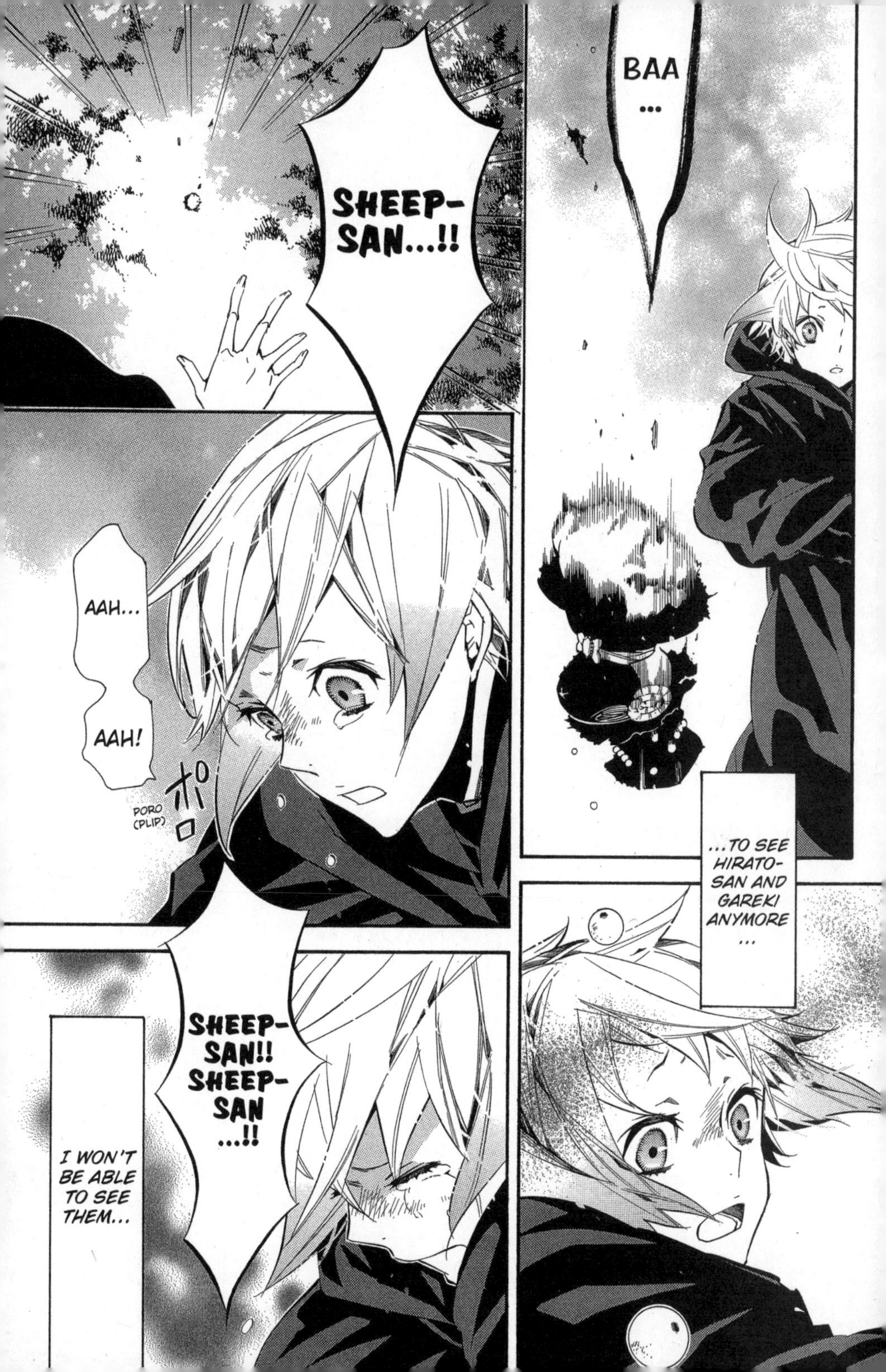
BAA ...
SHEEP-SAN...!!
AAH...
AAH!
ポロ
PORO (PLIP)
...TO SEE HIRATO-SAN AND GAREKI ANYMORE ...
SHEEP-SAN!! SHEEP-SAN ...!!
I WON'T BE ABLE TO SEE THEM...

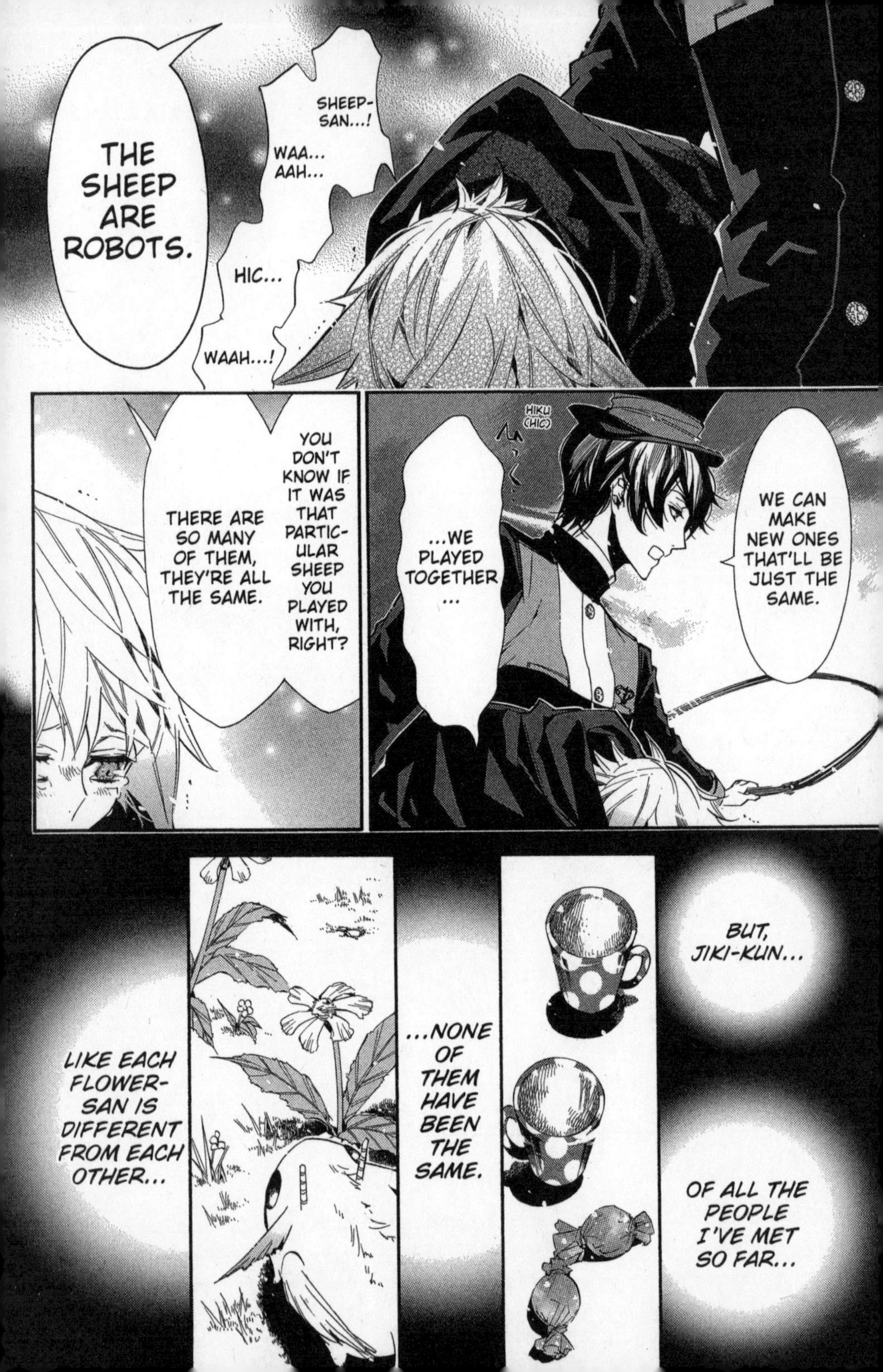
SHEEP-SAN...!
WAA... AAH...
HIC...
WAAH...!
THE SHEEP ARE ROBOTS.
HIKU (HIC)
WE CAN MAKE NEW ONES THAT'LL BE JUST THE SAME.
...WE PLAYED TOGETHER...
YOU DON'T KNOW IF IT WAS THAT PARTICULAR SHEEP YOU PLAYED WITH, RIGHT?
THERE ARE SO MANY OF THEM, THEY'RE ALL THE SAME.
...
BUT, JIKI-KUN...
OF ALL THE PEOPLE I'VE MET SO FAR...
...NONE OF THEM HAVE BEEN THE SAME.
LIKE EACH FLOWER-SAN IS DIFFERENT FROM EACH OTHER...

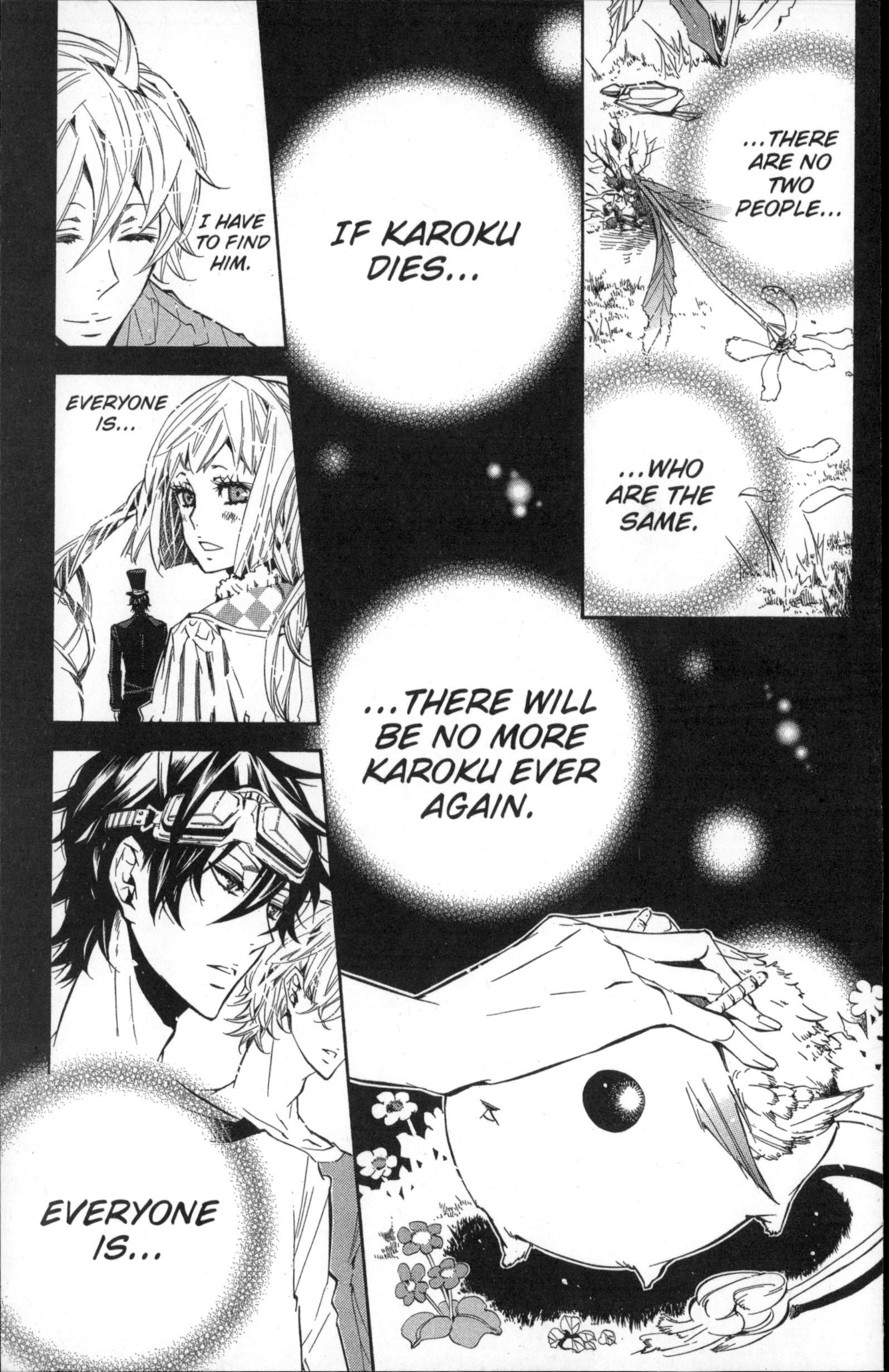
...THERE ARE NO TWO PEOPLE...
...WHO ARE THE SAME.
IF KAROKU DIES...
I HAVE TO FIND HIM.
...THERE WILL BE NO MORE KAROKU EVER AGAIN.
EVERYONE IS...
EVERYONE IS...

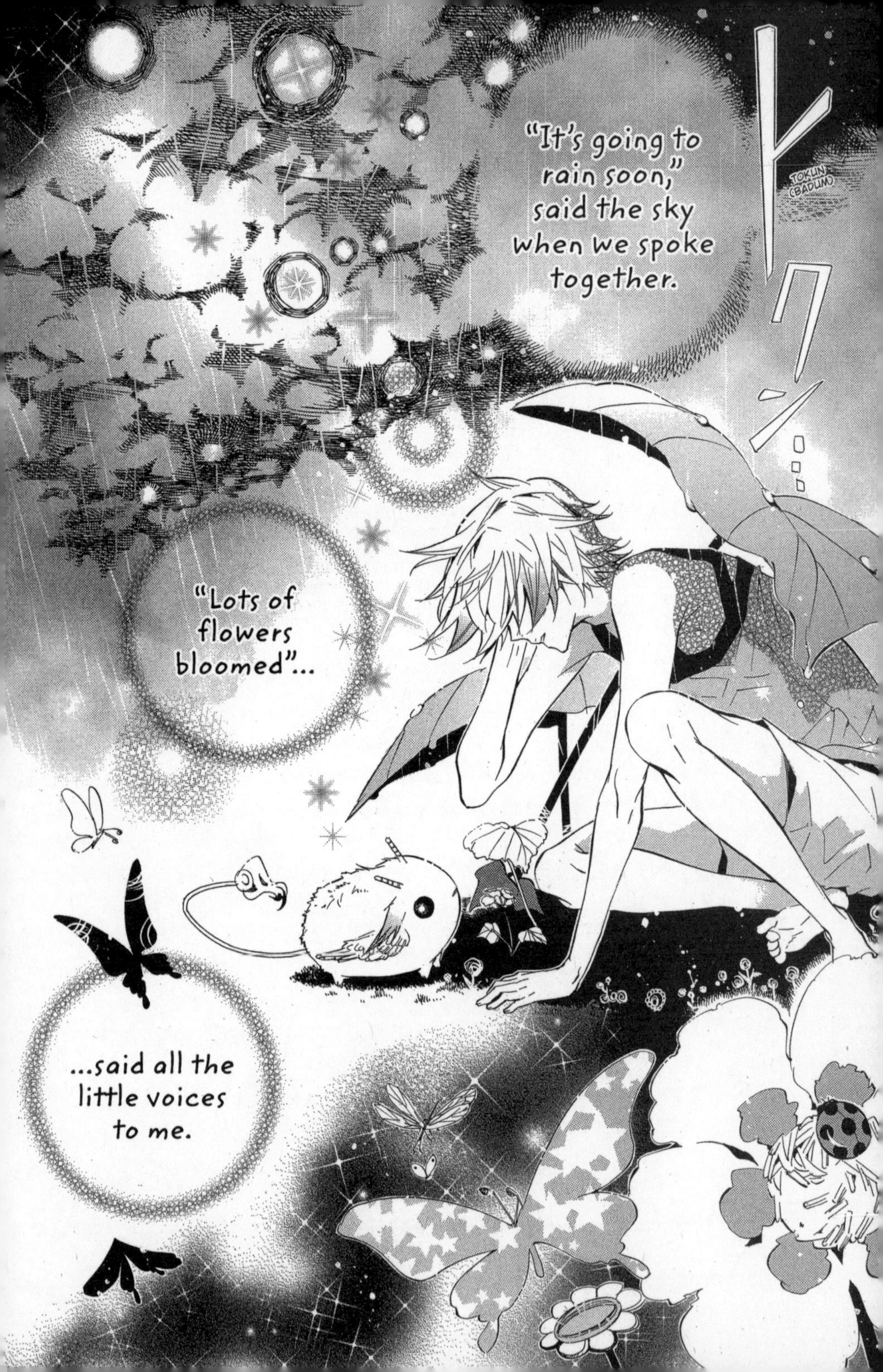

トクン…
TOKUN (BADUM)
"It's going to rain soon," said the sky when we spoke together.
"Lots of flowers bloomed"...
...said all the little voices to me.

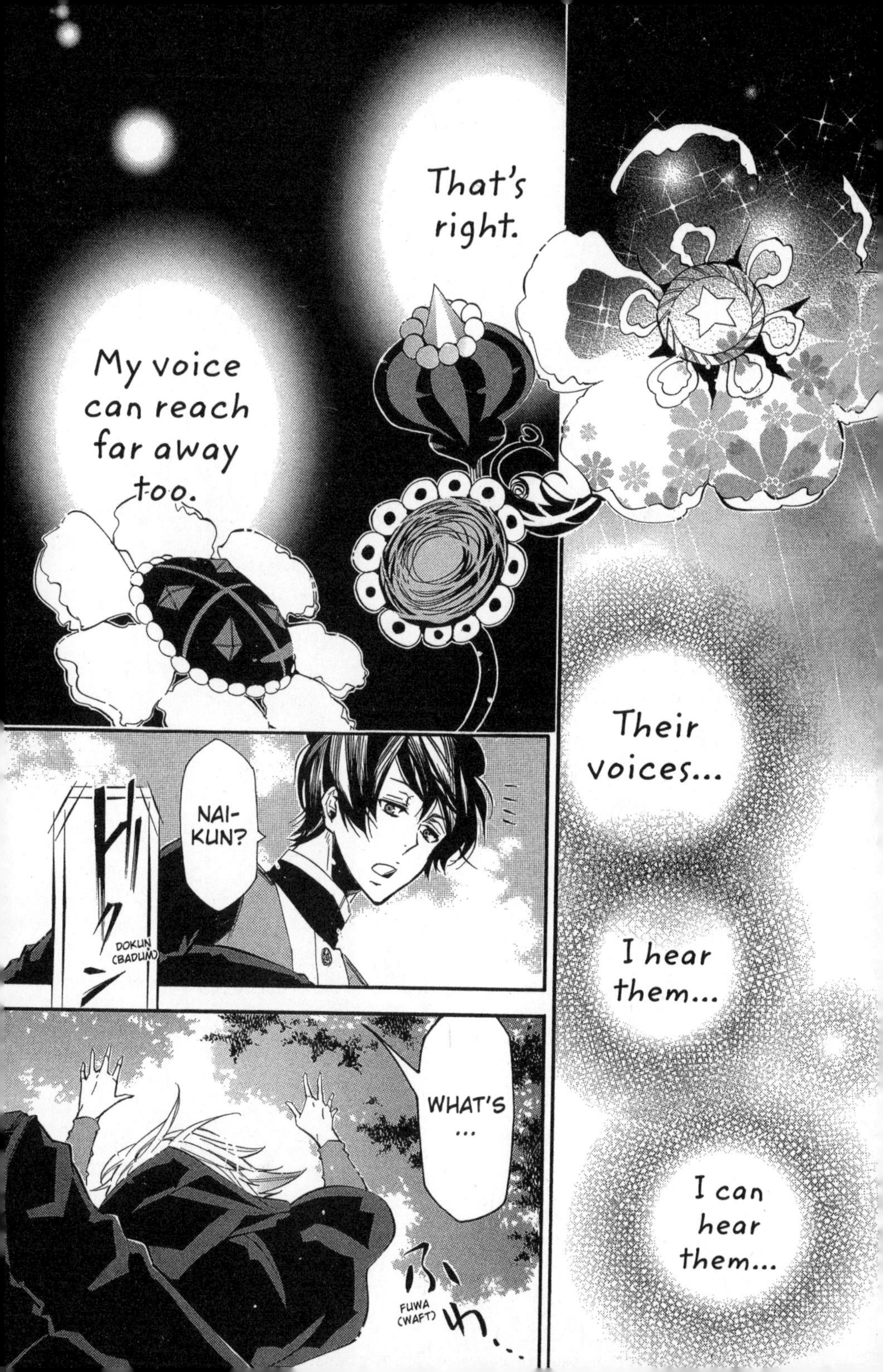
Their voices...
I hear them...
I can hear them...
That's right.
My voice can reach far away too.
NAI-KUN?
DOKUN (BADUM)
WHAT'S ...
FUWA (WAFT)

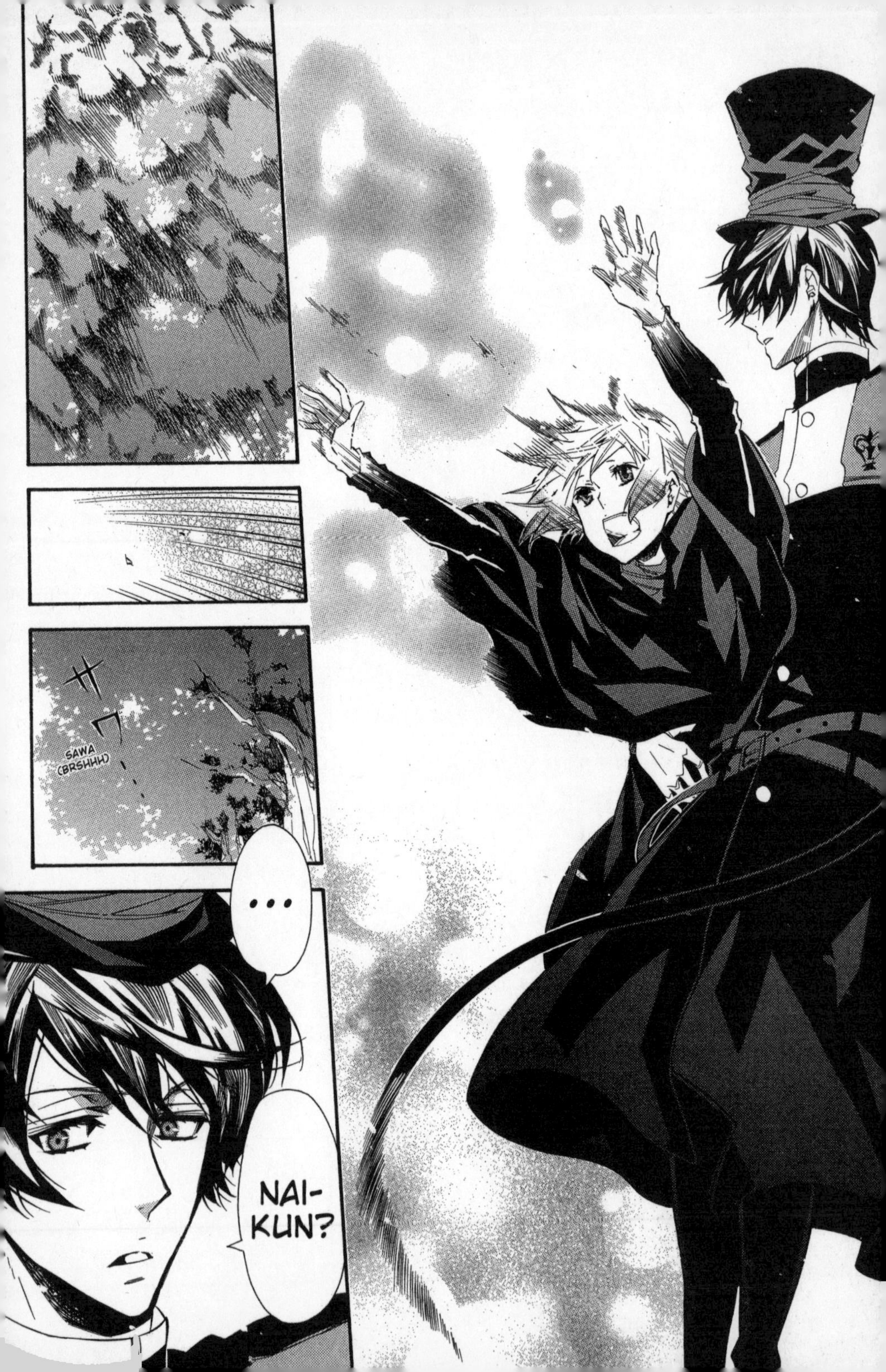
SAWA (BRSHHH)
...
NAI-KUN?

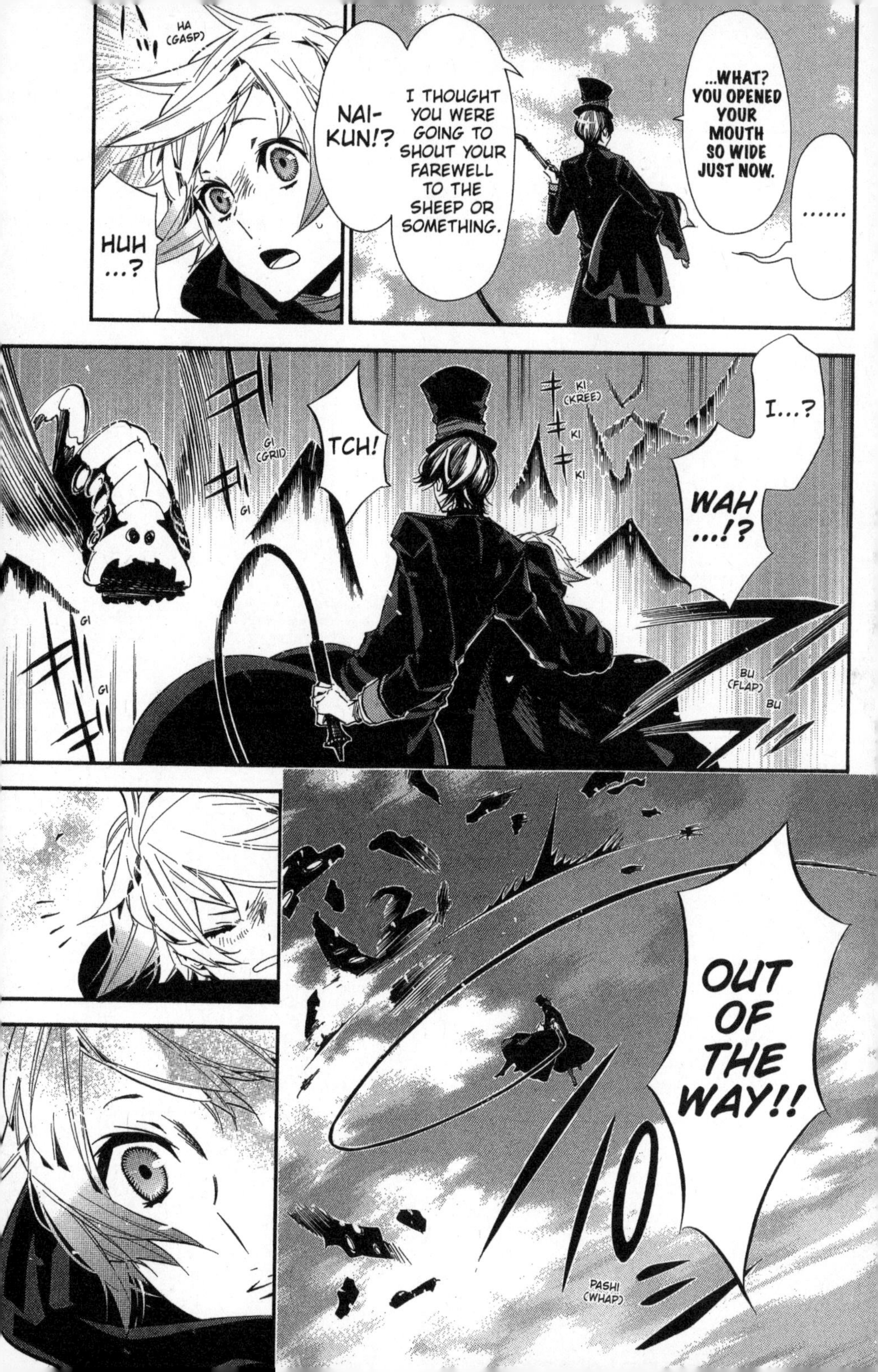
...WHAT? YOU OPENED YOUR MOUTH SO WIDE JUST NOW.
......
I THOUGHT YOU WERE GOING TO SHOUT YOUR FAREWELL TO THE SHEEP OR SOMETHING.
NAI-KUN!?
HA (GASP)
HUH ...?
I...?
WAH ...!?
KI (KREE) KI KI
TCH!
GI (GRID) GI
GI GI
BU (FLAP) BU
OUT OF THE WAY!!
PASHI (WHAP)

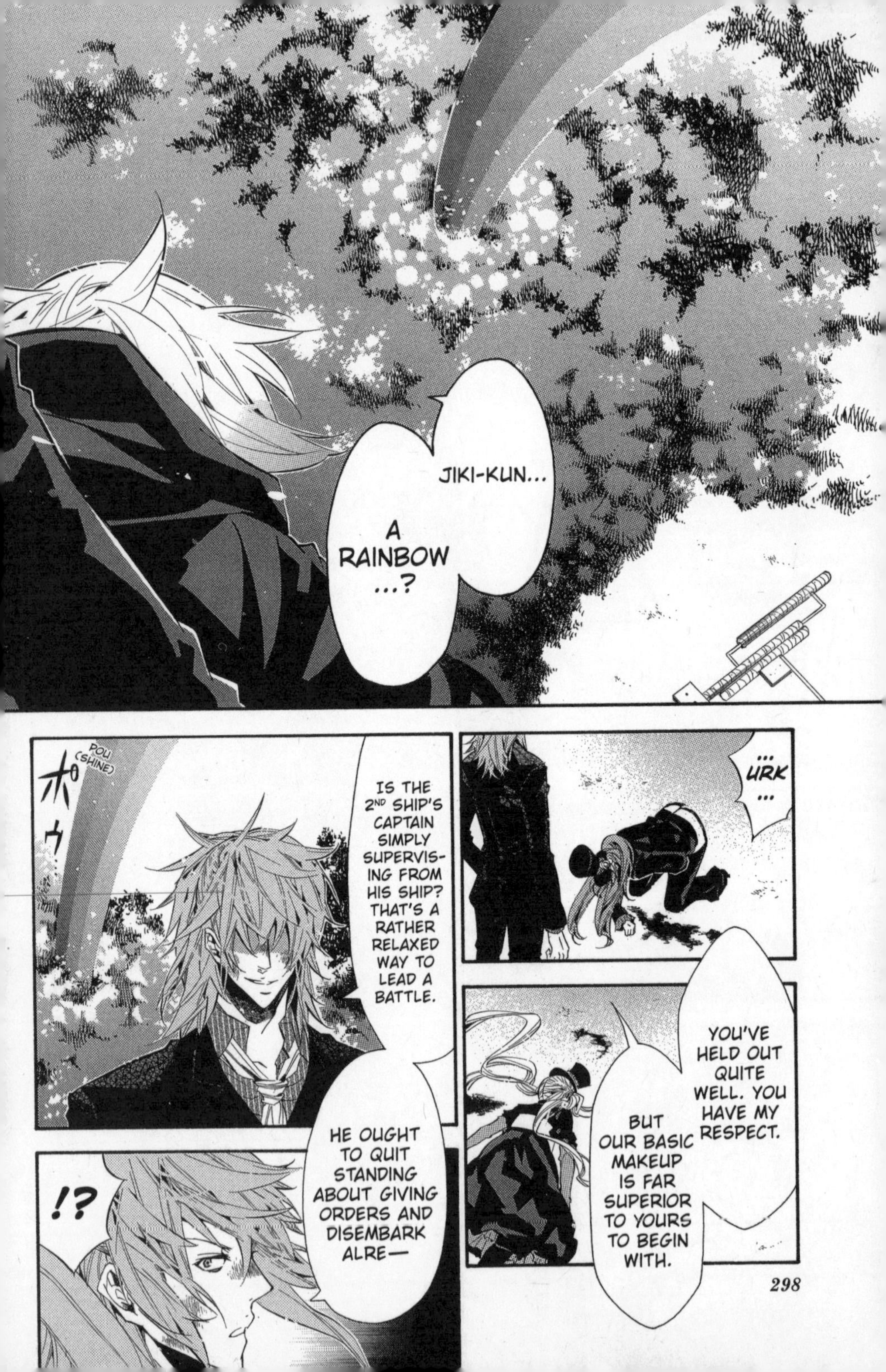
JIKI-KUN...
A RAINBOW ...?
... ÜRK ...
YOU'VE HELD OUT QUITE WELL. YOU HAVE MY RESPECT.
BUT OUR BASIC MAKEUP IS FAR SUPERIOR TO YOURS TO BEGIN WITH.
ポウ
POU (SHINE)
IS THE 2ND SHIP'S CAPTAIN SIMPLY SUPERVISING FROM HIS SHIP? THAT'S A RATHER RELAXED WAY TO LEAD A BATTLE.
HE OUGHT TO QUIT STANDING ABOUT GIVING ORDERS AND DISEMBARK ALRE—
!?

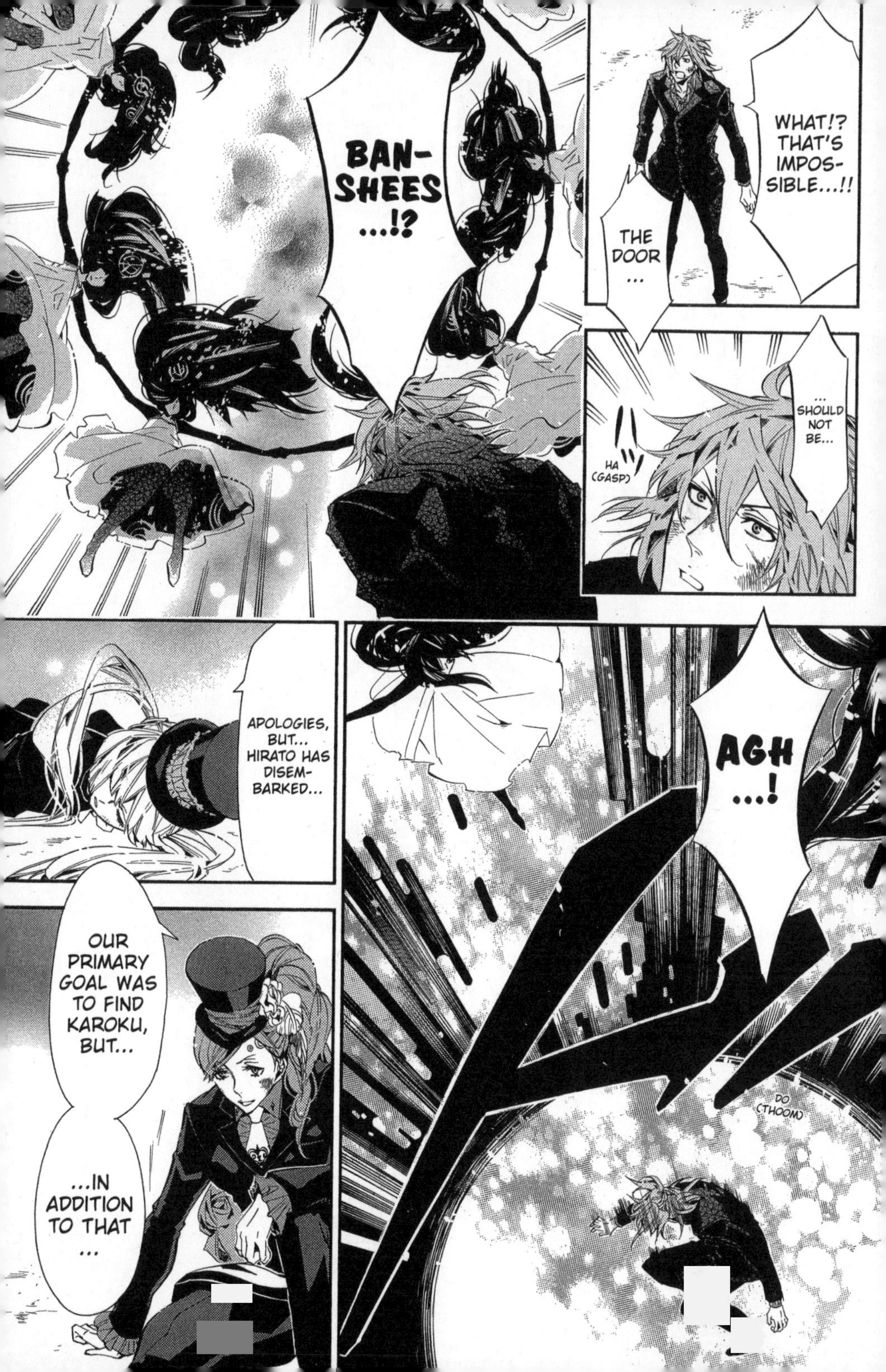
WHAT!? THAT'S IMPOSSIBLE...!!
THE DOOR ...
...SHOULD NOT BE...
HA (GASP)
BAN-SHEES ...!?
AGH ...!
DO (THOOM)
APOLOGIES, BUT... HIRATO HAS DISEMBARKED...
OUR PRIMARY GOAL WAS TO FIND KAROKU, BUT...
...IN ADDITION TO THAT ...

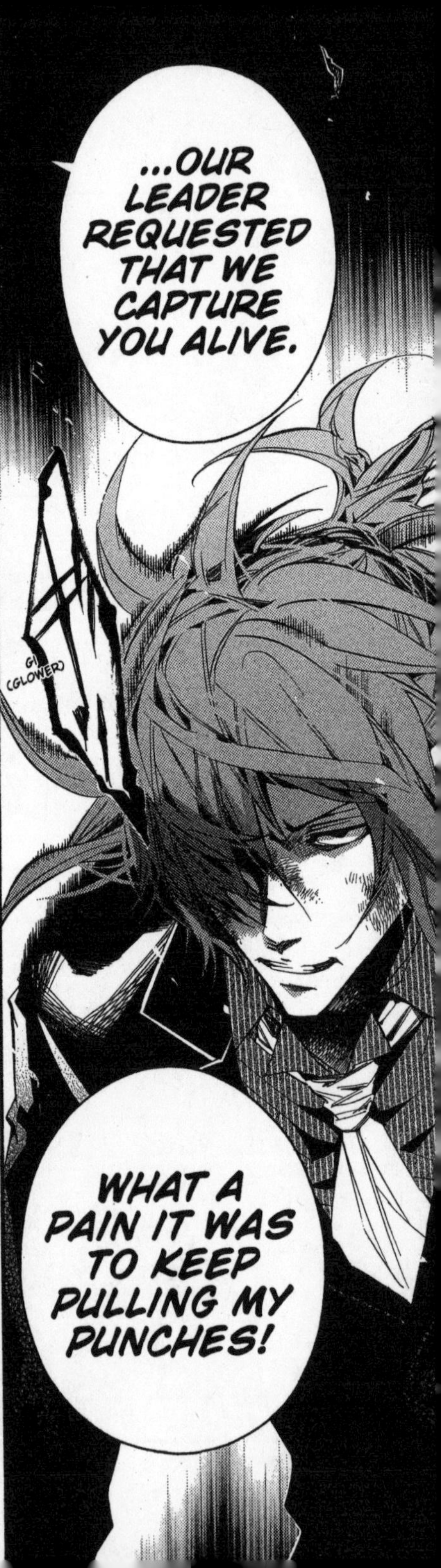
...OUR LEADER REQUESTED THAT WE CAPTURE YOU ALIVE.
GI (GLOWER)
WHAT A PAIN IT WAS TO KEEP PULLING MY PUNCHES!

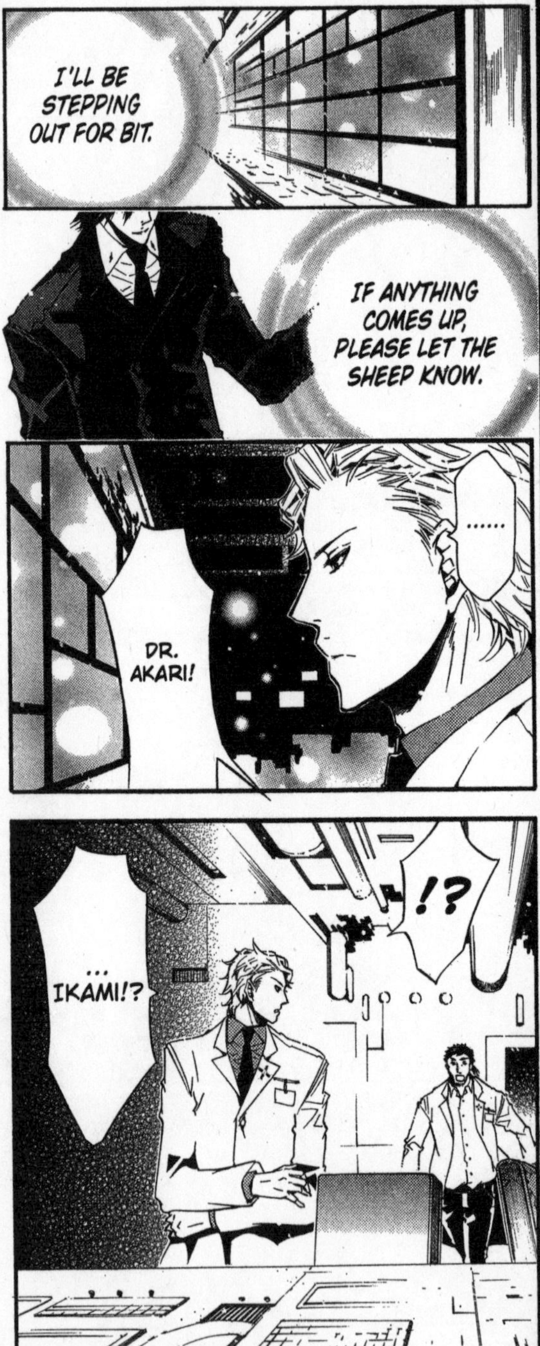
I'LL BE STEPPING OUT FOR BIT.
IF ANYTHING COMES UP, PLEASE LET THE SHEEP KNOW.
......
DR. AKARI!
!?
...IKAMI!?

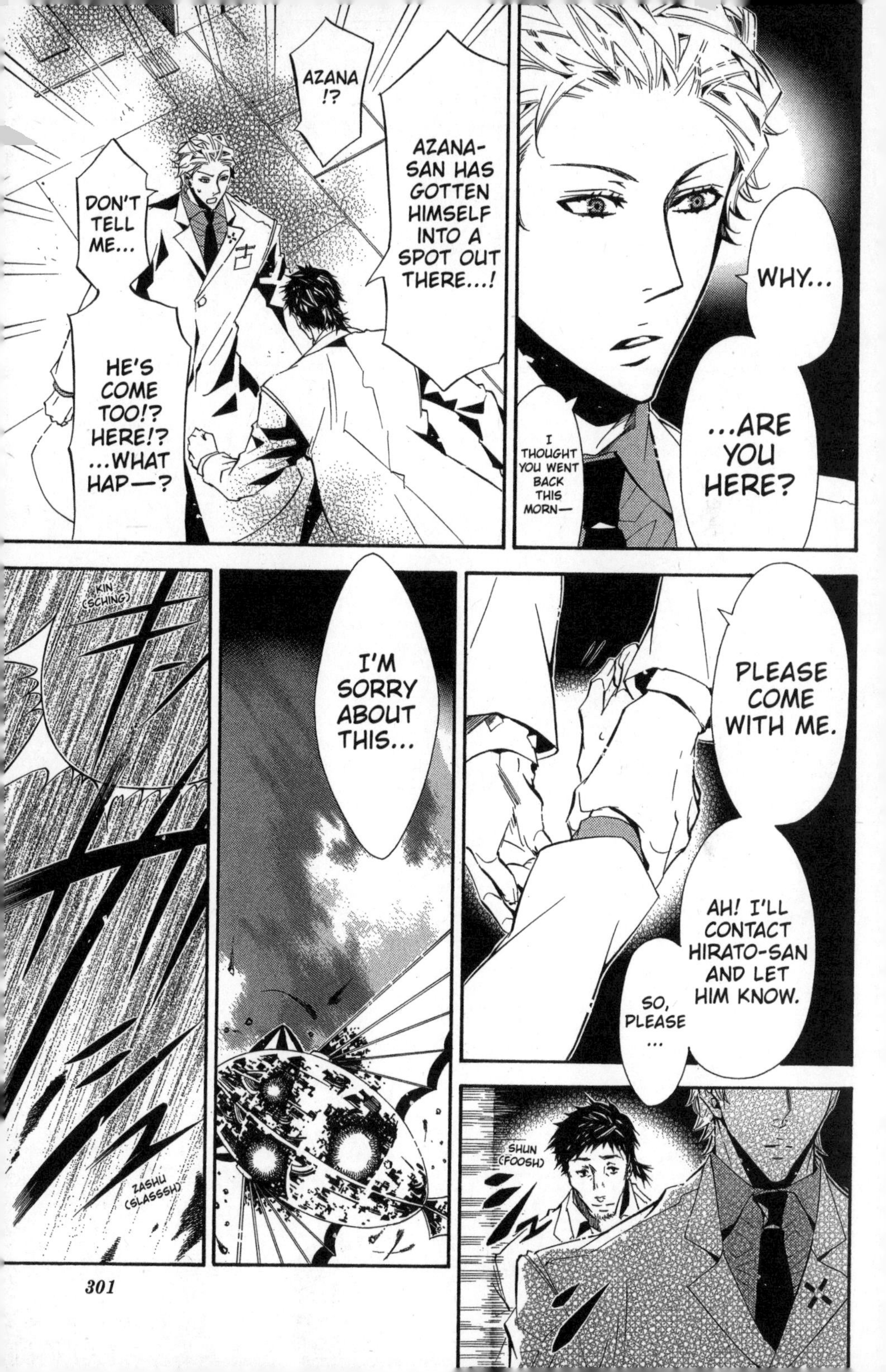
WHY...
...ARE YOU HERE?
I THOUGHT YOU WENT BACK THIS MORN—
AZANA!?
AZANA-SAN HAS GOTTEN HIMSELF INTO A SPOT OUT THERE...!
DON'T TELL ME...
HE'S COME TOO!? HERE!? ...WHAT HAP—?
PLEASE COME WITH ME.
AH! I'LL CONTACT HIRATO-SAN AND LET HIM KNOW.
SO, PLEASE ...
SHUN (FOOSH)
I'M SORRY ABOUT THIS...
KIN (SCHING)
ZASHU (SLASSSH)

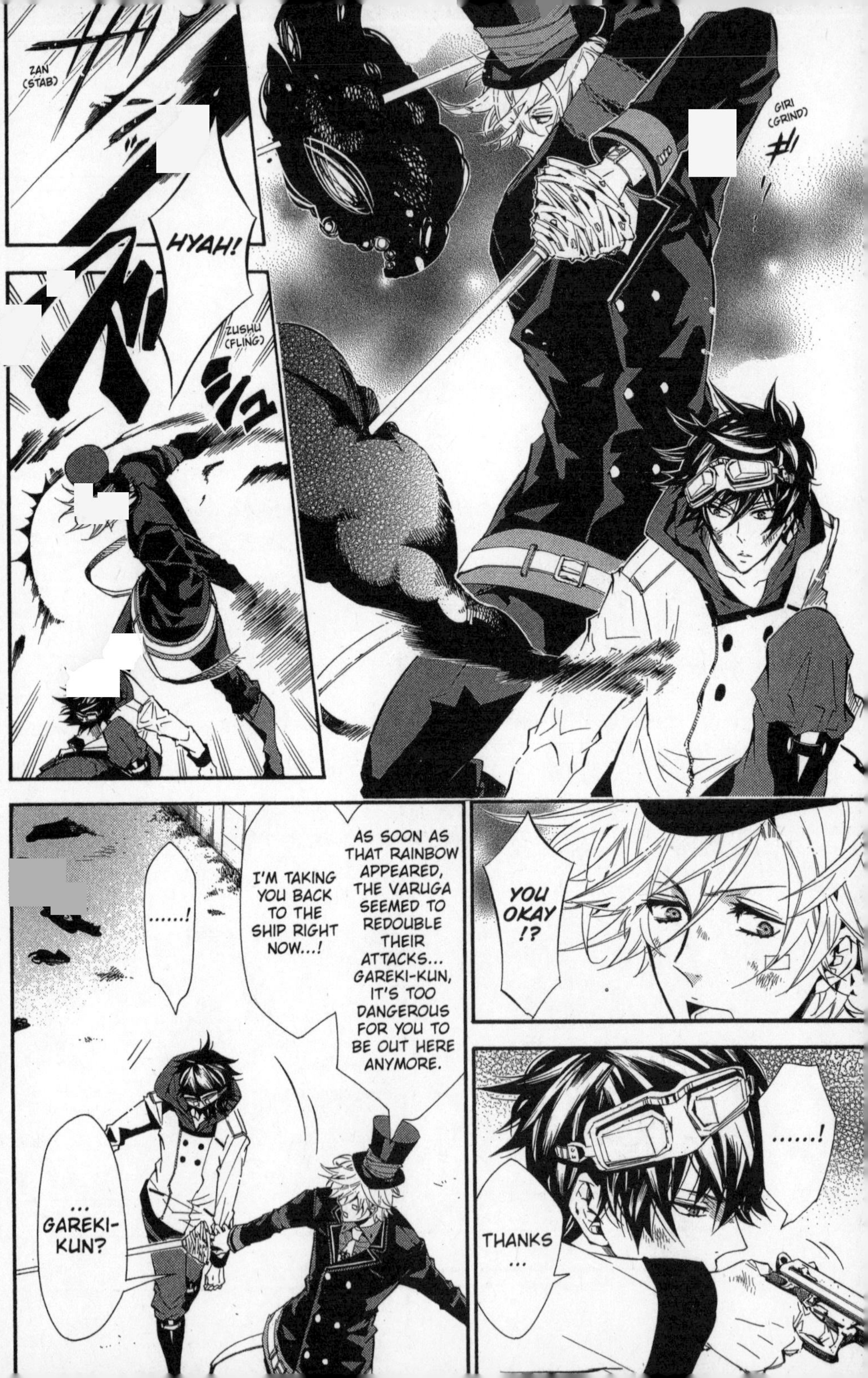
GIRI
(GRIND)
ZAN
(STAB)
HYAH!
ZUSHU
(FLING)
YOU OKAY!?
......!
THANKS...
AS SOON AS THAT RAINBOW APPEARED, THE VARUGA SEEMED TO REDOUBLE THEIR ATTACKS... GAREKI-KUN, IT'S TOO DANGEROUS FOR YOU TO BE OUT HERE ANYMORE.
I'M TAKING YOU BACK TO THE SHIP RIGHT NOW...!
......!
... GAREKI-KUN?

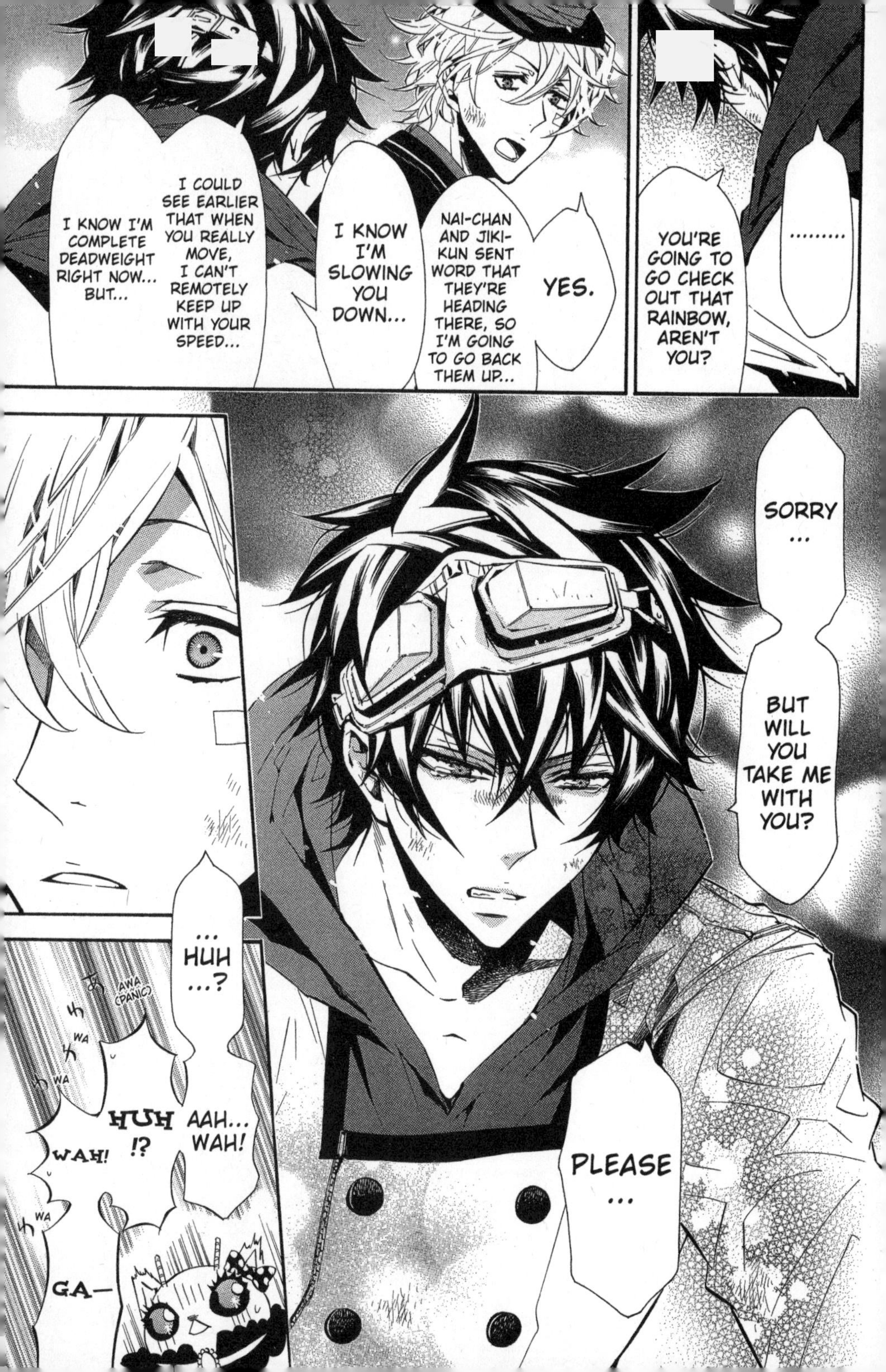
....
YOU'RE GOING TO GO CHECK OUT THAT RAINBOW, AREN'T YOU?
YES.
NAI-CHAN AND JIKI-KUN SENT WORD THAT THEY'RE HEADING THERE, SO I'M GOING TO GO BACK THEM UP...
I KNOW I'M SLOWING YOU DOWN...
I COULD SEE EARLIER THAT WHEN YOU REALLY MOVE, I CAN'T REMOTELY KEEP UP WITH YOUR SPEED...
I KNOW I'M COMPLETE DEADWEIGHT RIGHT NOW... BUT...
SORRY ...
BUT WILL YOU TAKE ME WITH YOU?
PLEASE ...
... HUH ...?
AWA (PANIC)
WA
WA
AAH... WAH!
HUH !?
WAH!
WA
GA—

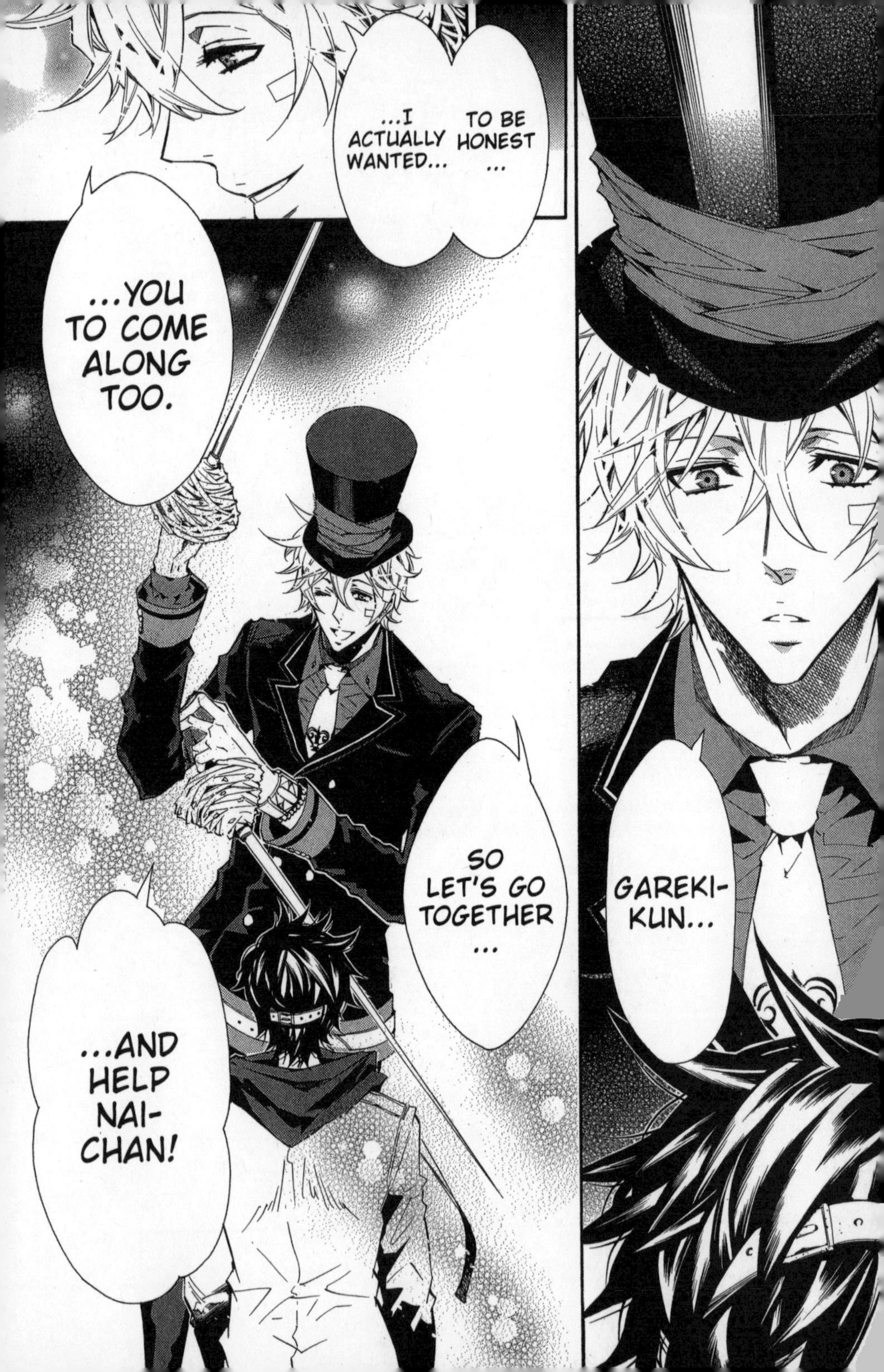
GAREKI-KUN...
TO BE HONEST ...
...I ACTUALLY WANTED...
...YOU TO COME ALONG TOO.
SO LET'S GO TOGETHER ...
...AND HELP NAI-CHAN!

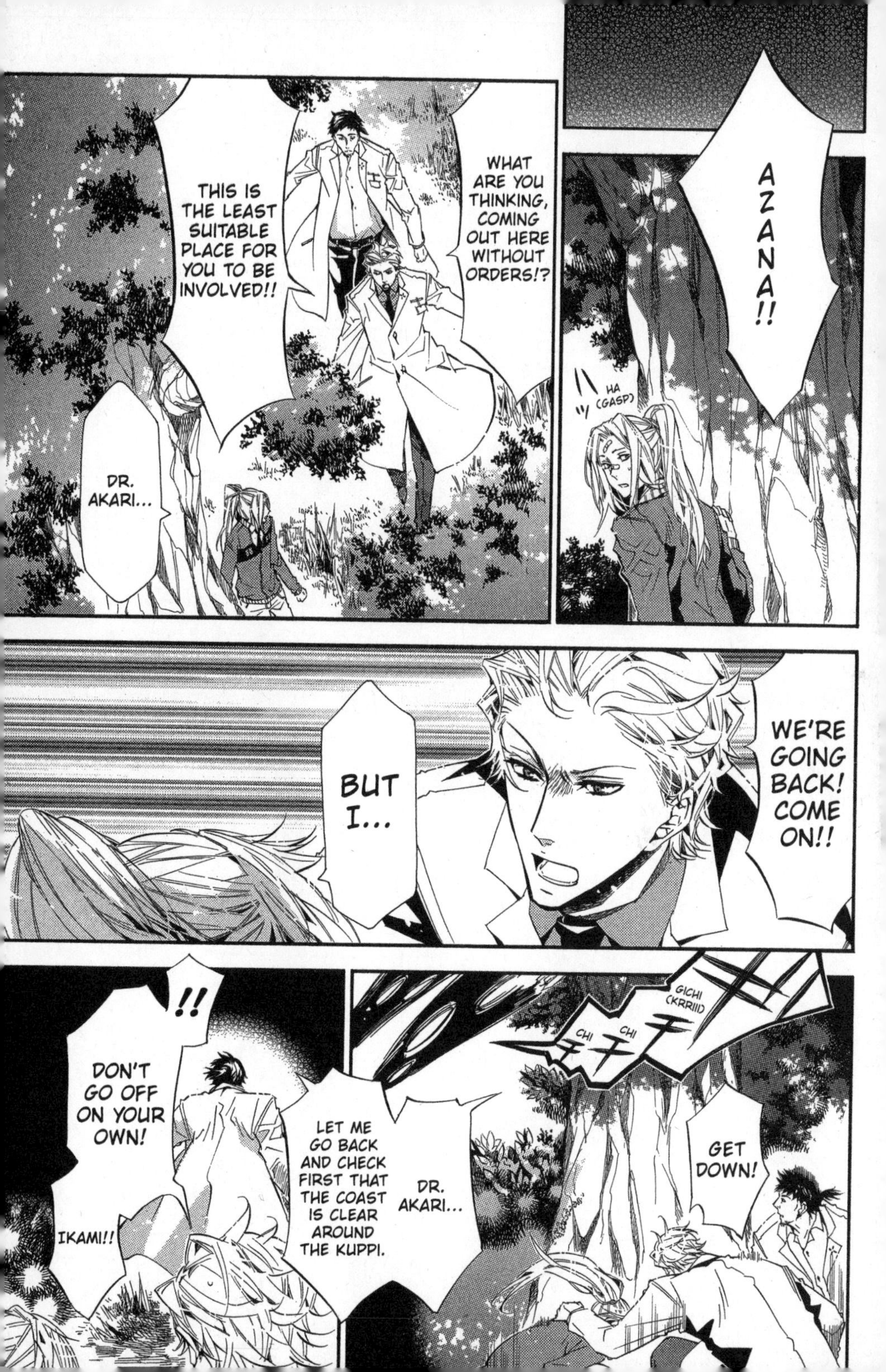
AZANA!!
HA (GASP)
WHAT ARE YOU THINKING, COMING OUT HERE WITHOUT ORDERS!?
THIS IS THE LEAST SUITABLE PLACE FOR YOU TO BE INVOLVED!!
DR. AKARI...
WE'RE GOING BACK! COME ON!!
BUT I...
GICHI (KRRIII)
CHI
CHI
GET DOWN!
DR. AKARI...
LET ME GO BACK AND CHECK FIRST THAT THE COAST IS CLEAR AROUND THE KUPPI.
!!
DON'T GO OFF ON YOUR OWN!
IKAMI!!

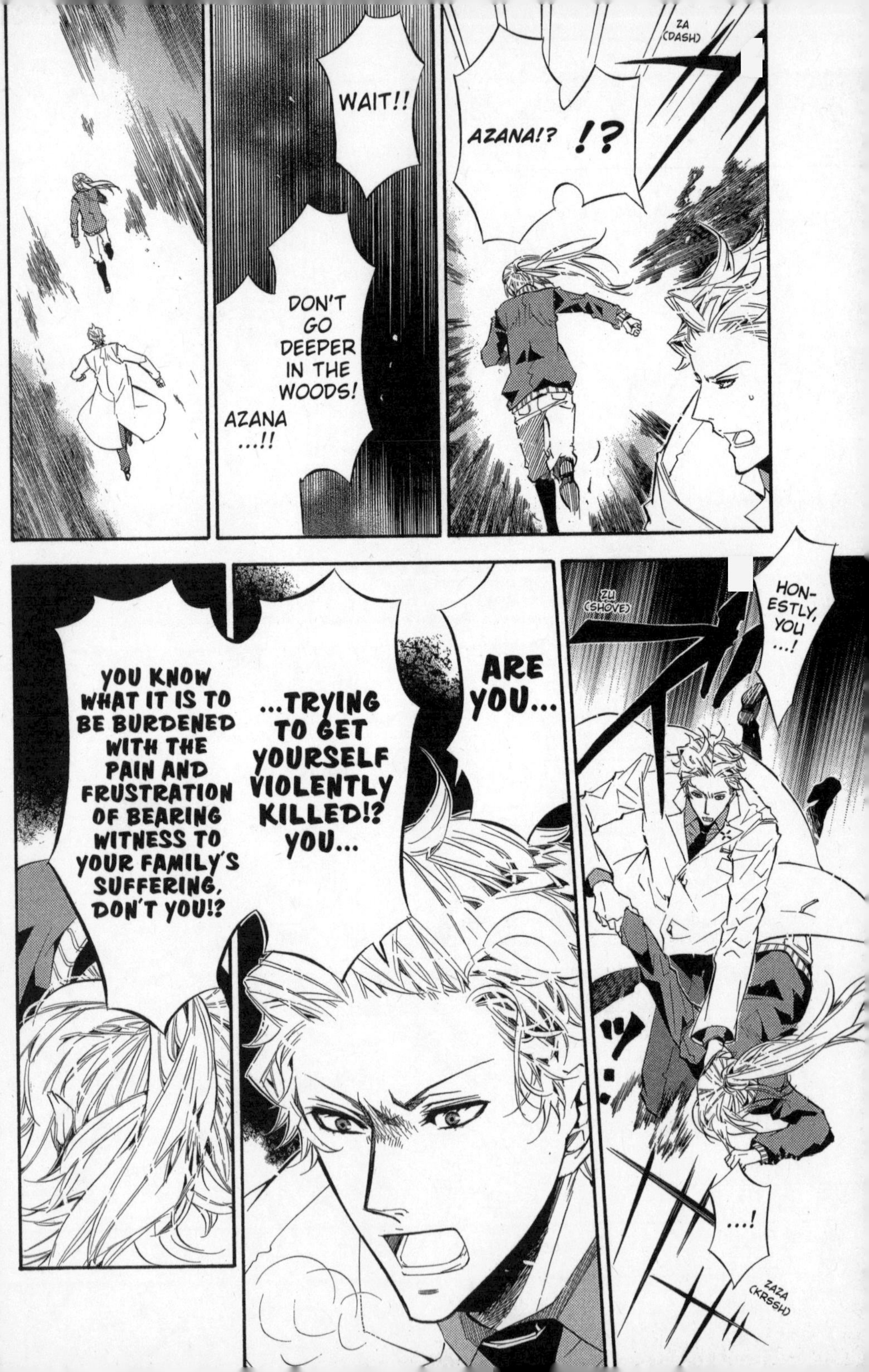
ZA (DASH)
AZANA!?
!?
WAIT!!
DON'T GO DEEPER IN THE WOODS!
AZANA ...!!
HON-ESTLY, YOU ...!
ZU (SHOVE)
!!
...!
ZAZA (KRSSH)
ARE YOU...
...TRYING TO GET YOURSELF VIOLENTLY KILLED!? YOU...
YOU KNOW WHAT IT IS TO BE BURDENED WITH THE PAIN AND FRUSTRATION OF BEARING WITNESS TO YOUR FAMILY'S SUFFERING, DON'T YOU!?

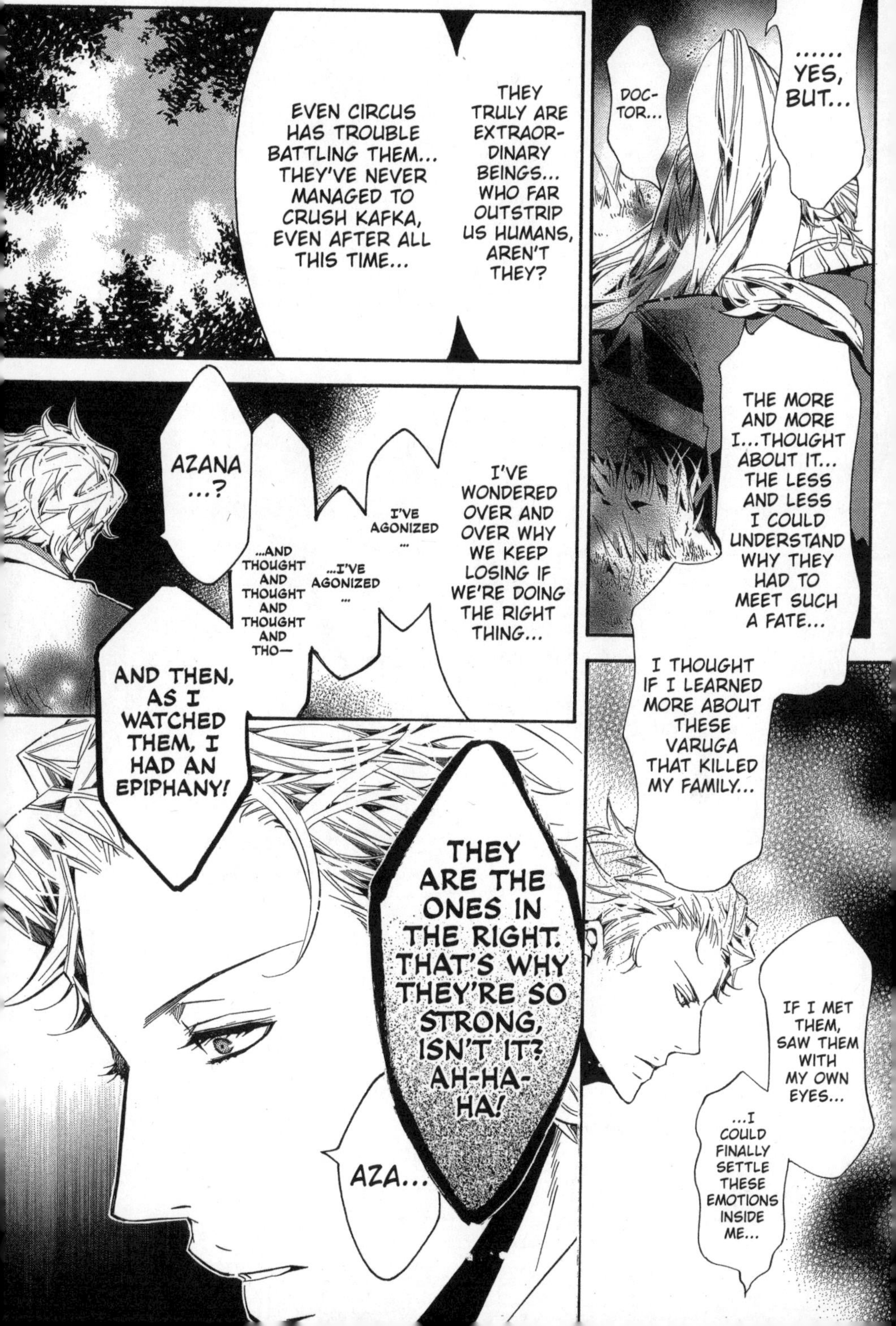
......YES, BUT...
DOC-TOR...
THE MORE AND MORE I...THOUGHT ABOUT IT... THE LESS AND LESS I COULD UNDERSTAND WHY THEY HAD TO MEET SUCH A FATE...
I THOUGHT IF I LEARNED MORE ABOUT THESE VARUGA THAT KILLED MY FAMILY...
IF I MET THEM, SAW THEM WITH MY OWN EYES...
...I COULD FINALLY SETTLE THESE EMOTIONS INSIDE ME...
THEY TRULY ARE EXTRAOR-DINARY BEINGS... WHO FAR OUTSTRIP US HUMANS, AREN'T THEY?
EVEN CIRCUS HAS TROUBLE BATTLING THEM... THEY'VE NEVER MANAGED TO CRUSH KAFKA, EVEN AFTER ALL THIS TIME...
I'VE WONDERED OVER AND OVER WHY WE KEEP LOSING IF WE'RE DOING THE RIGHT THING...
I'VE AGONIZED ...
...I'VE AGONIZED ...
...AND THOUGHT AND THOUGHT AND THOUGHT AND THO—
AZANA ...?
AND THEN, AS I WATCHED THEM, I HAD AN EPIPHANY!
THEY ARE THE ONES IN THE RIGHT. THAT'S WHY THEY'RE SO STRONG, ISN'T IT? AH-HA-HA!
AZA...

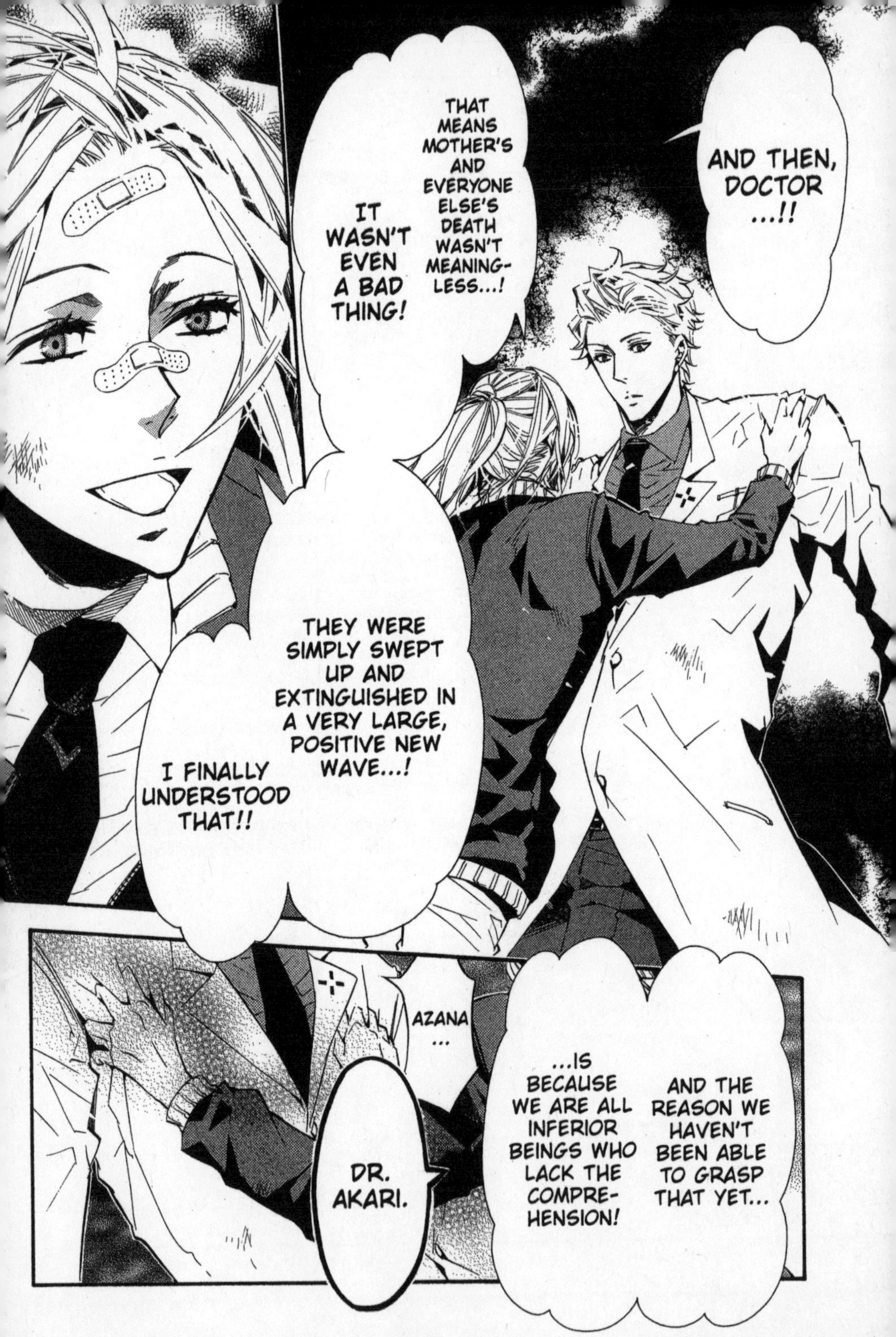
AND THEN, DOCTOR ...!!
THAT MEANS MOTHER'S AND EVERYONE ELSE'S DEATH WASN'T MEANING-LESS...!
IT WASN'T EVEN A BAD THING!
THEY WERE SIMPLY SWEPT UP AND EXTINGUISHED IN A VERY LARGE, POSITIVE NEW WAVE...!
I FINALLY UNDERSTOOD THAT!!
AND THE REASON WE HAVEN'T BEEN ABLE TO GRASP THAT YET...
...IS BECAUSE WE ARE ALL INFERIOR BEINGS WHO LACK THE COMPRE-HENSION!
AZANA ...
DR. AKARI.

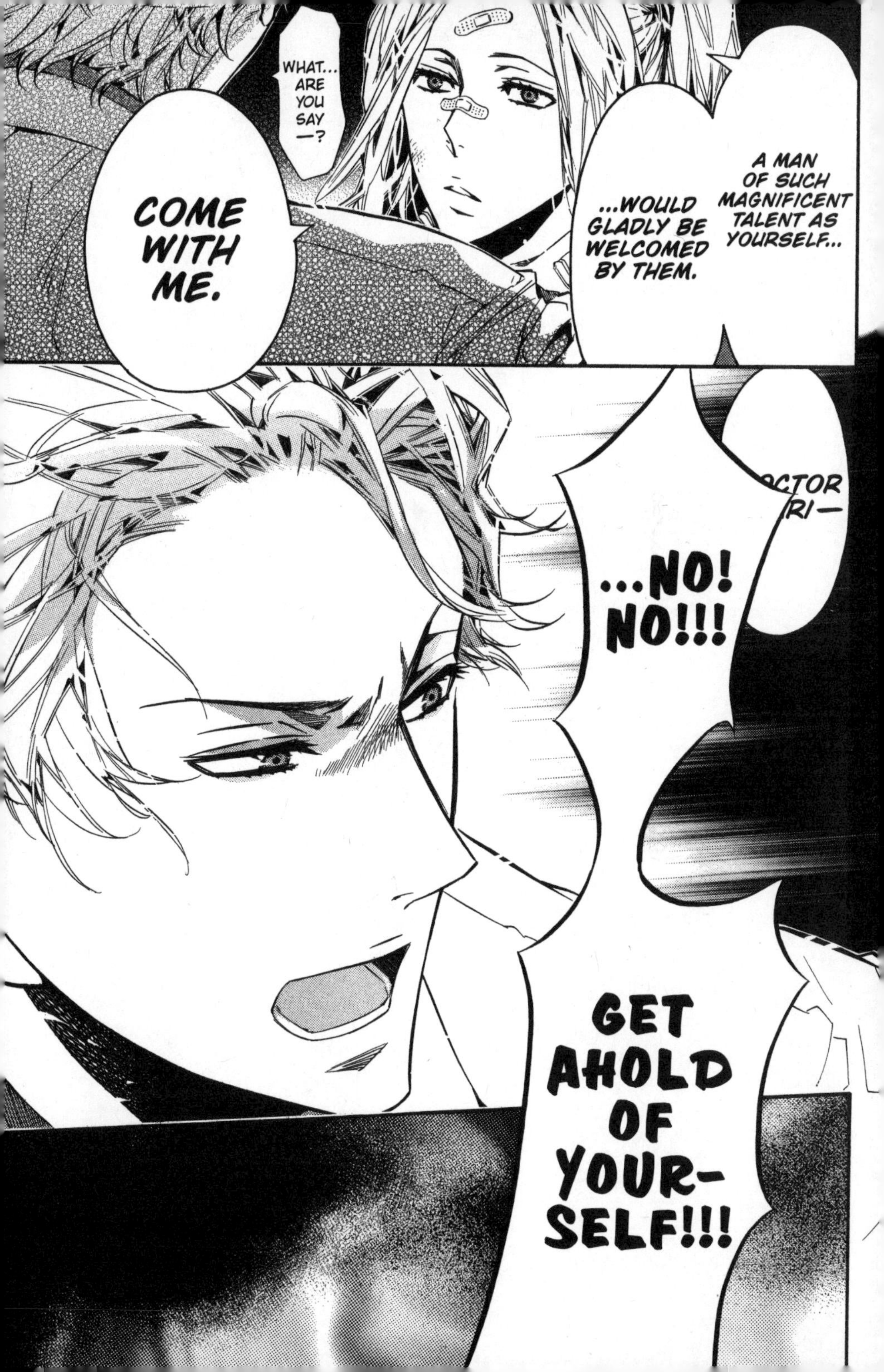
A MAN OF SUCH MAGNIFICENT TALENT AS YOURSELF...
...WOULD GLADLY BE WELCOMED BY THEM.
WHAT... ARE YOU SAY—?
COME WITH ME.
OCTOR
RI—
...NO! NO!!!
GET AHOLD OF YOUR-SELF!!!

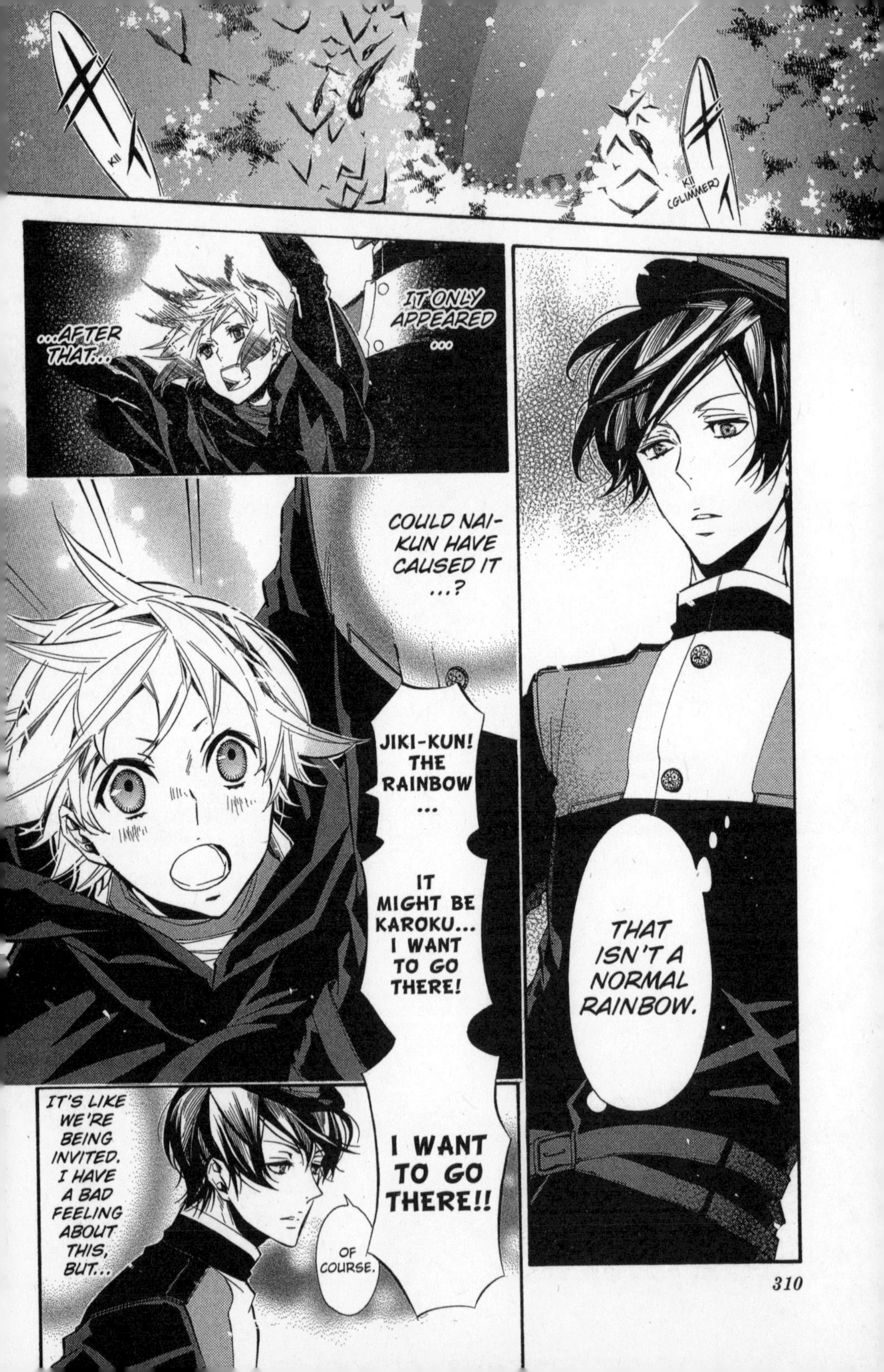
KII (GLIMMER)
KII
THAT ISN'T A NORMAL RAINBOW.
IT ONLY APPEARED...
...AFTER THAT...
COULD NAI-KUN HAVE CAUSED IT...?
JIKI-KUN! THE RAINBOW...
IT MIGHT BE KAROKU... I WANT TO GO THERE!
I WANT TO GO THERE!!
OF COURSE.
IT'S LIKE WE'RE BEING INVITED. I HAVE A BAD FEELING ABOUT THIS, BUT...

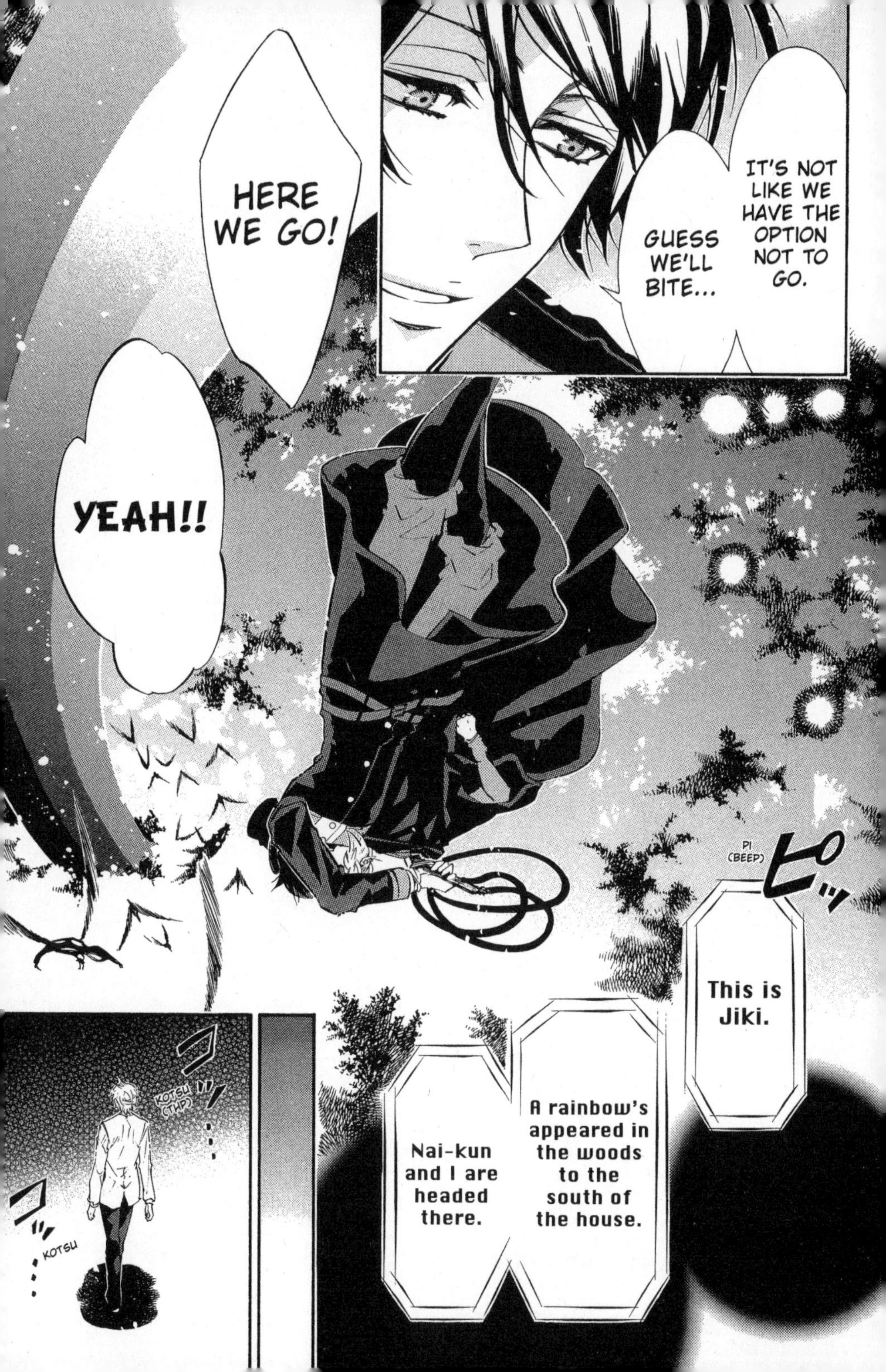
IT'S NOT LIKE WE HAVE THE OPTION NOT TO GO.
GUESS WE'LL BITE...
HERE WE GO!
YEAH!!
PI (BEEP)
This is Jiki.
A rainbow's appeared in the woods to the south of the house.
Nai-kun and I are headed there.
KOTSU (THP)
KOTSU

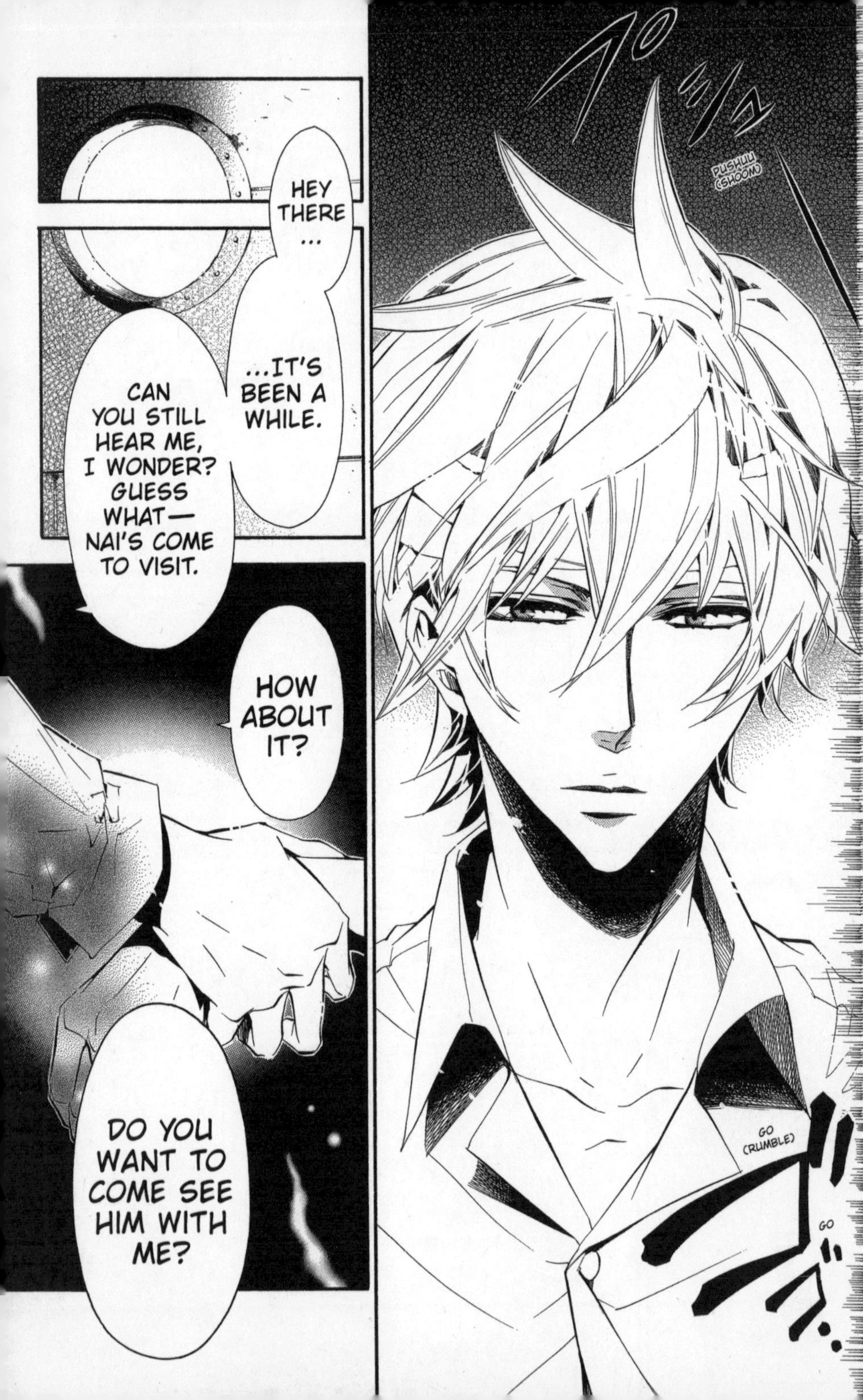
PUSHUU (SHOOM)
GO (RUMBLE)
GO
HEY THERE...
...IT'S BEEN A WHILE.
CAN YOU STILL HEAR ME, I WONDER? GUESS WHAT—NAI'S COME TO VISIT.
HOW ABOUT IT?
DO YOU WANT TO COME SEE HIM WITH ME?

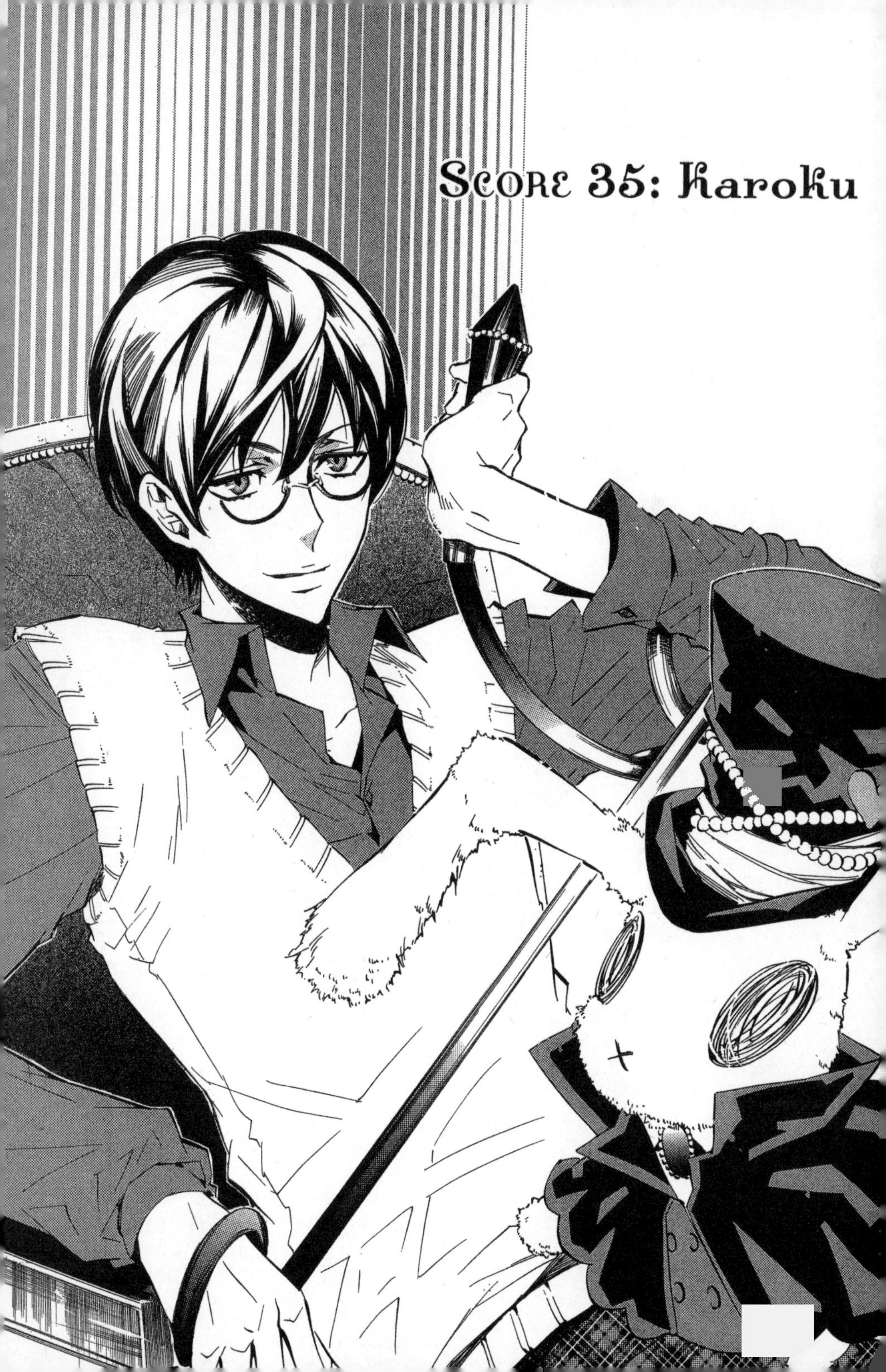
Score 35: Karoku

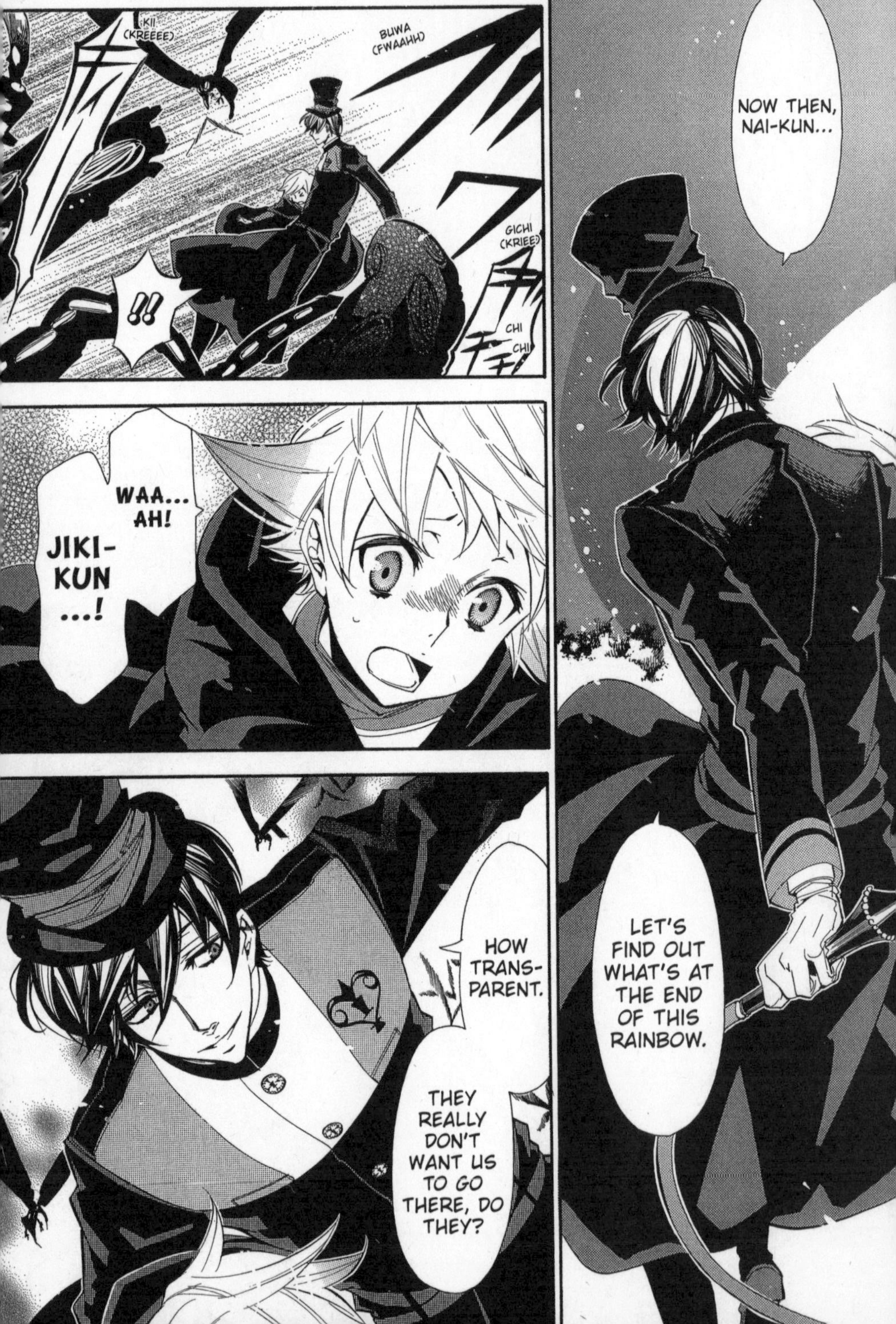
NOW THEN, NAI-KUN...
LET'S FIND OUT WHAT'S AT THE END OF THIS RAINBOW.
BUWA (FWAAHH)
KII (KREEEE)
GICHI (KRIEE)
!!
CHI CHI
WAA... AH!
JIKI-KUN...!
HOW TRANS-PARENT.
THEY REALLY DON'T WANT US TO GO THERE, DO THEY?

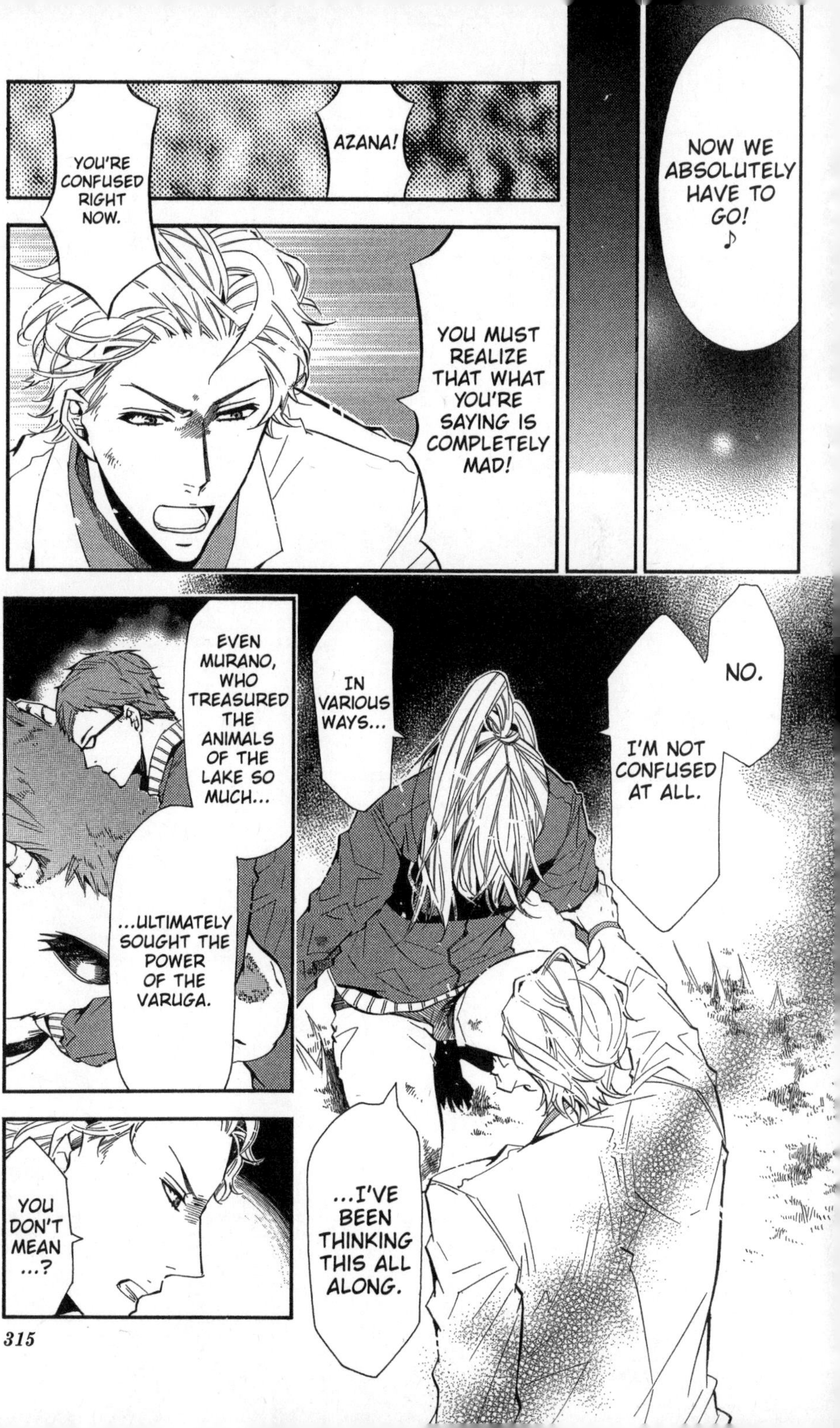
NOW WE ABSOLUTELY HAVE TO GO! ♪
AZANA!
YOU'RE CONFUSED RIGHT NOW.
YOU MUST REALIZE THAT WHAT YOU'RE SAYING IS COMPLETELY MAD!
NO.
I'M NOT CONFUSED AT ALL.
IN VARIOUS WAYS...
EVEN MURANO, WHO TREASURED THE ANIMALS OF THE LAKE SO MUCH...
...ULTIMATELY SOUGHT THE POWER OF THE VARUGA.
...I'VE BEEN THINKING THIS ALL ALONG.
YOU DON'T MEAN ...?

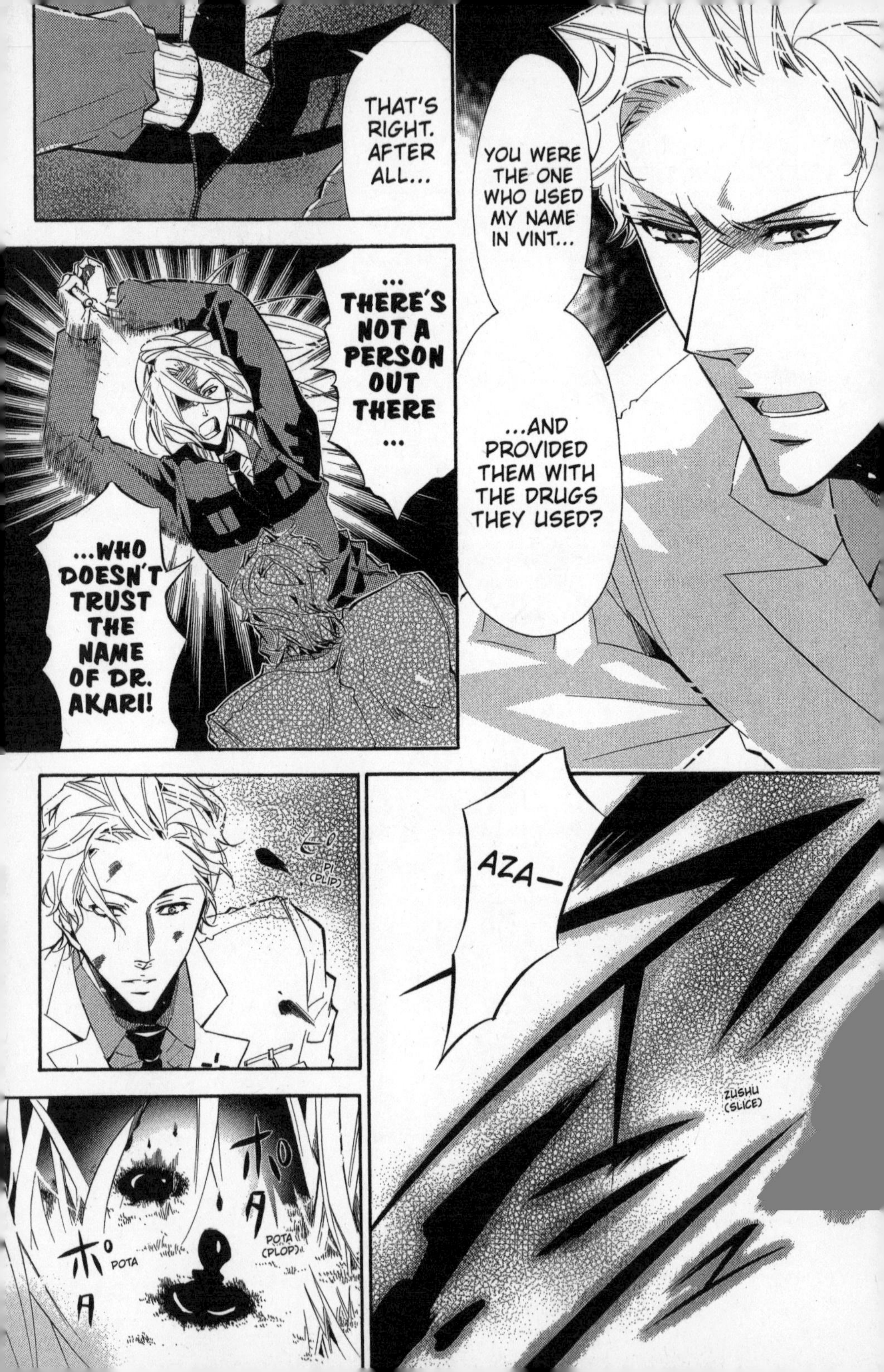
YOU WERE THE ONE WHO USED MY NAME IN VINT...
...AND PROVIDED THEM WITH THE DRUGS THEY USED?
THAT'S RIGHT. AFTER ALL...
...THERE'S NOT A PERSON OUT THERE...
...WHO DOESN'T TRUST THE NAME OF DR. AKARI!
AZA—
ZUSHU (SLICE)
PI (PLIP)
ポタ
POTA (PLOP)
ポタ
POTA

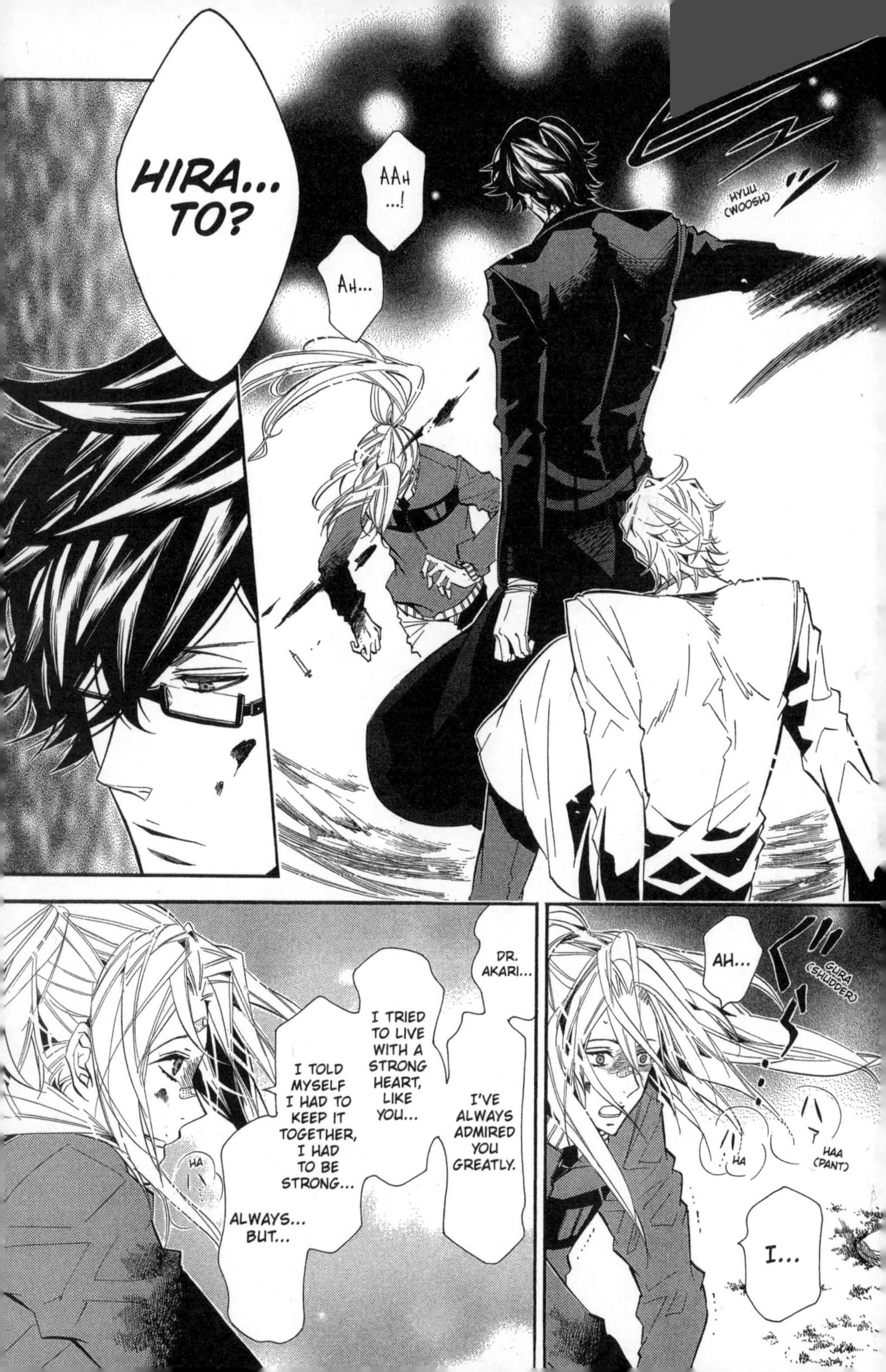
HYUU (WOOSH)
AAH ...!
AH...
HIRA... TO?
AH...
GURA (SHUDDER)
HA
HAA (PANT)
I...
DR. AKARI...
I'VE ALWAYS ADMIRED YOU GREATLY.
I TRIED TO LIVE WITH A STRONG HEART, LIKE YOU...
I TOLD MYSELF I HAD TO KEEP IT TOGETHER, I HAD TO BE STRONG...
ALWAYS... BUT...
HA

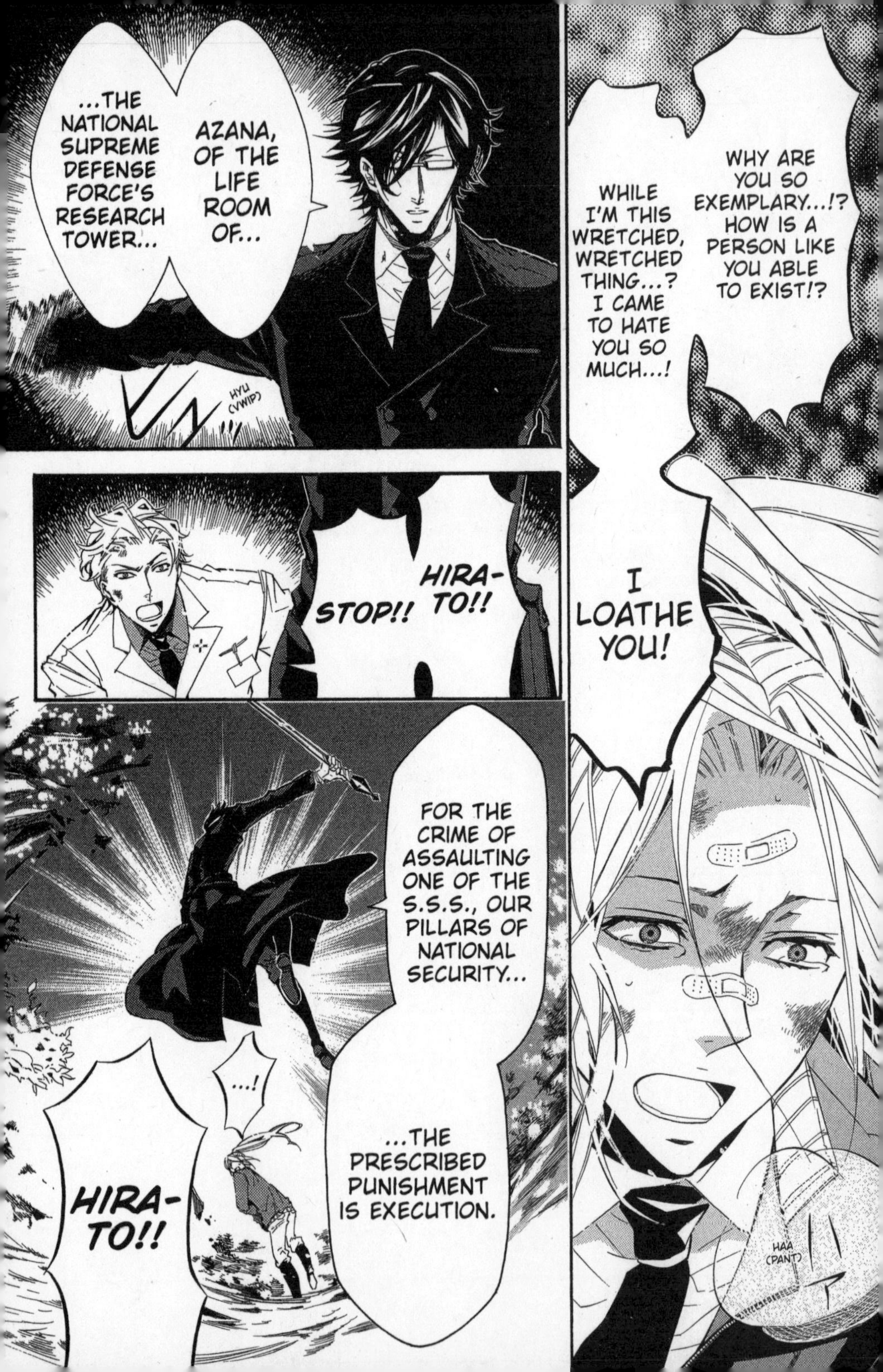
WHY ARE YOU SO EXEMPLARY...!? HOW IS A PERSON LIKE YOU ABLE TO EXIST!?
WHILE I'M THIS WRETCHED, WRETCHED THING...? I CAME TO HATE YOU SO MUCH...!
I LOATHE YOU!
HAA (PANT)
AZANA, OF THE LIFE ROOM OF...
...THE NATIONAL SUPREME DEFENSE FORCE'S RESEARCH TOWER...
HYU (VWIP)
HIRA-TO!!
STOP!!
FOR THE CRIME OF ASSAULTING ONE OF THE S.S.S., OUR PILLARS OF NATIONAL SECURITY...
...THE PRESCRIBED PUNISHMENT IS EXECUTION.
...!
HIRA-TO!!

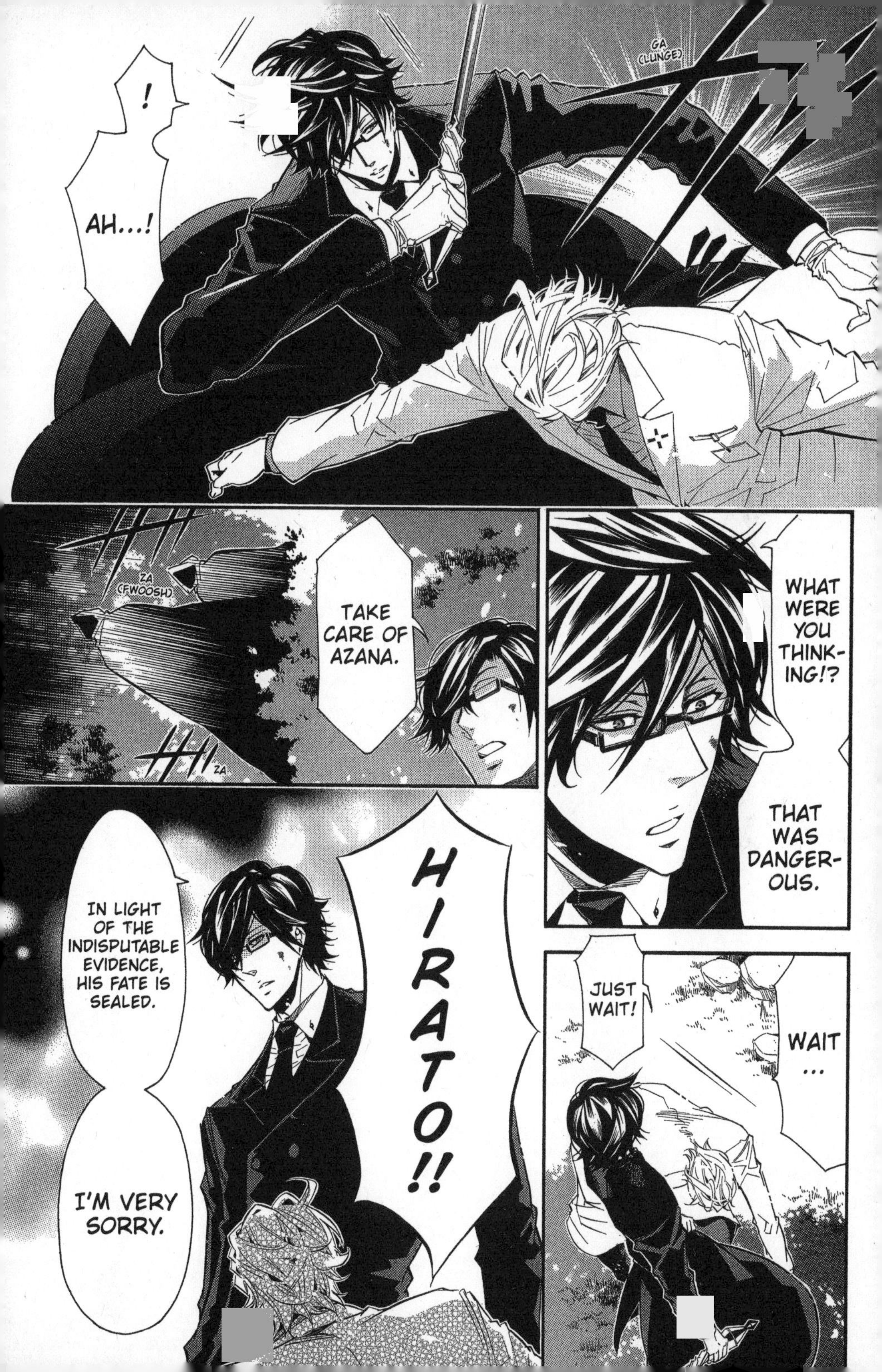
GA (LUNGE)
!
AH...!
WHAT WERE YOU THINKING!?
THAT WAS DANGEROUS.
TAKE CARE OF AZANA.
ZA (FWOOSH)
ZA
JUST WAIT!
WAIT...
HIRATO!!
IN LIGHT OF THE INDISPUTABLE EVIDENCE, HIS FATE IS SEALED.
I'M VERY SORRY.

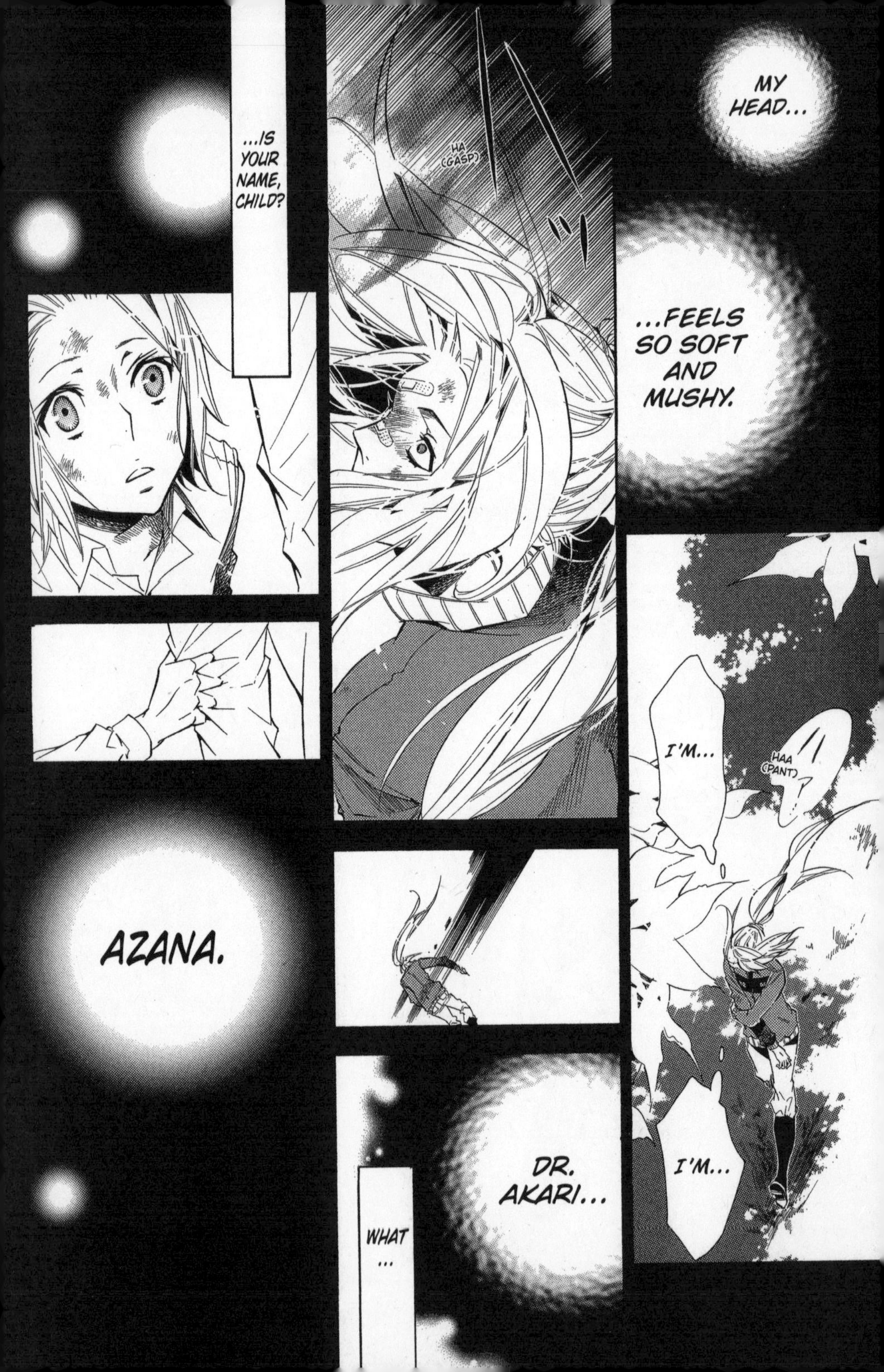
MY HEAD...
...FEELS SO SOFT AND MUSHY.
I'M...
HAA (PANT)
I'M...
HA (GASP)
DR. AKARI...
WHAT ...
...IS YOUR NAME, CHILD?
AZANA.

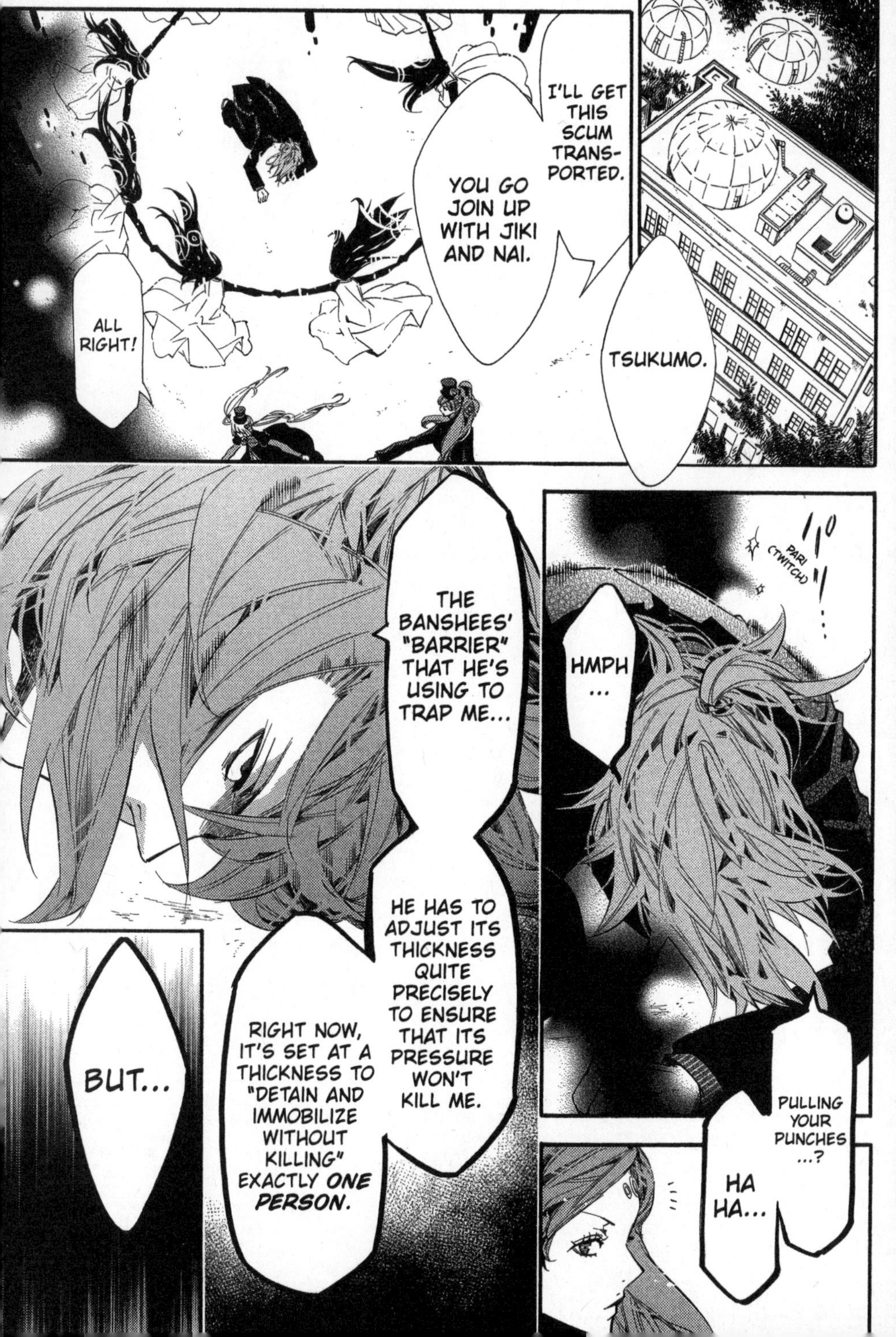
TSUKUMO.
I'LL GET THIS SCUM TRANSPORTED.
YOU GO JOIN UP WITH JIKI AND NAI.
ALL RIGHT!
PARI (TWITCH)
HMPH...
PULLING YOUR PUNCHES...?
HA HA...
THE BANSHEES' "BARRIER" THAT HE'S USING TO TRAP ME...
HE HAS TO ADJUST ITS THICKNESS QUITE PRECISELY TO ENSURE THAT ITS PRESSURE WON'T KILL ME.
RIGHT NOW, IT'S SET AT A THICKNESS TO "DETAIN AND IMMOBILIZE WITHOUT KILLING" EXACTLY ONE PERSON.
BUT...

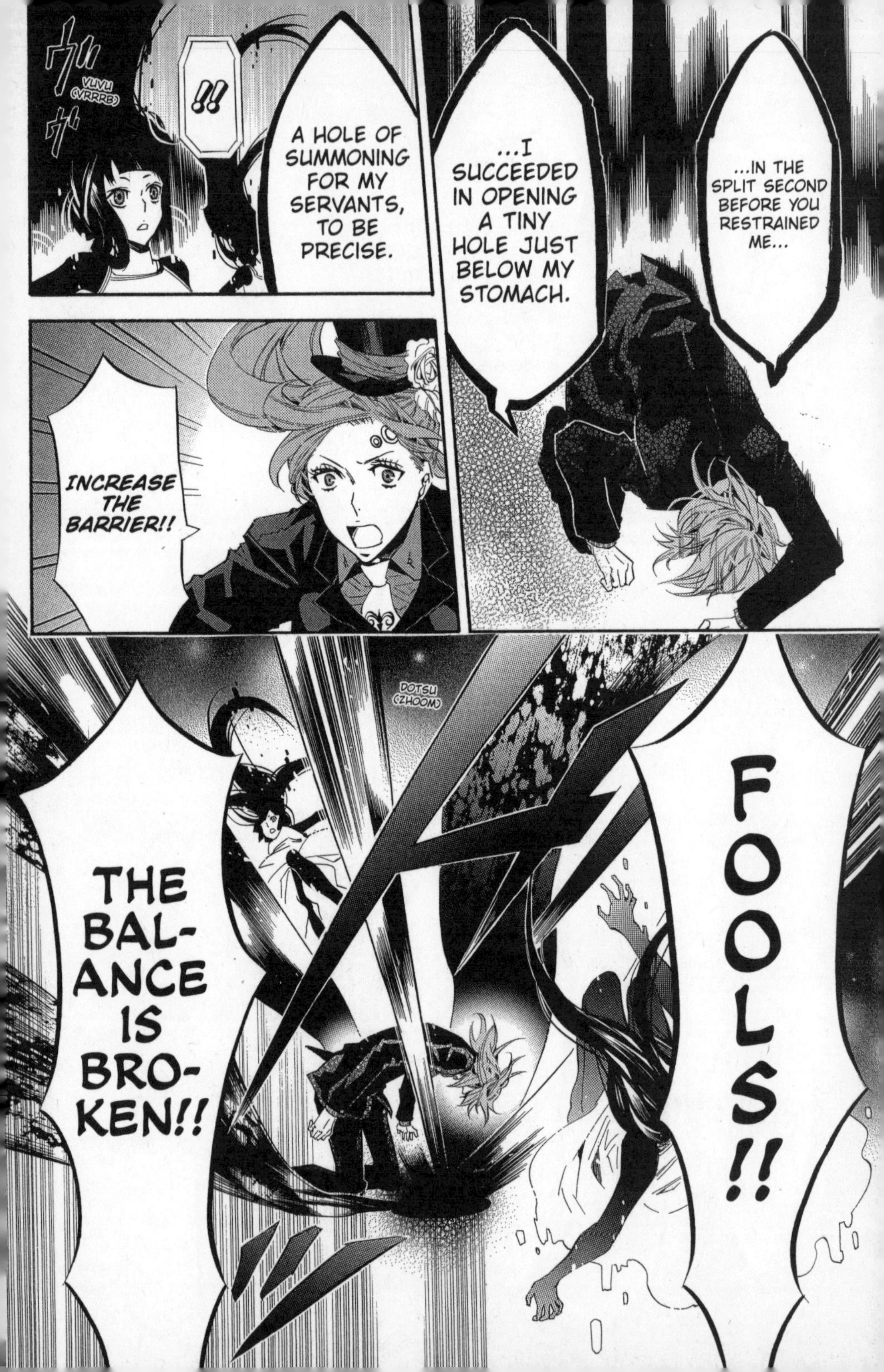
...IN THE SPLIT SECOND BEFORE YOU RESTRAINED ME...
...I SUCCEEDED IN OPENING A TINY HOLE JUST BELOW MY STOMACH.
A HOLE OF SUMMONING FOR MY SERVANTS, TO BE PRECISE.
!!
VUVU (VRRRB)
INCREASE THE BARRIER!!
FOOLS!!
DOTSU (ZHOOM)
THE BAL-ANCE IS BRO-KEN!!

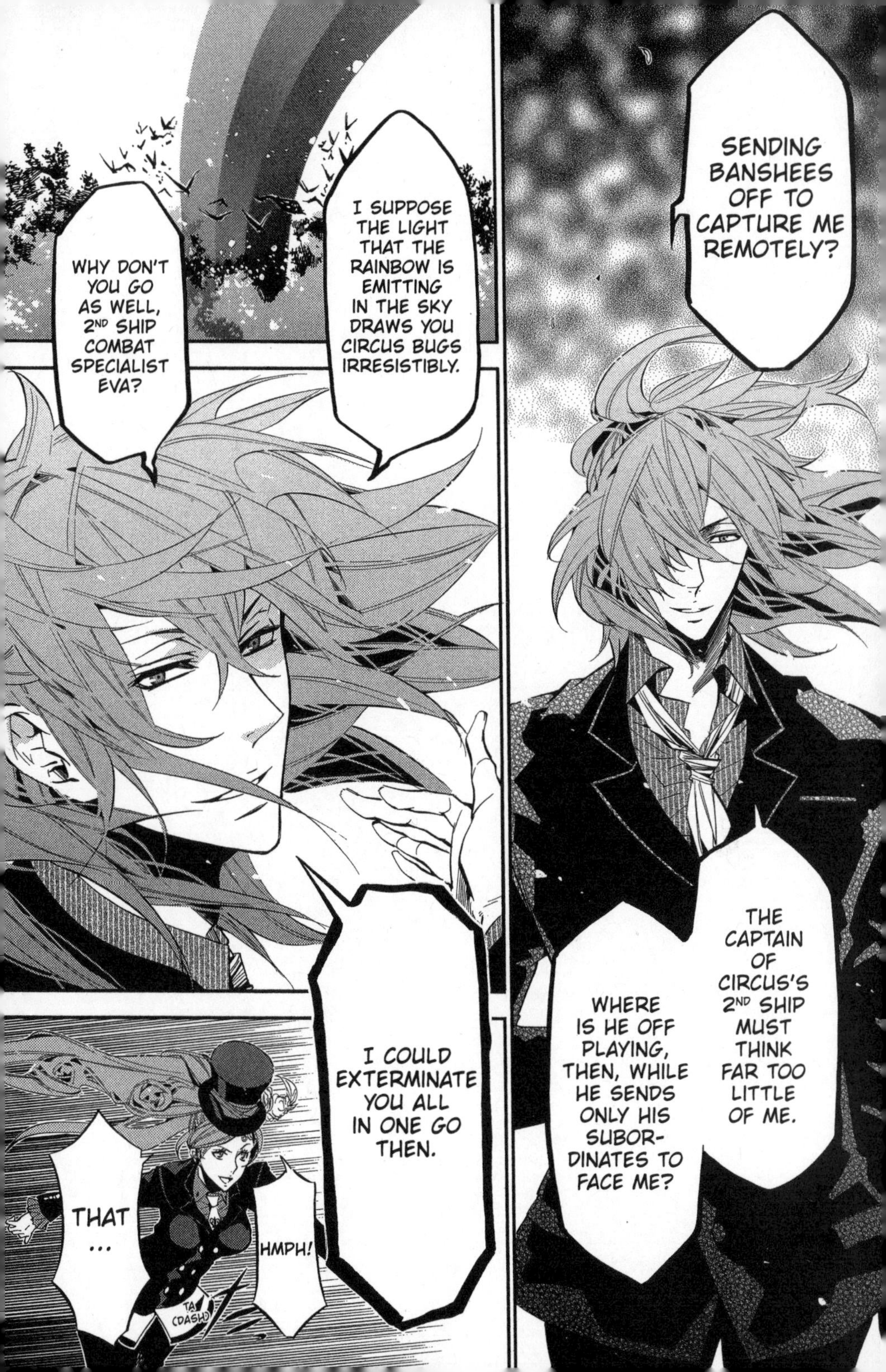
SENDING BANSHEES OFF TO CAPTURE ME REMOTELY?
THE CAPTAIN OF CIRCUS'S 2ND SHIP MUST THINK FAR TOO LITTLE OF ME.
WHERE IS HE OFF PLAYING, THEN, WHILE HE SENDS ONLY HIS SUBOR-DINATES TO FACE ME?
I SUPPOSE THE LIGHT THAT THE RAINBOW IS EMITTING IN THE SKY DRAWS YOU CIRCUS BUGS IRRESISTIBLY.
WHY DON'T YOU GO AS WELL, 2ND SHIP COMBAT SPECIALIST EVA?
I COULD EXTERMINATE YOU ALL IN ONE GO THEN.
HMPH!
THAT ...
TA (DASH)

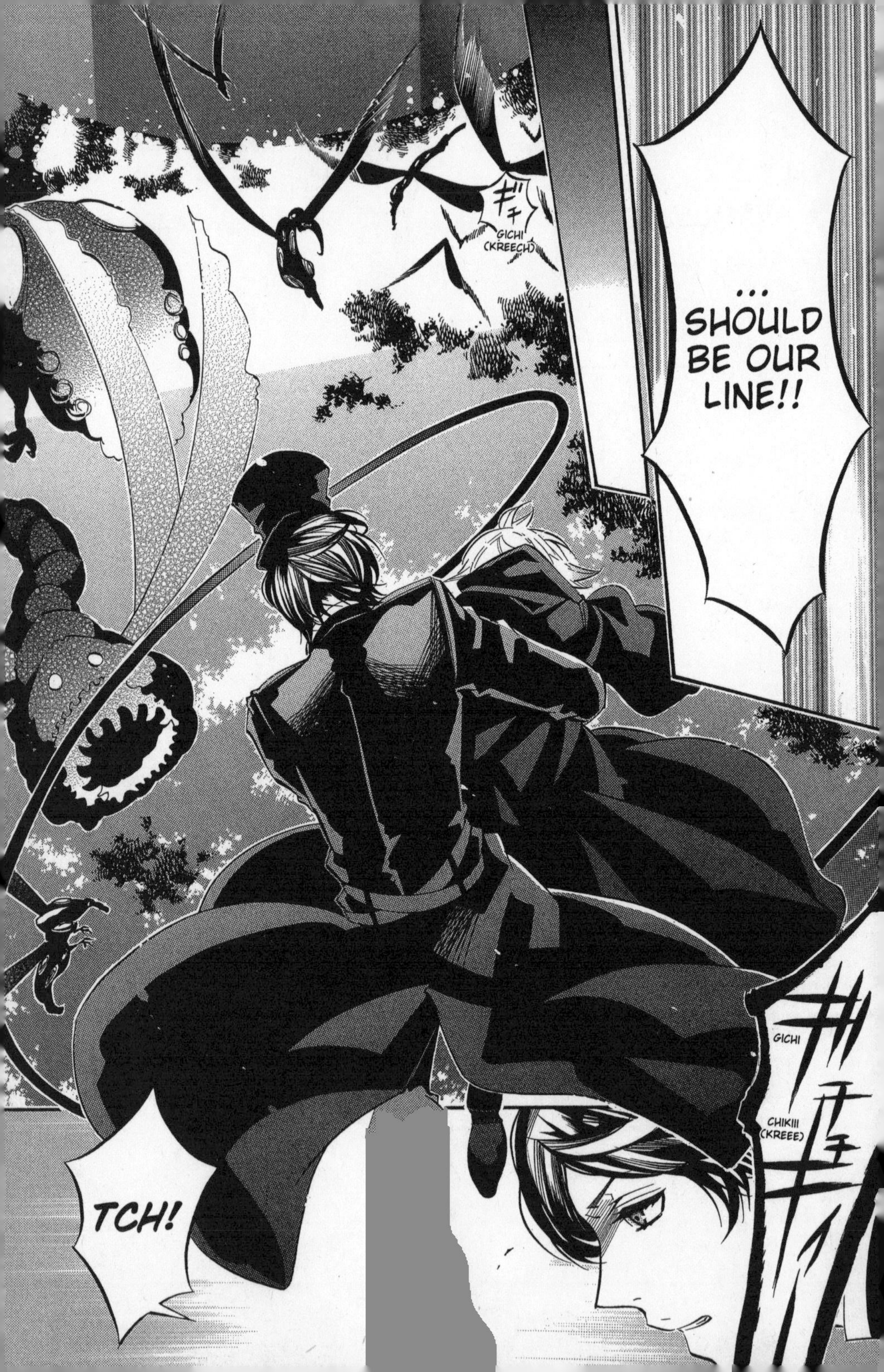

...SHOULD BE OUR LINE!!
ギチ
GICHI (KREECH)
GICHI
CHIKIII (KREEE)
TCH!

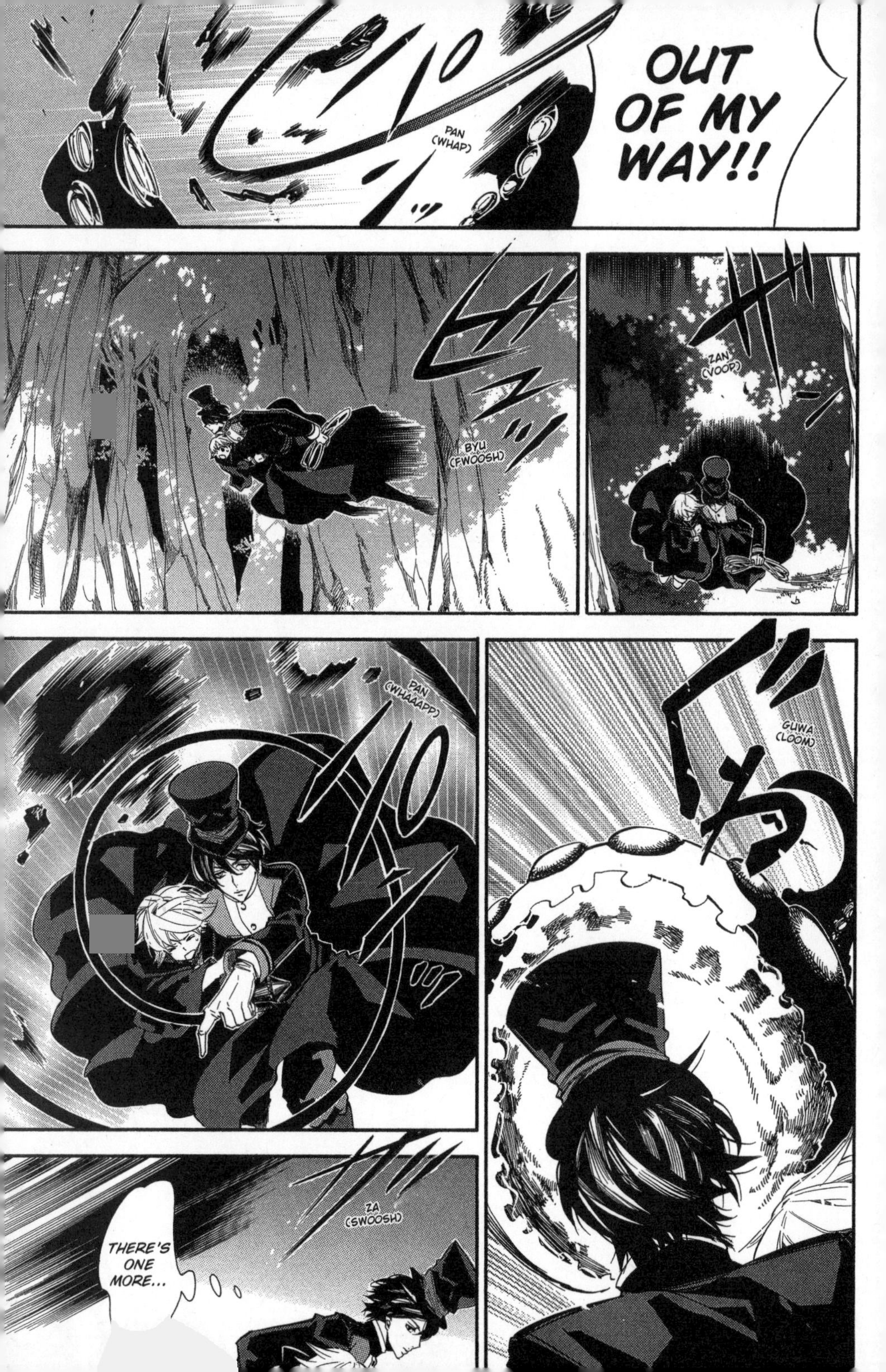
OUT OF MY WAY!!
PAN (WHAP)
ZAN (VOOP)
BYU (FWOOSH)
GUWA (LOOM)
PAN (WHAAAPP)
ZA (SWOOSH)
THERE'S ONE MORE...

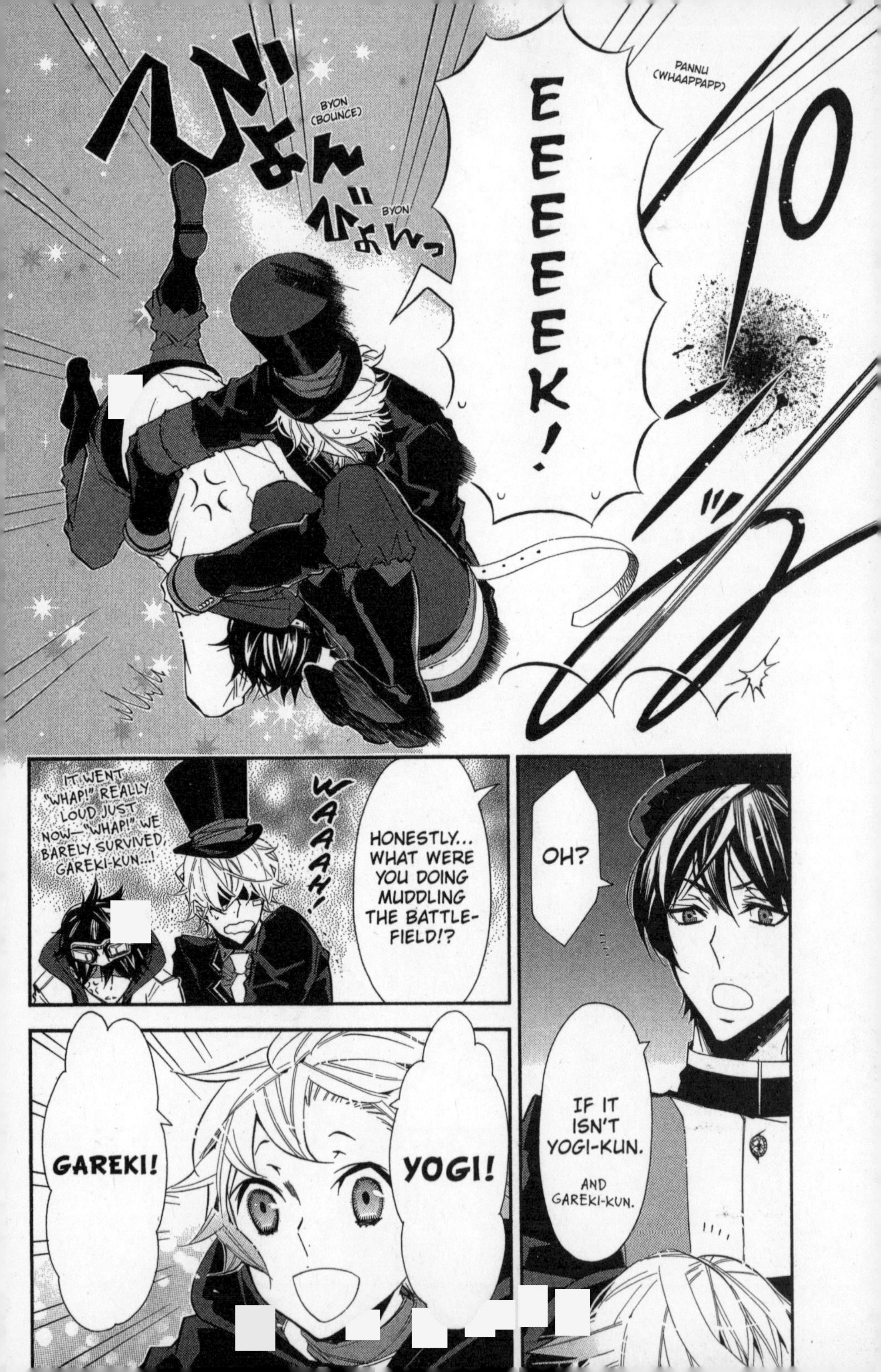

PANNU (WHAAPPAPP)
EEEEEEK!
BYON (BOUNCE)
BYON
OH?
IF IT ISN'T YOGI-KUN.
AND GAREKI-KUN.
HONESTLY... WHAT WERE YOU DOING MUDDLING THE BATTLE-FIELD!?
WAAAAH!
IT WENT "WHAP!" REALLY LOUD JUST NOW—"WHAP!" WE BARELY SURVIVED, GAREKI-KUN...!
YOGI!
GAREKI!

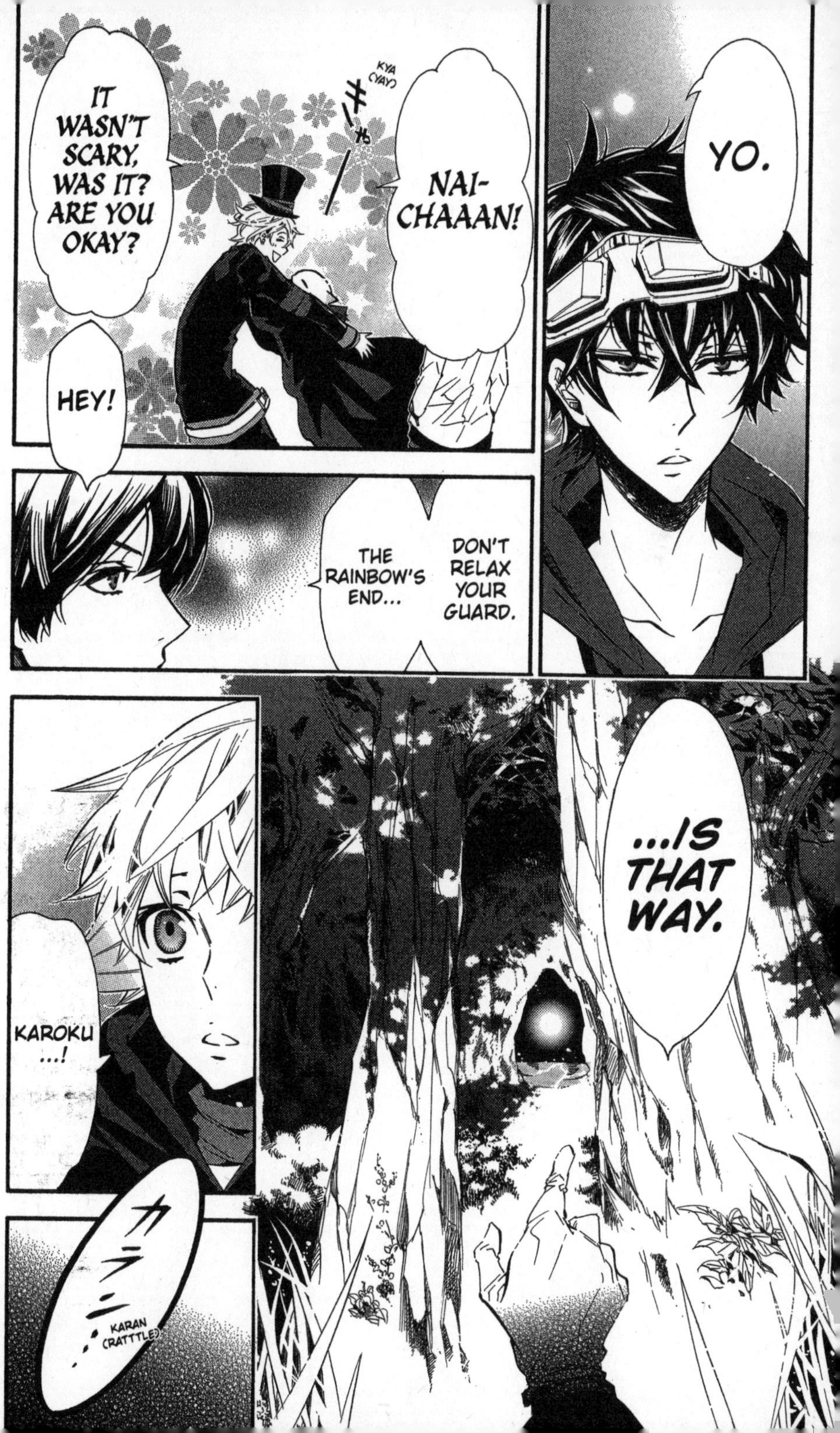
YO.
NAI-CHAAAN!
KYA (YAY)
IT WASN'T SCARY, WAS IT? ARE YOU OKAY?
HEY!
DON'T RELAX YOUR GUARD.
THE RAINBOW'S END...
...IS THAT WAY.
KAROKU ...!
KARAN (RATTLE)

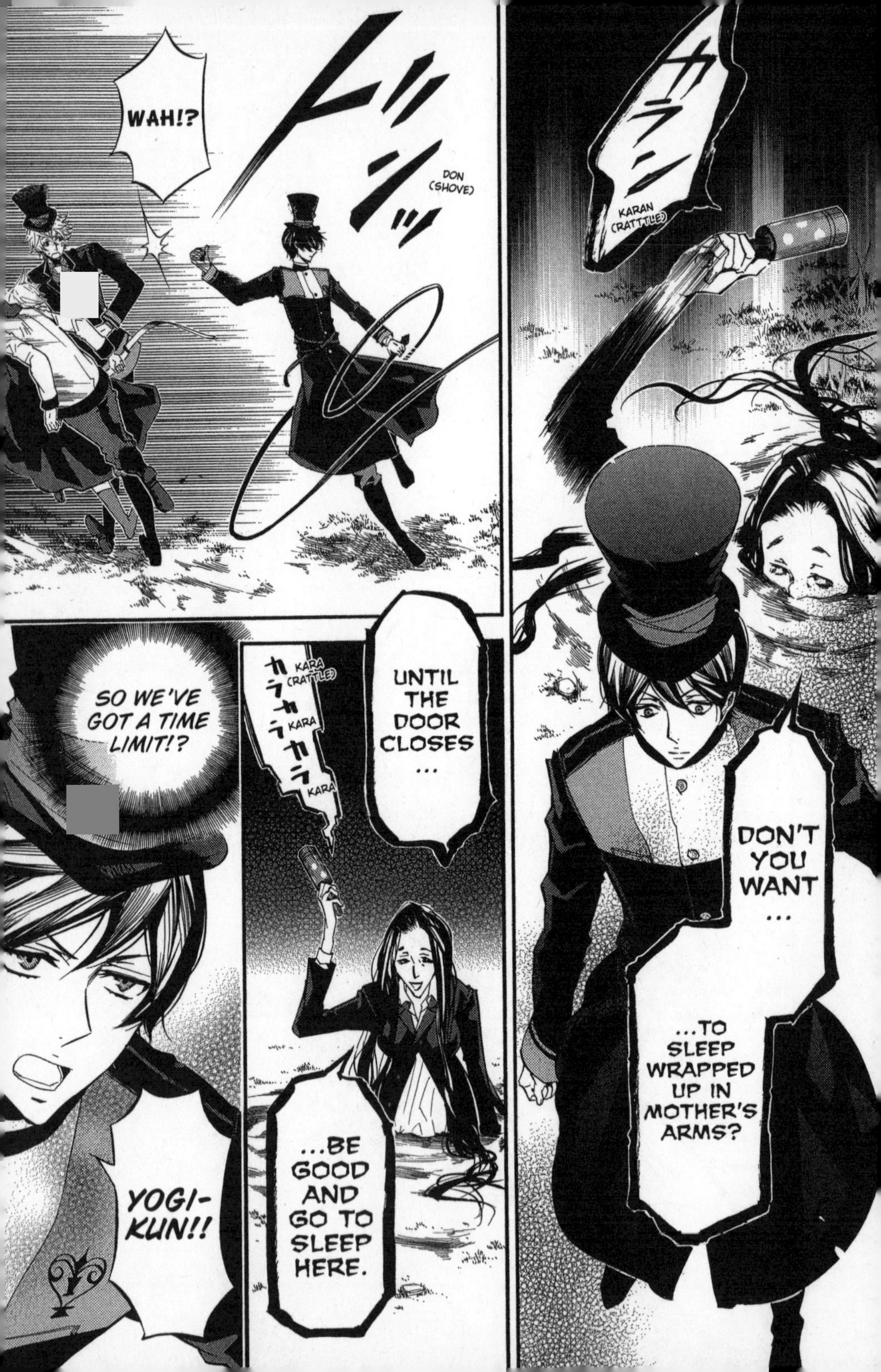

カラン
KARAN (RATTTLE)
DON'T YOU WANT...
...TO SLEEP WRAPPED UP IN MOTHER'S ARMS?
ドンッ
DON (SHOVE)
WAH!?
カラカラカラ
KARA (RATTLE) KARA KARA
UNTIL THE DOOR CLOSES...
...BE GOOD AND GO TO SLEEP HERE.
SO WE'VE GOT A TIME LIMIT!?
YOGI-KUN!!

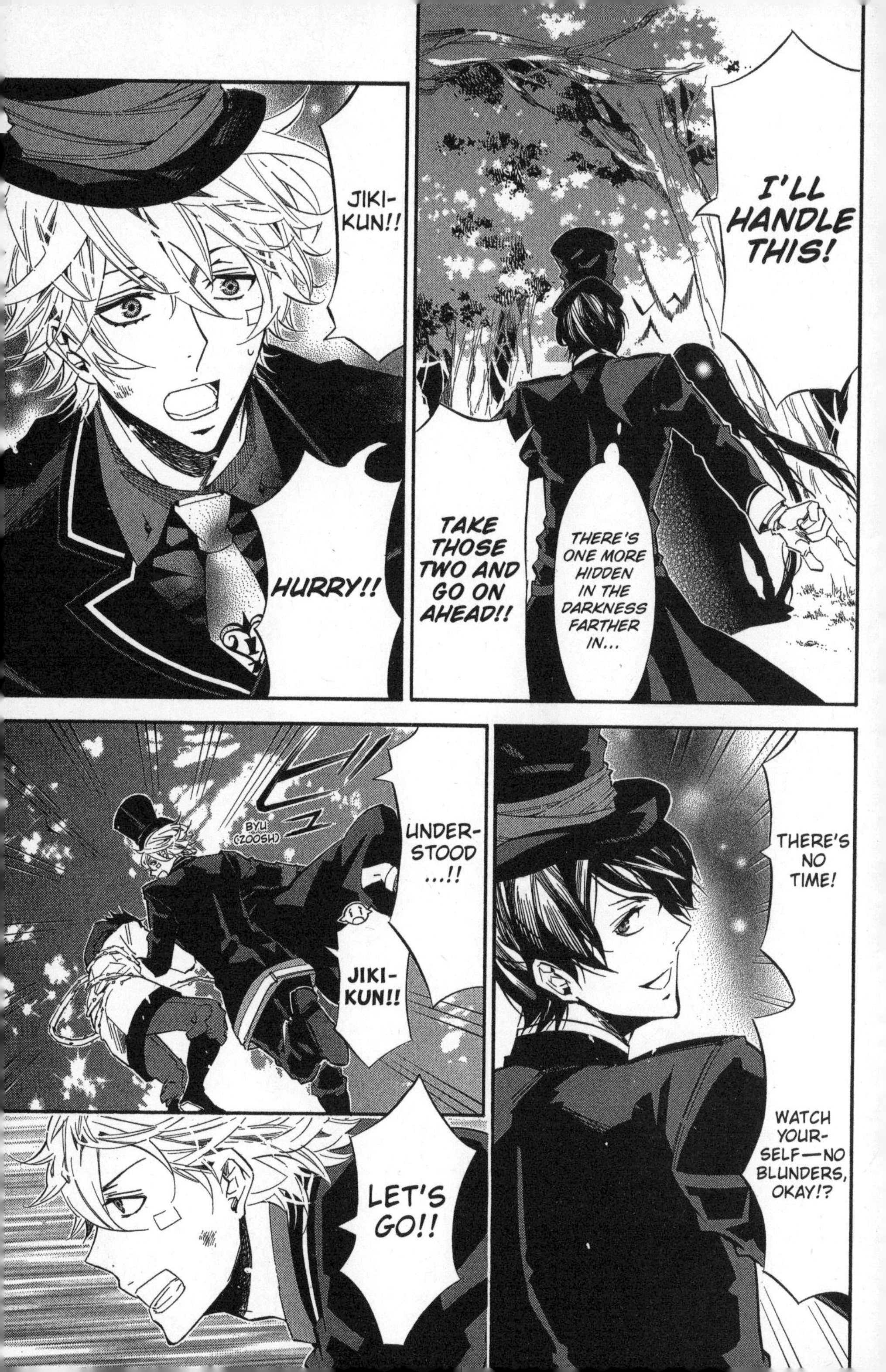
I'LL HANDLE THIS!
THERE'S ONE MORE HIDDEN IN THE DARKNESS FARTHER IN...
TAKE THOSE TWO AND GO ON AHEAD!!
JIKI-KUN!!
HURRY!!
THERE'S NO TIME!
WATCH YOURSELF—NO BLUNDERS, OKAY!?
UNDER-STOOD ...!!
BYU (ZOOSH)
JIKI-KUN!!
LET'S GO!!

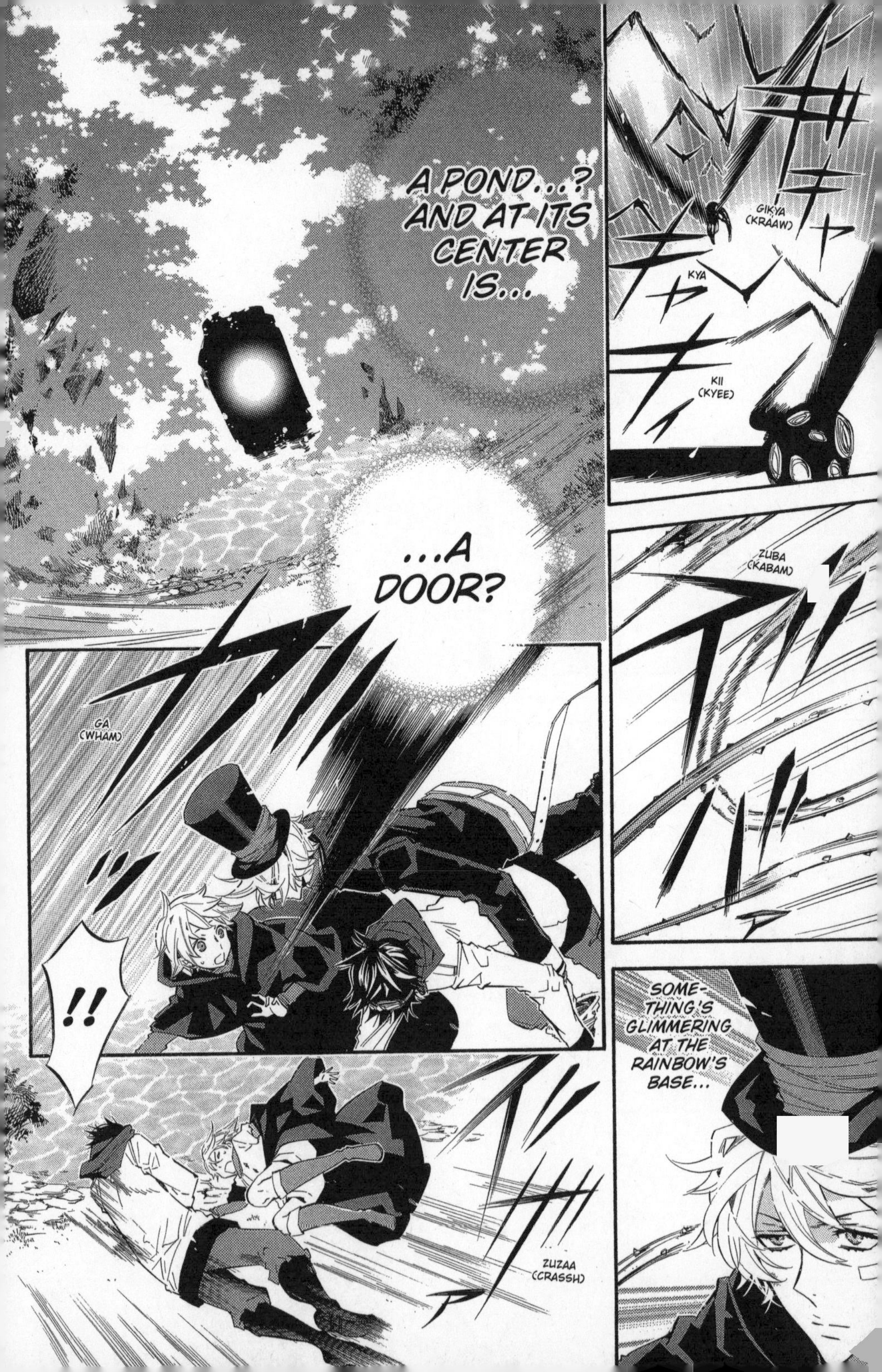
GIKYA (KRAAW)
KYA
KII (KYEE)
ZUBA (KABAM)
SOME-THING'S GLIMMERING AT THE RAINBOW'S BASE...
A POND...? AND AT ITS CENTER IS...
...A DOOR?
GA (WHAM)
!!
ZUZAA (CRASSH)

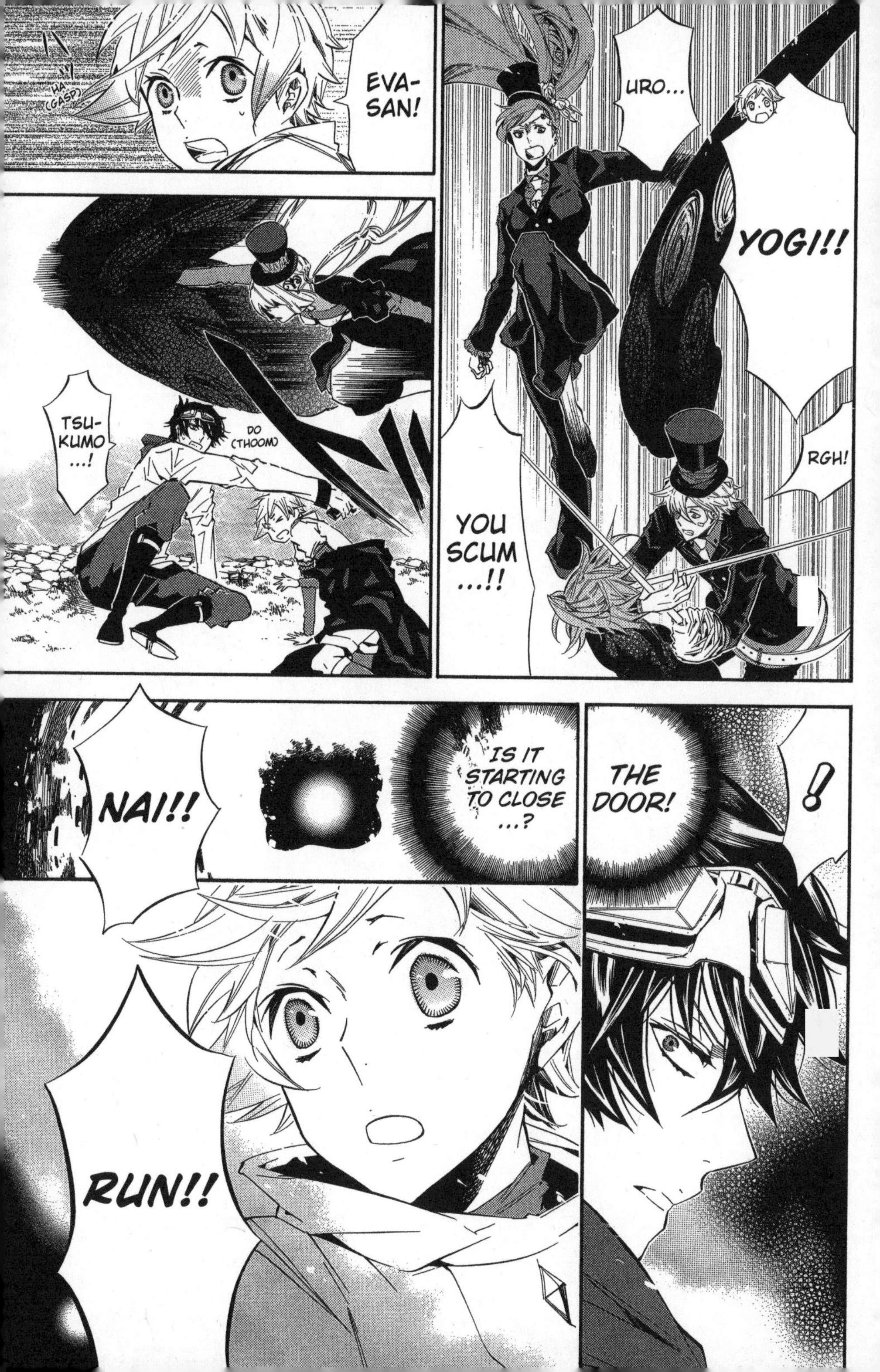

URO...
YOGI!!
RGH!
YOU SCUM ...!!
EVA-SAN!
HA (GASP)
DO (THOOM)
TSU-KUMO ...!
!
THE DOOR!
IS IT STARTING TO CLOSE ...?
NAI!!
RUN!!

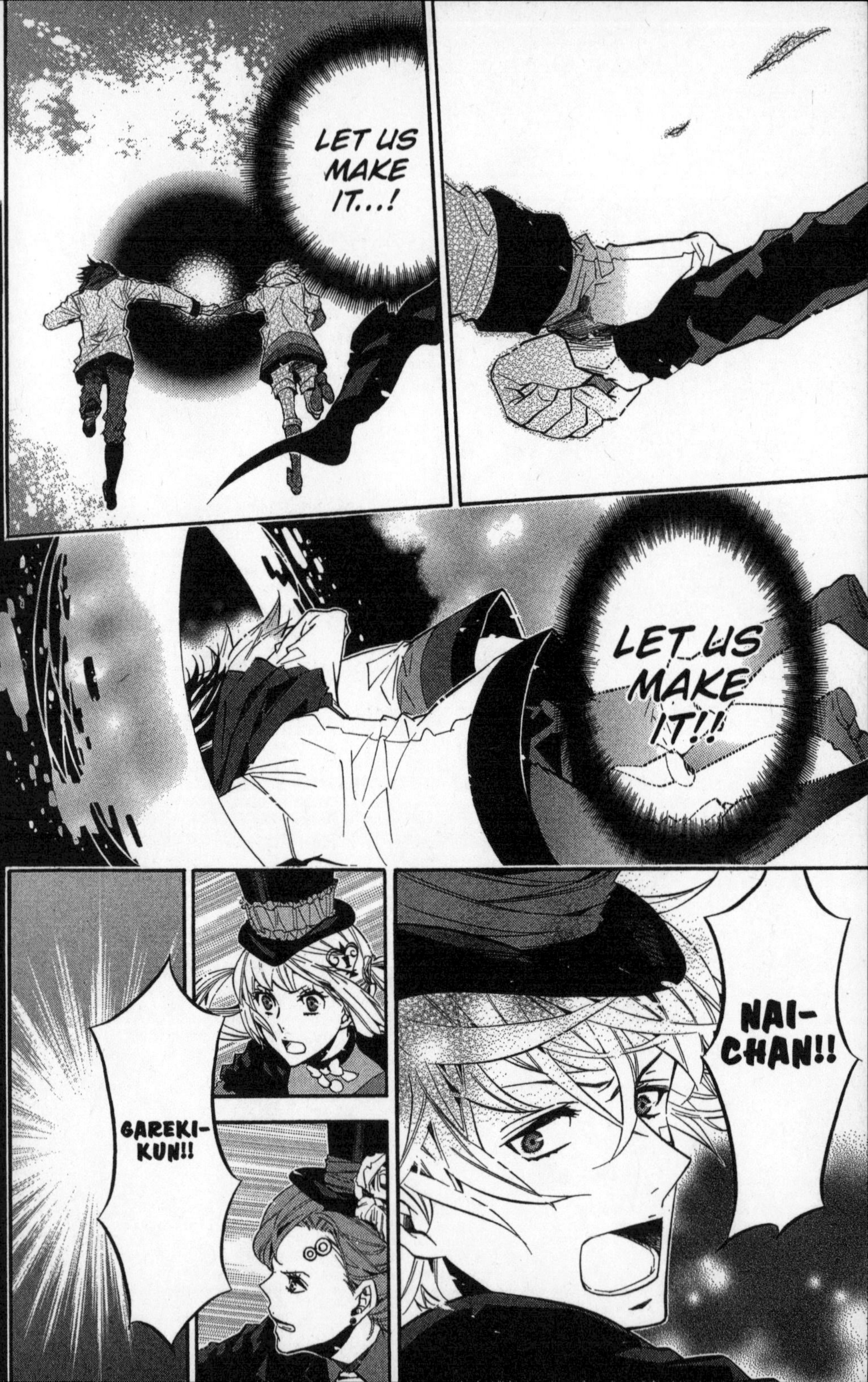
LET US MAKE IT...!
LET US MAKE IT!!
NAI-CHAN!!
GAREKI-KUN!!

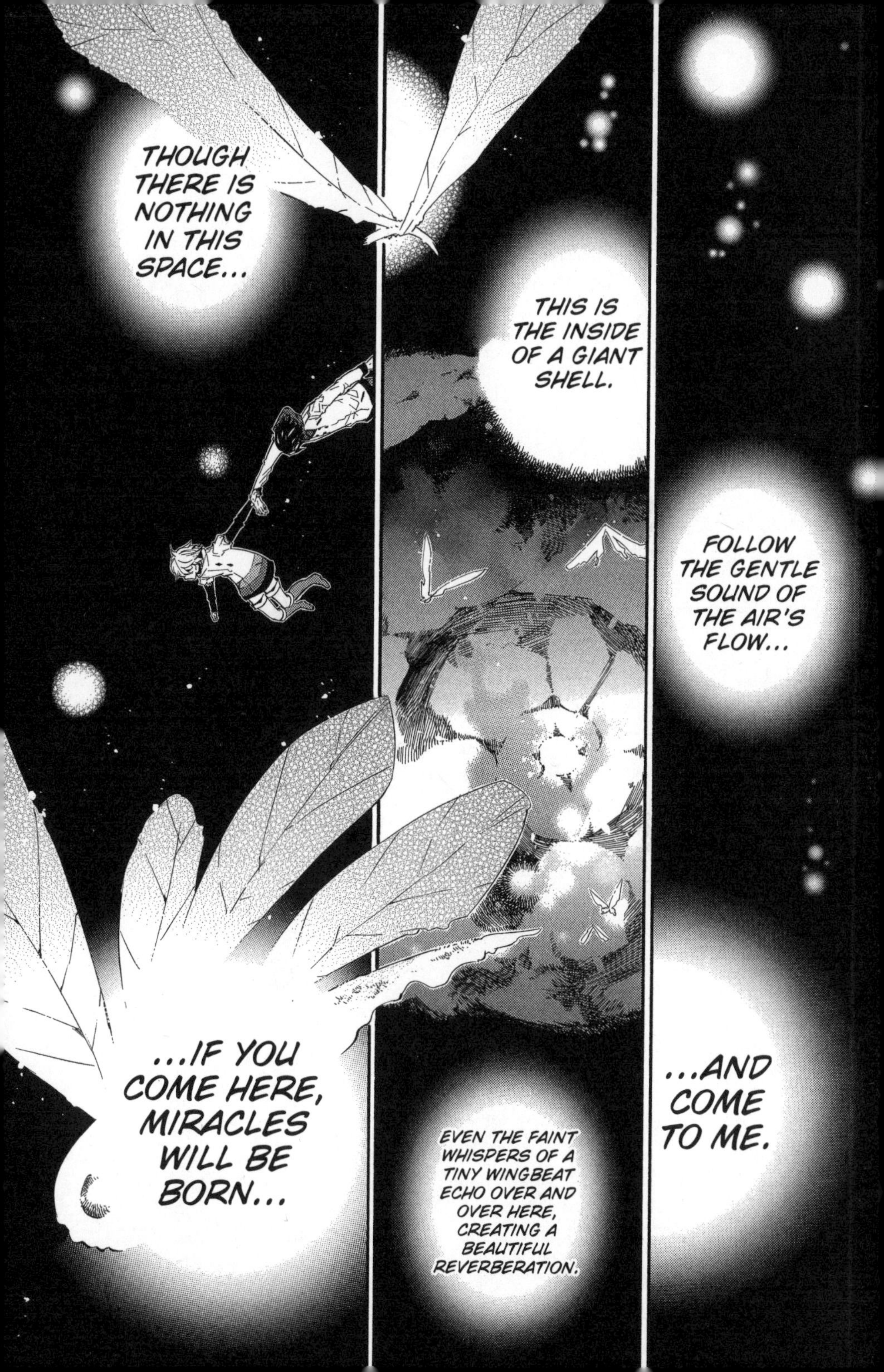
FOLLOW THE GENTLE SOUND OF THE AIR'S FLOW...
...AND COME TO ME.
THIS IS THE INSIDE OF A GIANT SHELL.
EVEN THE FAINT WHISPERS OF A TINY WINGBEAT ECHO OVER AND OVER HERE, CREATING A BEAUTIFUL REVERBERATION.
THOUGH THERE IS NOTHING IN THIS SPACE...
...IF YOU COME HERE, MIRACLES WILL BE BORN...

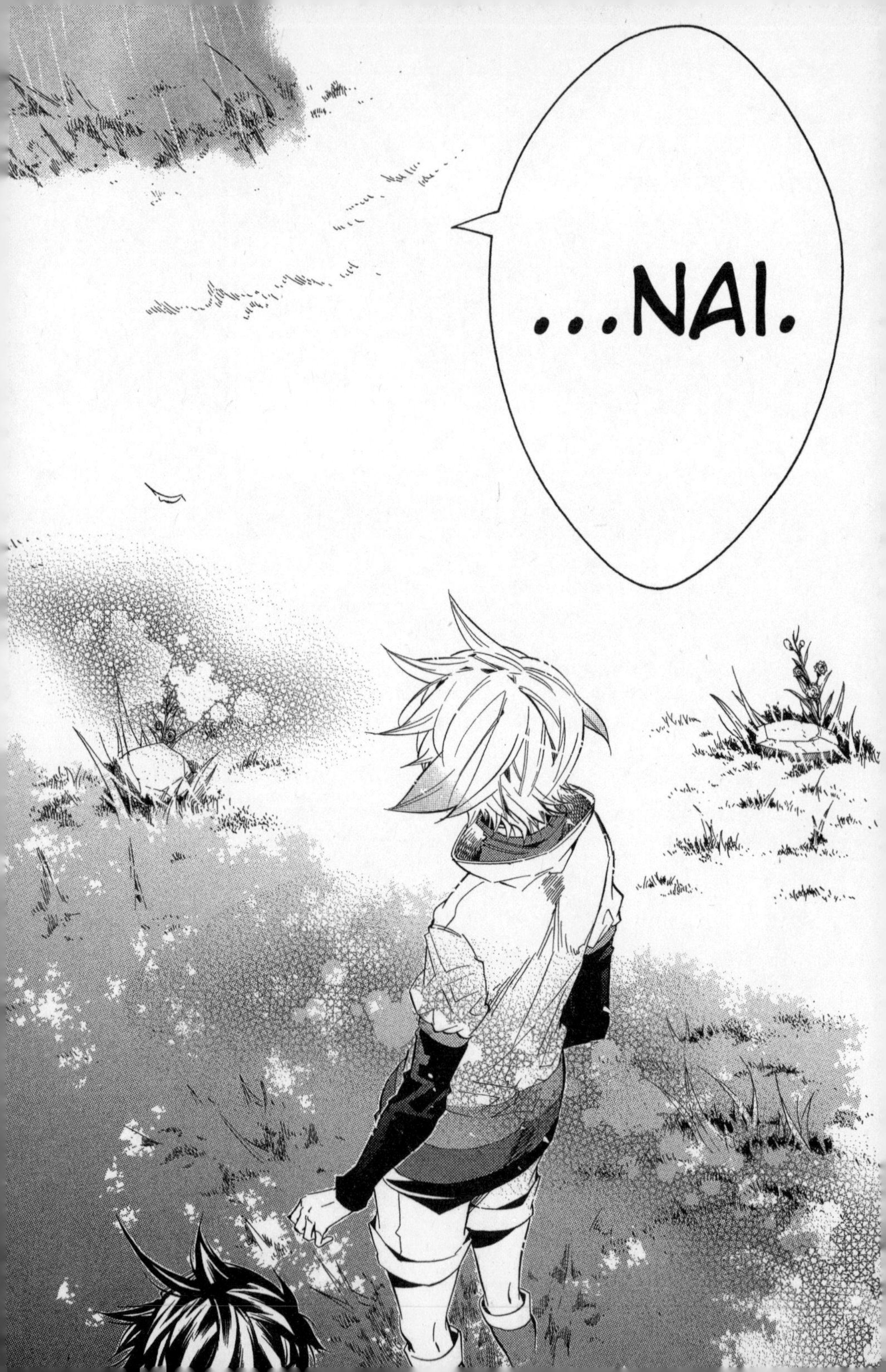
...NAI.

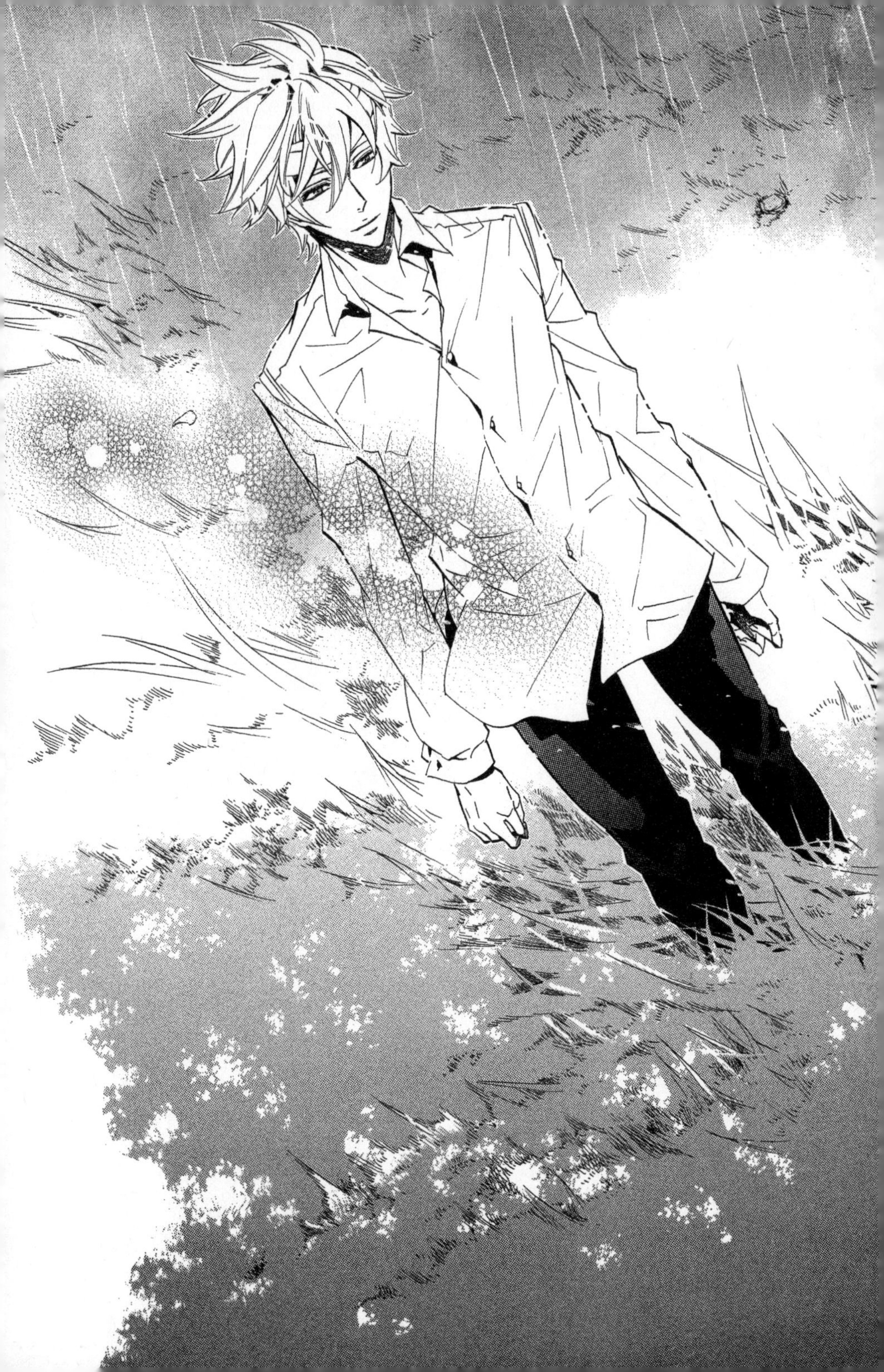

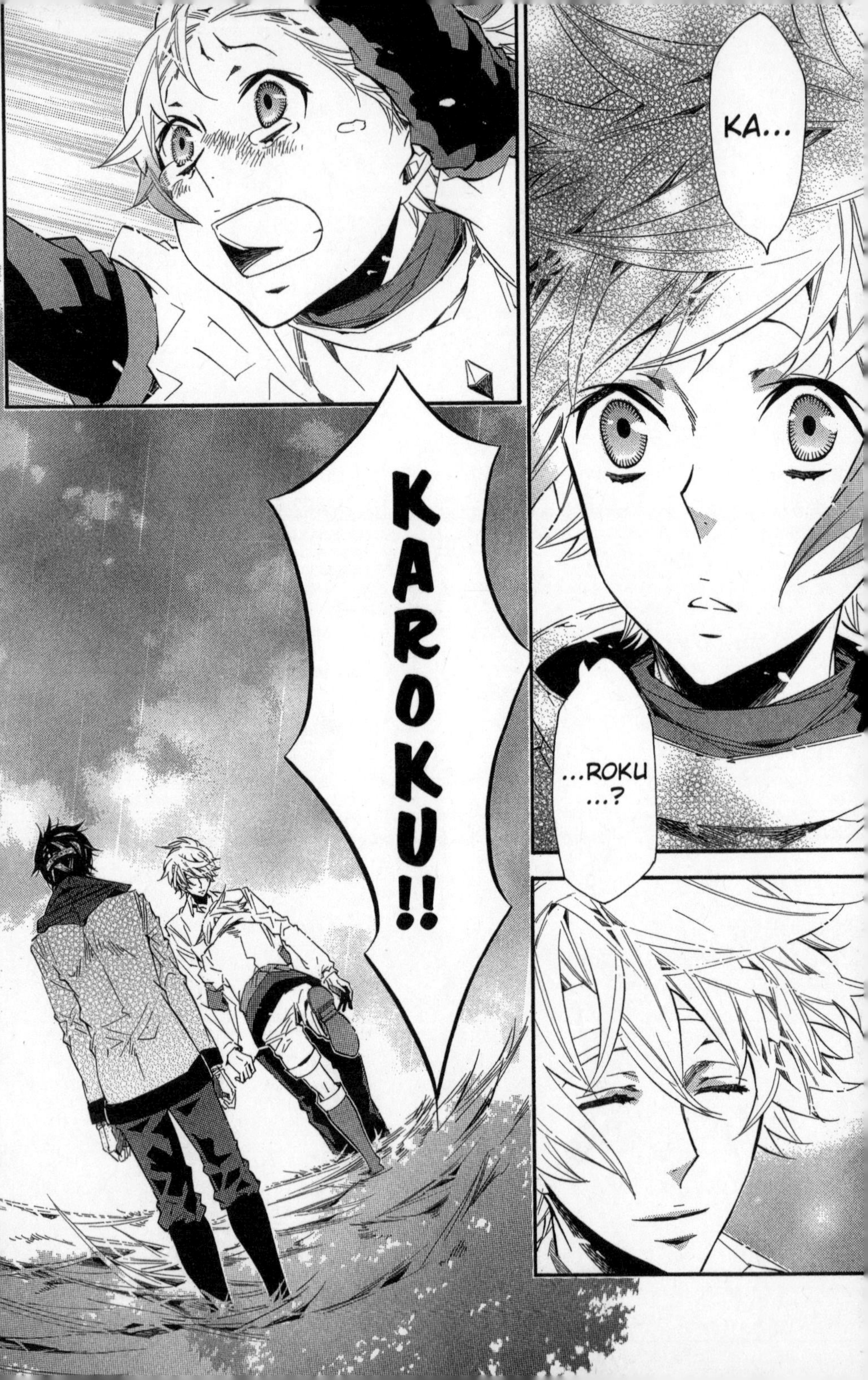
KA...
...ROKU ...?
KAROKU!!

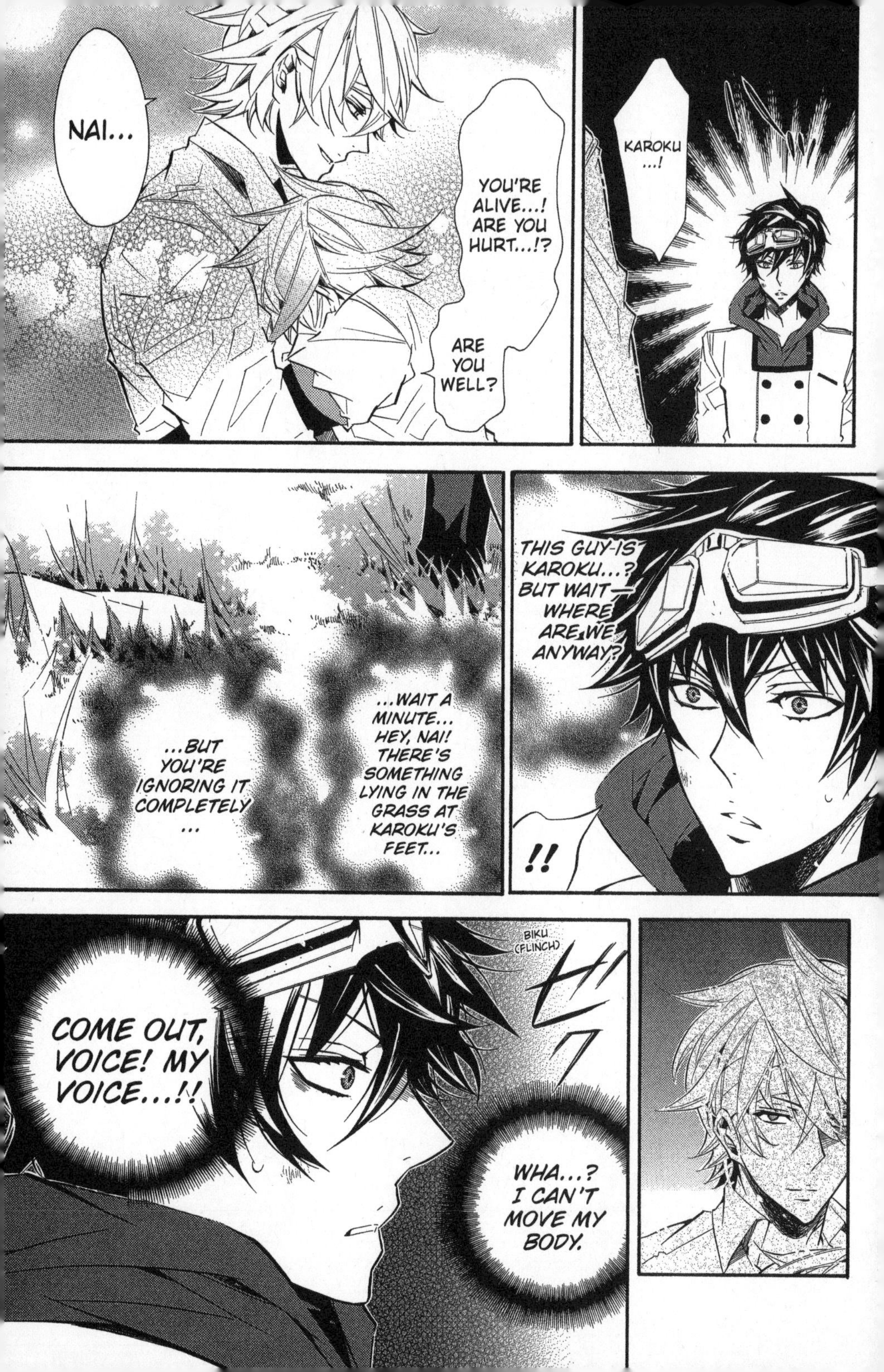
KAROKU ...!
NAI...
YOU'RE ALIVE...! ARE YOU HURT...!?
ARE YOU WELL?
THIS GUY IS KAROKU...? BUT WAIT— WHERE ARE WE ANYWAY?
!!
...WAIT A MINUTE... HEY, NAI! THERE'S SOMETHING LYING IN THE GRASS AT KAROKU'S FEET...
...BUT YOU'RE IGNORING IT COMPLETELY...
BIKU (FLINCH)
WHA...? I CAN'T MOVE MY BODY.
COME OUT, VOICE! MY VOICE...!!

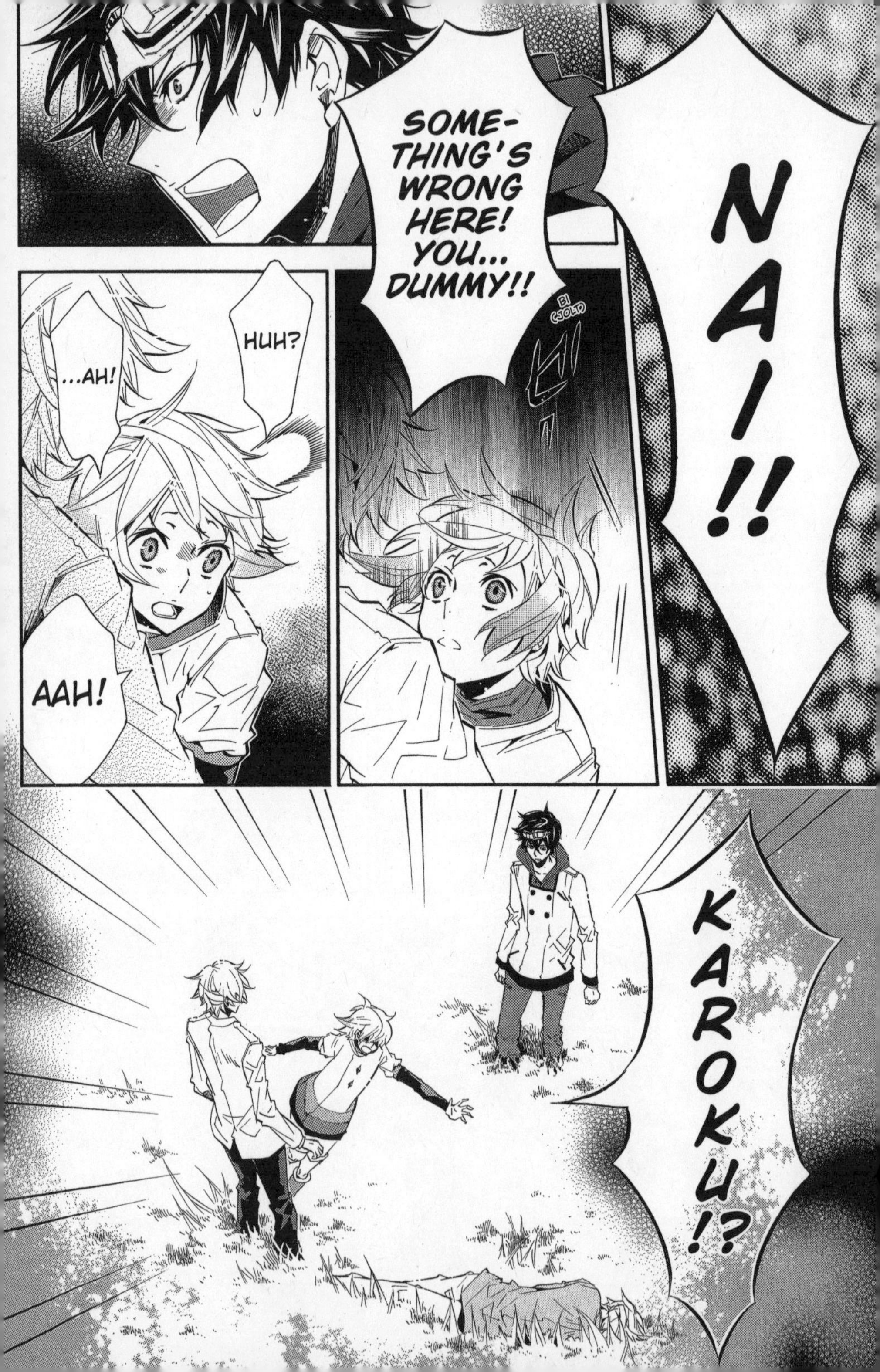
NAI!!
SOME-THING'S WRONG HERE! YOU... DUMMY!!
BI (JOLT)
HUH?
...AH!
AAH!
KAROKU!?

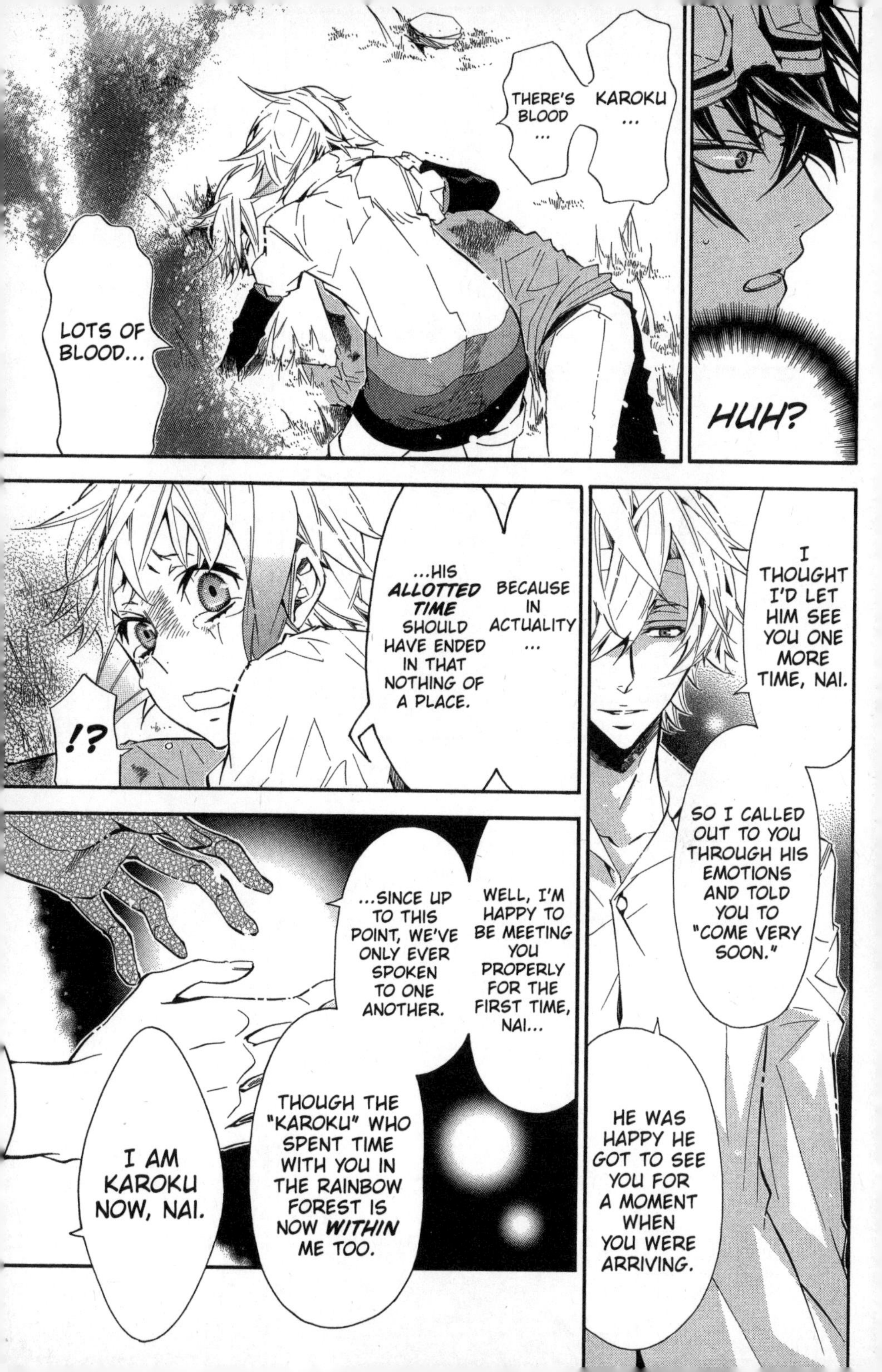
HUH?
KAROKU...
THERE'S BLOOD...
LOTS OF BLOOD...
I THOUGHT I'D LET HIM SEE YOU ONE MORE TIME, NAI.
BECAUSE IN ACTUALITY...
...HIS **ALLOTTED TIME** SHOULD HAVE ENDED IN THAT NOTHING OF A PLACE.
!?
SO I CALLED OUT TO YOU THROUGH HIS EMOTIONS AND TOLD YOU TO "COME VERY SOON."
HE WAS HAPPY HE GOT TO SEE YOU FOR A MOMENT WHEN YOU WERE ARRIVING.
WELL, I'M HAPPY TO BE MEETING YOU PROPERLY FOR THE FIRST TIME, NAI...
...SINCE UP TO THIS POINT, WE'VE ONLY EVER SPOKEN TO ONE ANOTHER.
THOUGH THE "KAROKU" WHO SPENT TIME WITH YOU IN THE RAINBOW FOREST IS NOW **WITHIN** ME TOO.
I AM KAROKU NOW, NAI.

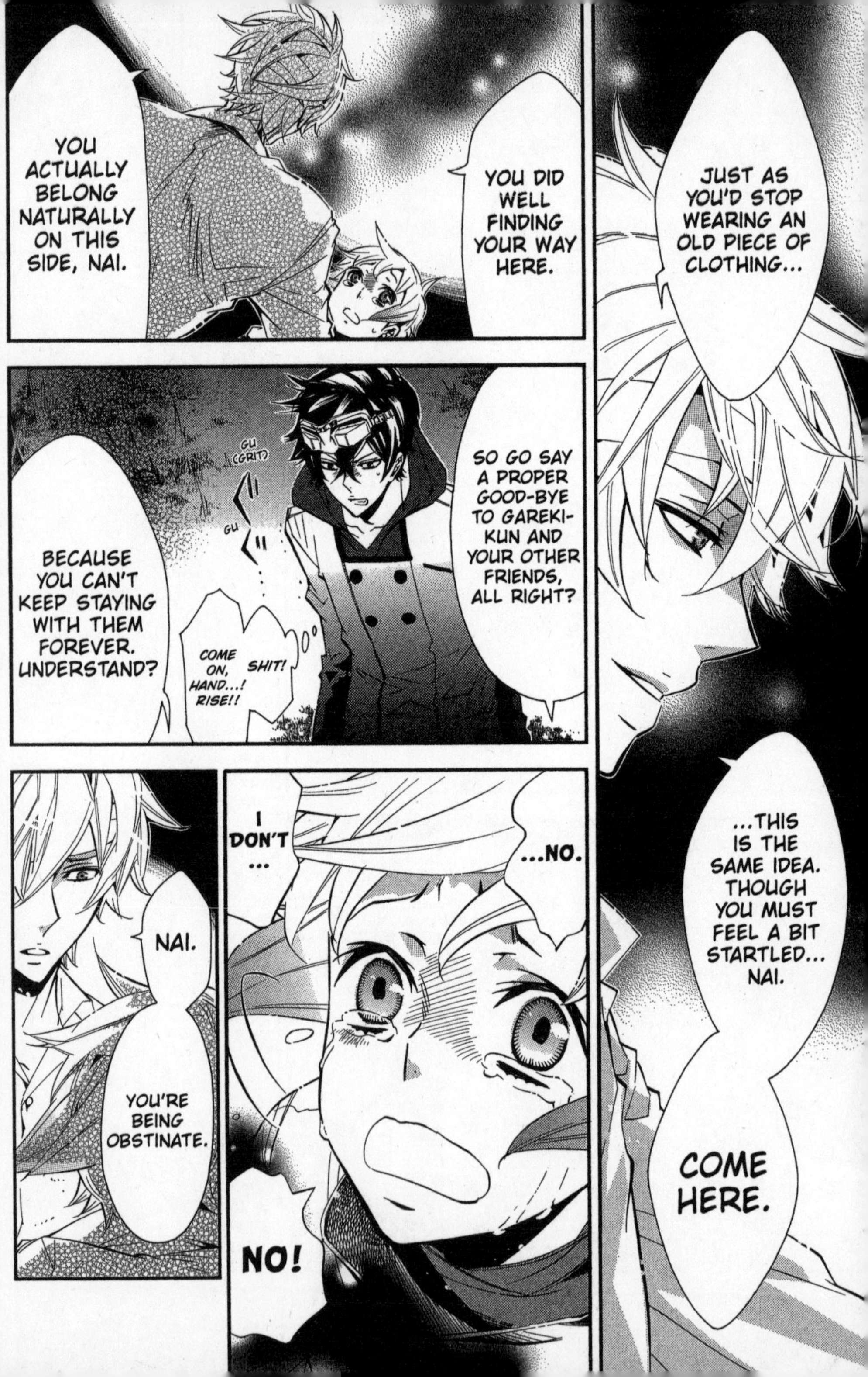
JUST AS YOU'D STOP WEARING AN OLD PIECE OF CLOTHING...
...THIS IS THE SAME IDEA. THOUGH YOU MUST FEEL A BIT STARTLED... NAI.
COME HERE.
YOU DID WELL FINDING YOUR WAY HERE.
YOU ACTUALLY BELONG NATURALLY ON THIS SIDE, NAI.
SO GO SAY A PROPER GOOD-BYE TO GAREKI-KUN AND YOUR OTHER FRIENDS, ALL RIGHT?
SHIT!
COME ON, HAND...! RISE!!
GU (GRIT)
GU
BECAUSE YOU CAN'T KEEP STAYING WITH THEM FOREVER. UNDERSTAND?
...NO.
I DON'T ...
NO!
NAI.
YOU'RE BEING OBSTINATE.

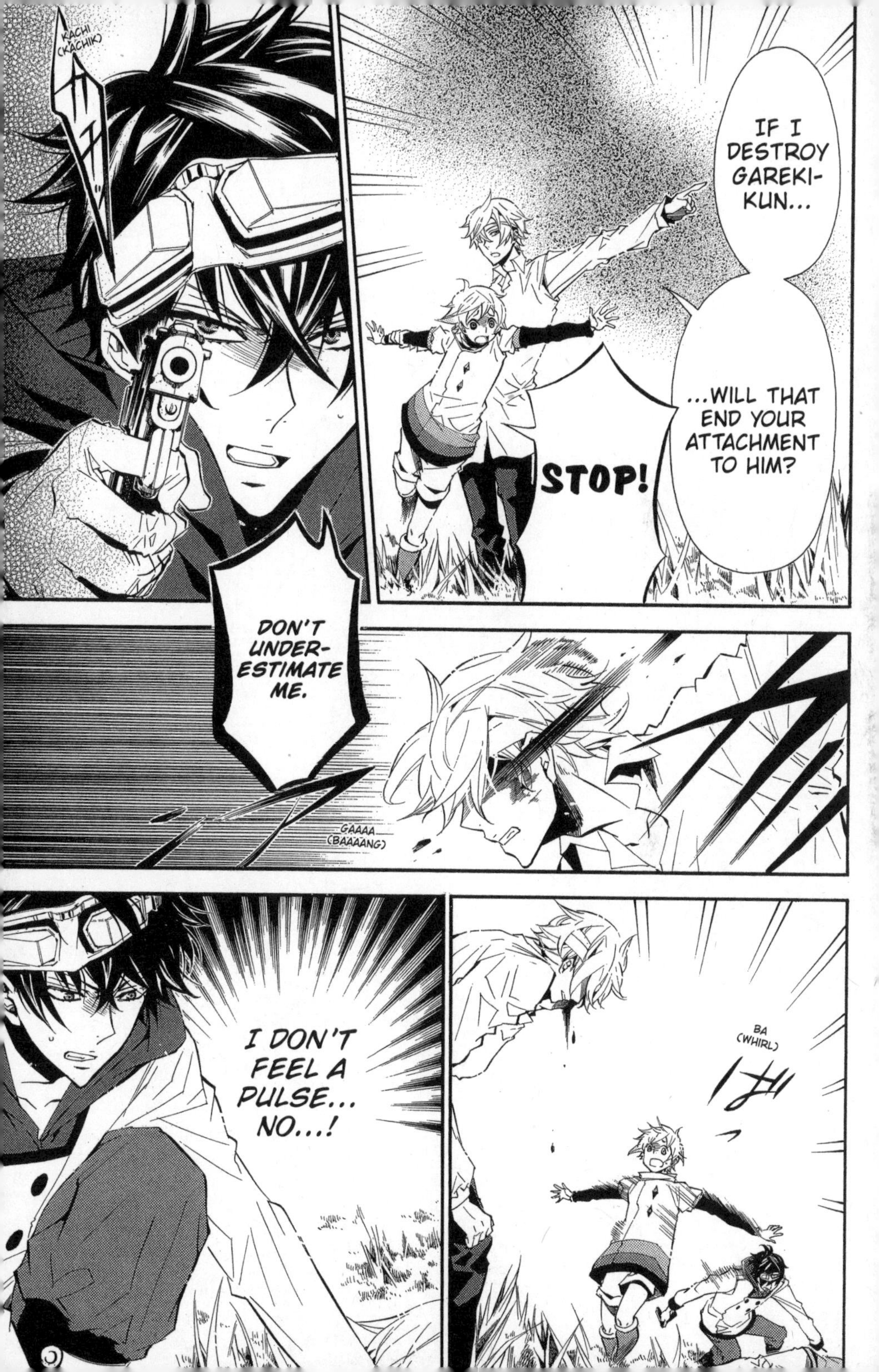
IF I DESTROY GAREKI-KUN...
...WILL THAT END YOUR ATTACHMENT TO HIM?
STOP!
KACHI (KACHIK)
DON'T UNDER-ESTIMATE ME.
GAAAA (BAAAANG)
BA (WHIRL)
I DON'T FEEL A PULSE... NO...!

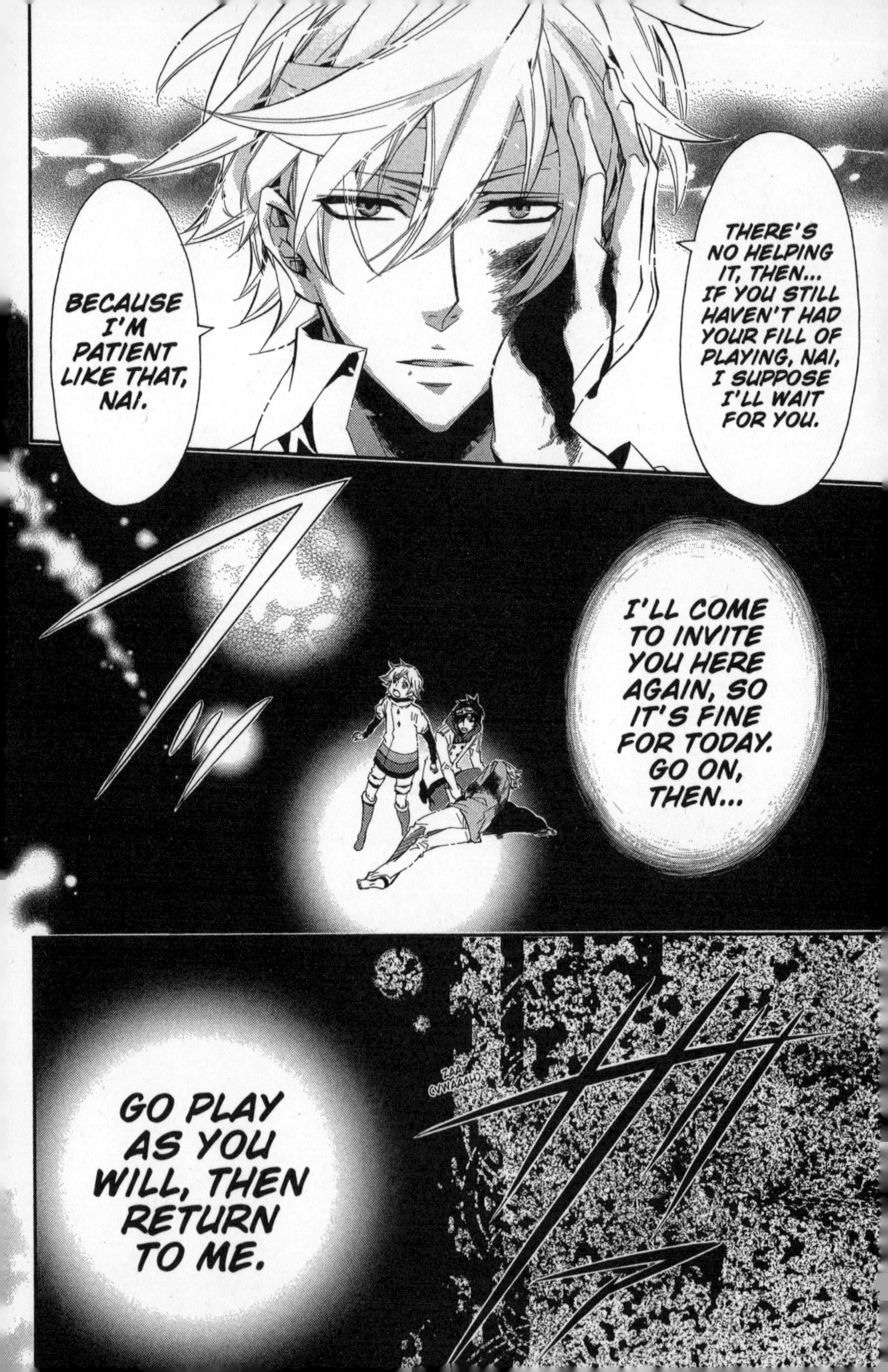
THERE'S NO HELPING IT, THEN... IF YOU STILL HAVEN'T HAD YOUR FILL OF PLAYING, NAI, I SUPPOSE I'LL WAIT FOR YOU.
BECAUSE I'M PATIENT LIKE THAT, NAI.
I'LL COME TO INVITE YOU HERE AGAIN, SO IT'S FINE FOR TODAY. GO ON, THEN...
ZAA (VWAAAH)
GO PLAY AS YOU WILL, THEN RETURN TO ME.

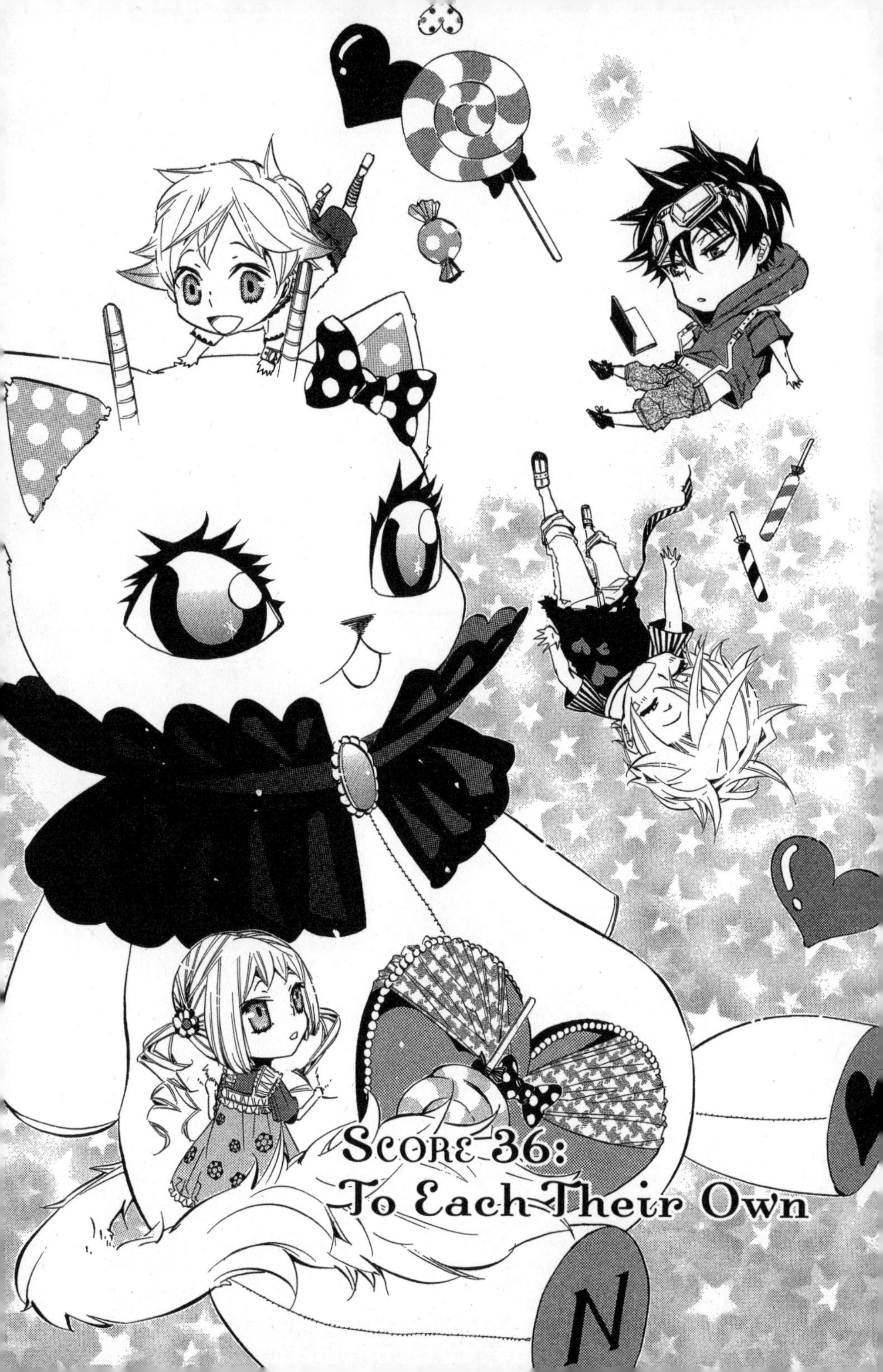
SCORE 36:
To Each Their Own

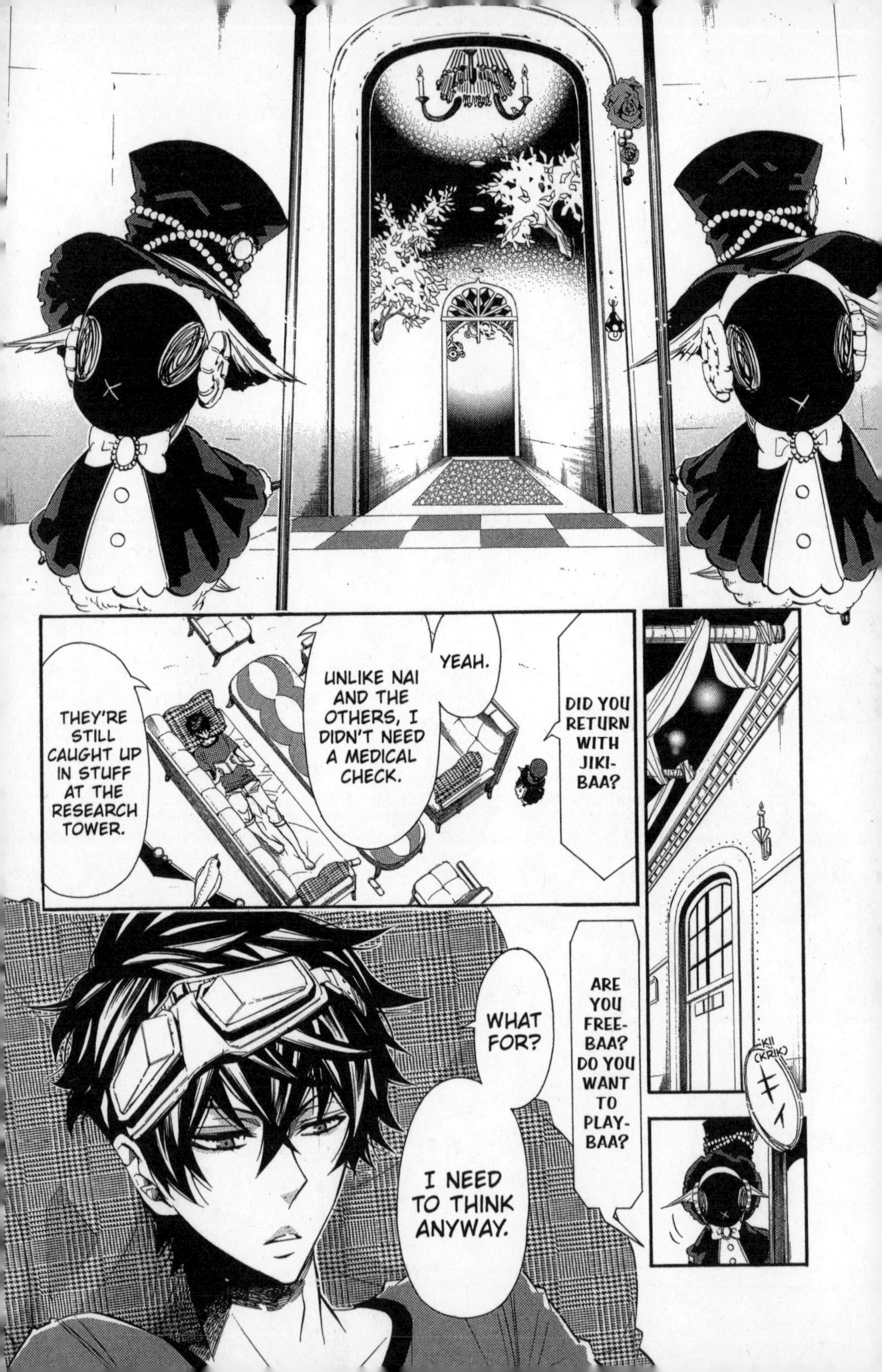
DID YOU RETURN WITH JIKI-BAA?
YEAH.
UNLIKE NAI AND THE OTHERS, I DIDN'T NEED A MEDICAL CHECK.
THEY'RE STILL CAUGHT UP IN STUFF AT THE RESEARCH TOWER.
KII (KRIK)
ARE YOU FREE-BAA? DO YOU WANT TO PLAY-BAA?
WHAT FOR?
I NEED TO THINK ANYWAY.

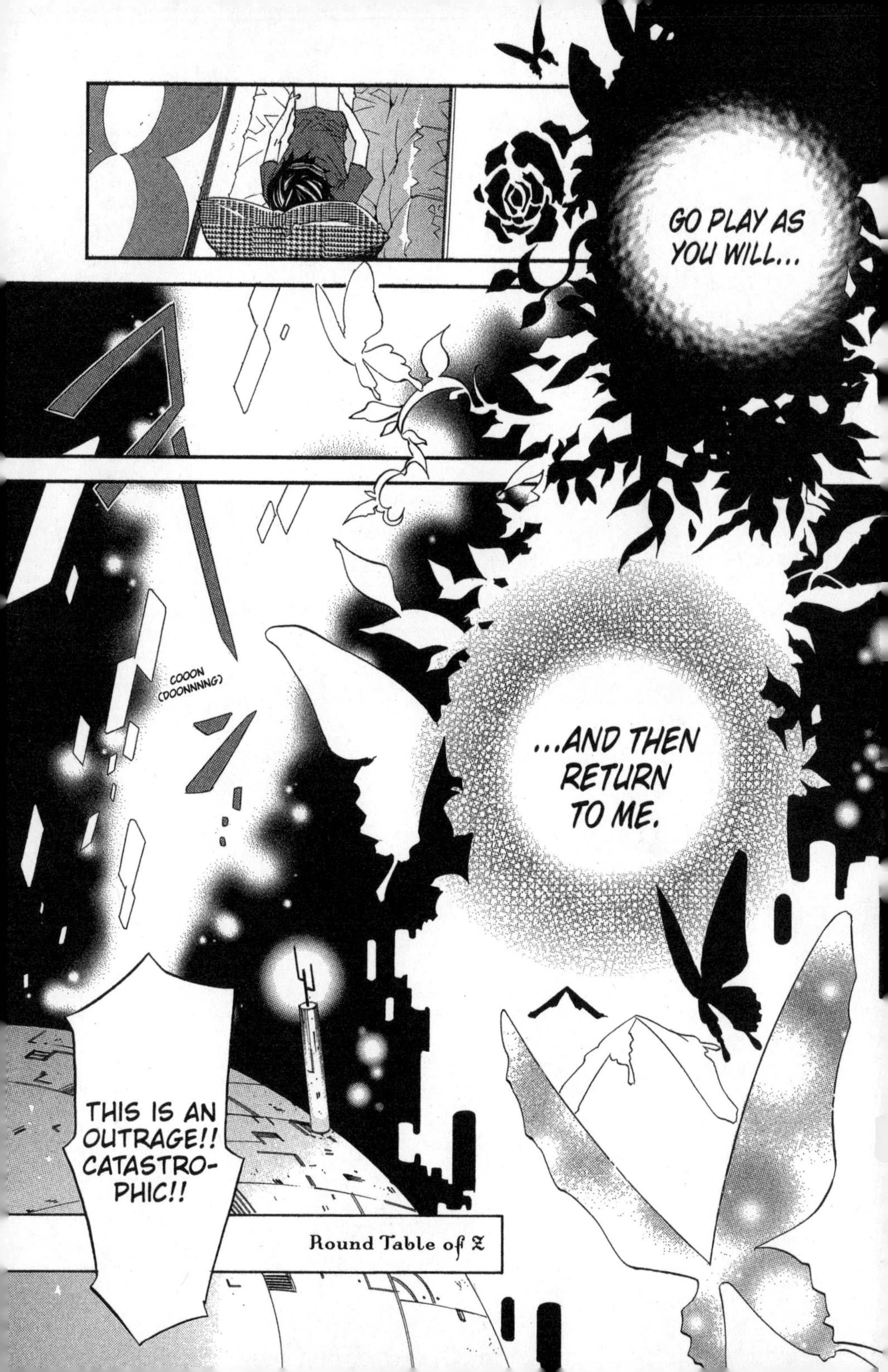
GO PLAY AS YOU WILL...
...AND THEN RETURN TO ME.
COOON (DOONNNNG)
Round Table of Z
THIS IS AN OUTRAGE!! CATASTRO-PHIC!!

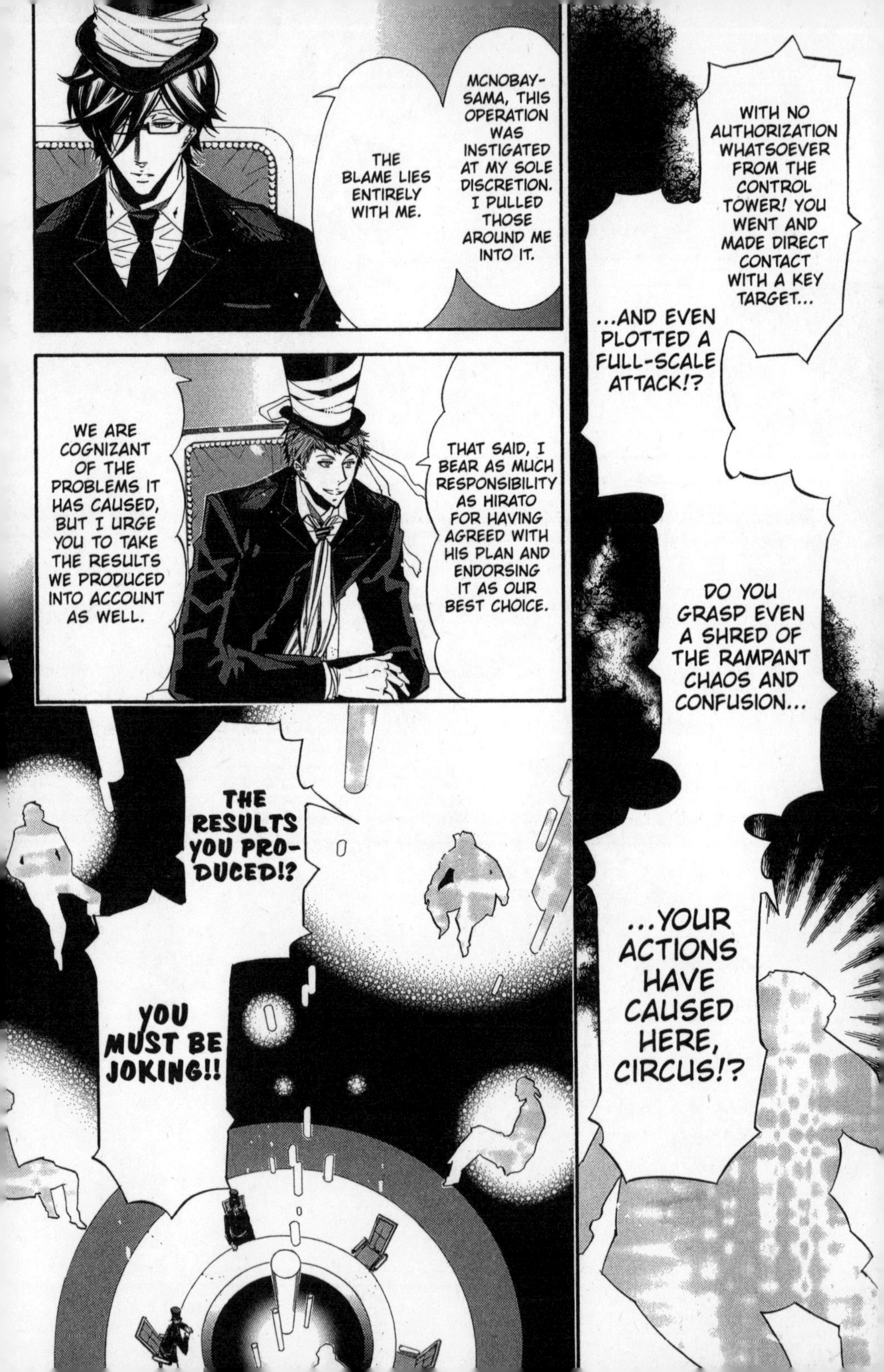
WITH NO AUTHORIZATION WHATSOEVER FROM THE CONTROL TOWER! YOU WENT AND MADE DIRECT CONTACT WITH A KEY TARGET...
...AND EVEN PLOTTED A FULL-SCALE ATTACK!?
DO YOU GRASP EVEN A SHRED OF THE RAMPANT CHAOS AND CONFUSION...
...YOUR ACTIONS HAVE CAUSED HERE, CIRCUS!?
MCNOBAY-SAMA, THIS OPERATION WAS INSTIGATED AT MY SOLE DISCRETION. I PULLED THOSE AROUND ME INTO IT.
THE BLAME LIES ENTIRELY WITH ME.
THAT SAID, I BEAR AS MUCH RESPONSIBILITY AS HIRATO FOR HAVING AGREED WITH HIS PLAN AND ENDORSING IT AS OUR BEST CHOICE.
WE ARE COGNIZANT OF THE PROBLEMS IT HAS CAUSED, BUT I URGE YOU TO TAKE THE RESULTS WE PRODUCED INTO ACCOUNT AS WELL.
THE RESULTS YOU PRO-DUCED!?
YOU MUST BE JOKING!!

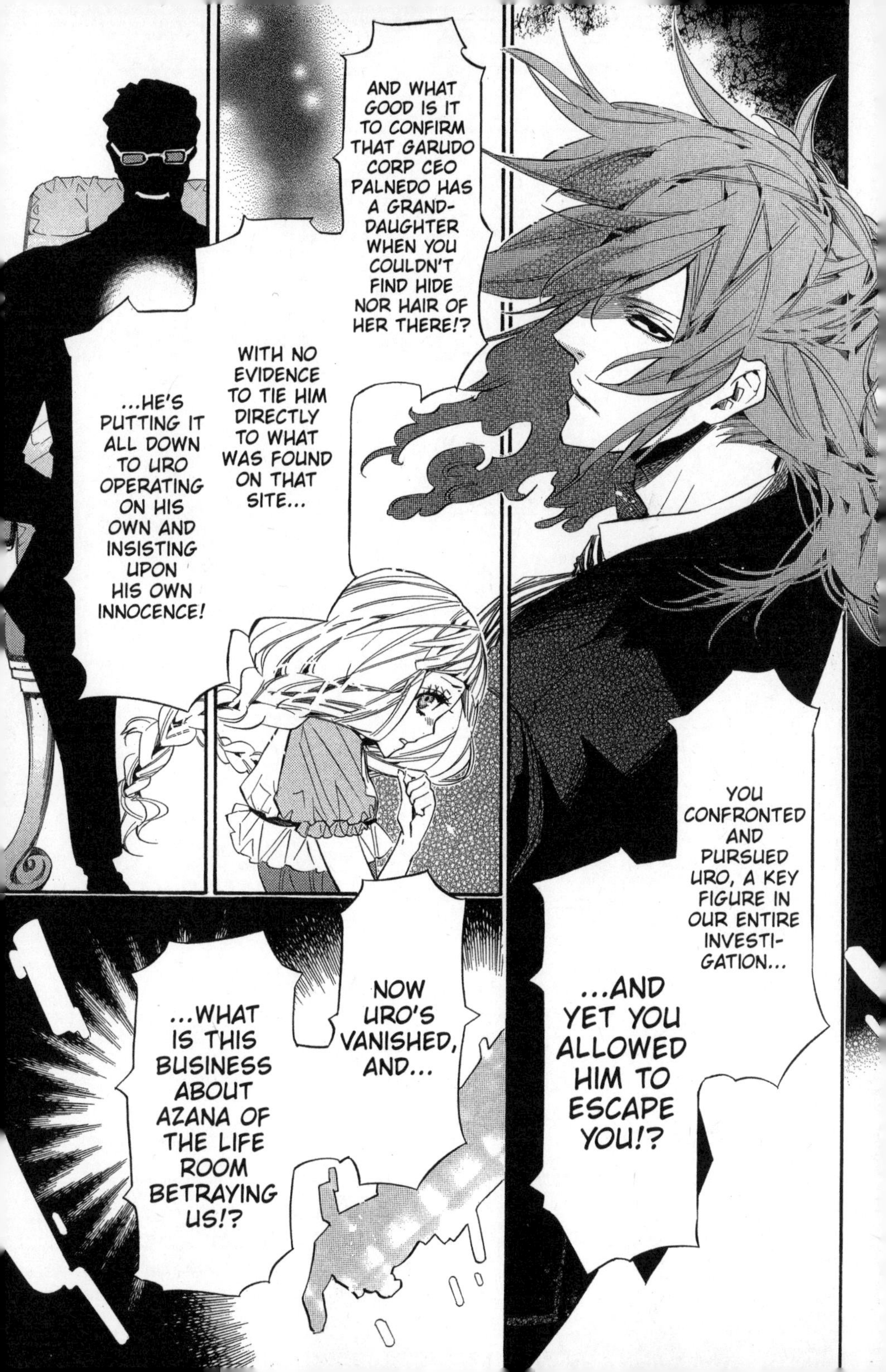
YOU CONFRONTED AND PURSUED URO, A KEY FIGURE IN OUR ENTIRE INVESTI-GATION...
...AND YET YOU ALLOWED HIM TO ESCAPE YOU!?
AND WHAT GOOD IS IT TO CONFIRM THAT GARUDO CORP CEO PALNEDO HAS A GRAND-DAUGHTER WHEN YOU COULDN'T FIND HIDE NOR HAIR OF HER THERE!?
WITH NO EVIDENCE TO TIE HIM DIRECTLY TO WHAT WAS FOUND ON THAT SITE...
...HE'S PUTTING IT ALL DOWN TO URO OPERATING ON HIS OWN AND INSISTING UPON HIS OWN INNOCENCE!
NOW URO'S VANISHED, AND...
...WHAT IS THIS BUSINESS ABOUT AZANA OF THE LIFE ROOM BETRAYING US!?

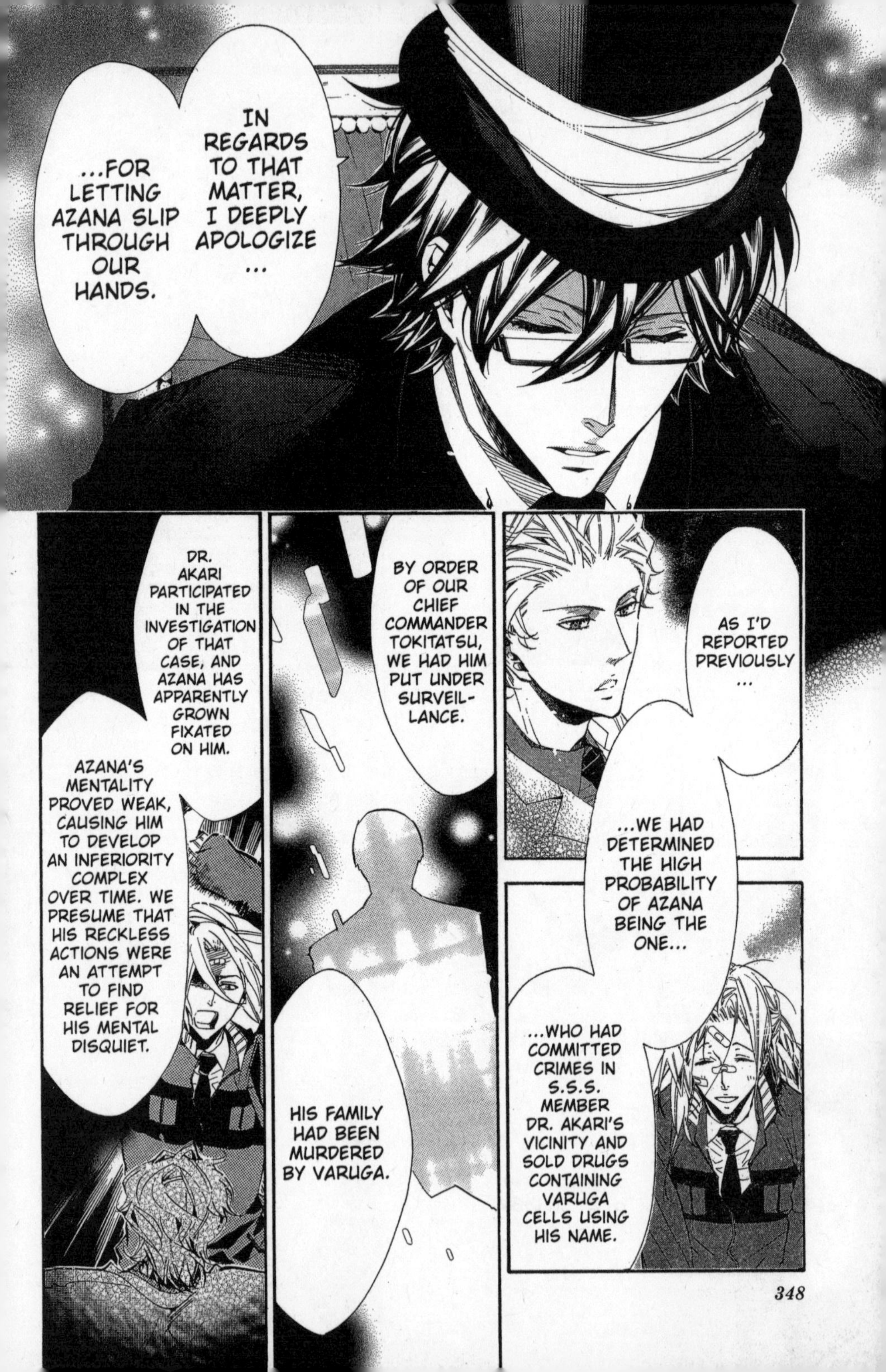
IN REGARDS TO THAT MATTER, I DEEPLY APOLOGIZE...
...FOR LETTING AZANA SLIP THROUGH OUR HANDS.
AS I'D REPORTED PREVIOUSLY...
...WE HAD DETERMINED THE HIGH PROBABILITY OF AZANA BEING THE ONE...
...WHO HAD COMMITTED CRIMES IN S.S.S. MEMBER DR. AKARI'S VICINITY AND SOLD DRUGS CONTAINING VARUGA CELLS USING HIS NAME.
BY ORDER OF OUR CHIEF COMMANDER TOKITATSU, WE HAD HIM PUT UNDER SURVEIL-LANCE.
HIS FAMILY HAD BEEN MURDERED BY VARUGA.
DR. AKARI PARTICIPATED IN THE INVESTIGATION OF THAT CASE, AND AZANA HAS APPARENTLY GROWN FIXATED ON HIM.
AZANA'S MENTALITY PROVED WEAK, CAUSING HIM TO DEVELOP AN INFERIORITY COMPLEX OVER TIME. WE PRESUME THAT HIS RECKLESS ACTIONS WERE AN ATTEMPT TO FIND RELIEF FOR HIS MENTAL DISQUIET.

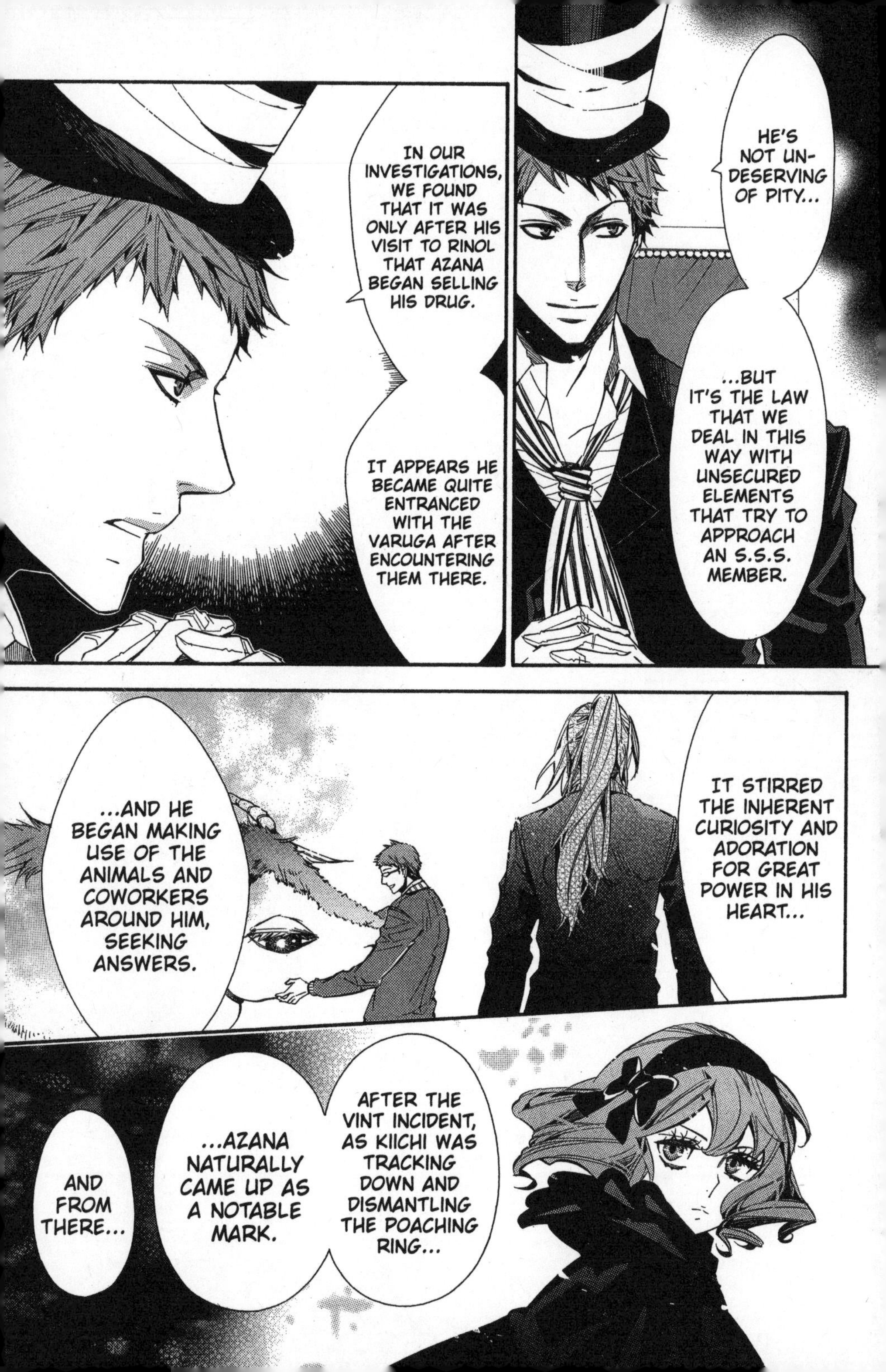
HE'S NOT UN-DESERVING OF PITY...
...BUT IT'S THE LAW THAT WE DEAL IN THIS WAY WITH UNSECURED ELEMENTS THAT TRY TO APPROACH AN S.S.S. MEMBER.
IN OUR INVESTIGATIONS, WE FOUND THAT IT WAS ONLY AFTER HIS VISIT TO RINOL THAT AZANA BEGAN SELLING HIS DRUG.
IT APPEARS HE BECAME QUITE ENTRANCED WITH THE VARUGA AFTER ENCOUNTERING THEM THERE.
IT STIRRED THE INHERENT CURIOSITY AND ADORATION FOR GREAT POWER IN HIS HEART...
...AND HE BEGAN MAKING USE OF THE ANIMALS AND COWORKERS AROUND HIM, SEEKING ANSWERS.
AFTER THE VINT INCIDENT, AS KIICHI WAS TRACKING DOWN AND DISMANTLING THE POACHING RING...
...AZANA NATURALLY CAME UP AS A NOTABLE MARK.
AND FROM THERE...

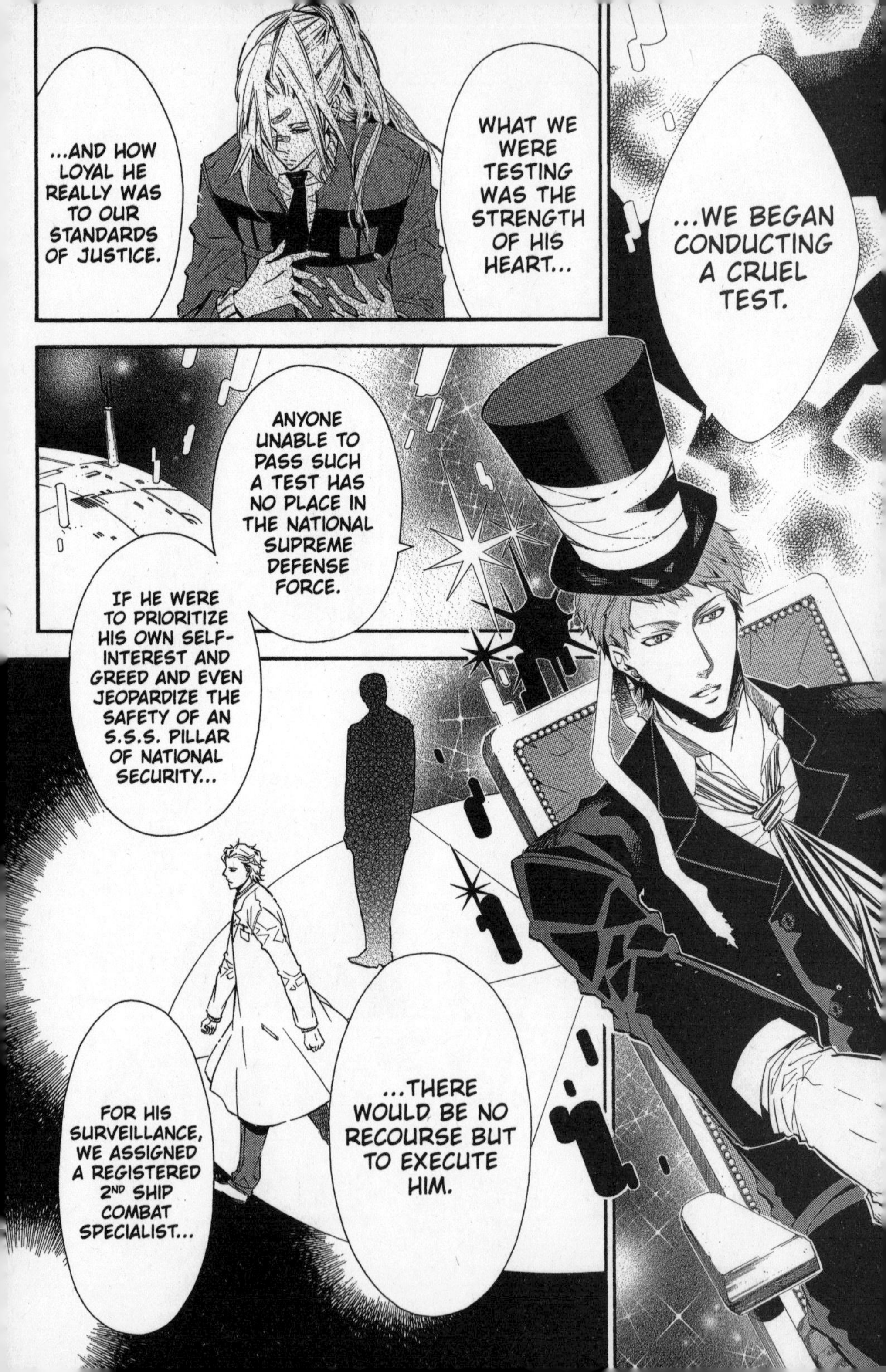
...WE BEGAN CONDUCTING A CRUEL TEST.
WHAT WE WERE TESTING WAS THE STRENGTH OF HIS HEART...
...AND HOW LOYAL HE REALLY WAS TO OUR STANDARDS OF JUSTICE.
ANYONE UNABLE TO PASS SUCH A TEST HAS NO PLACE IN THE NATIONAL SUPREME DEFENSE FORCE.
IF HE WERE TO PRIORITIZE HIS OWN SELF-INTEREST AND GREED AND EVEN JEOPARDIZE THE SAFETY OF AN S.S.S. PILLAR OF NATIONAL SECURITY...
...THERE WOULD BE NO RECOURSE BUT TO EXECUTE HIM.
FOR HIS SURVEILLANCE, WE ASSIGNED A REGISTERED 2ND SHIP COMBAT SPECIALIST...

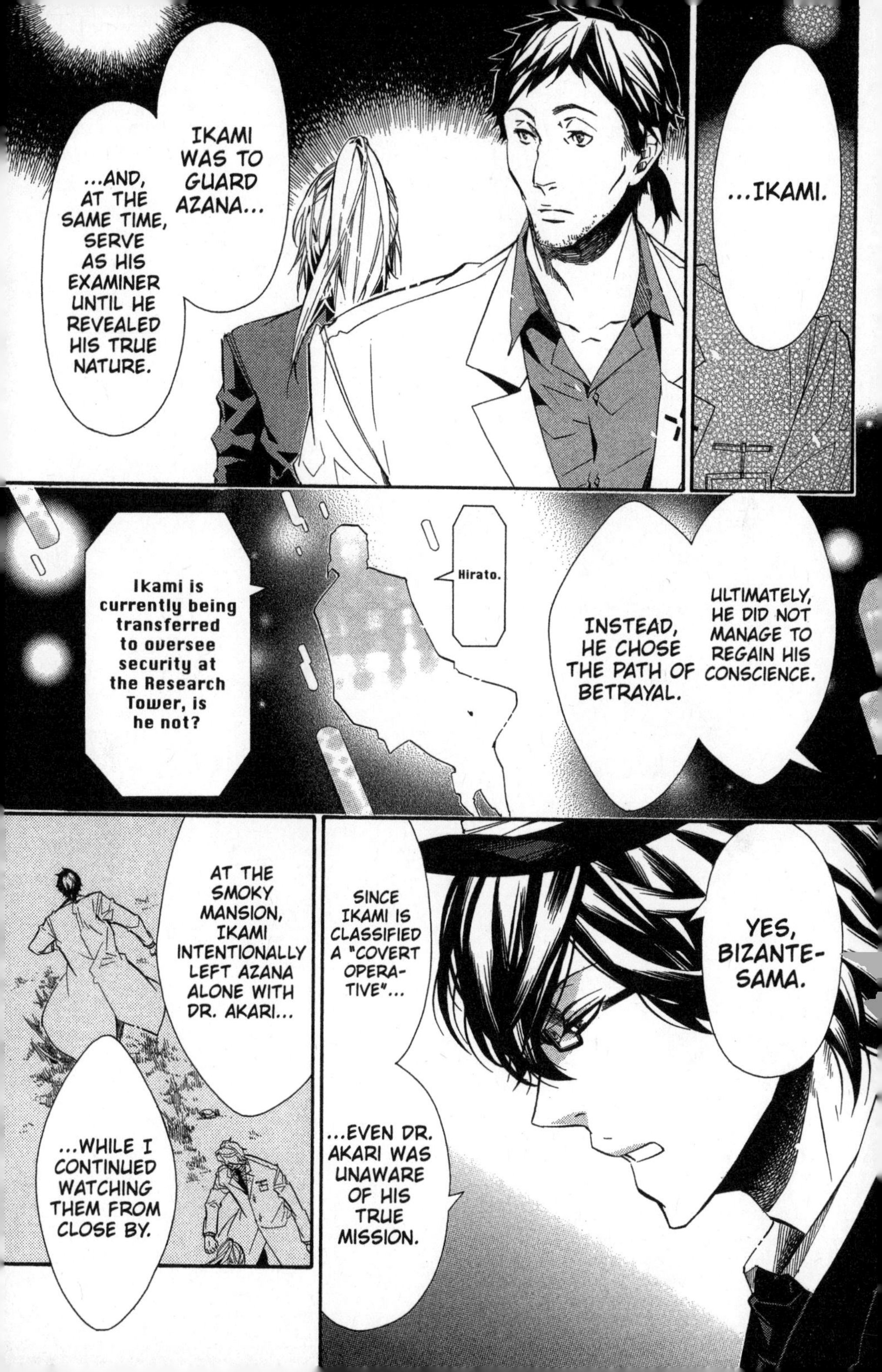
...IKAMI.
IKAMI WAS TO GUARD AZANA...
...AND, AT THE SAME TIME, SERVE AS HIS EXAMINER UNTIL HE REVEALED HIS TRUE NATURE.
ULTIMATELY, HE DID NOT MANAGE TO REGAIN HIS CONSCIENCE.
INSTEAD, HE CHOSE THE PATH OF BETRAYAL.
Hirato.
Ikami is currently being transferred to oversee security at the Research Tower, is he not?
YES, BIZANTE-SAMA.
SINCE IKAMI IS CLASSIFIED A "COVERT OPERATIVE"...
...EVEN DR. AKARI WAS UNAWARE OF HIS TRUE MISSION.
AT THE SMOKY MANSION, IKAMI INTENTIONALLY LEFT AZANA ALONE WITH DR. AKARI...
...WHILE I CONTINUED WATCHING THEM FROM CLOSE BY.

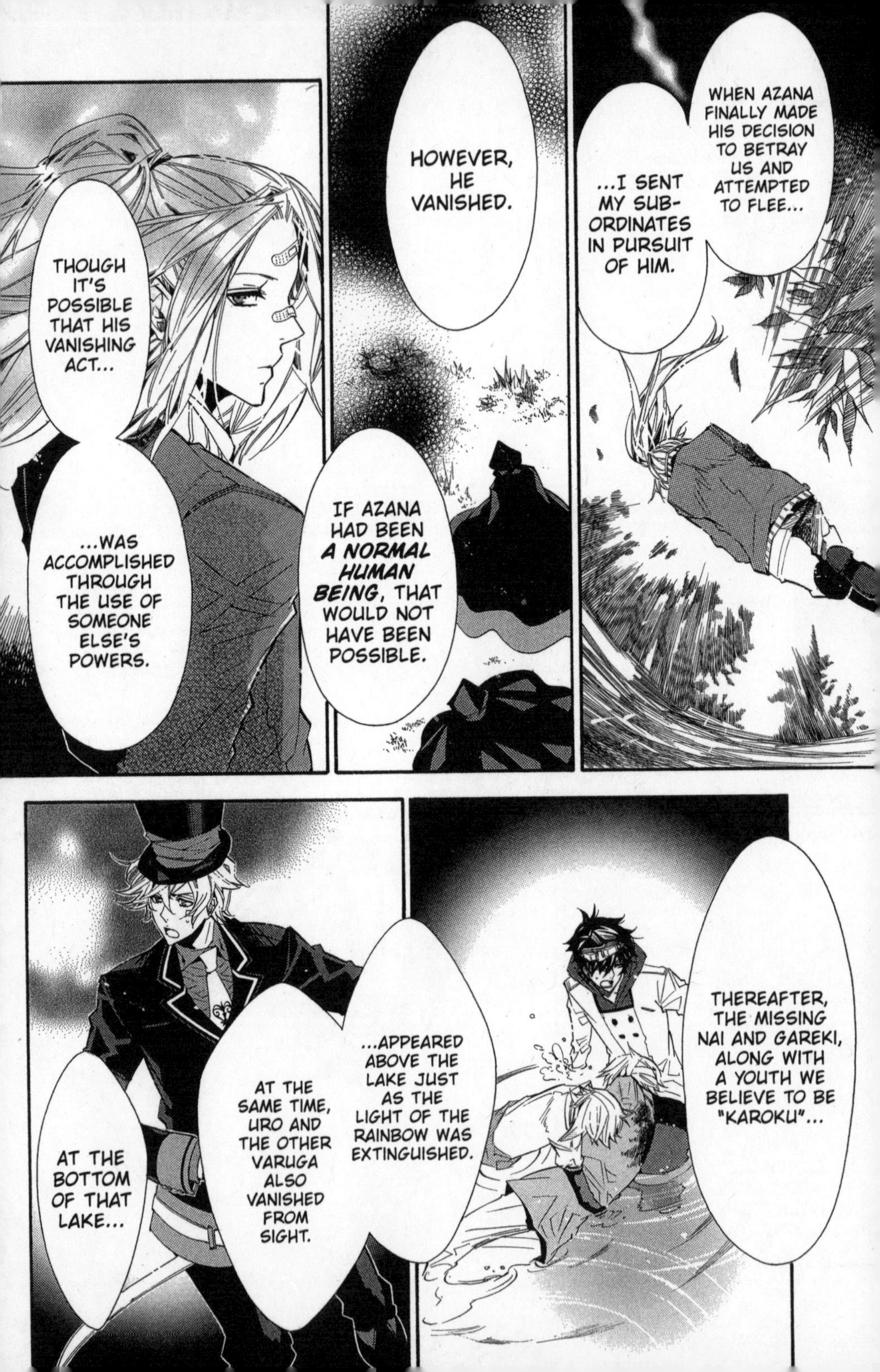
WHEN AZANA FINALLY MADE HIS DECISION TO BETRAY US AND ATTEMPTED TO FLEE...
...I SENT MY SUB-ORDINATES IN PURSUIT OF HIM.
HOWEVER, HE VANISHED.
IF AZANA HAD BEEN ***A NORMAL HUMAN BEING***, THAT WOULD NOT HAVE BEEN POSSIBLE.
THOUGH IT'S POSSIBLE THAT HIS VANISHING ACT...
...WAS ACCOMPLISHED THROUGH THE USE OF SOMEONE ELSE'S POWERS.
THEREAFTER, THE MISSING NAI AND GAREKI, ALONG WITH A YOUTH WE BELIEVE TO BE "KAROKU"...
...APPEARED ABOVE THE LAKE JUST AS THE LIGHT OF THE RAINBOW WAS EXTINGUISHED.
AT THE SAME TIME, URO AND THE OTHER VARUGA ALSO VANISHED FROM SIGHT.
AT THE BOTTOM OF THAT LAKE...

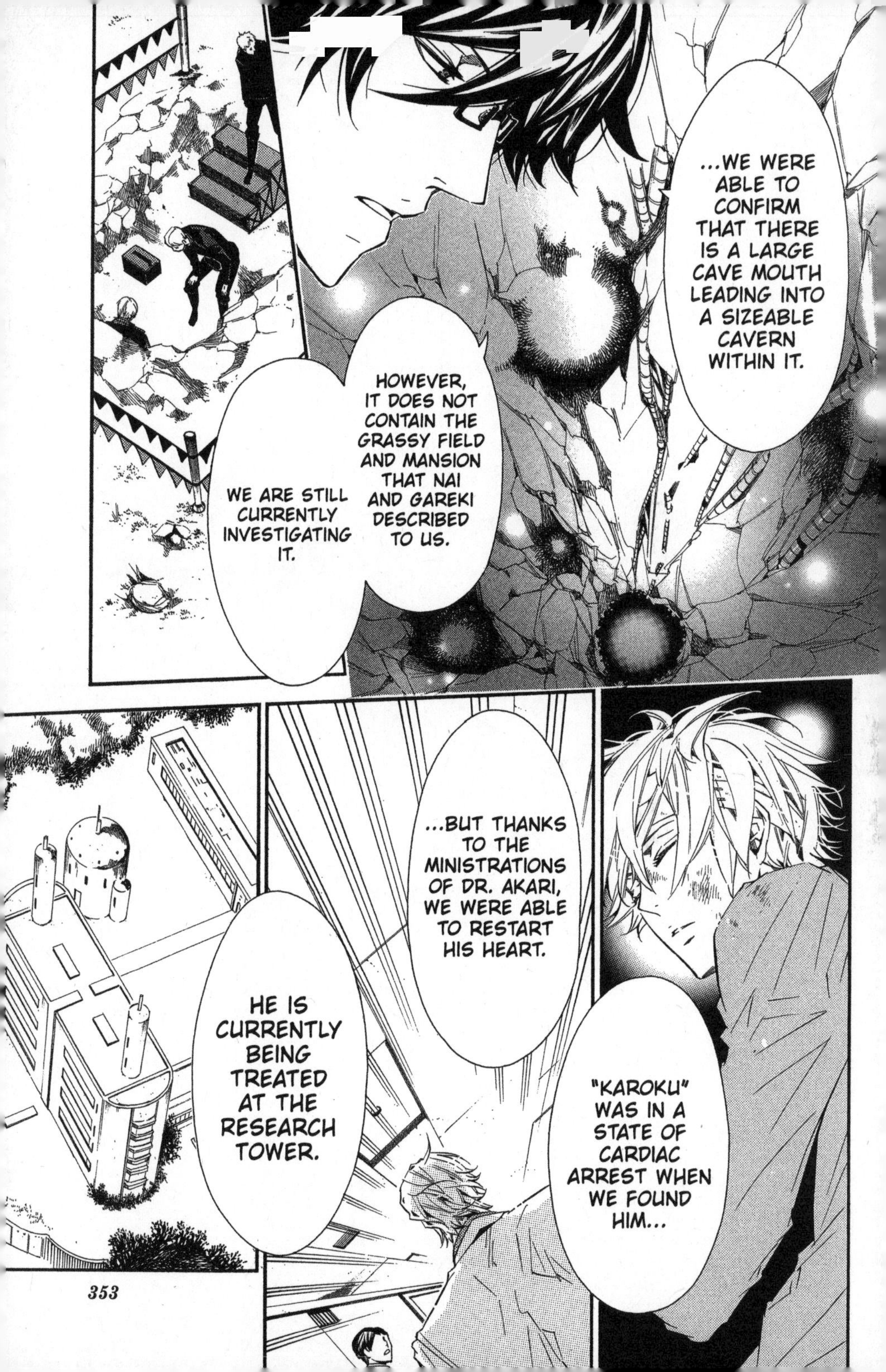
...WE WERE ABLE TO CONFIRM THAT THERE IS A LARGE CAVE MOUTH LEADING INTO A SIZEABLE CAVERN WITHIN IT.
HOWEVER, IT DOES NOT CONTAIN THE GRASSY FIELD AND MANSION THAT NAI AND GAREKI DESCRIBED TO US.
WE ARE STILL CURRENTLY INVESTIGATING IT.
"KAROKU" WAS IN A STATE OF CARDIAC ARREST WHEN WE FOUND HIM...
...BUT THANKS TO THE MINISTRATIONS OF DR. AKARI, WE WERE ABLE TO RESTART HIS HEART.
HE IS CURRENTLY BEING TREATED AT THE RESEARCH TOWER.

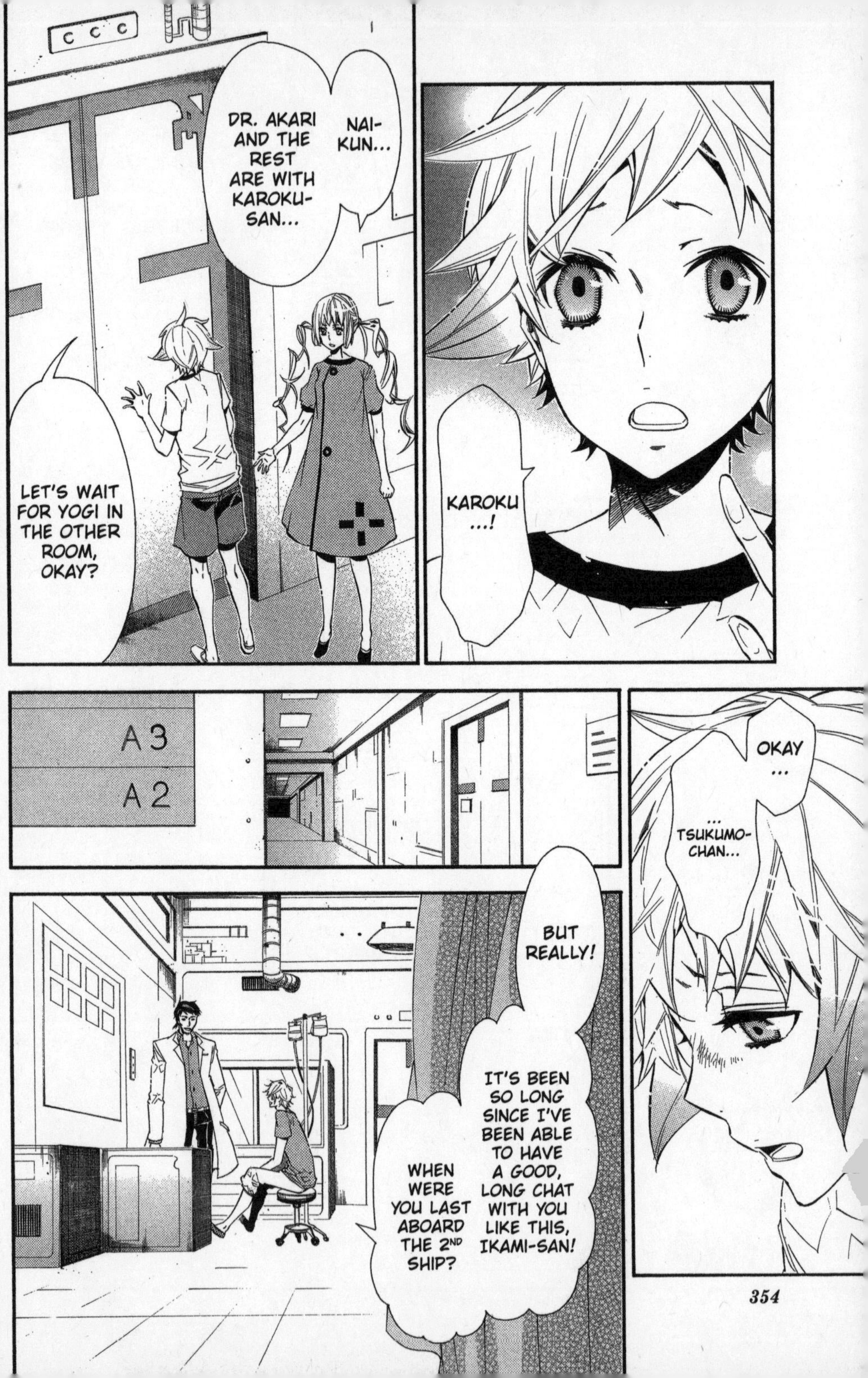
KAROKU ...!
NAI-KUN...
DR. AKARI AND THE REST ARE WITH KAROKU-SAN...
LET'S WAIT FOR YOGI IN THE OTHER ROOM, OKAY?
OKAY ...
... TSUKUMO-CHAN...
A3
A2
BUT REALLY!
IT'S BEEN SO LONG SINCE I'VE BEEN ABLE TO HAVE A GOOD, LONG CHAT WITH YOU LIKE THIS, IKAMI-SAN!
WHEN WERE YOU LAST ABOARD THE 2ND SHIP?

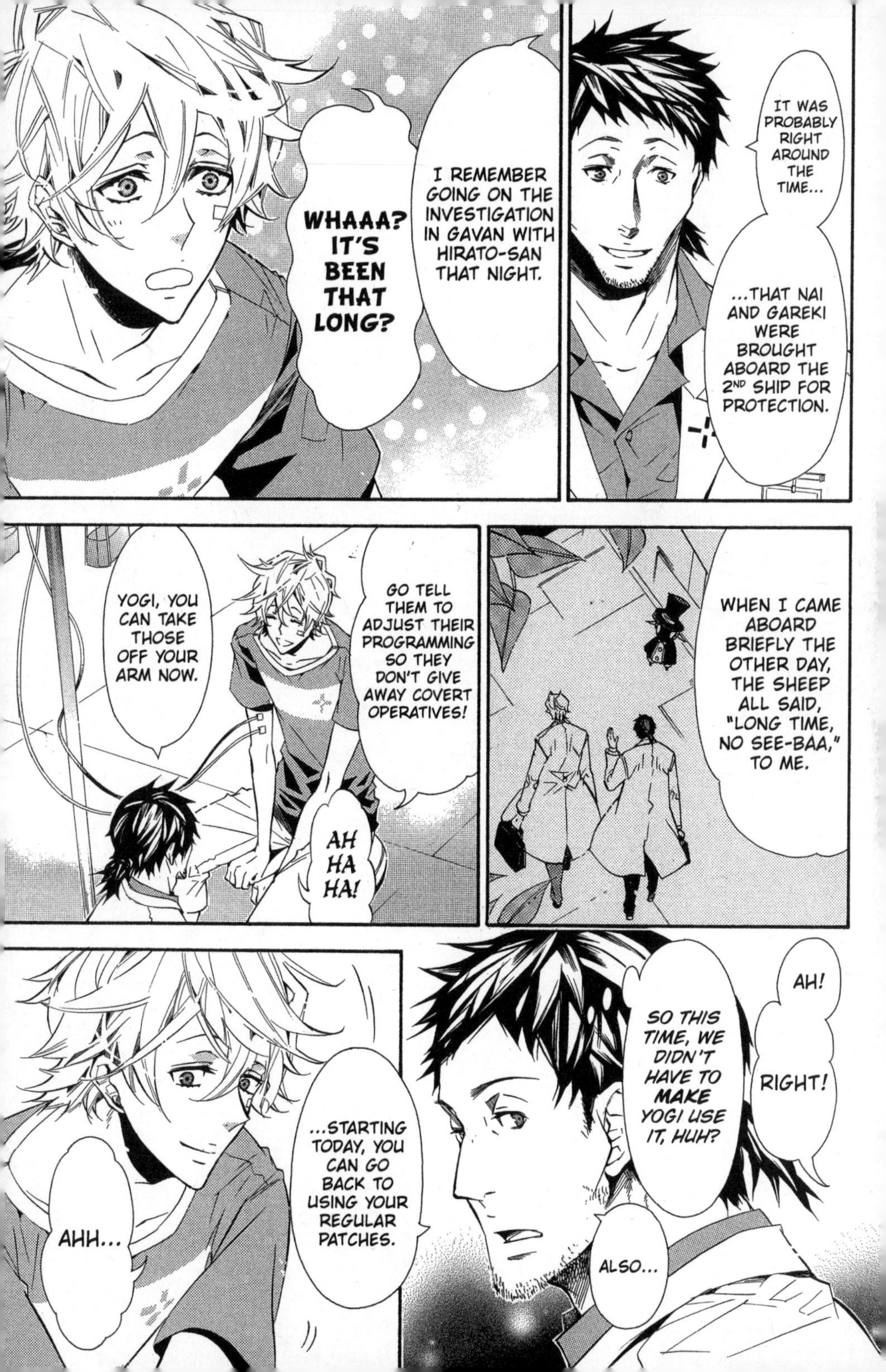
IT WAS PROBABLY RIGHT AROUND THE TIME...
...THAT NAI AND GAREKI WERE BROUGHT ABOARD THE 2ND SHIP FOR PROTECTION.
I REMEMBER GOING ON THE INVESTIGATION IN GAVAN WITH HIRATO-SAN THAT NIGHT.
WHAAA? IT'S BEEN THAT LONG?
WHEN I CAME ABOARD BRIEFLY THE OTHER DAY, THE SHEEP ALL SAID, "LONG TIME, NO SEE-BAA," TO ME.
GO TELL THEM TO ADJUST THEIR PROGRAMMING SO THEY DON'T GIVE AWAY COVERT OPERATIVES!
AH HA HA!
YOGI, YOU CAN TAKE THOSE OFF YOUR ARM NOW.
AH!
RIGHT!
SO THIS TIME, WE DIDN'T HAVE TO MAKE YOGI USE IT, HUH?
ALSO...
...STARTING TODAY, YOU CAN GO BACK TO USING YOUR REGULAR PATCHES.
AHH...

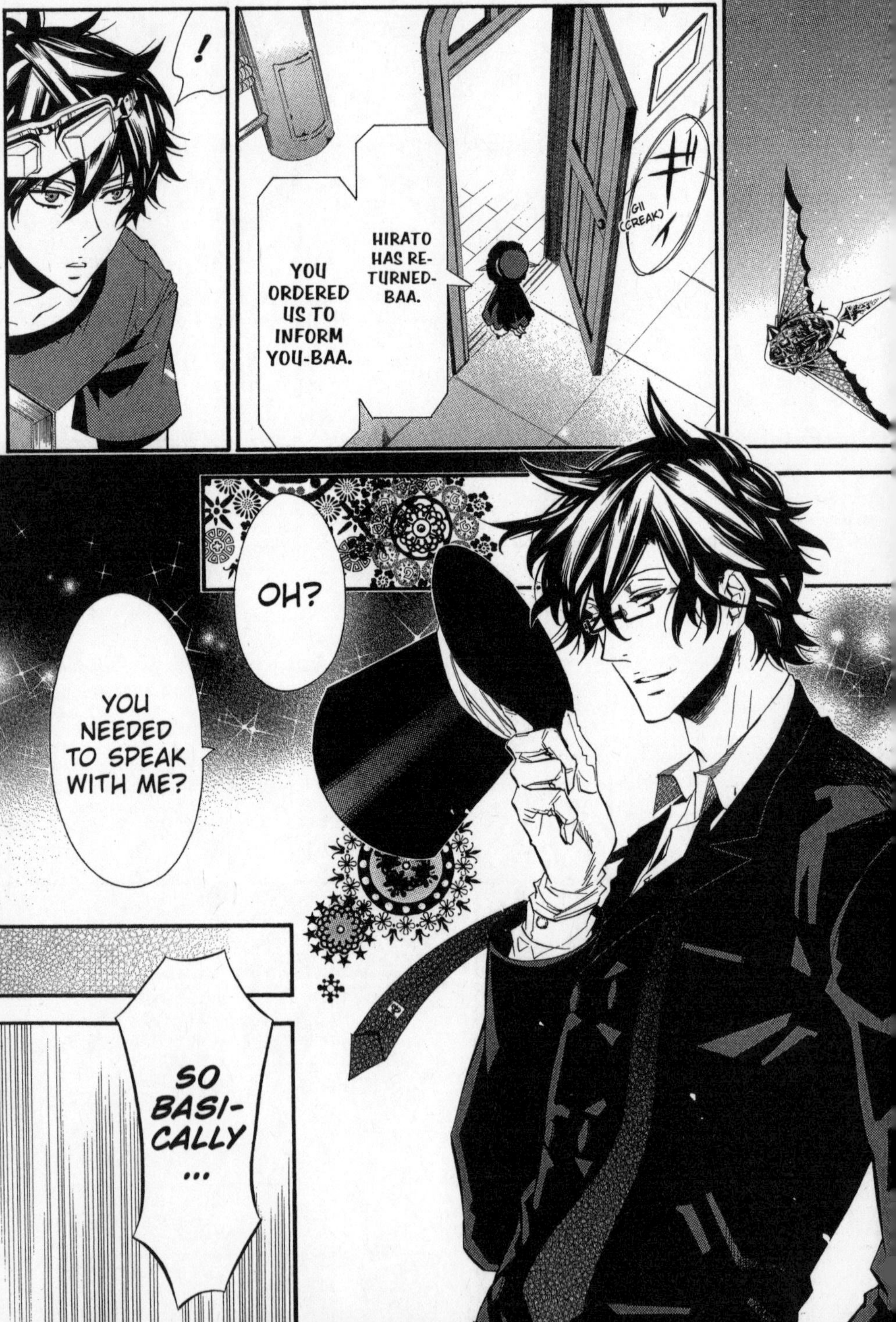
GII (CREAK)
HIRATO HAS RE-TURNED-BAA.
YOU ORDERED US TO INFORM YOU-BAA.
!
OH?
YOU NEEDED TO SPEAK WITH ME?
SO BASI-CALLY ...

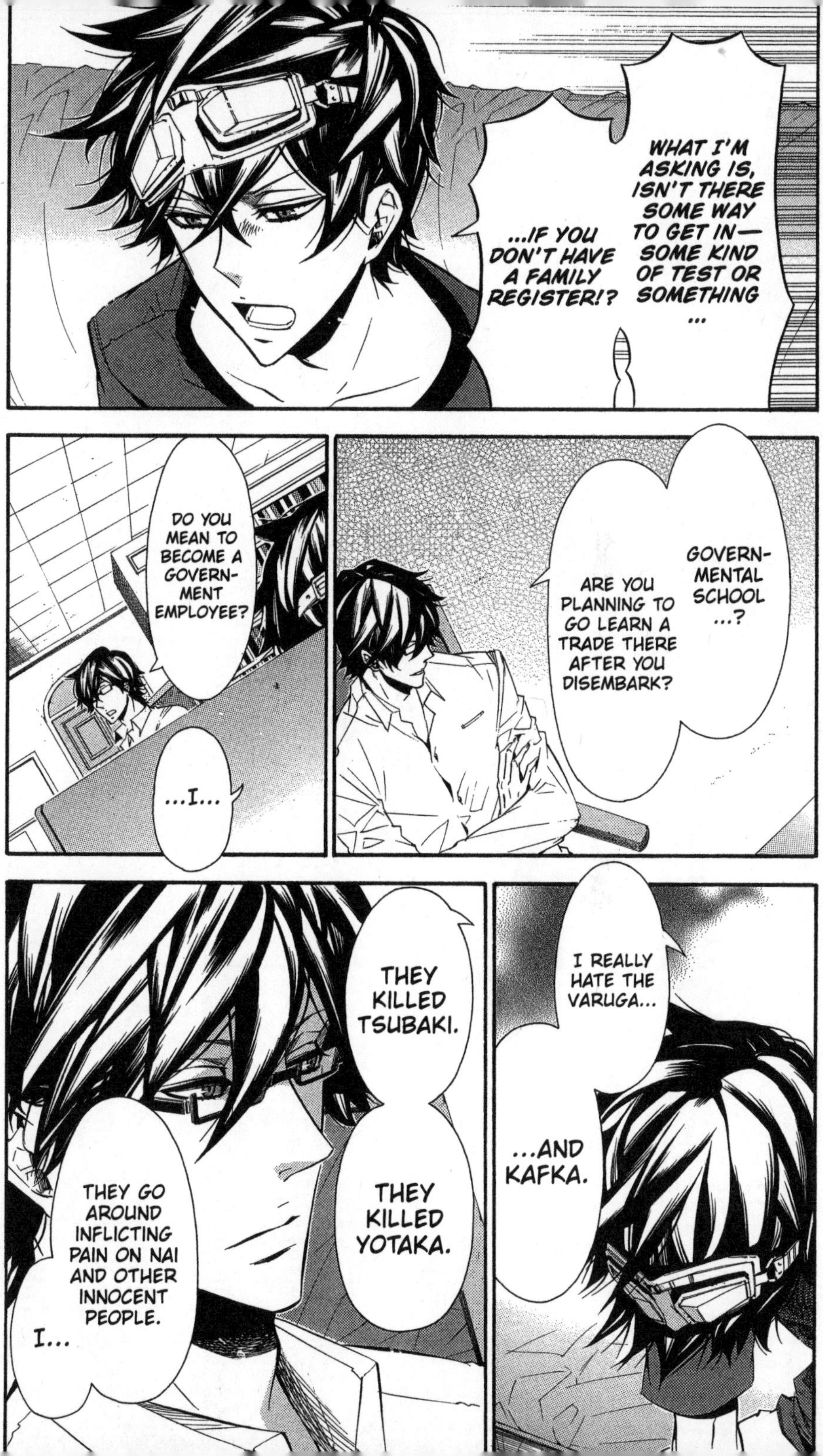
WHAT I'M ASKING IS, ISN'T THERE SOME WAY TO GET IN— SOME KIND OF TEST OR SOMETHING ...
...IF YOU DON'T HAVE A FAMILY REGISTER!?
GOVERNMENTAL SCHOOL ...?
ARE YOU PLANNING TO GO LEARN A TRADE THERE AFTER YOU DISEMBARK?
DO YOU MEAN TO BECOME A GOVERNMENT EMPLOYEE?
...I...
I REALLY HATE THE VARUGA...
...AND KAFKA.
THEY KILLED TSUBAKI.
THEY KILLED YOTAKA.
THEY GO AROUND INFLICTING PAIN ON NAI AND OTHER INNOCENT PEOPLE.
I...

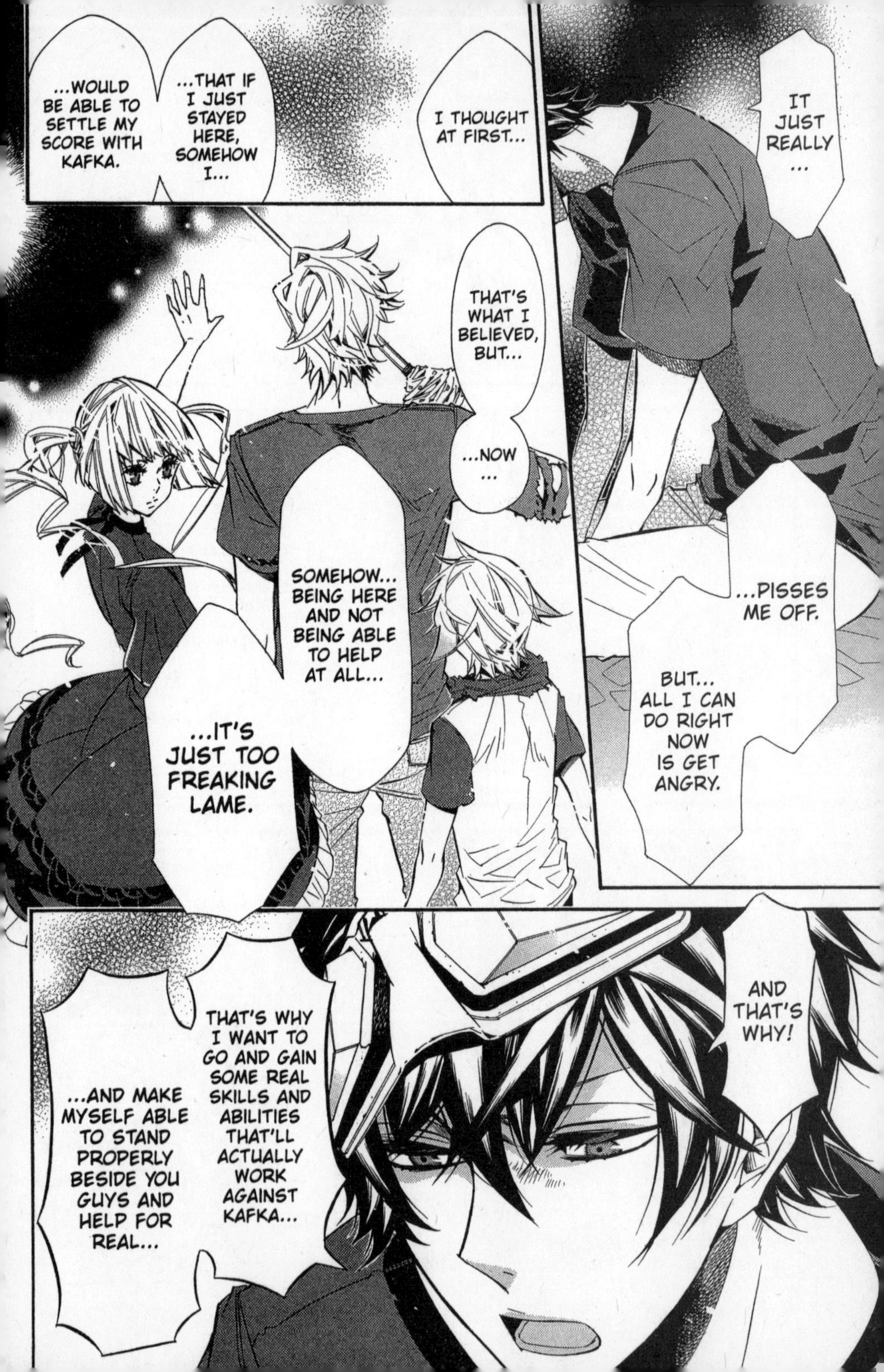
IT JUST REALLY...
...PISSES ME OFF.
BUT... ALL I CAN DO RIGHT NOW IS GET ANGRY.
I THOUGHT AT FIRST...
...THAT IF I JUST STAYED HERE, SOMEHOW I...
...WOULD BE ABLE TO SETTLE MY SCORE WITH KAFKA.
THAT'S WHAT I BELIEVED, BUT...
...NOW...
SOMEHOW... BEING HERE AND NOT BEING ABLE TO HELP AT ALL...
...IT'S JUST TOO FREAKING LAME.
AND THAT'S WHY!
THAT'S WHY I WANT TO GO AND GAIN SOME REAL SKILLS AND ABILITIES THAT'LL ACTUALLY WORK AGAINST KAFKA...
...AND MAKE MYSELF ABLE TO STAND PROPERLY BESIDE YOU GUYS AND HELP FOR REAL...

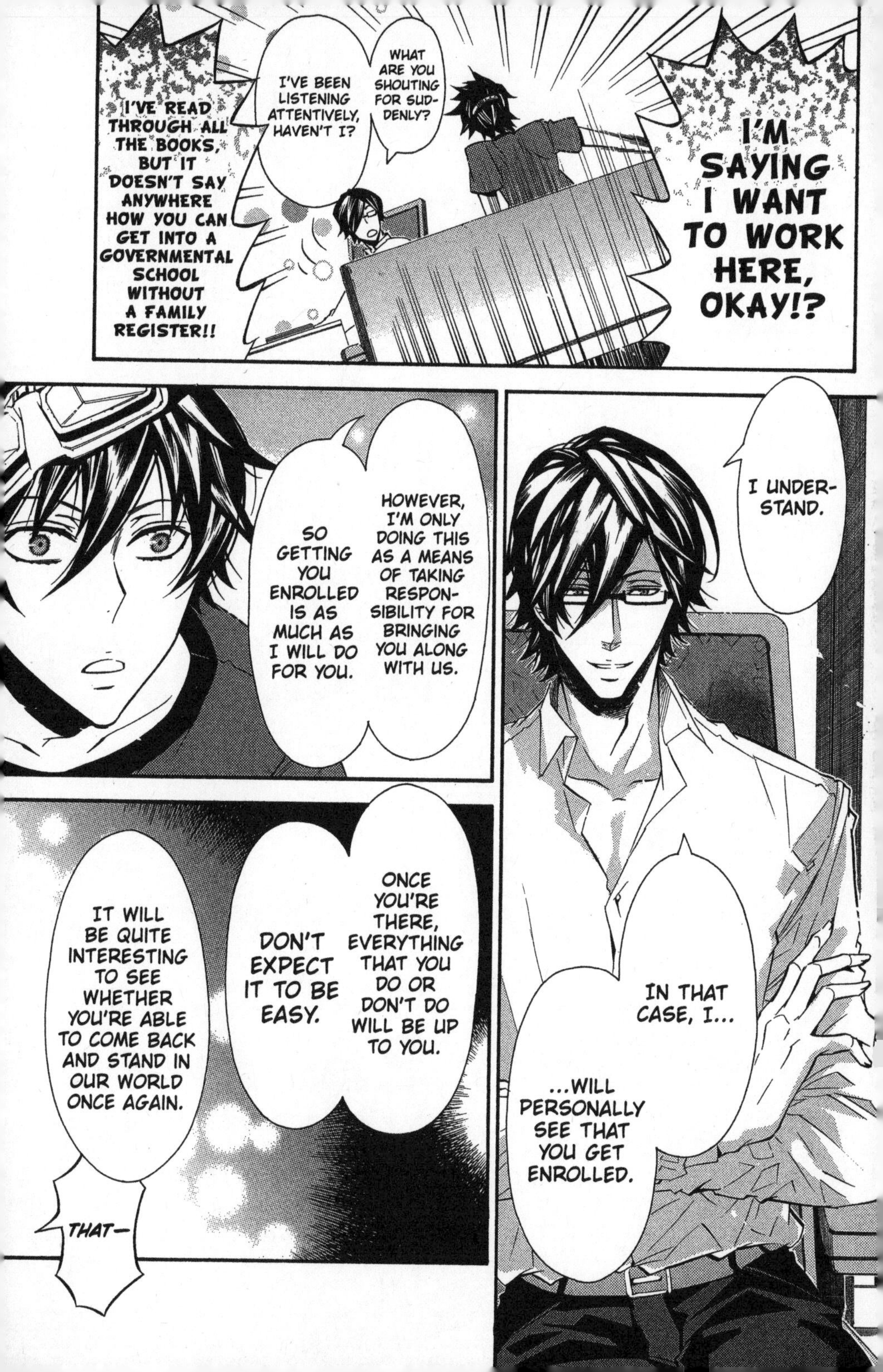
I'M SAYING I WANT TO WORK HERE, OKAY!?
WHAT ARE YOU SHOUTING FOR SUD-DENLY?
I'VE BEEN LISTENING ATTENTIVELY, HAVEN'T I?
I'VE READ THROUGH ALL THE BOOKS, BUT IT DOESN'T SAY ANYWHERE HOW YOU CAN GET INTO A GOVERNMENTAL SCHOOL WITHOUT A FAMILY REGISTER!!
I UNDER-STAND.
IN THAT CASE, I...
...WILL PERSONALLY SEE THAT YOU GET ENROLLED.
HOWEVER, I'M ONLY DOING THIS AS A MEANS OF TAKING RESPON-SIBILITY FOR BRINGING YOU ALONG WITH US.
SO GETTING YOU ENROLLED IS AS MUCH AS I WILL DO FOR YOU.
ONCE YOU'RE THERE, EVERYTHING THAT YOU DO OR DON'T DO WILL BE UP TO YOU.
DON'T EXPECT IT TO BE EASY.
IT WILL BE QUITE INTERESTING TO SEE WHETHER YOU'RE ABLE TO COME BACK AND STAND IN OUR WORLD ONCE AGAIN.
THAT—

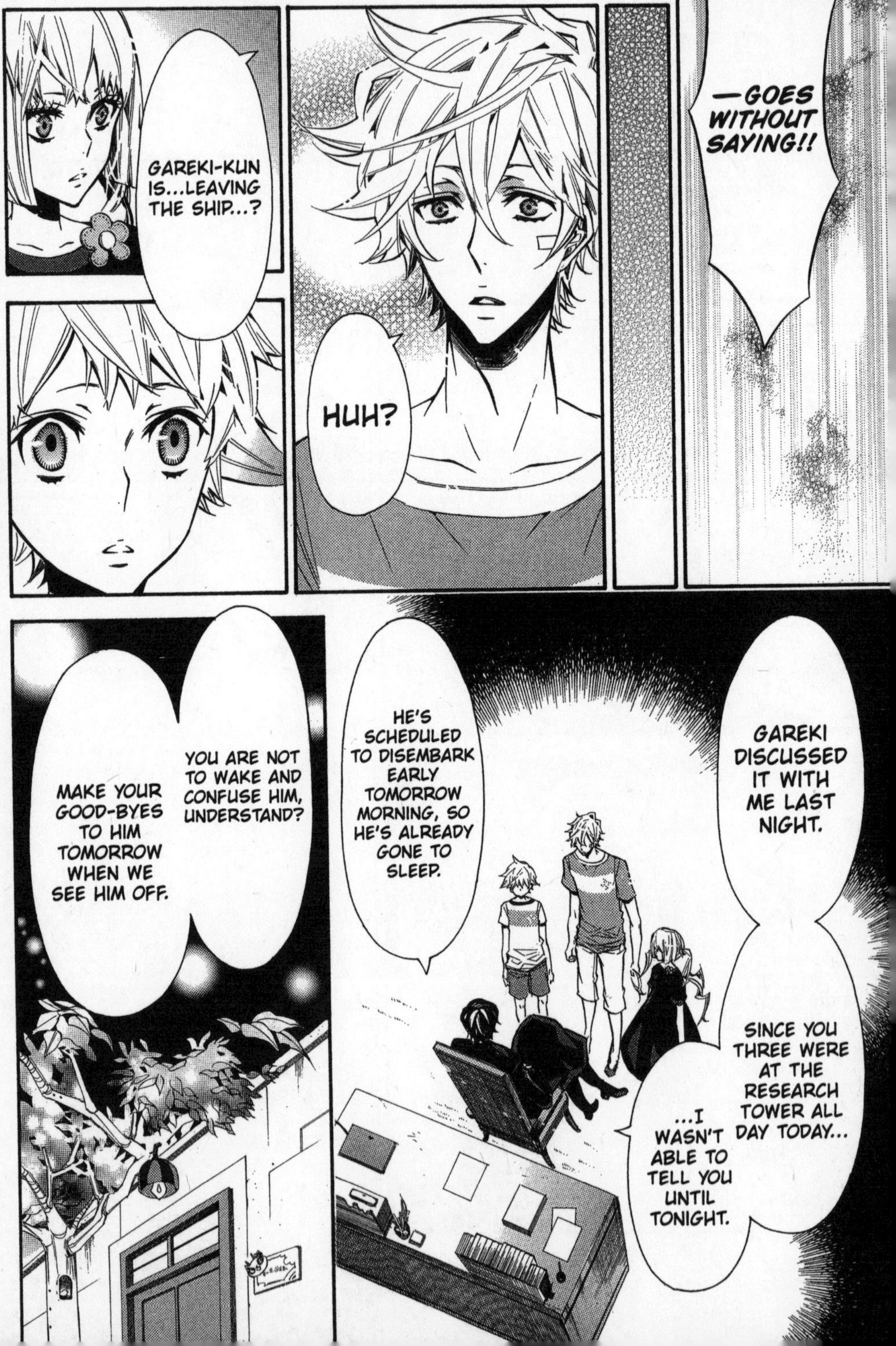
—GOES WITHOUT SAYING!!
HUH?
GAREKI-KUN IS...LEAVING THE SHIP...?
GAREKI DISCUSSED IT WITH ME LAST NIGHT.
SINCE YOU THREE WERE AT THE RESEARCH TOWER ALL DAY TODAY...
...I WASN'T ABLE TO TELL YOU UNTIL TONIGHT.
HE'S SCHEDULED TO DISEMBARK EARLY TOMORROW MORNING, SO HE'S ALREADY GONE TO SLEEP.
YOU ARE NOT TO WAKE AND CONFUSE HIM, UNDERSTAND?
MAKE YOUR GOOD-BYES TO HIM TOMORROW WHEN WE SEE HIM OFF.

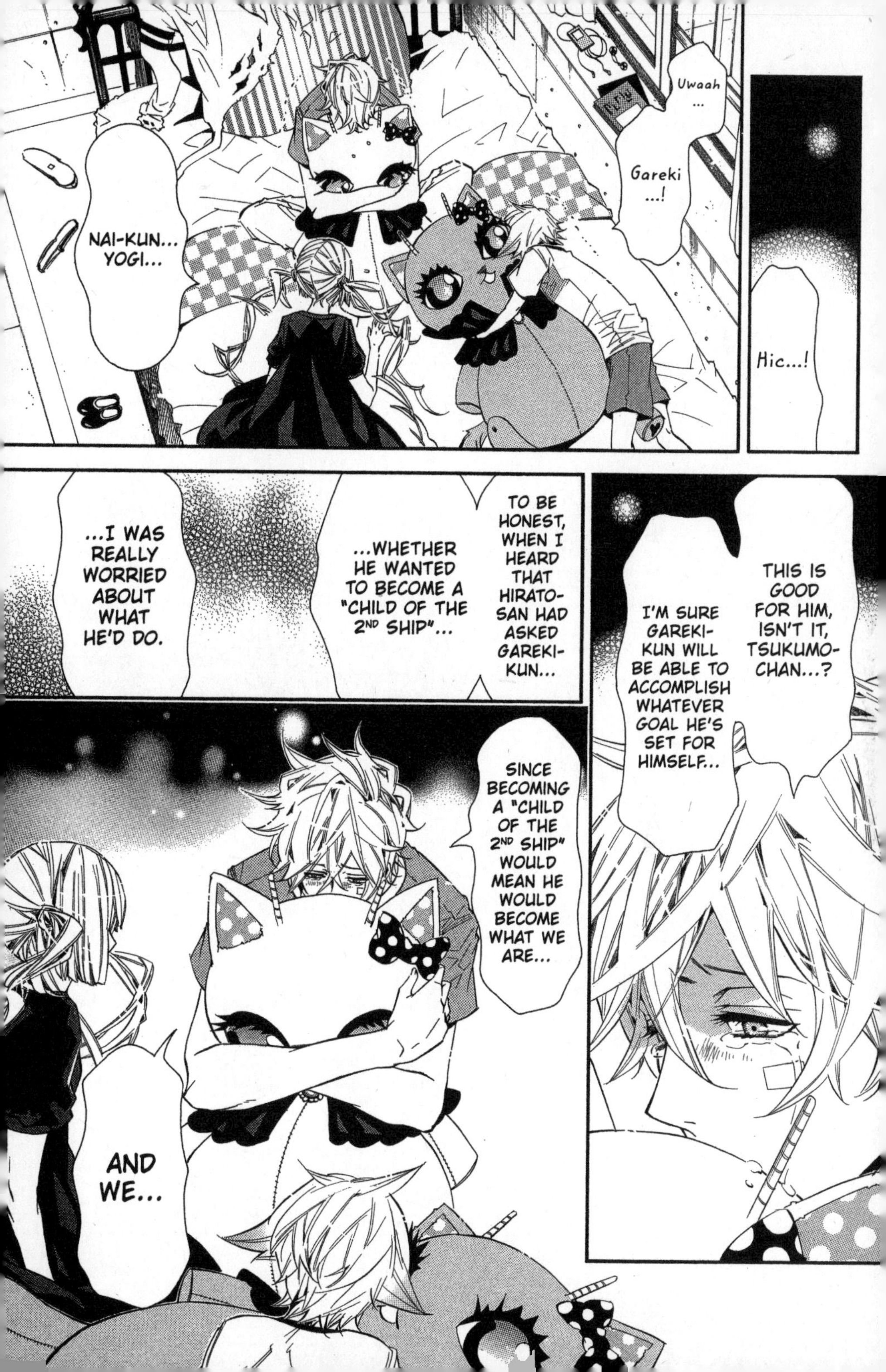
Hic...!
Uwaah ...
Gareki ...!
NAI-KUN... YOGI...
THIS IS GOOD FOR HIM, ISN'T IT, TSUKUMO-CHAN...?
I'M SURE GAREKI-KUN WILL BE ABLE TO ACCOMPLISH WHATEVER GOAL HE'S SET FOR HIMSELF...
TO BE HONEST, WHEN I HEARD THAT HIRATO-SAN HAD ASKED GAREKI-KUN...
...WHETHER HE WANTED TO BECOME A "CHILD OF THE 2ND SHIP"...
...I WAS REALLY WORRIED ABOUT WHAT HE'D DO.
SINCE BECOMING A "CHILD OF THE 2ND SHIP" WOULD MEAN HE WOULD BECOME WHAT WE ARE...
AND WE...

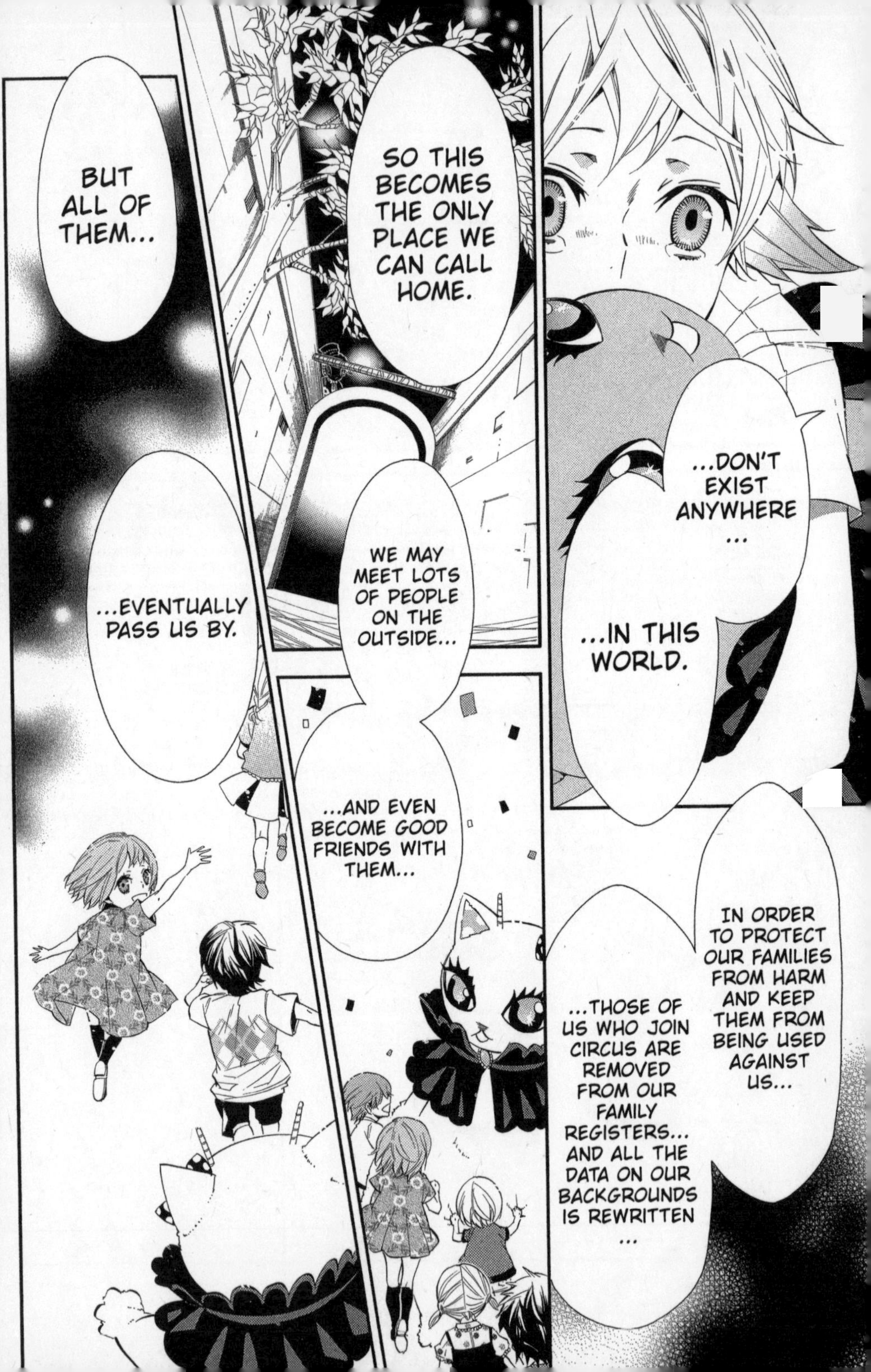
...DON'T EXIST ANYWHERE ...
...IN THIS WORLD.
IN ORDER TO PROTECT OUR FAMILIES FROM HARM AND KEEP THEM FROM BEING USED AGAINST US...
...THOSE OF US WHO JOIN CIRCUS ARE REMOVED FROM OUR FAMILY REGISTERS... AND ALL THE DATA ON OUR BACKGROUNDS IS REWRITTEN ...
SO THIS BECOMES THE ONLY PLACE WE CAN CALL HOME.
WE MAY MEET LOTS OF PEOPLE ON THE OUTSIDE...
...AND EVEN BECOME GOOD FRIENDS WITH THEM...
BUT ALL OF THEM...
...EVENTUALLY PASS US BY.

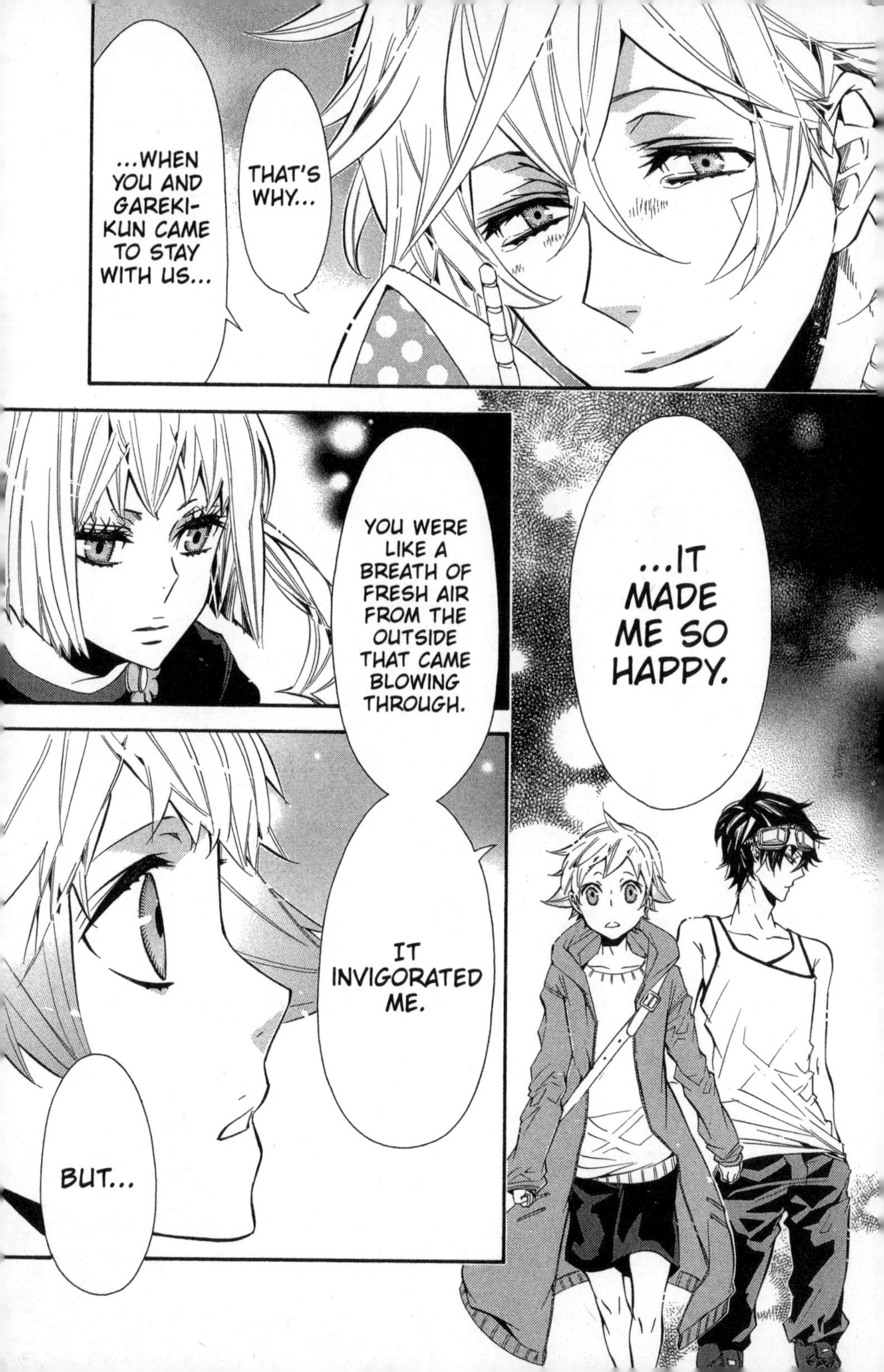
THAT'S WHY...
...WHEN YOU AND GAREKI-KUN CAME TO STAY WITH US...
...IT MADE ME SO HAPPY.
YOU WERE LIKE A BREATH OF FRESH AIR FROM THE OUTSIDE THAT CAME BLOWING THROUGH.
IT INVIGORATED ME.
BUT...

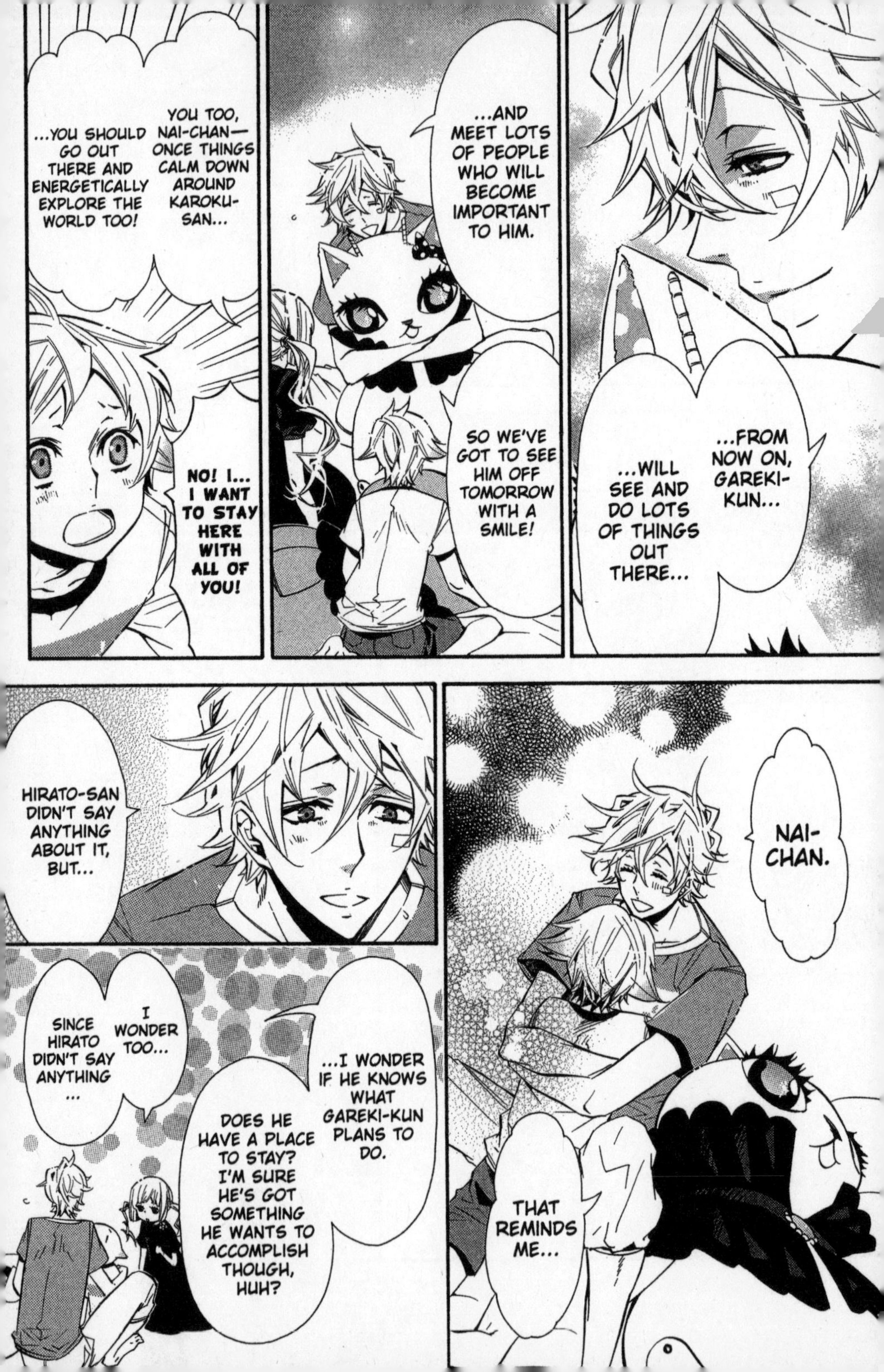
...FROM NOW ON, GAREKI-KUN...
...WILL SEE AND DO LOTS OF THINGS OUT THERE...
...AND MEET LOTS OF PEOPLE WHO WILL BECOME IMPORTANT TO HIM.
SO WE'VE GOT TO SEE HIM OFF TOMORROW WITH A SMILE!
YOU TOO, NAI-CHAN— ONCE THINGS CALM DOWN AROUND KAROKU-SAN...
...YOU SHOULD GO OUT THERE AND ENERGETICALLY EXPLORE THE WORLD TOO!
NO! I... I WANT TO STAY HERE WITH ALL OF YOU!
NAI-CHAN.
THAT REMINDS ME...
HIRATO-SAN DIDN'T SAY ANYTHING ABOUT IT, BUT...
...I WONDER IF HE KNOWS WHAT GAREKI-KUN PLANS TO DO.
DOES HE HAVE A PLACE TO STAY? I'M SURE HE'S GOT SOMETHING HE WANTS TO ACCOMPLISH THOUGH, HUH?
I WONDER TOO...
SINCE HIRATO DIDN'T SAY ANYTHING ...

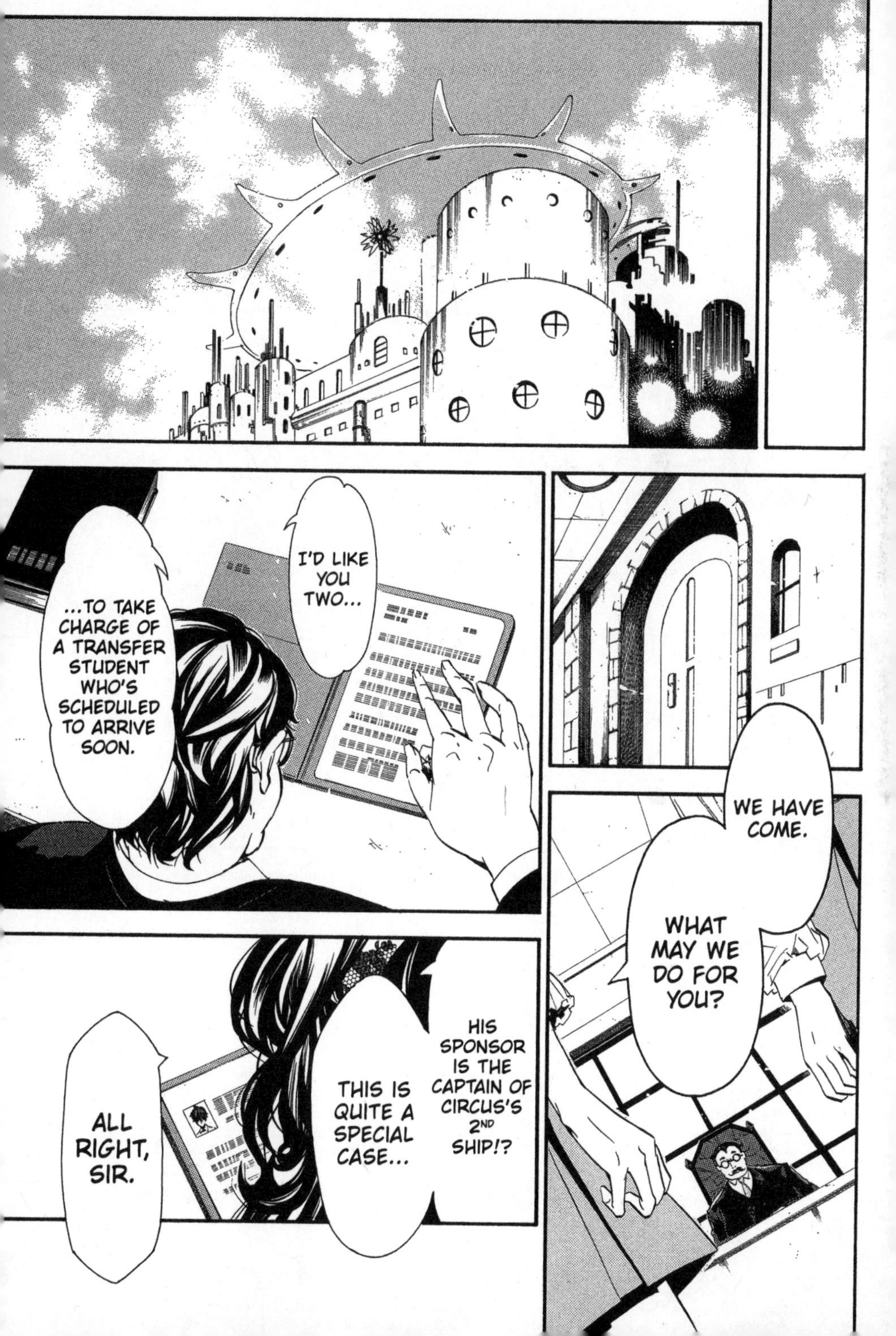
WE HAVE COME.
WHAT MAY WE DO FOR YOU?
I'D LIKE YOU TWO...
...TO TAKE CHARGE OF A TRANSFER STUDENT WHO'S SCHEDULED TO ARRIVE SOON.
HIS SPONSOR IS THE CAPTAIN OF CIRCUS'S 2ND SHIP!?
THIS IS QUITE A SPECIAL CASE...
ALL RIGHT, SIR.

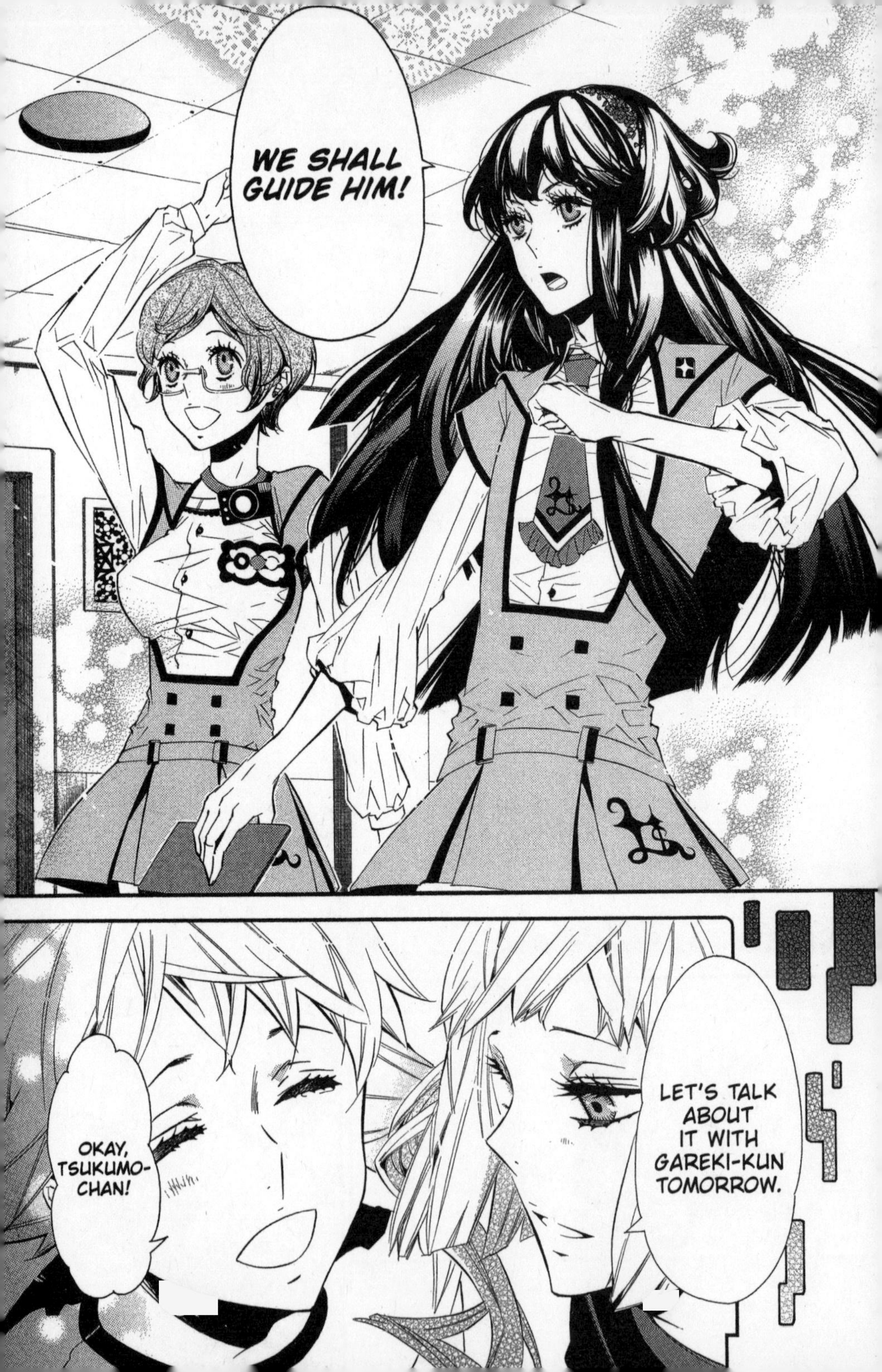
WE SHALL GUIDE HIM!
LET'S TALK ABOUT IT WITH GAREKI-KUN TOMORROW.
OKAY, TSUKUMO-CHAN!

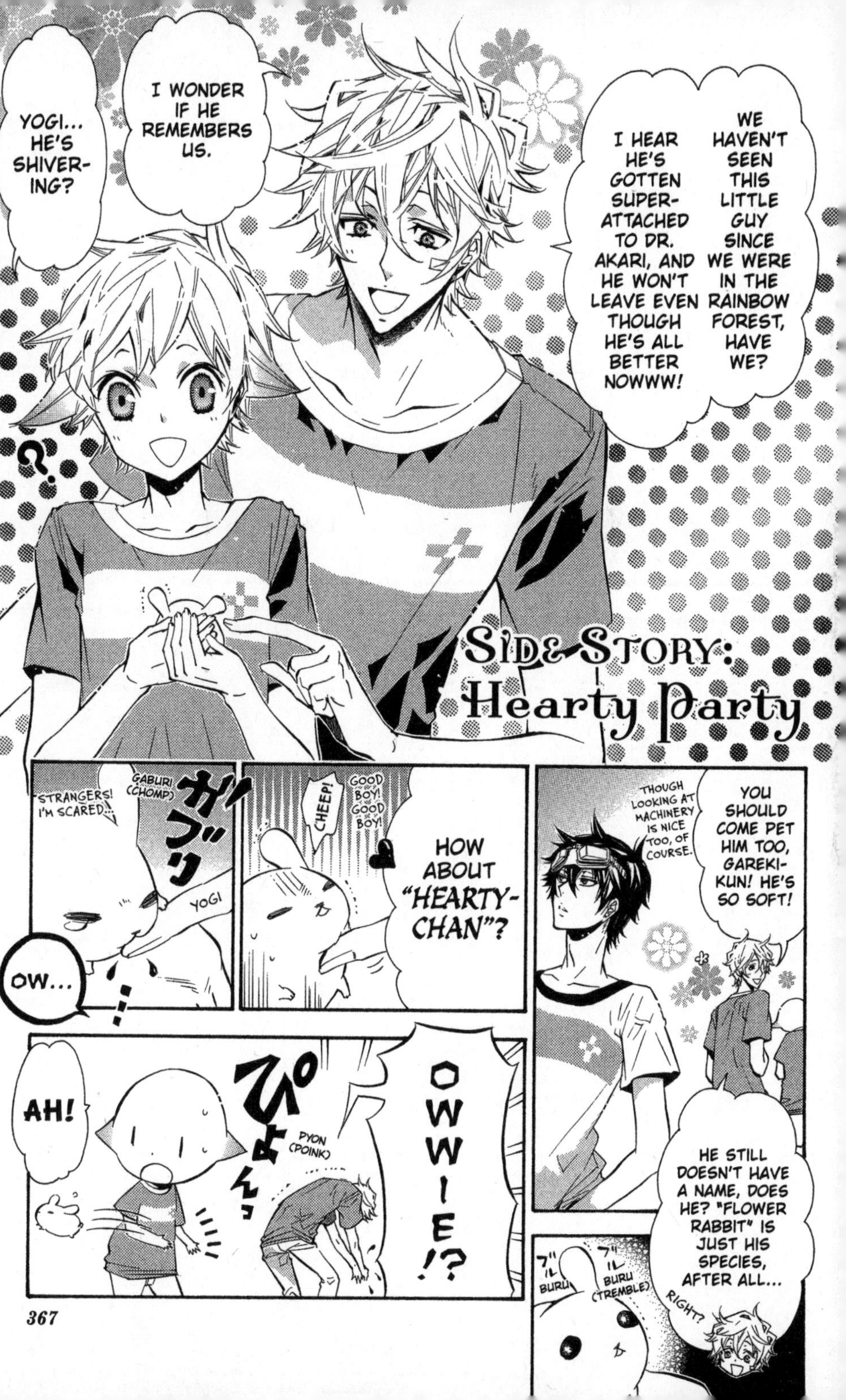
WE HAVEN'T SEEN THIS LITTLE GUY SINCE WE WERE IN THE RAINBOW FOREST, HAVE WE?
I HEAR HE'S GOTTEN SUPER-ATTACHED TO DR. AKARI, AND HE WON'T LEAVE EVEN THOUGH HE'S ALL BETTER NOWWW!
I WONDER IF HE REMEMBERS US.
YOGI... HE'S SHIVER-ING?
?
SIDE STORY: Hearty Party
YOU SHOULD COME PET HIM TOO, GAREKI-KUN! HE'S SO SOFT!
THOUGH LOOKING AT MACHINERY IS NICE TOO, OF COURSE.
HE STILL DOESN'T HAVE A NAME, DOES HE? "FLOWER RABBIT" IS JUST HIS SPECIES, AFTER ALL...
RIGHT?
ブル BURU
ブル BURU (TREMBLE)
HOW ABOUT "HEARTY-CHAN"?
GOOD BOY! GOOD BOY!
CHEEP!
ガブリ GABURI (CHOMP)
STRANGERS! I'M SCARED...
YOGI
OW...
...
OWWIE!?
ぴょん PYON (POINK)
AH!

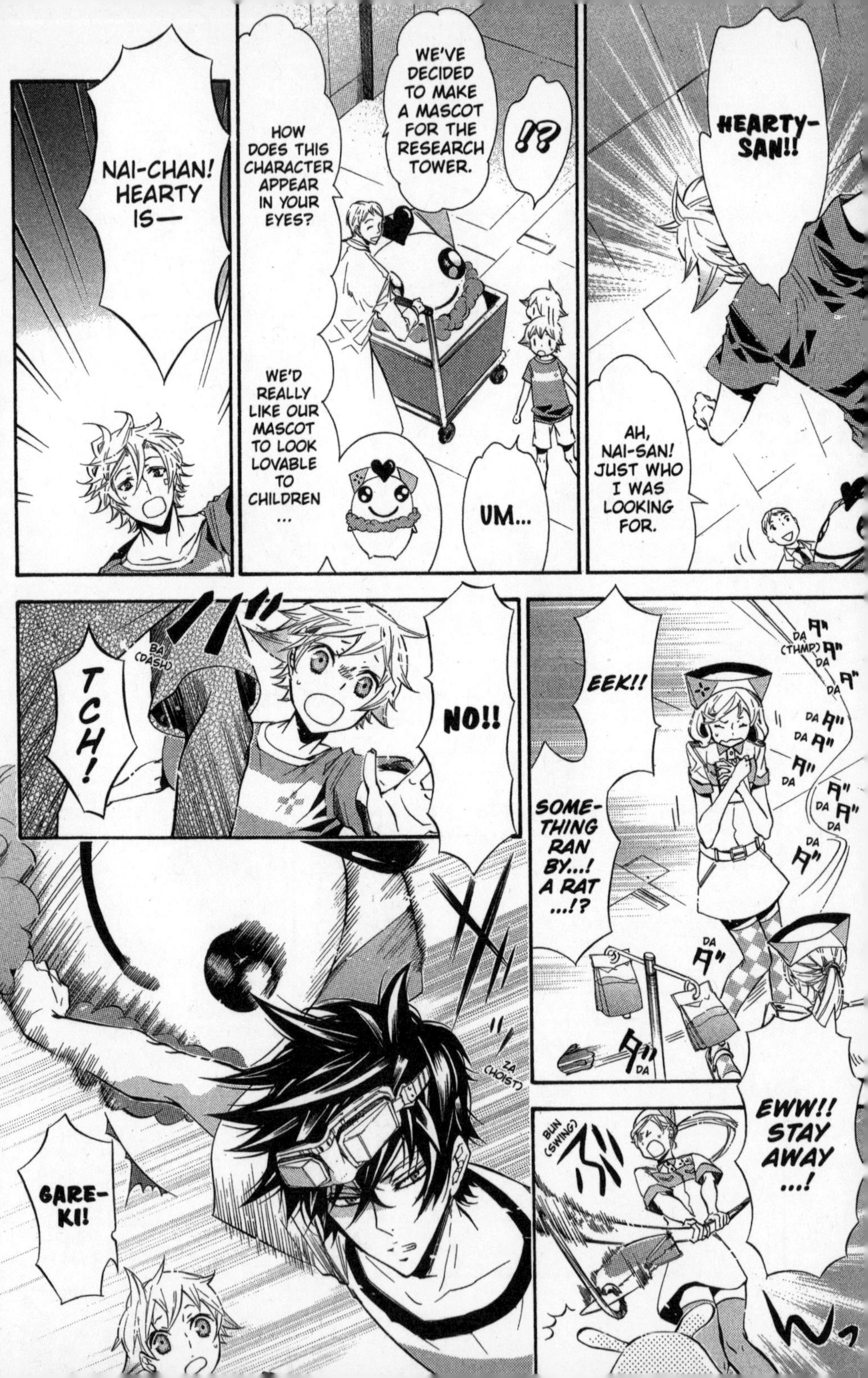
HEARTY-SAN!!
AH, NAI-SAN! JUST WHO I WAS LOOKING FOR.
WE'VE DECIDED TO MAKE A MASCOT FOR THE RESEARCH TOWER.
!?
HOW DOES THIS CHARACTER APPEAR IN YOUR EYES?
UM...
WE'D REALLY LIKE OUR MASCOT TO LOOK LOVABLE TO CHILDREN ...
NAI-CHAN! HEARTY IS—
DA (THMP) DA DA DA DA DA DA DA DA DA
EEK!!
SOMETHING RAN BY...! A RAT ...!?
DA
DA
EWW!! STAY AWAY ...!
BUN (SWING)
NO!!
BA (DASH)
TCH!
ZA (HOIST)
GARE-KI!

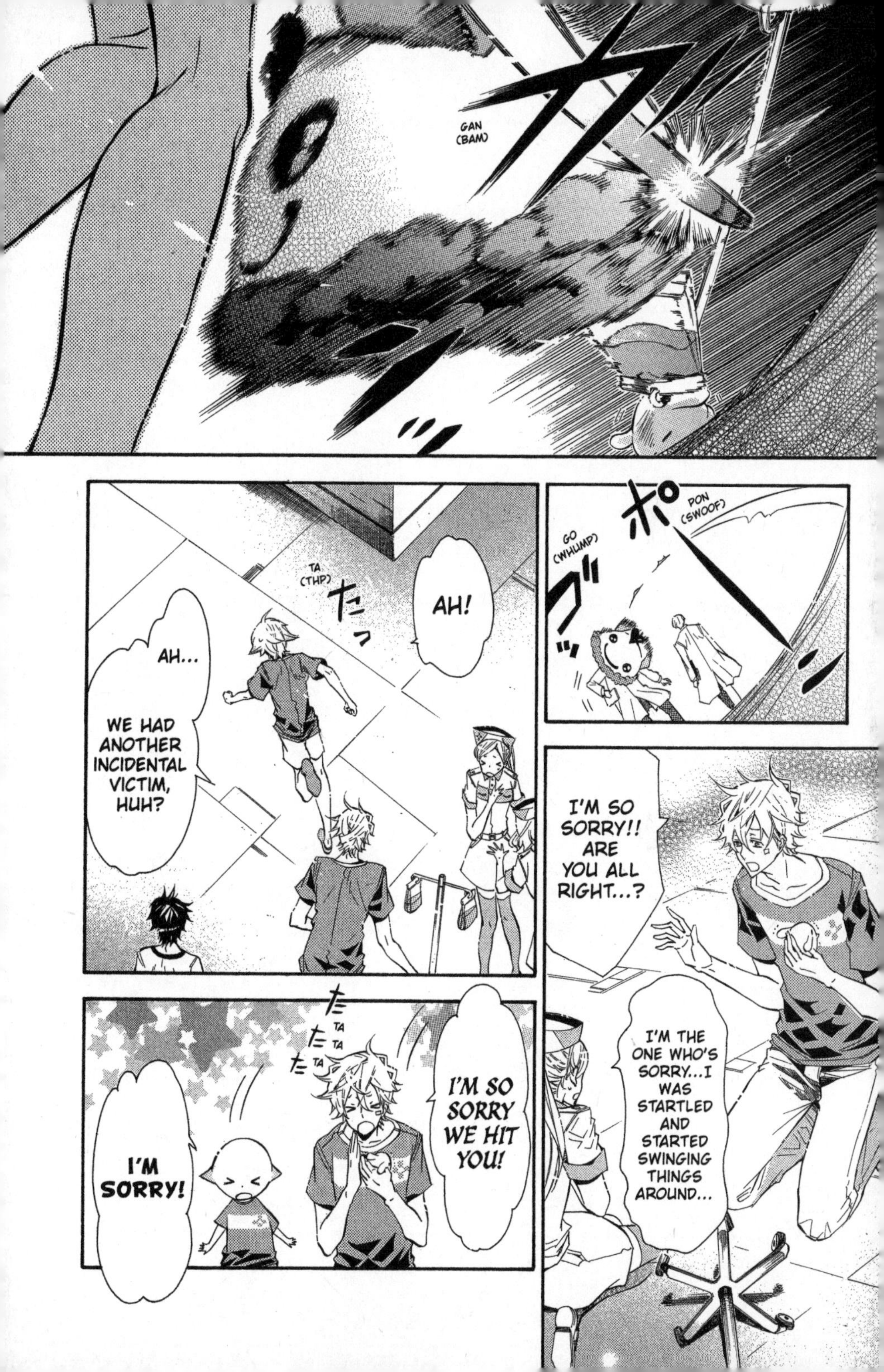
GAN (BAM)
PON (SWOOF)
GO (WHUMP)
AH!
TA (THP)
AH...
WE HAD ANOTHER INCIDENTAL VICTIM, HUH?
I'M SO SORRY!! ARE YOU ALL RIGHT...?
I'M THE ONE WHO'S SORRY...I WAS STARTLED AND STARTED SWINGING THINGS AROUND...
TA TA TA
I'M SO SORRY WE HIT YOU!
I'M SORRY!

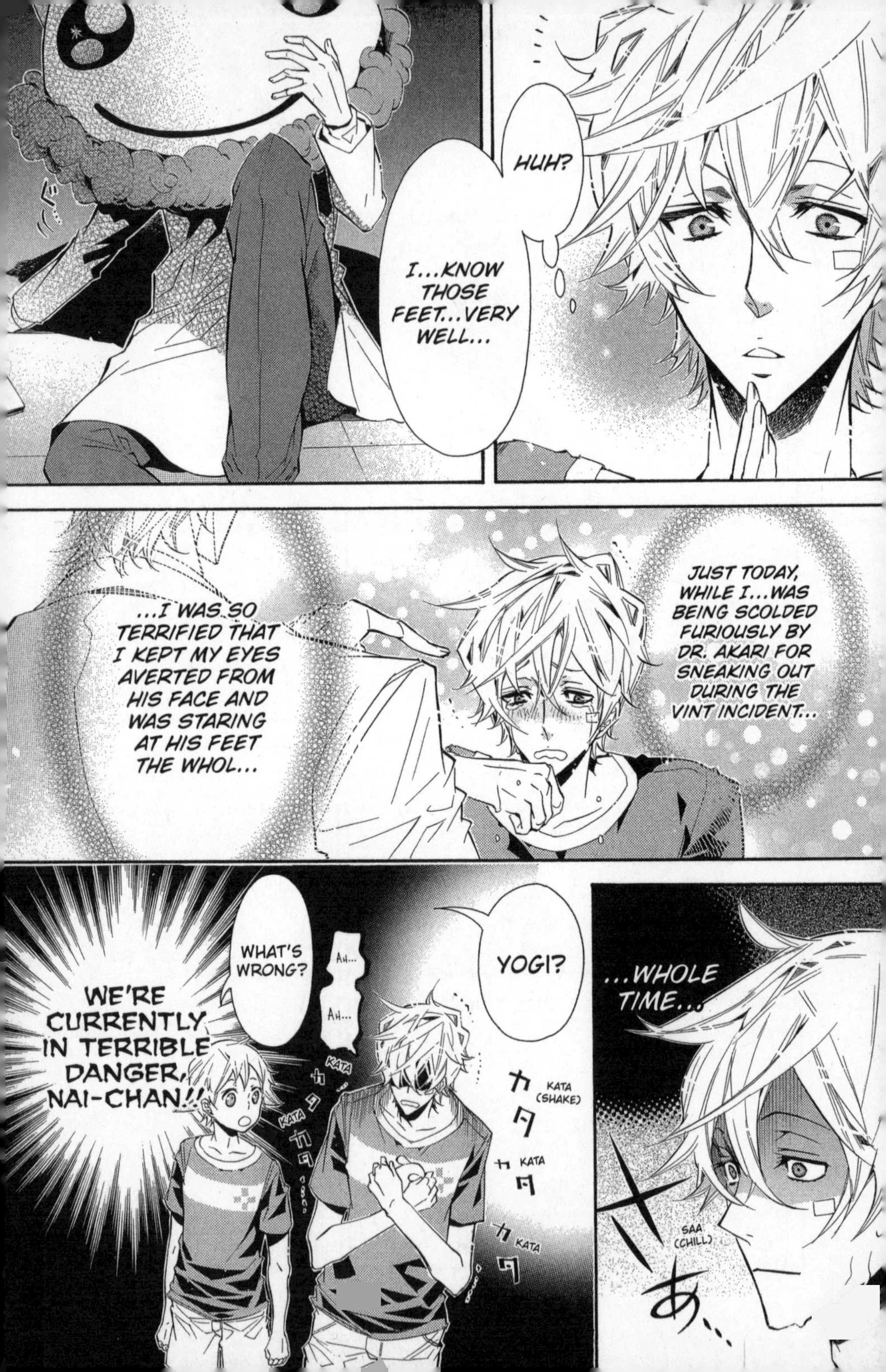
HUH?
I...KNOW THOSE FEET...VERY WELL...
JUST TODAY, WHILE I...WAS BEING SCOLDED FURIOUSLY BY DR. AKARI FOR SNEAKING OUT DURING THE VINT INCIDENT...
...I WAS SO TERRIFIED THAT I KEPT MY EYES AVERTED FROM HIS FACE AND WAS STARING AT HIS FEET THE WHOL...
...WHOLE TIME...
SAA (CHILL)
あ...
YOGI?
WHAT'S WRONG?
AH...
AH...
カタ
KATA (SHAKE)
カタ
KATA
カタ
KATA
KATA
KATA
WE'RE CURRENTLY IN TERRIBLE DANGER, NAI-CHAN!!

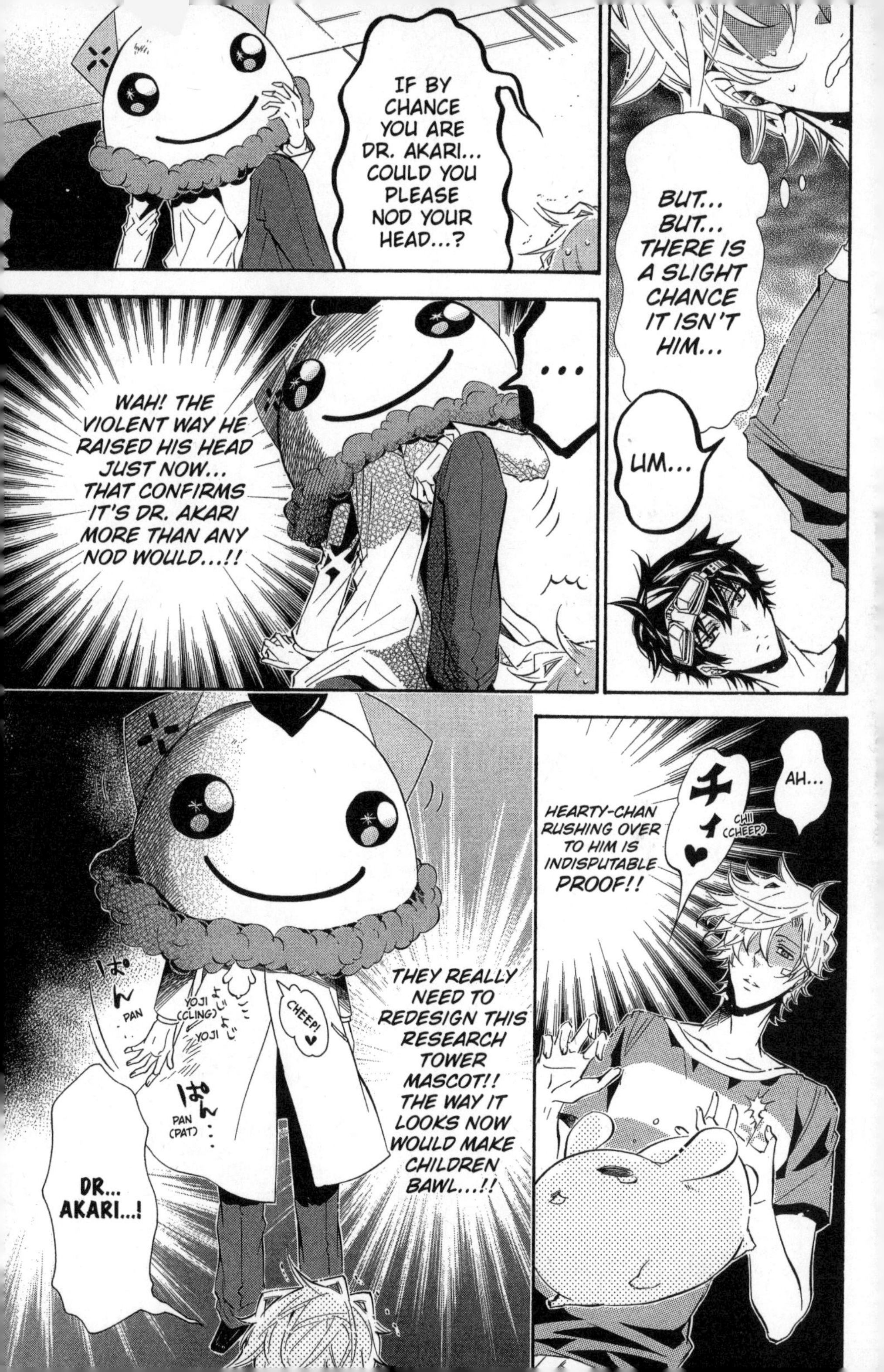
BUT... BUT... THERE IS A SLIGHT CHANCE IT ISN'T HIM...
UM...
IF BY CHANCE YOU ARE DR. AKARI... COULD YOU PLEASE NOD YOUR HEAD...?
...
WAH! THE VIOLENT WAY HE RAISED HIS HEAD JUST NOW... THAT CONFIRMS IT'S DR. AKARI MORE THAN ANY NOD WOULD...!!
AH...
チィ
CHII (CHEEP)
HEARTY-CHAN RUSHING OVER TO HIM IS INDISPUTABLE PROOF!!
THEY REALLY NEED TO REDESIGN THIS RESEARCH TOWER MASCOT!! THE WAY IT LOOKS NOW WOULD MAKE CHILDREN BAWL...!!
CHEEP!
よじよじ
YOJI (CLING) YOJI
ぽん
PAN
ぽん
PAN (PAT)
DR... AKARI...!

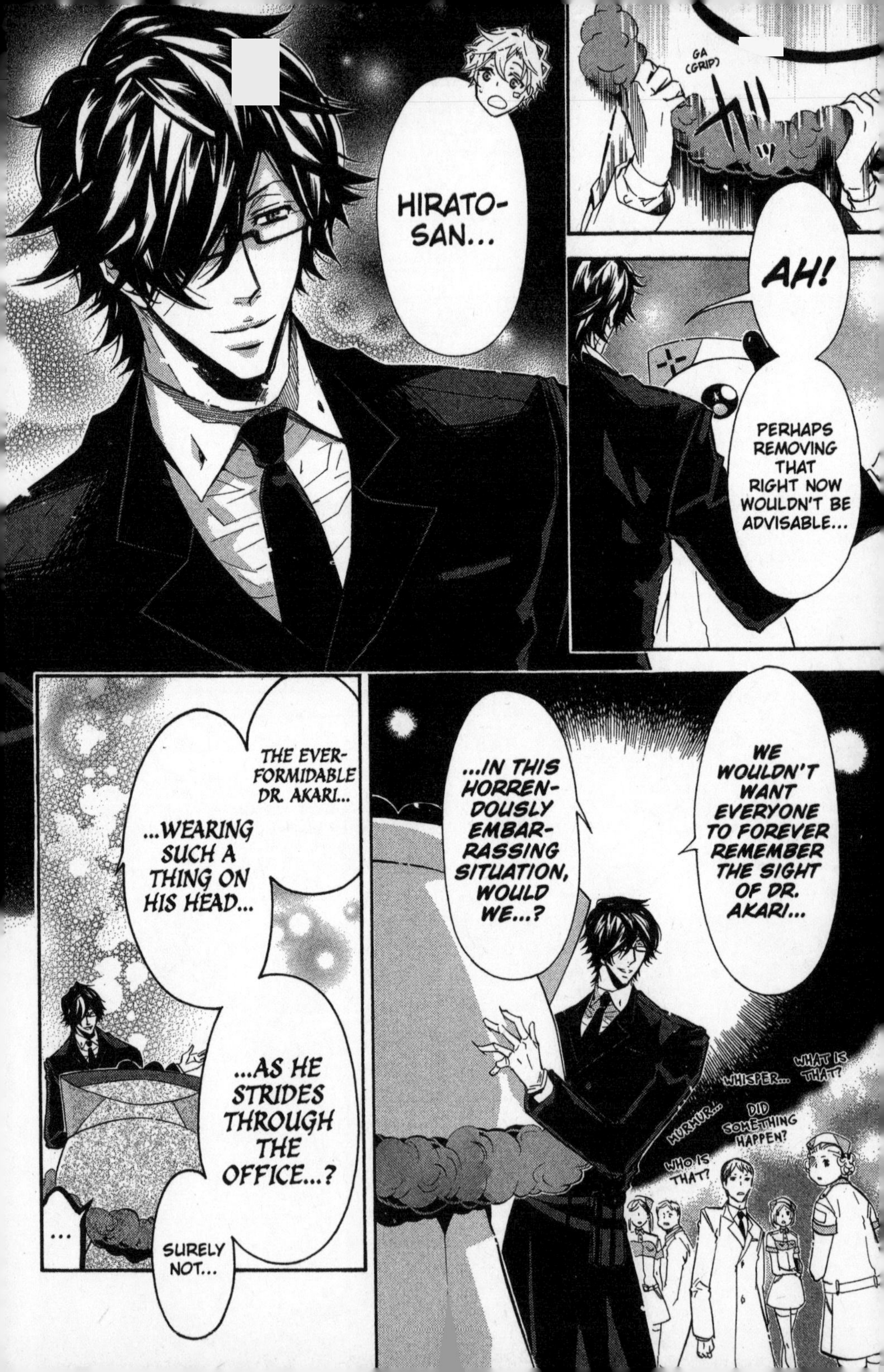
GA (GRIP)
AH!
PERHAPS REMOVING THAT RIGHT NOW WOULDN'T BE ADVISABLE...
HIRATO-SAN...
WE WOULDN'T WANT EVERYONE TO FOREVER REMEMBER THE SIGHT OF DR. AKARI...
...IN THIS HORREN-DOUSLY EMBAR-RASSING SITUATION, WOULD WE...?
WHAT IS THAT?
WHISPER...
DID SOMETHING HAPPEN?
MURMUR...
WHO IS THAT?
THE EVER-FORMIDABLE DR. AKARI...
...WEARING SUCH A THING ON HIS HEAD...
...AS HE STRIDES THROUGH THE OFFICE...?
...
SURELY NOT...

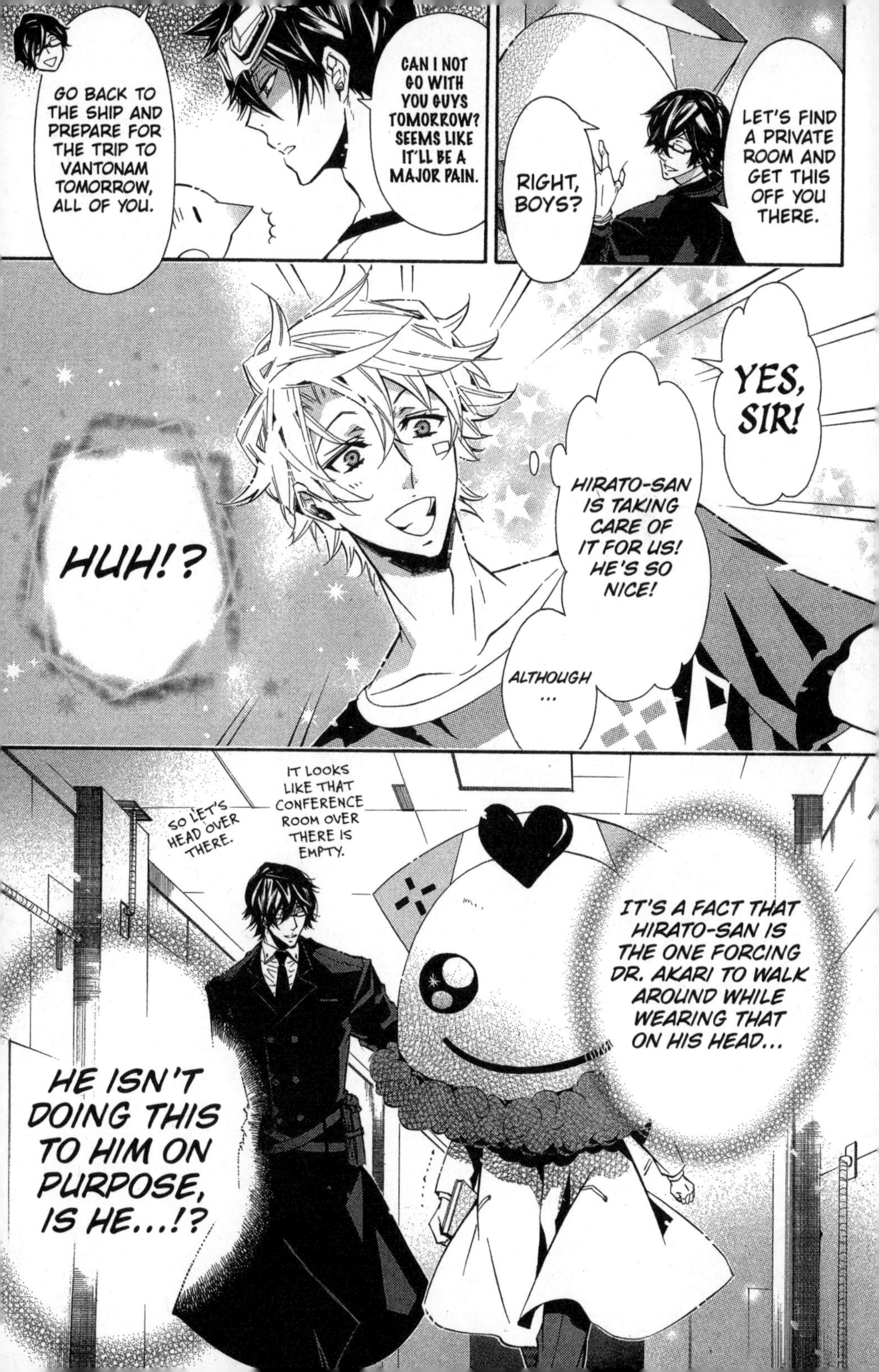
LET'S FIND A PRIVATE ROOM AND GET THIS OFF YOU THERE.
RIGHT, BOYS?
CAN I NOT GO WITH YOU GUYS TOMORROW? SEEMS LIKE IT'LL BE A MAJOR PAIN.
GO BACK TO THE SHIP AND PREPARE FOR THE TRIP TO VANTONAM TOMORROW, ALL OF YOU.
YES, SIR!
HIRATO-SAN IS TAKING CARE OF IT FOR US! HE'S SO NICE!
ALTHOUGH...
HUH!?
IT LOOKS LIKE THAT CONFERENCE ROOM OVER THERE IS EMPTY.
SO LET'S HEAD OVER THERE.
IT'S A FACT THAT HIRATO-SAN IS THE ONE FORCING DR. AKARI TO WALK AROUND WHILE WEARING THAT ON HIS HEAD...
HE ISN'T DOING THIS TO HIM ON PURPOSE, IS HE...!?

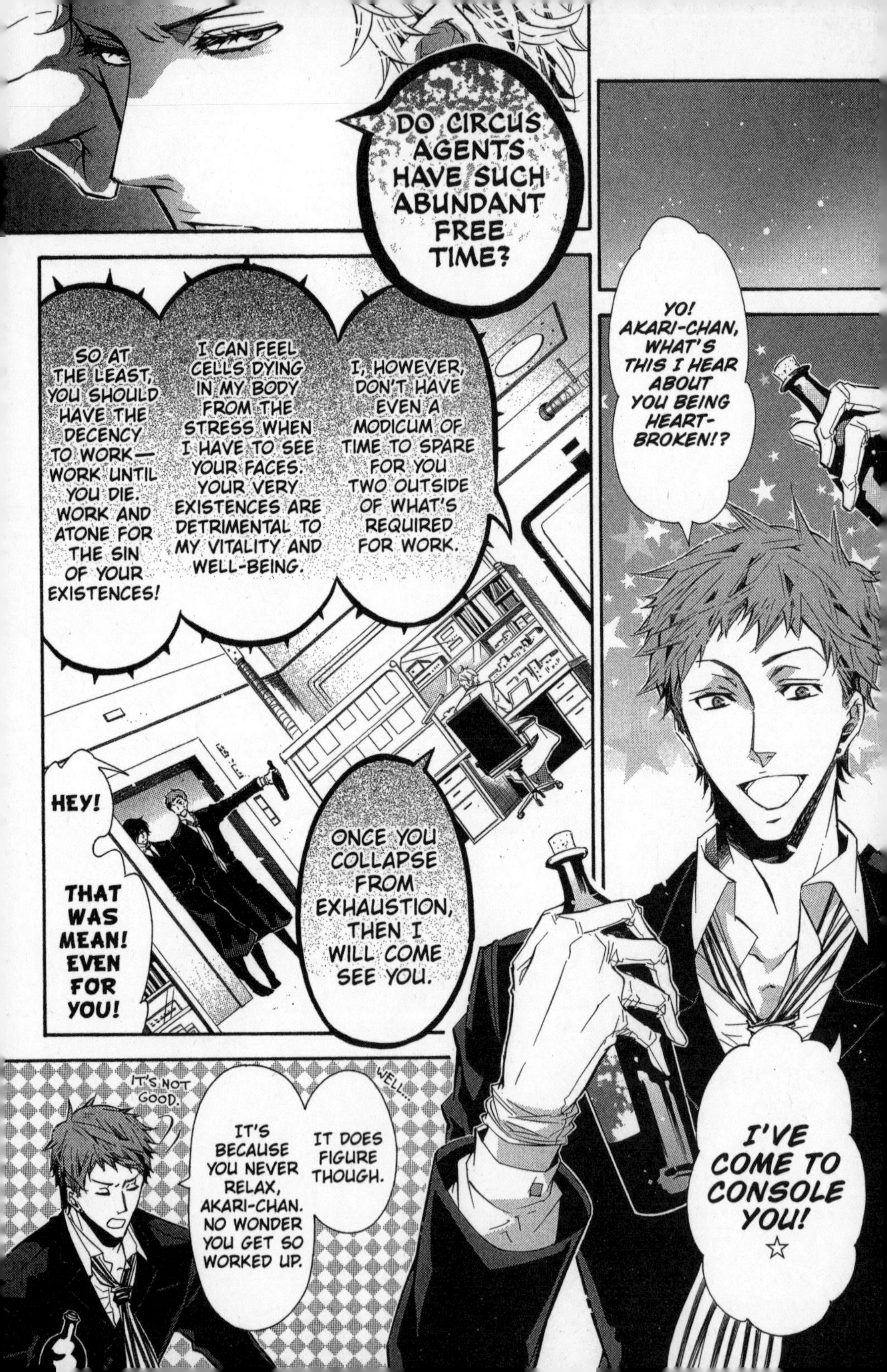
YO! AKARI-CHAN, WHAT'S THIS I HEAR ABOUT YOU BEING HEART-BROKEN!?
I'VE COME TO CONSOLE YOU! ☆
DO CIRCUS AGENTS HAVE SUCH ABUNDANT FREE TIME?
I, HOWEVER, DON'T HAVE EVEN A MODICUM OF TIME TO SPARE FOR YOU TWO OUTSIDE OF WHAT'S REQUIRED FOR WORK.
I CAN FEEL CELLS DYING IN MY BODY FROM THE STRESS WHEN I HAVE TO SEE YOUR FACES. YOUR VERY EXISTENCES ARE DETRIMENTAL TO MY VITALITY AND WELL-BEING.
SO AT THE LEAST, YOU SHOULD HAVE THE DECENCY TO WORK—WORK UNTIL YOU DIE. WORK AND ATONE FOR THE SIN OF YOUR EXISTENCES!
ONCE YOU COLLAPSE FROM EXHAUSTION, THEN I WILL COME SEE YOU.
HEY!
THAT WAS MEAN! EVEN FOR YOU!
WELL...
IT DOES FIGURE THOUGH.
IT'S BECAUSE YOU NEVER RELAX, AKARI-CHAN. NO WONDER YOU GET SO WORKED UP.
IT'S NOT GOOD.

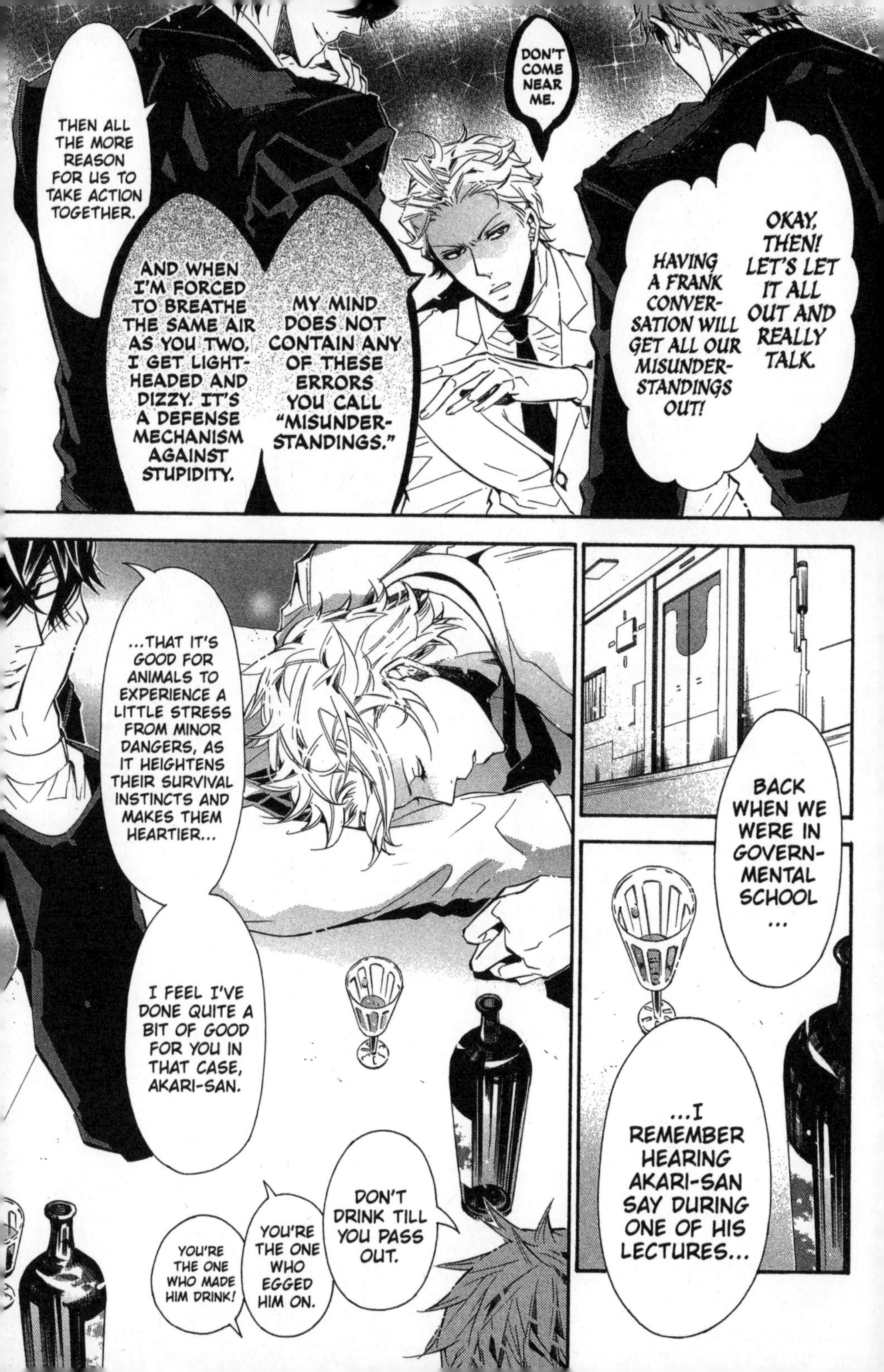
OKAY, THEN! LET'S LET IT ALL OUT AND REALLY TALK.
HAVING A FRANK CONVERSATION WILL GET ALL OUR MISUNDERSTANDINGS OUT!
DON'T COME NEAR ME.
MY MIND DOES NOT CONTAIN ANY OF THESE ERRORS YOU CALL "MISUNDERSTANDINGS."
AND WHEN I'M FORCED TO BREATHE THE SAME AIR AS YOU TWO, I GET LIGHT-HEADED AND DIZZY. IT'S A DEFENSE MECHANISM AGAINST STUPIDITY.
THEN ALL THE MORE REASON FOR US TO TAKE ACTION TOGETHER.
BACK WHEN WE WERE IN GOVERNMENTAL SCHOOL...
...I REMEMBER HEARING AKARI-SAN SAY DURING ONE OF HIS LECTURES...
...THAT IT'S GOOD FOR ANIMALS TO EXPERIENCE A LITTLE STRESS FROM MINOR DANGERS, AS IT HEIGHTENS THEIR SURVIVAL INSTINCTS AND MAKES THEM HEARTIER...
I FEEL I'VE DONE QUITE A BIT OF GOOD FOR YOU IN THAT CASE, AKARI-SAN.
DON'T DRINK TILL YOU PASS OUT.
YOU'RE THE ONE WHO EGGED HIM ON.
YOU'RE THE ONE WHO MADE HIM DRINK!

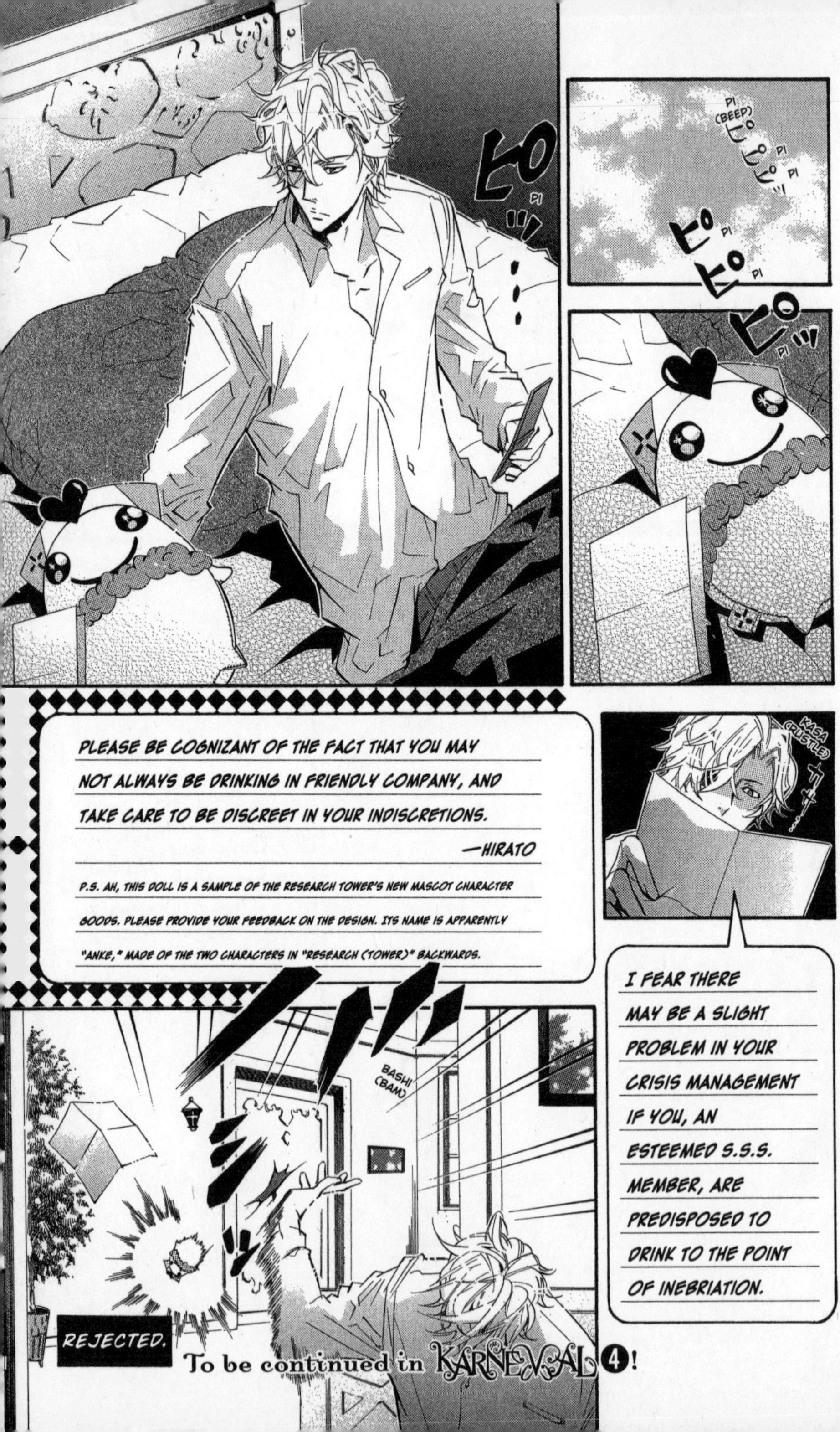
PI (BEEP)
PI
PI
PI
PI
PI
PI
KASA (RUSTLE)
I FEAR THERE MAY BE A SLIGHT PROBLEM IN YOUR CRISIS MANAGEMENT IF YOU, AN ESTEEMED S.S.S. MEMBER, ARE PREDISPOSED TO DRINK TO THE POINT OF INEBRIATION.
PLEASE BE COGNIZANT OF THE FACT THAT YOU MAY NOT ALWAYS BE DRINKING IN FRIENDLY COMPANY, AND TAKE CARE TO BE DISCREET IN YOUR INDISCRETIONS.
—HIRATO
P.S. AH, THIS DOLL IS A SAMPLE OF THE RESEARCH TOWER'S NEW MASCOT CHARACTER GOODS. PLEASE PROVIDE YOUR FEEDBACK ON THE DESIGN. ITS NAME IS APPARENTLY "ANKE," MADE OF THE TWO CHARACTERS IN "RESEARCH (TOWER)" BACKWARDS.
BASHI (BAM)
REJECTED.
To be continued in KARNEVAL 4!

KARNEVAL

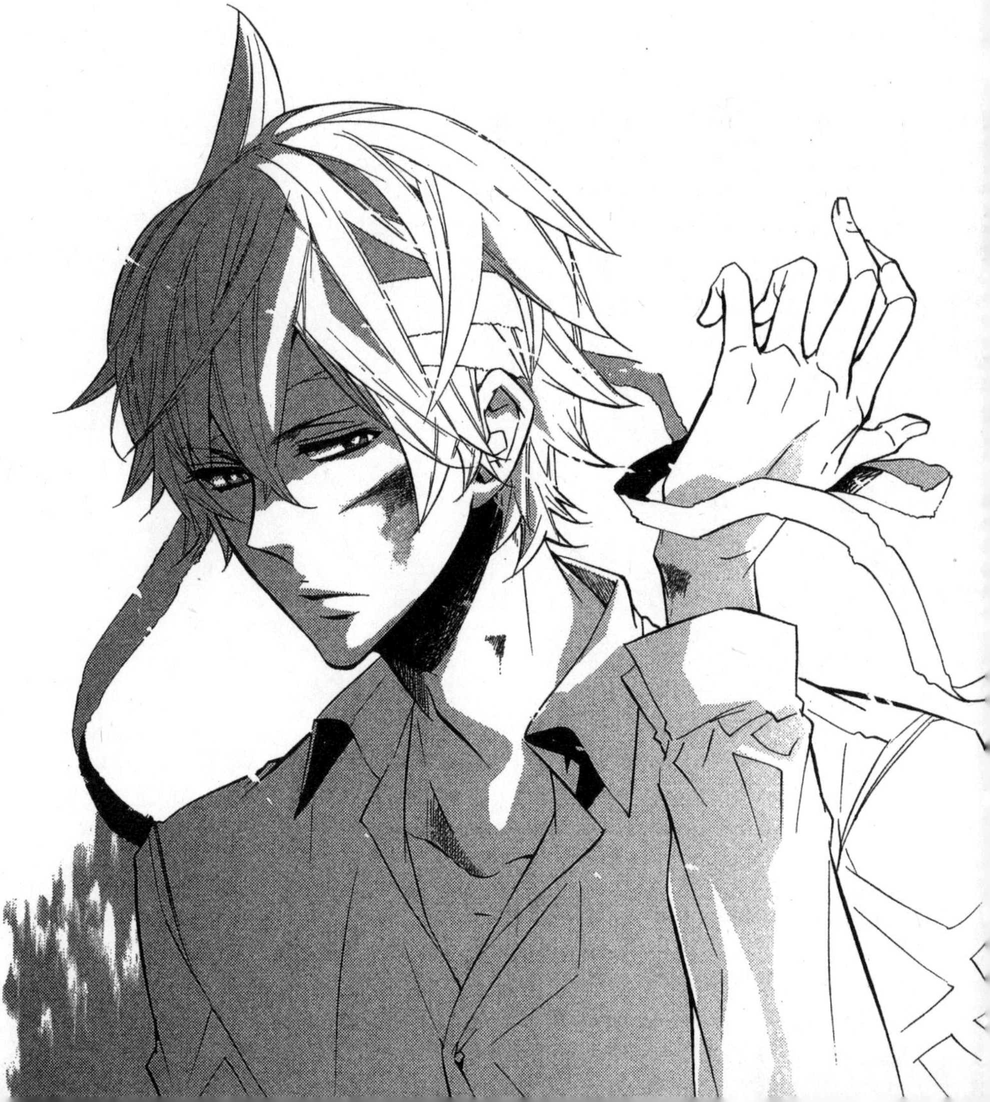

Bonus Comic 1 - Let's Have Fun Even in Our Dreams!

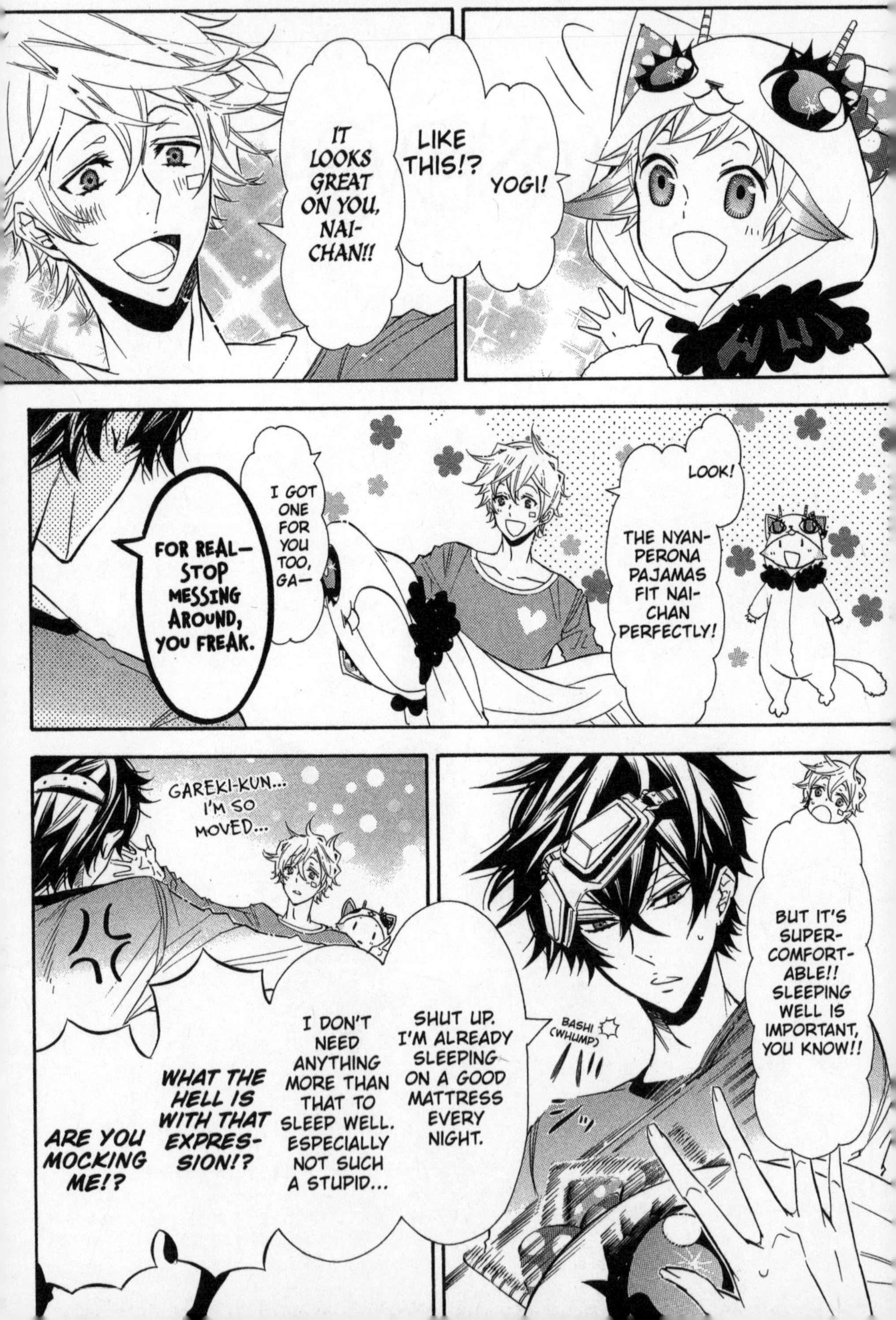
YOGI!
LIKE THIS!?
IT LOOKS GREAT ON YOU, NAI-CHAN!!
LOOK!
THE NYAN-PERONA PAJAMAS FIT NAI-CHAN PERFECTLY!
I GOT ONE FOR YOU TOO, GA—
FOR REAL—STOP MESSING AROUND, YOU FREAK.
BUT IT'S SUPER-COMFORTABLE!! SLEEPING WELL IS IMPORTANT, YOU KNOW!!
BASHI (WHUMP)
SHUT UP. I'M ALREADY SLEEPING ON A GOOD MATTRESS EVERY NIGHT.
I DON'T NEED ANYTHING MORE THAN THAT TO SLEEP WELL. ESPECIALLY NOT SUCH A STUPID...
GAREKI-KUN... I'M SO MOVED...
WHAT THE HELL IS WITH THAT EXPRESSION!?
ARE YOU MOCKING ME!?

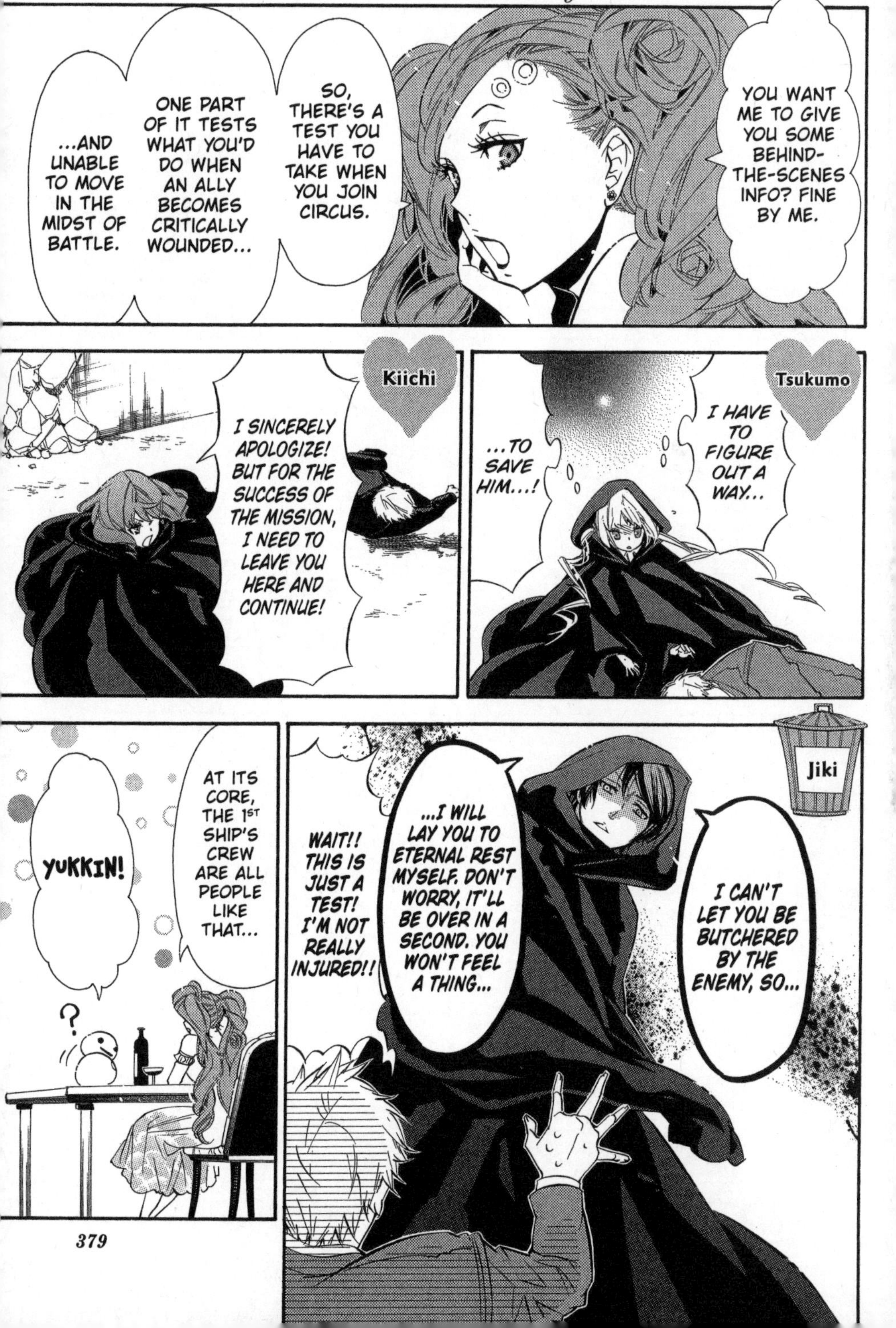
YOU WANT ME TO GIVE YOU SOME BEHIND-THE-SCENES INFO? FINE BY ME.
SO, THERE'S A TEST YOU HAVE TO TAKE WHEN YOU JOIN CIRCUS.
ONE PART OF IT TESTS WHAT YOU'D DO WHEN AN ALLY BECOMES CRITICALLY WOUNDED...
...AND UNABLE TO MOVE IN THE MIDST OF BATTLE.
Tsukumo
I HAVE TO FIGURE OUT A WAY...
...TO SAVE HIM...!
Kiichi
I SINCERELY APOLOGIZE! BUT FOR THE SUCCESS OF THE MISSION, I NEED TO LEAVE YOU HERE AND CONTINUE!
Jiki
I CAN'T LET YOU BE BUTCHERED BY THE ENEMY, SO...
...I WILL LAY YOU TO ETERNAL REST MYSELF. DON'T WORRY, IT'LL BE OVER IN A SECOND. YOU WON'T FEEL A THING...
WAIT!! THIS IS JUST A TEST! I'M NOT REALLY INJURED!!
AT ITS CORE, THE 1ST SHIP'S CREW ARE ALL PEOPLE LIKE THAT...
YUKKIN!
?

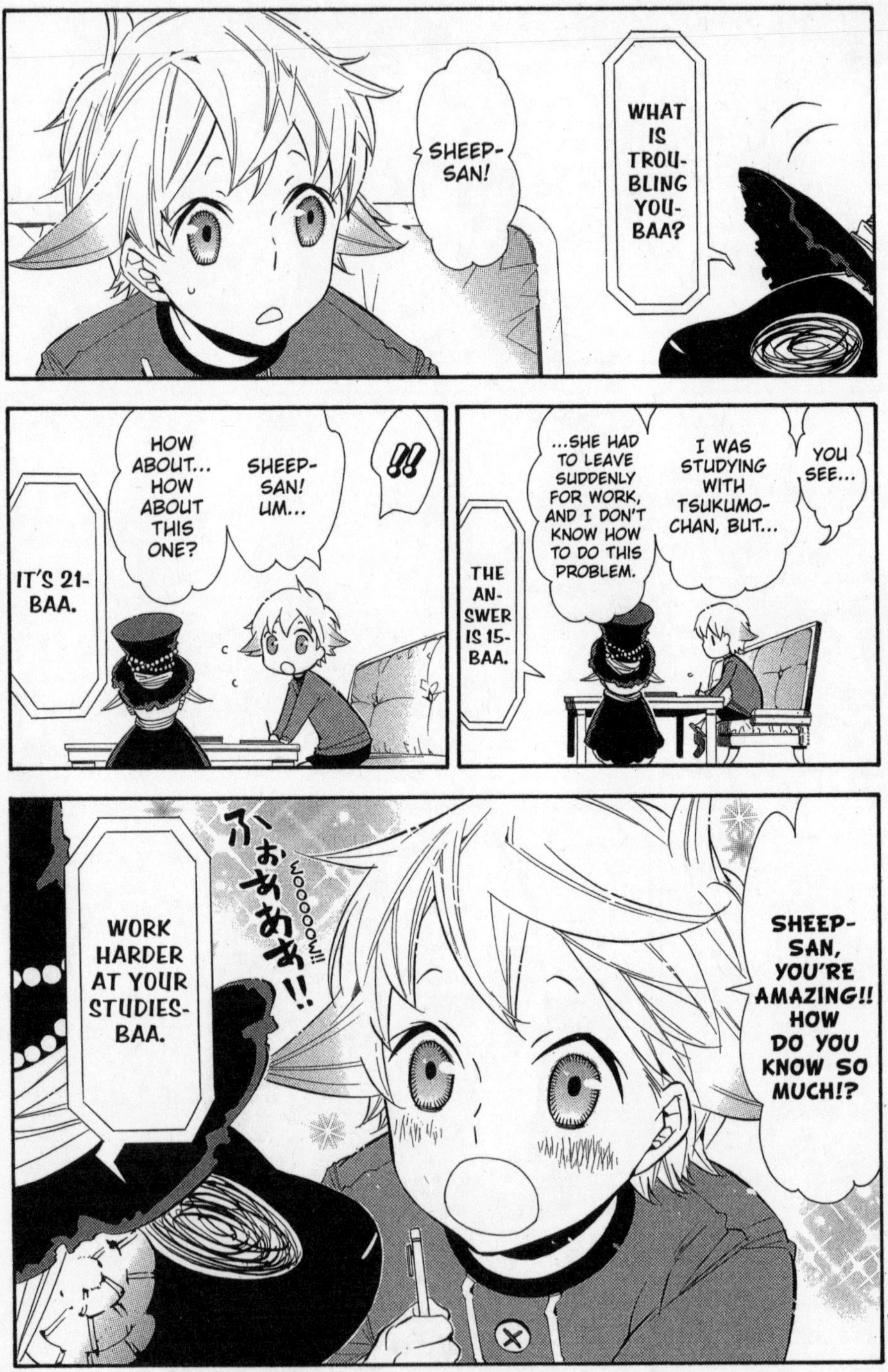
WHAT IS TROUBLING YOU-BAA?
SHEEP-SAN!
YOU SEE...
I WAS STUDYING WITH TSUKUMO-CHAN, BUT...
...SHE HAD TO LEAVE SUDDENLY FOR WORK, AND I DON'T KNOW HOW TO DO THIS PROBLEM.
THE ANSWER IS 15-BAA.
!!
SHEEP-SAN! UM...
HOW ABOUT... HOW ABOUT THIS ONE?
IT'S 21-BAA.
SHEEP-SAN, YOU'RE AMAZING!! HOW DO YOU KNOW SO MUCH!?
WOOOOOW!!
WORK HARDER AT YOUR STUDIES-BAA.

I'LL STUDY LOTS AND LOTS, SO PLEASE COME PLAY WITH ME IN VOLUME 4!! —NAI

The End

The Recording of the Drama CD
"KARNEVAL RINOL"!!☆

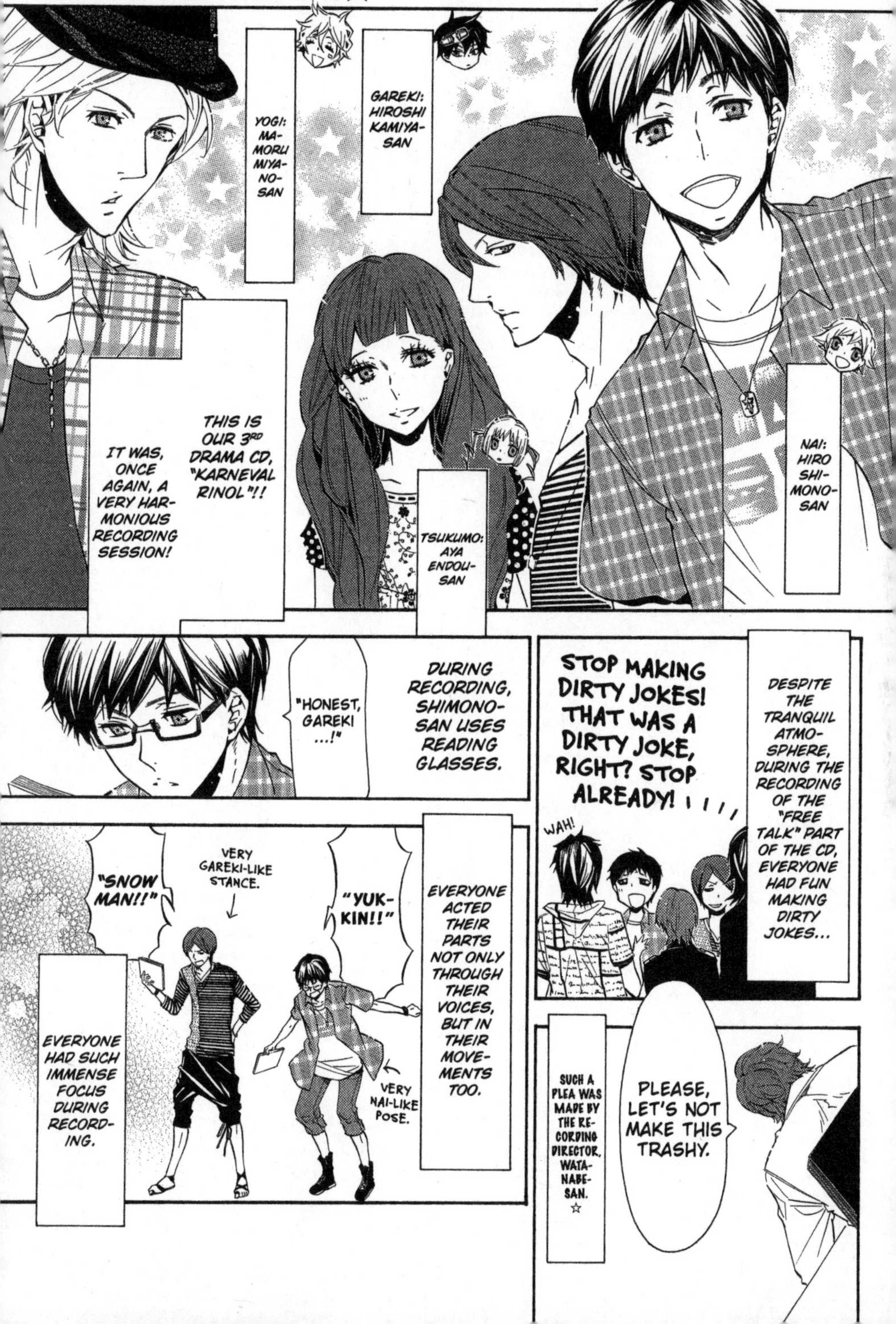
GAREKI: HIROSHI KAMIYA-SAN
YOGI: MAMORU MIYANO-SAN
NAI: HIRO SHIMONO-SAN
TSUKUMO: AYA ENDOU-SAN
THIS IS OUR 3RD DRAMA CD, "KARNEVAL RINOL"!!
IT WAS, ONCE AGAIN, A VERY HARMONIOUS RECORDING SESSION!
DESPITE THE TRANQUIL ATMOSPHERE, DURING THE RECORDING OF THE "FREE TALK" PART OF THE CD, EVERYONE HAD FUN MAKING DIRTY JOKES...
STOP MAKING DIRTY JOKES! THAT WAS A DIRTY JOKE, RIGHT? STOP ALREADY!
WAH!
PLEASE, LET'S NOT MAKE THIS TRASHY.
SUCH A PLEA WAS MADE BY THE RECORDING DIRECTOR, WATANABE-SAN. ☆
DURING RECORDING, SHIMONO-SAN USES READING GLASSES.
"HONEST, GAREKI ...!"
EVERYONE ACTED THEIR PARTS NOT ONLY THROUGH THEIR VOICES, BUT IN THEIR MOVEMENTS TOO.
"YUK-KIN!!"
VERY NAI-LIKE POSE.
VERY GAREKI-LIKE STANCE.
"SNOW MAN!!"
EVERYONE HAD SUCH IMMENSE FOCUS DURING RECORDING.

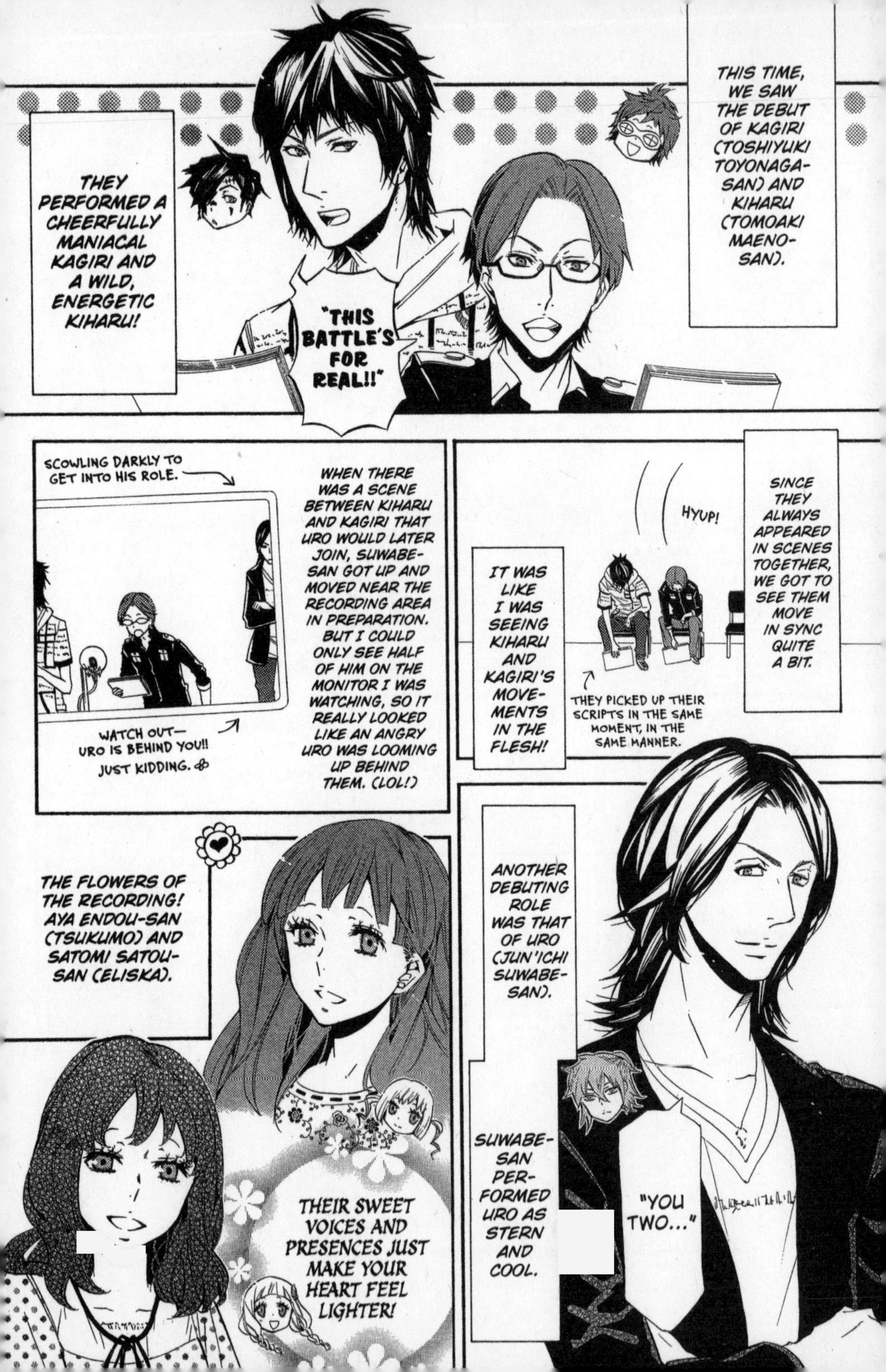
THIS TIME, WE SAW THE DEBUT OF KAGIRI (TOSHIYUKI TOYONAGA-SAN) AND KIHARU (TOMOAKI MAENO-SAN).
"THIS BATTLE'S FOR REAL!!"
THEY PERFORMED A CHEERFULLY MANIACAL KAGIRI AND A WILD, ENERGETIC KIHARU!
SINCE THEY ALWAYS APPEARED IN SCENES TOGETHER, WE GOT TO SEE THEM MOVE IN SYNC QUITE A BIT.
HYUP!
IT WAS LIKE I WAS SEEING KIHARU AND KAGIRI'S MOVEMENTS IN THE FLESH!
THEY PICKED UP THEIR SCRIPTS IN THE SAME MOMENT, IN THE SAME MANNER.
WHEN THERE WAS A SCENE BETWEEN KIHARU AND KAGIRI THAT URO WOULD LATER JOIN, SUWABE-SAN GOT UP AND MOVED NEAR THE RECORDING AREA IN PREPARATION. BUT I COULD ONLY SEE HALF OF HIM ON THE MONITOR I WAS WATCHING, SO IT REALLY LOOKED LIKE AN ANGRY URO WAS LOOMING UP BEHIND THEM. (LOL!)
SCOWLING DARKLY TO GET INTO HIS ROLE.
WATCH OUT— URO IS BEHIND YOU!! JUST KIDDING.
ANOTHER DEBUTING ROLE WAS THAT OF URO (JUN'ICHI SUWABE-SAN).
SUWABE-SAN PERFORMED URO AS STERN AND COOL.
"YOU TWO..."
THE FLOWERS OF THE RECORDING! AYA ENDOU-SAN (TSUKUMO) AND SATOMI SATOU-SAN (ELISKA).
THEIR SWEET VOICES AND PRESENCES JUST MAKE YOUR HEART FEEL LIGHTER!

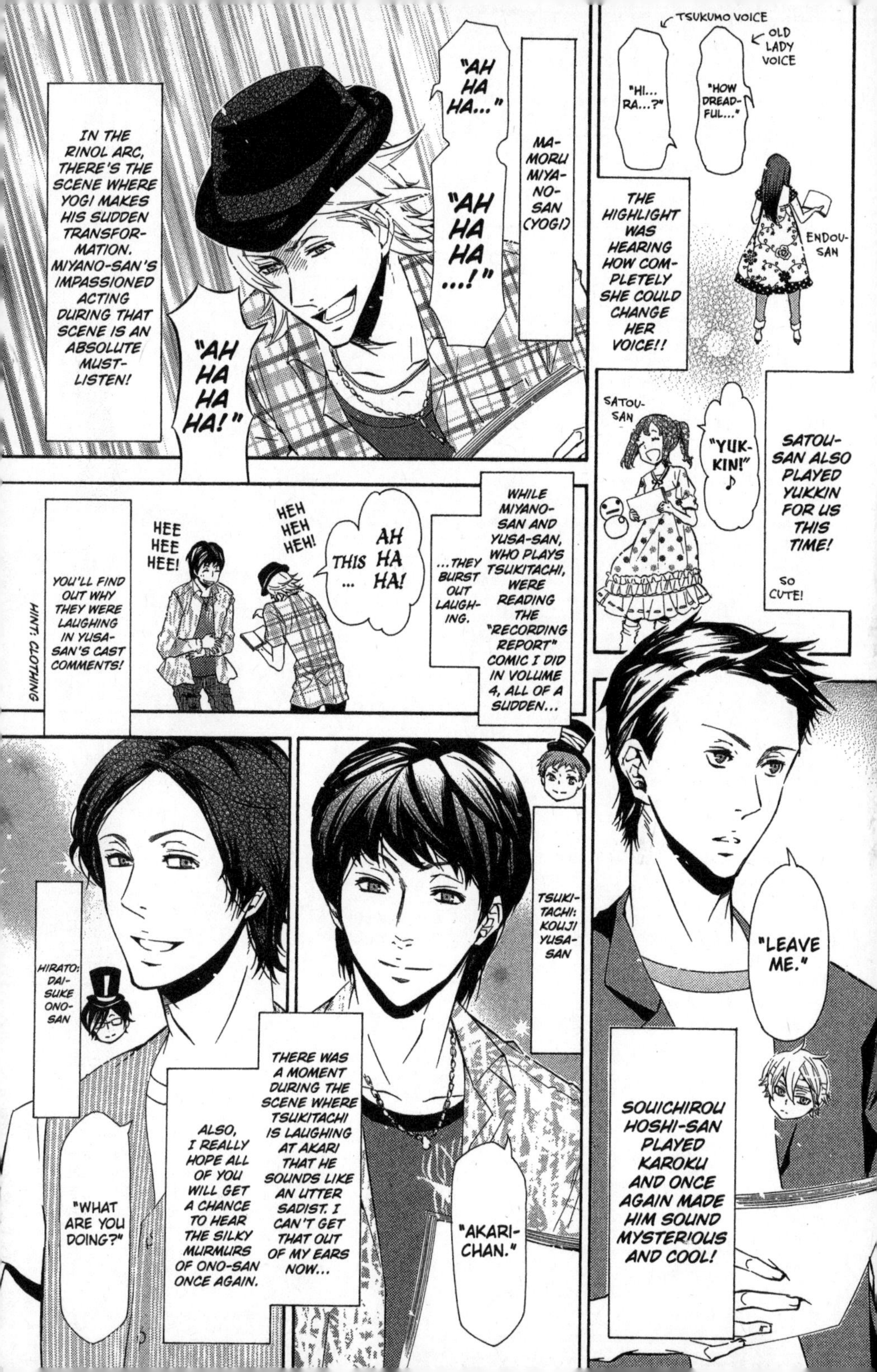

OLD LADY VOICE
"HOW DREADFUL..."
TSUKUMO VOICE
"HI... RA...?"
THE HIGHLIGHT WAS HEARING HOW COMPLETELY SHE COULD CHANGE HER VOICE!!
ENDOU-SAN
SATOU-SAN ALSO PLAYED YUKKIN FOR US THIS TIME!
SO CUTE!
"YUKKIN!" ♪
SATOU-SAN
MAMORU MIYANO-SAN (YOGI)
"AH HA HA..."
"AH HA HA...!"
"AH HA HA HA HA!"
IN THE RINOL ARC, THERE'S THE SCENE WHERE YOGI MAKES HIS SUDDEN TRANSFORMATION. MIYANO-SAN'S IMPASSIONED ACTING DURING THAT SCENE IS AN ABSOLUTE MUST-LISTEN!
WHILE MIYANO-SAN AND YUSA-SAN, WHO PLAYS TSUKITACHI, WERE READING THE "RECORDING REPORT" COMIC I DID IN VOLUME 4, ALL OF A SUDDEN...
...THEY BURST OUT LAUGHING.
AH HA HA!
THIS ...
HEH HEH HEH!
HEE HEE HEE!
YOU'LL FIND OUT WHY THEY WERE LAUGHING IN YUSA-SAN'S CAST COMMENTS!
HINT: CLOTHING
"LEAVE ME."
SOUICHIROU HOSHI-SAN PLAYED KAROKU AND ONCE AGAIN MADE HIM SOUND MYSTERIOUS AND COOL!
TSUKITACHI: KOUJI YUSA-SAN
"AKARI-CHAN."
THERE WAS A MOMENT DURING THE SCENE WHERE TSUKITACHI IS LAUGHING AT AKARI THAT HE SOUNDS LIKE AN UTTER SADIST. I CAN'T GET THAT OUT OF MY EARS NOW...
ALSO, I REALLY HOPE ALL OF YOU WILL GET A CHANCE TO HEAR THE SILKY MURMURS OF ONO-SAN ONCE AGAIN.
HIRATO: DAISUKE ONO-SAN
"WHAT ARE YOU DOING?"

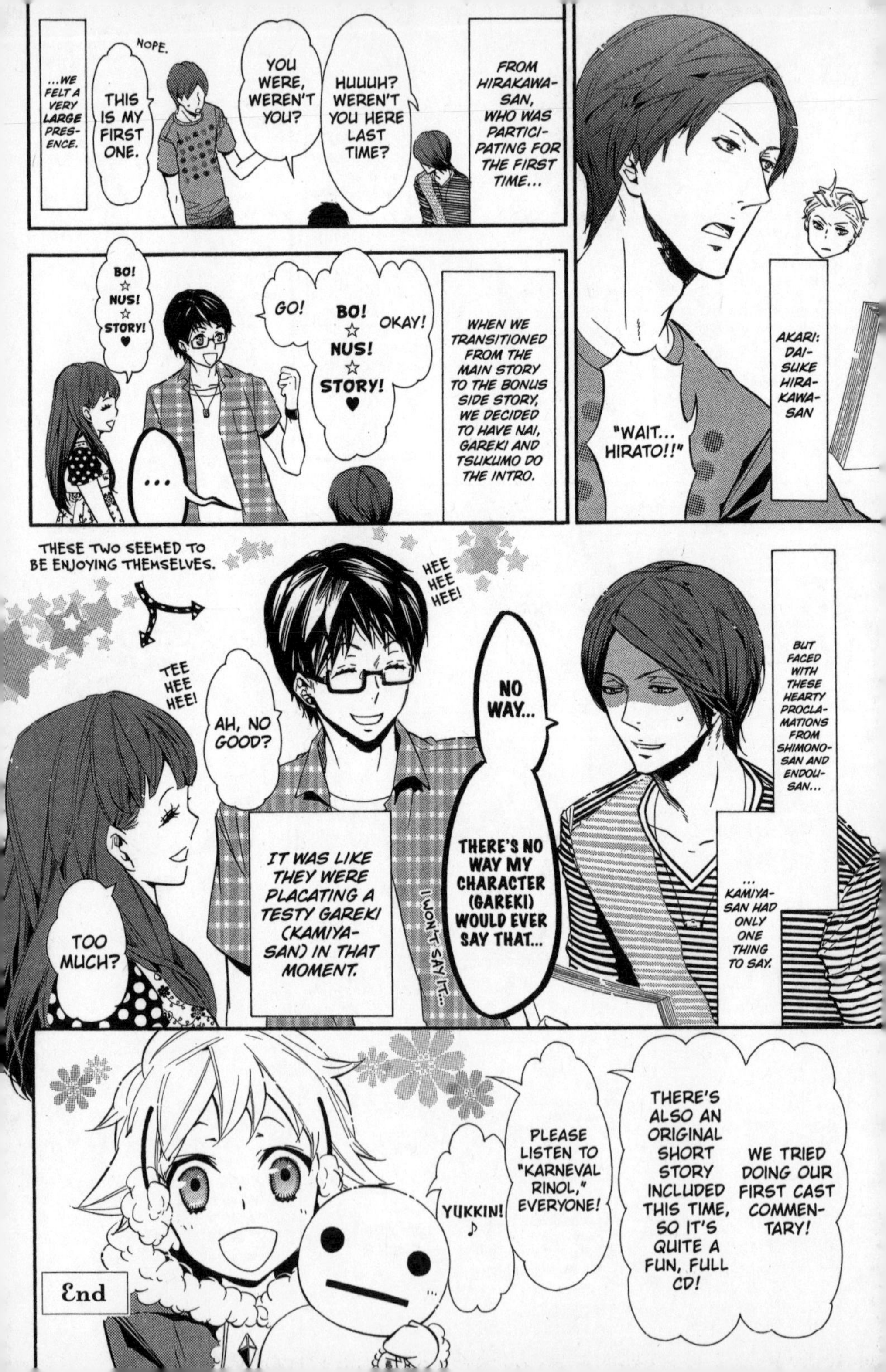
AKARI: DAISUKE HIRAKAWA-SAN
"WAIT... HIRATO!!"
FROM HIRAKAWA-SAN, WHO WAS PARTICIPATING FOR THE FIRST TIME...
HUUUH? WEREN'T YOU HERE LAST TIME?
YOU WERE, WEREN'T YOU?
NOPE.
THIS IS MY FIRST ONE.
...WE FELT A VERY LARGE PRESENCE.
WHEN WE TRANSITIONED FROM THE MAIN STORY TO THE BONUS SIDE STORY, WE DECIDED TO HAVE NAI, GAREKI AND TSUKUMO DO THE INTRO.
OKAY!
BO! ☆ NUS! ☆ STORY! ♥
GO!
BO! ☆ NUS! ☆ STORY! ♥
...
BUT FACED WITH THESE HEARTY PROCLAMATIONS FROM SHIMONO-SAN AND ENDOU-SAN...
... KAMIYA-SAN HAD ONLY ONE THING TO SAY.
NO WAY...
THERE'S NO WAY MY CHARACTER (GAREKI) WOULD EVER SAY THAT...
HEE HEE HEE!
I WON'T SAY IT...
IT WAS LIKE THEY WERE PLACATING A TESTY GAREKI (KAMIYA-SAN) IN THAT MOMENT.
AH, NO GOOD?
TEE HEE HEE!
TOO MUCH?
THESE TWO SEEMED TO BE ENJOYING THEMSELVES.
WE TRIED DOING OUR FIRST CAST COMMENTARY!
THERE'S ALSO AN ORIGINAL SHORT STORY INCLUDED THIS TIME, SO IT'S QUITE A FUN, FULL CD!
PLEASE LISTEN TO "KARNEVAL RINOL," EVERYONE!
YUKKIN! ♪
End

HELLO, MIKANAGI HERE! THIS TIME, THE VOLUME WAS MAINLY FILLED WITH BATTLES, SO I FELT LIKE THE STORY HAD A SOMEWHAT DIFFERENT ATMOSPHERE THAN USUAL. BUT WHAT DID YOU ALL THINK? THERE WERE LOTS OF SCENES I WANTED TO INCLUDE, BUT IT WOULDN'T HAVE ALL FIT, SO I TRIED TO GO THROUGH AND DECIDE WHICH SCENARIOS I MOST WANTED TO PRESENT TO MY READERS, AND WHICH I THOUGHT THEY WOULD MOST ENJOY.

YOU'VE GIVEN ME SO MUCH EXCITEMENT, ENERGY, AND COURAGE, AS WELL AS LOTS OF SUPPORT. OVER THE YEARS, I'VE RECEIVED SO MANY WONDERFUL FEELS FROM ANIME AND MANGA, SO THIS TIME, I WANTED TO BE THE ONE GIVING OUT THE FEELS. I CONTINUE DRAWING MANGA EACH DAY HOPING TO BECOME THE KIND OF MANGA ARTIST WHO CAN CREATE AND GIVE SUCH FEELINGS TO OTHERS. IF YOU WOULD CONTINUE ACCOMPANYING ME ON THIS JOURNEY, I'D BE SO HAPPY.

THANK YOU SO MUCH FOR CONTINUING TO SEND YOUR LETTERS! THOUGH I CAN'T USUALLY REPLY TO THEM, WITH EVERY LETTER I READ, I GAIN SO MUCH CHEER AND ENERGY. NOW THAT WE'VE RELEASED THREE WHOLE DRAMA CDS, I LOVE READING YOUR REACTIONS AND OPINIONS ABOUT THEM IN YOUR LETTERS TOO! THOUGH SOME THINGS HAD TO BE CUT OUT OF THE MOST RECENT ONE DUE TO TIME CONSTRAINTS, THE NEW DRAMA CD HAS SUCH GREAT LINES IN THERE, I REALLY CAN'T WAIT TO HEAR WHAT YOU ALL THINK ABOUT THEM TOO! ALSO, THE SHORT STORY WE INCLUDED ON IT IS ALL-NEW, SO PLEASE DEFINITELY GIVE IT A LISTEN!

IN ADDITION TO THE LATEST TANKOUBON AND THE NEW DRAMA CD, THERE ARE QUITE A FEW PIECES OF *KARNEVAL* MERCHANDISE AVAILABLE, SO PLEASE CHECK OUT MY BLOG FOR LINKS TO THOSE AS WELL AS GENERAL NEWS ABOUT THE SERIES. IF YOU SEARCH FOR "TOUYA MIKANAGI" ONLINE, MY WEBSITE SHOULD POP UP. IF YOU CHECK OUT MY BLOG ON YOUR CELL PHONE, YOU'LL GET TO SEE MY SPECIAL MOBILE SITE LAYOUT TOO!

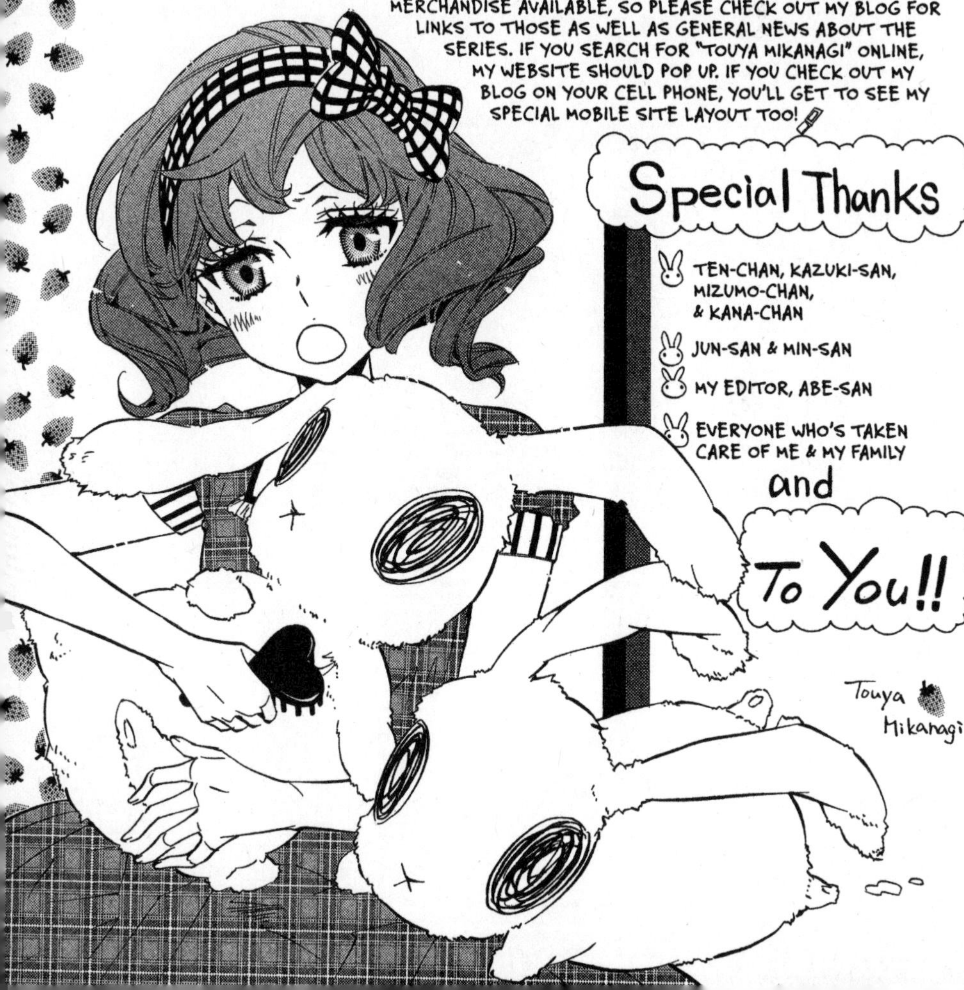

Special Thanks

- TEN-CHAN, KAZUKI-SAN, MIZUMO-CHAN, & KANA-CHAN
- JUN-SAN & MIN-SAN
- MY EDITOR, ABE-SAN
- EVERYONE WHO'S TAKEN CARE OF ME & MY FAMILY

and

To You!!

Touya Mikanagi

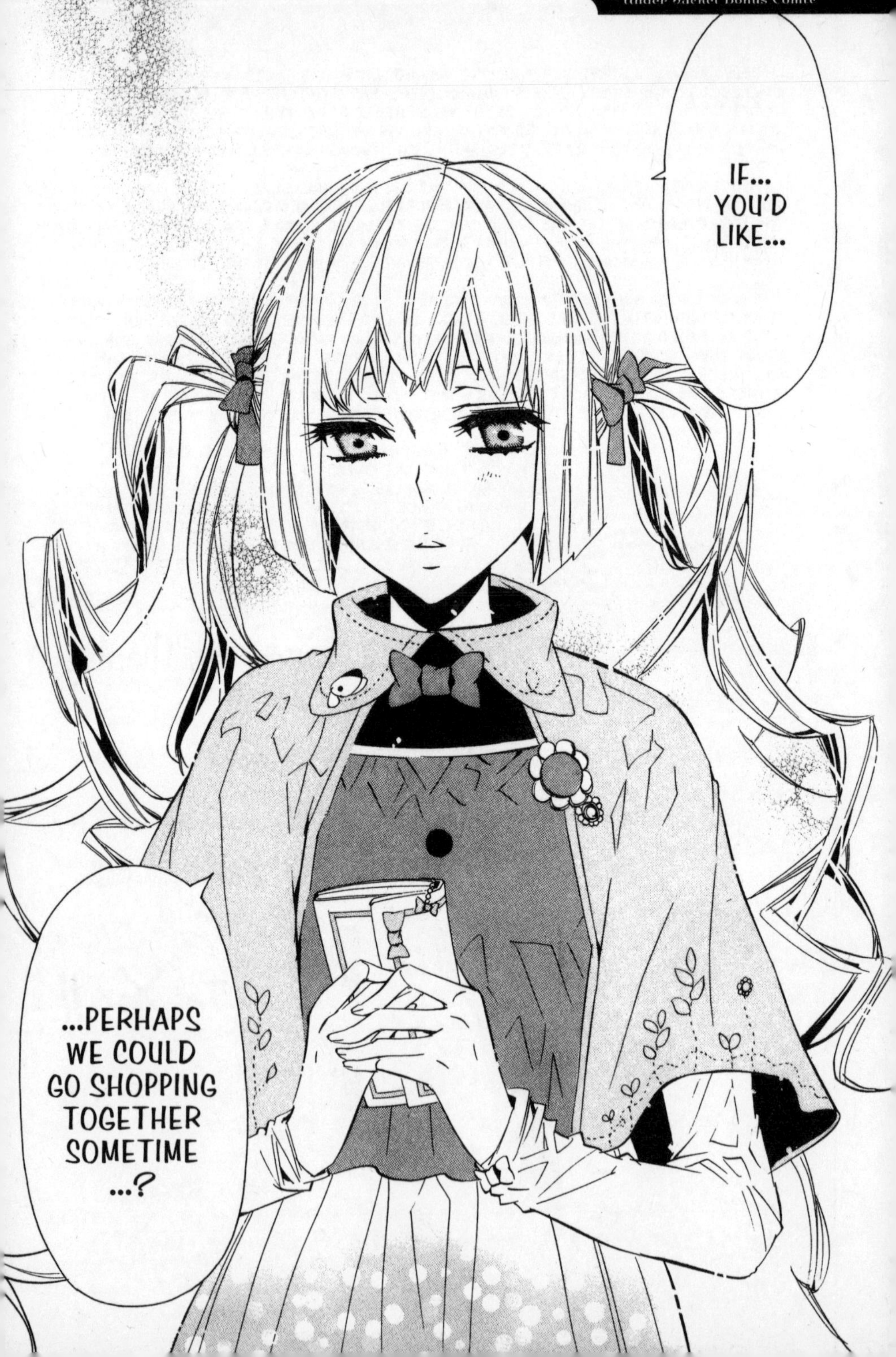
IF... YOU'D LIKE...
...PERHAPS WE COULD GO SHOPPING TOGETHER SOMETIME ...?

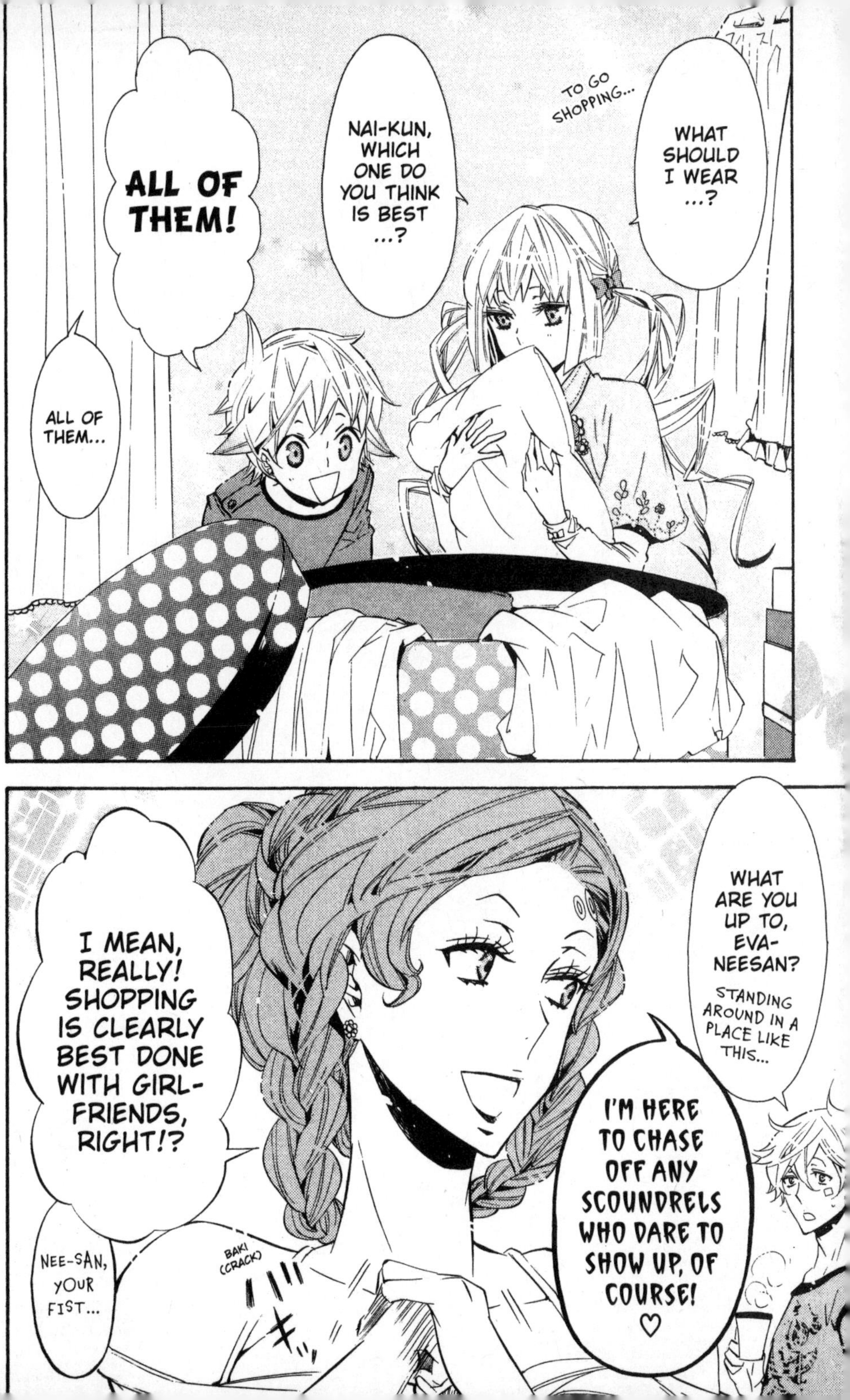
WHAT SHOULD I WEAR ...?
TO GO SHOPPING...
NAI-KUN, WHICH ONE DO YOU THINK IS BEST ...?
ALL OF THEM!
ALL OF THEM...
WHAT ARE YOU UP TO, EVA-NEESAN?
STANDING AROUND IN A PLACE LIKE THIS...
I'M HERE TO CHASE OFF ANY SCOUNDRELS WHO DARE TO SHOW UP, OF COURSE! ♡
I MEAN, REALLY! SHOPPING IS CLEARLY BEST DONE WITH GIRL-FRIENDS, RIGHT!?
BAKI (CRACK)
NEE-SAN, YOUR FIST...

Japanese Volume 6
Under Jacket Bonus Comic

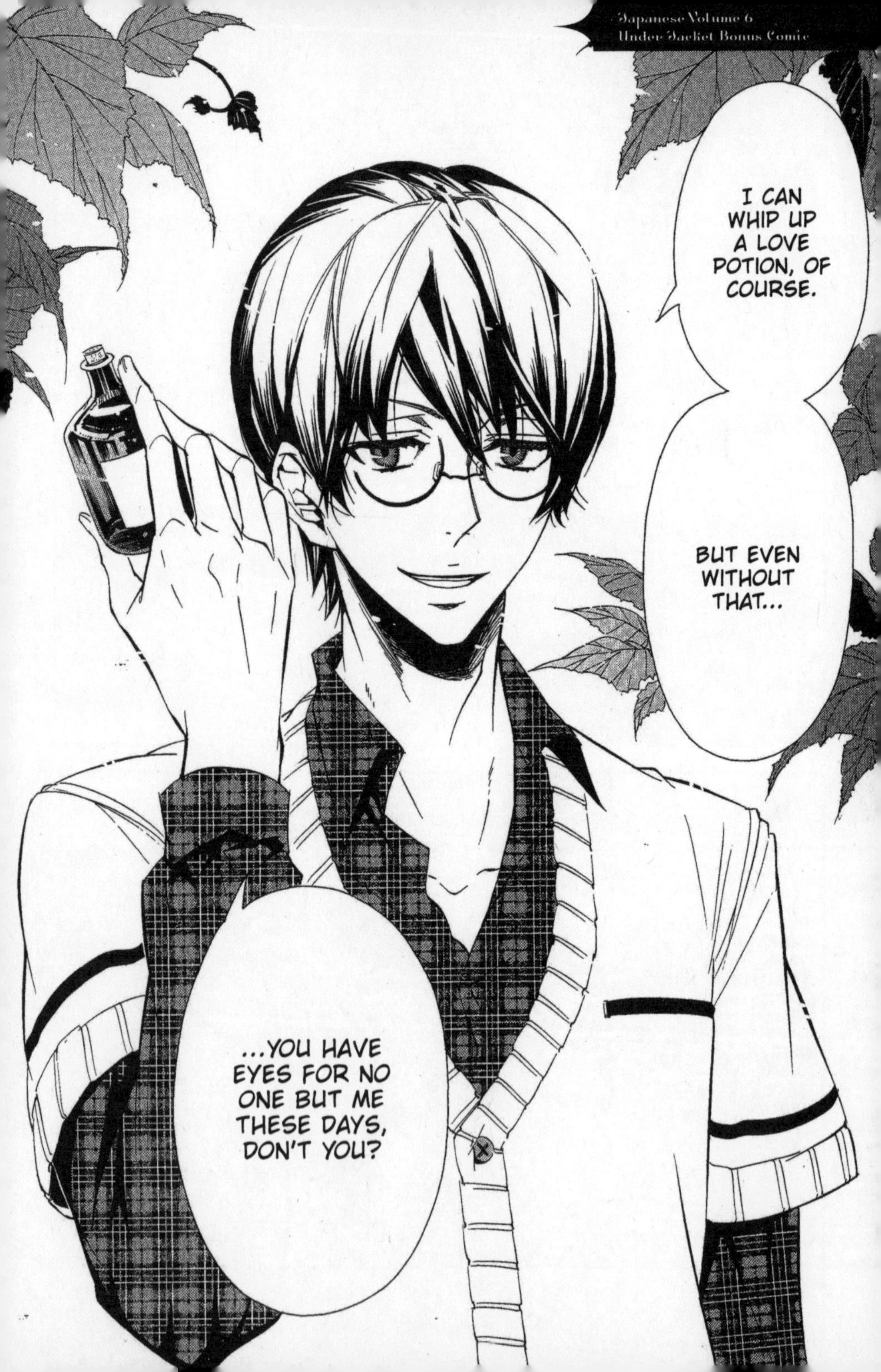
I CAN WHIP UP A LOVE POTION, OF COURSE.
BUT EVEN WITHOUT THAT...
...YOU HAVE EYES FOR NO ONE BUT ME THESE DAYS, DON'T YOU?

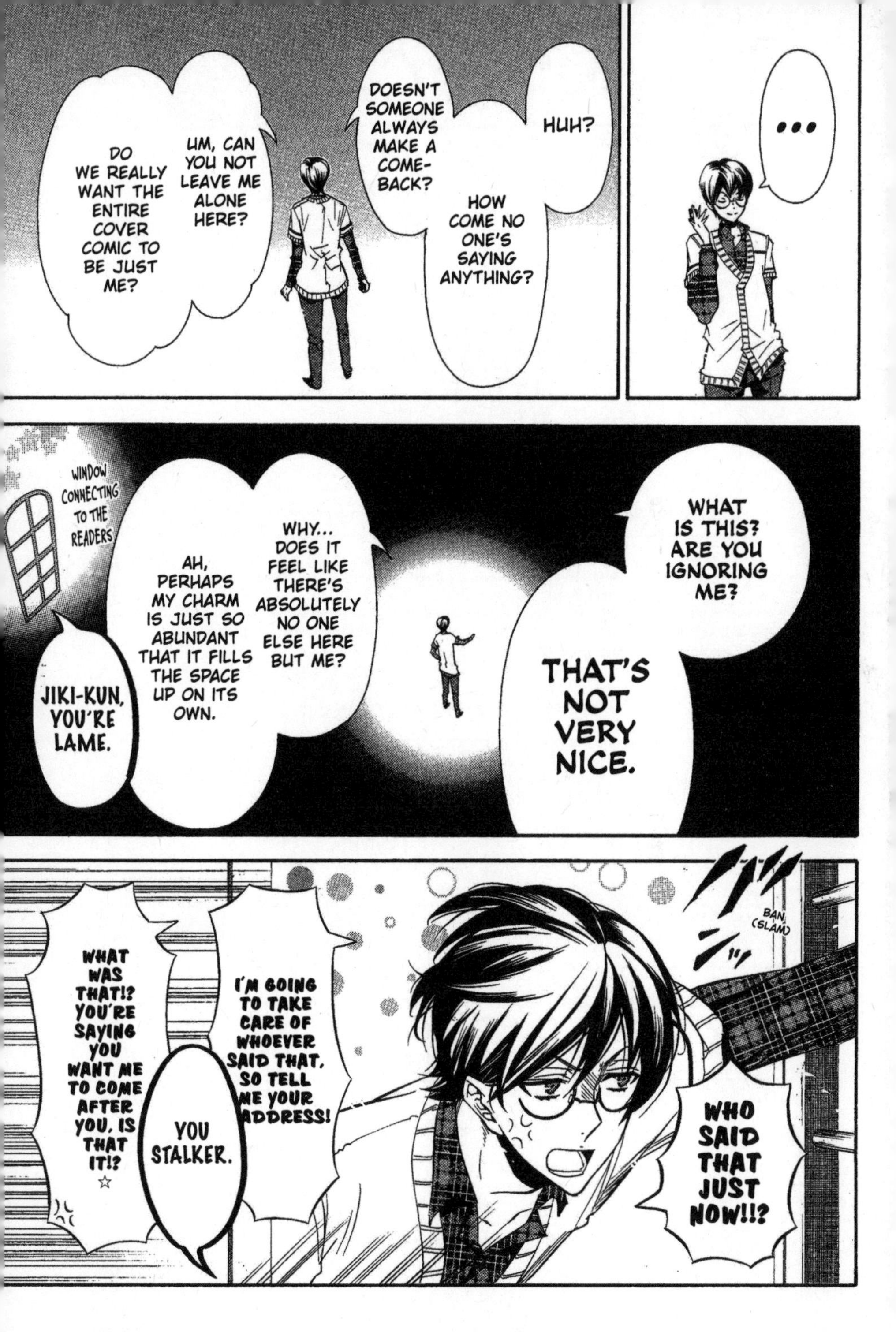
...
HUH?
HOW COME NO ONE'S SAYING ANYTHING?
DOESN'T SOMEONE ALWAYS MAKE A COME-BACK?
UM, CAN YOU NOT LEAVE ME ALONE HERE?
DO WE REALLY WANT THE ENTIRE COVER COMIC TO BE JUST ME?
WHAT IS THIS? ARE YOU IGNORING ME?
THAT'S NOT VERY NICE.
WHY... DOES IT FEEL LIKE THERE'S ABSOLUTELY NO ONE ELSE HERE BUT ME?
AH, PERHAPS MY CHARM IS JUST SO ABUNDANT THAT IT FILLS THE SPACE UP ON ITS OWN.
WINDOW CONNECTING TO THE READERS
JIKI-KUN, YOU'RE LAME.
BAN (SLAM)
WHO SAID THAT JUST NOW!!?
I'M GOING TO TAKE CARE OF WHOEVER SAID THAT, SO TELL ME YOUR ADDRESS!
YOU STALKER.
WHAT WAS THAT!? YOU'RE SAYING YOU WANT ME TO COME AFTER YOU, IS THAT IT!? ☆

KARNEVAL 3

Touya Mikanagi

Translation: Su Mon Han   Lettering: Alexis Eckerman

Karneval vols. 5-6 © 2010 by Touya Mikanagi. All rights reserved. First published in Japan in 2010 by ICHIJINSHA. English translation rights arranged with ICHIJINSHA through Tuttle-Mori Agency, Inc., Tokyo.

Translation © 2015 by Yen Press, LLC

Yen Press
1290 Avenue of the Americas
New York, NY 10104

www.YenPress.com

Yen Press is an imprint of Yen Press, LLC.
The Yen Press name and logo are trademarks of Yen Press, LLC.

The publisher is not responsible for websites (or their content) that are not owned by the publisher.

First Yen Press Edition: November 2015

ISBN: 978-0-316-26348-1

10 9 8 7 6 5 4 3

BVG

Printed in the United States of America